to follow these themes across types of exceptional pupils. The *Topical Contents* show how to take this noncategorical approach. They show how the themes are introduced in Chapter 1, presented in detail in Chapters 2 and 3, and then applied in Chapters 4 through 11 to each category of exceptional pupils protected by the laws; that is, how identification and planning, nondiscriminatory testing, individualizing instruction, and placement in the least restrictive environment each is carried out with the respective categories of exceptional pupils.

Educating Exceptional Pupils

Educating Exceptional Pupils

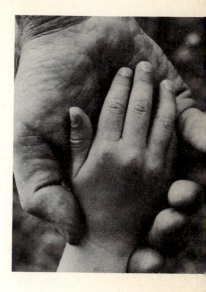

An introduction to contemporary practices

Kathryn A. Blake

Division for the Education of Exceptional Children
UNIVERSITY OF GEORGIA

**ADDISON-WESLEY
PUBLISHING COMPANY**
Reading, Massachusetts □ Menlo Park, California
London □ Amsterdam □ Don Mills, Ontario □ Sydney

This book is in the
ADDISON-WESLEY SERIES IN SPECIAL EDUCATION AND REHABILITATION

Sponsoring Editor: *Brian Walker*
Production Editor: *William J. Yskamp*
Book Design: *Vanessa Piñeiro*
Cover Design: *Robert A. Rose*
Cover Photograph and Book Logo: *Bruce Anderson*
Illustrator: *B. J. and F. W. Taylor*
Production Artist: *Lorraine A. Hodsdon*

Library of Congress Cataloging in Publication Data

Blake, Kathryn A
  Educating exceptional pupils.

  Bibliography: p.
  Includes index.
  1. Exceptional children—Education.   I. Title.
LC3965.B56   371.9   80-15222
ISBN 0-201-00083-0

Copyright © 1981 by Addison-Wesley Publishing Company, Inc. Philippines
copyright 1981 by Addison-Wesley Publishing Company, Inc.

ISBN 0-201-00083-0
ABCDEFGHIJ-DO-8987654321

Acknowledgments

The author expresses her gratitude to the organizations and individuals that courteously permitted us to reproduce materials appearing on the pages as listed under the following categories.

Photographs

5, 21, 52, 83, 106, 184, 194, 201, 301, and 384, Georgia Department of Education, Jane Lee and Glenn Oliver; 11, 65, 102, 111, 210, 215, 285, 373, 375, 376, and 377, from *Accepting Individual Differences*, © DLM—1977—7440 Natchez, Niles, Ill. 60648, Kathleen M. Hurley and John P. Starkel; 19 and 224, University of Georgia Toddler Learning Class, Warren Umansky and Walker Montgomery; 50, *Athens Banner Herald*, Wingate Downs; 69, University of Georgia Public Relations Department, Walker Montgomery; 96, Black Star, Charles Moore; 98 and 150, Media Services, Exceptional Child Center, Utah State University; 118 and 382, from *The Family Papers: A Return to Purgatory* by Burton Blatt, Andrejs Ozolins, and Joe McNally, copyright © 1979 by Longman, Inc., reprinted by permission of Longman, Inc., New York; 133 and 297, from *Teen Scenes*, © DLM—1979—7440 Natchez, Niles, Ill. 60648, Kathleen M. Hurley and John P. Starkel; 138, 444, 453, 462, and 465, Rutland Center—Developmental Therapy Institute, Mary M. Wood; 251 and 262 (bottom), Georgia Academy for the Blind, Richard Hyer; 253, Wisconsin School for the Visually Handicapped, Robert Rashid; 262 (top), Black Star, Don Rutledge; 262 (middle), Black Star, Jay Lurie; 314, *Athens Observer*, Bud Marshall; 320, Moss Rehabilitation Hospital, Philadelphia, Harry Finsberg and Lois Levy; 324, photograph © by Jill Krementz from *A Very Young Gymnast*, published by Alfred A. Knopf; 327, 331, 335, and 343, Black Star, Steve Shames; 392, 416, and 424, University of Georgia Diagnostic Clinic and Prep School, Dorothy D. Campbell; 407 and 421, Black Star, Robert H. Davis; 432, Athens Newspapers, Larry White.

Figures and Quoted Matter

4–8, Clara Claiborne Park, Elly and the Right to Education, *Phi Delta Kappan*, April 1974, 8:535–537.

30–32, Reprinted from *Exceptional Children*, What Is to Become of Katherine? by M. F. deBoor, by permission of The Council for Exceptional Children, © 1975, 41:517–518.

53, "Education's Latest Victim: The 'LD' Kid" by Diane Divoky. Reprinted by special permission of *Learning*, The Magazine for Creative Teaching, October 1974, © 1974 by Education Today Company, Inc.

74–75, L. R. Aiken, Jr., *Psychological Testing and Assessment* (3rd ed.), Boston: Allyn & Bacon, 1979.

77–79, T. J. Cottle, *Barred from School: 2 Million Children*. Copyright © 1976 by Thomas J. Cottle. Published by New Republic Books, Washington, D. C.

113–115, H. Moller, The Treatment of Childhood Schizophrenia in a Public School System, *Psychology in the Schools*, 1964, 1:297–304.

119–121, F. M. Hewett, The Orchestration of Success. In A. J. Pappanikou and J. L. Paul (eds.), *Mainstreaming Emotionally Disturbed Children.* Syracuse, N. Y.: Syracuse University Press, 1977, pp. 80–81.

121–122, S. Herr, The Right to an Appropriate Free Public Education. In M. Kindred *et al.* (eds.), *The Mentally Retarded Citizen and the Law.* Copyright © 1976 by The Free Press, a division of Macmillan Publishing Co., Inc.

122–123, F. J. Weintraub and A. Abeson, Appropriate Education for All Handicapped Children: A Growing Issue. *Syracuse Law Review,* 1972, 23(4):1044. Reprinted with permission of Syracuse Law Review.

127–128, B. H. Watts, Special Education in the Seventies: Promises and Problems, *Slow Learning Child,* 1975, 22:67–82.

149, 156, 157, 158, Charles Van Riper, *Speech Correction: Principles and Methods,* © 1978, pp. 5–6, 8, 18, 22, 24–25, 27, 30. Reprinted by permission of Prentice-Hall, Inc., Englewood Cliffs, New Jersey.

190–191, 193, 195–196, 198, From *Deafness and Learning, A Psychological Approach* by Hans G. Furth. © 1973 by Wadsworth Publishing Company, Inc., Belmont, California 94002. Reprinted by permission of the publisher.

235–238, A. M. Kidwell and P. S. Greer, *Sites, Perception, and the Non-Visual Experience: Designing and Manufacturing Mobility Maps.* New York: American Foundation for the Blind, 1973.

238–239, Shiro Fukurai, *How Can I Make What I Cannot See?* Tokyo: Kodansha Ltd., 1973.

284, Charles Van Riper, *Speech Correction: Principles and Methods,* © 1978, p. 392. Reprinted by permission of Prentice-Hall, Inc., Englewood Cliffs, New Jersey.

286–287, 396–398, A. P. Turnbull and J. B. Schulz, *Mainstreaming Handicapped Students: A Guide for the Classroom Teacher.* Boston: Allyn & Bacon, 1979.

316–318, 325, 332–334, 338–339, 340, 343–345, Audrey Grost, *Genius in Residence.* Englewood Cliffs, New Jersey: Prentice-Hall, 1970.

329–330, *The Autobiography of Bertrand Russell.* Copyright © 1969 by George Allen and Unwin, Ltd.

362, 363, 364, From Donald L. MacMillan, *Mental Retardation in School and Society.* Copyright © 1977 by Little, Brown and Company (Inc.). Reprinted by permission.

401–402, Janet W. Lerner, *Children with Learning Disabilities,* 2nd ed. Copyright © 1976 by Houghton Mifflin Company. Used by permission.

439–440, M. M. Wood, *Developmental Therapy Objectives.* Baltimore: University Park Press, 1979.

443, C. J. Kestenbaum, "Childhood Psychosis: Psychotherapy" in *Handbook of Treatment of Mental Disorders in Childhood and Adolescence,* © 1978, pp. 364–365. Reprinted by permission of Prentice-Hall, Inc., Englewood Cliffs, New Jersey.

448, J. M. Kauffman, *Characteristics of Children's Behavior Disorders.* Columbus, Ohio: Charles E. Merrill Publishing Company, 1977.

456–457, E. Mahon and D. Battin, "Therapeutic Nurseries" in *Handbook of Treatment of Mental Disorders in Childhood and Adolescence,* © 1978, pp. 73–74. Reprinted by permission of Prentice-Hall, Inc., Englewood Cliffs, New Jersey.

Table 1.1, pp. 12–13, R. J. Havighurst, *Developmental Tasks and Education* (3rd ed.), New York: McKay, 1972.

Fig. 1.2, p. 17, Dunlap, "The Education of Children with High Mental Ability," in Cruickshank/Johnson, *Education of Exceptional Children and Youth* (3rd ed.), © 1975, p. 156. Reprinted by permission of Prentice-Hall, Inc., Englewood Cliffs, New Jersey.

Fig. 2.2, p. 66, Reprinted from *Exceptional Children,* Clinical Evaluation and Coordination of Services, by E. D. Thomas and M. J. Marshall, by permission of The

Council for Exceptional Children, © 1977, 44:20.

Fig. 2.3, p. 68, S. Torres, *A Primer on Individualized Education Programs for Handicapped Children*, Foundation for Exceptional Children, 1920 Association Dr., Reston, Va. 22091.

Table 2.1, p. 72, L. R. Aiken, Jr., *Psychological Testing and Assessment*, 3rd ed. Boston: Allyn & Bacon, 1979.

Table 3.1, p. 93, Adapted courtesy of Ellidee D. Thomas M.D., Child Study Center, Section of Developmental Pediatrics, Oklahoma City, Okla.

Table 3.2, p. 95, J. W. Tawney, Programmed Language Instruction for the Severely Developmentally Retarded. From *The Directive Teacher*, Winter 1980. Reprinted by permission of the publisher.

Fig. 3.1, p. 96, Reprinted from *Exceptional Children*, Early Classroom-Based Intervention and the Role of Organizational Structure, by M. J. Guralnick by permission of The Council for Exceptional Children, © 1975, 42:25–31.

Fig. 3.2, p. 100, A. P. Turnbull and J. B. Schulz, *Mainstreaming Handicapped Students: A Guide for the Classroom Teacher*. Boston: Allyn & Bacon, 1979.

Table 3.3, p. 107, National Association of State Directors of Special Education.

Fig. 3.5, p. 118, J. D. Chaffin, Will the Real Mainstreaming Program Please Stand Up? *Focus on Exceptional Children*, 1974, 6(5):1–18.

Table 3.4, p. 120, B. M. Swanson and D. J. Willis, *Understanding Exceptional Children and Youth*. Copyright © 1979 by Rand McNally College Publishing Company.

Table 5.1, pp. 180–181, This checklist, prepared by Mary Wooten Masland, M. A., is reprinted with permission from January 1, 1970, *Volta Review*. Copyright © 1970 by Alexander Graham Bell Association for the Deaf, Inc., 3417 Volta Place, N. W., Washington, D. C. 20007.

Fig. 5.2, p. 182, Charles Van Riper, *Speech Correction: Principles and Methods*, © 1978, p. 409. Reprinted by permission of Prentice-Hall, Inc., Englewood Cliffs, New Jersey.

Fig. 5.3, p. 186, Hayes E. Newby, "Clinical Audiology" in Travis, *Handbook of Speech Pathology and Audiology*, © 1957, p. 353. Reprinted by permission of Prentice-Hall, Inc., Englewood Cliffs, New Jersey.

Table 5.2, p. 192, F. S. Berg, *Educational Audiology: Hearing and Speech Management*. New York: Grune and Stratton, 1976.

Fig. 6.2, p. 230, W. F. Hunter and P. L. LaFolette, *Directing Language Skills*. New York: Webster Division, McGraw-Hill Book Company, 1978, p. 11.

Fig. 6.7, p. 233, and Table 6.2, p. 234, Reprinted from "Eye Report for Children with Visual Problems" with permission of the National Society to Prevent Blindness.

Fig. 6.9, p. 255, Reprinted from *Large Type Books in Print* with permission of the R. R. Bowker Company. Copyright © 1978 by Xerox Corporation.

Fig. 9.1, p. 368, M. A. Fisher and D. Zeaman, Growth and Decline of Retardate Intelligence. In N. R. Ellis (ed.), *International Review of Research in Mental Retardation*, Vol. 4. New York: Academic Press, 1970, p. 163.

Fig. 10.1, p. 403, and Fig. 10.2, p. 409, H. Michael-Smith and M. Morgenstern, Learning Disorders—An Overview. In J. Hellmuth (ed.), *Learning Disorders*. Seattle: Special Child Publications, 1965. Used by permission.

Fig. 10.3, p. 410, S. A. Kirk; J. J. McCarthy; and W. D. Kirk, The Illinois Test of Psycholinguistic Abilities (rev. ed.), Urbana: University of Illinois Press, 1968.

Fig. 10.4, p. 411, S. A. Kirk and W. D. Kirk, *Psycholinguistic Learning Disabilities: Diagnosis and Remediation*. Urbana: University of Illinois Press, 1971.

Table 11.2, p. 442, H. L. Swanson and H. R. Reinert, *Teaching Strategies for Children in Conflict*. St. Louis: The C. V. Mosby Co., 1979.

Fig. 11.1, p. 450, J. M. Kauffman, *Characteristics of Children's Behavior Disorders*. Columbus, Ohio: Charles E. Merrill Publishing Company, 1977.

University of Georgia Public Relations Department, Walker Montgomery

In every child who is born, under no matter what circumstances and of no matter what parents, the potentiality of the human race is born again; and in him too, once more, is renewed in each of us, our terrific responsibility towards human life, towards the utmost idea of goodness, and towards a horror of error.

James Agee

Preface

It is interesting and, at first glance, somewhat amusing to observe that Margaret Mitchell Street and Martin Luther King, Jr. Drive meet at the State Capitol in Atlanta. As we think about it, however, we can see the fitness of this meeting. Figuratively speaking, King wrote the ending to *Gone With the Wind*, with that ending being guaranteed by law and rooted in the United States Constitution.

Now to be less metaphorical. Mitchell crystallized for a moment the *beginning* of the passing of the old system, a system of inequality in which opportunity and the valuing of people were based on the happenstance of birth and other characteristics that really do not matter. King symbolized and galvanized the *ending* of that system's passing and the beginning of the new system, a system of equality in which opportunity and the valuing of people are based on their rights as human beings and their citizenship in a society committed to the rule of law.

This tremendous shift in the spirit of our times toward egalitarianism, liberalism, and humanism has had an immediate impact on vulnerable populations, the handicapped among them. Today we are entering a period of unparalleled opportunity. Handicapped people's rights have been, and will continue to be, reaffirmed and protected through the laws. The twin ideals of *a free appropriate education* and *an equal educational opportunity* are our channels for carrying out these laws.

Knowledge certainly will not be a sufficient condition for this social improvement. But it certainly will be a necessary condition. This book is designed to present some of that knowledge. It pulls together concepts from special education, general education, psychology, and the law and applies these concepts to working with exceptional pupils. It is guided by six ideas.

1. *The pupils.* Exceptional pupils are youngsters whose patterns of growth and development differ so much from those of most other pupils that they need special help in learning the common tasks of our culture.

2. *The process.* Supplying this special help is a matter of fitting education to these pupils' extraordinary individual differences.

3. *The tools.* Regular education and special education have long had the tools for fitting education to pupils' extraordinary individual differences, i.e., classification, testing, individualizing instruction, and placement.

4. *The problems.* Previously, we have not always used these tools correctly, and some exceptional pupils have been hurt — either through lost opportunities for development or errors that distorted their development.

5. *The laws.* Now, to safeguard exceptional pupils from the problems, we have detailed laws governing our use of the tools for dealing with pupils' extraordinary individual differences so that their rights as citizens are not abused.

6. *The tasks.* Our present responsibility is to carry out four tasks needed to see that particular exceptional pupils get all of the rights and protections they are entitled to. These tasks essentially involve using the tools within the protections of the legal safeguards. In contemporary practice, they are called identification and planning, nondiscriminatory testing, individualizing instruction, and placing pupils in the least restrictive environment they can get along in effectively and comfortably.

In Part I, "Exceptional Pupils and Their Rights," we describe these six ideas in detail. Then, in Part II, "Special Needs of Exceptional Pupils," we apply them to exceptional pupils in categories protected by the laws — pupils who have speech and language impairments, hearing impairments, visual impairments, physical impairments, gifts and talents, mental retardation, learning disabilities, and emotional disturbances.

We all have the opportunity and the responsibility to help make the ideals of *a free appropriate education* and *an equal educational opportunity* a reality for particular youngsters. It's going to be a tough struggle. We will be limited by insufficient funds and too few people to do what human decency and the laws require. At the same time, as we try to decide how best to proceed, we will be distracted by disagreements. However, as happens in all social progress, we will muddle through — well-intentioned people doing the best we can despite our limitations and distractions. And the long view will reveal great progress in this era that is just beginning. The world for exceptional youngsters will change. It will be better, and we'll help make it better. It's a great time to be in the thick of the fray.

Athens, Georgia   K. B.
January 1981

Contents in Brief

Topical Contents

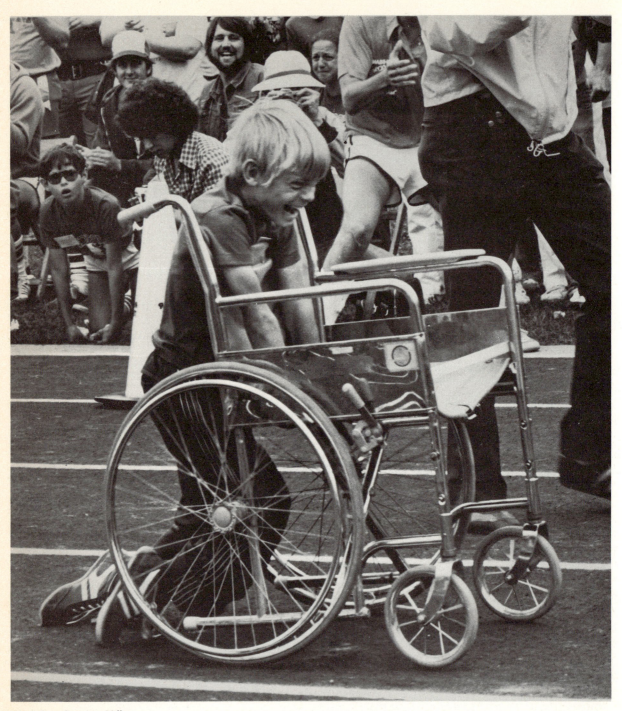

Black Star, Sue Ann Miller

Exceptional Pupils and Their Rights Part 1

At the outset of the Declaration of Independence, Jefferson wrote, and the Founding Fathers approved, this assertion:

> We hold these truths to be self-evident, that all men are created equal, that they are endowed by their Creator with certain inalienable Rights, that among these are Life, Liberty, and the pursuit of Happiness.

Since 1776, we have continued to move toward these ideals of equality and inalienable rights.

In Part I we show how this movement appears in the lives of exceptional pupils. We examine how extreme individual differences cause such a divergence in growth and development that pupils need special help in accomplishing cultural tasks required to meet their needs in socially approved ways. Then we consider how the traditional tools for delivering this special help — classification, testing, individualized instruction, and placement — have been so misused that the abuses violated youngsters' rights to equal treatment and their other rights as citizens. Finally, we see how instituting legal safeguards against these abuses has in contemporary practice led to a redefinition of the traditional tools into four tasks in guaranteeing pupils' entitlements and protections — identification and planning, nondiscriminatory testing, individualizing instruction, and placement in the least restrictive environment.

1

1

Exceptional Pupils

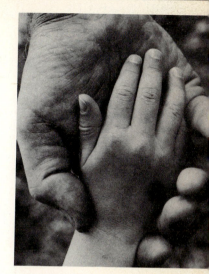

Understanding exceptional pupils

DEFINITION AND PREVALENCE

Every living thing is unique. Look around you. No two people are alike. One is taller, one shorter. One is more outgoing, one more shy. One is more intelligent, one less intelligent. In addition, any one person differs within. He or she may be highly intelligent, yet a motor moron and an average achiever in school. In education we call these differences *individual differences*.

If we all differ so much, who, then, are exceptional pupils? Definitions vary,* but essentially: Exceptional pupils are youngsters who show such *extraordinary* individual differences in their patterns of growth and development that they need special help in learning the common tasks in our culture as well as they might. Exceptional pupils include those who have gifts and talents as well as those who have handicaps, i.e., visual impairments, hearing impairments, physical impairments, mental retardation, learning disabilities, emotional disturbances, or speech and language impairments. Sometimes pupils have only one talent or handicap. Sometimes they have combinations.

Educating exceptional pupils — both the handicapped and the talented — is a major public concern of our time. Elly's experiences illustrate some reasons why we have had a revolution in special education and also some possibilities that lie before us.

> My daughter Elly is 15 now. It is 13 years since we first suspected something was wrong, 12 since we were given a name to paste on her strangeness and sum up the facts we lived with: that she didn't talk, didn't understand, didn't feed herself, didn't seem to see our faces, us, anything we did. There were other facts — the way she played, for example, with maddening repetitiveness and eerie precision — blocks lined up in parallels, chains snaked up and down, squares, triangles, circles, colors matched in a way to gladden the heart of an IQ tester — except that she seemed to recognize abstract shapes better than she recognized people.
>
> The name we were given was early infantile autism. (It is a rare condition although she shares most of her problems with many other kinds of special children, some with the emotionally disturbed, some with the retarded, some with the learning disabled, the aphasic, and the deaf.)
>
> Elly lives at home with us; she goes to the regional high school in our town, where she is in a small class for the emotionally dis-

---

* For example, Burgdorf (1980b) presents an extensive analysis of the etymology of "handicap" and the psychological, social, and legal meanings of the term.

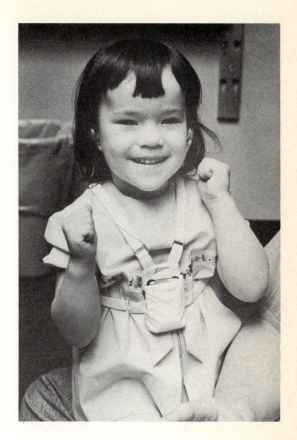

Educating exceptional pupils, both the handicapped and the talented, challenges the
commitment of a democratic society.

turbed. She goes on the bus with the others, and she doesn't come
back until school is over.

You will pardon me for recording these trivial facts; they are not
trivial to her or to us. Elly was 13 before she was in school for a full
school day — Elly, who had so much more to learn than a normal
child.

I am writing this in September, a September which approached
without anxiety. In another September, six years ago, Elly was 9
years old. The telephone call came on a Friday; she'd been in
school (mornings only) hardly three weeks. Monday, Elly wouldn't
be able to go back. She was too disruptive; she screamed; when the
teacher had decided she must share her special crayons, Elly had
erupted in autistic frustration and hit her.

What on earth had gone wrong? She had been in the special
class the previous spring, on trial; the teacher had been patient and
resourceful and things had gone reasonably well. Certainly there
had been some bad times, but nothing like this. What could I do to

help? I thought I could make her understand that she missed school when she behaved badly; I could certainly come and get her when she was disruptive. Would they give her another chance? There was no final answer that week, but the week stretched into another and another, and they added up to no. That was in 1967. There had been no Pennsylvania PARC* decision then, and we ourselves had not so much as formed the idea that our daughter had a right to be in school.

For five awful months Elly had nowhere to go, not even for those brief mornings. Nothing but a home teacher, two hours a week. It was back to what it had been when she was 2, when it was up to her family to invent and provide everything she needed to learn and grow. But in the second semester a place was found for her in a neighboring school system. Mornings only I drove her, a half-hour each way — hardly worthwhile going home in between. It was always clear that it was a temporary grace; children weren't supposed to be emotionally disturbed for more than two years. They were supposed to get well after that, or disappear. Elly made progress in that school, and the administrator was very good to have taken her in at all. But every September — and every February, and every June — we feared that the trapdoor would again open under our feet.

Elly had been in private school from 5 to 8 — nursery and kindergarten. Then they wouldn't keep her, and I took her to the public school superintendent's office. I had hoped to keep our private disaster from being a public burden. It seems incredible now, but I remember I thought of it that way. I would do it all differently today. I would have taken her to public school at 5, and I wouldn't have said she was autistic. I would have let them look at her as a child, not a case, see what she did and what she didn't and let their warm, teacherly instincts take over. Autistic? That was "emotionally disturbed." They had no class for that. I wished I hadn't mentioned her strange abilities — he was dubious about putting her with retarded children already. But I knew she could use that patient teaching. And she would be in school, and still be at home with us, because we loved her and taught her and played with her and worked with her, and we didn't want to send her away.

But were we doing the best thing for her, the superintendent asked. How could we hope to match what she'd get in a residential school? The state would give us money (and get her problems out of his district, though he didn't say that). But we'd spent eight years trying to make her love us, and now she did; what might it do to her to uproot her?

---

* Pennsylvania Association for Retarded Children v. The Commonwealth of Pennsylvania. This court decision requires that all handicapped pupils be admitted to public schools.

"I don't mean to offend you," said the superintendent, "but we do read the papers, and we see that your husband is going to India this summer, and you're willing to leave her to go there...."

I didn't get angry. A parent can't afford to — not at someone who has in his gift a commodity she and her child very much need. Keeping my voice steady, I explained that I wouldn't be accompanying my husband, that I had not been away from Elly for more than a day or so in four years. I didn't say that it seemed unfair to base one's impressions of a child's needs on local news items. I buttoned my lip, and that's how Elly got into the special class from which she was ejected the next September.

There were other conversations with that superintendent, for one wants to be helpful and cooperative. In one, I suggested that if Elly caused any problems in school, they call us — or if they couldn't wait for us to come, she could be sent home in a taxi. The superintendent erupted; I could hear in his voice the primitive terror of the abnormal. "But what if she threw herself out of the window of the cab?" Those terrible words — "emotionally disturbed," "mentally ill," "schizophrenic," and behind them, "insane" and "crazy" — had risen up between him and a little child and he simply couldn't see her. So when there was trouble there were no second chances, no alternative suggestions (a time-out room, even a broom-closet? a temporary relaxation in the teacher's demands? a telephone call home?). It was all over.

Today, Elly has been back in her own school system for three years, full time for a year and a half. That superintendent moved on to a bigger job, where presumably he has begun to learn what neither of us knew five years ago, that deviant children too have a right to be educated in their own community. I know of autistic children who are learning in classes for the retarded, the emotionally disturbed, the learning disabled, even in normal classes. What matters is not the classification but the resourcefulness and flexibility of the teacher. Elly has learned a lot in the special class: to read clear, factual material on a third-grade level, to substitute neat handwriting for her untidy capitals, to control herself when she's frustrated, to use a Kleenex. She has refined her primitive language with tapes. This year she's even composing sentences around her dictionary words.... She likes gym and art and cooking and sewing and math and typing, in all of which her performance is normal or better, and all of which she takes with normal teenagers. She tries hard, and most of the time successfully, to control her autistic outbursts so that she won't miss class next time. The teachers of these subjects are no longer bewildered and uncertain; they are confident and firm, the special teacher's effective auxiliaries.

There have been only little miracles. Only when Elly is silent, sketching a still life, using the sewing machine, completing a page *of simple algebra, could anyone mistake her for a normal teenager. Her speech is too strange, her postures and preoccupations are too bizarre. Any psychiatrist would still diagnose her as a psychotic youngster — of a degree of severity that 10 years ago no public school would have felt it could or should try to teach. Yet here are some excerpts from her reports:*

"Home economics: If Elly were a member of an eighth-grade class her work would merit a high B or a low A."

"Art: Elly is working in class with ninth-graders and doing remarkable work. Her mumblings, scribbling, and scratchings have ceased.

"Physical education: Elly has joined in the class activities very well. Her volley-ball skills are coming along nicely, but more important, she is able to function well as a team member with very little coaxing."

Her special teacher, who coordinates it all, is "most pleased with her progress." And so are we. (Park, 1974, pp. 535–537)

We need to know how many exceptional pupils exist so that we can plan for their education and find money to carry out these plans. There have been many studies of prevalence — by one count over 400. These different studies report different numbers of exceptional pupils. As a result, we cannot accept any single set of numbers as fact. Instead, all we can talk about is ranges of estimates and average estimates.

Roughly, the average estimates are that approximately 3% to 5% of school pupils are gifted and talented and that approximately 10% are handicapped. The differences among numbers of exceptional pupils reported happen primarily because of problems* in classification and testing (BEH, 1979, p. 12). One, people differ in how they define categories of exceptional pupils, and these different definitions cause differences in the numbers of pupils eligible for the categories. Two, people use different procedures to identify and test pupils, and these differences lead to different numbers of pupils' being identified.

A question related to prevalence is: Of the pupils eligible, how many are we serving? Since the early 1900s, we have seen a steady growth in the number of exceptional pupils served in special education. From the mid-1960s through the 1970s, this growth increased sharply; by the late 1970s about 7.4% were being served. Among other things, Park's comments show the human side of this sharp increase in the number of pupils we are identifying and serving.

---

* Chapter 2 has a discussion about how these and other problems in classification and testing lead to mistakes and disagreements in deciding which pupils are truly exceptional.

Figure 1.1 pulls together the information about prevalence estimates and the numbers of exceptional pupils we had identified and served as of the late 1970s (BEH, 1979, pp. 15–17, 162). The bars show the range of different prevalence figures reported in the 400 prevalence studies we alluded to above. The arrows show the average numbers of pupils the states reported they were serving in special education.

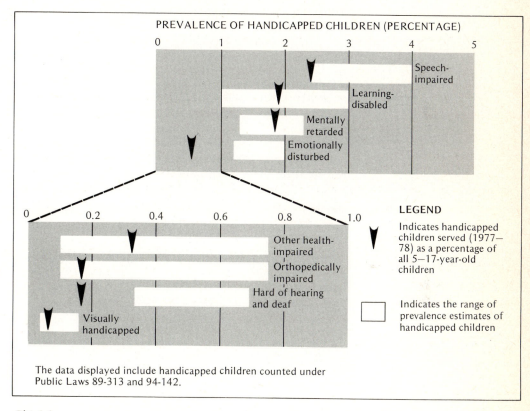

Fig. 1.1
Percentage of children served relative to various prevalence estimates. (Bureau for the Education of the Handicapped, 1979, p. 16.)

Figure 1.1 demonstrates clearly that we are serving many, but not all, pupils who need, and are eligible for, special attention. In more detail the chart shows that the different studies report numbers of speech-impaired pupils ranging from about 2½% to 4% and that the states report that they are serving about 2.4%. Summarizing the corresponding information for the rest of the chart: learning-disabled — 1% to 3% prevalence, 1.9% being served; mentally retarded — $1\frac{1}{2}$% to $2\frac{1}{2}$% prevalence, 1.8% being served; emotionally disturbed — $1\frac{1}{4}$% to 2% prevalence, 0.6% being served; other health-impaired (chronically ill) — 0.1% to 0.75% prevalence, 0.3% being served; orthopedically impaired (crippled) — 0.1% to 0.75% prevalence, 0.2% being served; hard of hearing and deaf — 0.35% to 0.65% prevalence, 0.2% being served; visually handicapped — 0.01% to 0.175% prevalence, 0.07% being served.

CENTRAL CONCEPTS

We have defined exceptional pupils as those who show such extraordinary individual differences in their patterns of growth and development that they need special help in learning the common tasks of our culture. Our understanding exceptional pupils defined this way and our providing the special help they need in the form of special education and related services* both are based squarely on our grasping relationships among three concepts — the cultural tasks, normal growth and development, and individual differences. We will look at the concepts separately and then at how they interrelate in leading to pupils' being designated exceptional.

Cultural Tasks   Cultural tasks are the knowledge and skills we must have to meet our needs in ways society approves of. A synonym for "cultural tasks" is "adaptive behavior." Most people accomplish these cultural tasks at particular chronological age periods. Some cultural tasks, such as learning to walk, arise mainly from physical maturation. Some such as learning to read, come mainly from environmental stimulation. Some, such as choosing and preparing for an occupation, come mainly from the person's values. Some, such as learning how to behave toward the opposite sex in adolescence, arise from all three sources — physical maturation, environmental stimulation, and personal values (Havighurst, 1972, pp. 2–6).

Many people have described tasks and the approximate ages when people accomplish them. Since Havighurst has long been a leader in teaching about cultural tasks, let's use his system as an example. He described representative tasks for infancy and early childhood, middle

---

* *Special education* is specially designed instruction to meet the unique needs of the pupil. *Related services* are therapy, transportation, and other services the pupil needs to help him or her profit from special education (PL 94-142, 1977, Sec. 121a.5). We consider these functions in detail in subsequent chapters.

Exceptional pupils need special help in learning
the common tasks of our culture.

childhood, adolescence, early adulthood, middle age, and later maturity. Table 1.1 summarizes some major tasks.*

The sequential relationship among the cultural tasks is crucial. Accomplishing a task at the usual age — especially the younger ages — is essential to accomplishing subsequent tasks at the expected times. Let's consider an example, using Havighurst's list of tasks. "1. Learning to walk and to use one's hands" in infancy and early childhood is essential to the child's accomplishing the following interacting† tasks at middle childhood.

1. Learning physical skills necessary for ordinary games.
2. Building wholesome attitudes toward oneself as a growing organism.
3. Learning to get along with age-mates.
4. Learning an appropriate masculine or feminine social role.
8. Achieving personal independence.

----

* The tasks in Table 1.1 are examples. Each of us has to master a very large number of cultural tasks at each stage of our development.

†Interacting means that the tasks at any one period affect one another: e.g., during middle childhood, learning physical skills can influence building wholesome attitudes, which in turn can affect learning to get along with age-mates, and so on.

TABLE 1.1 HAVIGHURST'S LISTS OF DEVELOPMENTAL TASKS.

Age Period		Tasks
Infancy and early childhood Ages birth–6	1.	Learning to walk and to use one's hands
	2.	Learning to take solid foods and to feed oneself
	3.	Learning to talk
	4.	Learning to control elimination of body wastes
	5.	Learning sex differences and sexual modesty
	6.	Forming concepts and learning language to describe social and physical reality
	7.	Getting ready to read
	8.	Learning to distinguish right and wrong and beginning to develop a conscience
Middle childhood Ages 6–12	1.	Learning physical skills necessary for ordinary games
	2.	Building wholesome attitudes toward oneself as a growing organism
	3.	Learning to get along with age-mates
	4.	Learning an appropriate masculine or feminine social role
	5.	Developing fundamental skills in reading, writing, and calculation
	6.	Developing concepts necessary for everyday living
	7.	Developing conscience, morality, and a scale of values
	8.	Achieving personal independence in eating, dressing, activities outside of the home, and so on
	9.	Developing attitudes toward social groups and institutions
Adolescence Ages 12–18	1.	Achieving new and more mature relations with age-mates of both sexes
	2.	Achieving masculine or feminine social role
	3.	Accepting one's physique and using the body effectively
	4.	Achieving emotional independence of parents and other adults

Age Period	Tasks
Adolescence Ages 12–18	5. Preparing for marriage and family life 6. Preparing for an economic career 7. Acquiring a set of values and an ethical system as a guide to behavior—developing ideology 8. Desiring and achieving socially responsible behavior
Early adulthood Ages 18–30	1. Selecting a mate 2. Learning to live with a marriage partner 3. Starting a family 4. Rearing children 5. Managing a home 6. Getting started in an occupation 7. Taking on civic responsibility 8. Finding a congenial social group
Middle age Ages 30–60	1. Assisting teenage children to become responsible and happy adults 2. Achieving adult social and civic responsibility 3. Reaching and maintaining a satisfactory performance in one's occupational career 4. Developing adult leisure-time activities 5. Relating oneself to one's spouse as a person 6. Accepting and adjusting to the physiological changes of middle age 7. Adjusting to aging parents
Later maturity Ages 60–	1. Adjusting to decreasing physical strength and health 2. Adjusting to retirement and reduced income 3. Adjusting to death of spouse 4. Establishing an explicit affiliation with one's age group 5. Adopting and adapting social roles in a flexible way 6. Establishing a satisfactory physical living arrangement

In turn, accomplishing these tasks at middle childhood is essential to accomplishing these interacting tasks at adolescence.

1. Achieving new and more mature relations with age-mates of both sexes.
2. Achieving masculine or feminine social role.
3. Accepting one's physique and using the body effectively.
4. Accepting emotional independence of parents and other adults.
5. Preparing for marriage and family life.
6. Preparing for an economic career.

This interdependency continues through the later stages of development. Finish the example by identifying which tasks at early adulthood, middle age, and later maturity follow from the tasks we pinpointed above starting with learning to walk in infancy and early childhood. In the same way, we can identify this interdependency among other sets of tasks. For example, we could start with "learning to talk" in early childhood or "achieving personal independence" in middle childhood and trace their roles in the youngster's learning and performing later cultural tasks.

Normal Growth and Development

Each infant starts with bodily structures that have particular functions necessary to survival. As time goes by, these structures and their functions grow and develop as a result of complex interactions of maturation (biological unfolding) and learning (environmental stimulation). As we watch the youngster, we see growth and development in motor (movement) skills, hearing behavior, visual behavior, intellectual behavior, speech/language behavior, emotional/social behavior, and speech/language (communication) behavior.

Growth and development in these functions follow an orderly sequence. Skills emerge at certain chronological ages. These skills become increasingly complex. That is, more mature skills are built on simpler skills. For example, a complex intellectual skill, such as problem solving, is built on simpler intellectual skills, such as attending to objects and events in the environment, noticing likenesses and differences when comparing two or more objects/events, keeping something in mind (i.e., remembering) something out of sight, and sensing inconsistencies or deficits.

"Normal" growth and development means that the skills emerge in the same sequence and, for most youngsters, at roughly the same rate. That is, certain skills appear at certain chronological ages.

"Individual differences" is the term we use to refer to the ways pupils vary in important characteristics. Individual differences are widely recognized (e.g., Tyler, 1969, 1974, 1978).

Individual Differences

> The uniqueness of the individual is a fundamental principle of life.... human beings differ anatomically, physiologically, and biochemically from one another in every characteristic for which measurements have been made.... (and) individuals show their own characteristic patterns of response to stressful situations. In short, if we consider many characteristics simultaneously, there is no "normal" person who might serve as a medical standard against which others can be evaluated.
>
> However, it is psychological individuality which is of the greatest importance to education. Each student in a classroom, no matter how carefully selected as a member of a "homogeneous" group, will of necessity react in his own unique way to the situation. There are differences in talents and aptitudes, in interests and motives, in habits and response styles, in emotional needs and vulnerabilities. In education as in medicine, there is really no "norm." When a teacher makes an assignment to a class of 30, it is actually 30 different assignments that are carried out. (Tyler, 1969, p. 639)

To illustrate individual differences, let's consider a representative class of pupils at about chronological age nine, the midpoint of the lower schoolyears. The pupils would differ on such characteristics as physical size, motor skills, intellectual ability, and social sensitivity. For example, consider intellectual ability. Table 1.2 is a summary for intelligence level (IQ) and mental-age level (MA), as measured by the Stanford-Binet Intelligence Test (SB) and the Wechsler Intelligence Scale for Children (WISC). Look carefully at the different levels of brightness and mental maturity this group's teachers must plan for and work with. For example, at the extremes, note that Martha H. has an IQ of 71 and a MA of 6-9, whereas Susie G. has an IQ of 153 and a MA of 14-3. And of course, pupils fall at levels throughout this 82-point IQ range and 6½-year mental-age range.

Table 1.2 shows us a cross section of individual differences at any one time. This cross-sectional view is important. In addition, the longitudinal view of the increasing spread of individual differences as time goes by is also quite important. Figure 1.2 illustrates this concept. It shows the snowballing of differences among individuals in one characteristic — intellectual level. It shows how pupils whose IQs differ at any one chronological age (CA) separate more widely from one another in mental age as they get older. For example, consider pupils at the extremes — with IQs of 80 and 180. At CA five in kindergarten, their MAs are 4-10 and 10-10 — a six-year difference. At CA

TABLE 1.2 ILLUSTRATION OF DIFFERENCES AMONG PUPILS — A CLASS OF CHRONOLOGICALLY NINE-YEAR-OLD PUPILS.

Pupils' Names	IQ	Status 9/81 MA (Approx.)*	Source of Evidence Procedure	Date Administered
Michael A.	112	10-7	SB	2/79
John A.	83	7-8	WISC	10/80
Gertrude B.	89	8-11	WISC	9/81
Mary B.	109	9-10	WISC	9/81
Steven C.	102	9-6	WISC	4/81
Paul C.	97	9-3	SB	9/80
Anna D.	79	7-7	WISC	12/80
Sandra D.	127	12-2	WISC	1/79
Rose D.	94	8-10	SB	5/80
Arthur E.	116	11-0	SB	5/79
Jimmy E.	121	11-10	SB	3/80
Harold F.	142	13-3	WISC	9/81
Clark F.	104	10-2	SB	2/79
Susie G.	153	14-3	WISC	10/80
Martha H.	71	6-9	WISC	5/80
Elizabeth J.	107	10-0	SB	6/81
Noel K.	129	12-0	SB	4/79
Fred L.	108	10-3	WISC	3/79
George Mc.	91	8-10	SB	6/80
Sam M.	104	9-8	SB	10/80
Bernard N.	118	11-5	WISC	4/81
Beth O. D.	125	12-0	SB	3/79
Sharill P.	101	9-5	SB	12/80
Jane R.	97	9-3	WISC	1/79
Lucille R.	86	8-4	WISC	4/81
Benjamin S.	111	10-9	SB	5/80
Clifford T.	137	13-2	WISC	9/81
Jack W.	75	7-0	SB	3/79
Arnold W.	124	12-0	WISC	2/81
Robert Y.	100	9-4	WISC	5/79
Joseph Z.	98	9-2	SB	4/80

*The numerals are in years and months, e.g., 10-7 means 10 years and 7 months.

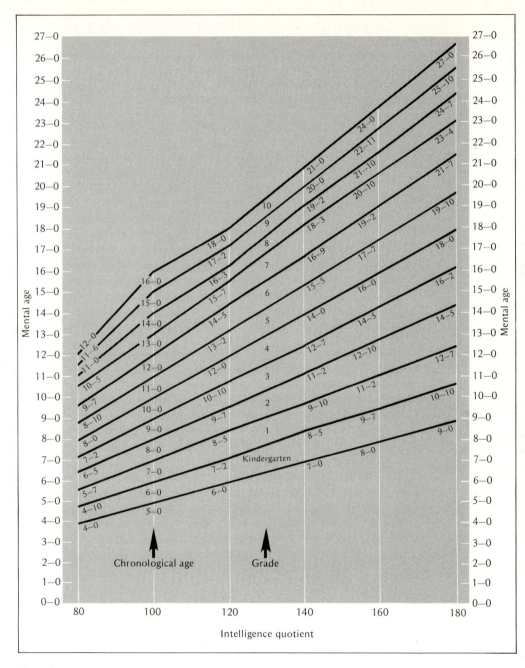

Fig. 1.2
Example of the increasing spread of individual differences. (From Dunlap, 1975, p. 156. Reprinted by permission.)

twelve in the sixth grade, their MAs are 9-7 and 21-7 — a twelve-year difference. At CA sixteen in the tenth grade, their MAs are 12-0 and 27-0 — a fifteen-year difference. Similar divergencies happen in other characteristics.

The essential point to note here is that we have differences among pupils in growth trends. As it always happens, averages are composites. Each individual has his or her own curves for growth and development, his or her own particular ages when skills emerge. These individual differences occur because children show different rates of development in characteristics such as physical size and different rates of benefit from teaching and other environmental stimuli. There are essentially three reasons for these individual differences in rates of development: (1) Children differ in inherited endowment. (2) They differ in environmental opportunities. (3) And, for some children, an insult occurs — e.g., destruction of the optic nerves transmitting visual sensations from the eyes to the brain — which deflects their growth and development from the trend it would have followed if their heredity and environments had been the only influences operating to shape them.

THE RELATIONSHIP AMONG THE CONCEPTS

The relationship among the three concepts — cultural tasks, normal growth and development, and individual differences — is the crux of the matter in understanding exceptional pupils and educating them. To put the process directly:

1. Learning and performing the cultural tasks are necessary for living successfully in our society.

2. Normal growth and development in certain crucial characteristics are necessary for learning and performing the cultural tasks through conventional means. These crucial characteristics are vision, hearing, physical structure and function, social/emotional function, intelligence, learning abilities, and speech and language.

3. A pupil's extraordinary individual differences in one or more of the crucial characteristics — his or her diverging extremely from normal growth and development — interferes with his or her learning and performing the cultural tasks through conventional means.

4. As time goes by, the pupil's increasing divergence from normal growth and development causes more and more delay and problems in his or her learning and performing the cultural tasks through conventional means.

5. As a result, the pupil needs special help — special education and related services — to enable him or her to master the cultural tasks.

6. This special help must begin early, before the increasing divergence over time leads to more — and often unnecessary — delay and problems in his or her learning and performing the cultural tasks.

This process happens with all characteristics: Some problem causes such extraordinary individual differences — i.e., deflection from normal growth and development — that the pupil has trouble mastering the cultural tasks. We can continue to use intelligence to illustrate. As time goes by, the youngster's central nervous system and other systems mature. At the same time, his or her environment provides general stimulation as well as more structured learning experiences. As a result, the child develops intellectual capabilities, such as attending, discriminating, seeing relationships (generalizing), remembering, and ultimately problem solving. These intellectual capabilities influence the youngster's learning and performing the cultural tasks. For example, according to Havighurst's list of tasks, intellectual behavior that is appropriately mature for a child's age level is necessary during infancy and early childhood for him or her to accomplish such tasks as learning to feed oneself, learning to

Special help for exceptional pupils' extraordinary individual differences must begin early, before opportunities for development are lost.

talk, learning to control elimination, learning sex differences and sexual modesty, and forming concepts and learning language to describe social and physical reality. In turn, appropriately mature intellectual behavior and mastery of these cultural tasks of infancy and early childhood are essential to mastering the cultural tasks of middle childhood. These effects continue to compound as the youngster goes into adolescence and the later ages.

Some youngsters are slow in developing intellectual skills; that is, the skills emerge at later chronological ages. As a result, these youngsters are not ready to learn the cultural tasks until *after* the expected chronological ages. They are slow in comparison to other pupils and are not able to act in ways that society expects people their ages to act.

On the other hand, some youngsters are fast in developing the intellectual skills; that is, the skills emerge at earlier chronological ages. As a result, these youngsters are ready to learn the cultural tasks *before* the expected chronological ages. They are fast in comparison to other pupils and, given appropriate learning experiences, are able to act in ways society expects from older pupils.

If these differences are extreme, that is, extraordinary, the pupils differ so much from other pupils that they have problems learning by conventional procedures. As a result, they need special education and related services to help them deal with their problems. In short, they are exceptional pupils. In the words of the Massachusetts Code for the education of exceptional pupils, they have special needs which must be taken care of if they are to profit as much as possible from education (Budoff, 1975).

To repeat for emphasis, we have used intelligence to illustrate the relationship among the cultural tasks, normal growth and development, and individual differences in pupils' being considered exceptional. The same process applies to other characteristics — vision, hearing, physical structure and function, speech and language, learning abilities, and social/emotional behavior. In any characteristic the pupil is designated exceptional when something causes him or her to diverge so much from normal growth and development that he or she cannot learn and perform the cultural tasks without special help — special education and related services.

Educating exceptional pupils

Educating exceptional pupils is a matter of providing for their individual differences in such a way that they diverge from normal growth and development as little as possible and learn to perform as many of the cultural tasks as they can. We work to keep a balance

between the need to adjust education to individual differences on the one hand and the need to work for and maintain normalization as much as possible on the other hand.

Educating exceptional pupils is a matter of providing for their individual differences.

The need to fit education to pupils' individual differences was recognized long ago in both regular education and special education. This need remains a continuing challenge to educators — especially to those of us concerned with exceptional pupils' extraordinary individual differences.

Our basic tools for fitting education to pupils' individual differences were developed quite early and have been used widely in both special education and regular education. The rest of this book is about those tools as they are now used in educating exceptional pupils. It is instructive to start with an overview of these tools — what they are, how they were used by those who went before us in history, problems created by their misuse in ways that harmed pupils, legal requirements we now have to protect pupils from that misuse, and finally the issues we are currently debating about how we should use these tools in serving exceptional pupils today.

TOOLS FOR FITTING EDUCATION TO PUPILS' INDIVIDUAL DIFFERENCES

We use two tools — *placement* and *individualizing instruction* — to fit education to pupils' individual differences. We support these tools with two additional tools — *testing* and *classification*.

Individualizing Instruction and Placement

Individualizing instruction is a tool for fitting teaching to *each pupil.* We select for a particular pupil the special education and related services he or she needs. Individualized instruction has long been used to deal with pupils' individual differences. Early versions were the Dalton (1920) and Winnetka (1919) plans, named after their places of origin in Massachusetts and Illinois, respectively. Later versions of procedures for individualizing instruction include: *processes* such as clinical teaching and diagnostic and prescriptive teaching; *forms of automated teaching* such as programed instruction, computer-assisted instruction, and computer-managed instruction; *instructional packages* such as the Science Research Associates materials, the Peabody Language Development Kits, and the DISTAR materials; and *systems* such as the Pittsburgh Individually Prescribed Instruction System, the PLAN System (Program for Learning in Accordance with Needs), and the Wisconsin Individually Guided Instruction System.

Placement, in the traditional definition, is a tool for getting *a group of pupils* who can be taught the same way (i.e., they can be treated as one) because they are alike on one or more characteristics important to learning. Pupils are selected through classification and are placed into groups for particular kinds of instruction.

Placement came into being for convenience in working with pupils. It is difficult to individualize instruction separately for each one of many pupils. Various kinds of groupings have been used to achieve greater similarity so that sets of pupils can be taught the same way. For example, by one count more than forty-two grouping schemes have been used in the schools (Shane *et al.*, 1971). Generally, the first approach was to divide pupils into chronological age levels and to divide the curriculum into graded sets from grades 1 to 12. This grouping helped, but even pupils within the age-grade levels continued to show wide individual differences, with these differences increasing as time went by. Therefore the next approach was to group pupils by achievement and ability levels in various ways.

Excluding pupils from public schools was a by-product of using placement for finding groups that could be taught alike. Pupils were not considered the schools' responsibility if they showed such extreme individual differences that they could not fit into any group and profit from the standard instruction given that group. Some excluded pupils stayed home. Some went to residential schools (e.g., institutions for the retarded) where pupils showing similar extreme individual differences were brought together from separate school districts into a regional or statewide center. Here again, after placement, sets of pupils were considered homogeneous groups and taught in a standard way.

Today placement is defined more broadly — at least in special education. It is a tool for locating a pupil so that we can conveniently deliver to that pupil the services he or she needs.

Classification is a tool to support placement and instruction. We use it in assigning pupils to a group. We put together in a category pupils who are alike in a characteristic important to learning and name the category, e.g., first graders, retarded pupils, deaf pupils, special-class pupils, middle-grade pupils, college prep pupils. The names signal the characteristic pupils are alike on, and they become shorthand in communication. They indicate the instruction the pupil probably needs and where we can place him or her so we can get that instruction to him or her conveniently. For example, the label "deaf" signals severe hearing impairment. It indicates that we probably will need to teach the pupil communication skills, among other things, and place him or her in situations where there are specially trained personnel, time, and facilities for teaching those communication skills.

Classification and Testing

Testing is a tool for measuring individual differences. Testing supports individualized instruction because we select instructional experiences to fit what tests tell us about where the pupil stands on characteristics important to learning the cultural tasks. For example, we use mathematics achievement test information in deciding what mathematics instructional objectives a pupil is ready for. Testing supports classification and placement because we assign pupils to groups also on the basis of what tests tell us about where the pupil stands on characteristics important to learning. In turn, we use test information in selecting instructional experiences for groups. For example, we classify a pupil moderately retarded and assign him or her to a group on the basis of information from intelligence tests, achievement tests, and adaptive-behavior scales. We also use this information and the same information on the rest of the group to fit instruction to the group.

USING THE TOOLS FOR FITTING EDUCATION TO INDIVIDUAL DIFFERENCES

Again, the four tools for fitting education to pupils' individual differences have been used for a long time in many countries. In other words, "with the exception of mental testing, Freudian psychology, and biochemical techniques, almost every current point of view in the education of exceptional children had by the nineteenth century found some level of expression" (Hewett and Forness, 1977, p. 47).

History

Also, we have seen a growing emphasis on training people to use these tools and on laws to enforce their proper use. Many people have written about this history. For example, Table 1.3 lists some milestones often pinpointed in histories of special education.

TABLE 1.3 MILESTONES IN THE HISTORY OF SPECIAL EDUCATION.*

Date	Event
1591	Swinburne proposed tests to diagnose mental retardation, e.g., asking the individual to measure a yard of cloth and to name the days of the week. (*Testing*)
1620	Juan Bonet developed procedures for teaching the deaf, based on finger spelling. (*Instruction*)
1651	Harsdorffer in Germany produced wax tablets the blind could write on, and Bernouilli in Switzerland invented a frame for guiding a pencil on paper. (*Instruction*)
1690	John Locke tried to distinguish between mental retardation and mental illness. (*Classification*)
1760	Abbé de l' Épée opened a public school for poor deaf children. (*Placement*)
1799	Itard started using intense sensory methods with Victor the Wild Boy of Aveyron, an apparently retarded boy who was found abandoned and living in the woods. (*Instruction*)
1817	Thomas Hopkins Gallaudet organized the first special education program in the United States. Gallaudet's school — the American Asylum for the Education and Instruction of the Deaf — is now called the American School for the Deaf. (*Placement*)
1829, 1832	Samuel Gridley Howe began the Perkins Institute for the Blind. (*Placement*)
1834	Louis Braille developed a system of embossed dots for blind individuals' use in reading and writing. (*Instruction*)
1837	Eduard Seguin started extending Itard's procedures to teaching the mentally retarded. (*Instruction*)
1840	Rhode Island passed the first state compulsory education law. (*Law*)
1840–80	Dorothea Dix called attention to deplorable treatment of the mentally ill and established more humane mental hospitals. (*Placement*)
1847	Following his introduction of embossed print for the blind, Valentine Huay proposed that the blind be taught to read by

Date	Event
	touch. In 1854 Huay adopted Braille's system of embossed dots. (*Instruction*)
1860	The first special class for retarded children was started in Germany. (*Placement*)
1869	Francis Galton published *Hereditary Genius: An Inquiry into Its Laws and Consequences* and followed this work with numerous treatises on measuring and developing intelligence. He, his students, and their students (e.g., Terman) taught that intelligence is inherited, fixed, and immutable and thus requires testing, selection, and eugenic planning. (*Testing/Classification*)
1886	Anne Sullivan started working with Helen Keller and got her first breakthrough: Helen indicated that she had made the first association between physical and symbolic entities when Sullivan poured water over her hands and finger-spelled the word in her hands. (*Instruction*)
	The Elizabeth, New Jersey, schools adopted a multiple-track system in which pupils were grouped according to the rate they could progress through academic material. (*Placement*)
1890	Maria Montessori began extending Seguin's work in teaching both retarded and normal children. (*Instruction*)
	Alexander Graham Bell's development of the telephone and other sound equipment led to hearing aids and emphasis on amplifying sound in teaching speech to the deaf. (*Instruction*)
	Freud began to get attention for his assertions about psychological bases of mental illness (in contrast to physical bases). (*Instruction*)
1891	The Cambridge Plan, whereby gifted pupils could progress through the first six grades in four years, was developed. (*Placement*)
1898	Edward L. Thorndike started as an assistant professor at Teachers college, Columbia University. His work served as a base for the development of intelligence and achievement tests and for many procedures for teaching — especially for teaching reading. (*Testing/Instruction*)
1900	Following Sigmund Freud's work, psychiatric conditions in children began to be recognized and described. (*Classification*)
1904	The French Ministry of Education commissioned Binet and Simon to develop a test for identifying pupils as mentally deficient and transferring them to special classes. (*Testing/Classification*)

(continued)

TABLE 1.3 *(continued)*

Date	Event
1910	The American Association on Mental Deficiency extended the traditional classification system involving "idiot" and "imbecile" to include "moron." Subsequently, there were attempts to differentiate educational and residential programs for people at different levels of mental retardation. (*Classification*)
1910–15	Psychologists criticized the Binet-Simon tests as being too narrow and for unfairly penalizing children with emotional and sensory problems and deprived backgrounds of experience. (*Testing*)
1911	Special classes for gifted pupils were started in cities throughout the country. (*Placement*)
	Alfred Binet and Theodore Simon revised their test and incorporated the concept of mental age, which they used to express a child's score in reference to age standards. (*Testing*)
1916	Lewis Terman at Stanford University translated the Binet-Simon test and established United States norms for what he called the Stanford-Binet Intelligence Test. He revised the test in 1937 and 1960. New norms were established in 1972. (*Testing*)
	Walter Lippmann and Lewis Terman engaged in a public debate about the roles of heredity and environment in intellectual development. (*Testing*)
1922	The International Council for Exceptional Children was founded. It later became the Council for Exceptional Children. The CEC is the professional organization for special educators and others who serve handicapped people and gifted and talented people. Among its other missions, the CEC has served as a clearinghouse for information and ideas about exceptional people and as an advocate for securing exceptional individuals' rights. (*Training/Law*)
1925–35	Sidney Pressey developed an array of ingenious and inexpensive devices that were among the first teaching machines that were to be used in individualizing instruction. He based his procedures on a view of learning that emphasized the role of meaning in learning. His approach contrasted with Skinner's more mechanistic ideas that served as a basis for Programmed Instruction. (*Instruction*)
1928, 1940	The National Society for the Study of Education devoted yearbooks to the roles of heredity and environment in intellectual development. (*Testing*)

Date	Event
1939	David Wechsler produced the Wechsler-Bellevue Intelligence Scale, the forerunner of the Wechsler Adult Intelligence Scale (1955) and his tests for children. (*Testing)*
1949	David Wechsler produced the Wechsler Intelligence Scale for Children. (*Testing*)
1950	The National Association for Retarded Citizens was organized primarily by parents of retarded individuals. The Association's purpose was to give mutual support and to advocate for retarded people's welfare. Subsequently, other parents formed similar advocacy groups, for example, the United Cerebral Palsy Association and the Association for Children with Learning Disabilities. (*Law*)
1954, 1964	In 1954, a judgment was handed down in *Brown* v. *Board of Education of Topeka, Kansas.* In 1964, the Civil Rights Act of 1964 was passed. These two actions guaranteed equal protection in education for black students. The actions were important precedents for the litigation and legislation that guaranteed handicapped pupils a free appropriate public education and an equal educational opportunity. (*Law*)
1957	The U.S. Office of Education started funding a number of programs for working with exceptional pupils. In the ensuing years, funds were used to support research on handicapped pupils and on gifted and talented pupils. Funds were also used to train teachers and counsellors to work with handicapped pupils and gifted and talented pupils. (*Training*)
1958	Marie Jahoda published *Current Concepts of Positive Mental Health*, demonstrating that there is not one agreed on definition of mental health and mental illness. (*Classification*)
	The USSR launched *Sputnik*, the first orbiting space vehicle. Many in the United States reacted to this event by saying that our country trailed the USSR culturally, scientifically, technologically, and militarily. They considered education the key to catching up. As a result, Congress allocated massive federal funds to the National Defense Education Act. The purpose was to train counsellors and teachers to identify and advise gifted and talented pupils and to teach them languages, mathematics, and the sciences. (*Training/Law*)
1961	Congress added funds to support preparation of teachers of deaf children and youth. (*Training/Law*)
1966	The Bureau for the Education of the Handicapped was or-

(continued)

TABLE 1.3 *(continued)*

Date	Event
	ganized within the U.S. Office of Education. It became a center for federal activities pertaining to the handicapped. (*Law*)
	Burton Blatt and Fred Kaplan published *Christmas in Purgatory: A Photographic Essay on Mental Retardation*. This collection of pictures portrayed squalid and inhumane conditions in institutions for the retarded. The impact was emotionally devastating. The work was an important force leading to the deinstitutionalization movement. (*Placement/Law*)
1968	Arthur Jensen reopened the controversy over the roles of heredity and environment in intellectual development. (*Testing*)
	After Lloyd Dunn spent years trying to get it published, *Exceptional Children* published his article, *Special Education for the Retarded: Is Much of It Justifiable?* In this essay, Dunn questioned the value — and perhaps the ethics — of assigning retarded pupils to special classes in the face of evidence indicating that retarded pupils in regular classes fared as well — or better — than retarded pupils in special classes. This widely quoted essay served as one main impetus to the mainstreaming movement of the 1970s. (*Placement/Law*)
1969	*The Six Hour Retarded Child* was published, demonstrating that a person can be handicapped for one purpose (school activities) and nonhandicapped for another purpose (out-of-school activities). (*Classification*)
1971	*Wyatt* v. *Stickney* was adjudicated, revealing deplorable conditions in institutions and leading to the requirement that inmates must be either treated with appropriate procedures or released. (*Placement*)
1972	Legal actions in Pennsylvania and in the District of Columbia initiated a national move to open and improve education for all exceptional pupils within the context of regular education to the fullest extent possible and with guarantees of due process and equal protection. The judgments were handed down in *Mills* v. *the District of Columbia Board of Education* and in *the Pennsylvania Association for Retarded Children* v. *the Commonwealth of Pennsylvania*. These judgments guaranteed handicapped pupils access to public education and other important rights. (*Law*)

Date	Event
1973	The American Association on Mental Deficiency redefined the term "mental retardation," thus demonstrating the arbitrary nature of classification. The definitional shift reduced the incidence of mental retardation from about 3% to 1%. About eight million people previously labeled mentally retarded were no longer so labeled. (*Classification*)
1973, 1975	Congress enacted two crucial laws — PL 93-112, The Vocational Rehabilitation Act of 1973 and PL 94-142, The Education of All Handicapped Children Act of 1975. These laws guarantee handicapped people a free appropriate public education, protection against discrimination, access to public facilities and, more broadly, to education, and equal opportunity in employment. (*Law*)
1977	The court ruled in *Mattie T. v. Holladay*, one of the first law suits seeking relief under Section 504 of PL 93-112. The judgment mandated that the law must be implemented without delay — that pupils must be given a free appropriate public education and an equal educational opportunity. (*Law*)
1979	Judge Peckham in *Larry P. v. Riles* declared a moratorium on California's using intelligence tests for classifying pupils as mentally retarded and placing them in special classes. He declared that intelligence tests are racially and culturally biased and violate rights and protections guaranteed pupils by the federal Constitution and laws. (*Testing, Classification, Placement, Law*)
1979–80	The Office of Education in the U.S. Department of Health, Education, and Welfare became a separate federal department — the U.S. Department of Education. At this time, the Bureau for the Education of the Handicapped was combined with the Rehabilitation Services Administration and became the Office of Special Education and Rehabilitation. (*Training*)
1980	The target date set by the U.S. Commissioner of Education for full educational opportunities to be available to all handicapped youngsters.

*Hewett and Forness (1977, pp. 12–61) was the main source consulted in developing this history.

Problems   By the end of the 1960s, we saw increasing concern about the tools we were using to fit education to pupils' individual differences (e.g., Tyler and White, 1979). Sometimes we did not use testing, classification, and placement *correctly*. And sometimes we did not use individualized instruction *sufficiently*. Further, we often made decisions about pupils' education *arbitrarily*, with little or no participation by someone to advocate for them — their parents, expert advisors, or the pupils themselves when they were able to participate. Thus we had few safeguards against decisions that might not be in the pupils' best interests. *Confidentiality* problems were coupled with all of these other problems, and advocates usually could not get control of, or even gain access to, the information used in decision making — to see whether it was right and whether it was needed for making the decisions.

These problems caused some pupils to develop in the wrong direction or to lose opportunities for development or both. And they sometimes placed an undue burden on parents. Katherine's story illustrates some of the problems and shows the terrible frustration and waste those problems caused.

What is to become of Katherine?

During the more than 20 years of her life, Katherine Jamieson has been diagnosed as retarded, borderline retarded, borderline, borderline normal, and every possible gradation between. Her IQ has tested between 70 and 90 over the years, and as the AAMD* definition of retardation fluctuated, so did the diagnosis. She has been in special classrooms, in sheltered workshops for adult retarded, in various types of training programs, in a mental hospital, in a residential facility — the list is endless. The pile of material collected by her father is remarkable for what it includes. Perhaps more remarkable is that it exists at all.

The material Mr. Jamieson has collected falls into several categories. There are the myriad little pieces of paper with lists of places and telephone numbers, presumably places that Mr. or Mrs. Jamieson called in an effort to find placement for Katherine. When I gave up counting, I had deciphered 20. There are many letters received over a period of years from counselors, therapists, and supervisors giving reports on Katherine's progress or, usually, the lack of it. At one point there is a letter to Katherine from her father, full of anguish and rage. "What will you do if you don't make it here? There is nowhere else for you to go; we have tried everything. Do what they tell you." Between the lines is the unwritten note, "Do it for us. We can't do any more for you." At the end of the file there is a series of letters from a workshop. The letters say things

---

* American Association on Mental Deficiency.

such as "On the bottle washing detail Katherine was unable to apply herself, likewise on the dishwashing detail, but she has done adequate or above adequate work in some other details." There is the reply from her father, "Thank you for your nice letter. It was so good to hear something positive about Katherine for a change."

There are letters from Katherine, long (13 pages) at times, barely legible, but coherent — letters home from a growing girl. Invitations designed for a spring party but never filled out and never mailed. A drawing, a long story. Notebooks with her algebra assignments and doodles. Signs of a girl growing up. Postcards to her brothers. Shoes put on layaway and never paid for.

Then there are all the bills, bills that every parent has (dentists, orthodontists) and bills that only Katherine's parents have. Mental health bills from psychologists and statements from the state hospital. Coupled with these are insurance forms, long letters to various agencies and insurance companies about forms that must be filled out. A statement from the state that Katherine is not qualified for disabled aid. A long letter to a state agency about the fact that the Jamiesons really cannot pay all these bills because they have other children who must not be deprived because of Katherine. The underlying message is clear; she is not their fault.

There are reports from many agencies. "Katherine is retarded." "Katherine will never be able to live alone." "We can't help her anymore." "She's untrainable and always has been." A school for the retarded wants extensive information before they will even consider Katherine. Could the parents go and look at the facility before they once again do all the work involved in collecting files? No, says the school, only afterward when it is possible that she will be admitted will they be allowed to look. So they do all the paperwork and the school turns them down.

An indication of the impotent rage appears in a letter to a bus company demanding refund for a ticket purchased for Katherine but never used. Mr. Jamieson has asked for this before but was sent a long form. He writes back an enraged letter about their "stupid form" and the "stupid rules" and says that if he does not get his money back he will go higher. When one is dealing with important questions, it is the little annoyances that really do one in.

When Katherine was evaluated this week at our facility, the conclusion was that she is not retarded at all. So what is she? Is she the victim of growing up in the 1950's when learning disability was just a word? Could she have been helped had she been born in 1970? Possibly. But instead there is Mr. Jamieson and his file, which he marched in with and deposited.

The fact that this file exists says a great deal. Many of us have files on our children, but we do not save every scrap of paper on which we have scribbled notes to call so and so, arrange this or that. Mr. Jamieson did. Most of us with children have doctor bills of all sorts, but we do not put them in a file marked with the child's *name. Mr. Jamieson did. Most of us do not make copies of the letters we send to our children, or the notes we sent to teachers, or the insurance forms we file when our child breaks his arm. Mr. Jamieson did, and the question is why?*

I think it is a matter of quantity. Katherine Jamieson had a problem that became evident at the age of 2. Presumably with confidence, the Jamiesons went to the first professional for help and were told something negative such as "She is retarded," but they were not told what to do about it. Perhaps they were told "There's nothing to do; it's very sad."

This file picks up the last 4 or 5 years, by which time everyone the Jamiesons talked to was telling them (a) "We will only look at your child after you filed 47 forms and let us look at everything concerned with Katherine, down to and including whether her grandmother had five toes or six," and then (b) either "Yes we will look at her" and "She is retarded and there is nothing to do" (not "We don't know what to do") or "No, we will not look at her." By this time Mr. Jamieson has started to keep a file. At least he will have that to show for all his labors, since his daughter has not benefited by them. He reaches the point where he exchanges notes with the state hospital about the wording of the records. This is after he has decided that he will keep the records himself so that he can send them out to each agency instead of always going through the red tape of release forms.

The final impression one gains from this file is that here is a father for whom the system has become the adversary. Rather than helping him and Katherine, the system is at war with them. If the time comes for the trial of the system against Katherine, Mr. Jamieson will have the evidence in his file. And he also has Katherine, now 21, unable to hold a job, promiscuous, unstable, happy only with her guitar. And the question which the Jamiesons asked 15 years ago is still unanswered: What is to become of Katherine? (de Boor, 1975, pp. 517–518)

Legal Safeguards*

The problems in using the tools required *legal* relief. Reforms had to be generated through the law for two reasons. First, the misused tools were very harmful to the pupils' present and future welfare. Second, through the years we had known about the misuse, but had not taken appropriate corrective steps. Today we are trying to keep such problems from occurring by guaranteeing certain entitlements and protections to each pupil (e.g., Burgdorf and Bersoff, 1980).

It helps to view the legal safeguards in the context of public policy. Public policy is the set of principles, plans, and procedures prescribing

---

* "Legal safeguards," "legal protections," and "procedural safeguards" are used interchangeably as synonyms throughout this book.

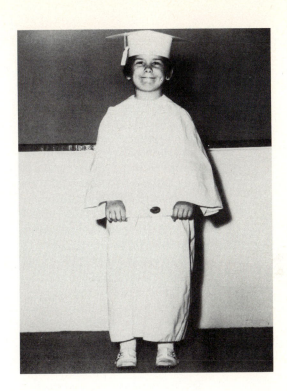

All pupils are now guaranteed a free appropriate public education and an equal educational opportunity.

how we deal with a common task — in our case educating exceptional pupils — and spend tax monies in carrying out those prescriptions. Public policy grows out of the context of thought and feeling existing in the society. To understand the scene in special education today, we need to understand the atmosphere in the United States and the world at large. To put it succinctly: "Almost every social and political issue of our times inevitably has become a legal and constitutional issue. The winds of social and political change blow through the courthouse and the legislative halls only shortly after they affect the atmosphere of social institutions, especially the schools" (Turnbull, 1977, pp. 61–62).

The winds of change have indeed blown through our society. Since World War II, we have seen a growth in liberalism, egalitarianism, and humanism. In addition, we have seen an increase in consumerism, with its stress on accountability accompanied by a readiness to bring lawsuits. Among other results, these trends have led to a quiet revolution (Dimond, 1973), and a not-so-quiet revolution, in our recognizing the rights of the individual — especially the vulnerable individual.

Now we are seeing changes in many of our cultural institutions — general education and special education among them.

As individuals and as groups, parents, advocates, and people in the helping professions have led in developing public policy on educating exceptional youngsters. The Associations for Retarded Citizens, the Council for Exceptional Children, and the Bureau for the Education of the Handicapped in the U.S. Office of Education* have been particularly active. The first approach was primarily through the courts. Success came, and given the tools and precedents provided by the judiciary, people worked effectively through the legislative and executive branches of government.

In the United States our recognizing and putting into practice vulnerable people's rights are anchored in the Fifth, Eighth, and Fourteenth amendments to the federal Constitution, especially the Fourteenth Amendment:

> All persons born or naturalized in the United States, and subject to the jurisdiction thereof, are citizens of the United States and of the State wherein they reside. No state shall make or enforce any law which shall abridge the privileges or immunities of citizens of the United States; nor shall any state deprive any person of life, liberty, or property, without due process of law; nor deny to any person within its jurisdiction the equal protection of the laws.

This brief passage is the basis for establishing certain requirements for governmental bodies (e.g., the schools), private bodies receiving federal subsidies (e.g., the airlines), and private bodies engaged in interstate commerce (e.g., motel chains). These requirements prevent governmental and private bodies from denying equal opportunities and service to people because of unalterable or uncontrollable characteristics such as age, sex, race, or handicap. In many cases these requirements call for affirmative action† to reduce the harm done by the unequal treatment protected people have experienced in the past (Turnbull and Turnbull, 1978, p. 33).

The keys to these requirements are in the four principal concepts in the Fourteenth Amendment.

1. *Each person is guaranteed national citizenship.* "All persons born or naturalized in the United States, and subject to the jurisdiction thereof, are citizens of the United States and of the State wherein they reside."

2. *National citizenship takes precedence over state citizenship.*

---

*Now the Office for Special Education and Rehabilitation in the U.S. Department of Education.

†*Affirmative action* is developing a plan for, and carrying out, activities to make up for the problems caused by discrimination, i.e., the lost opportunities, the wrong development, or both.

"No state shall make or enforce any law which shall abridge the privileges or immunities of citizens of the United States."

3. *Each person is guaranteed due process.** "Nor shall any state deprive any person of life, liberty, or property, without due process of law."

4. *Each person is guaranteed equal protection.†* "Nor (shall any state) deny to any person within its jurisdiction the equal protection of the laws."

These are indeed powerful concepts, and they apply widely.

Actions by the federal government and by state and territorial governments have translated these constitutional principles into particular practices we must observe. In education, even though some legal provisions have been made over the years since the early 1800s, a major shift came with the U.S. Supreme Court ruling in *Brown* v. *Board of Education of Topeka, Kansas* (1954) and regulations in the Civil Rights Act of 1964. These actions required that black pupils be given their right to equal protection in education. The precedents established are now extended and transferred to handicapped pupils, among others.

Handicapped people's civil rights have been reaffirmed in cases decided by the courts, in laws passed by the legislatures, and in regulations developed by the executive branches of governments. The range of these activities is remarkable. They pertain to such areas as definition and classification, equal educational opportunity, employment, access to buildings and transportation systems, freedom of choice (competency and guardianship), freedom from residential confinement, housing and zoning restrictions, equal access to medical services, procreation, marriage and rearing children, contracts, ownership and transfer of property, voting and holding public office, and miscellaneous other rights such as licenses, insurance, immigration and emigration, privacy, and recreational and athletic programs (e.g., Burgdorf, 1980a, pp. xvii–xxxiii). In addition, the number of court rulings, statutes, regulations and commentaries pertaining to these rights is prodigious. For example, the American Bar Association uses more than 250 categories to classify material on the legal rights of handicapped individuals (ABA, 1976, pp. 7–9). As Burgdorf (1980*a*,

---

* *Due process* means that we must give the person the chance to contest before a judge any decision which we as government officials make about him or her. And we must give him or her a chance to use lawyers and expert witnesses and to appeal each judgment to higher administrative levels of government and higher jurisdictional levels of the courts.

† *Equal protection* means that we must use the same rules, criteria, and procedures with everyone. We especially cannot use different rules, criteria, and procedures because people differ on unalterable or uncontrollable characteristics such as age, race, sex, or handicap.

p. v) put it in the preface to his 1127-page volume reviewing and analyzing legal rights of handicapped persons:

> I confess to having seriously underestimated the magnitude of this undertaking; early in the 1970's many of us advocates for handicapped people naively believed that all the "law" in this area could be toted around in a single file folder. The length of this book bears witness to the fact that there is actually a large and still-growing body of legal precedent and legislation dealing with the rights of handicapped individuals, and this relatively long volume resulted only after it was culled down from a manuscript over three times as extensive.

Two federal laws — Public Law 94-142 and Public Law 93-112 — bring together relevant precedents in the court rulings and statutes and apply them to exceptional pupils in schools. PL 94-142, The Education for All Handicapped Children Act of 1975, requires that handicapped youngsters from infancy through age twenty-one receive *a free appropriate public education* and *an equal educational opportunity*:

1. The pupil must have the special education and related services he or she needs at public expense under the direction and supervision of the local school system.
2. The pupil must have a written individualized education program (IEP) based on his or her special educational needs. The pupil's progress within the IEP must be reviewed at least annually and revised as appropriate.
3. The pupil must have nonacademic services (e.g., extracurricular activities) and physical education services.
4. The pupil must be placed in the least restrictive environment appropriate to his or her needs.
5. The pupil's advocates* must participate in all decisions.
6. The pupil and his or her advocates must have due process, equal protection, and confidentiality in identification, testing, instructional planning, and placement procedures.

In addition, we must engage in extensive searches for exceptional pupils who are unserved or inadequately served.

The means for enforcing PL 94-142 is in Section 504 of PL 93-112, The Vocational Rehabilitation Act of 1973. It prescribes that "no otherwise qualified handicapped individual in the United States... solely by reason of handicap can be excluded from participation in, be denied the benefit of, or be subjected to discrimination *under any*

---

*Parents, guardians, lawyers, and expert advisors and, if appropriate, the pupil.

program or activity receiving Federal financial assistance," [emphasis added]. In addition, PL 93-112 complements PL 94-142. It extends coverage to students eighteen to twenty-one and older who want basic education or other schooling. It prohibits discrimination in employment. And it requires barrier-free environments in public facilities or in private facilities getting governmental subsidies or engaging in interstate commerce.

These court rulings and laws are further backed up by Section 1983, Civil Action for Deprivation of Rights, U.S. Code, Title 42, the Public Health and Welfare:

> Every person* who ... subjects, or causes to be subjected, any citizen of the United States or other person within jurisdiction thereof to the deprivation of any *rights, privileges, or immunities secured by the Constitution and laws*, shall be liable to the party injured in an action at law, suit in equity, or other proper proceeding for redress. (Emphasis added)

Section 1983 means that we must not violate a pupil's civil rights either by failure to act (dereliction of duty) or by wrongly acting (malpractice). We are personally liable to a suit and money damages if we do not do what we as educators know is right, *or reasonably should know is right.* This duty extends to providing a pupil his or her rights to an education within the safeguards of equal protection, due process, and confidentiality as we use the four tools — classification, testing, individualizing instruction, and placement — because these entitlements and protections are now secured by both the Constitution and the laws. This potential liability will indeed serve as a powerful incentive to our putting the law into action with exceptional pupils.

However, it is difficult to carry out the law and serve exceptional pupils as we should. In education as in all social institutions, there is a continual tension and competition among the rights of one individual versus the rights of another individual, the rights of the individual versus the rights of the group, and the rights of the minority versus the rights of the majority. These age-old, and continuing, conflicts show up in obstacles to putting into practice PL 94-142 and other aspects of public policy respecting the handicapped. Several people have identified problems. For example:

☐ not enough money to meet the needs of both exceptional and nonexceptional pupils;

☐ not enough time and energy to do testing and planning with the care and attention to detail they need;

---

* "Every person" here includes people in all states and territories following any statute, ordinance, regulation, custom, or usage.

☐   not enough money and time for hiring enough people to offer expanded services; and

☐   not enough money and time to give as much service to uninformed clients as to those who are more experienced and resourceful. (Weatherly, 1977, pp. 9–13)

However, despite such obstacles, the force of the law grinds on. Lawsuits over enforcement of handicapped pupils' rights under PL 94-142, Section 504 of PL 93-112, and Section 1983 of 42 U.S.C. have reached the courts. Generally, the courts have reaffirmed pupils' rights and have ordered enforcement. In short, we must deal with the obstacles and implement the law.

To be sure that the pupil has a free appropriate public education and an equal educational opportunity, the law essentially requires that we:

☐   Use the traditional tools for adjusting education to pupils' individual differences — classification, testing, individualizing instruction, and placement; and

☐   Use procedural safeguards — advocate participation, due process, equal protection, confidentiality, and monitoring — with these traditional tools in order to prevent past problems from recurring.

We must accomplish four tasks to meet these requirements. In today's terminology, these tasks are identification and planning, nondiscriminatory testing, individualizing instruction, and placing the pupil in the least restrictive environment.

The rest of this book is organized around these four tasks. In Chapters 2 and 3 we look at the tasks noncategorically, that is, independent of any particular type of exceptional pupil. We define each task, look at ways it has been used wrongly in the past, and then examine current practices — ways the task is used within the safeguards of the law. The idea is that once we understand the tools thoroughly in isolation, we can better keep down mistakes in using the tools to deal with the very complex problems of the various types of exceptional pupils. Given this background, we then examine, in Chapters 4–11, how the tasks apply to each type of exceptional pupil. That is, we can see current practices in carrying out identification and planning, nondiscriminatory testing, individualizing instruction, and placement in the least restrictive environment with the respective types of exceptional pupils — the speech- and language-impaired, the hearing-impaired, the visually impaired, the physically handicapped, the gifted and talented, the mentally retarded, the learning-disabled, and the seriously emotionally disturbed.

A great, and healthy, thing about our nation is that we can contain so   **Issues**
much diversity of opinion among competent, well-intentioned people
as they go about meeting society's responsibilities. We certainly
see such honorable and healthy diversity among special educators'
opinions about the best ways to use classification, testing, individualized instruction, and placement to fit education to exceptional
pupils' individual differences. Table 1.4 summarizes major questions
and issues that we are currently wrestling with. In Chapters 2 and 3
we consider the nature of these issues as they cut across categories
of exceptional pupils. As we deal with each different type of exceptional pupil in the remaining chapters, we can see how these issues
show up over and over.

TABLE 1.4 CURRENT ISSUES IN SPECIAL EDUCATION.

Classification

Problem: To decide whether classification really helps us serve exceptional pupils better or whether it harms them.

At Issue: Answers to questions about categorization, labeling, and
definitions.

Categorization

1. Should we assign exceptional pupils to categories, e.g., mentally retarded or emotionally disturbed?

2. *Or* should we take a noncategorical approach and base
education on each pupil's strengths and weaknesses as we
find them?

3. If we categorize, should we categorize along strengths or
weaknesses?

Labeling

1. If we decide to put exceptional pupils in categories, should
we name those categories, e.g., emotionally disturbed or
blind?

2. *Or* should we avoid labeling exceptional pupils — especially
with negative labels?

3. What options exist for grouping without labels?

Definitions

1. If we decide to categorize exceptional pupils, what characteristics shall we use in defining the category? What cutting
points shall we use in deciding whether a pupil belongs in a
category?

2. When there are conflicting definitions, what definitions
shall we use? Are some definitions more functional than

(continued)

TABLE 1.4 *(continued)*

others? Does the usefulness of a definition depend on the purpose it is used for?

Testing

Problem: To decide what information we need and how can we get that information without mistakes that harm exceptional pupils.

At Issue: Answers to questions about validity, reliability, and standards for comparisons.

Validity

1. What information do we really need to identify and plan for exceptional pupils: What behavior should we measure?
2. What tests and other procedures give us true measures of that behavior? What tests should we discard as useless?

Reliability

1. What are the sources of error when we test exceptional pupils?
2. What tests and other procedures can we use to keep such mistakes at a minimum?

Standards for comparison

1. What standards should we use in judging exceptional pupils: Should we compare them to the requirements of the task to be accomplished? To normal pupils? To other pupils who have the same gifts/talents or handicaps?
2. What conditions cause us to discriminate against exceptional pupils when we compare them to normal pupils? That is, what are the sources of test biases?
3. What procedures can we use to deal with these discriminatory conditions?

Instruction

Problem: To decide what should be the nature of the educational and therapeutic programs for exceptional pupils.

At Issue: Answers to questions about objectives, schedules, procedures, settings, and therapies.

Objectives

1. What should we teach exceptional pupils: Academic content? Reading and other literacy skills? Survival skills? Perceptual processes? Linguistic processes? Daily living skills? Social skills? Emotional responses? Other material?

2. Should we reduce everything to be taught to behavioral objectives which we specify ahead of time?

Schedules

1. Should we allow an exceptional pupil to progress at his or her own rate? *Or* should we try to keep him or her on the group's schedule?

2. Should we eliminate objectives if an exceptional pupil does not have time to accomplish what other pupils do because he or she requires more time to learn? *Or* should we keep him or her in a grade longer or in school longer?

3. Should we add objectives if an exceptional pupil learns faster than others do? *Or* should we let him or her move through school in a shorter time?

Procedures

1. What methods should we use with exceptional pupils? How much should we use tutoring or solitary activity? How can we decide which methods are effective and yet not harmful to pupils?

2. Should we use behavior modification? For what purposes? What role do more humanistic procedures have?

3. What media and devices should we use with exceptional pupils? How can we decide which media and devices are effective and yet not harmful to pupils?

4. Is there an Aptitude × Treatment Interaction? That is, do pupils differ in the way they learn or only in how fast they learn and how far they can go? What does this mean for teaching?

Settings

1. What effect does the environment have? How can personnel and space be best arranged to be effective and helpful to exceptional pupils?

2. Should we structure and control the environment carefully? Should we allow it to be more fluid and flexible?

Therapies

1. How do we decide about priorities? Should some types of therapy be given precedence over other types? Over special education?

2. Are there common elements among the various types of therapy? Among the therapies and special education? How can the therapists and teachers reinforce each others' work?

(continued)

TABLE 1.4 *(continued)*

Placement

Problem: To find the best balance in decisions about where we should use scarce resources, what is best for the exceptional youngster, and what is best for other pupils.

At Issue: Answers to questions about right to education, early childhood special education, institutionalization, school location, transportation, facilities, extracurricular activities, and safety.

Right to education

1. Who is eligible for education at public expense? Should anyone have priority when resources become scarce?
2. Should we continue to provide education to severely/profoundly handicapped pupils if they do not show some learning after a reasonable period?

Early childhood special education

1. What behavior are we trying to train in infant stimulation and preschool education programs? That is, what instructional objectives should we have for young exceptional children?
2. Do infant stimulation and preschool education programs really give exceptional youngsters a head start? Would we accomplish as much if we delayed education until pupils were more mature?
3. Can we really influence characteristics such as intelligence, or are they fixed by inheritance?
4. What instructional procedures and settings are most beneficial and comfortable for young exceptional pupils?

Institutionalization

1. Should we prohibit placing an exceptional youngster in an institution?
2. *Or* should we base decisions about institutions on the ecology of the situation — the whole set of interacting forces around the exceptional youngster?
3. If we decide to keep residential schools, how can we ensure that they are helpful to the exceptional youngster?

School location

1. How can we determine what is the least restrictive environment which will enable an exceptional pupil to function with comfort and benefit?

2. Should ability grouping (special classes) ever be used with exceptional pupils? Full time? Part time? Under what conditions?

3. What does mainstreaming really mean? When is it helpful? Harmful? If we decide that it should be used, how can we make it work?

Transportation

1. How do we decide what a handicapped youngster's special transportation needs are? A gifted/talented youngster's? Is there a point of diminishing returns when the time a pupil spends in transportation to special centers for special education or therapy outweighs the value of the services he or she receives?

2. How much should special transportation be a public responsibility? How much a family responsibility?

Facilities

1. When do inappropriate facilities become barriers to handicapped youngsters' access to education and other public programs?

2. What is the public responsibility to provide equal access? Is it justifiable to send a youngster to a more distant facility with no barriers instead of modifying a nearby structure which has barriers?

Extracurricular activities

1. Should handicapped youngsters participate in extracurricular activities with other youngsters? How much should the activities be adapted to the handicapped youngsters' limitations and safety needs?

2. Should there be special extracurricular activities restricted only to handicapped youngsters? Only to gifted/talented youngsters?

Safety

1. Who is responsible for assuring a handicapped youngster's safety?

2. Is it ever justifiable to rule a program off limits to a pupil if it is extremely hazardous to him or her as, for example, using power machinery in industrial arts would be for a pupil who has hemophilia? If not, how can we guarantee the pupil's safety?

Summary

UNDERSTANDING EXCEPTIONAL PUPILS

Definition   Exceptional pupils are those who show such extraordinary individual differences in their patterns of growth and development that they need special help in learning the common tasks in our culture. They include gifted and talented pupils and handicapped pupils — those who have speech/language impairments, hearing impairments, visual impairments, physical impairments, mental retardation, learning disabilities, and emotional disturbances.

Prevalence   Different investigators report different numbers of pupils. The average estimates are 3% to 5% gifted and talented and 10% handicapped. Since the early 1900s and before, we have seen a steady growth in the numbers of exceptional pupils we serve. By the late 1970s, we were serving most exceptional pupils, even though we still had some to locate and serve.

Central Concepts   Cultural tasks, normal growth and development, and individual differences are central concepts in our understanding and serving exceptional pupils.

Relationships among the Central Concepts   Learning and performing the cultural tasks are necessary for living successfully in our society. Normal growth and development in certain crucial characteristics, such as hearing and intelligence, are necessary for learning and performing the cultural tasks through conventional means. A pupil's extraordinary individual differences — or diverging markedly from normal growth and development in one or more of the crucial characteristics — interferes with his or her learning and performing the cultural tasks through conventional means. As time goes by, the pupil's increasing divergence from normal growth and development causes more and more delay and problems in learning the cultural tasks. As a result, the pupil needs special help — special education and related services — to enable him or her to master the cultural tasks. This special help must begin early, before the increasing divergence over time leads to more — and often unnecessary — delay and problems in learning the cultural tasks.

EDUCATING EXCEPTIONAL PUPILS

Educating exceptional pupils is a matter of providing for their individual differences in such a way that they diverge from normal growth and development as little as possible and learn to perform as many of the cultural tasks as they can.

We use four tools to deal with pupils' extraordinary individual differences. These are placement, individualizing instruction, testing, and classification.

Tools

The four tools for fitting education to pupils' individual differences have been used for a long time in many countries. However, sometimes in the past the tools have been used incorrectly and insufficiently. Decisions about pupils have been made arbitrarily, and their confidentiality has been violated. These problems have harmed some exceptional pupils.

    The problems in using the tools required legal relief. In the United States, this legal relief is based in the federal Constitution — especially the Fourteenth Amendment, which guarantees national citizenship, the precedence of national citizenship over state citizenship, due process, and equal protection. Public Law 94-142 and Section 504 of PL 93-112 bring together the various court rulings and statutes and apply them to exceptional pupils in the schools. In sum, they guarantee a free appropriate public education, equal educational opportunity, equal public access, and equal employment opportunity to handicapped youngsters and adults. Section 1983 of Title 42, U.S. Code, backs up these laws by making personally liable anyone who violates another person's legal rights — through either malpractice or dereliction of duty. Carrying out the laws requires that we use the traditional tools for adjusting education to pupils' individual differences and, at the same time, that we protect pupils with the procedural safeguards against errors. In today's terminology these requirements mean that we must use identification and planning, nondiscriminatory testing, individualizing instruction, and placing the pupil in the least restrictive environment as our tools for providing for pupils' individual differences.

    Specialists working with exceptional pupils show a healthy diversity of viewpoints about many questions pertaining to classification, testing, individualizing instruction, and placement. The viewpoints we accept influence the way we use identification and planning, nondiscriminatory testing, individualizing instruction, and placing the pupil in the least restrictive environment.

Using the Tools for Providing for Individual Differences

2

Classification and Testing

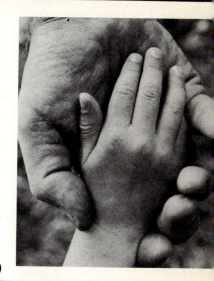

TOPICS

Identifying and planning for exceptional pupils

CLASSIFICATION AS A TOOL FOR DEALING WITH INDIVIDUAL DIFFERENCES

The classification process
Benefits of classifying exceptional pupils

LEGAL SAFEGUARDS IN CLASSIFICATION

Problems in classifying exceptional pupils
The law governing classification
Accountability

Nondiscriminatory testing of exceptional pupils

TESTING AS A TOOL FOR DEALING WITH INDIVIDUAL DIFFERENCES

Testing defined
Criterion-referenced tests
Norm-referenced tests

LEGAL SAFEGUARDS IN TESTING

Problems in testing exceptional pupils
The law governing testing

Identifying and planning for exceptional pupils

In contemporary practice, classification accompanied by the legal safeguards undergirds identifying exceptional pupils and planning for them. Identifying and planning for pupils is, of course, the first task in providing them with a free appropriate public education and an equal educational opportunity.

CLASSIFICATION AS A TOOL FOR DEALING WITH INDIVIDUAL DIFFERENCES

To review: Classification is a tool to support placement and instruction. We use it to identify pupils who need to be, and who can be, treated in a certain way because they are alike on important characteristics.

The Classification Process

As we have seen, diversity is a rule of life. Individuals vary among themselves and within themselves. Look at two trees. They differ in size, shape, color, leaves, bark, and so on. Look at any one tree. Two sections of bark are not the same, two leaves are not the same, and two limbs are not the same.

The human need to organize individual elements of the environment is also a rule of life. We form groups on important characteristics. For trees, we use characteristics such as size, shapes of leaves, makeup of bark, nature of root systems, and annual physiological cycles to form categories such as pine trees and oak trees. For school pupils, we use characteristics such as chronological age, intelligence level, academic achievement levels, and interests to form categories such as fourth graders, mentally retarded pupils, and physical science students.

This process of grouping individuals on one or more common characteristics is classification. Synonyms are concept formation, conceptualization, and categorization. Categories are groups of individuals classified on one characteristic or on several characteristics at one time. Synonyms are classes, groups, or, more generally, sets. Labels are the names of categories.

Learning and using concepts accurately is one of the most valued activities in education because classification is an important intellectual tool for organizing separate instances in our environment. We reduce the range of the individual differences we must deal with, and we identify regularities that enable us to communicate and agree on what actions we should take. For example, consider how you would react to these two comments: "There is a snake behind you" and

"There is a vine behind you." Further, consider your relative reactions to: "There is a rattlesnake behind you." "There is a garden snake behind you." "There is poison ivy behind you." "There is a grapevine behind you."

Classification can reduce differences and uncertainties, but it can never eliminate them. Individuals in a category still differ on characteristics not used to classify them, and these remaining differences influence their behavior. As a result, even after classification, we have some unknowns to investigate further. For example, we expect to move away from a rattlesnake. However, whether we actually move and how fast depends on such rattlesnake characteristics as whether it is satiated, dormant, ill, injured, defanged, milked, senile, or any combination of these characteristics not used in classification.

Now, in terms both more formal and more obviously fitting to exceptional pupils:

> Taxonomies have been developed for many years in a variety of disciplines to classify phenomena. They provide a way of simplifying complicated universes to make them easier to deal with — both conceptually and practically. Comprehensive and unambiguous classificatory systems can greatly enhance scientific advances. Historically, taxonomies were first developed in biology in the mid-1700s. The approach taken was inductive: Biologists observed and identified hundreds of plants and established criteria based on a specific purpose to group the plants. Their purpose was to classify plants so as to reflect their evolutionary development. Therefore, the purpose of the problem defined the criteria. Once set, criteria established the guidelines for the classification system which resulted. This same approach has also characterized the establishment of taxonomies in special education. (Armstrong, 1976, p. 105)

Our purpose for classifying pupils is to be sure that they get the special education and related services they need. We classify pupils by characteristics important in doing the cultural tasks because pupils who differ extraordinarily on these characteristics have special needs to which we must fit education so that they can learn and perform the cultural tasks. In practice, we usually classify pupils on one characteristic and label them by that characteristic, e.g., speech- or language-impaired or physically handicapped. Sometimes we classify on more than one characteristic and label pupils multihandicapped or with a compound name, e.g., deaf/blind.

As it happens in all classification, categorizing exceptional pupils reduces individual differences, but does not eliminate them. Pupils grouped on one characteristic, or even on more than one characteristic, still differ on other characteristics which also influence how

Classification is a tool for reducing, though not eliminating, differences among pupils.

quickly they learn, and how well they perform, the cultural tasks. For example, we classify into one group, and label "legally blind," pupils whose visual acuity is 20/200 or less in the better eye after correction and who have difficulty seeing print and other visual stimuli. By definition, blind pupils are alike on visual acuity and response to visual stimuli, and they are different from members of other groups on these classifying characteristics. At the same time, blind pupils are not necessarily alike on such other characteristics as physical maturity, intellectual ability, and emotional stability, which are not used in classifying them. One regularity — one thing that they are alike on — is that blind pupils have problems traveling independently because they cannot see where they are going, how to get there, and how to avoid dangers. They have special needs for training if they are to master the cultural tasks requiring independent travel, such as reaching their jobs or finding friends. Departing from this regularity, how quickly, and how well, they learn independent travel skills depends on how much vision they have left and can use, how hard they are willing to try, how quickly they learn, and similar characteristics.

Again, our purpose for classifying exceptional pupils is to be sure that they get the special education and related services they need. Classification helps accomplish this purpose because by categorization, we reduce the range of individual differences we must deal with, and we identify regularities that enable us to communicate and agree on what actions we should take. In practice, then, categories and labels have two benefits — as a focus for legal and philanthropic action and as indicators of treatment.

Benefits of Classifying Exceptional Pupils

Labels and categories have long been the focus for legal and philanthropic action. The granddaddy of voluntarism has been the March of Dimes campaign, started by F. D. Roosevelt to collect money to fight polio, which crippled him. Since then, we have had public subscription campaigns in many areas to raise money for working with various kinds of handicaps, e.g., campaigns against lung diseases, birth defects, muscular dystrophy, nephritis, and multiple sclerosis.

Labels and categories as a focus for action

Similarly, professional groups, parent groups, and handicapped people themselves have organized on the basis of their common interests. And the label for the handicap is often used in the organization's name. Among the many examples are the American Association on Mental Deficiency, American Association for the Gifted, American Foundation for the Blind, Association for Children with Learning Disabilities, United Cerebral Palsy Association, Muscular Dystrophy Association, National Association of the Deaf, National Society for Autistic Children, and Association for Retarded Citizens. We have national, state, and local organizations. As an example of the activities of such groups, it is interesting to note that in *Wyatt* v. *Stickney,* the landmark case so important in handicapped peoples' being guaranteed the right to treatment, *Amici Curiae** included not only the United States of America and the American Civil Liberties Union, but also the American Orthopsychiatric Association, the American Association on Mental Deficiency, the National Association for Mental Health, and the National Association for Retarded Citizens.

Finally, a good bit of law is tied to particular groups of exceptional pupils (e.g., Burgdorf, 1980*d*). These laws specify who will be treated, what order they will be treated in, and how they will be treated and protected. For example, PL 94-142 names the mentally retarded, deaf, hard of hearing, visually handicapped (blind, partially sighted), deaf/blind, orthopedically impaired, other health-impaired, seriously emotionally disturbed, specific learning-disabled, and speech-impaired. In PL 94-103 mental retardation, cerebral palsy, epilepsy, autism, and

---

* Friends of the Court, that is, people who help in the case even though they are neither the plaintiffs nor defendants in the lawsuit.

dyslexia are listed in the law for special attention as developmental disabilities. PL 95-561 specifically mentions the gifted and talented. Monies for education and other activities are limited to these groups. Agencies administering these laws must report by category label how many pupils have the exceptionality and how many are served before they can obtain federal funds and pass them through to local programs that use the money to pay for teachers, therapists, transportation, supplies, and other activities.

Labels and categories as indicators of treatment

"Every diagnosis is a prognosis" is a very old saying. It means that when we figure out what group to classify someone in (*diagnosis*), we know how to treat him or her and what response to expect (*prognosis*). For example, if we diagnose a pupil's disorder as diabetes, we know what kind of special dietary and other treatments to use and what help to expect from that treatment. Similarly, this treatment and expectation would differ from the treatment and expectation we would have for a pupil whose problem is diagnosed as epilepsy.

Beyond our using categories and labels as a focus for legal and philanthropic action, our sole justification for classifying pupils into groups such as emotionally disturbed, talented, or blind is to get indicators of treatment, that is, to get information that suggests special education and related services different from what we give to nonexceptional pupils or to other types of exceptional pupils.

Categories and labels serve as a focus for treating exceptional pupils.

LEGAL SAFEGUARDS IN CLASSIFICATION

The benefits of classification make it a powerful tool in serving exceptional pupils. However, at the same time, like any tool, classification can cause a lot of trouble if we misuse it or if desirable procedures become such routines that we use them mechanically and mindlessly.

Problems in Classifying Exceptional Pupils

> The children, all four-year-olds, are meeting school for the first time. They enter the gym with their mothers and are handed over to aides who will guide them through a labyrinth of *screening stations* for the next three-and-a-half hours.
>
> The work begins. Now, hop on your right foot. Satisfactory. Turn around. Satisfactory. Follow my finger with your eyes. Fail. Can you hear this noise? Is it higher or lower? Put your right hand on your left knee. Tell me the names of these pictures. Give me three blocks. What is a shoe made of? Make me a copy of this drawing.
>
> The battery of tests goes on: VMI, Frostig, Peabody, ITPA, WISC, House-Tree-Person, WRAT, Bender, Hooper. Visual acuity, perceptual motor, visual motor, audition. Tests to uncover dyslexia, dyscalculia, aphasia, agnosia, distractibility, mixed dominance, dyspractic movements, developmental lag, CNS damage, minimal brain dysfunction, or other new names indicating a variation from the magic norm of the diagnostician.
>
> In the next room, the mothers are busy relating family social and medical history to counselors, nurses, teachers, learning clinicians. Age your child walked? Weaned? Two-parent family? Child aggressive or very active or irritable? Discipline in home?
>
> When the mother and child finally depart the school, they leave behind an enormous mass of clues, conjectures, notes, guesses, scores, checklists, scales — all going to create a profile of the student the school expects the child to be in the fall. At the age of four, the child has acquired a set of labels and designations that could stay with him the rest of his life. (Divoky, 1974, p. 20)

Problems arising from the misuse of classification have long been recognized (e.g., Johnson, 1946). The particular problems we see operating in our work with exceptional pupils are limited relevance, arbitrary cutting points, false dichotomies, overgeneralization, labeling and stereotyping, and misclassification.

Limited relevance

We consider a category and a label to be relevant to an educational decision if it helps us choose a treatment and know what to expect from that treatment. For example, we teach braille to blind pupils, but not to sighted pupils. We provide speech and language therapy to deaf pupils and physical therapy to crippled pupils. In each case we expect the pupils to respond in a certain way, and we judge the success of the treatment by whether they do indeed respond as we expect them to.

However, the educational relevance of categories and labels is limited by two things. One, some of the categories and labels we use with exceptional pupils do not indicate how we should educate them. Two, individuals remain different on other characteristics even after we group them on a particular characteristic. Let's look at these two ideas and how they limit the relevance of categories and labels we use with exceptional pupils.

The idea that pupils should be treated differently, depending on their group membership, i.e., their handicaps or their talents, is based on a concept called Aptitude×Treatment Interaction.* This concept has been discussed and fought over for a very long time as the issue of quantitative differences versus qualitative differences in pupils' learning. *Aptitude×Treatment Interaction* means that treatments affect *one kind* of person one way and *another kind* of person another way.

The aptitudes involved determine how certainly we can identify interactions — what treatments work best for which groups. Sensory and physical characteristics (vision, hearing, muscular/motor function) and some language characteristics interact with certain instructional tasks (objectives), methods, and materials. For example, a deaf pupil learns better by visual methods than by verbal methods, whereas a hearing pupil does about as well with verbal methods as with visual methods. This notion of an Aptitude×Treatment Interaction for the physically and sensorially handicapped is based on common observation. We have little research on the matter.

Things are more uncertain for psychological characteristics such as emotional/social characteristics, general intellectual abilities, and specific learning abilities (Cronbach and Snow, 1977; Ysseldyke, 1973). We have considerable evidence from comparisons of groups such as the high anxious and low anxious; the intellectually retarded, normal, and superior; and the learning-disabled and nonlearning-disabled (e.g., Blake, 1976; Hammill and Larsen, 1974; Haring and Bateman, 1977). These comparisons do not reveal consistent Aptitude×Treatment Interactions. Such groups often differ in how quickly they learn a task, when they are ready to begin learning, and how much they can learn. However, they do not differ consistently in the way they respond to various treatments — to various methods and materials used to teach them. This unclear state of affairs is general to the whole area of study and action based on the interaction of psychological characteristics and treatments.

Aptitude refers to any characteristic used to group individuals. *Treatment* refers to any procedure used to work with individuals. *Interaction* refers to differences among groups in *how much* a treatment helps or hinders their learning or in *what way* a treatment helps or hinders them.

Categories and labels have limited relevance for educational decisions for another reason. As we have seen, pupils still differ on other characteristics important to learning even after we group them on one or two characteristics, as we do in identifying particular handicaps or talents. Therefore even though grouping reduces individual differences some and gives us some indication of treatment, especially for the physically and sensorially handicapped, we still have important differences among pupils that we must study and provide for.

The limited relevance of categories and labels is a *problem*, then, because they either help us only partly or not at all in making decisions about how to educate pupils. That is, for the physically and sensorially handicapped, we can use categories only as partial indicators of methods and materials for treatment. Although the range of uncertainty is reduced, even after classification, we must study each pupil and plan for him or her individually. For the psychologically exceptional, we cannot use categories as indicators of methods and materials for treatment. Instead, we must plan separately for each pupil, basing our decisions on his or her particular characteristics, not group membership.

"Cutting point" is the term for the test score* we use in separating individuals into different categories. Individuals whose scores are below the cutting point go into one group, and those whose scores are above the cutting point go into another group. The statistical concepts of normality and variation are helpful in understanding cutting points and their arbitrary nature. Consider a series of steps to review these ideas.

Arbitrary cutting points

☐ Suppose we measured the heights of 5000 nine-year-old boys who have histories of good health and adequate nutrition and who represent a cross section of genetic backgrounds.

☐ Suppose we plotted these boys' heights on a graph, with number of boys on the vertical axis and height on the horizontal axis.

☐ Suppose we drew a line through the points, showing the number of boys at each height.

Our result would be a bell-shaped curve, often called a *normal curve*.

We can describe the normal curve statistically. We can show the average for all individuals by an index of central tendency, such as the mean. We can show how some individuals differ from the average by an index of variation, such as the standard deviation. The normal curve has some very important regularities connected with the mean

---

* The test, of course, is one measuring the characteristic used in classifying the individuals.

and standard deviation. For example, 50% of the cases fall below the mean, 50% above; 34% of the cases fall between the mean and one standard deviation below the mean, 34% between the mean and one standard deviation above it (Fig. 2.1).

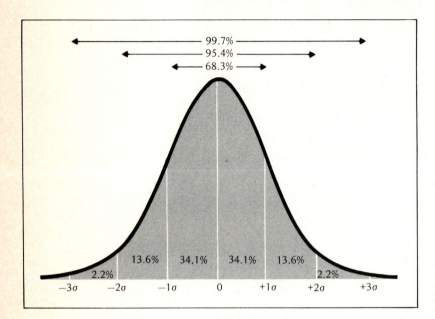

Fig. 2.1
The regularities in the normal curve.

The normal distribution holds for physical characteristics. We would also get normal curves for such features as the boys' weight, how fast they can run, how many pounds they can lift, and the ages at which they started walking. Stated another way, physical characteristics are distributed normally in the population. We do not know how psychological characteristics are distributed in the population. However, most psychological tests have been built to yield approximately normal distributions.

Now let's connect the statistical meanings of the terms normality and variation to the psychological meanings. Statistically, *variation, variant,* and *variance** refer to how individuals differ, or vary, from the average, the midpoint of the normal distribution. *Normality,* the state of being normal, refers to the middle of the range of scores on a characteristic. These statistical meanings begin to take on psychological meanings when we arbitrarily set cutting points and start

---

* *Deviation, deviant,* and *deviance* are synonyms for *variation, variant,* and *variance.* These synonyms suggest negative feelings and images to many people.

assigning pupils to groups. For example, in deciding about normality in nine-year-old boys' heights, we could say that normal is one standard deviation above and one standard deviation below the mean — the points 68% of the boys fall within. Or, just as arbitrarily, we could set the limits of normality at 1.96 standard deviations — the points 95% of the boys fall within. In the same way, we could select any other set of cutting points. Note three things very carefully.

1. Normality and variation are abstractions and arbitrary. That is, they are not concrete and independent from us, as, for example, a tree and a cat are. Instead, they are whatever we say they are and thus define with cutting points we select at will.

2. When we define *normal*, we at the same time define *not normal*, that is, *abnormal, variant,* or *deviant.* In other words, *normal* refers to individuals who fall within our arbitrary cutting points, and *abnormal, variant,* and *deviant* refer to individuals who fall outside of our arbitrary cutting points.

3. With usage over the years, values and attitudes have been attached to terms. *Normality* is reacted to as good or as desirable. *Abnormality, variant,* and *deviant* are reacted to as not good or as undesirable.

Now let's tie these statistical concepts and their psychological interpretations to exceptional pupils. Pupils are identified as exceptional when their scores on a measure of a characteristic fall outside the arbitrary cutting point dividing average from nonaverage. The AAMD's* actions in the recent past illustrate the arbitrary nature of cutting points dividing average from nonaverage. Different cutting points have been used in the succeeding versions of the AAMD *Manual on Terminology and Classification in Mental Retardation* (Grossman, 1973, 1977, in press; Heber, 1961). In the 1961 version the cutting point was IQ 84. In the 1973 and 1977 versions the cutting point was tied to two standard deviations below the mean on the Stanford-Binet Intelligence Test (IQ 68) or the Wechsler Scales (IQ 69). In the version currently being prepared, references to standard deviations have been dropped, and the cutting point has been placed at IQ 70.

Arbitrary cutting points can be a *problem.* Pupils can be harmed if people act as though normality and variation — and variation's hurtful synonyms — are real things instead of abstractions which can be changed at will. For example, mental retardation, i.e., mental deviance, is not real in itself; instead, it refers to a point on the range of

---

* American Association on Mental Deficiency.

intelligence. And related to this, confusion can occur when cutting points are changed. As we have seen, with a change in cutting points, a pupil can be classified and labeled as retarded one day and as normal the next day. That is, a person with an IQ of 70 would have been classified as retarded in 1961–1973, nonretarded in 1973–1980, and retarded again in 1980.

False dichotomies Dichotomizing is dividing individuals into groups that do not overlap. Dichotomizing is an old idea. However, there really are few true dichotomies. For example, being physically either *alone* or *not alone* is a true dichotomy. A person is either this or that. Beyond this, most things are a matter of degree. For example, we have degrees of strength. A person is never either *strong* or *not strong*.

With exceptional pupils, we use cutting points to identify groups as, for instance, either normal or not normal, retarded or normal, blind or sighted. Yet as we have seen, cutting points are arbitrary points we use for convenience. We can locate them anywhere we choose; therefore they do not yield true dichotomies in nature. As a result, falsely dichotomizing becomes a *problem* because our cutting points usually do not separate pupils who really differ in the sense of needing different instruction and placement (Haring, 1978).

To continue our example with the AAMD system, a youngster with a Stanford-Binet IQ of 90 would be classified normal, one with an IQ of 65 mildly retarded, one with an IQ of 40 moderately retarded, and one with an IQ of 15 severely/profoundly retarded. Does "either/or" thinking help us deal with these youngsters? If these categories were true dichotomies, we could expect the youngsters to be completely different — either this or that. And we could treat them accordingly with different instruction and placement. In practice, of course, we would find very little difference in the normal and mildly retarded youngsters and in the moderately and severely retarded youngsters, and in turn very little need to treat them too differently.

Overgeneralizations We overgeneralize when we take the characteristic pupils were grouped on, label them on the basis of that characteristic, organize all of our reactions around that one label, and ignore differences among pupils bearing the same label. We are all members of many categories. When these overlap or are closely related, it is difficult to attend to each separately and not focus on the most troublesome or distressing. Overgeneralizing is a *problem* because we do not consider *all* of the pupil's difficulties and assets and do our educational planning accordingly. For example, a pupil could, at the same time, be severely crippled, slightly visually impaired, intellectually gifted, articulate in speech and language, neglected by parents but cared for very well by grandparents, highly motivated, emotionally stable, socially isolated, and a very high achiever academically. To over-generalize by focusing on any of these characteristics — a strength or a weakness — would be to underrepresent the pupil's complexity, both the potentialities and the problems. Plans based on any one characteristic would be out of step with the other characteristics. In other words, the pupil needs multifaceted plans to fit his or her multi-faceted characteristics.

Sometimes we treat an abstraction as a thing. Sometimes we stereo-type by assigning a particular set of characteristics to a group and do not consider that individuals in that group might differ from one another. For example, thinking that he was dealing with IQs, "one Florida teacher gave his students more challenging assignments after noticing numbers ranging from 130 to 160 after their names; only later did he discover that they were locker numbers" (*Time*, 12/19/77, p. 89). This probably apocryphal, and certainly very old, story that keeps resurfacing means that the teacher treated the ab-stractions, the numerals, as the thing — in this case learning ability — and started acting according to a fixed idea about high intellectual ability.

Labels and stereotypes

As we deal with exceptional pupils, treating abstractions as things and stereotyping get mixed up with labeling. The situation is bad when it comes to a label such as genius, a kind of person most people would like to be or to associate with. The problem is profound when it comes to labels such as mentally retarded or emotionally disturbed, kinds of persons many people do not want to be or to associate with. The bad effects of labeling is an old issue in psychology and sociology as well as in special education. We have had many essays and research reports on the matter, and this material has been reviewed extensively (e.g., Murphy, 1976; Gottlieb and Siperstein, 1976). Essentially, the *problems* are: (1) putting down the pupil and causing him or her un-necessary pain; and (2) treating the pupil wrongly and causing him or her to learn inappropriate behavior. These problems show up in four assertions.

1. *Labels such as mentally retarded have a stigma attached.* Pupils may be isolated or rejected because they bear the label. Those of us who have had our consciousness levels raised about attitudes connected with being a woman, a he-man, a good Episcopalian, a black, a dutiful son, a warm teacher, and so on, know how classifica-tion, labeling, and society's expectations influence our reactions to ourselves and other people's reactions to us. If you doubt it, tell a

new acquaintance, a prospective spouse, or a potential employer that you have dyslexia, epilepsy, hemophilia, manic-depressive psychosis, incontinence, or any other difficult condition which other people cannot check easily by observation — and then watch what happens and see how you feel.

2. *Labeling sets up a circular process which becomes a self-fulfilling prophecy.* On the basis of the label, we expect pupils to act in certain ways. We treat them accordingly. In turn, they begin to act as we expect them to. That is, through learning, they become the label. For example, when pupils are labeled blind, people expect them to be helpless in certain situations and treat them as helpless in those situations. Given such treatment, these pupils do not learn to be independent, and therefore they stay helpless. That is, they learn to act blind and helpless because they are treated as blind and helpless.

3. *Pupils may suffer educational loss when they are classified and labeled and then placed in a special class designed for the labeled group.* Two things may happen. The pupils may not be exposed to as intensive instruction and motivation as they would get in a regular class with unclassified children. The longer they stay in a special class, the further behind they may fall. In a relatively short time, it becomes very difficult for them to return to the regular class.

4. *Pupils are often labeled and treated in an inappropriate special way in a special class.* This may happen when their problem is no impediment to school learning and special education is unnecessary. For example, a pupil who has hemophilia needs careful protection from physical wounds, but does not need special education in the sense of different objectives, schedules, procedures, or settings for instruction.

The evidence and opinions on these assertions conflict. Sometimes labeling is harmful, sometimes not. Many factors operate, e.g., what the label is, what experiences the pupils had before they were labeled, whether other pupils call them ugly names and make fun of them, and how their families react to the labels (e.g., MacMillan, 1977, pp. 277–278).

Misclassification

Wrongly classifying a pupil is a *problem* because it can lead to wrong placement and instruction. Misclassification often happens because it is difficult to specify categories and to measure characteristics.

Difficulties in specifying categories

As we have seen, individuals in the same universe may be classified in many ways. Thus the sorting criteria and cutting points we use depend on our purposes. For example, on thinking about trees to buy, we would use the criteria hardwood and softwood if we were interested in firebuilding, deciduous and evergreen if we were interested in avoiding leaf raking in autumn. This is as it should be because, again, classification is merely a tool. Troubles arise, however, when we are trying to get a basis for building a helping program. For example, many sets of criteria have been proposed for judging a person's mental health, and no one set of criteria completely separates healthy people from unhealthy people (e.g., Armstrong, 1976).

With different classification systems, we have different criteria, cutting points, and labels. In special education the difficulties are tremendous. We have several sets of categories for each type of handicapped pupil. For example, more than thirty-eight terms have been employed to describe or distinguish people classified as having minimal brain damage (Clements, 1971).

The many differences in classification systems and criteria are extremely serious. An individual might be considered handicapped under one system but not under another. Or the person might be considered to have one handicap under one system and another handicap under another system. This conflict leads to communication problems and difficulty in deciding about treatment and placement. Terrible mistakes can be made (e.g., Burgdorf, 1980 *a, b, c;* Burgdorf and Bersoff, 1980; Leviton, 1980; Shuger, 1980). For example, in the not too distant past, being labeled in some ways could result in a person's being institutionalized and perhaps subjected to such procedures as lobotomy or sterilization. And today certain categories and labels could result in a person's placement in certain special classes and on a track away from preparation for college or advanced technical school. In addition, we are currently hearing discussions about people in certain classifications being subjected to actions such as electroconvulsive therapy and various forms of drug therapy, loss of the right to vote, loss of the right to bear and rear children, and prohibition from entering into legal contracts.

Difficulties in measuring characteristics

Errors are highly likely when characteristics used in classification are difficult to measure. Many psychological characteristics used in classifying exceptional pupils — e.g., intelligence, emotional adjustment, language, learning abilities, reading achievement, and adaptive behavior — are very difficult to measure reliably and validly. Testing errors are frequently made, and they lead to frequent classification errors (e.g., *Larry P.* v. *Riles,* 1979). As we will see when we consider nondiscriminatory testing, many things can interfere with test performance.

As an illustrative preview, let's consider cultural bias. Cultural bias means that pupils from some cultures are penalized when they are judged by tests developed for a different culture. They simply have not had the teaching, and the chance to learn the information they need, to give the answers that the test questions require. A symptom of a problem here is the higher than expected number of black and chicano children classified and labeled as mentally retarded. Logically, we can expect intelligence to be distributed the same way whatever the racial or ethnic group, because intelligence tests are designed to yield normal distributions. Therefore we must suspect that the tests penalize some pupils when the percentage of minority groups classified as retarded exceeds the percentage of those groups in the total population (Songren, 1976).

The Law Governing Classification

Essentially, the court rulings say that we may classify exceptional pupils for legitimate educational purposes, but that we must not mis-classify them (e.g., McCarthy, 1976; Semmel and Heinmiller, 1977; Zettle and Abeson, 1978). As noted above, the public laws require classification in their administration. For example, PL 94-142 protects groups by name; these groups are labeled mentally retarded, deaf, hard of hearing, blind, partially sighted, seriously emotionally disturbed, physically handicapped, and learning-disabled. In addition, PL 94-142 and Section 504 of PL 93-112 require that we do systematic searches, called the *Child-Find*, to locate these types of exceptional pupils. Further, we must report on the number of pupils *in each disability category* located and served.

At the same time, the law has strict safeguards against the problems in classification. These safeguards, called *procedural safeguards*, require advocate participation, due process, equal protection, confidentiality, and monitoring when we classify pupils.

Advocate participation

Parents or guardians participate in the decisions about classification. They join in deciding what information about the pupil is needed, in evaluating how true that information is, and in deciding what it means for working with the pupil. To be sure that advocates participate, they are informed about all activities and invited to all meetings.

Due process

Advocates must agree to the procedures used in classification and to the final decisions. If they do not, they have the right to appeal through the administrative levels of the local and state school systems and through the jurisdictional levels of the federal courts.

Equal protection

The procedures used in classification must be nondiscriminatory. Errors that would penalize a pupil because of his or her handicap or racial, ethnic, or cultural background are guarded against. Pupils must be included in categories whose rights and protections they need, but not in categories whose rights and protections they do not need.

Information about procedures employed, data used, and decisions made in classification must be kept private. Only people who have a need to know have access to that information. Wrong information or unnecessary information is purged from the records.

Confidentiality

There is a continuing check at local, federal, and state levels to be sure that handicapped pupils who need services are found. And at the same time, there is close evaluation of procedures to be sure that the requirements for advocate participation, due process, equal protection, and confidentiality are observed.

Monitoring

In summary, people have wrestled with the issue of classifying exceptional pupils for quite a long time. Both benefits and problems in classification are recognized (e.g., Hobbes, 1975). Some have tried to avoid the undesirable effects of classification by being truly non-categorical. Others have sought to fall back on degree classifications, e.g., Special Needs (Level I); Special Needs (Level II), which are "*new* categorical not *non*-categorical" phrases (MacMillan, 1977, p. 246).

What we now have is a compromise. "Therefore, what may be required is a categorical aid formula administered in a non-categorical manner" (Blatt, 1972, p. 258). Translated into the terms of PL 94-142, such comments lead to a two-step process of identification and planning within the procedural safeguards. That is, we use categories and labels to identify protected pupils and then go further to build a program of special education and related services for each pupil, based on his or her characteristics, while at the same time we observe the protections against errors. Beyond this, we need to use common sense, tolerance, and a willingness to value each individual (Warren, 1976, pp. 91–92).

Accountability is the current term for our responsibility to do our duty and to do it accurately. Antonyms are negligence, dereliction of duty, nonfeasance, misfeasance, and malpractice. We have two areas of responsibility with exceptional pupils (e.g., Gee and Sperry, 1978; Turnbull, 1975).

Accountability
The concept of accountability

1. *Pupil protection.* We must forsee risks and safeguard pupils from physical danger.
2. *Program adequacy.* We must use correct procedures as we work with pupils. At a minimum, correct procedures are those guaranteed in the United States Constitution and court rulings or specified in the laws.

Sanctions are penalties for failure to meet responsibilities covered by accountability requirements. We have three kinds of sanctions: loss of public monies, disciplining of public officials, and personal liability.

1. *Loss of public monies.* As we have seen, the laws guarantee the pupil's civil rights — access to school, protection in evaluation and placement, confidentiality, due process, advocate participation, and a free appropriate education. Quite simply, school systems that do not comply face loss of monies to help pay for special education, related services, and other school costs.

2. *Disciplining of officials.* Public officials may be held in contempt of court when the court rules that some action must be taken and the official refuses or fails to take that action. Penalties for contempt are fines, jailing, or both.

3. *Liability for damages.* Institutions, or individuals within institutions, may be penalized through liability for damages. That is, they may be sued for their actions, and if they lose, they may have to pay damages. Sometimes officials have personal liability and must pay damages with their personal money. As noted in Chapter 1, Section 1983 of 42 U.S. Code holds that we may be sued for personal damages if we violate a person's rights that are guaranteed through the United States Constitution and court rulings or through laws. Exceptional pupils' rights are guaranteed through the federal Constitution and through subsequent laws and court rulings. Therefore they are covered through Section 1983 of 42 U.S. Code, and we may be sued if we violate their rights through neglect or wrong practices (Turnbull, 1976, pp. 362, 366).

The doctrine of sovereign immunity is frequently cited as exempting institutions and public officials from personal liability as a sanction. This is an important issue for educators, since we are public officials.*

Sovereign immunity means that the government and its representatives cannot be sued for damages. The doctrine has a long history under English common law. Following from the idea of the divine right of kings, the sovereign had absolute immunity — "the king can do no wrong." This immunity covered public officials because the actions of the sovereign's subordinates were considered to be the sovereign's actions.

Over the years, sovereign immunity became more limited. As things now stand, at least in civil rights cases, we are liable if our

---

* The analysis here is based on Henning (1976) and Turnbull (1976).

actions violate a person's constitutional rights. This ruling applies even if we acted in good faith when we failed to act or acted wrongly. The crucial test is whether we knew, or *reasonably should have known*, that our actions violated the pupil's rights.

This restriction of sovereign immunity and expansion of personal liability to public officials will have tremendous effects in our dealing with exceptional individuals. It is one thing when state agencies, institutions, and school systems are being sued as organizations. It is another thing when we are being sued as individuals who will have to pay off with our own money.

It is the law. We must ensure that the pupil gets an equal educational opportunity and a free appropriate public education. To carry out the law, we must find out whether the pupil qualifies for one of the protected categories and if so, we must extend special education and related services along with the procedural safeguards against discrimination and error. We use the Child-Find and the IEP as our guides for accountability in carrying out the law.

Accountability through the Child-Find and the IEP

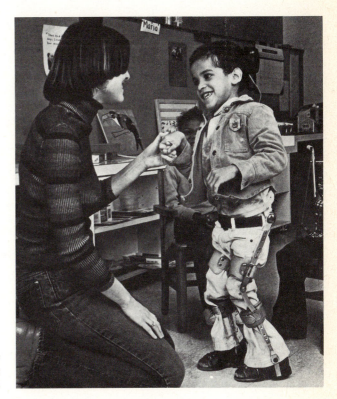

The Child-Find guarantees accountability in classifying exceptional pupils; the IEP, in providing them with the services they need.

Child-Find is the label for the active searches we must do to locate exceptional pupils. Essentially, we classify the pupil into one of the groups protected by the laws. Different people use different procedures; however, most use three stages: awareness, screening, and referral. In the *awareness* phase we use TV, radio, personal contacts, and other media to help the public realize the kinds of problems exceptional pupils have, the services available to them, and the need to get them in touch with helping programs. In the *screening* phase we look at the pupils' characteristics to see whether they possibly have problems. In the *referral* phase we arrange for pupils with possible problems to be studied further by appropriate specialists. Figure 2.2 portrays areas that usually need to be assessed and specialists who do

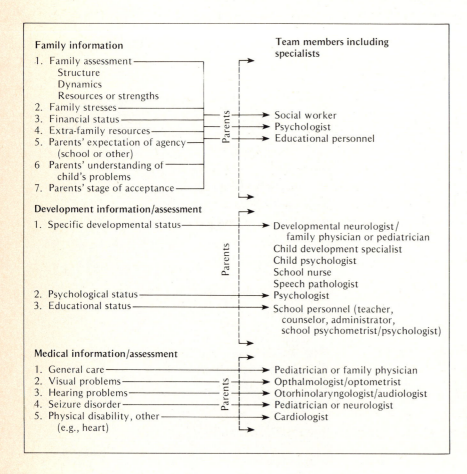

Fig. 2.2
Areas assessed in the referral phase of the Child-Find and specialists who do that assessment. (Swanson and Willis, 1979, p. 16, adapted from Thomas and Marshall, 1977, p. 20.)

that assessment. This diagnosis has two purposes: (1) to get information for deciding whether the referred pupils should be classified into one of the categories protected by the laws; and (2) to get information for deciding how best to work with the pupils and their families.

Once we classify the pupil, we use the *Individual Education Program* (IEP) as a management tool for organizing the testing, individualized instruction, placement, and procedural safeguards he or she needs (Torres, 1977; National Advisory Committee on the Handicapped, 1976). In PL 94-142 the IEP is defined as:

1. A written statement for each handicapped pupil

2. Developed in a meeting by

a) A representative of the local education agency (LEA), or an intermediate educational unit (IEU) who shall be qualified to provide, or supervise the production of, specially designed instruction to meet the pupil's unique needs,

b) the teacher,

c) the pupil's parents or guardians, and

d) whenever appropriate, the pupil.

3. The statement includes:

a) the pupil's present levels of educational performance,

b) annual goals, including short-term instructional objectives,

c) the specific educational services to be provided to the pupil (i.e., instructional services, nonacademic services, related services, and services to ensure the procedural safeguards),

d) the extent to which the pupil will be able to participate in regular education programs,

e) the projected date for initiation and anticipated duration of the services,

f) appropriate objective criteria and evaluation procedures, and

g) a schedule for determining, at least annually, whether instructional objectives are being achieved.

Figure 2.3 shows the activities required to develop an IEP and the people who are responsible for doing these activities. Appendix 1 has IEP's illustrating how these activites may be carried out for particular handicapped pupils. The first IEP is for an emotionally disturbed youngster named Tommy (Wood, 1979, pp. 45–47). The second IEP is for a learning-disabled youngster named John (Turnbull *et al.*, 1978, pp. 81–84).

Parent approval and IEP educational services started

Review, revise, and redesign the IEP when appropriate

Initiated by parents or professionals

Parents/service provider

Determination of actual placement; finish IEP and secure signatures from the parents

Administrator of special education

Meetings conducted to determine written statements that include:

- A statement of the present levels of educational performance of the child
- A statement of annual goals, including short-term instructional objectives
- A statement of specific educational services to be provided to the child, and the extent to which the child will be able to participate in regular educational programs
- The projected date for initiation and anticipated duration of such services, and appropriate objective criteria and evaluation procedures and schedules for determining, on at least an annual basis, whether instructional objectives are being achieved (Section 602(19))
- Proposed type of program placement or alternatives

- A representative of the local educational agency, other than the child's teachers, who is qualified to provide, or supervise the provision of, special education
- The child's teacher or teachers, special or regular, or both, who have a direct responsibility for implementing the child's individualized education program
- One or both of the child's parents
- Where appropriate, the child
- Other individuals, at the discretion of the parent or agency

Parents contacted; IEP meeting date, time, and location mutually convenient established

Administrator of special education or designee

Assessment conducted and eligibility criteria are met; child is determined to be handicapped

Multidisciplinary team members, chosen on basis of need for assessment data of student

Fig. 2.3
Tasks and responsibilities — developing an individualized education program (IEP). (Reprinted by permission from Torres, 1977.)

Nondiscriminatory testing of exceptional pupils

Testing carefully bounded with the legal safeguards has in today's practice become nondiscriminatory testing. Nondiscriminatory testing is the second task in providing the exceptional pupil with his or her rights to a free appropriate public education and an equal educational opportunity.

TESTING AS A TOOL FOR DEALING WITH INDIVIDUAL DIFFERENCES

As we have seen, testing is a tool for measuring individual differences. It supports individualizing instruction because we use test information in deciding how to fit teaching and related services to a particular pupil. It supports placement because we use test information in classifying pupils who can be grouped together to be taught alike and in deciding what special education and related services to use in that group teaching.

Testing, a tool for assessing individual differences, supplies evidence for decision making.

Testing Defined

To work most helpfully with a pupil, we need to know what he or she is like, what his or her characteristics are (e.g., Bertrand and Cebula, 1980). As in getting to know anyone, we can get to know a pupil best by being with him or her over a long period, observing closely how he or she responds to a wide variety of situations and then comparing these responses to an external standard — to particular tasks the pupil needs to accomplish or to other pupils' responses to the same situations. We use tests, for one reason, because we do not have enough time to get to know a pupil as well as we should.

A *test* is a procedure for systematically taking samples of a pupil's behavior. Tests include standardized aptitude and achievement instruments, diagnostic and evaluative devices, interest inventories, personality inventories, projective instruments and related clinical techniques, and many kinds of personal history forms (APA, 1974, p. 2). We can organize these procedures in many ways. Legally, distinguishing criterion-referenced tests from norm-referenced tests is important.

Criterion-Referenced Tests

Criterion-referenced tests are measures of competence — what a person *does* — in contrast to measures of ability — what a person *can do* (Tyler, 1978). In a criterion-referenced test a pupil's performance is compared to the instructional or therapeutic objectives for an area being tested (Moran, 1978). Instructional objectives contain or are accompanied by a statement of content and behavior and a criterion for mastery. For example:

General statement	*Criterion behavior*
The student will associate number in expanded notation with the numeral (hundreds, tens, and ones).	Given ten numbers in expanded notation form and four choices for each, the student will select the correct number for the expanded form, with 90% accuracy.

The test for this objective is clear-cut (Fig. 2.4). A pupil who performs nine items correctly has mastered the objective. One who gets seven items correct has not.

Note that there is no comment here about how well other pupils perform. The emphasis is on the pupil's performance of an objective for instruction or therapy.

We must observe an important condition when we use criterion-referenced tests. *And note well:* if we cannot meet this condition, we

Directions: Select the correct numeral for each expanded form. Minimum: 9 SCORE_____	Mathematics 4. 1. 3 C 11. 1. 1. 1. 1. 11. 2. 23. 40. 11 Pretest

1.   3 hundreds + 2 tens + 1 one =
    a) 3210   c) 6
    b) 321   d) 312
 	
2.   5 hundreds + 4 tens + 2 ones =
    a) 542   c) 11
    b) 5042   d) 524
 	
3.   4 hundreds + 7 tens + 9 ones =
    a) 4079   c) 479
    b) 20   d) 4790
 	
4.   8 hundreds + 5 tens + 7 ones =
    a) 857   c) 20
    b) 8570   d) 8057
 	
5.   1 hundred + 6 tens =
    a) 7   c) 106
    b) 160   d) 1060
 	
6.   2 hundreds + 4 tens + 5 ones =
    a) 245   c) 2450
    b) 2045   d) 11
	7. 1 hundred + 9 tens + 7 ones =
	    a) 197 c) 17
	    b) 1097 d) 1970
	
	8. 3 hundreds + 8 tens + 4 ones =
	    a) 384 c) 3084
	    b) 15 d) 3840
	
	9. 6 hundreds + 5 tens + 3 ones =
	    a) 6530 c) 653
	    b) 6053 d) 14
	
	10. 4 hundreds + 7 tens + 2 ones =
	    a) 13 c) 4750
	    b) 472 d) 4072

Fig. 2.4
Illustration of a criterion-referenced test. (Duval County, Florida, Public Schools.)

cannot give the test to the pupil without a high chance of making errors. The condition is that the pupil must receive the test items under the circumstances stated in the instructional or therapeutic objectives, and he or she must make the responses specified. If this condition is not observed, the test items may become different. In turn, we make errors because the pupil cannot show what he or she is capable of doing on the instructional or therapeutic objectives we think we are testing.

In a norm-referenced test a pupil's performance is compared to other pupils' performance (e.g., Salvia and Ysseldyke, 1978). The emphasis is on how well pupils perform in relation to one another, not on how many instructional or therapeutic objectives pupils have mastered.

Norm-Referenced Tests

Ability tests are a major category of norm-referenced tests. In ability testing we sample behavior with activities such as defining words and drawing circles and diamonds. For example, Table 2.1 shows the names of test activities on the Wechsler Scales — very frequently used intelligence tests. We interpret pupils' scores on such tests' activities by comparing them to the scores that other pupils make, i.e., we infer that they are average, above average, below average, and so on. We use these score interpretations to predict how well pupils should do in areas we think are related to intelligence, e.g., reading, success in a training program such as the regular-class program, or success on a job. For example, we expect a pupil who has above average intelligence to have above average arithmetic achievement. If the pupil is not above average in arithmetic, we consider that he or she is underachieving and start looking for problems and what we can do about those problems.

TABLE 2.1 SUBTESTS IN THE WECHSLER SCALES, LISTED IN THE ORDER OF ADMINISTRATION.

Wechsler Adult Intelligence Scale (WAIS) (Ages 16 Years +)	Wechsler Intelligence Scale for Children—Revised (WISC-R) (Ages 6–16 Years)	Wechsler Preschool and Primary Scale of Intelligence (WPPSI) (Ages 4–6½ Years)
Information (V)	Information (V)	Information (V)
Comprehension (V)	Picture Completion (P)	Animal House (P)
Arithmetic (V)	Similarities (V)	(Animal House Retest) (P)
Similarities (V)	Picture Arrangement (P)	Vocabulary (V)
Digit Span (V)	Arithmetic (V)	Picture Completion (P)
Vocabulary (V)	Block Design (P)	Arithmetic (V)
Digit Symbol (P)	Vocabulary (V)	Mazes (P)
Picture Completion (P)	Object Assembly (P)	Geometric Design (P)
Block Design (P)	Comprehension (V)	Similarities (V)
Picture Arrangement (P)	Coding (P)	Block Design (P)
Object Assembly (P)	(Digit Span) (V)	Comprehension (V)
	(Mazes) (P)	(Sentences) (V)

"V" denotes tests on the Verbal scale; "P" on the Performance Scale.
Source: Aiken (1979, p. 114).

We have absolutely no justification for giving intelligence and other norm-referenced tests if we do not make inferences and predictions. However, making inferences and predictions requires that we go beyond the test scores we obtain. It is a process open to many errors, especially when we deal with exceptional pupils. Key points to watch are validity, reliability, and norms.

Validity refers to how much test items are true samples of the behavior they are supposed to sample. We are concerned with three types of validity* — how well a test samples a given body of academic material, e.g., reading, how well a test samples behavior we can never see directly, e.g., intelligence, and how well a test's scores predict other behavior, e.g., intelligence test scores predict reading test scores.

Reliability refers to how accurate the test scores are. All measurement is plagued by chance errors. These chance errors cause scores we obtain to bounce around the pupil's true score. Reliability coefficients and standard errors of measurement based on reliability coefficients indicate how susceptible a test is to chance errors of measurement.

Norm comes from the word "normal"; it is a standard of performance which shows the levels of responses by pupils in a group defined in a certain way. If the norm group is defined by chronological age, we have an age norm; by school grade, a grade norm. For example, suppose that a pupil's performance leads to a grade placement score of 4.2 on the reading portion of a test such as the Metropolitan Achievement Tests. That means that the pupil is reading at a level attained by pupils in the norm group at the second month of the fourth grade. It does not tell us anything about what reading skills he or she can or cannot perform.

Norm groups are sometimes called *standardization groups*, meaning the groups on which the standards are based. They have a particular status on characteristics which can influence performance on the test, e.g., chronological age, brightness, socioeconomic background, and educational background. And they receive the test under particular, i.e., *standard*, instructions and procedures. Norms are usually based on samples of pupils from throughout the nation. Test builders use a simple procedure: They define the characteristics of a group, administer the tests in the standard way, figure levels of performance, and express these levels as scores. Most authors try to norm their tests on a cross section of the population. The more the norm group represents the total population, the more widely we can generalize the test results; in other words, the more individuals we can compare the pupil we test to.

We must observe two conditions before we can use a norm-referenced test with a pupil, that is, before we can compare a pupil to the norm group. *Again, note well.* If we cannot meet these conditions,

---

* Technically, these types of validity are labled content validity, construct validity, and predictive (criterion-related) validity, respectively.

we cannot give the test to the pupil without a high chance of making errors.

The *first condition* pertains to standard procedures of testing. The pupil being tested and the pupils in the norm group must have the same directions, use the same way for responding, and generally receive the test under the same circumstances. The norms do not apply if we violate this condition and do not give the test under the standard procedures. The test may be easier or harder for the pupil being tested than it was for the pupils in the norm group. In turn, this could make scores wrong in indicating what the pupil is really able to do.

The *second condition* in using norms in norm-referenced tests pertains to the pupil's background of experience with the language and materials in the test. The pupil being tested must have had the same chance as pupils in the norm group to learn the language used in the test and to learn how to use materials like those in the test items. If the pupil being tested has had either restricted experience or different experience, for him or her the test items are not accurate ways to sample the behavior they are supposed to sample. He or she may be more capable than he or she shows up on the test. For example, answer the questions below and see how well you can do with a test sampling the knowledge and language used there. What does this have to do with your experience background?

*Items from the Dove Counterbalance Intelligence Test**
The following ten items were selected from a test reportedly developed by Watts social worker Adrian Dove to measure intelligence as the term applies in lower-class black America:

1. A "Gas Head" is a person who has a: (a) fast moving car; (b) stable of "lace"; (c) "process"; (d) habit of stealing cars; (e) long jail record for arson.

2. If you throw the dice and "7" is showing on the top, what is facing down? (a) seven; (b) "snake eyes"; (c) "boxcars"; (d) "little Jones"; (e) eleven.

3. Cheap chitlings (not the kind you purchase at a frozen food counter) will taste rubbery unless they are cooked long enough. How soon can you quit cooking them to eat and enjoy them? (a) 15 minutes; (b) 2 hours; (c) 24 hours; (d) 1 week (on a low flame); (e) 1 hour.

4. "Bird" or "Yardbird" was the "jacket" that jazz lovers from coast to coast hung on: (a) Lester Young; (b) Peggy Lee; (c) Benny Goodman; (d) Charlie Parker; (e) "Birdman of Alcatraz."

*Source: Aiken (1979, p. 145).

5. Hattie Mae Johnson is on the County. She has four children and her husband is now in jail for nonsupport, as he was unemployed and was not able to give her any money. Her welfare check is now $286.00 per month. Last night she went out with the highest player in town. If she got pregnant, then nine months from now how much more will her welfare check be? (a) $80.00; (b) $2.00; (c) $35.00; (d) $150.00; (e) $100.00.

6. A "handkerchief head" is: (a) a cool cat; (b) a porter; (c) an Uncle Tom; (d) a hoddi; (e) a preacher.

7. "Money can't get everything it's true _____."
(a) but I don't have none and I'm so blue; (b) but what it don't get I can't use; (c) so make with what you've got; (d) but I don't know that and neither do you.

8. Which word is out of place here? (a) splib; (b) Blood; (c) grey; (d) Spook; (e) Black.

9. How much does a show dog cost? (a) $0.15; (b) $2.00; (c) $0.35; (d) $0.05; (e) $0.86 plus tax.

10. Many people say that "Juneteenth" (June 10) should be made a legal holiday because this was the day when: (a) the slaves were freed in the USA; (b) the slaves were freed in Texas; (c) the slaves were freed in Jamaica; (d) the slaves were freed in California; (e) Martin Luther King was born; (f) Booker T. Washington died.

Answers: 1(c); 2(a); 3(b); 4(d); 5(a); 6(c); 7(b); 8(c); 9(a); 10(b).

LEGAL SAFEGUARDS IN TESTING

Problems in Testing Exceptional Pupils

Errors in testing

There is a great deal of controversy about whether we should use tests or, if we use them, how we should use them. The basic problem is that using tests to collect evidence is fraught with error (e.g., Flaugher, 1978; *Larry P.* v. *Riles*, 1979; Tyler and White, 1979).

Chance errors befall all measurement. They are usually small, and they may be either positive (overestimates of the true score) or negative (underestimates). The theory is that the positive and negative errors cancel each other out. Information about test reliability helps us judge these chance measurement errors. For most tests we expect the pupil's scores to bounce around, i.e., to change, from five to ten points every time he or she takes a test.

Nonchance errors also frequently occur. These errors are caused by problems such as a deprived language background or emotional illness. They are usually negative, i.e., underestimates of what the individual is potentially able to do. They may be quite large. For example, a person's intelligence test scores may change over the years — sometimes as much as 25 to 100 points during the age span two through eighteen years, with continuing changes through middle age (e.g., Fisher and Zeaman, 1970; Hopkins and Bracht, 1975).

Nonchance errors are very complex, but essentially two things might happen. On the one hand, the test scores may be wrong. A pupil may be more intelligent than a test indicates, may have a higher level of academic achievement, may have more or less anxiety, and so on. On the other hand, at a particular time the tests sometimes yield fairly accurate measures of characteristics, such as intelligence, which theoretically should be relatively stable. However, the measures may change and become wrong as the person and his or her situation changes. To see a human side to these abstractions, consider this excerpt from a study conducted over a period of years.

> In 1966 a group of 24 Black children completing grade 4 were selected for a special class grouping for gifted children.* If conventional IQ and achievement criteria (e.g., 130 IQ and "superior" achievement) had been the only criteria for selection, only one of the students would have qualified. Interviews and teacher and peer nominations were the main bases for selection of these students...
>
> (The authors presented statistical evidence about the pupils' responses to the stimulation and opportunities they received in the special class for the gifted. The pupils made much larger gains in academic achievement than they were expected, on the basis of test evidence, to show; the intelligence and achievement test scores they obtained before the program were very poor in predicting scores on tests given during the program. Also, pre-program intelligence test scores changed during the program. The authors went on to show that after they left school the pupils did better than would be expected on the basis of their earlier test scores. They attended first-rate colleges and won many academic prizes and honors.) (Baldwin, 1977, pp. 620–621)

The situation shown here is the type of thing most of the furor over testing has been all about. Such testing errors are profoundly serious because they can lead to wrong decisions: "...it happens that this issue of bias in testing is currently appearing in public forums, including courts of law, and decisions are being made that have an impact on critical issues such as who shall be educated and who shall be employed" (Flaugher, 1978, p. 671).

We can tie the problem to the decisions we make in fitting an exceptional pupil's education to his or her individual differences.

1. Wrong test information can lead to mistakes in identification decisions. Such misclassification might lead us to deny some

---

* "Giftedness" is defined in the school district as "intellectual and academic excellence."

pupils special help they need or to put some students in special-help situations they do not need.

2. Wrong test information can lead to mistakes in decisions about individualizing instruction. We might select the wrong special education experiences and the wrong related services.

3. Wrong test information can lead to mistakes in placement decisions. We might place a pupil in an environment more or less restrictive than he or she needs.

4. Wrong test information can lead to mistakes in accountability decisions. We might change programs when we should not change them, or we might leave programs standing when we should change them.

Wrong decisions can cause losses of time and opportunity in a pupil's life, losses that are very difficult to make up. Also, wrong decisions can cause harm to the pupil's intellectual, emotional, and social well-being — harm that it is very difficult to remedy.

The story of B. J. Harris shows the impersonality, inefficiency, and perhaps dishonesty that a pupil and his or her family can encounter, and at the same time it shows the bewilderment and emotional trauma they may experience.

Small, frail-looking, a boy of few expressions, B. J. Harris has done his school work as diligently as he could, but usually with minimal success. "He tries," his mother says, looking up toward the ceiling as if to make certain God too has heard her. "I see the way he's worked, I know he tries. But it's never enough. If they paid a little more attention to him, maybe that would help. I think maybe it would too, you know. B. J. never has a problem passing his subjects, it's when he thinks he could do better than all right that things start coming down on his head. You take last year. There never was the slightest complaint from his teachers. I used to go there and talk with them and they'd always say he was doing fine. Not excellent, you understand, just fine. That was good enough for his father and me, you know what I mean? We knew he wasn't a genius like his sister Doreen. All we wanted was for him to pass on to the next grade and make sure no one put him in with the serious problem children. They got retarded children in the school. Children who don't learn so fast as the others. No problem, no problem, the teachers told us. We'd always smile, you know. Just as long as he was keeping up with the other children. Didn't want him to repeat any time, that's all we were praying for, you understand.

"So, the year finished up, and we were told he did good enough to pass. They weren't saying fine this time, just good enough to pass. . . .

"This September he goes to school and everything's all right for a week, two weeks maybe. Boy comes home from school looking all right — he's never one to let you know how he's feeling, like his father in that way — and I don't worry about anything. All I think about is that he did it. Then one day he comes home and says he ain't going to be with his friends anymore, in the same class. 'You flunk?' I asked him. I mean, I was surprised 'cause I had went to the school, and they said everything was all set for the next year. B. J. said he didn't flunk. Exactly. That's what he said, 'exactly.' 'What'd you do?' I asked him. I figured he made trouble. 'They got me in a special class,' he says. 'What kind of special class?' I ask him. 'I don't know,' he says. 'Just a special class with different kids.' 'They got you in the fourth grade, B. J.?' I ask him. 'I think so,' he says. 'I think it's the fourth grade.' 'What do you mean you think it's the fourth grade? Don't you know what grade you're in?' I knew, see, that he wasn't about to be moving up an extra grade. 'You go back there tomorrow' I told him, 'and you ask those people what grade you're in. I don't understand how a child can be in school and he don't even know what grade he's in. You do that for me, B. J.!' "

…[The next day B. J. reported:] " 'It ain't the fourth grade or the third grade. It's a special grade.' At first I thought he didn't know what he was talking about. 'You got to be in one grade or the other,' I told him. I remember shouting at him. We couldn't figure it out. Mr. Harris and I were getting ready to get to the school and find out for ourselves, 'cept you hate to go there all the time 'cause it makes the boy think you don't believe him.

"Then I understood. They got him in the special class with the problem children. That's what the boy was trying to tell me. He didn't want to come right out and say special class, 'cause he was disappointed and beginning to feel real bad. You can understand that. I understood. Women I was sitting with they understood too. But I felt ashamed. Something was wrong with the boy, and we never knew it. I thought everybody would think we were hiding his problem, making believe he could go to the same school with everyone else. But like I say, when school was out last year I went there and asked the teacher and they said everything was fine. 'You're sure now?' I said. They were sure. So that's where he is. They got him in their special class. They say if he does well maybe they can put him back where he belongs, with his friends, you know, in the real fourth grade."

After two months in his special class, however, B. J. Harris had stopped going to school. The class was tiring him, which was his word for boring him, and causing him to feel anxious. Each day there was less and less for him to do. Several children in the class, he reported, felt the same way. They would do some reading with a teacher, but then she would have to attend to the others for whom the written word meant little. It was days before they resumed *work together. B. J. found himself killing time, sitting in the same corner of the room watching the teacher and the other children. Most upsetting, he began to believe that school was making him act like the other children in class who he knew were far worse off than he. His belief was only confirmed by the reactions to him of his friends in the regular classes. After all, if he had been put in a special class, there must be something wrong with him. Trying to account for the change in B. J.'s status, they might have thought that he was a little weird to begin with....*

(Further investigation and arrangement for further testing revealed that B. J.'s test scores were in error and that he was wrongly placed in a special class. He returned to the regular class.) (Cottle, 1976, pp. 125–138)

We need to know where the testing errors come from so that we can prevent them. Major sources of errors in testing exceptional pupils are failure to meet the tests' conditions, poor tests and test users, and temporary pupil problems (e.g., Mercer, 1974; Soeffing, 1975).

Three situations — cultural differences, language differences, and pupil handicaps — can cause failure to meet the conditions for norm-referenced testing. In turn, this failure to meet conditions causes the test's norms to be wrong for a pupil and consequently leads to errors in measuring what he or she can really do in relation to the norm group.

Failure to meet the conditions for norm-referenced testing

Cultures differ in many ways, e.g., the amount of stimulation and attention given to children, the kinds of materials children have to work and play with, and the way language is used. The role of *cultural differences* in causing errors in testing is one of the oldest controversies in education and psychology. Earlier, the issue appeared as the nature-nurture controversy (e.g., National Society Study of Ed., 1928; 1940*a, b*). Today it has come around again in the arguments about race and intelligence (e.g., Cronbach, 1975; Gage, 1972*a, b*; Jensen 1972, 1979*a, b*).

On the one hand, some hereditarians maintain that characteristics such as intelligence are inherited, that a person's status on these characteristics does not change, that environmental influences have little impact on intellectual behavior (and intelligence test performance), that compensatory programs to counteract the harmful effects of environment have little value, and that eugenic planning and control are needed to reduce the number of people who have what they consider inherited weaknesses. On the other hand, some environmentalists maintain that to the contrary, intelligence is not inherited, that a person's status on such characteristics does change, that environmental influences have a great deal of impact on intellectual behavior (and performance on tests standardized with white, middle-class individuals from more privileged environments), that pupils can be trained in compensatory education programs to show more mature intellectual behavior (including intellectual skills sampled by intelligence tests), and that eugenic planning and control are unnecessary and ethically wrong.

Probably a middle ground is more appropriate in that champions are born to be made. That is, both heredity and environment make important contributions to a person's behavior. At any rate, the question cannot be answered unless we can meet the conditions required in using norms to judge pupils' behavior. And when the cultural background of the pupil being tested differs from that of the norm group, we violate condition 2, requiring a common background of experience and opportunity for learning to use the language and materials in the test. The scores will be wrong because they will not show what the pupil can really do in relation to the norm group.

Beyond the problem of cultural differences between the individual and the norm group, we have *language differences*. Quite simply, the necessary communication between the testee and the tester will suffer when the testee does not speak English or speaks English poorly or when the two give different meanings to the same words. Errors are highly probable when the tester cannot portray the directions and test items in a way the testee can understand them and the testee cannot portray the answers in a way the tester can understand them. Again, we violate condition 2 when the pupil's language background differs from that of the norm group. And the scores will be wrong because they will not show what the pupil can really do in relation to the norm group.

Pupil handicaps also cause pupils to differ from the norm group. Most obviously, handicaps might interfere with our using the standard procedures for testing, as required in condition 1. For example, blind pupils cannot see the test materials well enough to respond. Therefore they cannot take manual tests such as the performance items on the Wechsler scales, paper-and-pencil tests such as the Metropolitan Achievement Tests, performance and paper-and-pencil components of tests such as the Stanford-Binet, and tests requiring responses to visual materials such as the Peabody Picture Vocabulary Test and the Rorschach Ink Blots. Such problems render the tests' norms inappropriate for judging handicapped pupils. The tests' scores will not show how capable pupils really are; they just become additional measures of the pupils' handicaps.

Less obviously, handicaps might interfere with pupils' having the common background of experience and opportunity for learning to use the language and materials in the test that condition 2 requires. To illustrate: Blind pupils are restricted in independent travel and in learning about the visual stimuli which lie behind many words and concepts. For instance, one item on the Stanford-Binet requires knowledge about bicycle riding. Most young blind children have not had experience riding bicycles themselves or seeing other people on bicycles. Again, the pupil might be quite capable in relation to the norm group, but not have the test materials to show that capability on.

In sum, the *tests* are not appropriate because the *norms* are not appropriate when cultural differences, language differences, and pupil handicaps interfere with meeting the conditions required for norm-referenced testing. In a word, the test materials and procedures are discriminatory/unfair because they do not allow the pupil to show what he or she is capable of doing in relation to the norm group. Consequently, we may make errors and misjudge the pupil when we use a test that we cannot meet the conditions for.

Inappropriate criteria are a source of error in criterion-referenced tests. Sometimes pupils' handicaps interfere with meeting the condition that the pupil receive the test items under the circumstances stated in the instructional or therapeutic objectives and that they make the responses specified. For example, blind pupils could not respond to items based on an instructional objective requiring reading and writing, as in the following.

Failure to meet the conditions for criterion-referenced testing

General statement	*Criterion behavior*
The pupil will supply the spelling of consonant sounds in the initial, medial, and final positions of words.	Given sixty unique words written with consonant letters omitted from the initial, medial, or final position, the pupil will write the missing letters with 90% accuracy.

If pupils were given the material in oral form, the items would be harder than they would be in the written form. Further, pupils are penalized if they do not understand the language or if they have not had experience with materials and situations like those used in the test.

To be more explicit, the *tests* are not appropriate because *criteria* are not appropriate when pupil handicaps interfere with meeting the condition required for criterion-referenced testing. That is, the test materials and procedures are discriminatory/unfair because they do not allow the pupil to show what he or she is capable of doing in relation to the instructional or therapeutic objective the test is designed to sample.

Poor tests and test users Within the test situation, test users may be unqualified or careless. Tests may be unreliable, invalid, or faulty.

Unqualified test users Test use requires high qualifications. Test administration, scoring, interpretation, and beyond this, using test information in decision making are very complex, requiring extensive training and experience. Some procedures, e.g., using tests such as the Stanford-Binet to assess intelligence and devices such as the Rorschach to study personality, require special certification. People without proper qualifications often make errors. In addition, people testing handicapped pupils need training and experience working with those pupils. For example, anyone testing deaf pupils must understand deafness, how it affects pupils' communication abilities, and how it affects their psychological functioning. Many errors can be made in the absence of such knowledge.

Careless test users Test use requires extreme caution. Every test administration requires close attention to the standard procedures. And every test scoring requires safety double-checks to catch and eliminate errors. People who do not use proper caution often make errors.

Unreliable tests Tests must be reliable. With low reliability, we have a higher likelihood of chance error. In turn, we make wrong statements about a pupil's true score.

Invalid tests Tests must be valid. With low test validity, we are not measuring the characteristic we think we are measuring. In turn, we make wrong statements about a pupil's status on that characteristic.

Faulty test materials Test materials must be adequate. Sometimes directions or test items have errors and unclear parts. These problems interfere with the pupil's responding to the test and lead to errors.

Temporary pupil problems Sometimes pupils go through periods of physical or emotional problems. For example, pupils may be malnourished, or anemic or have any number of chronic health problems which make them weak. Similarly, pupils may go through periods of high anxiety, school phobia, and other emotional states which cause them pain and distract them.

Such weakness and distraction can interfere with test performance. They may wrongly depress test performance and thus lead to error. Later when these problems — and pupils' weaknesses or distractions — are removed, the causes of the depression in test performance are removed, and test performance may change.

The law guarantees nondiscriminatory testing to protect pupils.

Court rulings have provided safeguards to protect pupils in testing (e.g., Sorgren, 1976; Turnbull and Turnbull, 1978). Legislative statutes have extended these rulings to specific procedures we must follow. Essentially, the laws guarantee equal protection in evaluation, supported by participation and due process for advocates and pupils and confidentiality of information (PL 88-352, 1964; PL 93-112, 1973; PL 94-142, 1975).

The Law Governing Testing

Equal protection in evaluation means that test materials and the way they are administered must be fair. We must meet these requirements:

1. Standard instructions and directions provided by the test producers must be used.

2. Test materials and directions and the pupil's responses must be in the pupil's native language or other mode of communication (e.g., sign language).

3. Care must be taken to ensure that the pupil's handicap does not interfere with his or her showing what he or she is capable of doing.

4. Evaluation must not be limited to a single intelligence test. A wide range of characteristics must be sampled, e.g., health, vision,

hearing, social/emotional status, general intelligence, academic performance, communication status, and motor abilities, as appropriate.

5. The tests must be valid for the purpose they are used.

6. Evaluation must be done by an interdisciplinary team including at least one person trained in the handicap of the pupil tested.

Due process procedures essentially provide that the advocates: (1) *must* give consent for the evaluation; (2) *may* have access to all evaluation results; (3) *may* challenge any evaluation results and have redress; and (4) *must* participate in decision making based on evaluation data.

Confidentiality restricts the availability of the test information. Three concerns about test information are that it will not be available to the pupil and his or her advocates, that it will be available to people who have no business seeing it, and that it will be kept and jeopardize the pupil later in school and in getting admitted to college, getting a job, or in such activities as getting financial credit. The Privacy Act of 1974 has very strict regulations about confidentiality. These regulations were put into PL 94-142 to protect the confidentiality of the exceptional pupil. Essentially, they guarantee access, challenge and redress when the test information is questionable, and they guarantee destruction of test information that is incorrect and test information that is no longer relevant to planning for the pupil.

We can anticipate even more stringent protections in testing in the near future. This tightening will come as a result of the final judgment in *Larry P. v. Riles* (1979). *Larry P.* is a class-action suit in which the plaintiffs, six black elementary school children, asked that the defendant, the California State Education Department, be prohibited from using intelligence tests for placing pupils in classes for the educable mentally retarded. Federal District Court Judge Robert Peckham's ruling imposed a permanent moratorium on California's using intelligence tests for placement. This excerpt from Judge Peckham's summary illustrates the issues discussed above.

> This court finds in favor of plaintiffs, the class of black children who have been or in the future will be wrongly placed or maintained in special classes for the educable mentally retarded, on plaintiffs' statutory and state and federal constitutional claims. In violation of Title VI of the Civil Rights Act of 1964, the Rehabilitation Act of 1973, and the Education for All Handicapped Children Act of 1975, defendants have utilized standardized intelligence tests that are racially and culturally biased, have a discriminatory impact against black children, and have not been validated for the purpose of essentially permanent placements of black children into educationally

dead-end, isolated, and stigmatizing classes for the so-called educable mentally retarded. Further, these federal laws have been violated by defendants' general use of placement mechanisms that, taken together, have not been validated and result in a large over-representation of black children in the special EMR classes.

Defendants' conduct additionally has violated both state and federal constitutional guarantees of the equal protection of the laws. The unjustified toleration of disproportionate enrollments of black children in EMR classes, and the use of placement mechanisms, particularly the I.Q. tests, that perpetuate those dispropor-tions, provide a sufficient basis for relief under the California Con-stitution. And under the federal Constitution, especially as interpreted by the Ninth Circuit Court of Appeals, it appears that the same result is dictated. (Peckham in *Larry P. v. Riles*, 1979, pp. 3–4)

If this judgment is sustained on appeal, the precedent established could markedly limit people's using standardized intelligence tests with handicapped pupils — especially handicapped pupils who have different cultural and language backgrounds.

Summary

CLASSIFICATION AS A TOOL FOR DEALING WITH INDIVIDUAL DIFFERENCES

The Classification Process

Classification is the process of grouping individuals on one or more common characteristics. Our purpose for classifying exceptional pupils is to be sure that they get the special education and related services they need. We classify pupils by characteristics important in doing the cultural tasks, and arrive at groups such as speech-/language-impaired, physically handicapped, and so on. Classifying exceptional pupils reduces individual differences, but it does not eliminate them.

Benefits of Classifying Exceptional Pupils

Categories and labels serve as a focus of legal action and philanthropic action. For some groups, categories and labels partially indicate how to treat a youngster and what to expect from that treatment.

LEGAL SAFEGUARDS IN CLASSIFICATION

Problems in Classifying Exceptional Pupils

There are problems in classification that can cause harm to excep-tional pupils. These problems are limited relevance, arbitrary cutting points, false dichotomies, overgeneralization, labeling and stereo-typing, and misclassification resulting from difficulties in specifying categories and difficulties in measuring characteristics.

The Law Governing Classification
The courts have ruled that we may classify exceptional pupils for legitimate educational purposes, but that we must not misclassify them. The public laws require classification in their administration. At the same time, the law has strict procedural safeguards against the problems in classification. These safeguards are advocate participation, due process, equal protection, confidentiality, and monitoring.

Accountability
Accountability is the term for our responsibility to do our duty and to do it accurately. With exceptional pupils, we are accountable for pupil protection and program adequacy. Failure to meet our accountability requirements can lead to three kinds of sanctions: loss of public monies, disciplining of officials, and liability for damages. The doctrine of sovereign immunity does not protect us from personal liability if we violate a pupil's constitutional rights.

The Child-Find and the IEP are our guides, or channels, for carrying out the law — for finding out whether the pupil qualifies for one of the protected categories and, if so, for extending special education and related services along with the procedural safeguards against discrimination and error. Child-Find is the name for the active searches we do to locate exceptional pupils. The individual education program is a management tool for organizing decisions about testing, individualized instruction, placement, and the procedural safeguards for each pupil.

TESTING AS A TOOL FOR DEALING WITH INDIVIDUAL DIFFERENCES

Testing Defined
A test is a procedure for systematically taking samples of a pupil's behavior. Tests include a wide variety of instruments and devices.

Criterion-Referenced Tests
In criterion-referenced tests a pupil's performance is compared to the instructional or therapeutic objectives for an area being tested. An essential condition in criterion-referenced testing is that the pupil must receive the test items under the circumstances stated in the instructional or therapeutic objectives and that he or she must make the responses specified.

Norm-Referenced Tests
In norm-referenced tests a pupil's performance is compared to other pupils' performance. We use norm-referenced tests to make inferences about the pupil and to predict what he or she can do in areas related to the tests. To make such inferences and predictions, we must use tests that have high reliability, high validity, and appropriate norms.

Two essential conditions in norm-referenced testing are that the pupil receive the test under the standard conditions of testing used with the norm group and that the pupil's background of experience with the language and materials in the test be like that of the pupils in the norm group.

LEGAL SAFEGUARDS IN TESTING

All measurement has chance errors. We estimate these with reliability coefficients. In addition, tests are subject to nonchance errors: test scores may be wrong, originally correct measures may become wrong as the person changes. Wrong test information can cause us to make erroneous decisions in classification, individualizing instruction, placement, and accountability. In turn, these errors cause loss of time and opportunity in the pupil's life and harm to the pupil's well-being. The major reasons for error are poor tests and test users, temporary pupil problems, and failure to meet the tests' conditions because of pupils' handicaps, cultural differences, or language differences.

Problems in Testing Exceptional Pupils

Court rulings and legislative statutes have provided safeguards and specific procedures we must use to protect pupils in testing. These laws guarantee equal protection in evaluation supported by participation and due process for advocates and pupils and confidentiality of information.

The Law Governing Testing

3

Instruction and Placement

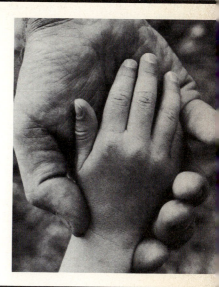

Individualizing instruction for exceptional pupils

Today, as in the past, individualizing instruction is the keystone for all of the activities needed to fit education to pupils' individual differences. The process, along with its procedural safeguards, is the third task in guaranteeing exceptional pupils a free appropriate public education and an equal educational opportunity.

INDIVIDUALIZING INSTRUCTION AS A TOOL FOR DEALING WITH INDIVIDUAL DIFFERENCES

To review: Individualized instruction* is a tool for fitting instruction to each pupil. We look at the pupil's strengths and problems and then choose the special education and related services he or she needs. Tom's case illustrates the process.

> When seven-year-old Tom entered the Lab School of the Kingsbury Center in Washington, D.C., he brought a mind above average in intelligence. Testing in some areas like verbal reasoning had placed him in a superior range for his age. He used adult vocabulary correctly, but he often twisted his tongue on certain syllables. He might say, "I gather this decision is umanimous" or "The emenies are encroaching upon us!"
>
> Tom could discuss the galaxies with the ease of a knowledgeable ten-year-old, yet he couldn't name the days of the week or the seasons. Nor could he count to ten correctly. Although his eyesight was normal, Tom could not perceive the difference between a straight line and a curved one. Symbols like dollar signs or percent marks made no sense to him. He was unable to link sound and symbol in order to recognize letters, much less words. He could not spell, follow simple directions, or interpret things beyond the most literal sense. He seldom paid attention in class because a very little noise or movement distracted him. And he was inflexible and unwilling to try new things to the point of bringing the same kind of sandwich to school every day for one year.
>
> None of these problems was apparent. On the surface, Tom appeared to be a typical, bright, attractive seven-year-old. His was the hidden handicap of learning disabilities. Medical specialists had found no brain damage, but they concluded that minimal brain dysfunction was evident. They recommended special education.

---

* An important distinction to note: Individualizing instruction means doing a separate plan for each pupil according to his or her needs, and it includes various settings. It does not mean teaching that pupil by himself or herself. Solitary activity is undesirable from both the pupil's and the teacher's viewpoints, and it should be used only when absolutely necessary.

Tom spent five years at the Lab School before he began to read and another two before he could read above grade level and catch up in math skills. But at the same time that he was struggling through the laborious process of reading readiness, Tom was being challenged in intellect and imagination. He was learning history, geography, and civics. Mainly through ingenious use of drama and all the arts in the Lab School's academic clubs, Tom was covering material from the Old Stone Age through the Renaissance to Discovery of the New World. Through "talking books" and tapes in the Lab School Media Center he was encountering literature like A Tale of Two Cities. At various times he was building a desk and chair, xylophone, go-cart, and a six-foot boat in the woodwork shop, following every step of planning, measuring, and constructing. In addition, as tangible proof of success in each project, Tom taught another child how to do the same thing. . . .

Always restless, Tom was constantly crashing into doors or falling into holes in the ground — partly because he wasn't looking where he was going and partly because he was impulsive and did not judge the space around him properly. Like a child of two or three on unfamiliar turf, Tom had no sense of what was in front, behind, above, or below. He couldn't tell left from right. . . .

After a few years Tom began to plan better and move more effectively. His use of space on paper also improved. The orderly placement of math problems on a page was real progress from his past practice of crowding all the problems down one side of the paper. He could follow some directions like "Write your name in the upper left-hand corner of the page."

In all his arts activities, the Logic Lab where games of logic and strategy are played, the Media Center, the academic clubs, and in special projects, Tom was developing central skills in reasoning, language, and general knowledge. In everything he did he was learning how to organize. He was asked to order his belongings, time, work, space, body, and — above all — his mind. In effect, a filing system was being created in his brain so that information could be slotted and retrieved at will. Tom had to be taught, step by step and over and over again, what most children can do automatically by school age. No opportunity was lost. Even the simple routine of lining up to leave a room became a game in which Tom and his classmates each represented a day of the week and proceeded to get into proper sequence in a line. In dozens of ways every day, Tom was immersed in patterns and asked to sort out and classify information into some order. . . .

All through his Lab School years, Tom worked in art, woodwork, dance, drama, music, film-making, and academic club projects to learn and refine academic and readiness skills necessary to advance in school. The special education was what Tom needed. Today, at 18, he is a senior in a regular high school and he's making plans for college. His SAT scores in English place him nationally in the 99th percentile and those in math put him in the 93rd percentile. He still has trouble with spelling. To cover this weakness, Tom organizes his work to allow extra time for the dictionary. Most of all, thanks to the years of painstaking guidance in Lab School classes and projects, Tom has embarked on a lifetime of learning — a problem he has learned how to handle. (Smith, 1978, pp. 18–23)

The Process of Individualizing Instruction

The process for individualizing instruction has been widely described. Writers differ somewhat on details, but they agree on essential elements. There are four phases: *testing* — finding out about the pupil's strengths and problems; *prescription* — on the basis of the test information, planning educational services; *teaching/therapy* — using the prescription with the pupil; *evaluation and revision* — determining how well the teaching/therapy worked and replanning as appropriate (e.g., Gartner and Riessman, 1977; Haring *et al.*, 1976; Larsen and Poplin, 1980; Wehman and McLaughlin, 1981). Table 3.1 shows examples of what specialists would consider as they plan the testing and educational services needed to individualize instruction for exceptional pupils.

It is easy enough to individualize instruction. However, it is time-consuming. Therefore ready-made materials for teachers have been developed by private individuals and by people using funds from the federal government. As a result, we have available an extremely large number of systems for individualizing instruction. In *regular education* these systems go under such labels as Individually Prescribed Instruction (IPI), Programs for Learning in Accordance with Needs (PLAN), Individualized Mathematics Curriculum Project, and Mastery Learning (Gronlund, 1974; Hambleton, 1974). Individualized instruction has, of course, long been proposed as the *raison d'être** for *special education.* It is labeled with various terms such as "clinical teaching" and "diagnostic and prescriptive teaching" (e.g., Flaherty, 1976; Gillespie and Sitko, 1975; Laycock, 1980; Weisberger, 1975). In addition, we have many systems developed by special educators, e.g., the Peabody Language Development Kits, the Guide to Early Developmental Training, and the CAMS — Curriculum and Monitoring System (Dunn and Smith, 1965; Wabash Center, 1977; Utah State University, 1977, respectively).

Special Education

"Special education is specially designed instruction to meet the unique needs of the pupil" (PL 94-142, 1977, Sec. 121a.5). In designing instruction any educator — a special educator or a regular

---

* "The reason for being."

TABLE 3.1 EXAMPLES OF FACTORS CONSIDERED IN INDIVIDUALIZING INSTRUCTION.

Sample Disability	Professionals for Specific Care	Special Teaching Techniques Required?	Likely to Affect Vocational Choice?	Likely to Affect Independent Living Choice?	Likely to Affect Social and Recreational Choices?
Visual disability/ blindness	Ophthalmologist Optometrist Optician Educator	Yes	Yes	Possibly	Yes
Hearing disability/ deafness	Otorhinolaryn- gologist Audiologist Educator	Yes	Yes	Possibly	Yes
Seizure disorder	Primary care M.D./develop- mental neurologist Educator	Possibly	Possibly	Possibly	Possibly
Mental retarda- tion	Psychologist Psychometrist Educator	Yes	Yes	Possibly	Probably
Cerebral palsy	Primary care M.D. Developmental neurologist Physical therapist Educator	Yes	Possibly	Possibly	Probably

Source: Swanson and Willis (1979, p. 17), adapted courtesy of Ellidee D. Thomas, M.D., Child Study Center, Oklahoma City.

educator — works with four components: instructional objectives, schedules, procedures, and settings. To the extent that special education is special, we make selections for exceptional pupils different from those we make for normal pupils. We select different objectives, different schedules, different procedures, or different settings. What testing reveals about the pupil's characteristics determines what selections we make and whether these selections differ from the selections we make for normal pupils. Sometimes we select only different objectives; sometimes only different schedules; sometimes only different procedures; or sometimes only different settings. And

sometimes we make different selections for more than one component. Again, the selections depend on the pupil's characteristics.

☐ A young mildly retarded pupil may have the same objectives, procedures, and settings as normal pupils, but proceed through the
objectives on a slower schedule.

☐ An older blind pupil may have the same objectives, schedules, and
settings as normal pupils, but use different media, e.g., textbooks
done in braille.

☐ An emotionally disturbed pupil may have the same objectives and
procedures as normal pupils, but a different schedule and different settings.

☐ A severely physically handicapped pupil may have different objectives, procedures, schedules, and settings from those which
normal or less handicapped pupils have.

Instructional objectives   Instructional objectives are statements about what the pupil should
be able to do if he or she learns through instruction. They perform
two crucial services. They guide selecting instructional procedures
because the instructional procedure should lead to the behavior/
content specified in the instructional objective. They guide selecting
testing procedures because the tests should enable the pupil to
demonstrate whether he or she has attained the behavior/content
specified in the instructional objective (Padzersky and Gibson,
1974).

Exceptional pupils might be able to deal with objectives taught in
the schools, or they might need instruction in areas nonexceptional
pupils learn outside of the school, for instance, self-help skills such as
tooth brushing (e.g., Callahan, 1978; Wehman and McLaughlin, 1980;
Simon and O'Rourke, 1977). It all depends on their characteristics.

☐ A moderately retarded nine-year-old might need instruction in
beginning arithmetic, reading, and other such content.

☐ A highly intelligent deaf sixteen-year-old might need instruction
in advanced English grammar, trigonometry, and similar college-
preparatory subjects.

☐ A severely spastic (cerebral palsied) six-year-old might need
instruction in oral communication, self-help skills, and similar
domains.

☐ A severely mentally retarded eighteen-year-old might need instruction in independent travel, interpersonal skills, and similar
domains.

We call a set of objectives a *curriculum*. Exceptional pupils use curricula developed in regular education. In addition, we have many, many curricula developed especially for exceptional pupils, such as the Social Learning Curriculum, the Project Mathematics Material, and the I CAN Curriculum for physical education (respectively, Goldstein, 1974; Cawley, 1978; Knowles, 1975). For example, Table 3.2 shows topics covered by objectives in the *Programmed Environments Curriculum* for severely developmentally retarded pupils (Tawney, 1980).

TABLE 3.2 SCOPE OF THE PROGRAMMED ENVIRONMENTS CURRICULUM FOR SEVERELY DEVELOPMENTALLY RETARDED PUPILS.

Area	Skills
Receptive skills	
Responding to social interaction	Responding to signal words
Attending to voice	Identifying objects
Following cued commands	Identifying body parts
Attending to own name	Identifying people
Expressive skills	
Making sounds	Shaping words
Responding vocally to model	Naming actions
Indicating preferences	Naming objects
Producing sounds on requests	
Cognitive skills	
Focusing attention	Putting objects in sequence
Attending to objects	Lining up objects
Responding to teacher model	Sorting
Repeating teacher model	Selecting equivalent amounts
Finding hidden objects	Matching equal sets
Finding source of sound	Counting rationally
Imitating actions	Selecting a specified quantity
Matching	
Identifying simple pictures	

Source: Tawney (1980, p. 11. Reprinted with permission.)

Instructional schedules

Schedules are based on rate of instruction — the amount of time an exceptional pupil works toward an objective, or stated differently, the amount of direct teaching and independent practice he or she needs

Exceptional pupils might be able to deal with objectives taught in the schools, or they might need instruction in areas that nonexceptional pupils learn outside of the schools.

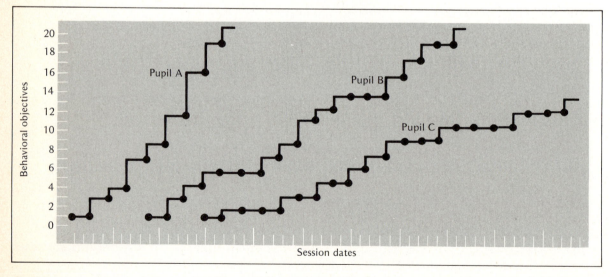

Fig. 3.1
Results of three exceptional children's working through a particular preschool intervention curriculum at different rates. (Reprinted by permission from Guralnick, 1975.)

to reach an objective. Adjusting schedules means: (1) planning time so that each pupil has the appropriate time — no more and no less — than he or she needs to master an instructional objective; and then (2) moving on to the next objective in the instructional sequence.

Requiring all pupils to master the same objectives while allowing each one to proceed at his or her own rate is a very old technique for individualizing instruction. Regular educators label this technique "the continuous-progress approach" or "mastery learning." We use the technique widely in special education.

> The graph [Fig. 3.1] shows three hypothetical though representative results of three children who have worked through a particular curriculum at different rates. The numbers on the vertical axis reflect the number of sessions or lessons. Vertical increments indicate that the child has reached criterion on the probe questions for that lesson unit. As illustrated, Child A proceeded quite rapidly through the 20 steps of the curriculum, never failing a lesson and frequently reaching criterion on two or more objectives in a single lesson period. Child B proceeded at a moderate rate, finding difficulty only at certain points, while Child C learned at a slow rate with considerable problems at various points in the curriculum. (Guralnick, 1976, pp. 27–28)

Instructional procedures are the means we use to help exceptional pupils attain their instructional objectives. These procedures include methods, media, and equipment.

Methods are recurrent patterns of teacher behavior (e.g., Berliner and Gage, 1976; Gardner, 1977). Major teaching methods used throughout education are:

□ *Teacher presentation:* Lectures, demonstrations, and recitation

□ *Student problem solving:* Inquiry training, brainstorming, and experimenting

□ *Group work:* Discussion, debates, and symposia

□ *Individual work:* Tutoring, independent learning, and solitary activity

□ *Direct experience:* Field trips, consultants, events

□ *Behavior modification:* Modeling, precision teaching.

We use these methods with exceptional pupils as much as with non-exceptional pupils.

Media are materials and machines we use (Jamison *et al.,* 1974). Major media used throughout education include:

□ *Print media:* Textbooks, trade books, and workbooks — singly and in kits.

Instructional procedures

    □   *Audio, visual and audiovisual media:* Photographs, radios, audiodiscs, tapes, cassettes, films, filmstrips, TV, videotapes, videodisc, object models

    □   *Prototypes:* Games and simulations

    □   *Programs:* Programed learning devices, programed teaching devices, and computer-assisted instruction.

Media used with nonexceptional pupils are appropriate for many exceptional pupils; in addition, a large number of items have been developed especially for exceptional pupils (e.g., DLM, 1979; Lance, 1977; Mann *et al.*, 1980; Treffinger *et al.*, 1976; Withrow, 1976).

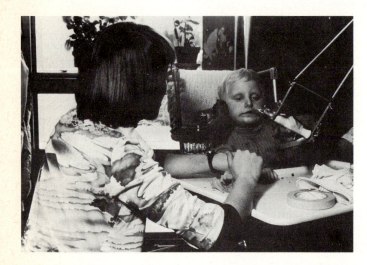

Sometimes we use different methods, different media, and different equipment to individualize instruction for exceptional pupils.

Instructional settings   *Special equipment* includes a wide variety of devices to compensate for particular handicaps (Sorbye, 1977; Wexler, 1978). A few examples are wheelchairs for crippled pupils, special amplifiers for deaf pupils, machines to write braille for blind pupils, and communication boards for pupils who have severe speech handicaps.

Settings are the ways personnel and space are arranged for instruction.

    Allocation of personnel refers to how pupils, teachers, and teacher aides are organized. The commonest patterns are:

    □   Individual tutoring — a pupil is taught alone

    □   Independent study — a pupil uses a self-instructional system or undertakes to write a paper, solve a problem, or do a project alone or with a group of other pupils

□   Solitary activity — a pupil works alone

□   Small groups — two or more pupils work together by themselves or under the guidance of a peer tutor or an adult; these groups are put together on the basis of mutual interest or a mutual level of achievement; and

□   Large groups — one entire class or several classes join together in a common activity.

All of these staffing patterns are used with exceptional pupils (e.g., Rich, 1980). For instance, it is frequently recommended that gifted pupils be encouraged to carry out independent studies and small-group activities. The idea is that they can use these opportunities for enrichment, i.e., for pursuing a topic at a level of complexity beyond the level that the majority of the class chooses to do. However, the value of the staffing patterns depends on their wise use. It is a common-sense notion that smaller pupil-teacher ratios and tutoring are more beneficial to the student. Nevertheless, sometimes pupils do better when they receive stimulation from the group or other pupils (e.g., Rosenshine, 1976).

Differentiated staffing means teams working together to deliver services to the pupil. The people on the teams have different kinds and levels of training and responsibility.

□   The paraprofessional keeps records, assists pupils physically, and sees that the classroom housekeeping activities are done.

□   The teacher or therapist does some of the assessment and delivers the instruction specified in the individual education programs.

□   The master teacher or master therapist leads in the development of the individual education programs and coordinates those providing services to pupils.

Team teaching is a related idea. Here two or more teachers work with larger groups. Each teacher takes the lead on a different topic. Differentiated staffing and team teaching are very useful in our work with handicapped pupils — especially the severely and profoundly handicapped. It will become more necessary as we plan and carry out more individual education programs.

Allocation of space refers to how facilities are arranged for instruction. *Common areas* are used for larger group activities. *Carrels* are small enclosed spaces pupils can retire to for working free from distraction. *Special centers* are areas with materials devoted to particular functions, e.g., mathematics centers contain activities and media that enable pupils to work independently on learning arith-

1. Identifying poster
2. Materials container
3. Concept cards
4. Manipulative materials

5. Drill cards
6. Task card
7. Extended activities
8. Reinforcing activity

Fig. 3.2
A mathematics learning center.
(Reprinted by permission from
Turnbull and Schulz, 1979.)

metic objectives (Fig. 3.2). *Depositories* are areas for keeping books, films, tapes, learning packages, and other materials.

Instructional settings can be organized as needed in working with particular groups of exceptional pupils. For example, note the organization portrayed in Fig. 3.3.

The Related Services   "Related services are therapy, transportation, and other services the pupil needs to help him/her benefit from special education" (PL 94-142, 1977, Sec. 121a.5). The related services are supplied primarily by speech pathologists, audiologists, psychologists, social workers, physical therapists, physicians, and vocational rehabilitation specialists (e.g., Connolly, 1980; Jenkins and Odle, 1980).*

---

* Transportation is described later in this chapter.

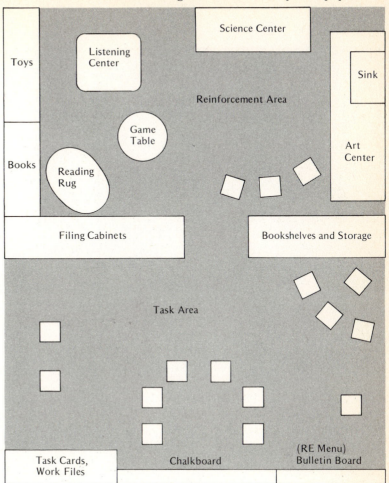

Fig. 3.3
Illustration of space allocations —
location of work centers in the
classroom. (Reprinted by permission from Turnbull and Schulz,
1979.)

Speech pathologists diagnose pupils' speech and language problems. Then they provide therapy appropriate for these problems.

Audiologists diagnose pupils' hearing problems. They advise
parents and others about pupils' needs for hearing aids, auditory
training, and other services.

Psychologists assess pupils' intellectual, academic, social, and
emotional characteristics. They also supply counseling to pupils and
parents.

Physical therapists evaluate pupils' capabilities for standing,
sitting, and ambulation. They work to strengthen pupils' muscle functions, train pupils in balance and movement, and train them to use
braces, wheelchairs, and other ambulation aids.

Occupational therapists evaluate pupils' capabilities for performing activities of daily living, such as feeding themselves or dressing

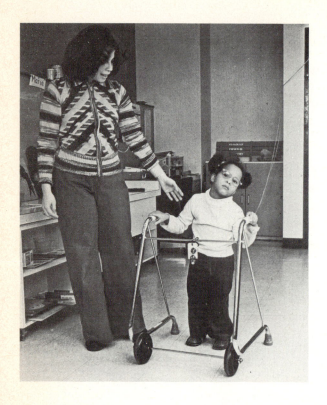

Related services help pupils benefit
from special education.

themselves. And they train pupils to perform the activities of daily living.

School social workers help families locate services and arrange for their payment. They also provide crisis intervention and other counseling services.

Physicians diagnose medical problems and provide treatment with drugs, surgery, prostheses,* and other procedures. The specialists most often working with exceptional pupils are psychiatrists, neurologists, otologists, ophthalmologists, and such internal medicine specialists as cardiologists, urologists, and hematologists.

Vocational rehabilitation specialists assess youngsters' potentialities and possible limitations for occupational training and performance. They also supply information and counsel to youngsters and their parents about jobs, and they arrange for services and training to prepare youngsters for jobs. If needed, they also help youngsters locate jobs.

---

* Prostheses are artificial replacements for bodily structures. Dentures are a familiar prosthetic device.

LEGAL SAFEGUARDS IN INDIVIDUALIZING INSTRUCTION

For many years, we have had procedures for individualizing instruction to help pupils overcome their handicaps or develop their talents. We have accomplished a great deal. Yet as we saw in "What is to become of Katherine?" (Chapter 1), many pupils do not function as well as they could, or should, in the academic, physical, social, emotional, and self-help areas. Two problems are functional exclusion and confusing instruction and placement. These problems have joined with other problems to lead to terrible frustration and waste.

Problems in Individualizing Instruction for Exceptional Pupils

> Schools fail, however, less because of maliciousness than because of mindlessness. Like Procrustes stretching his guests or cutting off their limbs to make them fit the standard-sized bed his inn provided, educators and scholars, frequently with the best of intentions, have operated on the assumption that children should be cut or stretched or otherwise "adjusted" to fit the schools, rather than adjusting the schools to fit the children. And most of us have tended to accept this without question. (Silberman, 1970, p. 81)

Actual exclusion means not allowing a pupil in school. We consider this problem in discussing placement. *Functional* exclusion is also a serious problem and an insidious one. It means not teaching a pupil as well and as fully as we should (e.g., Turnbull and Turnbull, 1978, p. 109). As a result, the pupil does not achieve what he or she should. There are two reasons for functional exclusion.

Functional exclusion

One reason is that it is difficult to deal with handicaps and talents. It takes a lot of time and hard work to learn skills to compensate for a handicap or to learn to function in spite of a handicap. And it takes a lot of time and hard work to develop a talent to a high level. For example, think about the time and effort it takes for a crippled youngster to learn to walk and to travel independently. Or think about how long and how much work it takes to develop a truly creative musician's skills. In the face of such difficulty, teachers and pupils often give up. As a result, teachers might follow the easiest course and not adjust instruction to pupils' needs, or pupils might not work as hard as they should to learn.

Another reason for functional exclusion is that we do not expect enough of pupils. We may not recognize the implications of their handicaps or talents. Or conversely, we may react to labels and underestimate pupils. Either way, we do not sufficiently fit instruction to pupils' needs, and they do not learn as much as they should.

Placement and individualizing instruction are separate but complementary tools for dealing with individual differences. In the past we relied on placing pupils in homogeneous classes and teaching them

Confusion about instruction and placement

as groups. Recently we have started to emphasize individualizing instruction for each particular pupil.

> Much as we favor adaptation of schooling, we have had to retreat from the simple concept of "placement decisions"... Instructional decisions must be based on a whole complex of student characteristics and teacher actions. There is no such thing as a homogeneous group of students or a specifiable "method" of instruction. Educational practice over the next decade or two — if not eternally — will have to make its adaptations informally and judiciously not by an actuarial technology of cutting scores and regression equations. (Cronbach and Snow, 1977, p. viii)

However, we still have a great deal of confusion about both the roles and the values of individualizing instruction and placement in fitting education to pupils' individual differences.

First, consider the roles of the two tools. *Individualized instruction* is teaching, i.e., starting with the pupil's present performance levels and fitting special education and related services to those present performance levels. *Placement* is assigning a pupil to a location for conveniently delivering the individualized instruction to him or her. An example of an instructional activity is to select certain instructional objectives for mathematics and to teach through individual tutoring with the procedures and materials in Cawley's Project Mathematics Material. An example of a placement option is to assign the pupil to a resource room for this instruction.

Second, consider the values of the two tools. As a result of instruction, pupils should learn. As a result of placement, pupils and their teachers should be more comfortable and efficient as they go about learning and teaching.

Third, consider the distinction between the two tools. The distinction between instruction and placement for delivering that instruction is a very important one. Nevertheless, this distinction is often not made. On the one hand, people have substituted placement for instruction. For example, they have placed pupils in self-contained special classes, but have neglected to select related services or objectives, schedules, procedures, and settings for instruction appropriate for those pupils' present performance levels. On the other hand, people have tried to adjust instruction without proper placement. For example, they have tried to use an individualized instructional system such as the Wisconsin System of Mathematics Skill Development without having enough teachers and aides to give guidance to the pupils. In both cases they have been frustrated, and negligent, when pupils have not learned as they should.

This confusion between placement and instruction has long been recognized and decried (Goodlad and Klein, 1974; Meyen, 1972). Solutions have been identified. Simply, we must *first* plan the pupil's individualized instruction, and we must *second* find the placement, the most enabling environment, where we will deliver that individualized instruction to him or her (Zettle and Abeson, 1978, p. 215).

As we have seen, it is a very old idea to deal with individual differences by treating each pupil differently on the basis of his or her particular strengths and problems. Now individualized programs are required by law for handicapped individuals and other individuals, such as public offenders, in publicly funded facilities. The labels used by different disciplines vary somewhat, for example: individual education program (special education), individual habilitation plan (developmental disabilities), individual service plan (mental health), and individual instruction plan (vocational education). However, all of these involve the same things — testing, prescription, teaching, and evaluation/revision — all accompanied by procedural safeguards. The requirement is clear whatever the difference in labels and terminology (e.g., Odle and Galtelli, 1980; Zettle and Abeson, 1978, p. 214).

The Law Governing Individualizing Instruction

The legal basis for individualized instruction is equal educational opportunity (e.g., Coleman, 1966, 1969; McCarthy, 1976; Semmel and Heinmiller, 1977). The concept of what constitutes equal educational opportunity has evolved over the last century. Prior to the mid-1800s, it was considered the state's responsibility to provide a free education within the local tax base, with local peers, and a uniform curriculum. In turn, it was considered the pupil's responsibility to take advantage of this provision. In the late 1800s the doctrine of "separate but equal" was put forth. This meant that if they remained equal, separate facilities could be established for particular groups; in fact, the two races (*Plessy* v. *Ferguson*, 1890). In the mid-1900s the separate-but-equal doctrine was struck down (*Brown* v. *Board of Education*, 1954). Equality was interpreted to mean not only parity in facilities, methods, media, and curricula, but also exposure to fellow students with diverse educational backgrounds. In the late 1960s the emphasis began to shift from putting the burden on the pupil to benefit from equal offerings to putting the burden on the school to supply the pupil with remedial treatment or differentiated instruction. For example, the Supreme Court held that "there is not equality of treatment merely by providing students with the same facilities, textbooks, teachers, and curriculum" (*Lau* v. *Nichols*, 1973, pp. 563, 566). And the Civil Rights Act of 1964 — P.L. 88-352, Sec. 601 — clearly requires providing a program suitable to the needs of the pupil, that is, "providing individuals with equal access to differing resources for differing objectives" (Weintraub and Abeson, 1972, p. 1056). This is sometimes called "equal diversity of opportunity" (Cronbach and Snow, 1977).

PL 94-142 requires that we individualize instruction within the individual education program. It does not leave much open for interpretation or different approaches. It explicitly states that we must get information about the pupil's present performance levels and, on this basis, specify annual goals, including short-term objectives, name educational services,* state how progress will be evaluated, and supply schedules for instruction, evaluation, and revision. The law goes on to specify that the advocates must participate in planning and revising the instruction. And they must have due-process rights to appeal if they disagree with any decisions. Table 3.3 shows specialists who might participate in the decision making here. Actual participants depend on the pupil's particular needs.

PL 94-142 requires that we individualize instruction through the individual education program.

As we carry out this law, we must make a clear distinction between accountability for program adequacy and accountability for pupil achievement. Accountability for program adequacy means that we are responsible for guaranteeing the pupil's rights. Accountability for pupil achievement means that we are responsible for guaranteeing

* These educational services include instructional services, nonacademic services, related services, and services to ensure the procedural safeguards.

TABLE 3.3 POSSIBLE PARTICIPANTS IN PLANNING FOR EXCEPTIONAL PUPILS.

Person	Permanent Members	Recommended on Core Committees	Consulting Members
School administrator	X		
Special education administrator	X		
Referring/receiving teacher		X	
Parent		X	
Psychologist			X
Educational diagnostician			X
Speech pathologist			X
Physical therapist			X
Occupational therapist			X
Audiologist			X
School nurse			X
Social worker			X
Guidance counselor			X
Curriculum specialist			X
Methods and materials specialist			X
Physician			X
Ophthalmologist/ optometrist			X
Vocational rehabilitation counselor			X
Other consultants			X

Source: Based on the Swanson and Willis (1979, p. 18) adaptation of the National Association of State Directors of Special Education (1976, p. 16).

that the pupil will attain particular instructional objectives, often called a minimum standard of pupil achievement. Earlier we considered accountability for program adequacy. We ensure this accountability through the Child-Find and the IEP. Now let's examine accountability for pupil achievement.

Legal accountability for attaining at least a minimum standard of pupil achievement is an emerging area of education (e.g., Saretsky, 1973; Gee and Sperry, 1978). The idea is that we are responsible for teaching pupils at least certain basic skills and for holding pupils back in school unless, and until, they learn those skills. Accountability for a minimum standard of pupil achievement is an attractive and commonsense notion to many people. However, it is very difficult to put into practice. His or her learning is determined by influences both within and outside of the pupil. At our present level of knowledge and technology in education and the behavioral sciences, it is almost impossible to separate the effects of those influences and to prove who and what are responsible for a pupil's learning or not learning (Abel and Conner, 1978; Cox, 1977). These problems are present when we deal with nonexceptional pupils. They are increased mightily when we deal with exceptional pupils, with all of their particular difficulties and their various special education and related services (e.g., Cook, 1972; Jones, 1973).

PL 94-142 recognizes our responsibility for program adequacy and at the same time exempts us from accountability for pupil achievement:

> Each public agency must provide special education and related services to a handicapped child in accordance with an individualized education program. However, Part B of the Act does not require that any agency, teacher, or other person be held accountable if a child does not achieve the growth projected in the annual goals and objectives.
>
> *Comment:* This section is intended to relieve concerns that the individualized educational program constitutes a guarantee by the public agency and the teacher that a child will progress at a specified rate. However, this section does not relieve agencies and teachers from making good-faith efforts to assist the child in achieving the objectives and goals listed in the individualized education program. Further, the section does not limit a parent's right to complain and to ask for revisions of the child's program or to invoke due process procedures, if the parent feels that these efforts are not being made. (PL 94-142, Sec. 121a. 349)

To stress: We *are not* accountable for a minimum standard of pupil achievement. We *are* responsible for program adequacy as planned, implemented, and maintained through the Child-Find and the IEP.

Placing exceptional pupils in the least restrictive environment

The traditional tool of placement coupled with the procedural safeguards to protect the pupil has become, in contemporary practice, placement in the least restrictive environment. Placing pupils is the fourth task in guaranteeing them a free appropriate public education and an equal educational opportunity.

PLACEMENT AS A TOOL FOR DEALING
WITH INDIVIDUAL DIFFERENCES

Formerly placement was a tool for getting a group that could be taught the same way because its members were classified to be alike on one or more characteristics important to learning. Today placement is defined more broadly to mean a tool for locating a pupil for conveniently delivering services to him or her.

Placement options are the plans for organizing pupils and teachers to deal with individual differences. Various plans have emerged as school populations have changed.

Placement Options

In the 1700s and early 1800s geographical areas were sparsely populated, and education was not compulsory. Therefore only a small number of youngsters, varying widely in chronological age and other characteristics, were brought together in any one place for education. In such "one-room schools" individual tutoring and small-group instruction were used to accommodate individual differences.

The mid-1800s saw the beginning of both compulsory education and a large population growth resulting from immigration from abroad and movement within the country. The number of youngsters increased, and the one-room school became impossible. Dealing with individual differences became a problem.

Educators sought more similarity by assigning pupils to groups by chronological age, i.e., apparently by maturity levels. At the same time, the total curriculum to be learned was divided into sets graded roughly by difficulty level and assigned to the several chronological age levels, e.g., the first-grade curriculum went to six-year-old pupils, the second-grade curriculum to seven-year-old pupils, and so on. As pupils increased in age, year by year, they were exposed to, and expected to progress through, the sets of graded objectives. In this way the chronological age-grade lockstep was developed to deal with the wide individual differences that occurred with greatly expanded enrollments.

Chronological age-grade grouping certainly reduced the range of individual differences. At the same time, it did not do the job completely. Marked individual differences among and within pupils of a given chronological age in a grade remained and, as we have seen, increased as pupils grew older. Stated more simply, pupils mastered the graded objectives at different rates. Some pupils did not master some objectives.

Various plans were developed for working with these individual differences within chronological age-grade groupings. These plans may be classified into six patterns. We still use some of them.

Outside public day schools   Some pupils leave home to go to *residential schools* designed especially for their problems — blindness, deafness, mental retardation, emotional illness (e.g., O'Connor and Sitkei, 1975). Some who have chronic illnesses or relatively long-term illnesses receive *home instruction*, or *hospital instruction*, or both for the time necessary (e.g., Lee, 1975). So do some pupils recovering from surgery.

Preschool programs   In some cases infants and children below CA 6 are enrolled in preschool programs which have special services for those with problems. We have examined how a difference in a characteristic such as vision occurring early in the youngster's life can deflect his or her growth and development of behavior in that area so that he or she becomes progressively different from other youngsters. At the same time, this divergence affects his or her accomplishing the cultural tasks — again with an earlier divergence leading to progressively wider differences at later ages. Preschool programs, then, are designed to stimulate children during early critical periods in growth and development in order to prevent problems and to build on strengths. Preschool programs may be delivered in homes, schools, or community centers (e.g., Allen *et al.*, 1978; Gallagher, 1976; Stanley, 1973).

Achievement/ability grouping   In some cases similarity in achievement and ability are sought by moving brighter pupils forward across CA levels to put them with older pupils and by holding duller pupils back across CA levels to put them with younger pupils. Colloquially, these practices are known as grade-skipping and failing students; more formally, as *acceleration* and *retention*.

In some cases similarity in achievement and ability are sought by keeping pupils together by chronological age but dividing them according to ability and achievement levels. In the lower schools this practice is called *grouping, homogeneous grouping, tracking,* and *streaming.* In the secondary schools it is done through such practices as *course selection* (e.g., algebra versus general math) and, more broadly, by *program selection* (e.g., college preparation versus general preparation).

For exceptional pupils who show more extraordinary individual differences, these homogeneous achievement and ability groups are called *self-contained special classes* — for the gifted, the retarded, the physically handicapped, the emotionally disturbed, the learning disabled, the hearing impaired, or the visually impaired (e.g., Jackson, 1975; Koons, 1976–1977; Stanley, 1976).

Within chronological age grouping   Here pupils are first classified by chronological age. Then individual differences in achievement and ability are dealt with by: (1) grouping within class as needed for various objectives; (2) tutoring by specialists such as reading teachers, special education teachers, speech therapists, and other related services personnel; and (3) independent learning. These techniques may be carried out by one teacher or by a differentiated staff consisting of a master teacher and helpers, plus specialists. These procedures are labeled *regular classes* and *remedial teaching*. The specialists are sometimes called itinerant teachers, resource room teachers, and remedial teachers. Sometimes the specialist works with the pupil in his or her homeroom; sometimes in a resource room or clinic. The labels "continuous-progress plans" and "nongraded plans" are used to describe those settings where pupils are allowed to work on, and master, the objectives at their own rates, with grade levels ignored (e.g., Childs, 1975; Vernon and Prickett, 1976).

The combined plans are designed to get the benefits of each option without its problems. Pupils are assigned to special classes (ability groups) for training in citizenship (social studies) and literacy (reading, writing, spelling, and math). In the lower schools they are assigned to regular classes (CA groups) for general cultural subjects

Combined ability and CA grouping

Normalization — enabling a person to participate in society as much as possible and as independently as possible — serves as a basis for mainstreaming.

such as physical education, literature, the arts, and consumer education. In the secondary schools they self-select for specialized training in such areas as higher mathematics and science, computer technology, and metal working. This approach is labeled a *dual-progress* plan in regular education (Stoddard, 1961) and an *integrated* or *part-time special-class plan* in special education (Deno, 1970).

No grouping   Individual differences are dealt with by allowing, encouraging, and leading the pupil to explore freely and to engage in objectives appropriate to his or her interests and capabilities. Spontaneous groups may emerge, but no particular groups are imposed. The contemporary version of this approach is labeled *open education* (Barth, 1976–1977; Knoblock, 1973; Wright, 1975).

The Least Restrictive   The practice of the least restrictive environment is based on the con-
Environment   cept of the least restrictive alternative. This concept is applied widely in government.

> The principle of the least restrictive alternative rests on the apple-pie premise that people should in general be free to live as they please. If you accept this elementary moral premise, the principle of the least restrictive alternative easily follows; that is, when government does have a legitimate communal interest to serve by regulating human conduct, it should use methods that curtail individual freedom to no greater extent than is essential for securing that interest. When you swat a mosquito on a friend's back, you should not use a baseball bat. (Chambers, 1976, p. 486)

We have applied the least-restrictive-alternative concept of handicapped individuals' residential placement and school placement (e.g., Deno, 1978; Roos *et al.*, 1980). The principle of normalization is the basis for this application. Normalization means enabling a person to participate in society as much as possible and as independently as possible. The application of the normalization principle has been the subject of considerable discussion and some disagreement (e.g., Burton *et al.*, 1977; Roos, 1977; Blatt, 1979; Childs, 1979*a, b*; Warren, 1979).

Residential   Applied to residential placement, normalization involves arranging
placement   housing and services so that the handicapped individual can, as much as possible, live in the community as nonhandicapped individuals do, participating socially and physically in school, church, recreation, and other activities (Apolloni *et al.*, 1980). Possible residential settings can be arranged roughly from the least to the most restrictive. The individual can move among these options as his or her needs and capabilities for self-management change. For example

(Glenn, 1976, pp. 506–512):

    developmental homes (foster homes)
    children's intensive training residences
    adolescent intensive training residences
    family living residences
    intensive adult training residences
    adult minimum supervision residences
    room and board homes
    adult boarding
    cluster apartments
    co-resident apartments
    counseled apartments
    independent living (counseling available)
    five-day residences
    behavior shaping residences
    developmental maximization units*
    crisis homes
    structured correctional residences
    structured rehabilitation residences

Educational placement

We apply the principle of normalization to educational placement in a similar way (Anderson *et al.*, 1980; Laycock, 1980). We arrange things so that the handicapped pupils can participate in school activities as much as possible as nonhandicapped pupils do. The key is flexibility. We have flexibility with environments in which the pupil moves back and forth between more and less restrictive environments as his or her needs and capabilities change. And we have flexibility of services whereby the pupil stays in one environment and we move more and less specialized services in and out as his or her needs change.

    This description of an emotionally disturbed boy's progress illustrates the flexibility notion in more human terms.

    Joseph was an only child living with his mother and father. He had difficulty in kindergarten and first grade and was referred for psychiatric study. In the hospital's report, he was described as having potentially superior intelligence, but not being able to function on his level because of emotional confusion.... The hospital confirmed that he was much too disturbed to attend public school, and recommended a small private school and prolonged treatment for the entire family.

      Joseph went to a small private school in the second grade, but his parents refused to continue. He was then returned to the Arling-

---

* For severely and profoundly handicapped individuals who need close medical supervision and intensive training in self-care, communication, etc.

ton Public Schools for the third grade, presumably on trial. There, he was reported to be annoying the other children, but he did reasonably well academically....

In the fourth grade Joseph was expelled again from public school with the following report: "Grabs children, runs around the room during class lessons, makes loud noises without any reason, yells, is lying, biting and taking children's books, pencils, and other belongings." The school then provided a home tutor for one hour daily. In the fifth grade, Joseph was permitted to return to school for 1½ hours daily but there was no improvement. At the end of the fifth grade, he was referred to the newly created Psychological Counseling Department. Although Joseph had had no individual therapy for the previous 2½ years, a small group had been formed around him for therapeutic purposes under the aegis of a children's agency....

The decision not to refer Joseph to a state hospital for psychotic children was made partly to capitalize on the parents' desire for Joseph's public school attendance, and partly to utilize the therapeutic resources inherent in an educational environment. Therefore, an experimental treatment plan was worked out with the school as the integrating agency of all therapeutic efforts. The senior psychologist was to become Joseph's therapist and see him twice weekly, the school social worker was to meet the parents once weekly, and the school's principal, teacher, tutor, and school nurse became part of the team. He was to attend school a short time each day, with the understanding that his time in the classroom would be increased as soon as he showed that he could behave as other boys do. A new elementary school was chosen in which the principal and 6th grade teacher were willing to accept this disturbed boy, and they were given the assurance that he would be withdrawn if he proved too disturbing for the class....

[Joseph, other class members, and the teacher had difficulties. Additional conferences among the psychological/educational team were held. In the beginning, Joseph could tolerate only three hours a day in school without exploding into disruptive behavior. After a while, his tolerance, and thus his time in school, increased. All concerned decided he was ready to try junior high school.]

Junior high school attendance proved to be a frightening experience for Joseph in the beginning, and he became very uncontrolled at times. After the first few weeks, it became clear that a full school day was more than he could endure. A new academic program was worked out, which let Joseph attend only four sessions in the morning, but covering all his major subjects. He was promised a full day again, when he was ready. He accepted this and seemed relieved, realizing that he was still different from the other students. Three months later, another change appeared advisable, *because in two of his four sessions he did very poorly, behaviorally and academically. It was decided to transfer him to two different sections, both of which were scholastically higher and therefore academically more challenging....*

In September, he had gained sufficient security and control to be enrolled in a full 8th grade program. He received grades of B in all subjects, except C's in Latin and Art. His highest aim was to get on the honor roll, and he suddenly adopted an extremely competitive attitude in school.

The club leader of the Boston Children's Services who had continued to see Joseph in a group through four years also let us know that Joseph had made a "fantastic" improvement; he now was going along with suggestions made for the group without his usual testing out and objecting. He had also learned to treat the weaker members of the group of seven boys with more consideration.

Socially, intellectually, and academically, Joseph has made outstanding gains during the last three years, so much so that his principal and his teachers have no reservations to recommend him for a full academic program in high school. The therapeutic team, however, is aware of his extreme vulnerability in any crisis situation mainly because of the pathology at home. To forestall his succumbing to his tendency to "act out" rather than to "think out," there is a continuing need for the supportive environment provided by the firm structure of the school and for the personal concern of his therapist. (Moller, 1964, excerpts)

To illustrate this flexibility, people have used various diagrams showing environments and services in a straight line with arrows indicating directions of movement among more and less specialized options as pupils' needs change. These are valuable ideas and illustrations. However, we must be careful. Sometimes showing environments and services in a line can narrow our thinking about where more severely handicapped pupils should be placed for instruction. Such narrowing contradicts the original intent to keep the pupil in the least restrictive environment possible (Sontag, 1976). Perhaps a better metaphor would be a circular arrangement of services (Hyer, 1979). (Fig. 3.4) This arrangement would suggest that all placement options are equally valuable and that all are equally accessible to a pupil as his or her needs change and consequently the environment which is most enabling to him or her changes.

We have had considerable confusion about the relationship among the least restrictive environment, mainstreaming, and placement in the regular class. As we have seen, placement in *the least restrictive environment* means applying the principle of normalization to educational placement, i.e., arranging things so that the handicapped pupil can participate in school activities as much as possible as nonhandicapped pupils do. *Mainstreaming* is a synonym.

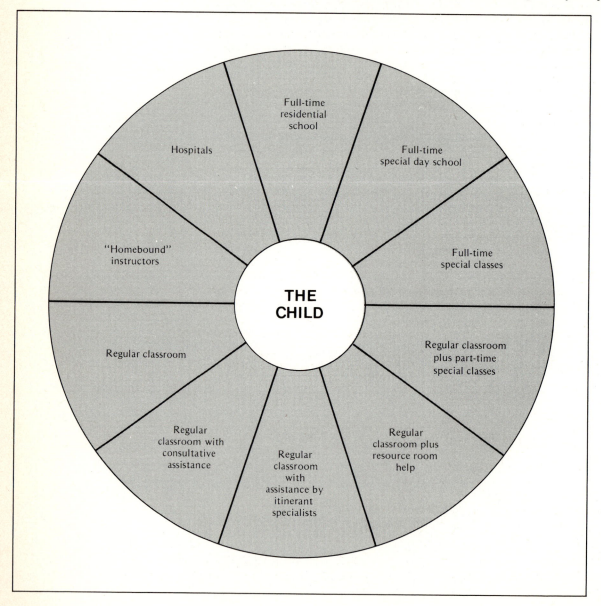

Fig. 3.4
The circular arrangement of services suggests that all placement options are equally valuable and that all are equally accessible to a pupil as his or her needs change.

The Council for Exceptional Children uses this definition:

> Mainstreaming is a belief which involves an educational placement procedure and process for exceptional children, based on the conviction that each such child should be educated in the least restrictive environment in which his educational and related needs can be satisfactorily provided for. This concept recognizes that exceptional children have a wide range of special educational needs, varying greatly in intensity and duration; that there is a recognized continuum of educational settings which may, at a given time, be appropriate for an individual child's needs; that to the maximum extent appropriate, exceptional children should be educated with nonexceptional children; and that special classes, separate schooling, or other removal of an exceptional child from education with nonexceptional children should occur only when the intensity of the child's special education and related needs is such that they cannot be satisfied in an environment including non-exceptional children, even with the provision of supplementary aids and services.* (CEC, 1976, p. 43).

Regular class placement is not a synonym for mainstreaming or the least restrictive environment. Instead, it is only one option among several for placement. That is, "regular class" refers to self-contained classes of twenty-five to thirty-five pupils grouped by CA and no other criteria — especially not achievement level and ability to learn. When the pupil is placed in the regular class, the regular-class teacher has the primary responsibility. The special education teacher, along with the reading specialist and other specialists, does team teaching with the regular-class teacher. These specialists do three things: give advice, supply supporting help (e.g., testing), and tutor the pupil either in the regular classroom or in a separate room. The work in the resource room may be *random*, i.e., work as needed by the pupil on particular skills from time to time. Or it may be *regular* for various periods to cover particular parts of the pupil's instructional program (for example, Fig. 3.5).

"Mainstreaming," "placing pupils in the least restrictive environment," and "placing pupils in regular classes" are watchwords. They signal a desirable goal — ending a youngster's isolation and enabling him or her to engage in life with other children. At the same time, they signal a difficult, demanding task — putting a youngster in a position in which he or she must accomplish the same cultural tasks other youngsters are accomplishing even though his or her deficits, by definition, interfere with the accomplishment of those cultural tasks. This is rather like throwing a baseball player into a game with a ping

---

* Mainstreaming is widely advocated, e.g., Agard *et al.* (1978), Baldwin *et al.* (1978), and MacMillan and Becker (1977).

INDIRECT	I-1	Consultation and observation
	I-2	Formal and informal testing assistance
	I-3	Supply instructional materials
DIRECT	D-1	Resource room random
	D-2	Tutorial regular class (1—6 weeks)
	D-3	Contracted services
	D-4	Resource room regular (6 weeks or more, 1—2 periods)
	D-5	Resource room regular (6 weeks or more, 2—4 periods)
	D-6	Other alternative (e.g., special placement)

Fig. 3.5
The service hierarchy proposed by Chaffin (1974, pp. 13–15). (Reprinted by permission.)

Conditions at some institutions have been execrable.

pong paddle for a bat. These comments do not argue against main-streaming and, if appropriate, regular-class placement. Instead, they argue for a thoughtful interpretation of "least restrictive environ-ment" to mean the most *enabling* environment for the pupil, not an automatic assignment to a regular class. Table 3.4 illustrates some concerns about mainstreaming that we must consider and also some strategies for dealing with those concerns.

Even with careful planning and good support, placing handi-capped pupils in regular classes must be done very carefully. So far, the evidence indicates that young handicapped children benefit most, whereas older handicapped children, especially the retarded, may suffer in regular classes — even under the best circumstances (e.g., Fredricks *et al.*, 1978; Kaufman *et al.*, 1978; Reynolds and Birch, 1977). This evidence is just another sign of the relationship that we keep stressing. That is, individual differences get larger and larger as time goes by and pupils' rates of growth and development continue to diverge. This increasing diversity shows in different levels of ability to meet the demands of society by mastering the increasingly complex cultural tasks. Our main hope is to find and to work with youngsters early, before their differences have time to become so large and the cultural tasks they must master have time to become such complex syntheses of earlier cultural tasks. In sum, then, mainstreaming — a desirable end — is a very complicated process to accomplish in a way that pupils will be helped rather than harmed. We must consider a number of questions. These comments about emotionally disturbed children provide examples.

A student in a class of mine asked to see me in my office. She was interested, she said, in discussing a current phenomenon she under-stood was happening on a national basis in special education. "I think it's called 'streamlining,' " she said. I looked puzzled. "No, maybe it's 'mainlining,' " she added. I smiled and said, "I'll bet you mean 'mainstreaming.' " And indeed she did. This humorous inter-action actually is more telling than it first might appear. As we find ourselves caught up in the middle of mainstreaming, many educa-tors, both special and regular, may well be equally as confused with respect to what this current phenomenon actually means.

Basically, the mainstreaming movement aims at guaranteeing all exceptional children, including the disturbing and disturbed child, the *right* to a public school education and the *opportunity* for a better education than many of them may now be receiving. It is the latter with which I am particularly concerned. For, if broadening and normalizing the disturbed child's educational experience through involvement with the regular education program does not provide a better education, then we are hardly making progress.

TABLE 3.4 MAINSTREAMING CONCERNS AND STRATEGIES.

Concerns	Strategies
Our present and past teacher training programs provide little opportunity for regular teachers to become competent in meeting the needs of varied handicapped students.	Regular teaching training programs must undergo change to provide the increased understanding and competency needed in working with the handicapped.
Teacher training programs frequently place greater emphasis on methodology than on interpersonal needs of children in the classroom. Handicapped youngsters frequently have greater adjustment problems.	Greater emphasis on the social and emotional needs of *all* youngsters in the classroom is required.
Many youngsters are currently mainstreamed in regular classes but do not receive adequate services. Failure, frustration and social isolation are a consequence.	Careful, periodic evaluations need to be made of the benefits each child derives from the mainstreamed setting. Individual performance criteria must be examined.
Many prejudices and misconceptions exist concerning handicapped youngsters.	Personal values and present knowledge will need re-examination so as not to interfere with total commitment to all students as required in the teaching profession.
Mainstreaming will "dump" many handicapped children into the regular classroom as reluctance to make special class assignments grows.	Careful pre-assessment of a child's needs and capacity for success in the regular setting must be determined before foregoing special class placement.
Assessment procedures are controversial with regard to their effectiveness in determining needs of students.	Appropriate assessment procedures must be further identified and used by only those skilled in adequate interpretation.
Children are often inappropriately labeled as handicapped or overlooked as in need of special services because of differences in professional opinions.	A team approach must be utilized in determining if a child is in need of special services, what services are to be provided and how best to provide such services. The classroom teacher serves as a member of the professional team, working with other appropriately designated professionals.
Given current class sizes, individual differences among students are already great and preclude the teacher's adaptation to the even greater differences that would be present if handicapped children were included.	Class size needs to be restricted to a realistic number (perhaps eighteen to twenty-two students) in the elementary setting so that individual needs can be met.

Source: Swanson and Willis (1979, p. 32), compiled from Brenton (1974), Martin (1976), and USOE (1975).

There are many unanswered questions still to be pondered regarding the effects of mainstreaming. Exactly what does a regular classroom have to offer the disturbed child? What are the likely positive and negative effects of integration on the child? What about other children? Will they gain or lose in relation to their rights for a good education? And the regular teachers? How ready are they to extend their ranges of tolerance for academic and behavioral differences within classrooms which will be required if the mainstreaming process is to be successful? These are only a few of the issues that must be dealt with as mainstreaming is implemented. (Hewett, 1977, pp. 80–81)

These questions can be generalized beyond emotionally disturbed pupils to include all pupils. Also, to keep things in perspective, we must remember that *mainstreaming* and *regular class* are terms coming from special education. For a long time, many nonspecial educators have tried as hard as they can to get away from regular classes — the automatic assignment of pupils by their chronological ages (e.g., Anderson, 1973; Goodlad and Klein, 1970).

Transportation and Facilities

Proper transportation and facilities are two key factors in placing exceptional pupils (Aiello, 1976; Hill and Ponder, 1976). *Transportation* includes the pupil's travel to and from school, between schools, between schools and therapy sites, and in and about school buildings. Schools provide special transportation if the pupil cannot use regular transportation.

Facilities means the physical structure of the environment. They include general rooms, laboratories, lavatories, cafeterias, auditoriums, libraries, gymnasiums and showers, entrances/exits, hallways, stairways, and so on. Facilities where exceptional pupils work and play need special attention.

LEGAL SAFEGUARDS IN PLACEMENT

Problems in Placing Exceptional Pupils

We have had some terrible difficulties in using the placement options to deal with individual differences in both regular education and special education. There is an enormous number of essays and research reports describing these difficulties. The major problems have centered on arbitrary placement, exclusion from school, institutionalization, ability grouping, and facilities and transportation. These problems have had a frightful human cost.

Summarily suspended in the third grade, Derrick was to spend several years floating through Washington, D.C., institutions before a federal judge compelled the school authorities to resume their educational responsibilities to him. By then he was 13 years old.

At the time of his expulsion, there had been great upheaval in Derrick's life. His father had recently died, he had problems with his siblings, and he was said to be "acting up" in school. One day he was told by his classroom teacher to get out and not come back anymore. Derrick's mother was to receive neither notice nor a hearing nor even the reasons for her son's dismissal.

Derrick's mother was left with an eight-year-old child to take care of and educate. As a working mother earning four to five thousand dollars, what was she to do?

Eventually she went to the welfare department hoping to find a tuition grant for psychiatric-oriented schooling. The welfare department accepted Derrick as a ward, representing to his mother that the result would be therapeutic treatment, training, and an educational experience for Derrick.

Instead, Derrick was placed in Junior Village, a massive custodial "warehouse" for the District's dependent children. Four days after his arrival there, Derrick was sexually assaulted by other boys and ran home. When a ward runs away from a public institution, upon recapture, he can be transferred to a security facility. Thus, for nearly three months Derrick found himself behind the prisonlike bars and barbed wire fences of Oak Hill. Again, there was no educational program available to him. Although the very justification for declaring him a ward was his need for education, the outcome of this strategy was only a barren custodial care.

Before his plight was aired in Washington's daily newspapers and a congressional committee hearing, Derrick had made a most demoralizing odyssey: through three juvenile correctional institutions, St. Elizabeth's mental hospital, D.C. General Hospital, and Junior Village. (Herr, 1977, p. 253)

Arbitrary placement   Formerly, school people could, and often did, at their own discretion deny pupils admission or assign them anywhere in the schools. They were not required to consult the parents, the pupils, or other advocates. Nor were they required to document the rightness of their decisions (e.g., Chiba and Semmel, 1977). Sometimes sound decisions were made. Sometimes capricious acts led to errors and abuses.

Harris, my only son, is ten and is somewhat small for his age but has always been very active, playing with friends in the neighborhood. Last spring I got a note asking me to come to school. The pupil adjustment counselor told me that Harris and another boy, who had been his friend, had been fighting and that Harris was not to return to school for a week. When he returned to school he was immediately sent home again for no specific length of time, but with the message that he couldn't return again until he "learns to behave." When I again went to school to see his teacher, I learned that Harris had been placed in a class for retarded children since last year. I became very upset because I had never been told of this.

I did get a note from someone last year saying that Harris was receiving some special help with his studies, but it said nothing about a class for retarded children. I visited the school several times about this and asked to see Harris's records and test scores, but was told that I couldn't because the information was "confidential." The teacher did say that Harris's work had been better than the others, and that he could be smart when he wanted to, and that she didn't really understand him. It seemed as though he had been placed in the class because of his behavior. Since I wasn't satisfied, I had him tested at a private clinic and was told by the psychologist that he had an IQ of 96, a normal score and that he definitely should not be in a class for mentally retarded children since that probably would only cause him to act up more, rather than helping him. Finally, a lawyer at the agency called the principal and the Director of the Department of Special Classes (for mentally retarded), and got Harris into a regular class. I'm happy now and Harris is doing better, but a neighbor told me that several other parents whose children go to Harris's school are upset because their children also have been put in those classes. (Weintraub and Abeson, 1972, p. 1044)

Such arbitrariness prevented independent checks on whether the right placement decision was being made.

Exclusion from school

PL 94-142 states the congressional finding that "one million handicapped children in the United States are excluded entirely from the public school system and will not go through the educational process with their peers" (PL 94-142, Sec. 3, b, 4). Traditionally, youngsters have been excluded from school if they do not conform to the norm fairly closely (e.g., Task Force on Children Out of School, 1970; Children's Defense Fund, 1974).

One justification for school exclusion pertained to how school monies should be spent. *One argument* was that school monies should be spent for education but not for training. That is, it was considered educationally legitimate to teach a pupil reading, writing, and the other academic skills. It was not considered legitimate to teach the pupil more rudimentary topics, such as dressing, eating, and other self-help skills. This kind of thinking led to the distinction between the educable retarded child and the trainable retarded child and the exclusion of the trainable child from public day schools. *Another argument* was that school monies should be spent for educators but not for attendants. That is, a pupil should be able to move about unaided and to manage his or her personal needs, e.g., eating. This kind of thinking led to the exclusion of many retarded and physically handicapped pupils. *Still another argument* was that scarce school funds should not be diverted from the normal majority to the handicapped minority. Special services are quite expensive — increasingly so the more severe the handicap. Greater return can be obtained by spending money on the nonhandicapped, where it will go further to more pupils who can profit from it better. This kind of thinking led to exclusion — or insufficient services for — all severely handicapped pupils, including the deaf, blind, and severely speech-impaired.

Another justification for school exclusion pertained to whether a pupil's behavior was potentially harmful. That is, pupils could not be in school if their behavior was disruptive to other pupils' learning, if their behavior interfered with their own learning, or if they were dangerous to themselves or to others. This kind of thinking led to the exclusion of children with emotional and social problems and children with hyperactivity associated with learning disabilities.

Some excluded pupils stayed at home. Others went to day treatment facilities provided by health departments, parent groups, philanthropic organizations, or all three.

Exclusion from public education is harmful to handicapped youngsters because when they are out of school, they are not learning the skills they need for existing in society. In addition, exclusion is an unfair burden to the parents.

> [Handicapped children need more extensive and more intensive education than normal children, yet they] are more frequently either misplaced in school or thrown back on their parents, who then are faced with a total responsibility beyond their bearing. To the child's initial handicap, which may have been beyond our human power to prevent, are then added two man-made injuries — the deprivation for the child of the benefits of any societal education and the burden to the parent which is greatly aggravated in the social, economic, and emotional senses. (Boggs, quoted in Herr, 1977, p. 254)

Inadequate institutions   Institutions are twenty-four-hour residential facilities. Sometimes they are called hospitals; sometimes training schools. Historically, we have had institutions for every type of handicapped individual. These institutions have been large enough to serve entire states or regions within states.

Institutions for the blind and deaf generally have been run in a satisfactory way. Or at least they have had very little criticism. Some institutions for the mentally retarded and for the emotionally and socially disturbed do an adequate job. Inmates and their families benefit, or at least they are not hurt too much. Some institutions have more problems. At best, conditions in some problem institutions do not help the inmate. At worst, conditions in some problem institutions are inhuman, degrading, and dangerous to inmates' psychological and physical health (e.g., Blatt and Kaplan, 1966; Blatt *et al.*, 1979; Braginsky and Braginsky, 1974; Tebeest and Dickie, 1976; Vitello, 1976).

A. And I noticed one of the residents was in a camisole tied to a bench. A camisole is a restraining device in which the hands and arms are held roughly in this position. I asked the charge attendant about this, why it was necessary; and she explained that this was necessary because this girl sucked her hands and her fingers. And I asked the attendant how long this girl had been in a camisole; the attendant indicated as long as she, the attendant, had been on that unit, which I ascertained was the last nine years.

Q. Doctor, let me interject — is the behavior that you have just described, sucking fingers, is that able to be modified, within your experience?

A. Yes sir; this behavior can both be created, encouraged, supported, or eliminated. Not unusual — it is not unusual to find people developing this behavior when they are out in such a deprived environment that they have to find something to do to keep themselves occupied.

Q. Thank you. Would you please continue.

A. About this time, I observed a small group of girls who had already been put to bed for the evening, and several of these were tied to the bed. One was restrained by both wrists in a spreadeagle fashion with the barest possible amount of leeway for movement of the arms.

Q. Doctor, did you go to another building after you visited the Girls 2 Building?

A. We visited a unit of mildly retarded teenage and young adult girls. This was a unit which was defined as a rehabilitation unit. These girls were very verbal, spoke with me at length. They were concerned because they had little or no contact with boys. Girls of that age should now typically show some interest in that type of activity. They indicated that they viewed the facility as a prison, which was the word they used. They demanded loudly and strongly to be discharged. I found the bathroom facility for these girls to contain two toilets with no partition, with no attempt to give these girls any type of privacy. The girls spoke to me of punishment and discipline, including having to sleep on the floor, being deprived of dinner, being deprived of entertainment such as movies and shows, and in some instances being sent to a building housing profoundly retarded girls and being assigned there as a working resident.

Q. Were you able to ascertain whether this statement was accurate or not?

A. I was. I reviewed some of the files and found that indeed there were notations there indicating that some of these girls were sent to these low-level dormitories as punishment.

Q. Thank you, Doctor. Please continue.

A. I queried the staff as to the degree of contact they had with the families of these girls, and found they had almost none; that they had no meaningful contacts with the families. I also asked them about the degree of access they had to medical reports, psychological reports, social service reports, things to this type; and they indicated they had no access to these reports. They were not familiar with these types of reports; they were not involved in making any recommendations, in any of the decisions that influenced the lives of these children, even though they expend the major part of the day with them. I might say in passing that several of the girls in this unit were totally misplaced; that they were not retarded at all; and that being in a facility of this type would tend to have a devastating effect on their functioning as human beings. I did follow through on this and noted, for example, at least one of these girls on the Wechsler Adult Intelligence Scales, on which they have been evaluated, scored in the dull-normal range of intelligence, performing in essence better than fifteen percent of the population.

Q. Doctor, did you have occasion to visit at one of the other cottages?

A. I went to one of these units defined as a nonambulatory unit — that is a unit where a lot of the residents are in bed — and I observed this facility during the luncheon meal.

Q. Doctor, could you identify what unit that was, or cottage?

A. It was Cottage 3. The unfortunate residents of the cottage were being fed in bed by working residents. Essentially, they were being fed a blended diet by these working residents. I found that the charge attendant did not seem to be familiar with the residents. I asked her the name of one of the residents, and she had to look at the written name on the head of the crib before she could answer my question. There seems to be little understanding as to the nature of the residents' disabilities. I could get no explanation of why some of these individuals were unable to walk. The attendants seemed to accept at face value the notion that these residents would be unable to develop; that they would never be able to walk, to ambulate, that they would never be able to talk. A classic example of a self-fulfilling prophecy. I found, for example, that one of the residents was tied to the crib by the ankle — very short, I might say; the foot was quite cyanotic. I asked why, and I was told that this resident had a tendency to stand in the crib and that there was danger that he might fall and hurt himself, so by being tied down, this would eliminate the possibility of his standing. (Roos, 1973, pp. 469–473)

Such conditions are execrable.

People have devoted more essays and studies to ability grouping than to almost any other topic in education. Comments and studies have come from both regular education and special education.

The problem of ability grouping and special classes is complex, and arguments abound. This complexity and ambiguity are illustrated in Watts's (1975, pp. 2–3) comments on Bruinicks and Rynders's (1971, pp. 2–3) earlier summary of arguments pro and con ability grouping of the mentally retarded. These ideas pertain also to other types of handicapped pupils.

Pro	Con	Comment
Research evidence indicates that mentally retarded children in regular classrooms are usually rejected by more able classroom peers.	Special class placement isolates retarded child from normal classroom peers.	*Does physical proximity ensure societal interaction since peer attitudes are determined partly by system values. One must ask whether the system (segregated or integrated) offers the child the opportunity to reveal himself as a person with the myriad characteristics of persons or whether it limits him to revealing himself as less than adequate in areas that are highly valued by system, teacher and peers.*
Mentally retarded children in regular classroom experience loss of self-esteem because of their inability to compete with more able classroom peers.	Special class placement results in stigmatizing the retarded child, resulting in a loss of self-esteem and lowered acceptance by other children.	*Stigma may arise under either circumstance. What is done in either setting to foster self-esteem; particularly how do teachers in special or regular schools perceive the child? In which setting, under what conditions, is the more able mentally retarded child likely to gain.*
It is logically absurd to assign children to instruction without considering differences in ability or achievement levels.	There is little evidence to support the practice of ability grouping for retarded or normal children.	*Ability grouping per se is not the critical issue; the critical issue is what occurs after grouping has been achieved. To what extent do teachers capitalize on the opportunities made available?*
Evidence on the efficiency of special classes is inconclusive since most studies possess significant flaws in research design.	Mildly retarded children make as much or more academic progress in regular classrooms as they do in special classrooms.	*There is little available research evidence in Australia particularly on broad samples. Academic progress is certainly an extremely important goal, there are other goals also which must be taken into account in evaluation.*

Pro	Con	Comment
Criticisms of special classes are based ostensibly upon examples of poorly implemented programs.	There is little point in investing further energy in improving special classes, since this arrangement poorly serves the social and educational needs of children.	*(Con) This seems an unwarranted conclusion.*
The alternatives to present practices are less desirable and would lead to a return to social promotion as an approach to dealing with mildly retarded children.	Other more flexible administrative and curricula arrangements should be developed to supplement or supplant special classes.	*Both are true.*
Properly implemented special classes are optimally suited to deal with the major learning problems of retarded children.	Special class arrangements inappropriately place the responsibility for academic failure on children rather than upon schools and teachers.	*What is the research evidence for the Pro statement?* *(Con) Need this be so? The philosophy of the education system is implicated here.*
Special class arrangements should not be unfairly indicted for mistakes in diagnosis and placement.	The very existence of special classes encourages the misplacement of many children, particularly children from minority groups.	*The first step in referral and ultimate special school placement of children is most frequently carried out by the teacher (Mercer, 1973). Won't teacher attitudes which prompt referral continue in the regular classroom?*
A democratic philosophy of education does not dictate that all children have the same educational experiences, but that all children receive an equal opportunity to learn according to their individual needs and abilities.	Special class placement is inconsistent with the tenets of a democratic philosophy of education because it isolates retarded from normal children, and vice versa.	*What is democracy? It seems that the protagonists and antagonists of many positions can equally invoke "democracy."*

The abstractions above are pretty powerful. However, we must remember that there is a human dimension also. These comments, excerpted from the text of *Guadalupe* v. *Tempe Elementary School District,* show a youngster's pain.

It really don't have to be the tests, but after the tests, there shouldn't be no separation in the classes. Because, as I say again, I felt good when I was with my class, but when they went and separated us — that changed us. That changed our ideas, our thinking, the way we thought about each other and turned us to enemies toward each other — because they said I was dumb and they were smart.

When you first go to junior high school you do feel something inside. You have been from elementary to junior high, you feel great inside. You say, well daggone, I'm going to deal with the *people* here now, I am in junior high school. You get this shirt that says Brown Junior High or whatever the name is and you are proud of that shirt. But then you go up there and the teacher says — "Well, so and so, you're in the basic section, you can't go with the other kids." The devil with the whole thing — you lose — something in you — like it just goes out of you. (Cited in Levine, 1973, p. 105)

On the other hand, the human side of the ambiguity and complexity of special class versus regular-class placement could as easily be illustrated by citing how a youngster feels when facing the competition and hurly-burly of the regular class and of an unprotected environment in general — especially during the adolescent years.

These comments all point to one conclusion. As it happens in most complex issues, placing pupils in regular classes and placing them in special classes both have benefits and drawbacks. Neither is clearly superior. Different pupils need different placements, depending on their characteristics beyond their handicaps or talents.

Transportation and facilities share problems of stigmatizing, access, and safety (e.g., McGaughey, 1976; Morgan, 1976; Nelson, 1977; Van Vechten and Pless, 1976).

Inadequate transportation and facilities

Stigmatizing can happen if we set apart or unduly mark facilities used for resource rooms, special classes, and related services. For example, it may occur as putting a special class for adolescents in an elementary school, devoting one wing of a building to all special services, using signs such as "special class" or "visually handicapped resource room." Stigmatizing is a problem that is minor now because it is fast disappearing.

Access problems are more complex. Section 504 of PL 93-112 now requires that new public buildings be free of barriers. However, facilities designed before the 1970s have many barriers which will require time, money, and effort to correct or compensate for. These old buildings become serious problems as normalization leads handicapped people to more and more public places. For example, the *physically handicapped* encounter physical barriers because of the way buildings are constructed. Many buildings have more than one story. Some have elevators and some do not. Doors, which are hard to manage from wheel chairs or crutches or because of unsteady balance, are in entrances to buildings, rest rooms, and other rooms. Water fountains are difficult to reach from wheel chairs. Cafeteria lines are difficult to deal with. Public telephones are high to reach. Outside curbs, steps, and sharp inclines are difficult to manage. Parking for cars is often difficult to find.

Schools have, of course, always been responsible for the *safety* of pupils on the premises and enroute to and from school. And handicapped pupils have always merited special caution. However, again, the potential problems have increased as normalization causes mainstreaming and other activities connected with the least restrictive environment. Pupils' handicaps make them particularly vulnerable (Klimert, n.d.; Russon, 1974). Again, an illustration: Hearing-impaired individuals have difficulty hearing warning sounds in their environment, e.g., an oncoming car as they leave the school bus, the fire alarm signal, or the shout of warning about an oncoming baseball. In addition, their language impairments may make it difficult for them to understand safety warnings and rules. For instance, they may not understand, and thus not heed, such rules as: no horseplay may occur when the teacher is absent, safety goggles must be worn in the shop, no running by or around the stairs.

The Law Governing Placement

A great deal of legal attention has been devoted to placement.[*] Court rulings clearly require treatment in institutions or release, access to public education, placement in the least restrictive environment, equal protection, due process, confidentiality, and advocate participation in decision making. Also, these requirements are written into the statutes. Regulations to guide enforcing the statutes have detailed procedures for carrying out these requirements.

One thing we need to consider clearly. Understanding the concept of the least restrictive environment is very important in carrying out the requirements for placement. Again, the least restrictive environment is not an absolute place; it is not a synonym for a regular class, a self-contained group of twenty-five to thirty pupils who are about the same on chronological age and possibly different on other characteristics. Rather, it *is* a relative place. It is the most enabling environment, the location where pupils can function most effectively and comfortably at a particular time, with the understanding that they can be, and must be, moved as their needs change. The principle is that we must not separate exceptional pupils from nonexceptional pupils any more than necessary to fit instruction to their characteristics. Each pupil must be placed in a situation that is as nonspecialized as possible.

---

[*] *Hobson v. Hansen* and *PARC v. Commonwealth of Pennsylvania* are examples of the court rulings; PL 94-142 and PL 93-112, of the statutes. Descriptions of, and comments on, the growing body of litigation and legislation are in such sources as Abeson (1976), Burgdorf and Bersoff (1980), Burt (1976), Chambers (1976), Federal Programs Advisory Service (1980), Kirp (1974a,b), *Michigan Law Review* (1973).

This definition and principle translate into essential points we must observe when we provide the least restrictive environment for the pupil.

☐ Each pupil's educational placement must be reevaluated yearly or more often.

☐ Placement decisions must be made by a group of persons who know about the pupil, the meaning of the evaluation information, and the placement options.

☐ The team must consider, as appropriate, evaluation information from a variety of sources, including aptitude and achievement levels, physical condition, social and cultural background, and adaptive behavior.

☐ Placement options must include a continuum of alternative placements, facilities, and services. These include: (1) placements in a hierarchy from the least specialized to the most specialized; and (2) facilities and services that enable the pupil to function in the least specialized placement possible.

☐ The exceptional pupil must be educated with nonhandicapped pupils as much as possible.

☐ The pupil may be placed in a special class or otherwise removed from the regular class only if he or she cannot get along in regular class, given all of the supplementary aids and services appropriate.

☐ In turn, the pupil may be placed in a special day school only if he or she cannot profit from a special class given all of the supplementary aids and services appropriate.

☐ Further, a pupil may be placed in a residential school only if he or she cannot get along in the available special classes and special day schools, given all of the supplementary aids and services appropriate.

☐ The placement must be based on the pupil's individual educational plan. It must be in the school the pupil would attend if he or she were not handicapped, unless the IEP indicates otherwise.

☐ Pupils may not be denied any placement because facilities are not accessible to, or usable by, handicapped people. Old facilities must be altered as needed to be appropriate to the handicapped. New facilities must be designed to be appropriate.*

---

* These comments are a summary and paraphrase of requirements in PL 94-142 and PL 93-112.

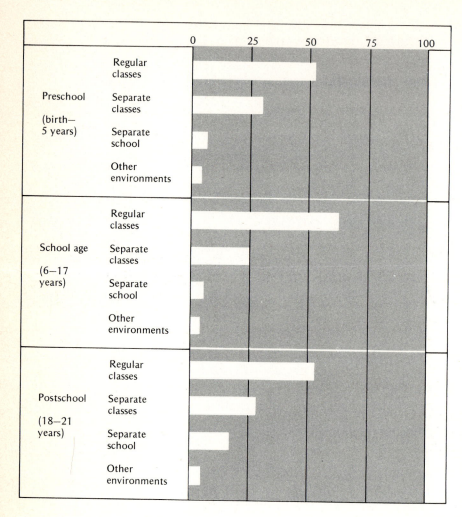

Fig. 3.6
Most frequent placements of handicapped pupils reported by the states in the late 1970s. (Based on information in BEH, 1979, pp. 169–180.)

Figure 3.6 shows the placements being used in the late 1970s as we were beginning to progress toward fully observing these requirements.

In addition, the team deciding about placement must identify and plan for the pupil's transportation. As the pupil's needs require, these transportation plans cover the pupil's movement within the school, from home to school, and from school to places where the pupil gets therapy, if these sites are outside the school.

Finding appropriate extracurricular activities is an essential part of placement.

Teachers and other personnel who officially work with exceptional pupils must supervise these pupils' conduct and all of their activities and protect them from all forseeable risks. Failure to supervise makes the teacher liable for damages (e.g., Gee and Sperry, 1978). The following situations are examples of what the duty to supervise covers.

☐ The teacher should be present with the pupils. The teacher should foresee that injury can occur during his or her absence.

☐ The teacher must instruct the student about, and enforce, rules for hazardous situations, such as shop work and hazardous athletic events.

☐ The teacher must not allow a pupil to engage in hazardous or strenuous activities if he or she is physically unfit to do so.

☐ The teacher must not use unreasonable procedures when disciplining a student.

☐ The teacher must not put a student in a hazardous situation and then fail to supervise his or her activities.

Bus drivers and other school employees must exercise caution during official transportation. These principles are examples.

☐ The driver must operate the bus safely, e.g., maintain lawful and appropriate speeds.

□ The pupils must be discharged to a place safely and cautioned about possible dangers. In addition, all signals must be in operation until the student is out of danger.

□ Safe conditions must be maintained inside the vehicle, e.g., horseplay must be prevented.

The school building and grounds (facilities) must be safe. Pupils should be warned against, and protected from, possible dangers. For example:

□ Defects (e.g., broken playground equipment) should be identified and repaired.

□ Dangerous situations (e.g., steep stairways) should be pointed out.

□ Rules of conduct (e.g., no horseplay) should be made, disseminated, and enforced.

Summary

INDIVIDUALIZING INSTRUCTION FOR EXCEPTIONAL PUPILS

Individualizing Instruction as a Tool for Dealing with Individual Differences

The process of individualizing instruction

Individualizing instruction is fitting instruction to each pupil by looking at his or her strengths and problems and then choosing the educational services he or she needs. The four phases are testing to determine the pupil's strengths and weaknesses, prescribing special education or related services, doing the teaching or therapy prescribed, and evaluating and revising the prescription in the light of the pupil's progress. In special education the process is labeled with such terms as clinical teaching and diagnostic and prescriptive teaching.

Special education

Special education is specially designed instruction to meet the unique needs of the pupil. When we prescribe, or design, instruction, we work with four components: instructional objectives, schedules, procedures, and settings. For each component, we make selections appropriate for the pupil's characteristics. These selections may or may not differ from selections we make for other pupils.

The related services

Related services are therapy, transportation, and other services the pupil needs to benefit from special education. These services are supplied by speech pathologists, audiologists, psychologists, social workers, vocational rehabilitation specialists, physical therapists, and physicians.

We have had procedures for individualizing instruction for a long time. Although we have accomplished a great deal, many youngsters are still not functioning as well as they could or should. One problem is functional exclusion — not teaching a pupil as well and fully as we should because it is so difficult to deal with handicaps and talents and because we do not expect enough of pupils. Another problem is confusion about instruction and placement — placing a pupil but failing to individualize instruction so that he or she can learn in that setting *or* individualizing instruction but failing to place the pupil in a setting where that instruction can be delivered effectively.

Now individualized programs are required by law for handicapped individuals and other vulnerable individuals. The legal basis for this requirement is the concept of equal educational opportunity. This concept has evolved until it now means that the individual must be provided equal access to differing resources for differing objectives. PL 94-142 explicitly requires that we individualize instruction — get information about pupils' present performance levels and on that basis specify annual goals and short-term objectives, name all educational services, state how programs will be evaluated, and supply schedules for instruction, evaluation, and revision. At the same time, we must provide for advocate participation and due process. As we carry out the law here, we must be clear about accountability. We are accountable for program adequacy, which we ensure through the Child-Find and the IEP. We are not accountable for the pupil's attaining a minimum standard of achievement.

PLACING EXCEPTIONAL PUPILS IN THE LEAST RESTRICTIVE ENVIRONMENT

Placement is a tool for locating a pupil for conveniently delivering services to him or her. Placement options are the plans for organizing pupils and teachers to deal with individual differences. Originally, pupils were not grouped. Then chronological age-grade grouping was used to reduce individual differences in groups teachers dealt with. Since individual differences still remained, further plans were developed: *outside public day schools* (residential schools, home instruction, hospital instruction), *preschool programs, achievement/ability grouping* (acceleration and retention, homogeneous grouping, course selection, and program selection), *within chronological age grouping* (regular classes with resource teachers and resource room procedures, nongraded plans, and continuous

Legal Safeguards in Individualizing Instruction

Problems in individualizing instruction for exceptional pupils

The law governing individualizing instruction

Placement as a Tool for Dealing with Individual Differences

Placement options

progress plans), *combined ability and CA grouping* (part-time special classes), and *no grouping* (open education).

The least restrictive environment

The widely recognized legal concept of the least restrictive alternative has been applied as the least restrictive environment in handicapped people's residential placement and school placement. The basis for this application is the principle of normalization — enabling a person to participate in society as much and as independently as possible. Applied to residential placement, normalization involves arranging housing and services so that the handicapped individual can, as much as possible, live in the community as nonhandicapped individuals do, participating socially and physically in school, church, recreation, and other activities. Applied to education, normalization involves arranging things so that the handicapped can participate in school activities as much as possible as nonhandicapped pupils do. The key is flexibility — flexibility of placements where pupils move back and forth between more and less restrictive environments as their needs and capabilities change and flexibility of services where pupils stay in one environment as we move more and less specialized services in and out as their needs and capabilities change.

There is some confusion about the relationship among placement in the least restrictive environment, mainstreaming, and placement in the regular class. Placement in the least restrictive environment and mainstreaming are synonyms. Regular-class placement is one option on a continuum of options used in placing pupils in the least restrictive environment. The option of regular-class placement for handicapped pupils must be used very carefully. The goal is to get pupils to the most *enabling* environment for them to learn and perform the cultural tasks.

Transportation and facilities

Transportation and facilities are key concerns in placing exceptional pupils. Transportation includes all of pupils' travel. Facilities refer to the physical structure of the environment. Many handicapped pupils require special transportation and facilities.

Legal Safeguards in Placement

Problems in placing exceptional pupils

We have had some great difficulties in using the placement options to deal with individual differences in both regular education and special education. The major problems have centered on arbitrary placement, exclusion from school, institutionalization, ability grouping, and facilities and transportation. These problems have had a frightful human cost.

Much legal attention has been devoted to placement. The litigation and the legislation now clearly require treatment in institutions or release, access to public education, placement in the least restrictive environment, equal protection, due process, confidentiality, and advocate participation in decision making. In addition, appropriate transportation and facilities must be provided, as well as protection of pupils against foreseeable risks.

The law governing placement

Rutland Center — Developmental Therapy Institute, Mary M. Wood

Special Needs Part
of Exceptional Pupils

2

Hillel, the great Rabbi, was once asked to very briefly give the meaning of Judaism. His reply: "Love God and your fellow man. All the rest is explanation."

So it is with other great principles — civil rights principles among them. We have to consider many details when we apply highly distilled, and simply stated, ideas to specific cases.

In Part II we consider some details about how we apply the principles of equality and inalienable rights to ways we serve exceptional youngsters. We use this approach. In Part I we saw how the traditional tools for fitting education to pupils' individual differences have in contemporary practice become four tasks in guaranteeing pupils' entitlements and protections — identification and planning, non-discriminatory testing, individualizing instruction, and placement in the least restrictive environment. Now, in Part II, we examine how these tasks are applied to categories of exceptional pupils protected by the laws — pupils who have speech and language impairments, hearing impairments, visual impairments, gifts and talents, mental retardation, learning disabilities, and emotional disturbances.

TOPICS

Identifying and planning for speech-/language-impaired pupils

Special Needs of Speech-/Language-Impaired Pupils

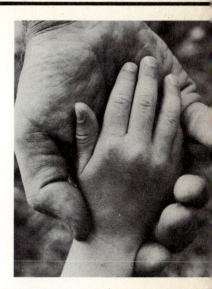

ACCOUNTABILITY

> Identifying and planning for speech-/language-impaired pupils

> Observing the procedural safeguards for speech-/language-impaired pupils

Nondiscriminatory testing of speech-/language-impaired pupils

PROBLEMS IN TESTING SPEECH-/LANGUAGE-IMPAIRED PUPILS

PROCEDURES FOR TESTING SPEECH-/LANGUAGE-IMPAIRED PUPILS

Individualizing instruction for speech-/language-impaired pupils

SPEECH/LANGUAGE THERAPY

> Articulation problems
> Voice problems
> Fluency problems

Language problems
Multiple problems

OTHER RELATED SERVICES

Audiology
Medical services
Psychological services
Vocational rehabilitation
Physical therapy

SPECIAL EDUCATION

Placing speech-/language-impaired pupils in the least restrictive environment

PLACEMENT OPTIONS
EXTRACURRICULAR ACTIVITIES
TRANSPORTATION AND FACILITIES
SAFETY

Identifying and planning for speech-/language-impaired pupils

Identifying and planning constitute our first task in guaranteeing that speech-/language-impaired pupils receive a free appropriate public education and an equal educational opportunity. Here we conduct the Child-Find and develop the individual education program. At the same time, we observe the procedural safeguards. Our doing these activities requires that we understand normal speech and language, speech and language impairments, and the impact of these impairments on pupils' characteristics.

NORMAL SPEECH AND LANGUAGE

Adequate structure and functioning of the central nervous system, the ears, and the speech apparatus are essential to normal development of speech and language behavior. Normal speech and language development, in turn, is essential to accomplishing the cultural tasks.

Structure and Functioning of the Speech Apparatus*

Figure 4.1 shows the speech apparatus. The structures work together to control three essential functions — phonation, articulation, and resonation. *Phonation* is producing voiced sounds. The muscles in the rib cage contract to begin the outward flow of air. This airflow is shaped as it goes through the larynx, pharynx, and mouth structures. *Resonation* is reinforcement and prolongation of sound by the sound waves' bouncing and vibrating as they pass through the larynx, pharynx, mouth, nose, and sinuses. *Articulation* is shaping the speech sounds as the resonant sound waves go through the patterns of the throat, jaws, and tongue muscles acting together with one another and with the teeth. Phonation, resonation, and articulation coordinate to control sound production. In addition, phonation controls pitch (high/low), intensity (loud/soft), and fluency (inflection and the flow of speech) (e.g., Hixon and Abbs, 1980).

Development of Normal Speech and Language Behavior

"*Communication* is the process of exchanging messages using any system (not confined to language) and various media (e.g., speech, gesture, facial expression). *Language* is a conventional system of

---

* We will consider the structure and functioning of the ear in Chapter 5 and the central nervous system in Chapter 7.

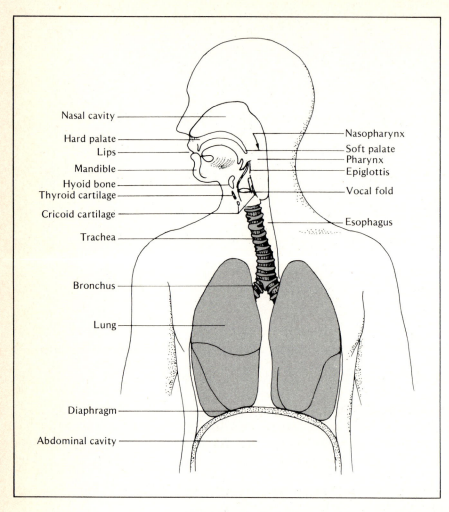

Nasal cavity

Hard palate
Lips
Mandible
Hyoid bone
Thyroid cartilage
Cricoid cartilage

Trachea

Bronchus

Lung

Diaphragm

Abdominal cavity

Nasopharynx
Soft palate
Pharynx
Epiglottis

Vocal fold

Esophagus

Fig. 4.1
The structure of the speech
apparatus.

phonological, syntactic, and semantic rules* for decoding experience. *Speech* production is the vocal-motor channel of language performance" (American Speech and Hearing Association, 1978).

The infant cries at birth. Moving from this generalized sound production, speech and language skills differentiate as the child matures neurologically and physically and learns (e.g., Rees, 1980; Shelton and

---

* *Phonology* refers to the sound units (phonemes), i.e., vowels and consonants. *Syntax* refers to: (1) indivisible meaning units (morphemes), e.g., the (s) plural or the (un) prefix, as they are combined to make words; (2) parts of speech (form classes), e.g., nouns; and (3) sentence patterns, e.g., questions. *Semantics* refers to word meanings. We have literal meanings and figurative meanings. For example, literally "green" refers to a color, as in "a green tree"; figuratively, it refers to an inexperienced person, as in "a green baseball player, who still needs to learn when he can steal bases."

Wood, 1978). Table 4.1 shows some milestones in the form of the chronological ages when some skills emerge in the process of normal speech and language development. Note especially how more complex skills at the later ages are built on the simpler skills at the younger ages. For example, "joins sentences together" at four to five years requires such earlier developed skills as:

☐ "Talks in sentences of three or more words" at three to four years,

☐ "Joins vocabulary together in two-word phrases," at two to three years,

☐ "Says successive simple words to describe an event," at one to two years, and

☐ "Repeats some vowel and consonant sounds," below one year.

TABLE 4.1 MILESTONES IN DEVELOPING SPEECH AND LANGUAGE BEHAVIOR.

Age (Months)	Understanding Speech and Language	Producing Speech and Language
	Responds to speech by looking at speaker.	Makes crying and noncrying sounds.
	Responds differently to aspects of speaker's voice (for example, friendly or unfriendly, male or female).	Repeats some vowel and consonant sounds (babbles) when alone or when spoken to.
0–12	Turns to source of sound.	Interacts with others by vocalizing after adult.
	Responds with gesture to *hi, bye-bye,* and *up,* when these words are accompanied by appropriate gesture.	Communicates meaning through intonation.
	Stops ongoing action when told *no* (when negative is accompanied by appropriate gesture and tone).	Attempts to imitate sounds.
	Responds correctly when asked where (when question is accompanied by gesture).	Says first meaningful word.
		Uses single word plus a gesture to ask for objects.

(continued)

TABLE 4.1 *(continued)*

Age (Months)	Understanding Speech and Language	Producing Speech and Language
12–24	Understands prepositions *on, in,* and *under.* Follows request to bring familiar object from another room. Understands simple phrases with key words (for example, *Open the door,* or *Get the ball*). Follows a series of 2 simple but related directions.	Says successive single words to describe an event. Refers to self by name. Uses *my* or *mine* to indicate possession. Has vocabulary of about 50 words for important people, common objects, and the existence, non-existence, and recurrence of objects and events (for example, *more* and *all gone*).
24–36	Points to pictures of common objects when they are named. Can identify objects when told their use. Understands question forms *what* and *where.* Understands negatives *no, not, can't,* and *don't.* Enjoys listening to simple storybooks and requests them again.	Joins vocabulary words together in two-word phrases. Gives first and last name. Asks *what* and *where* questions. Makes negative statements (for example, *Can't open it*). Shows frustration at not being understood.
	Begins to understand sentences involving time concepts (for example, *We are*	Talks in sentences of three or more words, which take the form agent-action-object

Age (Months)	Understanding Speech and Language	Producing Speech and Language
	going to the zoo tomorrow). Understands size comparatives such as *big* and *bigger*.	(*I see the ball*) or agent-action-location (*Daddy sit on chair*). Tells about past experiences.
36–48	Understands relationships expressed by *if… then* or *because* sentences. Carries out a series of 2 to 4 related directions. Understands when told, *Let's pretend.*	Uses "s" on nouns to indicate plurals. Uses "ed" on verbs to indicate past tense. Refers to self using pronouns *I* or *me*. Repeats at least one nursery rhyme and can sing a song. Speech is understandable to strangers, but there are still some sound errors.
48–60	Follows three unrelated commands in proper order. Understands comparatives like *pretty, prettier*, and *prettiest.* Listens to long stories but often misinterprets the facts. Incorporates verbal directions into play activities. Understands sequencing of events when told them (for	Asks *when, how*, and *why* questions. Uses modals like *can, will, shall, should*, and *might.* Joins sentences together (for example, *I like chocolate chip cookies and milk*). Talks about causality by using *because* and *so.* Tells the content of a story but may confuse facts.

(continued)

TABLE 4.1 *(continued)*

Age (Months)	Understanding Speech and Language	Producing Speech and Language
	example, *First we have to go to the store, then we can make the cake, and tomorrow we will eat it).*	
60–72	Demonstrates pre-academic skills.	There are few obvious differences between child's grammar and adult's grammar.
		Still needs to learn such things as subject-verb agreement, and some irregular past tense verbs.
		Can take appropriate turns in a conversation.
		Gives and receives information.
		Communicates well with family, friends, or strangers.

Source: Hayden and Smith (n.d., pp. 126–133).

Speech and Language and the Cultural Tasks

In our interactions with other people we certainly communicate nonverbally — through facial expressions, bodily positions, and movements. However, we do most of our communicating — especially our clearest communicating — through speech and language. We communicate directly in face-to-face situations and indirectly through devices such as the telephone, audiotapes, and TV. Consequently, speech and language are central to our accomplishing the cultural tasks which require exchanging information. Look back at Table 1.3 and decide how many cultural tasks like those listed there require speech and language for learning them and performing them. Also consider how accomplishing later tasks rests on accomplishing earlier tasks.

> When we deal with speech, we deal with the essence of man. Only human beings have mastered speech. It is what sets us apart from all other species. Because we can speak, we can think symbolically; and it is this which has enabled man to conquer the world and space and every other creature...
>
> We who have spoken so much so easily and for so long find it hard to comprehend the miraculous nature of speech — this peculiarly human tool. It seems as natural and as easy as breathing. (It is utterly vital and necessary) to human existence. Not only do we use it in thinking and in the sending and receiving of messages, we also build our very sense of self out of word-stuff. We need speech to command and restrain ourselves. Our words are our means for controlling others. Verbally we express our loves and hates. It is the safety valve of our emotions, the medicine of psychotherapy.
>
> The good things of life must be asked for, must be earned by the mouth as well as the hands. The fun of companionship, the satisfaction of earning a good living, the winning of a mate, the pride of self-respect and appreciation, these things come hard to the person who cannot talk. Often he must settle for less than his potential might provide, were it not for his tangled tongue. Speech is the "Open Sesame," the magical power. When it is distorted, there is small magic in it — and much frustration.
>
> We need safety valves for emotion. When we can express the angry evils within us, they subside; when we can verbalize our grief, it decreases. A fear coded into words and shared by a companion seems less distressing. A guilt confessed brings absolution....
>
> (We use) speech as the expression of self.... Most of us talk about ourselves most of the time. We talk so people will notice us, so we can feel important. This egocentric speech is highly important in the development of the personality.... If you will listen to the people about you or to yourself, you will discover how large a portion of your talking consists of this cock-a-doodle-dooing. When we speak this way we reassure ourselves that all is well, that we are not alone, that we exist and belong. (Van Riper, 1978, pp. 8, 24–25)

SPEECH AND LANGUAGE IMPAIRMENTS

Sometimes problems interfere with the structure and function of the speech apparatus, the central nervous system, or the ears. These problems can cause disruption to the normal development of speech and language behavior. We call this disruption an impairment when it is bad enough to interfere with a youngster's learning and performing the cultural tasks. These principles are applied in the legal definition we use to identify speech- and language-impaired youngsters quali-

Legal Definition and Prevalence

fied for the rights to special education services and related services and to the protections of the procedural safeguards guaranteed under PL 94-142. "A speech impairment is a communication disorder, such as stuttering, impaired articulation, a language impairment, or a voice impairment, which adversely affects a child's educational performance" (PL 94-142, Sec. 121a.5).

The information in Fig. 1.1 shows that 2.5% to 4.0% of school pupils have speech/language impairments. About 2.4% of these pupils were receiving services in the late 1970s.

Finding Speech-/ Language-Impaired Pupils

Public *awareness* campaigns are an important part of the Child-Find for locating pupils whose speech/language impairments qualify them for the entitlements and protections guaranteed in the laws. Again, early detection is crucial because early skills are so important to later development.

Adults in contact with the pupil do *screening* for signs of speech/language impairments. Parents and teachers are key people in screening because they see the youngster in so many different situations. In addition, one responsibility of the speech pathologist is to screen

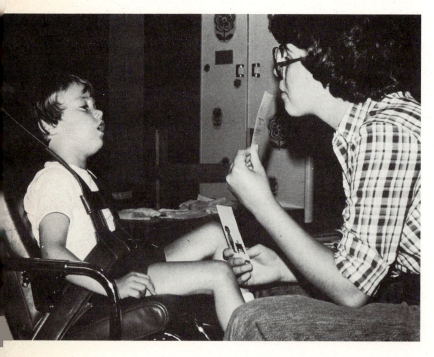

Speech and language problems may adversely affect a pupil's development.

pupils for problems. Examples of signs of problems are:

☐ The pupil does not talk very often, seldom volunteering to speak or not responding when spoken to.

☐ Other pupils make fun of the pupil's speech and language.

☐ The pupil consistently mispronounces certain sounds. His or her speech may be very difficult to understand.

☐ The pupil's voice is inappropriate, e.g., too loud or soft for the circumstances, too high-pitched or low-pitched for his or her age and sex, too harsh or breathy, or too nasal or denasal.

☐ The pupil has garbled speech even in periods of little stress. He or she talks too fast and adds too many extra syllables and words.

☐ The pupil has an excessive number of repetitions, prolongations, and pauses for his or her age and also may engage in struggle behavior when trying to speak.

☐ The pupil has trouble using words, appearing not to understand words or having difficulty producing words for objects. At the same time, he or she has difficulty producing written symbols in writing or understanding written symbols in reading.

☐ The pupil's level of language is behind the levels reached by other pupils his or her age. His or her vocabulary is unduly limited, or his or her grammar is unduly rudimentary.

Parents and teachers seeing such symptoms make *referrals*, sending the pupil to the speech/language pathologist for further study. Depending on the problem, the speech/language pathologist refers the pupil to several specialists: an *audiologist* for a fuller evaluation of hearing; an *otologist* for a fuller evaluation of the ear's anatomy and functioning; an ear, nose, and throat specialist for a fuller evaluation of the anatomy and functioning of the speech apparatus; and a neurologist for a further evaluation of how well the central nervous system is functioning.

Speech impairments include articulation problems, voice problems, and fluency problems. Language impairments include aphasia and delayed language (Filter, 1977).

Articulation problems are wrong productions of sounds. *Substitution* is using a different sound in place of the conventional one. *Distortion* is mispronouncing the sound. *Omission* is leaving out a sound, and *addition* is putting in an extra sound (Shelton, 1978a).

Diagnosis: Classifying Pupils by Type of Speech/Language Impairment

Articulation problems

The following are examples of commonly occurring articulation problems.

1. *Substitution:* /f/ for the voiceless /th/; /v/ for the voiced /th/. "Muvver, I hurt my fumb" for "Mother, I hurt my thumb."
2. *Distortion:* the lateral lisp in producing the *s,* as in "LLLLick LLLam" (L's whispered) for "Sick Sam."
3. *Omission:* leaving out initial sounds in words, as in "A I eep the oor?" for "May I sweep the floor?"
4. *Addition:* putting in medial sounds, as in "Puh lease hit the buh all" for "Please hit the ball."

Voice problems   *Voice problems* result from wrong phonation and resonation. They include pitch, intensity, and voice-quality disorders (Boone 1977, 1980; Damste and Lerman, 1975; Shelton, 1978*b*).

One type of *pitch disorder* occurs when the person's voice is higher or lower than we expect of someone his or her age and sex. Another occurs when a person uses an improper inflection pattern, such as a monotone or a persistent ending of sentences with a rising inflection.

One *intensity problem* is persistent aphonia, i.e., loss of voice, whereby the person's voice becomes a whisper. A related problem is when the voice is too soft for the situation, especially when there are signs of strain. The opposite problem is when the voice is too loud for the situation, again especially when there are signs of strain.

Voice-quality problems include several difficulties. *Nasality* refers to how the air is resonated in the nose and nasal sinuses. *Hypernasality* happens when too much air goes through the nose when the person produces the vowels and all of the consonants except the m's, n's and ng's. *Hyponasality*, or denasality, occurs when too little air goes through the nose. This is the cold-in-the-nose sound. Other, more ambiguous voice problems include excessive harshness and excessive hoarseness.

Fluency problems   *Fluency problems* are difficulties in phonation. Stuttering and cluttering are the main disorders we see in which speech loses fluency (Dalton and Hardcastle, 1978; Perkins, 1980; Wingate, 1978; Zwitman, 1978).

Primary stuttering is excessive hesitations or prolongations (e.g., t———table) or excessive repetitions (e.g., t-t-t-table) of sounds during speech. It is sometimes called dysfluency. *Secondary stuttering* is the added-on grimaces, head movements, or gestures indicating a struggle to speak accompanying the primary stuttering. Some people block and stutter randomly; some, on particular sounds; and some, on particular words.

Cluttering is fast speech garbled with extra sounds or mispronounced sounds and sometimes mixed-up sentence structure. For example, "Can I-I mean-uh May I — uh-uh-g-g-go to the — May I run over to the store to-to-to-uh uh-buy one-two-one pound of lice — oh no darn it — I mean rice."

Aphasia means loss* of ability to express meanings in language or to receive meanings through language once language has developed. For example, the pupil may know what the actions of running and walking are, but be unable to say the words for the meanings. Or, conversely, he or she may be able to say words but not to attach them to the objects or situations they stand for. This difficulty in expressing or receiving messages through speech may occur alongside difficulty in receiving messages through reading (dyslexia) or producing messages through writing (agraphia). That is, the pupil has a general difficulty dealing with symbols in communication (Agranowitz and McKeown, 1975; Eisenson, 1972; Hubbell, 1978; Wiig and Semmel, 1976).

Aphasia

Delayed language is the failure of language skills to appear at the ages when they ordinarily appear. That is, the youngster may not be able to understand what someone says to him or her or may not be able to convey a message through speech and language. For example, look back at the milestones in Table 4.1. The youngster who has not mastered skills such as producing three-word sentences by age three to four is showing delayed language development.

Delayed language

All of the speech/language impairments occur alone. In addition, they occur in sets in association with cleft palate/cleft lip and other handicaps.

Multiple speech/ language impairments

Clefts in the palate, the lip, or both happen early in fetal development. The palate, or lip, or both fail to fuse at the midline (Ewanowski, 1980). When there is a cleft in the palate, the youngster cannot resonate properly and also expells air through his or her nose. The result is a voice problem — hypernasality — and an articulation problem — improper pronunciation of sounds that require storing up air pressure, for example, unvoiced sounds such as /th/ in *breath* and consonant blends such as /st/ in *stop*. A cleft in the lip and upper gum ridge causes problems in articulating sounds usually made in the front of the mouth, such as /b/, /d/, /t/, /p/.

Cleft palate/cleft lip

---

* Some children never develop the ability. This condition is called congenital aphasia.

*Cerebral palsy** The cerebral palsied youngster will have speech impairments if the muscles of his or her rib cage, throat, and mouth do not move properly. He or she will have trouble with articulation if the tongue, lip, and throat muscles are cerebral palsied. He or she will have fluency problems showing up as labored speech if the rib cage muscles are cerebral palsied, i.e., speech will be halting and then come in bursts (Aronson, 1980). In addition, the youngster may show aphasia if the brain injury that causes the movement disturbances also causes disturbances in his or her ability to use symbols. And it sometimes happens that he or she may show delayed language development because of the restriction of experience often accompanying severe cerebral palsy.

Hearing impairment Deaf youngsters have difficulty with all areas — articulation, voice quality, fluency, and language — because they cannot hear to learn the conventional speech patterns and language meanings. Nor can they rely on their hearing for feedback and monitoring their speech — its articulation, fluency, and voice quality (Bloodstein, 1979).

Mental retardation Mental retardation leads to several problems. By definition, mentally retarded youngsters have a slow rate of intellectual development. This delay affects how quickly they learn speech and language. Therefore retarded youngsters show more articulation problems and more delayed appearance of speech and language structures when they are compared to other children their chronological ages.

Diagnosis: Classifying Pupils by Cause of Speech/Language Impairment
Organic problems

Organic problems and functional problems are traditional ways of classifying causes of speech and language problems (Filter, 1977).

Organic disorders result from deformities in the speech apparatus, damage to the brain, or damage to the cranial nerves serving the speech apparatus.

Brain injury is the cause of aphasia. Brain injury also causes problems in muscle function, which in turn lead to the speech problems of cerebral palsied youngsters.

Deformities of the lips, gums, and palate lead to articulation and voice problems associated with cleft palate and cleft lip.

Injury to the cranial nerves serving the nose, mouth, throat, or rib cage or injury to those structures themselves can lead to problems in articulation, voice quality, and rhythm. So can a laryngectomy, an operation to remove the larynx.

Functional problems Functional problems occur when speech and language go wrong, but no organic problems are apparent. That is, the problems are due to the

---

* A movement disturbance resulting from brain injury.

pupil's not learning to use conventional ways of speaking or conventional language structures. He or she may have come from a deprived language environment, may not have had the appropriate models to imitate, may have made errors that were not corrected and thus became habits, may have emotional problems that affect speech and language, or may have been rewarded for improper patterns, e.g., a lisp may have been considered, and treated, as cute.

We do not know what causes some problems. For example, stuttering requires special consideration. People differ in their ideas about the cause of stuttering. Some believe that stuttering is organic, e.g., improper dominance relationships between the hemispheres of the brain. Some believe that stuttering is learned, e.g., a child who is dysfluent by chance is labeled a stutterer and treated as one until ultimately he or she persists in the dysfluency and builds up the secondary stuttering pattern.

Unknown causes

People from different ethnic and racial groups and different geographical regions sometimes use different dialects (Naremore, 1980). Some groups speak more rapidly than the norm, some more slowly. Some have different articulation and inflection patterns. For example, New Englanders' substitutions, additions, and distortions appear in such patterns as "Ayeh, I sawr him in the yaad in Bawstin," and Southerners are notorious for their omissions and distortions as in such patterns as "Thays out yonder huntin wif th houn dawgs."

The Distinction between Dialects and Speech Problems

When do these differences become problems and the concern of the speech/language pathologist? This question has generated much controversy — especially as it pertains to black dialect. One viewpoint is that the pupil should be taught to speak standard English. Another viewpoint is that the dialect is a complete language and appropriate for the culture in which the pupil learned it. Still another viewpoint is that the pupil should be taught to discriminate between his or her dialect and standard English and to choose and use either one at will, depending on how he or she wishes to speak and on what is appropriate for the particular situation. For example, one might use dialect at a family reunion and standard English at an interview for a job in a large national corporation.

IMPACT OF SPEECH/LANGUAGE IMPAIRMENTS ON PUPILS' CHARACTERISTICS

To recap: A speech or language impairment — i.e., a disruption in normal speech and language development — interferes with the pupil's accomplishing the cultural tasks that must be mastered to

Introduction

meet his or her needs in socially approved ways. Sometimes this interference is direct. Sometimes it is indirect through the speech and language impairments affecting other primary characteristics, such as emotional function, which in turn affect the youngster's accomplishing the cultural tasks. These comments illustrate ways speech impairments interfere and the pain this interference causes.

> *The worst feature of my brain injury was the frustration. I would know exactly what I wanted to say, but it would come out of my mouth differently. If I wanted to say "Please pass the cake," my mouth might say, "Please part the ice," which didn't make sense to anyone else or even to my own ears. A hundred times a day this would happen. I'd find myself crying or cursing or frozen into some stiff posture or making some meaningless movements with my leg, and I knew that these were just my ways of trying to handle the complete feeling of inability that characterized my life. (Van Riper, 1978, pp. 31–32)*

> *My friends tell me I'm attractive, but I can count all the dates I've had on the fingers of one hand. Boys don't want to go out with girls who talk through their nose like I do. The doctors fixed my cleft lip so you can't hardly see the scar, but my voice is nasal and they say they can't help with that. In grade school the kids called me "Honker" or "Nosey" and mocked the way I talked. People don't do that now, but they look at me funny and shy away. Or they are extra kind to me and that's worse. I don't want pity. I just want to live like everybody else. I wonder how many nights I've cried myself to sleep over these miserable years. (Van Riper, 1978, p. 5)*

Emotional/Social Characteristics   One definition used by speech language pathologists is that speech is abnormal when it deviates so far from the speech of other people that it calls attention to itself, interferes with communication, or causes the speaker or his or her listeners to be distressed. This definition recognizes that since oral communication is so central to human interaction, speech/language impairments can interfere with interaction so much that they cause social/emotional problems, which in turn interfere with youngsters' accomplishing the cultural tasks. Youngsters may be laughed at, rejected, or devalued in many ways. The examples that follow come from autobiographies of youngsters who stutter. However, similar experiences could be cited by individuals who have other types of speech/language problems.

> *Most clerks look away when I get stuck and begin to force. It always infuriates me that they don't even have the decency to look at me.*

Once I even went to the manager of a store about it, and he looked away too.

My father wouldn't ever listen to me when I stuttered. He always walked off. I finally got so I'd say everything to him by having mother give him the message.

People do not usually laugh at my other kinds of stuttering, but when I begin to go up in pitch, they always smile or laugh right out loud. I was phoning a girl today and hung up when I heard her snickering. (Van Riper, 1978, p. 18)

Some youngsters take such treatment in stride and do not show undue social emotional stress. However, some do show more problems. Some youngsters react to the psychological pain with anger, and this anger causes themselves and other people more problems.

Ivan, whom we straightway named "The Terrible," was a very agile little boy of six with completely unintelligible speech. He was a holy terror. Other mothers would sweep their children back into the house when Ivan came tricycling up the sidewalk. No baby-sitter ever sat twice at his house. His mother worked days, probably in self-defense; and the boy was cared for by his grandfather and grandmother, who lived upstairs.... (Van Riper, 1978, p. 22)

Some youngsters react to the psychological pain with fear of speech situations. This fear can easily generalize to become anxiety, a free-floating feeling of dread that is not tied to anything real.

Edward had undergone many operations for his cleft palate, but the scars on his face and the speech that came from his mouth bore testimony of his difference. Throughout his elementary and secondary school years, he had appeared a carefree, laughing, mischievous child. He was the happy clown, the gay spirit, and by this behavior, he had managed to gain much acceptance. Then suddenly, in the final semester of his senior year in high school, he underwent a marked personality change. He laughed no longer; he became apathetic, quiet and morose. Our intensive study of this boy revealed that he had always lived with anxiety, that his gay behavior was adaptive but spurious. Underneath he had always ached. The compensatory pose of gaiety had brought him rewards, but it had not allayed the anxiety. When faced with the necessity for leaving school and earning a living, the anxiety flared up too strongly to be hidden, and the change of personality took place. (Van Riper, 1978, p. 27).

Some youngsters react to the psychological pain with feelings of guilt. They may feel as though they have done something evil and thus deserve the pain they encounter. Or, they may feel remorse for the pain that their parents and others feel about their speech/language problems.

> *Even when I was a little girl I remember being ashamed of my speech. And every time I opened my mouth, I shamed my mother. I can't tell you how awful I felt. If I talked, I did wrong. It was that simple. I kept thinking I must be awful bad to have to talk like that. I remember praying to God and asking Him to forgive me for whatever it was I must have done. I remember trying hard to remember what it was, and not being able to find out. (Van Riper, 1978, p. 30)*

Anger, anxiety, and guilt can aggravate the youngster's speech and language problems. And these emotions can be turned inward to cause self-hate and psychosomatic illnesses such as asthma. Generally, they can spill over to interfere with the child's mastering the cultural tasks.

Other Characteristics   What are the physical, visual, auditory, intellectual, and academic achievement characteristics of speech-impaired pupils? The answer to the question depends on the cause of the speech/language impairments.

First, let's consider organic speech/language impairments caused by abnormalities in the speech-production system (e.g., cleft palate), brain injury (e.g., cerebral palsy), hearing impairment, or mental retardation. Sometimes these causes lead to problems not only in speech/language, but also in physical, visual, auditory, intellectual, and academic achievement characteristics. And so youngsters here may be multihandicapped by having not only speech/language handicaps, but also physical handicaps, learning disabilities, or some other problems, depending on the etiology, or cause, of the problem.

Second, let's consider functional speech/language impairments caused by the pupil's learning improperly. There is no reason to expect these pupils to have problems in physical, visual, auditory, intellectual, or academic functioning.

ACCOUNTABILITY

Accountability procedures ensure that people use correct procedures in identifying and planning for speech-/language-impaired pupils and in observing the procedural safeguards protecting those pupils.

Assertive searches for speech-/language-impaired pupils are integral parts of services for them. Reports on these searches describe the procedures we use for fostering public awareness about speech/language impairments, screening for speech/language impairments, and referring pupils who apparently have speech/language impairments to audiologists and others for further examination. Also, these reports show how many speech-/ and language-impaired pupils we locate and serve.

Once pupils are classified as speech-/language-impaired and thus entitled to services and protections guaranteed by law, their individual education programs are prepared. These IEPs include descriptions of pupils' present performance levels in all areas related to progress in speech/language therapy, long-term goals and short-term objectives for the speech/language therapy, the procedures for reaching those goals and objectives, and a schedule for evaluating pupils' progress and making any needed revisions in the plans. The team preparing the IEP includes the advocates, teachers, psychologists, representatives of the school systems, the speech/language pathologists, and other specialists as needed.

We observe the procedural safeguards closely in conducting the Child-Find for speech-/language-impaired pupils and in developing and carrying out their individual education programs.

The pupils' parents/guardians have the right to participate as advocates in all decisions involved in identifying and classifying the pupils as speech-/language-impaired, testing their present performance levels in characteristics related to progress in speech/language therapy, setting the goals and objectives for the therapy and related special education, placing them in the least restrictive environment for delivery of therapy, and evaluating and revising their programs. The advocates may have as consultants experts who have special training and experience in dealing with speech/language impairments. If pupils' parents/guardians choose not to participate in decision making, surrogates for them are appropriate.

Speech-/language-impaired pupils' advocates have due process rights. That is, they may seek redress if they do not agree with any decision about the pupils' identification and classification, testing, therapy, and placement. The channels for this appeal are through administrative levels of the schools and through the jurisdictional levels of the federal courts.

Identifying and Planning for Speech-/Language-Impaired Pupils

Documenting the Child-Find

Developing the individual education program

Observing the Procedural Safeguards for Speech-/Language-Impaired Pupils

Advocate participation

Due process

Equal protection   Speech-/language-impaired pupils have the rights of equal protection in identification and planning, testing, therapy, and placement. That is, the same rules, criteria, and procedures apply to speech-/language-impaired pupils as to all pupils, regardless of their particular problems or other characteristics. Equal protection in evaluation through nondiscriminatory testing is especially crucial because of the ways in which speech and language problems can interfere with, and thus bias, test performance.

Periodic reevaluation   Speech-/language-impaired pupils are reevaluated periodically to find out whether we made errors in previous evaluations which we need to remedy. And objective criteria and evaluation procedures are used for checking the pupils' progress and deciding what steps come next.

Confidentiality   Strict confidentiality procedures surround information about the speech-/language-impaired pupils' problems, characteristics, placement, and progress. This information is completely open to the pupils' advocates, but is closed to all others except those who have a need to know and the advocates' clearance to see the information. Further, files are purged of information that is contested as wrong or irrelevant. And all except actuarial information is destroyed after the speech-/language-impaired pupils progress through school and therapy and their cases are closed.

Nondiscriminatory testing of speech-/language-impaired pupils

The second task, once the pupil has been identified as speech-/language-impaired, is to use nondiscriminatory testing to get information about characteristics that will influence the pupil's response to speech/language therapy specifically and to the cultural tasks in general.

PROBLEMS IN TESTING SPEECH-/LANGUAGE-IMPAIRED PUPILS

The dangers in testing most handicapped pupils are certainly present when we assess pupils who have communication problems. Briefly, the tests may become just additional measures of the pupils' speech/language problems rather than of whatever characteristics we are purporting to measure.

The pupils' speech/language problems might interfere with meeting the requirement about standard conditions of testing. For example, a pupil who omits the first part of every word could leave the examiner mystified about what his or her answers are. The communication problem is especially difficult on timed items. For example, one item at the ten-year mental age on the Stanford-Binet Intelligence Test requires saying at least twenty-eight words in one minute. Both the Binet and the Wechsler Intelligence Scales require saying digits forward or backward at a rate of about one per second. What can a pupil who stutters do with items like those? Changing the way the pupil responds would violate the requirement of standard conditions of testing and consequently destroy the tests' norms.

The pupil's problems might also interfere with meeting requirements about his or her language and experience backgrounds in comparison to the norm group's language and experience backgrounds. For example, a pupil with aphasia, who by definition cannot use symbols, certainly cannot be judged by a test like the Stanford-Binet, which is based on manipulating symbols in solving problems. Using this test would be a measure of the pupil's aphasia — not his or her intelligence. A similar example would be with the pupil whose language is delayed. There is no way to legitimately compare him or her to norms for language-based tests.

A more subtle danger is in the way that speech/language problems affect pupils' approaches to the test situation. Tests are stressful. They make most of us feel afraid. Pupils with communication problems may feel even more afraid. This fear could distract them and interfere with performance or cause them to withdraw from the situation and not try.

PROCEDURES FOR TESTING SPEECH-/LANGUAGE-IMPAIRED PUPILS

Information needed for planning comes from a range of questions about the pupil's medical background, growth and development, psychological functioning, and therapeutic history (e.g., Darley and Spriesterbach, 1978; Emrich and Hatten, 1979; Nation and Aram, 1977). Answers to these questions come from a variety of procedures:

☐ conducting interviews with, and eliciting questionnaire responses from, parents, siblings, and others who deal with the pupil;

☐ reviewing the reports and records of physicians, therapists, teachers, and other specialists who work with the pupil; and

☐ observing the pupil in representative settings and completing anecdotal records, rating scales, checklists, and other devices for reporting observations.

In addition, standardized tests can be used if the conditions for using norms to judge the pupil can be met.

Information-collection procedures are surrounded with safeguards against dangers which could lead to errors in judging what the pupil's characteristics are and what they mean for his or her functioning. Among the cautions is that only qualified people do the assessment and interpretation of what the assessment information means. Another caution is that we use only reliable and valid instruments which are appropriate in view of the pupil's speech/language impairment, i.e., the impairment does not prevent comparing the pupil to the norms of a norm-referenced test or the criteria of a criterion-referenced test.

Individualizing instruction for speech-/language-impaired pupils

Individualizing instruction is the third task in providing the speech-/language-impaired pupil with the rights and protections he or she qualifies for under the law. We engage in speech/language therapy, elicit special education support if it is needed, and select related services.*

SPEECH/LANGUAGE THERAPY

The general process applies here too. In speech/language therapy the sequence of activities is to diagnose present performance levels, use test information to plan therapy, do the therapy, assess the pupil's response to that therapy, and revise the procedures as appropriate. The therapy itself involves setting goals fitting the pupil's problems and selecting procedures appropriate for reaching those goals. We have a great deal of information about procedures for speech/language therapy. The overview that follows has examples organized by type of problem.

Articulation Problems   Here the goals are to have the pupils pronounce correctly whatever sounds they are mispronouncing. Five types of procedures are commonly used.

1. *Sound stimulation.* This procedure teaches pupils to recognize the sounds and then to produce them. There are four steps: *auditory training* to recognize the correct ways to produce the sounds and the

---

* This presentation is based on information in sources such as Allen (1980), Eisensen and Ogilvie (1977), Filter (1977), Gregory (1978), Mower (1978), Polow (1975), Schieffelbusch (1977, 1978), and Van Riper (1978).

incorrect ways which they do them; *production in isolation* to make the sounds in their single states independent of words; *production in context* to make the sounds in combination with other sounds in syllables, words, sentences, and contextual speech; and *carryover* to make the sounds in speech situations beyond the speech-therapy sessions.

2. *Paired sounds.* This procedure teaches pupils to use key words as models of the sounds correctly produced in words. Pupils have their own particular keys containing the sounds they mispronounce. They remember these keys and retrieve them as guides whenever the speech situation involves the mispronounced sounds. The pupils learn to do this by pairing the key words with a series of words containing their mispronunciations. By matching the model, the pupils learn to pronounce more and more words with the problem sounds. Ultimately, they learn to remember and to retrieve the model at will.

3. *Behavior shaping.* Essentially, this approach involves reinforcing pupils when they make the sounds correctly. The procedure is to expose pupils to many stimuli including the sounds they mispronounce and to reinforce them for correctly producing the sounds. At first, the sounds they mispronounce are placed in simple isolated syllables and words. Progressively, they are placed in more and more complex speech situations.

Early identification and treatment of speech and language problems are essential.

4. *Placing articulators.* Here the pupils learn how to place their tongues, teeth, lips, etc., to correctly produce each sound they mis-articulate. Training is done by physically placing the articulators as they should be to produce the sound correctly, telling pupils about correct placements, showing pupils pictures, diagrams, and models of the correct placement, or using combinations of these procedures.

5. *Distinctive features.* A sound is made by blending more than one component. These components are called "distinctive features" of the sound. Work with distinctive features is a part/whole approach. It involves teaching pupils to hear what features they mispronounce, to correctly produce these features, and to integrate them into the correct production of the whole sound.

Voice Problems

The goal of voice therapy is to teach the pupil to produce a kind of voice quality, a level of loudness, or a level of pitch appropriate for his or her age and surroundings and comfortable for his or her speech-production mechanism. Procedures vary somewhat with the type of problem and its cause. However, it is well to remember that the three types of problems are interrelated; thus to clear up a problem in one area sometimes requires work on related areas, e.g., to clear up an intensity problem, we might have to help the pupil change his or her pitch level.

Voice quality

Medical treatment is the first step if the nasality, denasality, breathiness, or harshness has physical causes such as cleft palate or vocal nodes. After the best physical repair possible, vocal training is in order. There are several stages.

1. The therapist helps the pupil recognize that his or her voice quality is not appropriate and that he or she needs to work on it.

2. The pupil learns how to recognize when the inappropriate voice quality occurs in his or her speech.

3. The pupil learns to speak with an appropriate voice quality. That is, the pupil learns the breath control and muscle movements necessary to produce a range of appropriate voice patterns, and he or she chooses the levels that he or she likes best.

4. The pupil continues to produce the new voice until it becomes stable and until he or she can use it widely in situations beyond the speech/language therapy sessions.

Loudness

Again, the first step is to identify the cause. If the cause is physical, e.g., hearing impairment or spasticity of the throat muscles, it must be treated by a physician or other specialist, such as an audiologist. If the cause is psychological, e.g., extreme anxiety, it must be treated by a psychiatrist or a clinical psychologist. Once the cause has been recognized and, if possible, alleviated, the next step is speech/language therapy.

1. The pupil is helped to recognize that his or her voice level is not appropriate — too loud or too soft.
2. The pupil learns to relax his or her speech muscles — especially the throat muscles — and to control them more adequately.
3. The pupil learns to breathe properly for speech.
4. The pupil learns to speak with the correct intensity. After reaching a comfortable level, the pupil fixes it and learns to use it in situations beyond therapy.

Again the first step is to look for physical causes, such as delayed maturation, or psychological causes, such as excessive tension, and to treat those problems medically and psychologically. Once the cause is under control, speech therapy predominates.

Pitch

1. The therapist gives the pupil ear training in recognizing that his or her pitch is inappropriate, e.g., unusual, like a monotone, or too high or low for his or her sex and age.
2. The pupil learns to vary his or her pitch and to discriminate between different pitch levels. In this process the pupil learns to control his or her breathing and muscles.
3. The pupil adopts an appropriate pitch level and learns to use it in various situations outside of therapy.

The goal in working with cluttering is to teach the pupil to speak more slowly and to leave out extra sounds and words. The procedure here is to help the pupil become aware of his or her problem and to consciously slow down and organize his or her speech.

Fluency Problems

Cluttering

There are two goals. One goal is to enable pupils to eliminate all forms of secondary stuttering, i.e., struggle behavior such as grimaces and head shaking, when they try to speak. The other goal is to enable pupils to speak with a minimum of dysfluency. There are many specific techniques, but essentially two basic forms of therapy are used: desensitation and behavior modification.

Stuttering

In *desensitation therapy* the idea is to modify the form of stuttering, i.e., to get rid of secondary struggle behavior and to help the pupil become more fluent by teaching him or her to stutter easily. The pupil learns to relax and bobble easily when the block comes before or during speech. At the same time, the pupil learns to not avoid speech situations and to not use artificial tricks, such as talking with an accent so that he or she is distracted enough not to stutter.

In *behavior modification therapy* the idea is to eliminate the stuttering. Fluent speech is elicited and reinforced by reward. Procedures for eliciting fluent speech include getting the pupil to speak slowly, getting him or her to use particular rhythms, or using delayed auditory feedback.

Language Problems

The general goal with language problems is for the pupil to learn language appropriate for his or her mental age level. Specific goals vary with the type of language problem.

Aphasia

The goal is for the pupil to learn to formulate, understand, and express meanings through language. "Aphasic therapy consists of building bridges from the things the patient can do to those he cannot do" (Van Riper, 1978, p. 381). Many different techniques are available. Choices depend on the specific variety of aphasia the person shows, as well as his or her other characteristics, e.g., interests and skills available to be built on. Examples with young children are teaching them to memorize nursery rhymes, working with flash cards, or telling stories about pictures. Whatever the approach, care must be taken to keep down stress in the form of pressure on the pupil to produce and respond to language before he or she is ready or too quickly at any one time.

Delayed language

The goal is to help the pupil learn to understand and produce words and connected discourse using syntax and word structures and meanings appropriate to his or her mental age. Specific techniques vary, but three basic approaches are generally used: the developmental (natural/discovery) approach, the behavior modification approach, and the cognitive approach.

In the *developmental approach* the idea is to use training activities that parallel the natural sequence of language development. For example, the speech/language therapist helps the pupil learn and in turn produce single words; two-word sentences (noun/verb); longer, more complex sentences; and so on.

In the *behavior modification approach* the speech/language therapist elicits correct language patterns and then reinforces them. This procedure continues until the pupil learns a variety of words and language structures consistently and applies these widely — again to a level appropriate for his or her mental maturity level.

In the *cognitive approach* the pupil is taught phoneme (sound) pronunciations, word meanings, and grammar (prefixes, suffixes, and grammatical rules). At the same time, he or she is taught skills underlying language use, e.g., perception, selective attention, and inner verbalization.

Multiple Problems

Speech and language problems resulting from cleft palate/cleft lip, cerebral palsy, hearing impairment, and mental retardation are very complex to deal with. Treatment differs, depending on the type of problem.

Cleft palate/cleft lip

The first step in treatment is to surgically repair the cleft as much as possible. In cleft palate a prosthesis may then be used if some opening remains in the roof of the mouth. Essentially, pliable materials such as plastics are molded to serve as a cover for the gap that remains in the palate.

After the medical repair, speech therapy begins. The goals are to decrease misarticulations and hypernasality. Misarticulations are reduced by the pupil's learning compensatory movements of his or her tongue tip, lips, and jaws as well as appropriate contractions of the soft palate and pharynx. At the same time, excessive nasality is reduced by the pupil's learning to direct the airflow through breath and muscular control.

Cerebral palsy

Medical treatment to facilitate relaxation may be in order. After that, speech therapy can begin. Goals depend on the pupil's particular problems. Generally, they include reduction of misarticulations, labored speech, specific language disabilities, and aphasia. Therapists use procedures to help pupils learn muscle relaxation, appropriate breathing, and appropriate movements of the muscles controlling articulation, resonation, and phonation. And they use procedures to help the pupil learn language structures and meanings appropriate to his or her mental age. If the pupil's cerebral palsy is severe, prognosis for his or her communication through speech may be so poor that therapists may need to teach him or her alternative communication systems. For example, the pupil may learn to send messages through answering questions with particular facial or bodily movements, e.g., eye closing for "yes" and lip clenching for "no." Or, the pupil may learn to use communication boards for relaying essential messages.

Hearing impairment

We use extensive procedures to teach communication skills to deaf pupils. These procedures are described in Chapter 5.

Mental retardation   The goal is to train the mentally retarded pupil to articulate and to use language structures and meanings appropriate for his or her *mental age** level. Speech/language therapy parallels that used with non-retarded pupils. It just proceeds more slowly and with procedures appropriate for the pupil's mental age level.

OTHER RELATED SERVICES

In addition to speech and language therapy, youngsters may need other related services. These include audiological, medical, and psychological services as well as physical therapy and vocational rehabilitation.

Audiological Services   Audiologists' goals are to determine whether a hearing problem contributes to the communication problems and to work with the pupil on using hearing aids if aids are needed. Audiological services are especially important parts of dealing with pupils who have severe problems with articulation, loudness, voice quality, or delayed speech/language. And, of course, audiological monitoring is central in working with obviously hearing-impaired pupils.

Medical Services   Medical diagnosis and treatment come first when pupils have speech/language problems caused by organic disorders. The goal is to reduce the physical problems, e.g., to repair a cleft palate. If a cure is not possible, the alternative goal is to reduce the problem's harmful effects, e.g., by using drugs to relax severely spastic muscles.

Psychological Services   If psychological problems cause the speech/language difficulty, for example, as it happens in hysterical aphonia, the psychotherapist's or psychiatrist's goal is to reduce the problem. This problem reduction needs to be done before too much time and energy are devoted to speech/language therapy. The psychiatrist or psychotherapist has a somewhat different goal when the pupil has psychological problems caused by the frustrations and penalties attendant on severe speech/language problems. Here the goal is to help the pupil make a constructive and mature response to the pain he or she feels as a result of his or her communication problems.

Psychologists and psychiatrists may also need to counsel the pupil's family. The goal is for the family to change its ways if family members are causing a pupil to have psychological problems which

---

* This gearing of difficulty to mental age rather than to chronological age is discussed in Chapter 9, "Special Needs of Mentally Retarded Pupils."

in turn are causing speech/language problems. Or, the goal is for the family to learn ways to support the pupil whose speech/language problems are accompanied by, and made worse by, psychological pain resulting from his or her communication problems.

School psychologists assess the pupil's intellectual functioning if there is a possibility that mental retardation is contributing to delayed language. The goal is to supply the speech/language therapist with information to use in deciding what level of speech/language maturity to work toward and what rates of progress to expect.

Vocational rehabilitation specialists work with youngsters whose speech and language problems remain a barrier to their communication in the late adolescent and young adult years, with the expectations that those problems probably will remain a barrier. The goal is to provide occupational assessment, information, and counseling. In this process the specialist, a youngster, and the youngster's parents study the youngster's aspirations, interests, and capabilities in the context of job requirements and possibilities. After the youngster makes some decisions, the vocational rehabilitation specialist helps marshall the services needed to help prepare the youngster for the chosen occupation. Subsequently, he or she may help the youngster locate employment, if appropriate.

Vocational Rehabilitation

Physical therapists work mainly with cerebral palsy pupils whose speech/language problems are caused by wrongly functioning muscles. The goal is to teach a pupil to relax his or her muscles and to approximate normal movements as much as possible.

Physical Therapy

SPECIAL EDUCATION

The speech/language pathologist delivers therapy, and the teacher's role is to back him or her up. That is, the two can work closely as a team. The pathologist describes how the pupil's problem shows up in the various speech situations, what the therapy goals are, and what the teacher can do to help the pupil transfer what he or she learns in therapy to the classroom. The teacher creates a climate which encourages communication and provides activities in which the pupil can use his or her new speech and language skills.

For example, if a pupil's problem is too soft a voice, the teacher can see to it that the pupil uses in the classroom the appropriately loud voice he or she is learning to use in therapy. In addition, if the cause of the problem is fear in speech situations, the teacher can supply a wide range of nonthreatening situations and at the same time give the pupil emotional support as he or she talks in those situations.

Consider another example. Suppose that the pupil's problem is a substitution, such as /w/ for /r/. Again, the teacher can ensure that the pupil uses the correct pronunciation in his or her speech contacts in the classroom. In addition, the teacher can watch related areas, such as reading or spelling, to be sure that the erroneous learning that caused the articulation problem does not cause problems in the pupil's reading or writing with the problem sounds in them.

Placing speech-/language-impaired pupils in the least restrictive environment

Placement is our final area of decision making as we plan for the speech-/language-impaired pupil. In doing this fourth task, we attend to placement options, extracurricular activities, transportation and facilities, and safety.

PLACEMENT OPTIONS

We must identify true speech/language problems as early as possible and begin therapy. The idea is to prevent any disruption in the children's developing normal communication. Such disruption can have increasingly devastating effects on their growth and development and their accomplishing important cultural tasks.

Nevertheless, we must be very careful with early treatment because the self-fulfilling prophecy can cause problems. Sometimes young children have temporary misarticulations or nonfluencies that disappear as the youngsters mature. Undue attention to such temporary problems may cause emotional complications which in turn make speech/language problems worse.

Figure 4.2 shows how frequently the various placement options were being used in the late 1970s. For the most part, speech/language therapy is delivered in the regular environment of the school the pupil attends.

The speech/language pathologist usually works with one pupil at a time or with groups of pupils who have the same problem. The pupil usually goes to a separate room for therapy and then returns to his or her classroom. A pupil with a more severe problem or a more difficult problem may go to a speech and hearing clinic for therapy. There are several labels for these approaches to delivering therapy.

1. *Itinerant therapists.* The speech/language pathologist travels from school to school in a school district or intermediate educa-

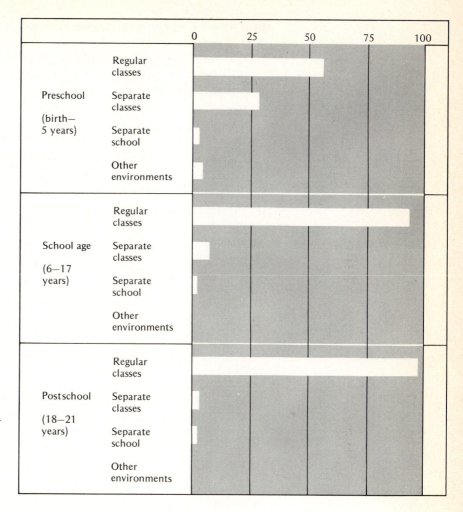

Fig. 4.2
Most frequent placements of speech-/language-impaired pupils reported by the states in the late 1970s. (Based on information in BEH, 1979, pp. 169–180.)

tion agency. This plan is used in sparsely populated areas where there are not many pupils with speech/language problems. In addition, itinerant therapists may deliver services to pupils confined to their homes or to hospitals.

2. *Resource room.* The speech/language therapist has a separate station in the school. Pupils go to that resource room for therapy. This plan is used in larger schools where there are many pupils with problems.

3. The resource room and itinerant plans may be combined. That is, several schools may have resource rooms, and the itinerant therapist may move among them.

4. *Special centers.* Pupils travel to a centrally located facility. These may be speech/language clinics in universities or hospitals. Or they may be special schools run by volunteer organizations such as the Junior League.

5. *Consultant services.* The speech/language pathologists do not give direct services to pupils with problems. Instead, they give advice to parents or teachers about the best procedures and materials for working with pupils' speech/language problems. In turn, the parents or teachers work with the pupils.

EXTRACURRICULAR ACTIVITIES

Speech-impaired pupils generally do not have any restrictions in extracurricular activities. However, depending on the stage of therapy, they may need some emotional support to enter into the social interactions surrounding these extracurricular activities.

Language-impaired pupils have more restrictions — especially if their problems are severe. They may have difficulty understanding the language used in giving instructions for, and carrying on the business of, activities such as basketball, cheerleading, 4-H Club, or the school newspaper. In turn they may have difficulty communicating their ideas in such extracurricular activities.

In practice, then, the goal is to find activities for pupils in which their communication problems are not a barrier to their participation. At the same time, we must be careful not to get them in solitary situations or ones involving little social interaction and communication.

TRANSPORTATION AND FACILITIES

Speech/language therapy is usually conducted in the pupils' schools. Consequently, transportation is not too much of a problem. However, special transportation may be needed if the pupils have to attend a special clinic.

Special arrangements for transportation to and from school may be required for pupils whose problems are sufficiently severe that they cannot understand directions from other people or make other people understand their wishes and needs. Pupils who may need such special treatment include those who have language problems or younger pupils who have more severe articulation and fluency problems.

Special arrangements in facilities are not necessary if speech/language impairments are the pupils' only problems.

SAFETY

As is true in other aspects of placement, most speech-/language-impaired pupils do not need special attention in safety beyond the provisions made for all pupils. However, younger pupils who have severe speech impairments and most pupils who have language problems need more monitoring. For example, someone must be sure that they can communicate their needs during distress and that they understand safety rules. If they cannot meet these safety requirements, they need close supervision and protection.

Summary

IDENTIFYING AND PLANNING FOR SPEECH-/LANGUAGE-IMPAIRED PUPILS

Normal Speech and Language

Adequate structure and function of the speech apparatus, the central nervous system, and the ears are required for normal speech and language. As the youngster matures neurologically and physically and has appropriate learning experiences, his or her speech and language grow increasingly complex. Normal development of speech and language is essential to learning and performing the cultural tasks requiring communication.

Speech and Language Impairments

Sometimes problems interfere with the structure and function of the speech apparatus, the central nervous system, and the ears. These problems cause disruption of normal development of speech and language. The pupil is considered speech-impaired when this disruption is serious enough to interfere with his or her learning and performing the cultural tasks. The Child-Find to locate speech-/language-impaired pupils qualified for special protection under PL 94-142 includes public awareness, screening, and referral for further diagnosis and treatment. Types of speech/language impairments include articulation, voice, and fluency problems, aphasia, delayed language, and multiple speech/language problems, such as those accompanying cleft palate/cleft lip. Organic and functional problems are the two traditional ways of classifying causes of speech/language problems. We do not know the causes of some problems. Dialects are not speech/language problems. Most people recommend that pupils learn standard English to use in place of the dialect when it is appropriate to do so.

Impact of Speech/ Language Impairments on Pupils' Characteristics

Speech and language impairments may lead to emotional pain, which the youngster may react to with anger, guilt, or anxiety. Speech/ language impairments do not cause secondary problems in other characteristics. However, other problems may coexist with speech/ language problems which have organic causes.

Accountability

We use accountability procedures to ensure correct procedures in identifying speech-/language-impaired pupils and planning their IEP's. At the same time, we observe the procedural safeguards protecting them — advocate participation, due process, equal protection, periodic reevaluation, and confidentiality.

NONDISCRIMINATORY TESTING OF SPEECH-/LANGUAGE-IMPAIRED PUPILS

Problems in Testing Speech-/Language-Impaired Pupils

Speech/language impairment may interfere with the pupil's responding to tests, and thus the tests may become just additional measures of the impairment. The dangers are that the impairment may interfere with the requirement that the testee must be like the norm group in receiving the standard conditions of testing and in having a common language and experience background. Also, the pupil's fear in the test situation might interfere with his or her performance.

Procedures for Testing Speech-/Language-Impaired Pupils

Information needed for planning comes from interviews, questionnaires, records, reports, pupil observation, and sometimes standardized tests if the necessary conditions can be met. Information-collection procedures must be surrounded with safeguards against the dangers in testing speech-impaired pupils.

INDIVIDUALIZING INSTRUCTION FOR SPEECH-/LANGUAGE-IMPAIRED PUPILS

Speech/Language Therapy

In speech/language therapy the sequence of activities is to diagnose present performance levels, use that diagnostic information to plan therapy, do the therapy, assess pupil response to that therapy, and revise the procedures as appropriate. The therapy itself involves setting goals fitting the pupil's problems and selecting procedures appropriate for reaching those goals. There are particular goals and procedures for articulation problems, voice problems, fluency problems, language problems, and multiple problems.

Other Related Services

Audiologists, physicians, psychologists, and sometimes vocational rehabilitation specialists and physical therapists supply diagnosis and treatment which complement the speech/language pathologists' work.

Teachers help pupils transfer what they learn in therapy to the classroom. They also create a climate that encourages communication.

Special Education

PLACING SPEECH-/LANGUAGE-IMPAIRED PUPILS IN THE LEAST RESTRICTIVE ENVIRONMENT

Speech/language problems must be identified and treated early to reduce or prevent disruption of normal growth and development of communication skills. Speech/language therapists usually work with individuals or small groups in the school. The names of the plans for delivering therapy are itinerant therapists, resource rooms, special centers, and consultant services.

Placement Options

Speech-impaired pupils usually do not have any restrictions in extracurricular activities, transportation, facilities, and safety. However, they might need emotional support. Language-impaired pupils have more difficulty because of their limited understanding and ability to make their needs known. They require more special attention, supervision, and protection.

Extracurricular Activities, Transportation, Facilities, and Safety

TOPICS

Identifying and planning for hearing-impaired pupils

NORMAL HEARING

> Structure and functioning of the ear
> Development of normal hearing behavior
> Hearing and the cultural tasks

HEARING IMPAIRMENTS

> Legal definition and prevalence
> Finding hearing-impaired pupils
> Audiometric procedures
> Diagnosis: Classifying pupils' hearing impairments

IMPACT OF HEARING IMPAIRMENTS ON PUPILS' CHARACTERISTICS

> Introduction
> Physical characteristics
> Speech and language characteristics
> Intellectual characteristics
> Social/emotional characteristics
> Academic achievement
> Vocational characteristics

Special Needs of Hearing-Impaired Pupils

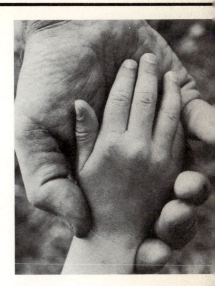

RELATED SERVICES

    Medical services
    Audiological services
    Speech/language services
    Psychological services
    Vocational rehabilitation services
    Family information and counseling

Placing hearing-impaired pupils in the least restrictive environment

PLACEMENT OPTIONS
EXTRACURRICULAR ACTIVITIES
TRANSPORTATION AND FACILITIES
SAFETY

Identifying and planning for hearing-impaired pupils

In order to provide the hearing-impaired pupil with a free appropriate public education and an equal educational opportunity, we must begin with our first task — identifying whether the pupil qualifies for a protected category and, if so, developing the individual education program all within the limits of the procedural safeguards. The knowledge we need for these activities is an understanding of normal hearing, hearing impairments, and the impact of these impairments on pupils' characteristics.

NORMAL HEARING

The structure and functioning of the ear and the central nervous system must be adequate if normal development of hearing is to occur (e.g., Glattke, 1980; McClelland, 1978; Skinner, 1978). In turn, normal development of hearing is necessary for the youngster to accomplish many of the cultural tasks necessary to meet his or her needs in socially acceptable ways.

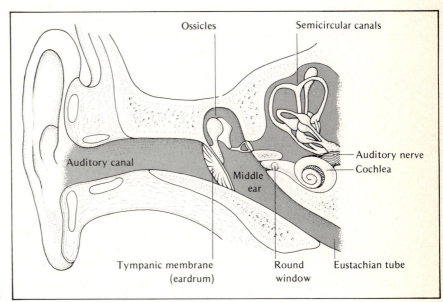

Fig. 5.1
The structure of the ear.

Figure 5.1 is a cross section of the ear's structure. The hearing process works this way. Sound stimuli enter the outer ear and go through the ear canal to the eardrum, which vibrates within the middle ear. The

Structure and Functioning of the Ear*

---

* We consider the structure and functioning of the central nervous system in Chapter 7.

chain of three small bones — the hammer (malleus), anvil (incus), and stirrup (stapes) — conducts these vibrations to the oval window, which leads to the inner ear. In addition, sound is conducted to the inner ear through the bones in the skull. Once they get to the inner ear, vibrations go through the semicircular canals to the cochlea. Here the vibrations are translated into electrical signals which go through the auditory nerve to the brain.

Development of Normal Hearing Behavior

An infant shows his or her sensitivity to sounds at birth by the startle reflex at loud noises. Subsequently, hearing becomes more differentiated. Table 5.1 lists milestones in the development of normal hearing. Again, note how earlier, simpler skills serve as a foundation for later, more complex skills.

TABLE 5.1 MILESTONES IN DEVELOPING NORMAL HEARING BEHAVIOR.

Age	Behavior
3–6 months	Awakens or quiets to the sound of familiar adults' voices. Typically turns eyes and head in the direction of the source of sound.
7–10 months	Turns head and shoulders toward familiar sounds, even when he or she cannot see what is happening. Such sounds do not have to be loud to cause the infant to respond.
11–15 months	Shows understanding of some words by appropriate behavior; for example, points to or looks at familiar objects or people, on request. Jabbers in response to a human voice, is likely to cry when there is thunder, or may frown when scolded. Imitation indicates that he or she can hear the sounds and match them with his or her own sound production.
1½ years	Some children begin to identify parts of the body. Child should be able to show his or her nose or eyes. Should be using a few simple words. They are not complete or pronounced perfectly, but are clearly meaningful.
2 years	Should be able to follow a few simple commands without visual clues. Most two-year-olds enjoy being "read to" and shown simple pictures in a book or magazine and will point out pictures when you ask them to.

Age	Behavior
	Should be using a variety of everyday words heard at home and in the neighborhood.
	Refers to himself or herself by name.
	Many two-year-olds show interest in radio and TV by word or action.
	Produces "sentences" even though they are not usually complete or grammatically correct.
2½ years	Many children can say or sing short rhymes or songs and enjoy listening to records or to people singing.
	A child who has good hearing and gets pleasure from these events usually reacts to the sound by running to look or telling someone what he or she hears.
3 years	Understands and uses some simple verbs, pronouns, prepositions, and adjectives, such as *go, me, in,* and *big.*
	Locates the source of a sound.
	Uses complete sentences some of the time.
4 years	Gives a connected account of some recent experiences.
	Carries out a sequence of two simple directions.
5 years	Has intelligible speech, although some sounds may still be mispronounced.
	Most children of this age can carry on a conversation if the vocabulary is within their experience.
	Uses some pronouns correctly.
	Most of the time, his or her grammar matches the patterns of grammar used by the adults in the family and neighborhood.

Source: Adapted from Masland (1970, pp. 40–42).

Hearing and the Cultural Tasks

Hearing is our avenue for perceiving auditory stimuli — their loudness, pitch, and rhythm. Consequently, hearing connects us with our immediate environment.

Hearing is perhaps our most versatile and valuable sense. Uniquely designed as a high-fidelity stereo system, it personalizes or decodes much of the world in which we live. It reaches behind, under, above, around the corners, through walls, and over hills, bringing in the crackling of a distant camp fire, the bubbling of a nearby stream, the closing of a door, the message of a voice — the myriad of sound which identifies much of our experience. (Berg, 1976, p. 7)

For example, Fig. 5.2 shows some of the sounds that a normally hearing person responds to with no difficulty — often as background noise.

Among all of the sounds important for us to receive, those crucial to communication perhaps rank first. Hearing is the primary medium through which we learn speech and language. Further, it is central to our receiving and sending messages in face-to-face situations, through media such as telephones and television, and more indirectly

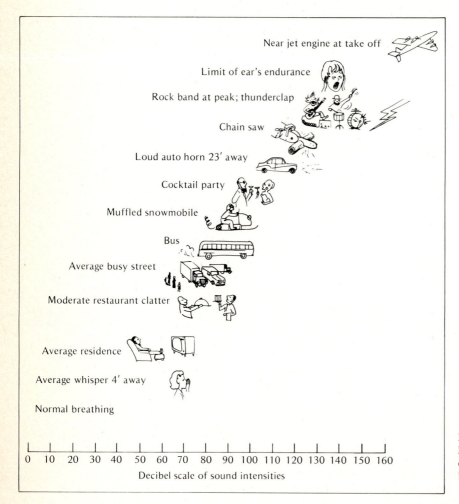

Near jet engine at take off

Limit of ear's endurance

Rock band at peak; thunderclap

Chain saw

Loud auto horn 23' away

Cocktail party

Muffled snowmobile

Bus

Average busy street

Moderate restaurant clatter

Average residence

Average whisper 4' away

Normal breathing

0 10 20 30 40 50 60 70 80 90 100 110 120 130 140 150 160

Decibel scale of sound intensities

Fig. 5.2
Loudness (decibels, or dB) of common sounds. (Reprinted by permission from Van Riper, 1978, p. 409.)

through print media. In short, hearing is a very important tool in our performing the cultural tasks to meet our needs in socially approved ways. Again, refer to the cultural tasks described in Table 1.1. Consider how important hearing and, more specifically, speech and language are to our performing these and similar tasks. Note also how accomplishing the simple earlier tasks is prerequisite to accomplishing the later, more complex cultural tasks.

HEARING IMPAIRMENTS

Legal Definition and Prevalence

Defects in the structure and function of the ear and the central nervous system can cause the development of the youngster's hearing behavior to deviate from normal. We consider this disruption to be an impairment when it is extensive enough to interfere with his or her mastering the common tasks of our culture. This relationship is recognized in the legal definition of the hearing-impaired categories we use for identifying youngsters qualified for the rights to special education and related services and the protections of the procedural safeguards guaranteed by PL 94-142. The law provides for hearing-impaired pupils at two levels of severity:

Deaf   A hearing impairment which is so severe that the child is impaired in processing linguistic information through hearing, with or without amplification, which adversely affects educational performance.

Hard of hearing   A hearing impairment, whether permanent or fluctuating, which adversely affects a child's educational performance but which is not included under the definition of "deaf" in this section. (PL 94-142, 1977, Sec. 121a.5)

Look back at the prevalence estimates in Fig. 1.1. About 0.3% to 0.65% of school pupils are hearing-impaired. About 0.17% were being served in the late 1970s.

Finding Hearing-Impaired Pupils

At the outset, the Child-Find locates pupils qualified for the entitlements and protections of the laws governing the way we treat handicapped pupils, in this case hearing-impaired pupils. *Awareness* campaigns through direct contacts and the newspapers and other media inform the public not only about the need to detect hearing-impaired pupils early in order to protect them from secondary problems developing, but also about the rights and protections pupils are entitled to.

Screening is the next step. Severe hearing impairments are obvious while the child is still quite young. Less obvious impairments are more subtle and are easy to confuse with other problems such as

Audiometric procedures are crucial in working with hearing-impaired pupils.

mental retardation. Symptoms that parents, teachers, and others should look for are signs that the pupil is unaware of some environmental stimuli. For example:

1. *Speech/language symptoms*
   a) Sounds pronounced incorrectly
   b) Voice too loud or too soft for the circumstances
   c) Voice excessively nasal
   d) Difficulty understanding or producing some language structures and vocabulary — especially vocabulary

2. *Behavioral symptoms*
   a) Apparent inattentiveness and daydreaming
   b) Confusion and difficulty grasping and following directions
   c) Frequently asking for repetition of comments made to him or her
   d) Fearfulness, irritability, hyperactivity, and other signs of straining to keep up with what is going on

3. *Physical symptoms*
   Frequent earaches, sinus congestion, and allergies.

Referral for further study follows observing signs of hearing impairment. Several specialists participate in this further study. An audiologist uses appropriate hearing-evaluation procedures to determine whether a hearing impairment actually exists and, if so, its type and severity. An ear specialist or an ear/nose/throat specialist looks for medical problems such as otitis media (infection of the middle ear) and prescribes treatment. Speech/language pathologists and specialists in educating the deaf assess the pupils' articulation, voice quality, fluency, and language maturity. Teachers of the deaf and school psychologists assess academic achievement, intellectual, and social/emotional characteristics. Vocational rehabilitation specialists assess older hearing-impaired pupils' occupational potentialities.

Audiometry means measuring hearing. Essentially, we identify how loud a sound has to be before the person can hear it at various pitch levels (e.g., Lloyd and Kaplan, 1978; Newby, 1979; Rose, 1979; Wiley, 1980). Loudness (intensity) is measured in decibel (dB) units. Pitch (frequency in cycles per second) is measured in hertz (Hz) units. Zero is the minimal hearing threshold level — the lowest intensity level that normally hearing people can hear.[*]

Audiometric Procedures

During testing, audiologists vary loudness from 0 to 110 dB and pitch from a low pitch level of 125 Hz to a high pitch level of 8000 Hz, with special attention to 500 to 2000 Hz — the speech range. Sounds are generated through various types of audiometers. In air conduction tests sound vibrations are transmitted through earphones on the right and left ears. In bone conduction tests sound vibrations are transmitted through terminals fixed on the mastoid and forehead bones.

Testing results are plotted on an audiogram. In air conduction tests o---o in red designate the right ear and x---x in blue designate the left ear. In bone conduction tests < indicates the left ear and > the right. (See Fig. 5.3.)

The four main types of audiometric procedures are pure-tone audiometry, speech audiometry, electrodermal (GSR) audiometry, and auditory brainstem response (ABR) audiometry:

1. In *pure-tone audiometry* audiologists use tones without content. These are transmitted through earphones. The testee signals when he or she hears the tone.

2. In *speech audiometry* audiologists use two-syllable words called Spondee words transmitted through earphones. The speech-

---

[*] This standard is identified as ISO because it was adopted by the International Organization for Standards.

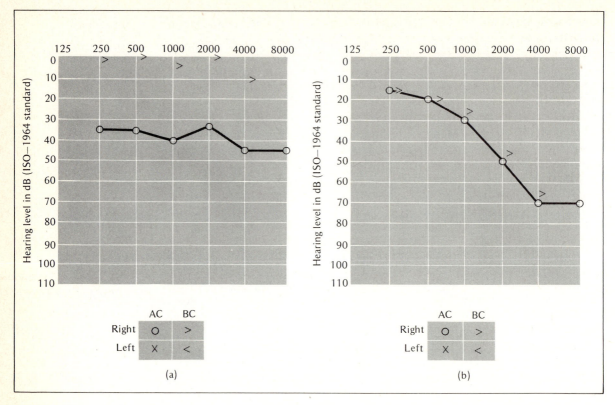

Fig. 5.3
Audiograms illustrating conductive and sensorineural hearing losses: (a) conductive loss; (b) sensorineural loss. (Reprinted by permission from Hayes A. Newby, Clinical Audiology. In L. E. Travis (ed.), *Handbook of Speech Pathology and Audiology*. Prentice-Hall, 1971, p. 353. Reprinted by permission of Prentice-Hall, Inc., Englewood Cliffs, New Jersey.)

reception threshold (SRT) is the level at which the testee can understand half of the words presented.

3. In *electrodermal audiometry* audiologists use conditioning. Electrodermal audiometry is sometimes called GSR audiometry because it is based on the galvanic skin response. A conditioned response is established by following a sound with an electric shock. The unconditioned response, sweating palms/hands, soon occurs when the person hears a sound because he or she expects the shock. Thus sweating palms becomes the response conditioned to the sound. Then, by noting whether palm sweating occurs as sounds are fed in at the various loudness and pitch levels, the audiologist can assess what sounds the testee is hearing.

4. In *auditory brainstem response (ABR) audiometry* the audiologists measure brain wave response to sounds. Electrical terminals are fixed to the scalp, as in any electroencephalographic examination. Sounds at the various loudness and pitch levels are sent through earphones to the testee. A computer differentiates brain waves caused by the sounds from those caused by other environmental stimuli. The audiologist can determine which sounds the testee hears by noting whether he or she has brain waves when the various sounds are sent through the earphones.

We classify pupils' hearing impairments in three ways, depending on our purposes. We classify by cause of hearing loss for decisions about medical treatment, by type of hearing loss for decisions about hearing aids and other amplification procedures, and by degree and age of onset of hearing loss for decisions about communication training and other educational matters (e.g., Bess, 1977; Davis and Silverman, 1978; Hodgson, 1978).

Diagnosis: Classifying Pupils' Hearing Impairments

Three sets of problems cause hearing impairments. These are congenital problems, infections, and traumatic injuries.

Classification by cause of hearing loss

1. *Congenital problems.* Sometimes hearing impairment is inherited. There is a transmission of incomplete hearing structures or a tendency toward conditions such as otosclerosis, a condition in which the stapes, one bone in the middle ear, fuses to the oval window and thus does not move as necessary to transmit vibrations through the middle ear.

Rh incompatibility,* measles during the first trimester of pregnancy, and other problems leading to brain injury also frequently lead to deafness if the injury occurs in the part of the brain controlling hearing.

2. *Infections.* Infections such as meningitis and encephalitis may destroy nerve tissue and in turn lead to hearing impairment. Otitis media — infection of the middle ear — also is a common problem. It leads to congestion that interferes with sound transmission and can sometimes lead to destruction of middle ear structures, which of course leads to permanent hearing impairment. Sometimes allergies lead to otitis media, and the condition is referred to as serous otitis media.

3. *Traumatic injuries.* Punctures or blows to the head that damage the hearing apparatus, the auditory nerve, or the brain may cause hearing impairment. Also, very loud sounds, such as a jet plane engine

---

* Rh incompatibility happens when the mother has an Rh negative factor in her blood and the fetus has an Rh positive factor. This difference triggers a chain of events which leads to brain injury.

at take-off or high-intensity music, can destroy structures in the inner ear and cause hearing impairment.

Classification by type of hearing loss

We have two types of hearing loss. These are conductive losses and sensorineural losses (Fig. 5.3).

1. *Conductive losses.* Conductive losses happen because the sound vibrations in the air cannot get through the outer ear or the middle ear to the sensory end organs and the auditory nerve. An obstruction or malformation of the outer or middle ear structures causes the block. However, sound vibrations can get through the skull bones. Therefore conductive losses rarely exceed 60 to 70 dB. On an audiogram conductive losses show up as little loss when hearing is tested with bone conduction procedures coupled with a marked loss when hearing is tested with air conduction procedures (Fig. 5.3a). Pupils with conductive losses have a good prognosis for benefiting from hearing aids and other amplification procedures because the nerves are intact and can function once the vibrations get beyond the area where the block occurs.

2. *Sensorineural losses.* Sometimes called perceptive losses, sensorineural losses happen because the sound sensations are not transmitted through the nerves. They are caused by problems in the brain, the auditory nerve, or the structures in the inner ear — especially the hair cells of the organ of Corti — the sensory end organ for the auditory nerve. Sensorineural losses show up on the audiogram as similar levels of losses on both bone conduction and air conduction tests (Fig. 5.3b). Amplifying sound with hearing aids and other procedures does no good when the pupil has a sensorineural loss, because sensations do not get transmitted through the nerves.

Classification by degree and age of onset of hearing loss*

How much hearing the pupil has lost and when it happened are critical for educational decisions. This is so because speech/language learning and performance are critically affected by age of onset and degree of loss.

1. *Age of onset.* Currently, age of onset is keyed to language development. *Prelingual* impairment is present at birth or happens before the child spontaneously learns speech and language. *Postlingual* impairment happens after the child spontaneously learns speech and language. A pupil whose deafness is postlingual has intact language

---

* The categories reported here were developed by an ad hoc committee of the Conference of Executives of American Schools for the Deaf. The committee was called the Committee to Redefine Deaf and Hard of Hearing for Educational Purposes (Frisina, 1974).

and speech. His or her main tasks are to learn ways to receive other people's speech and to keep his or her own speech intelligible. Prelingual deafness is a more extensive problem. The pupil has to consciously learn language, speech, and other methods to receive and convey language.

2. *Degree of hearing loss.* There are various systems for classifying degree of hearing loss. The following are two useful ones. They are keyed to understanding speech and to instruction and placement.

a) *Keyed to speech*

(1) *Deaf.* The hearing loss (usually 70 dB ISO or greater) prevents understanding speech through the ear alone, with or without using a hearing aid.

(2) *Hard of hearing.* The hearing loss (usually 35 to 69 dB ISO) hinders, but does not prevent, understanding speech through the ear alone, with or without a hearing aid.

b) *Keyed to instruction and placement*

(1) *Level I,* 35 to 54 dB ISO. Pupils require special speech and hearing help. They should be able to function in regular classes.

(2) *Level II,* 55 to 69 dB ISO. Pupils require special speech, hearing, language, and educational help. They may need special-class placement.

(3) *Level III,* 70 to 89 dB ISO. Pupils require special speech, hearing, language, and educational help. They most likely need special-class/special-school placement, at least until they learn to communicate.

(4) *Level IV,* 90 dB ISO and beyond. Pupils require special speech, hearing, language, and educational help. They need special-class/special-school placement.

IMPACT OF HEARING IMPAIRMENTS ON PUPILS' CHARACTERISTICS

Hearing impairment directly interferes with a person's communication. It reduces his or her receiving messages through speech and other human sounds, such as laughter, and through nonhuman environmental signals and sounds, such as an automobile horn, a doorbell, an alarm clock, or a dog growling. In addition, if this reduction in auditory stimulation occurs early enough in the child's development, it interferes with his or her learning speech and language. These direct effects of hearing impairment can, but not necessarily

Introduction

do, lead to indirect effects — on intellectual functioning, social/emotional behavior, and motivational tendencies. It follows that hearing impairment can interfere with a person's learning and performing cultural tasks which depend on speech and language and on intellectual functioning, social/emotional behavior, and motivation.

The following upbeat description of some deaf adults' activities illustrates the direct effects of hearing impairment which are dealt with in such a way that the indirect effects do not occur and in turn many cultural tasks are managed well.

Quite probably, unknown to you, deaf people live within a few miles of your home. Let us look at their life, particularly at their activities and communications at home and during leisure times. Such a visit can be as intellectually and emotionally rewarding as any trip to a foreign country. The first striking difference is of course the elaborate use of gestures. Contrary to what you may have thought, the typical deaf person communicates primarily by means of visible movements of the hands, fingers, face and whole body. Here is a young deaf mother in lively conversation with a visiting deaf friend. They are reminiscing about the residential school they both attended — about mutual friends, impressions of teachers and other adults, interesting excursions, and activities of various kinds. At times during the heat of conversation, both women talk and listen at the same time. Among deaf persons such simultaneous activities are easier and create less interruption than with us, because talking is done by gestures and listening by sight.

The conversation is taking place in the kitchen-dining area while the mother prepares dinner. The three-year-old son plays in an adjacent room, and mother keeps an eye on him. The little boy catches his mother's eye and exclaims, "I am starving." He accompanies his speech by moving his right hand down his chest toward his stomach. You observe the child's normal and clear articulation and rightly infer that he is not deaf. He is using signs all the same to make himself understood by his deaf parent. The mother replies by gesturing and making a sound that you can guess is meant to stand for "Just wait a little."

Shortly afterwards a bell rings, whereupon the boy excitedly cries out, "Daddy, daddy," and points to a flashing light connected to the bell. The mother notices the light and presses the button that opens the door downstairs. In a few moments the father enters the apartment and expresses delight at seeing an old school friend. He picks up his son, settles down in a chair with the boy on his lap, and joins the conversation with eagerness and interest. On his part, he reports some less happy news about the car accident of a mutual acquaintance, told to him by a deaf fellow worker at the plant.

Every now and then the little boy participates, but mostly he nudges his mother toward the stove....

[When dinner is over, the mother] puts the child to bed after playing with him for a little while. Attached to the bed is a microphone that transmits sound above a certain level of loudness to a light signal in the living room, to which the two other adults have retired. In this manner the deaf parents can "hear" distress signals from their child and can keep in touch with him. Modern technology makes the life of deaf persons easier. You think of hearing aids. Only the man wore an aid, and he removed it as soon as he was at home and does not put it on later when he goes out again. Your guess that hearing aids cannot be a simple answer to the problem of hearing loss is reasonable. The man wears the aid chiefly to become aware of sudden noises at work, whereas the two others have found that hearing aids are of no functional benefit and they never wear them. The man leaves now to attend a meeting of the Deaf Athletic Club, of which he is an active member, both as organizer and as tennis player. As he gets into the car and drives to the clubhouse you may wonder that a deaf person is allowed to drive at all.

Again, this is a normal reaction. A deaf person would not hear the sound of a horn in another car or even the warning signal of a fire truck or a police car. For these and similar reasons deafness used to be a legal obstacle to getting a driving license in many states and countries, although today a deaf person can obtain a license in all the United States and Canada. However, insurance is a major problem, as it is for many people with physical disabilities. The deaf community in the U.S. has solved this problem in typical fashion, first by creating their own association for purposes of life insurance and then by lobbying as an association for their legal rights. What about their driving record? Does not a lack of hearing contribute to a greater accident rate? The facts show that deaf drivers have a better record than others. The small disadvantage of not hearing is apparently more than compensated for by greater visual vigilance. Consider for a moment: if you could not hear the siren, you would still notice the peculiar reaction of the other cars and would behave accordingly. (Furth, 1973, pp. 2–5)

Physical Characteristics

Hearing impairment does not affect pupils' physical characteristics. Hearing-impaired pupils show the same range of structures and abilities that hearing pupils do.

Deaf pupils may have some problems with organized physical activities. These problems happen because their speech/language impairments interfere with their dealing with rules and signals during the games, not because they lack physical skills.

Speech and Language Characteristics   In oral communication the producer starts with an idea, encodes a message, and transmits it through speech. The receiver gets the message through listening and decodes it. The child learns oral language skills by participating in a hearing/speaking environment. He or she learns to use and to understand both language and speech sounds and to talk with a normal voice quality, loudness level, pitch, and rhythm.

A child who cannot hear cannot participate in a hearing/speaking environment. Being shut out of this learning opportunity, his or her oral communication skills suffer. This child does not learn to use and to understand language and speech sounds. Nor does he or she learn to talk with a normal voice quality, loudness level, speech, and rhythm. Using the types of problems considered in Chapter 4, we can say that the hearing-impaired pupil has delayed language, articulation problems, voice problems, and rhythm problems. Table 5.2 lists some examples — language problems shown by first grade pupils with various degrees of hearing loss.

TABLE 5.2 EXPECTED RELATIONSHIP BETWEEN DEGREE OF HEARING LOSS AND LANGUAGE, PARTICULARLY VOCABULARY, DEVELOPMENT.

Hearing Loss for Better Ear in dB	Characteristic Language Problem of Hearing-Impaired First Graders
26–40 (mild)	Only 1800–2100 of the 2500 normally spoken words are uttered. For example, the child may not say the word *binocular*, which is typically in the spoken vocabulary of the first grader.
41–70 (moderate and moderate to severe)	Only 1200–1800 of the 2500 words are spoken. Morphemes like the *s* plural and possessive endings are also omitted, i.e., the child says "The boy hat" instead of "The boy's hat."
71–90 (severe)	Only 200–1200 of the 2500 words are spoken, and the plural and possessive form *s* is not used. In addition, unstressed words may be omitted. For example the deaf first grader may say "Finished went home" instead of "When he was finished, he went home."

(Reprinted by permission from Berg, 1976, p. 19.)

Intellectual Characteristics   In considering the learning and thinking characteristics of deaf pupils, we must make a clear distinction between intellectual processes and the content we apply these processes to. Intellectual processes include such activities as learning associations, learning concepts, and solving problems. These processes may be applied to an infinite variety of content — sounds, movements, objects, quantities, feelings, and so on as well as to the words labeling these things.

Hearing impairment does not interfere with deaf pupils' learning and thinking when they are using the intellectual processes with nonverbal (physical) content. For example, deaf pupils can do as well as hearing pupils in forming concepts about physical materials such as colors. Hearing impairment does interfere with deaf pupils' learning and thinking when they are using the intellectual processes with verbal (symbolic) content. For example, deaf pupils do less well than hearing pupils in forming concepts about symbolic materials such as numbers and geographic directions (Hoemann and Ullman, 1976).

Learning and thinking

> If we wish to investigate the thinking processes of deaf persons, particularly children, we must use procedures that do not contain in themselves or in their instructions a strong linguistic component. Otherwise, we would observe nothing but the poor linguistic knowledge of deaf children, which would be as unfair to deaf persons as judging a normal person's thinking skill by means of a verbal test conducted in a language he does not understand. Once he realizes that deaf children are not at home in the English language, one will think twice before accepting results of verbal tasks as evidence for an alleged inferiority in anything but language. (Furth, 1973, p. 56)

Again, we must watch the role of language and distinguish between nonverbal and verbal tests. In sum, deaf youngsters and hearing youngsters do not differ on nonverbal tests. But deaf youngsters do less well on verbal tests.

Intelligence test performance

> The cognitive skills of deaf children and youth have been extensively investigated. The question of singular importance concerns the impact of auditory deprivation on intellectual development and functioning. Since deafness is almost synonymous with linguistic retardation, the question reduces to the relationship between linguistic facility and cognitive development. A large number of investigations conducted during the last 50 years has conclusively demonstrated that intellectual development and functioning are not dependent on language skills and that deaf persons possess normal intelligence. This is a very important conclusion because it implies that deaf persons have the potential to achieve to the same degree as hearing persons. (Bolton, 1976*a*, p. 3)

Hearing impairment does not directly affect pupils' social/emotional characteristics. It does have an indirect effect on their social maturity, emotional control, and motivation (Meadow, 1976).

Social/Emotional Characteristics

Social maturity   Many, but not all, deaf youngsters are considered socially immature, i.e., they do not have some skills that hearing youngsters their ages have. As we have seen, speech and language are crucial tools for interacting with other people and for performing many social tasks. Therefore deaf pupils are more often left out when they are among hearing people. For example, they cannot participate in activities that require verbal communication, such as playing cards. Also, deaf youngsters' communication problems interfere with their mastering such skills as traveling independently. In sum, their limitations and restrictions interfere with their acquiring common knowledge and basic social skills that many hearing people have. "This delayed personal-social development can be attributed to growing up in a sheltered, over-protected environment, and not to deafness per se" (Bolton, 1976a, p. 3).

It is often difficult for hearing-impaired pupils to learn language-based academic content.

Some, but not all, deaf individuals show difficult behavior such as excessive temper tantrums and other acting-out behavior, excessive dependency, or excessive withdrawal. Many of these problems are traceable to the poor self-concepts related to a disability, to frustration resulting from communication problems, and to the effort required to interact socially or to perform tasks when an individual has a language problem.

Behavior control

As with other handicapped pupils, motivational problems may be an indirect effect of deafness. Deaf pupils have to work so hard to communicate. And they can never be sure how other people will react to them. Therefore they may show a reluctance to undertake new activities, a reluctance to persist in the face of difficulty, and a reluctance to act independently. Of course, some deaf youngsters may go to the other extreme. They may try to undertake more activities than they can handle and may show extreme independence and marked persistence in the face of difficulty.

Motivation

In past studies deaf pupils have scored considerably below hearing pupils on tests sampling reading, arithmetic, and other subjects. These trends are not too surprising when one considers the extensive effects of language impairments and the amount of time pupils must devote to learning language and ways to communicate (e.g., Lane, 1976).

Academic Achievement

Hearing-impaired pupils' language problems interfere with their becoming literate, i.e., their learning to read and write. In turn, oral communication, reading, and writing are crucial tools in learning academic subjects, the arts, and vocational subjects in which most of the content is transmitted through language. Also, many sports and games require language to learn the rules and to relay signals to make the activity progress. Consequently, hearing impairment handicaps pupils in all of these subjects.

Most of deaf pupils' time — especially during the early school years — must be devoted to developing language and communication techniques for oral language. This time must be taken from instruction in the academic topics.

> Here in a nutshell is the problem of education of deaf children. The one educational objective to which all energies are tuned is language. The colossal reading failure reflects a deficiency in the knowledge of language and not, as would be the case with hearing children, a reading disability. These results caused no excitement when they were published. Any large school for deaf children that does not select its pupils has lived with these facts, and surveys have never reported an appreciably different picture. A person who has been

profoundly deaf from birth and who can read at grade 5 or better is invariably an exception. (Furth, 1973, pp. 92–93)

Vocational Characteristics

People have to be able to use language to learn and to perform most jobs above the unskilled level. Many of these jobs also require speaking and understanding speech. Deaf people are at a disadvantage in these situations. As a result, a disproportionate percentage are either unemployed or underemployed in the sense of being in jobs which are less skilled than the individuals are able to master (e.g., Bolton, 1976 *b*; Lassiter, 1974).

ACCOUNTABILITY

The accountability requirements involve monitoring whether correct procedures are used for identifying and classifying hearing-impaired pupils, developing their individual education programs, and observing the procedural safeguards which protect them.

Identifying and Planning for Hearing-Impaired Pupils

Documenting the Child-Find

There must be active searches for hearing-impaired pupils — public awareness campaigns about hearing impairment, screening pupils for signs of hearing impairments, and referring pupils who appear to have hearing problems for further evaluation. Reports must document the procedures used for these activities and the results in terms of the number of hearing-impaired pupils found and served.

Developing the individual education program

A pupil who qualifies for protection as hearing-impaired must have an individual education program to provide the services needed. The IEP is based on the pupils' present performance levels in all characteristics which influence his or her response to special education and training in communication. It contains long-term goals and objectives for special education and communication training, instructional procedures to help the pupil reach these goals, placement in the least restrictive environment for conveniently delivering that special education and communication training, and a schedule of times for periodically reevaluating his or her progress in response to the special education and communication training. The IEP team consists of the representative of the school system, the advocates, the audiologists, the teachers, the therapists who will assist in communication training, and other specialists as needed.

Observing the Procedural Safeguards for Hearing-Impaired Pupils

In identifying hearing-impaired pupils and planning their individual education programs, we at the same time scrupulously observe the procedures safeguarding their civil rights.

Again, advocates participate in the decisions about identifying and classifying pupils as hearing-impaired, testing their present performance levels in characteristics related to progress in communication training and special education, setting goals and objectives for communication and special education, selecting methods and materials for the special education and communication training, placing them in the most appropriate environment for delivering special education and communication training, and evaluating their progress and revising their special education and communication programs as necessary. If the parents/guardians choose not to participate in the process, surrogates stand for the pupil. As consultants, the parents/guardians or their surrogates may have experts in hearing impairment — its effects and treatment.

Advocate participation

The hearing-impaired pupils' advocates have rights for redress when they disagree with decisions about the hearing-impaired pupils. They may appeal through administrative channels of the school systems and the jurisdictional channels of the federal courts.

Due process

Hearing-impaired pupils are entitled to equal protection in identification and planning, testing, special education and related services, and placement. We must treat them by the same rules, criteria, and procedures used for all pupils, regardless of their other characteristics. The direct and indirect effects of their communication problems require special vigilance for possible errors in testing them.

Equal protection

We must reevaluate the hearing-impaired pupils at reasonable intervals. Again, this reevaluation is to catch any errors made previously. And periodic reevaluation helps find out whether objective criteria and evaluation procedures show that pupils are progressing satisfactorily toward their goals and objectives for communication and special education. Depending on that progress, we make decisions about what new goals and objectives to choose for their special education and communication training or what revisions in methods and materials are needed.

Periodic reevaluation

Hearing-impaired pupils have the right to strict confidentiality in all information about their hearing impairments, their related characteristics, their responses to communication training and special education, and about the bases for their placement for the delivery of instruction and therapy. The confidentiality procedures ensure that the advocates have access to the information, say-so over its release to all other parties, and the right to have wrong or irrelevant information purged from the records. Further, after the hearing-impaired pupils progress through the programs and their files are closed, all but actuarial information is discarded.

Confidentiality

Nondiscriminatory testing of hearing-impaired pupils

Nondiscriminatory testing of hearing-impaired pupils means collecting evidence within the protection of procedural safeguards against biases which may happen because of the hearing impairment. It is the second task in providing hearing-impaired pupils with their entitlements and protections in education.

PROBLEMS IN TESTING HEARING-IMPAIRED PUPILS

The goal in testing hearing-impaired pupils is to identify their characteristics, independent of the effects of the hearing impairment which might mask those characteristics.

> ... we must ask ourselves, what is the purpose of testing deaf children? What do we want to know? Perhaps the most unjust question is impossible to answer: How would the child have scored if he had not been deaf? This is the kind of question that is nearly as unanswerable as the quest for the true innate potential. (Furth, 1973, p. 88)

The direct effects of hearing impairment pose dangers in testing hearing-impaired pupils. The pupils' communication problems interfere with their test taking. At the speech and hearing level, they may have trouble understanding the instructions and presenting their answers in an understandable way. For example:

> At the primary grades, many achievement tests are adding sections that must be dictated orally to meet the methods of motivation that are primarily oral and to be a better test for educationally disadvantaged children. To use these test items for the deaf, the standardization may be altered if they are given sign language or fingerspelling. If standard procedures are used, lipreading skills are tested in addition to the subject matter of the test. A spelling test given in fingerspelling cannot be considered a test of spelling ability. (Lane, 1976, p. 102)

At the language level, they may have trouble understanding the vocabulary and the ideas in the tests. For example:

> An example of language confusion in arithmetic reasoning is the interpretation of "more" which means addition to the deaf child. However, if a problem states that John has five dollars and Bill has three dollars and then asks how much *more* money does John have, his answer may be eight dollars. (Lane, 1976, p. 104)

The indirect effects of hearing impairment can also lead to several problems. For example, hearing impairment and the resulting communication blocks can lead to tremendous frustration and anxiety.

These negative emotions, in turn, can distract the pupil so that he or she may not respond as well as possible in test situations.

These direct and indirect effects of hearing impairment can cause errors in getting evidence about what the pupil is like. In turn, these testing errors can cause judgments that the pupil is less capable, has accomplished less, or is less well adjusted than is actually the case. Such misjudgments can lead to wrong decisions and missed opportunities. We must consider these dangers when we select evaluation procedures and when we observe due process and equal protection in evaluation.

PROCEDURES FOR TESTING HEARING-IMPAIRED PUPILS

It is important to get evidence about the pupil's present performance levels on all characteristics important in learning the cultural tasks — especially efficiency in communication and the characteristics indirectly affected by hearing impairment. This evidence about the special needs of hearing-impaired pupils comes from answering assessment questions about the pupils' medical background, growth and development, psychological functioning, and educational capabilities.

We can certainly use with deaf pupils some of the same procedures we use with normally hearing pupils. For example, we use reports and records of past history, interviews and questionnaires, and observations of pupils in various situations. In addition, we may use standardized tests if we can meet the conditions about standard procedures and common background of experience. And we may use criterion-referenced tests if we can meet conditions specified in referenced tests if we can meet conditions specified in the criteria.

As we use these procedures, we must, of course, use procedures that will help us guard against errors. These procedures include involving a team of specialists who are qualified by knowing about not only testing and evaluation, but also hearing impairment, its effects, and its implications for individualizing instruction and placement. In addition, we must not use tests if we cannot meet their conditions nor must we use adaptations of tests which would destroy the test norms.

Individualizing instruction for hearing-impaired pupils*

We turn to our third task, individualizing instruction, once we have identified the pupil as hearing-impaired and have used nondiscrimi-

---

* The material in this section is based on information from such sources as Bloodstein (1979), Christopher (1976), Hoemann (1978), Kretschmer (1978), Moores (1977), Ross (1978), Streng (1978), Van Riper (1978), and Wier (1980).

natory testing to assess his or her present performance levels. We use the test information to plan how we will differentiate the special-education components and select related services. Then we put the plan into operation, evaluate how well it works, and change it as appropriate.

To start with, we need to survey methods hearing-impaired pupils use to communicate as a background for describing special education and related services they need. Then we can consider special education and related services.

SURVEY OF COMMUNICATION PROCEDURES

As it is for us all, language is the foundation of hearing-impaired people's communication. They transmit and receive this language through several media — speech production, speech reading (lip-reading), amplified sounds, residual hearing, and manual communication (finger spelling and sign language). In addition, they use reading and writing for written/printed messages. Generally, they combine these media into four communication methods: auditory, aural/oral, Rochester, and total communication (sometimes called the simultaneous method). For more than 200 years, deaf educators have disagreed about what methods are best, or at least what methods we should teach deaf pupils.

Language

As we have seen, language is a set of conventions for vocabulary and grammar (morphemes, form classes, and sentence patterns). Our goal is to teach hearing-impaired pupils to use these language conventions at an appropriate maturity level. We use several procedures. The generative grammar method and the natural method are representative.

In the *generative grammar method* we systematically teach pupils morphemes and rules for combining them into words and also form classes and rules for combining them into sentences. At the same time, we teach literal and figurative word meanings in vocabulary study.

In the *natural method* we expose pupils to a rich language environment. Then we rely on their acquiring grammatical knowledge and word meanings by unconsciously inferring them, as hearing pupils do.

The Communication Media

Speech production

Speech production is sending messages by talking. Our goal is to teach hearing-impaired pupils to produce words and sentences orally with the appropriate articulation, voice quality, and rhythm. The primary methods for teaching speech to hearing-impaired pupils are

Hearing-impaired pupils transmit
messages by oral, written,
and manual means.

through the visible speech, oral, acoustic, concentric, and tactile/
visual/auditory (TVA) methods.

The *visible speech method* essentially involves portraying how
parts of the speech mechanism operate to produce sounds in words
and sentences. The idea is that the youngster learns to copy what he
or she sees. Alexander M. Bell, a phonetician, developed the original
visible speech method. His son, Alexander Graham Bell, the telephone's inventor, extended the system. Others built on the Bells'
work and ultimately incorporated electronic devices which show
speech visibly, e.g., an oscilloscope, which translates sound patterns
into light patterns, the Bell Telephone Visible Speech Translator, and
the Instantaneous Pitch-Period Indicator. The teacher makes the
correct sound, and it appears on the display. The pupil continues to
modify his or her sound production until the sound patterns approximate the teacher's. Thus the pupil learns by successive approximation and proprioceptive feedback (biofeedback).

In the *oral method* the pupil learns to pronounce syllables and
then to combine them into words with the appropriate accent. The
teacher emphasizes not only correct pronunciation, but also rhythm,
accent, and breath control.

In the *acoustic method* the pupil learns to analyze and to interpret sound vibrations in speech, music, and pure tones, using touch and vision to perceive the sound sensations and what they mean for speech. That is, the pupil learns to associate particular patterns of vibrations and visual pictures with particular words, pitches, rhythms, accents, inflections, and intensities (loudness).

In the *concentric method* the pupil concentrates on a limited number of sounds. He or she learns to produce these sounds orally and with simultaneous finger spelling to help prevent ambiguities in expression or understanding. He or she proceeds to the next round of sounds after mastering the first round. He or she continues until the necessary sounds are produced with the correct articulation, voice quality, and rhythm.

The *tactile/visual/auditory* method is a multisensory one, as the name indicates. The pupil learns to produce sounds by associating tactual and visual cues, and also auditory cues if he or she can hear anything at all.

Speech reading   Speech reading is often called lipreading. The person decodes words by watching and interpreting primarily lip movements and more generally jaw, throat, facial, and bodily movements. The person has to learn to use very minimal cues, for two reasons. Movements are very similar for some sounds, e.g., /d/, /t/, and /n/. Also, some sounds, such as /h/, involve so little movement that they are difficult to recognize visually.

Our goal is for the youngster to read different people's speech when they converse at a normal rate. We have several methods for teaching speech reading. Essentially, however, the youngster begins with the more visible sounds and proceeds to the less obvious. At the same time, the youngster works on wholes — patterns of movements that indicate multiple sounds in a word, phrase, or sentence.

Amplifying sounds   Amplifying sounds means increasing their loudness. This is done by electronically boosting their intensity. Most people have seen hearing aids worn by hearing-impaired people to amplify sounds. Essentially, hearing aids have a microphone to receive the sound, a power source to boost the sound, and wires and earphones to carry the sound vibrations to the ear or to the bones in the ear area. Monaural hearing aids serve one ear; binaural hearing aids, both ears. Today, with miniaturization, hearing aids are less cumbersome and more feasible.

Sometimes we use what is called group hearing aids. The teacher speaks into a microphone, and sound is amplified and sent to multiple receivers — sets of earphones worn by pupils in a group. These sounds may be transmitted through wires, or they may be sent without wires, as radio signals.

Our goal is for the youngster to use hearing aids comfortably. Training methods here include teaching the pupil to care for his or her hearing aid, to put it in place and to remove it, to adjust volume to levels comfortable and effective for various listening situations, and to control static and random or painful noise.

Residual hearing is that remaining beyond the hearing loss. By definition, hard-of-hearing youngsters have residual hearing. In addition, many deaf pupils have some residual hearing — especially after they learn to use hearing aids and other procedures for amplifying sounds. Youngsters can learn skills to help them better use this residual hearing. These skills, called listening skills, help them to attend closely and to operate on more minimal cues.

Using residual hearing

Our goal in teaching listening skills is for the youngster to become sensitive to minimal cues and to learn to interpret them. Methods for teaching listening skills include teaching the pupil general skills, such as attending closely and concentrating, and specific skills, such as recognizing individual sounds and recognizing whole words and phrases.

Using the *manual alphabet* is sometimes called *finger spelling.* We have finger/hand patterns for each of the twenty-six letters (Fig. 5.4). The finger speller holds one hand in front of his or her chest and spells out words and combinations of words. Conversation by sending and receiving finger spelling is done at about the rate of an oral conversation.

Manual communication

In *sign language* we use more complex configurations to represent complete ideas. These complex configurations are developed through combinations of hand positions, patterns, and movements. Examples from one system of sign language, American Sign Language (Ameslan), are shown in Fig. 5.5.

Our goal is for the youngster to learn to send and receive messages through manual communication at about a normal conversational rate. The procedures for helping the pupil learn manual communication include teaching him or her to associate hand signals with letters and signs with the meanings they stand for, to produce the letters and signs singly and in combinations, and to read the letters or signs produced by someone else.

To recap: The communication methods are the combinations of the communication media which hearing-impaired people use to communicate the central language core. They include the auditory, the oral/aural, the Rochester, and the total communication methods.

The Communication Methods

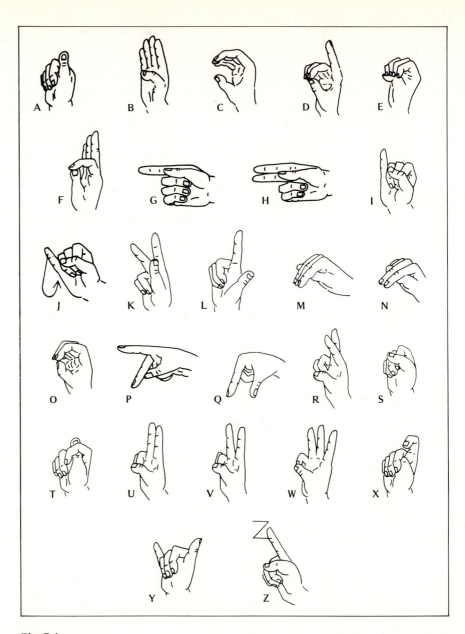

Fig. 5.4
Side view of the American manual alphabet. (Reprinted by permission from Riekehof, 1978, p. 15.)

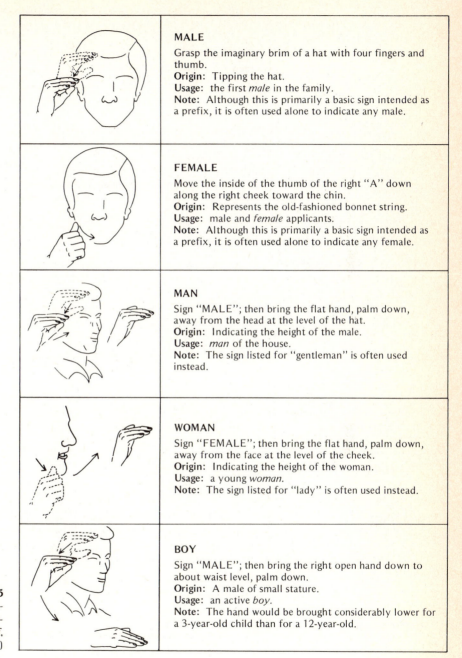

MALE

Grasp the imaginary brim of a hat with four fingers and thumb.
Origin: Tipping the hat.
Usage: the first *male* in the family.
Note: Although this is primarily a basic sign intended as a prefix, it is often used alone to indicate any male.

FEMALE

Move the inside of the thumb of the right "A" down along the right cheek toward the chin.
Origin: Represents the old-fashioned bonnet string.
Usage: male and *female* applicants.
Note: Although this is primarily a basic sign intended as a prefix, it is often used alone to indicate any female.

MAN

Sign "MALE"; then bring the flat hand, palm down, away from the head at the level of the hat.
Origin: Indicating the height of the male.
Usage: *man* of the house.
Note: The sign listed for "gentleman" is often used instead.

WOMAN

Sign "FEMALE"; then bring the flat hand, palm down, away from the face at the level of the cheek.
Origin: Indicating the height of the woman.
Usage: a young *woman*.
Note: The sign listed for "lady" is often used instead.

BOY

Sign "MALE"; then bring the right open hand down to about waist level, palm down.
Origin: A male of small stature.
Usage: an active *boy*.
Note: The hand would be brought considerably lower for a 3-year-old child than for a 12-year-old.

Fig. 5.5
Signing family relationships. (Reprinted by permission from Riekehof, 1978, pp. 17–18.)

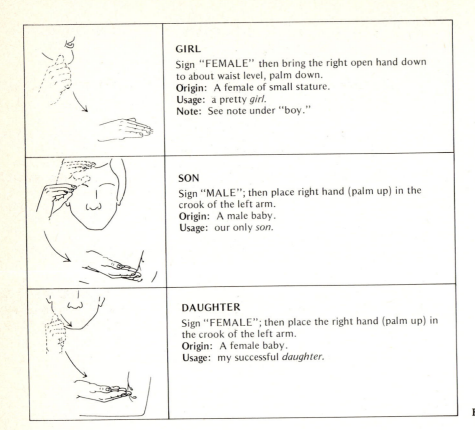

GIRL
Sign "FEMALE" then bring the right open hand down to about waist level, palm down.
Origin: A female of small stature.
Usage: a pretty *girl*.
Note: See note under "boy."

SON
Sign "MALE"; then place right hand (palm up) in the crook of the left arm.
Origin: A male baby.
Usage: our only *son*.

DAUGHTER
Sign "FEMALE"; then place the right hand (palm up) in the crook of the left arm.
Origin: A female baby.
Usage: my successful *daughter*.

Fig. 5.5 *continued*

The auditory method   Youngsters using the auditory method learn to use amplified sound and their residual hearing to get messages. They do not learn to use speech reading or manual communication. The corollary is that they will learn normal speech production unconsciously as hearing youngsters do as they interact in a hearing world. If they do not learn normal speech production naturally, they are given speech training. Instruction in reading and writing are delayed until pupils learn oral communication. The idea is to motivate youngsters to rely on oral communication until they become sufficiently skilled.

The oral/aural method   Youngsters using the oral/aural method learn to get messages through amplification and residual hearing. They also learn to use speech reading. In addition, they are intensively trained in speech production, but are not trained in manual communication. Also, reading and writing instruction are delayed until pupils learn oral communication.

In the Rochester method finger spelling is combined with the oral/ aural method. Pupils learn to receive messages by using amplification, residual hearing, speech reading, *and* finger spelling together. They learn to send messages by using speech and finger spelling together. At the same time, they receive intensive instruction in using reading to receive messages and writing to send messages.

The Rochester method

Youngsters using the total communication method, sometimes called the simultaneous method, employ oral/aural media and manual communication at the same time. They receive messages through amplification, residual hearing, speech reading, finger spelling, and sign language. They send messages through speech, finger spelling, and signs. At the same time, they learn to receive messages through reading and to send messages through writing.

The total communication method

Most people agree that hard-of-hearing youngsters and those classi- fied as deaf but who have sufficient hearing to do so should learn to communicate through the auditory method or, if necessary, the oral/ aural method. That is, pupils should not learn to rely on manual com- munication unless they need it.

The methods controversy

The controversy arises over which methods we should teach youngsters who are so deaf that they do not have residual hearing. This old and bitter controversy has roots in Europe. It reached a high in the United States with the disagreement between Alexander Graham Bell, who advocated oral/aural methods, and Thomas Gallaudet, who advocated manual methods.

The oralists maintain that deaf people must learn to live in a hearing environment. They consider that to teach youngsters to rely on manual methods or reading and writing would lead to their iso- lation from hearing people because they lack the necessary tools for easy communication at a normal rate. The manualists contend that some youngsters are not able to learn oral/aural methods ever or in a reasonable time. They consider that forcing such a pupil to rely on oral/aural methods deprives him or her of communication too severely and too long. That is, they think that using manual com- munication, with all of its restrictions, is preferable to no communi- cation or to communication deferred for too many of the precious early years when the youngster should be learning language and basic emotional and social patterns.

We have a lot of research on which of the four methods is most beneficial to pupils' social/emotional well-being, language adequacy, academic achievement, and vocational adjustment. Generally, pupils fare best when they use manual communication in combination with the oral/aural methods as much as possible. Though the controversy still goes on and we have pure oralists and pure manualists, many deaf educators today recommend studying the pupils' capabilities and then teaching them the methods they can best learn — always trying to prepare them to function in the least restrictive environment possible.

SPECIAL EDUCATION

In special education we differentiate the four components — instructional objectives, schedules, procedures, and settings. The particular ways we differentiate depend on each hearing-impaired pupil's characteristics.

Instructional Objectives

As all pupils do, hearing-impaired pupils have objectives for communication, academic content (e.g., mathematics, physical science, and health), the fine arts, vocational information and skills, and leisure skills. However, first priority must be given to communication.

Specially trained teachers of the deaf, speech pathologists, and audiologists working with the parents and regular educators teach pupils language and the communication media. Teaching language and the communication media is a complex, laborious process requiring years of systematic work. Such teaching usually begins in infancy, but it overlaps into the school years. Consequently, for hearing-impaired youngsters — especially deaf ones — we add objectives to those ordinarily pursued by hearing youngsters.

How adults working with the pupil stand on the oralism/manualism controversy determines what media they teach — speech production, speech reading, using sound amplification and residual hearing, finger spelling, and using signs. Once they select the media, they of course select the goals and objectives appropriate for each medium. For example, when they are teaching the pupil to use residual hearing, the goal is for the pupil to detect and interpret speech and other common environmental signals under quiet and noise conditions. Depending on the pupil's characteristics and needs, they have specific objectives for listening skills, such as locating the sources of sounds and attending closely.

The skills for communicating through written language — reading and writing (grammar, rhetoric, spelling, composition, handwriting/typing) — have a very high priority, second only to language and the communication media. As we have seen, the literacy skills are a problem for deaf pupils because they are the visual analog of the oral communication skills in transmitting messages through language. Consequently, the literacy goals and objectives for a particular pupil will depend on how much the hearing impairment has influenced his or her language and communication skills.

Once the goals and objectives for language, the communication media, and literacy are brought fairly well under control, we can be concerned about objectives for academic content, the fine arts, vocational subjects, and leisure skills. Hearing-impaired pupils have the same objectives for these curricular areas that hearing pupils do. However, we may have to select among objectives, taking only the most crucial and dropping others if hearing-impaired pupils do not have time for all objectives because they have to devote so much time to objectives for language, communication media, and literacy skills.

Generally, we need to differentiate schedules for deaf pupils when we individualize their instruction. This happens because with deaf pupils, as with others, we must base schedules on when they are ready to learn and how quickly they can proceed. The impact of deafness on their communication can affect when they are ready for certain material and how quickly they can learn it.

Instructional Schedules

The most desirable thing is for hearing-impaired pupils to be identified early — in infancy or as soon as the loss occurs if it happens after birth — and for training in language and communication skills to begin immediately. Among other benefits, this early identification and treatment might help the pupil to be ready for school learning as soon as his or her hearing peers are. And it follows that hearing-impaired pupils would not need different, i.e., special, schedules. If they have not acquired sufficient language and communication skills by school age, pupils do need special schedules; other objectives have to be delayed until the pupils acquire sufficient language and communication media to interact with other people and to serve as foundation for learning in other curricula areas.

When we are scheduling instruction, we must attend carefully to how quickly hearing-impaired pupils can proceed. We may need to plan for their proceeding more slowly if they have not mastered language and the communication media sufficiently. It takes longer to exchange ideas with pupils whose language and communication skills are inadequate. And more subtly, we need to devote more time to digressing to teach material that is necessary to proceed, but which pupils have not mastered. For example, refer back to the comment about deaf pupils' interpreting "more" to mean add. We must take the time to clarify the multiple special meanings of "more" if we wish to teach the pupil to do math problems of the "How much more is X than Y?" variety.

Instructional Procedures

We use special methods for teaching language and the communication media to hearing-impaired youngsters. We described these methods above in discussing communication procedures.

In the curricular areas beyond language and the communication media, we use with hearing-impaired pupils the same *methods* we use with hearing pupils, i.e., teacher presentations through lecture, etc., group work, individual work, direct experience, and student problem solving. Of course, as we use these general methods, we are careful to use language and communication skills appropriate for the pupil. For example, if he or she depends on speech reading and finger spelling, we use finger spelling and keep illumination, the pupil's position, and the teacher's position right for speech reading.

The instructional *media* depend on how much the pupil can get messages by using amplification and residual hearing. However, to reduce strain as much as possible, we generally use visual media as much as we can. Two important types of media here are the captioned films and other media for the deaf and also films and videotapes that have an interpreter simultaneously finger spelling and signing the speaker's comments. There is a federally subsidized Captioned Films and Media Program for the Deaf. Qualified people can get items on loan from the Library of Congress directly and through local and regional libraries. In addition, there are many other specially prepared media; e.g., see the *Index to Media and Materials for the Deaf, Hard of Hearing, and Speech Impaired* (1978).

Visual media and concrete materials are especially important for hearing-impaired pupils.

Generally, we use about the same instructional settings with deaf pupils that we use with hearing pupils. In *allocating personnel* we provide for individual tutoring, solitary activity, independent study, small groups, and large groups. In *allocating space* we provide common areas, carrels, special centers, and depositories.

Again, we must be very careful about the physical arrangements if pupils depend on residual hearing, speech reading, finger spelling, and signing. We must let them move to where they can hear the speaker or recorder, and we must be sure that environmental noise does not interfere unduly. For example, passing buses can block a pupil's sound reception if he or she has a high-frequency hearing loss, because the low tones he or she depends on are masked by a bus's low-frequency motor noise.

RELATED SERVICES

A hearing-impaired pupil may need a fairly wide range of related services, depending on the nature of his or her hearing impairment and its impact on his or her language, communication skills, and other characteristics. The pool of probably needed services includes medical, audiological, speech/language, psychological, vocational rehabilitation, and family information and counseling services.

The first step after we identify the pupil's hearing problem is to get services from an otologist, or an ear/ nose/ throat specialist. These physicians diagnose the cause of the hearing impairment and provide the treatment (surgery, drugs) to clear up that cause as much as possible. Periodically, the physician rechecks the pupil's problem and decides whether further treatment is necessary.

The audiologist takes over where the physician leaves off, assessing the degree of hearing loss and the feasibility of a hearing aid. The audiologist both fits the hearing aid and helps the pupil learn to use it. Periodically, the audiologist rechecks the pupil's hearing, how well the hearing aid is working, and how well the pupil uses it.

Usually, the specially trained teacher of the deaf is the primary person responsible for teaching the hearing-impaired pupil language, communication media, and literacy skills. The speech/language pathologist provides backup consultation and help for the deaf educators. However, the speech/language pathologist may take the lead role if the pupil's problem is not severe enough to require a teacher of the deaf. In such cases the speech/language pathologist works with the pupil on language and communication media while the classroom teacher serves as the backup. At the same time, the speech/language pathologist serves as consultant and backup to the teacher who trains the pupil in the literacy skills and other content areas (such as history).

Psychological Services Clinical psychologists and psychiatrists assess how the hearing impairment affects the pupil's social/emotional and intellectual functioning. They also provide counseling to the pupil and his or her family if counseling is needed.

School psychologists assess how the hearing impairment affects the pupil's intellectual functioning and academic achievement. In turn, they provide educational recommendations.

Vocational Rehabilitation Services Vocational rehabilitation specialists enter the picture in the adolescent and young adult periods. They assess the hearing-impaired youngster's capabilities and limitations. Then they provide information about occupations — their duties, benefits, and requirements. A VR specialist also provides counseling to the hearing-impaired youngster and his or her parents. Together, they consider the youngster's interests, aspirations, and capabilities in relation to possible occupations. Once the youngster makes some choices, the VR specialist helps him or her locate appropriate training agencies and services he or she needs to take that training. If appropriate, the VR specialist also helps the trained youngster find employment.

Family Information and Counseling The family must make many decisions during the course of the pupil's identification and treatment. At the same time, they must deal with the impact of a handicapped child and his or her needs on their structure and activities. In order to carry out these tasks, they need a great deal of information about hearing impairment — its causes, effects, identification, and treatment — and about the services available to the pupil and his or her rights to those services. They also need counseling to help them deal with psychological stresses and problems in the situation. Social workers, teachers, and the specialists who provide the various related services are responsible for delivering that information and counseling.

Placing hearing-impaired pupils in the least restrictive environment

After we have identified the special education and related services pupils need, our next task is to decide where they should be located for the delivery of those services. Our decisions here pertain to placement options, extracurricular activities, transportation and facilities, and safety.

PLACEMENT OPTIONS

Early treatment is so very important for any handicapped children. It certainly is important for hearing-impaired children (Simons and Martin, 1976). Medical correction and, beyond that, auditory stimulation and communication training must begin in infancy. No time must be lost in the pupils' learning to communicate. Nor must we allow them to suffer psychological and social trauma or deprivation because of their problems in dealing with sounds in the world. Again, pupils' growth and development can diverge quickly, and they can suffer almost irremedial losses in accomplishing the cultural tasks so essential to their well-being.

At the primary, intermediate, and later school levels, we have a variety of placement options. These include:

☐ the regular class with team teaching arrangements among the regular-class teacher, the teacher of the deaf, and the speech/language pathologist;

☐ the regular class with part time in a resource room for intensive work on communication and tutoring in subjects which depend heavily on communication;

☐ the special class for deaf pupils; and

☐ the residential school for deaf pupils.

Figure 5.6 shows how frequently each option was being used across the country in the late 1970s. School-age pupils most often attended regular classes with team teaching arrangements and resource rooms available. Preschool pupils and postschool pupils attended the various settings about equally.

In placing a particular pupil, the placement option we choose depends, of course, on what the pupil's level of communication is, whether he or she has associated problems, and his or her readiness to interact with hearing pupils and tolerate stress. As the pupil's status on these characteristics improves, we must be prepared to shift the pupil's placement to less specialized situations (e.g., Birch, 1975; Leslie and Clark, 1980; Yater, 1977).

EXTRACURRICULAR ACTIVITIES

The hearing-impaired pupils' communication problems make finding extracurricular activities essential but demanding. Access should be no difficulty with activities such as tennis and swimming, which do not require too many signals or very much communication. However, again, we must be careful that such individual activities by their very accessibility do not draw us off into decisions which will lead to further isolating the pupil from other pupils.

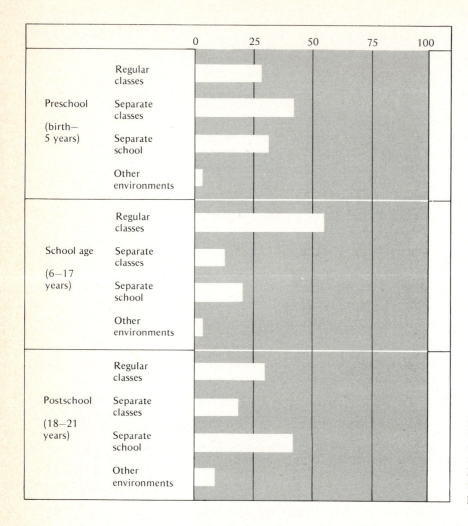

Fig. 5.6
Most frequent placements of hearing-impaired pupils reported by the states in the late 1970s. (Based on information in BEH, 1979, pp. 169–189.)

Activities involving more communication require more planning and arranging. For example, the deaf pupil should be able to play on the baseball team, given that the players and coaches rely on hand signals rather than words. Also, deaf pupils should be able to get along quite well in such activities as 4-H clubs and the school annual if the leaders and the hearing pupils can work out or learn some procedures for communicating with them.

TRANSPORTATION AND FACILITIES

We need to make special arrangements for deaf pupils' *transportation* around the school and to and from school until they learn sufficient communication skills to travel independently. Buddies need to be assigned to them until they learn their ways around school. Bus drivers need to be alerted to their problems and trained to communicate with them. And deaf pupils need to know their addresses and how to communicate distress.

Access to *facilities* is not a particular problem for deaf pupils. However, we need to be sure that warning signals such as fire alarms and storm alerts are visual as well as auditory. For example, a fire should be signaled by flashing lights as well as bells, buzzers, or sirens.

SAFETY

We have three concerns about deaf pupils' safety. One concern is that they really understand safety rules and procedures. Because of their communication problems, we need to be very careful that they grasp dangers and how to avoid them.

Another concern is that they be aware of warning signals. These include not only fire and storm alerts, but also situations such as flying balls and oncoming cars.

Still another concern is that deaf pupils know how to inform someone when they are in distress. For example, the ill pupil needs to be able to communicate the location, nature, and severity of his or her pain.

Hearing-impaired pupils can participate in many activities with other pupils.

Summary

IDENTIFYING AND PLANNING FOR HEARING-IMPAIRED PUPILS

Normal Hearing

The structure and function of the ear must be adequate if normal development of hearing behavior — and secondarily speech and language — is to occur. In turn, normal development of hearing behavior — and speech and language — is necessary for the youngster to learn and perform many cultural tasks.

Hearing Impairments

Defects in the structure and function of the ear and the central nervous system can cause the development of the youngster's hearing behavior to deviate from normal. We consider this disruption to be an impairment when it is extensive enough to interfere with the youngster's mastering speech and language and the cultural tasks.

Deaf and hard-of-hearing pupils are protected by the laws. In the Child-Find we conduct public awareness activities, stressing early discovery, screening for signs of impairment, and referral of youngsters with possible problems for further study by audiologists, otologists, and other specialists.

Audiometric procedures are used to measure hearing. The four main types of audiometric procedures are pure-tone audiometry, speech audiometry, electrodermal audiometry, and auditory brain-stem response audiometry. When we classify by cause of hearing problems, we identify whether a pupil's problem is caused by congenital problems, infections, or traumatic injuries. Classification by type of hearing loss involves categorizing by conductive losses or sensorineural losses. In classification by age of onset we identify whether the loss is *prelingual* (before language developed) or *postlingual* (after language developed). One system for classifying pupils by degree of hearing loss is keyed to whether the pupils can understand speech through the ears with or without hearing aids. Another system is keyed to what kind of instruction and placement for schooling pupils need.

Impact of Hearing Impairments on Pupils' Characteristics

Hearing impairment directly interferes with a person's receiving messages through sound. If it is severe enough and occurs early enough, hearing impairment also interferes with speech and language development. If intensive training is not started early, the hearing impairment and the speech and language impairment can cause secondary problems in the pupils' performing organized physical activities, learning and thinking tasks, intelligence tests, academic tasks, and vocational tasks that involve language and speech. Further, the hearing-impaired youngsters' frustrations and the ways they are treated may lead to social/emotional immaturity and problems.

Accountability requirements involve our documenting the Child-Find and developing IEP's to be sure that correct procedures are used in identifying and planning for hearing-impaired pupils. At the same time, we ensure advocate participation, due process, equal protection, periodic reevaluation, and confidentiality in observing procedural safeguards for the pupils.

Accountability

NONDISCRIMINATORY TESTING OF HEARING-IMPAIRED PUPILS

Nondiscriminatory testing of hearing-impaired pupils means that we collect evidence within the protections of the procedural safeguards against biases resulting from the hearing impairment. Hearing impairment — and accompanying speech and language problems — interfere directly and indirectly with pupils' showing what they can really do or what they are really like on tests. In short, if we cannot meet the conditions of criterion-referenced and norm-referenced tests, tests often become another measure of the hearing impairment.

Problems in Testing Hearing-Impaired Pupils

To collect the information needed for planning, we use some testing procedures, e.g., interviews and questionnaires, that we use with all pupils. In addition, we can use norm-referenced and criterion-referenced tests if we can satisfy the conditions for these tests. All information collection is carefully circumscribed with the procedural safeguards.

Procedures for Testing Hearing-Impaired Pupils

INDIVIDUALIZING INSTRUCTION FOR HEARING-IMPAIRED PUPILS

Language is the foundation for hearing-impaired people's communication. They transmit and receive language through several communication media — speech production, speech reading (lipreading), amplified sounds, residual hearing, and manual communication (finger spelling and sign language), as well as through conventional reading and writing. They combine these communication media into four communication methods — the auditory method, the aural/oral method, the Rochester method, and the total communication (simultaneous) method. Educators of the deaf have long disagreed about which methods are best and which we should teach deaf pupils.

Communication Procedures

Today many deaf educators recommend studying the pupils' capabilities and teaching them the methods they can best learn — always trying to prepare them to function in the least restrictive environment possible.

Special Education
As all pupils do, hearing-impaired pupils have *objectives* for language, communication skills, academic content, fine arts, vocational information and skills, and leisure skills. First priority must be given to objectives for language and the communication skills. If the objectives for language and the communication skills require more time than usual, we might have to omit objectives in other areas. If hearing impairment can be identified in infancy and training in language and the communication skills started early, pupils may be ready for school learning when their peers are. If not, we need to adjust *instructional schedules* especially to the deaf pupils' readiness to progress.

We use special *methods* in teaching language and the communication skills to deaf youngsters. Beyond this, we use the same methods we use for other youngsters, with special attention to communication. We use some oral *media* if youngsters can get messages through amplification and their residual hearing. Beyond that, we use visual media as much as possible. We use about the same *instructional settings* with hearing-impaired pupils as we use with other pupils. In doing so we pay careful attention to circumstances that might help and circumstances that might hinder communication.

Related Services
A hearing-impaired pupil may need a wide range of related services, depending on the nature of his or her hearing impairment and its impact. The services probably needed include medical, audiological, speech/language, psychological, vocational rehabilitation, and family information and counseling services.

PLACING HEARING—IMPAIRED PUPILS IN THE LEAST RESTRICTIVE ENVIRONMENT

Placement Options
Training programs for infants and preschool hearing-impaired pupils are crucial. After that, we use a variety of placement options, depending on the pupils' language and communication skills and other characteristics. These options include the regular class with the deaf educator team teaching or consulting as appropriate, the regular class with part-time resource room work with the deaf educator, the special class for hearing-impaired pupils, and the residential school for hearing-impaired pupils.

Extracurricular activities need to be chosen with care to be sure that the hearing impairment and communication problems do not penalize the pupil. At the same time, we need to be sure that the protected or special activity does not lead to the pupil's undue social isolation.

Extracurricular Activities

We need to provide especially for transportation until the pupil learns to communicate adequately. Access to facilities is not a problem for deaf pupils. However, we need to provide carefully for safety.

Transportation, Facilities, and Safety

TOPICS

Identifying and planning for visually impaired pupils

NORMAL VISION

Structure and functioning of the eye
Development of normal visual behavior
Vision and the cultural tasks

VISUAL IMPAIRMENTS

Legal definition and prevalence
Finding visually impaired pupils
Diagnosis: Classifying pupils by cause of visual impairment
Diagnosis: Classifying pupils by degree of visual
impairment

**IMPACT OF VISUAL IMPAIRMENTS ON PUPILS'
CHARACTERISTICS**

Introduction
Physical characteristics
Social/emotional characteristics
Speech and language characteristics
Intellectual characteristics

Special Needs of Visually Impaired Pupils

Academic characteristics
Vocational characteristics

ACCOUNTABILITY

Identifying and planning for visually impaired pupils
Observing the procedural safeguards for visually impaired pupils

Nondiscriminatory testing of visually impaired pupils

PROBLEMS IN TESTING VISUALLY IMPAIRED PUPILS

PROCEDURES FOR TESTING VISUALLY IMPAIRED PUPILS

Individualizing instruction for visually impaired pupils

SURVEY OF COMMUNICATION MEDIA

SPECIAL EDUCATION

Instructional objectives
Instructional schedules
Instructional procedures
Instructional settings

RELATED SERVICES

> Medical services
> Peripatology/physical therapy
> Occupational therapy
> Speech/language therapy
> Psychological services
> Vocational rehabilitation services
> Family information and counseling

Placing visually impaired pupils in the least restrictive environment

PLACEMENT OPTIONS

EXTRACURRICULAR ACTIVITIES

TRANSPORTATION AND FACILITIES

SAFETY

Identifying and planning for visually impaired pupils

With visually handicapped pupils, as with all handicapped pupils, our first task in guaranteeing each pupil a free, appropriate education and an equal educational opportunity is to conduct the Child-Find and to organize the individual education program — both within the requirements of the procedural safeguards. To do so, we must understand normal vision, how it becomes impaired, and how these impairments affect pupils' characteristics.

NORMAL VISION

Normal development of visual behavior depends on an intact eye and central nervous system and on adequate functioning of those structures (e.g., Rosenthal, 1975). In turn, accomplishing many cultural tasks depends on normal development of visual behavior.

Figure 6.1 is a cross section showing the anatomy of the eye. The *cornea*, the outside covering of the eye, bends the visual stimuli to focus them. The *aqueous humor* is a liquid that keeps the eye clear and lubricated in its socket. The *iris*, the colored portion of the eye, screens the light. The *pupil* is the opening in the iris, expanding and contracting to control the amount of light going into the eye. The *lens* focuses the stimulus through the *vitreous humor* to the retina. The *retina* consists of nerve fibers that transmit the sensations to the *optic nerve*, which transmits the sensations to the brain. The visual stimuli, in the form of light sensations, pass through each structure

Structure and Functioning of the Eye*

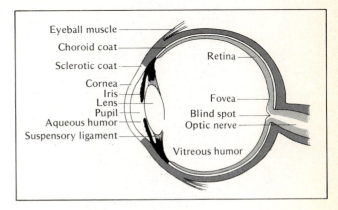

Fig. 6.1
The structure of the eye.

* We consider the central nervous system in Chapter 7.

in turn as they move from the outside to the brain. For this process to occur, the eyeball must be directed toward a stimulus. This direction is controlled by muscles that hold the eye steady or turn it in horizontal and vertical directions.

Development of Normal Visual Behavior

In the beginning the infant apparently does not respond to visual stimuli. Very quickly, however, as maturation and learning occur, he or she begins to attend to visual stimuli and to respond to them in increasingly complex ways. Table 6.1 lists some important milestones in the development of visual behavior. Again, note how the earlier, simpler skills serve as a foundation for the later, more complex skills.

Vision and the Cultural Tasks

Vision is important in our perceiving physical stimuli — their lightness/darkness, sizes, colors, shapes, positions, and movements (e.g., Fraiberg, 1977; Scott *et al.* (1977). We use our vision to get direct information about the characteristics of phenomena *within the reach* of our hearing, touch, temperature perception, kinesthesis and proprioception, smell, and taste. We also, and especially, use vision to get direct information about phenomena *beyond the reach* of our other senses. These phenomena are almost endless. They range from the print on the page before us, to the wind, to the plane flying at 40,000 feet, to the smiling person in the moon, to the pattern of colors

Vision is extremely important to our gaining information about the world and ourselves and to our using that information as we solve problems in living.

TABLE 6.1 MILESTONES IN DEVELOPING NORMAL VISUAL BEHAVIOR.

Age	Behavior
Birth	Corneal reflex to touch. Pupil reaction to light. Reflex closing of both eyelids to bright light shone in face. Lids tighten to same stimulus during sleep.
2 weeks	Rudimentary fixation on objects. May only be using one eye at a time (has "walleyed" appearance).
3 months	Stares at light source. Follows moving objects, to midline first, then past midline. Fascinated by lights and bright colors. Cries real tears. *Advancing:* Fixation ability. *Emerging:* Convergence. Will converge on objects as close as 5″, progressing to 3″. Binocular coordination. Begins to look within designs, instead of fixating on one spot along perimeter. Hand regard, usually to side favored by tonic neck reflex.
5 months	Fixates on objects at 3 feet. Macular development at its peak. Peripheral vision poor; field is only about one-third of adult's. Acuity nearly equal to adult's. *Advancing:* Inspection of hands. Central vision. *Emerging:* Accommodation at distances of 5–20 inches. Alternates gaze from hand to object and from object to object (rapid movement).
5–7 months	Eye-hand coordination developed ("top-level reaching"). Fixation fully developed. Discrimination of forms. Convergence occurs consistently. Most binocular reflexes coordinated.
11 months	Interest in tiny objects. Tilts head to look up. Smooth visual pursuit (i.e., follows with eyes and not necessarily head). *Emerging:* Depth perception.
12 months	Discriminates geometric forms. Fixates on facial expressions (and imitates). Binocular vision developed.
12–18 months	Identifies likenesses and differences. Interested in pictures. Marks and scribbles. Vertical orientation develops.
18 months–3 years	All optical skills smooth. Accommodation developed. Visual images recalled.
3–4 years	Copies geometric figures. Eye-hand coordination good.
4–5 years	Color recognition; shadings; differentiations. Sharpness and clarity of detail. Depth perception fully developed.

Source: Ferrell (n.d., pp. 2–5).

we call an impressionist painting, to the car approaching at a high speed, to a multitude of other events. Note that from where you sit or stand, you can identify many more stimuli by sight than you can by hearing and the other senses. Similarly, you can imagine (recall images of) more visual phenomena than auditory, tactual, taste, thermal, or olfactory phenomena.

The point is that vision is extremely important to our gaining information about the world and to our using that information as we solve the problems in living — from walking to the kitchen for a drink of water, to mowing the lawn, to learning the physics required for college entry, to many other activities. It is a tool we use in performing the cultural tasks, i.e., in dealing with the physical and social environments to meet our needs in socially acceptable ways. Look again at the cultural tasks listed in Table 1.1. Consider how crucial adequate vision is to a youngster's learning and performing tasks like those. And consider too how important mastering the earlier, simpler tasks is to acquiring the later, more complex tasks.

VISUAL IMPAIRMENTS

Legal Definition and Prevalence

Normal development of visual behavior goes awry when problems occur in the structure and function of the eye or the central nervous system. An impairment exists when these visual deviations make it very difficult or impossible for the youngster to accomplish cultural tasks dependent on vision. These contingencies are expressed in the legal definition of the visually impaired category, which we use in identifying youngsters qualified for the rights to special education and related services and the protections of the procedural safeguards guaranteed by PL 94-142. That is, "a visual handicap is defined as a visual impairment which after correction, adversely affects a child's educational performance. The term includes both partially seeing and blind children" (PL 94-142, 1977, Sec. 121a.5). In Fig. 1.1 we saw that 0.17 of 1% of pupils are expected to be visually impaired. As of the late 1970s, 0.07% had been located and were being served.

Finding Visually Impaired Pupils

In the Child-Find we identify a pupil who apparently has a visual problem and then determine whether he or she is qualified for the visually handicapped category and therefore protected by the laws governing education for exceptional pupils.

Awareness campaigns here are like those used with other types of handicaps. Campaigns go on through media, notices, and contact with people. The emphasis is on early detection and treatment of visually impaired pupils so that the harmful secondary effects of visual impairments can be prevented.

Screening is done at the preschool and in-school levels. Parents, families, teachers, and nurses carry the primary responsibility for picking up signs of visual problems (e.g., Ritty, 1979). Severe visual impairments are obvious. Symptoms of less severe impairments are various signs of eyestrain (Bishop, 1971, pp. 18–19). For example:

1. *Appearance of the eyes*
   a) Swollen or red-rimmed eyelids
   b) Crusts near the lashes
   c) Frequent sties
   d) Unusual discharge in the eyes or along the lids
   e) Reddened or watery eyes
   f) Eyes that do not appear straight (one or both turn in, out, up, or down; especially, and sometimes only, when the child is tired).
   g) Pupils of different sizes
   h) Eyes that move constantly
   i) Clouding of the pupillary opening
   j) Drooping eyelids
2. *Visual behavior*
   a) Complaints of aches or pains in the eyes; excessive headaches; dizziness or nausea after close eye work
   b) Squinting, blinking, frowning, facial distortions, constant rubbing of the eyes or attempts to brush away a blur, tilting of the head when seeing; closing or covering one eye when looking or reading
   c) Undue light sensitivity
   d) Holding of reading material relatively close or relatively far away; frequently changing the distance of reading material from near to far
   e) Head thrust forward or body tense when viewing distant objects
   f) Inattentiveness during reading; inability to read for long periods without tiring
   g) Tendencies toward reversals of letters and words or confusion of letters or numbers with similar shapes
   h) Constant loss of place in a sentence or on a page
   i) Stumbling over objects
   j) Poor spacing in writing, with inability to "stay on the line."

Sometimes we do further screening with the Snellen Chart to get a rough index of the pupil's visual acuity or, conversely, degree of visual impairment.

Referral for further study comes next if in screening we find that the pupil has physical signs of pathology, a reduced visual field, or reduced visual acuity, or any combination of these. We refer the pupil to an ophthalmologist — a *physician* specializing in the eye — for medical diagnosis and, if needed, treatment. We refer the pupil to *school psychologists* and *special education personnel* for study of his or her psychological, physical, social/emotional characteristics and their effects on his or her learning the cultural tasks. We may also need assessments by *physical therapists, occupational therapists,* and *peripatologists* — orientation and mobility specialists — to get an assessment of the pupil's capabilities and needs in the self-help skills and independent travel. And for older pupils, we need to work with vocational rehabilitation/vocational education specialists.

Diagnosis: Classifying Pupils by Cause of Visual Impairment

The structure and function of the eye are complex, and many things can go wrong to cause visual impairments. Three important categories of impairments are refraction errors, muscular imbalance, and pathology of the eyeball and nervous tissue. Commonly seen problems in each category are defined below (Merck, 1972; Rosenthal, 1975).

Refraction errors

Refraction errors influence how the light rays strike the retina. Refraction refers to the eye's ability to bend (refract) light rays entering it in order to form an image on the retina.

Hyperopia, or farsightedness, happens when the pupil's eyeball is abnormally short from front to back. Thus the light rays converge behind the retina. As a result, the pupil can see items clearly when they are off at a distance, but not when they are close up.

Myopia is nearsightedness. The pupil's eyeball is abnormally long from front to back. The light rays converge in front of the retina. The pupil can see items clearly when they are nearby, but not when they are far off.

Astigmatism is blurred vision. A structural defect in the lens prevents light rays from converging on a single focal point on the retina. As a result, the images are indistinct and distorted.

Muscular imbalance

Muscular imbalance happens when the muscles controlling eye movement and position do not maintain the appropriate amounts of pull (tension). As a result, the pupil cannot focus his or her eyes on a point and hold that focus.

Nystagmus is a continuous, often rapid, movement of the eyeballs. They may go in a circular movement, or they may move side to side in a left-right direction.

Strabismus happens when the muscles pull unequally on a lateral plane. Internal strabismus is a directing of the eyeballs inward toward the nose. External strabismus is a directing of the eyeballs outward toward the ears. One eyeball may be in balance and the other out of balance. Both eyeballs may be out of balance. Or, as in alternating strabismus, one or both eyeballs shift among the balanced, internal, and external positions. More rarely, there is a muscular imbalance on a vertical plane. Then the eye may shift upward or downward.

Amblyopia ex anopsia is a functional blindness that occurs along with strabismus. The strabismus may lead to double vision. To reduce the confusion, the brain suppresses the image from one eye, and the youngster uses only one eye. If the problem is not corrected, the suppression may become permanent blindness in the affected eye.

Pathology of the eyeball and nervous tissue results from damage from various sources. The effect on vision depends on the parts of the eye or the nerves which are injured.

Pathology of the eyeball and nervous tissue

Destruction of nervous tissue in the optic nerve or in the part of the brain controlling vision can lead to blindness. Such destruction can result from tumors. It also can result from viral infections associated with encephalitis in the child or with the mother's having rubella during the first trimester of pregnancy.

Traumatic injuries are damage to any part of the eye from such events as puncture wounds and severe blows in the regions of the eyes.

Congenital anophthalmos is the incomplete development of the eye and the visual area of the brain.

Retrolental fibroplasia is the formation of scar tissue behind the lens. This scar tissue interferes with the passage of light rays through to the retina and optic nerve. The condition results from excessive oxygen being given to premature infants.

Congenital glaucoma happens when there is an increase in pressure within the eyeball. In turn, there is damage to the retina and the optic nerve, and visual impairment results.

Cataracts are a condition in which the lens becomes opaque. As a result, light images cannot get through, and visual blurring and blindness result.

Diagnosis: Classifying Pupils by Degree of Visual Impairment   The conditions causing visual impairment can lead to various degrees of impairment. Degrees of impairment are described in terms of visual acuity and field of vision (Lowenfeld, 1974). (Illustrations from the viewpoint of the visually impaired person are given in Figs. 6.2–6.6.)

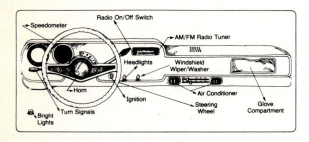

Fig. 6.2
A page of print as seen by a pupil who has normal vision. (Reprinted by permission from W. F. Hunter and P. L. LaFollette, *Directing Language Skills.* New York: Webster Division, McGraw-Hill Book Company, 1978.)

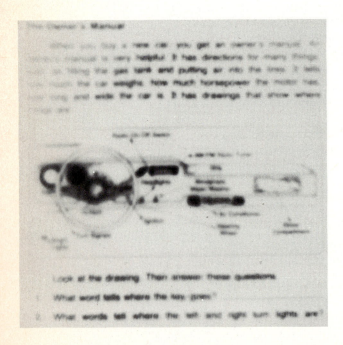

Fig. 6.3
A page of print as seen by a pupil who has astigmatism. (Idea for this presentation is from Scott, Jan, and Freeman, 1977.)

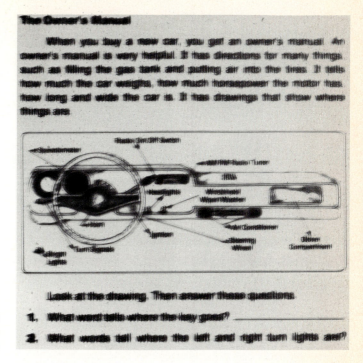

Fig. 6.4
A page of print as seen by a pupil who
has nystagmus.

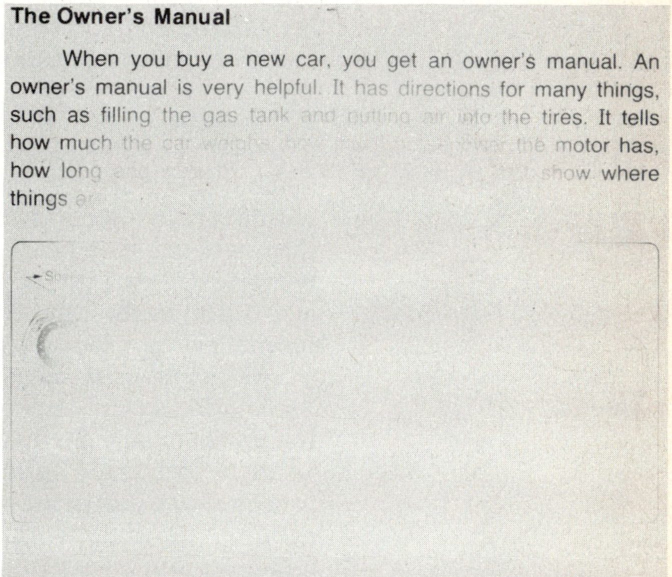

Fig. 6.5
A page of print as seen by a pupil who
has impaired central vision.

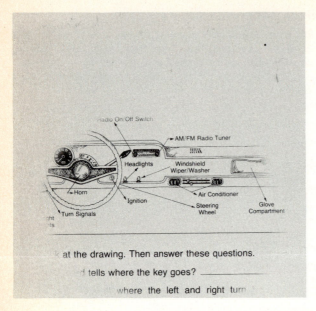

Fig. 6.6
A page of print as seen by a pupil who
has tunnel vision — impaired
peripheral vision.

Measuring vision   We describe visual acuity in terms of distance vision and near vision
(e.g., Aubuchon, 1973; Kugel, 1972).

Distance vision is measured primarily by a Snellen chart, which
has lines of letters, numbers, and symbols graded in size according to
Snellen measurements. Each size is labeled with the distance at
which it can be read by the normal eye. For distance vision, the pupil
is tested at 20 feet away from the chart. The results of the test are
usually described as a ratio. The denominator refers to what the
normal eye can see at a given number of feet; the numerator, to what
the eye being tested can see. For example, 20/100 means that the eye
being tested can see at 20 feet what the normal eye can see at 100
feet; 5/200 means that the eye being tested can see at 5 feet what the
normal eye can see at 200 feet.

Near vision is measured several ways. The American Medical
Association's (AMA) special Snellen chart with the reference set at 14
inches is one way. For example, 14/40 means that the pupil can see at
14 inches what the normal eye can see at 40 inches. Another way, the
Jaeger chart, has print or type of various sizes. Each print/type size
is numbered and described by points. For example, the average book
for adults is printed in 9-point type. A person's near vision is described
by the size the print must be for the person to read it.

The perimeter is used to map out the *field of vision* in 360 degrees.
Central vision is the middle of the visual field. Peripheral vision is

vision above and below and to the sides of the central vision. Figure 6.7 illustrates the charts used to record the field of vision in the right and left eyes.

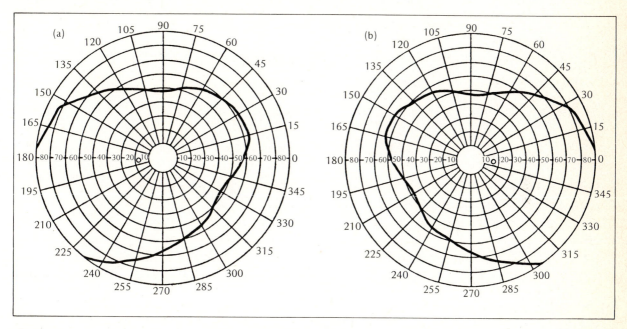

Fig. 6.7
The field of vision in the (a) right and (b) left eyes. (Reprinted by permission from the National Society to Prevent Blindness, n.d.)

Legal categories

For legal purposes, we are concerned with legal blindness and partial sightedness. *Legal blindness* is central visual acuity of 20/200 or less in the better eye with correcting glasses. Or, *legal blindness* is a contraction of the visual field to an angle of 20 degrees or less. This definition holds regardless of central visual acuity — it may or may not be greater than 20/200. *Partial sightedness* is central visual acuity between 20/70 and 20/200 in the better eye after correction.

Visual efficiency

A legal standard of blindness is important as a focus for legal and philanthropic action. "A whole system of social benefits is accessible only to those who are classified as blind.... These benefits, including education, health care, welfare, rehabilitation services, aids and appliances, employment, and recreation, are paid for, in part, out of tax funds and philanthropic contributions. (Rusalem, 1972, p. 12)

However, the legal definitions do not indicate how much vision a pupil has for learning important cultural tasks. For example, few people are totally blind in the sense of complete blackness, with no visual stimuli coming through. Most blind people have some residual vision. Table 6.2 portrays visual efficiency corresponding to the measures of distance and near vision. The smaller type sizes referred to in Table 6.2 are frequently seen. The larger type sizes are the following (*Large Type Books in Print*, 1978).

14 pt. Fourteen

16 pt. Sixteen

18 pt. Eighteen

20 pt. Twenty

24 pt. Twenty-four

Some educators prefer not to use the terms "blind" and "partially sighted." Instead, they prefer definitions in terms of behavior: "Learns only through listening"; "Learns through braille"; "Learns through

TABLE 6.2 VISUAL EFFICIENCY CORRESPONDING TO VISUAL ACUITY NOTATIONS.

Distant Snellen	AMA	Near Jaeger	Metric	% Central Visual Efficiency for Near	Point*	Usual Type Text Size
20/20 (ft)	14/14 (in.)	1	0.37 (M.)	100	3	Mail-order catalog
20/30	14/21	2	0.50	95	5	Want ads
20/40	14/28	4	0.75	90	6	Telephone directory
20/50	14/35	6	0.87	50	8	Newspaper text
20/60	14/42	8	1.00	40	9	Adult text books
20/80	14/56	10	1.50	20	12	Children's books 9–12 y
20/100	14/70	11	1.75	15	14	Children's books 8–9 yr
20/120	14/84	12	2.00	10	18 ⎫	Large-type text
20/200	14/140	17	3.50	2	24 ⎭	
12.5/200	14/224	19	6.00	1.5		
8/200	14/336	20	8.00	1		
5/200	14/560					
3/200	14/900					

* Point refers to type size. For example, 3-point type is the size ordinarily used in mail-order catalogs; 5-point, in want ads.
(Reprinted by permission from the National Society to Prevent Blindness, n.d.)

large print." Yet there are still problems. Therefore, as we have seen repeatedly, we need to use classifications for legal purposes to get the pupil to the services and protections guaranteed by law. Then we need to deal with each pupil as an individual, assessing his or her visual impairment (and residual vision) and its impact on those characteristics important in learning the cultural tasks.

IMPACT OF VISUAL IMPAIRMENTS ON PUPILS' CHARACTERISTICS

Visual impairment has a tremendous impact on a pupil's getting along in the world and accomplishing the cultural tasks. This impact can be both direct and indirect.

Introduction

> Above all else, blindness is a barrier between the individual and the unseen environment. In many respects, our world is a visual world. Most of its activities are initiated by visual stimuli and brought to a culmination by behaviors responsive to those stimuli. It is a world to be seen and, having seen it, the individual interacts with, controls, savors, and derives additional stimulation from it. To see the world is to be part of it. On the other hand, those who are deterred from seeing can become readily disengaged from it. This disengagement has both physical and psychosocial implications. (Rusalem, 1972, p. 15)

To get an idea what the blindness barrier can be like, look at Figs. 6.3–6.6, photographs of what a visually impaired person may or may not see. (This series of photographs uses the idea in the series presented by Scott *et al.*, 1977, pp. 17–26.)

Let's consider orientation and mobility in order to get a feeling of the impact of such visual impairments on a youngster's performing the cultural tasks. Consider the following interview with a blind young adult who has superior intellectual ability.

> **Intent:** *To find out what information would be useful on a map for blind persons and what orientation and mobility cues a blind person uses.*
>
> **PARTICIPATING:** *Scott, age 21, Harvard senior, Social Relations major, congenitally blind.*
>
> **Scott:** *I have little conception of any kind of urban or suburban environment. I have no conception of Boston, but I know in some places the streets are north-south or east-west and the reason when they're not. I'm often disturbed when I think of the little conception I have of campuses. I'm congenitally blind.*
>
> **Authors:** *Do you have a conception of a block?*
>
> **Scott:** *No, I think of it as one big piece of macadam between two streets. I don't have much more of a conception than that of a city*

block. I had problems conceptualizing when I was working with my mobility instructor in high school. He found it was easier to make me learn things by rote memory than to get me to conceptualize things because it was so impossible for me to conceptualize almost anything. I seem to have the kind of mind that tends to memorize as opposed to thinking of larger patterns or relationships.

Authors: *It may also be because no one has lucked into a good way of describing these things.*

Scott: *Maybe.*

Authors: *Where do you generally go when you're around Harvard? Do you stay here most of the time?*

Scott: *No, I go into Boston quite a bit. Usually it's appointments. Yesterday I went in for a haircut.*

Authors: *What are the cues that you look for?*

Scott: *I memorize everywhere I go. One important thing is landmarks. For example, when I went to get a haircut, I walked out of the subway at Washington Street. As I got off the escalator I knew I had to make a left turn to go out of the subway. Then I walked straight. I knew when to cross the street because of echo perception. Everyone has echo perception. When you're outside tapping a cane, the sound from the wall nearest you will bounce back to you. So if I were about to walk into the wall, chances are that I would know. I would know that I was going to hit the wall even before I hit it. Mobility instructors are requiring now more and more that students have their senses stimulated like that. When I went out the door I knew when to cross because the wall which is on my left discontinued and then I just turned right and crossed the street and went down one block and crossed there and went down to the next corner (a rounded corner) and turned right. I knew where the door was because Fanny Farmer, which is right before the door, has an exhaust fan. Smell is an aid. What's important is, is the cue going to be there all the time? The exhaust fan is there year around so it's a reliable factor. If smell is seasonal, then it's risky.*

Authors: *When you first went to the haircut place, did you go by yourself or did someone show you?*

Scott: *When I first went to the haircut place, someone showed me. Once in a while I teach myself how to get places, but not as often as people show me. It's easier that way....*

Authors: *What method do you use to cross streets? What do you do at an intersection?*

Scott: *Intersections around here are often all messed up. I'm used to lights that are red and then green, as opposed to yellow. When the light is against you, and therefore perpendicular traffic is moving, parallel traffic is idling. Hopefully, you can hear someone idling his engine. The minute he guns his engine to go down that street, you* *step out into the street to prevent him from turning down your street. That was the method I was taught to cross streets. Other methods are less desirable, like "bluffing" cars. I do that too.*

Authors: *Does the recommended method work?*

Scott: *Not around Cambridge. In practice, I'm very unhappy about all the crossings around here. I think they're dangerous. There is one I use all the time which I'm convinced is dangerous. It's right by Krackerjacks. There are crosswalks there, but I think cars come whipping around the corner so fast that they really can't see the person who's crossing. I wait for a break in traffic or now I'm beginning to learn to estimate distances. How fast is a car coming at me and can I get across? I've just started learning how to do this. If a car is coming rapidly, can I still get across or do I have to wait for him? I'm not too good at it yet, but I'm better than I was two years ago. I'm still very cautious about those kinds of things, but I'm getting better. I've learned if there's a whole line of cars coming through, just to inch my way out into the traffic, which is condemned from a mobility point of view. My instructor told me never to do that, that it was very dangerous. It was only my fault if I got hit. Sometimes it seems it's the only thing to do. You're forced to do it. There's no one around to help....*

Authors: *Does it help to identify corners by the direction of traffic?*

Scott: *Sure. If the streets were one way, this would do it. If the map had directions of traffic, it would help. It's easy to perceive traffic direction.*

It's good to know entrances of stores out of which people come quickly, like a department store. You need to use a shorter cane technique there so you won't trip people. It's helpful to know that there is a revolving door since there is a technique for getting through it. You might map the reference point, i.e., where I can put my hand on the part of the door that doesn't revolve, so that I can take my other hand and feel the door "swish, swish."

Authors: *Is it necessary to pinpoint entrances or tell what kind it is?*

Scott: *It's nice to know if you're walking down the street that it's the fifth door on the right or third recessed entrance on the right as opposed to a non-recessed entrance. It's frustrating because when you ask people directions, they don't know this.*

With me it would be better to put too much on a map than too little because I can rule out extraneous things. It might make the map more interesting.

Authors: *What kind of visual dreams do you have, if you have such things?*

Scott: *I have dreams, but they're not visual dreams at all. They're sound or texture or smell or taste. No visual imagery.*

Authors: *But you've mastered visual concepts because they have*

meanings in other senses as well. You've mentioned several:
parallel, perpendicular, right, left.
Scott: *"Visualizing" has an overlap of meaning. I'm visualizing it,*
but I'm not visualizing. (Kidwell and Greer, 1973, pp. 88–91)

To get an idea of some other psychological effects of visual impairment, look at this report of a blind pupil's inaccurate perception of a dog, as shown through his work with clay.

"Sensei, could you come here a minute?" called a ninth grade boy
who always nodded his head and showed the whites of his eyes as
he spoke. His blindness was congenital. I was surprised that he
had called me because he usually gave me excuses for not working.
The clay figure on his desk was shaped like an airplane, two by
three inches.
    "What is this?"
    "Sensei, you should understand it."
    "I wonder what it could be."
    "You don't know?"
    Silence.
    "It's a dog."
    "Do you have a dog?"
    "Yes, that's why I know what he's like."
    "Tell me which part is which?"
    "These are his arms and these are his legs. This is the tail."

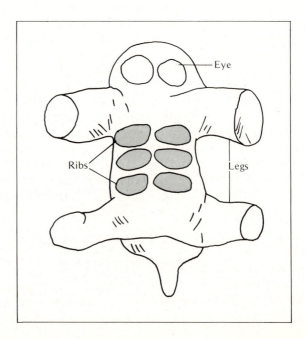

What he meant by "arms" and "legs" were the front and hind legs of the figure which were attached to the torso as though his work represented a stretched animal skin.

But what I couldn't understand were six small pieces of clay in two rows along the torso.

"What are these button-like things?"

"Oh, you know, when you pat a dog, you feel them."

"What part of the dog do you mean?"

"Oh, these bumpy places," he said, taking my hand and moving it down one side of his skinny chest. I could feel his ribs.

Those small pieces of clay represented the dog's ribs!

Of course anyone who holds a dog can feel his ribs, although a child with normal vision never tries to express what is beneath the fur. This was the unique understanding, this was the special domain of the blind. I could now see their sightless world....

The little boy remained intrigued with the idea of representing his dog in clay. Several weeks later he brought me another figure. This time it was three-dimensional but its torso made it look like a desk with crooked legs.

"Because he gallops as he runs, his hind legs must be longer than his front legs...."

Once again before he graduated, he brought me a clay dog, again one with long hind legs. (Fukurai, 1973, pp. 44–45)

How seriously the visual impairment affects the pupil's functioning depends on how early the impairment begins. *Congenital impairment* — that which occurs at birth — is more serious than *adventitious impairment*, which occurs later, after the pupil has had a chance to get an idea about how his or her environment looks. The seriousness of the impact also depends on the amount of vision the pupil has left. Other things, such as motivation, being equal, the more remaining vision, the less the impact of the impairment.

Physical Characteristics

By itself, visual impairment does not interfere with the pupil's physical structure and function. It does affect his or her eye-hand coordination and movement in space and in relation to objects. Consequently, visual impairment interferes with pupils' orientation/mobility and tool use and, in turn, all of the cultural tasks requiring orientation/mobility and tool use (e.g., Lowenfeld, 1974; Warren, 1974).

Orientation/mobility

Orientation is getting lined up toward a goal and in relation to the environment in general. Mobility is moving from one place to another. Visual impairment interferes with orientation and mobility in several ways. Pupils cannot orient themselves toward a goal when they cannot see the goal or the obstacles in between. And of course they cannot move toward a goal if they cannot get headed in the right direction. In addition, they cannot learn by imitation, because they cannot see others to imitate. Nor are they stimulated to move toward a goal they cannot see. Further, and quite realistically, they may hold back because they fear getting hurt on obstacles they cannot see. And we may have to restrict their mobility to protect them from injury. It follows from all of this that visually impaired pupils are limited in independent travel on foot or by vehicles such as bicycles, cars, and public transport. They require systematic, long-term training. How well pupils respond to mobility training for independent travel depends on other characteristics such as:

☐ Their sensitivity to, and ability to orient themselves by, environmental cues which to seeing people are often unnoticed. For example, echoes, temperature variations, and constant sounds, such as street noises or running water in particular spots, all give cues to locations needed in independent travel.

☐ Their residual vision. Other things being equal, the more sight pupils have, the easier they will learn independent travel.

☐ Their intellectual ability. Other things being equal, the more intelligent pupils will be better able to perceive and to remember the minimal cues, the reckonings of distance by number of steps traveled, and the general layouts of areas.

☐ Their motivation to learn independent travel. As in other difficult tasks, maximum learning of independent travel is influenced by how hard pupils are willing to work, their persistence, their acceptance of the need for learning independent travel, and their willingness to endure pain.

Tool use   Severe visual impairment also interferes with pupils' using tools. They have limited eye-hand coordination, i.e., limited ability to see and purposefully manipulate objects in relation to one another in performing tasks. In addition, as with mobility, their learning by imitation is limited, they have less stimulation to try tool-use activities they cannot see, they often encounter uncertainty and injury in new and unfamiliar situations, and they have to be restricted with some tools (e.g., knives) for their own and other people's protection. As a result, they have problems using a great variety of tools, ranging from pencils, books, eating implements, hammers, and so on, through the myriad implements we use in our culture. They must have systematic, long-term training. Their responses to this training depend, again, on their sensitivity to cues through other senses, their remaining vision, their intellectual ability, and their motivation to learn.

"Blindisms" is a label for some mannerisms which visually impaired pupils engage in apparently for self-stimulation (e.g., Eichel, 1978 Stratton, 1977). These mannerisms include such activities as eye pressing, rocking, spinning around in a circle, staring at light, and finger play.

Blindisms

> "Eyes are buttons to push" was Kaare's reply when asked what his eyes were for. Pressing on one or both eyes is the most common of what are known as mannerisms. Apparently, pressure on the eyeball results in a pleasurable sensation to the child, who finds it both entertaining and relaxing. When a visually impaired child is around twelve months of age his parents may notice he seems to rub his eyes a good deal, and they naturally assume he is sleepy or his eyes are uncomfortable. By eighteen months of age the habit is well established and each child may practice three or four variations on the theme. He may put the tip of his thumb up under the bone above his eye and press with his knuckle on the eye itself, he may use his bent forefinger in much the same way, or he may like to lie on the floor with his head resting either on the back knuckles of both hands or on his closed fists. He may favor one eye or press them both. Very few blind children have been observed sucking their thumbs and the few who do are not pressers. These children press their eyes on the same occasions when others would suck their thumbs, that is, when they are tired, anxious, bored, or in any situation where they need comforting. (Scott *et al.*, 1977, pp. 74–77)

Visually impaired pupils do not show any more emotional maladjustments than sighted pupils do. However, they may have trouble in social interaction (e.g., Kinnane and Suziedelis, 1974; Scholl, 1974). Because they cannot see to imitate, they often do not learn and use nonverbal communication through facial expressions and body language. They are often left out of social activities, such as playing tennis, because they cannot see to participate. And some people reject visually impaired youngsters because they do not have the security, skills, and understanding to deal with these youngsters comfortably.

Social/Emotional Characteristics

Visually impaired people also have potential problems in motivation (Scholl, 1974). Of course, they face more insecurity than sighted people do, because they face more dangers, e.g., getting run down by a car or getting lost. And they are called on to work harder because it takes more effort to carry out activities in spite of blindness. Beyond these problems, though, rests the problem of the dependency we encourage by overprotecting visually impaired people; in Scott's (1969) words, we make men blind by treating them as being helpless. This is the self-fulfilling prophecy we studied in connection with problems arising from labeling pupils.

Speech and Language Characteristics

Generally, visually impaired pupils have no difficulty with the language we learn through *hearing*, that is, the sounds, structures, and functions of words and sentences as well as longer connected discourse. Nor do they have trouble with words and concepts learnable through touch, smell, temperature, kinesthesis, and taste. The myriad examples here range from the sound of /a̅/ through the concept of salty.

The visually impaired do have language restriction, however, with words and concepts that signify some concrete stimuli and with concepts experienced through vision (e.g., Henderson, 1974). As a result, they have trouble using many words with meaning. For example, consider how much a blind person could really understand: "In the fall, the huge ginko trees are beautiful as they spread their yellow fans." The term *verbalism* is used to refer to blind pupils' using words without meanings, i.e., words for phenomena they have had no direct sensory experience with.

This language restriction can be a tremendous problem and have many subtle effects. Language is one mediator, along with visual imagery, for much of what we remember and what we think. For example, suppose that in economic geography you are studying the importance of physical terrain and water supply in population distribution. It is easier to understand the principles and their applications to the Rocky Mountain states, the Middle Atlantic states, and the Pacific Coast states if you can visualize, and verbalize about, heavy mountain terrain, dry areas, and large waterways.

Use of language as a mediator shows up in two places: in readiness for new learning and in responding to tests, such as intelligence tests, which help us make judgments about the pupil's future learning capability based on what he or she has previously learned as a result of experience. A visually impaired pupil's language restriction can interfere with his or her readiness and test performance.

Intellectual Characteristics

Learning is a change in behavior as a result of experience. Visual impairment restricts pupils' gaining experience. Restriction in experience, in turn, diminishes learning. As a result, visual impairment can interfere with pupils' intellectual development and performance (Barraga, 1974; Lowenfeld, 1974; Scholl, 1974). Three areas are conceptual behavior, specific intellectual abilities, and intelligence test performance.

Conceptual development

To review: We form concepts by grouping instances on one or more common characteristics. Take an example of a *concrete* concept — one from biological science. *Trees* is a high-order concept referring to a large class of diverse objects which have in common a certain kind of structure and a certain kind of physiological function. Trees differ from birds, which have their own particular structure and physiology. Within the class trees are many subclasses, depending on what dimension(s) our purpose requires that we sort by, e.g., pine, oak, holly; evergreen and deciduous; ornamental and food-producing. Now take an example of a more *abstract* concept — one from mathematics. *Rate* is a concept referring to unit change in one dimension as a function of unit change in another. This concept describes a large number of instances. One instance is the normal curve and the area-frequency relationships described by the mean and standard deviation. (We considered this concept in Chapter 2.)

Such concrete and abstract concepts are easy enough for sighted pupils, but are much more difficult for visually impaired pupils to *really* grasp. Visually impaired pupils often cannot see the characteristics of many concrete stimuli and the likenesses and differences in those stimuli. The problem is especially acute with stimuli beyond the range of touch, e.g., color and space. However, the problem appears to be in the content of the concepts, not the process of concept formation. Visually impaired pupils can classify nonvisual stimuli and respond to training in conceptualization as well as seeing pupils can (e.g., Freidman and Pasnak, 1973).

Specific abilities/disabilities

To the extent that their vision is restricted, visually impaired pupils by definition are limited in specific abilities such as visual memory and visual processing. The question remaining is: Do visually impaired pupils have special abilities? According to one idea, visually impaired people have better acuity in such senses as hearing, smell, and touch. This idea is groundless. They have no more raw ability than anyone else does. What happens is this: Some, but not all, visually impaired people develop more sensitivity in the auditory, tactual, and other areas because they have to depend more on these senses (e.g., Barraga, 1974; Stephens, 1972).

Intelligence test performance

There has been considerable concern about this question: What are visually impaired pupils' intelligence levels compared to sighted pupils' levels? This is an improper question. The proper question, if one has to ask it, is: How do visually impaired pupils compare to sighted pupils in those areas where visual impairment does not interfere with their performance? Generally, both the logic and the evidence indicate that visually impaired pupils perform as well as sighted pupils do if they have a similarly rich educational background and if they are given tests that do not penalize them for their visual impairment (e.g., Bauman, 1974*a, b*).

Academic Characteristics

Some visually impaired pupils achieve lower academically than sighted pupils do. This is not surprising when we consider their problems with concepts and potentially with motivation and when we consider how much of their school time goes into learning skills such as tool use and mobility, which sighted pupils learn before they come to school. However, there is little reason to expect underachievement in areas such as reading, math, and science if we start training pupils early enough so that they are ready for school learning when they reach school age and if we use procedures for teaching which circumvent their visual impairments.

Vocational Characteristics

Of course, visual impairment makes it impossible for youngsters to qualify for occupations where they could endanger themselves and others. For example, a blind person cannot be an airline pilot or sailor. However, many occupations remain after we remove those requiring vision. For example, given appropriate tools, such as magnifiers, which enlarge print, or the optacon scanner, which converts print to tactual stimuli, visually impaired people can perform a large number of jobs, ranging from the law to business.

Despite their potentialities and opportunities, many visually impaired pupils remain unemployed or underemployed. This happens because some visually impaired youngsters do not acquire characteristics — such as personal independence and persistence in the face of frustration — required for occupational success. Of course, these problems cause many seeing youngsters to have job difficulties. It is just that visual impairment makes visually impaired youngsters more prone to such secondary problems if we do not carefully train them to act otherwise.

ACCOUNTABILITY

We are accountable for using correct procedures for identifying and classifying visually impaired pupils, developing their individual education programs, and extending to them the protections of the procedural safeguards.

Identifying and Planning for Visually Impaired Pupils
Documenting the Child-Find

We must actively look for visually impaired pupils by using awareness campaigns and screening procedures. Once we have pupils who have potential problems, we of course refer them for further study. In our documentation we report the Child-Find activities we used and the number of visually impaired pupils we located and served.

Preparing the individual education program is the next step we take once we have pupils classified as visually impaired and thus qualified for the special education, related services, and protection. We test their present performance levels in all characteristics related to their progress in special education, orientation and mobility training, and training in using tools. Given this information, we set goals and objectives, select instructional procedures for reaching the goals and objectives, and then we decide about the best placement for delivering special education and other training to the visually impaired pupils and set times to monitor their progress. The team doing the IEP includes representatives from the school system, the advocates, the teachers, and the therapists who will deliver related services.

Developing the individual education program

The procedural safeguards must permeate all of our activities in serving visually impaired pupils, from the first identification to the final dismissal.

Observing the Procedural Safeguards for Visually Impaired Pupils

Someone must advocate for the visually impaired pupils. Ideally, the advocates are the pupils' parents or guardians. If they refuse the role, we must locate surrogates to substitute for them. The advocate must participate in all decisions about identification and classification, testing, special education and related services, placement, and periodic evaluation. If they wish, they may bring along as consultants specialists in visual impairment — its nature, impact, and treatment.

Advocate participation

The advocates must agree in all decisions about the visually impaired pupils. If they do not, they have redress — the right to appeal through the administrative levels of the school system and the jurisdictional levels of the federal courts. We must, of course, inform them about these rights and the procedures to follow in appeal.

Due process

Visually impaired pupils have the right to be treated by the same rules, criteria, and procedures that we follow with all pupils. They especially must not be discriminated against because of their visual impairments or other unalterable characteristics. And of course we must be particularly vigilant in testing to be sure that they are not treated unfairly because of their visual impairments.

Equal protection

Quite frequently and systematically, we must reevaluate visually impaired pupils' progress. We must check whether we made errors in our earlier evaluations and if so, change our earlier decisions. And we must use objective criteria and evaluation procedures to check the pupils' responses to special education and related services. With

Periodic reevaluation

satisfactory responses, we set new goals. With unsatisfactory responses, we revise our goals and procedures with the idea of getting better results.

Confidentiality   We must treat information about visually impaired pupils' problems, characteristics, and progress with strict confidentiality. Their advocates, of course, have complete access to the information and control over who else has access. Further, they have the right to have wrong or irrelevant information purged from the pupils' records and to have the files destroyed after the pupils are dismissed from the special education and related services.

Nondiscriminatory testing of visually impaired pupils

Once the pupil is identified as visually impaired, our next task is to use nondiscriminatory testing to get information to use in deciding about his or her instruction and placement. Evaluating visually impaired pupils is a very complex undertaking. We need to be very careful about the dangers involved and the procedures to deal with these dangers (e.g., Bell, 1975; Currie, 1975; Monbeck and Mulholland, 1975).

PROBLEMS IN TESTING VISUALLY IMPAIRED PUPILS

Pupils are referred to us because they obviously or apparently have visual problems which interfere with their benefiting from education. In collecting information our evaluation task is to get evidence about what the pupil is able to do in the areas being tested and to infer what this ability means for his or her learning the cultural tasks. Doing this evaluation task requires that we separate what the pupil can do from the effects of visual impairment which may hide what he or she can do.

> The most pressing question for the examiner is to determine what degree of test failure can be attributed to impaired visual functioning and what to an inability to perform the task. Unless the examiner can assess to what degree a particular test item or task is tapping a client's visual ability, failure may be incorrectly recorded as a basic task failure rather than a deficit in visual ability (Scholl and Schnur, 1976, p. 6)

When we carry out the evaluation task, we must be sensitive to two *dangers* — one obvious and one not so obvious (e.g., Bauman, 1974*a*, *b*). These dangers are dangers because they cause testing errors by interfering with a pupil's showing in a test situation what behavior he or she is capable of showing. For example, he or she may be more intelligent, know more academically, or be better adjusted emotionally/socially than the tests show.

The *obvious danger* is that visual impairment interferes with pupils' taking tests, just as it interferes with their performing other cultural tasks. Visually impaired pupils cannot see test materials as well as sighted pupils can. This impairment interferes with or prevents their taking manual tests such as the performance items on the Wechsler scales, paper-and-pencil tests such as the Metropolitan Achievement Tests, both the performance and paper-and-pencil components on tests such as the Stanford-Binet, and tests requiring responses to visual materials such as the Peabody Picture Vocabulary Test and the Rorschach.

The *not so obvious* danger rests in the way visual impairment can affect pupils' development. As we have seen, visual impairment can lead to such problems as limited mobility and tool use, which in turn can restrict pupils' opportunities to learn through a wide range of experiences, limited conceptual development, limited language development, and overdependency. These problems can also interfere with the pupils' showing what they are capable of on tests.

These dangers can interfere with our meeting the conditions for norm-referenced and criterion-referenced testing. As a result, we may underestimate a pupil. Such underestimates because of testing errors are harmful to a pupil because they can cause him or her to be denied, and thus to miss, opportunities for development. Therefore the procedural safeguards — due process, equal protection in evaluation, and confidentiality — are crucial. The difficulties are legion.

> ... the total science of psychological evaluation leaves even its most ardent practitioners unsatisfied with the lack of appropriate and proven tools to answer some kinds of questions, while the younger and less developed field of evaluation of the visually handicapped is still struggling with the development of materials and procedures especially appropriate to both children and adults who have either no or very limited vision. (Bauman, 1974, p. 95)

PROCEDURES FOR TESTING VISUALLY IMPAIRED PUPILS

As with all pupils, we need to be sensitive to the pupil's present performance levels on all of the characteristics important to learning the cultural tasks — physical status, vision, hearing, speech and language, learning style, motivation, personality and adjustment, specific abilities, experience background, and previous academic achievement. We need to be particularly attentive to visual efficiency and to characteristics that are vulnerable to the impact of visual impairment. In sum, considering the potential special needs of visually impaired pupils, we need to collect evidence to answer many assessment questions about the pupil's medical background, growth and development, psychological functioning, and educational/therapeutic history.

Some assessment procedures we use with other pupils are also appropriate with visually impaired pupils. These include examining records and reports, using questionnaires and interviews, and observing the pupil in many different situations.

We must be very careful when we go beyond these general procedures to criterion-referenced educational tests or to norm-referenced educational and psychological tests. Review the dangers described above which may cause us to underestimate what a pupil is capable of. To repeat: The pupil may not be able to see the test materials well enough to respond to them; the impact of visual impairment on other characteristics such as motivation may interfere with the pupil's test performance.

Again, we plan the assessments on a child-by-child basis. We do not routinely try to answer every question or to use a particular battery of tests. Of course, the parent/advocate, the ophthalmologist, and the teacher take part in this assessment process. Depending on the pupil's problems, other participants may include a peripatologist, a physical therapist, an occupational therapist, a speech/language therapist, a psychologist, and a social worker. And as we carry out this careful assessment, we must observe the procedural safeguards for advocate participation, equal protection, due process, periodic reevaluation, and confidentiality.

Individualizing instruction for visually impaired pupils

We know a great deal about special education and related services for visually impaired pupils (e.g., Hanninen, 1975; Russell, 1978; Weisgerber, 1974, 1975). Therefore once we have pinned down a visually impaired pupil's special needs, our next task is to individualize instruction by selecting particular special education and related services appropriate to those special needs. Our sequence of activities is the usual one. We take test information and use it as a basis for our prescriptions. We use those prescriptions with the pupil. Then we evaluate how well the teaching/therapy worked and revise our prescriptions appropriately.

The categories sighted, partially sighted, and blind are not true dichotomies. Therefore we must identify each pupil's special needs. Some partially sighted pupils can function as easily as sighted pupils if materials are well enough lighted, magnified, and intensified. Some partially sighted pupils need more help with tool use, orientation and mobility, and other functions. Some legally blind pupils have enough vision to operate as partially sighted pupils, given appropriate illumination, magnification, and intensification. Other blind pupils cannot operate as partially sighted pupils, and they need special techniques for tool use, orientation and mobility, and so on. Again, categories only put us in the ballpark. We must go further to determine for each pupil individually what his or her particular special needs are.

SURVEY OF COMMUNICATION MEDIA

To get a background for discussing instruction, we must diverge briefly to consider communication media. Messages can be conveyed through auditory materials, magnified and intensified visual materials, and embossed/tactual materials (e.g., Library of Congress, 1972; Margach *et al.*, 1975; Suen and Beddoes, 1975).

We can convey most information auditorily through speech and other sounds. These materials may be experienced directly and the

We can use electronic aids
to process visual materials.

blind youngster can record them and reproduce them when he or she so desires. In addition, a large number of items are recorded especially for the visually impaired. Sometimes called "talking books," these media often have compressed speech, i.e., a speeding up of a recording to a degree that saves time but does not distort the speech.

We can easily magnify and intensify print, pictures, and other visual materials (Fig. 6.8). We can use already produced materials such as books done in larger than usual print/type. For example, look back at Table 6.2 to see the type sizes appropriate at the respective levels of visual efficiency. Also, we can use magnifying glasses or projectors that can produce the materials in any size necessary and can enlarge and intensify materials ourselves.

We can use embossing to transfer materials from the visual to the tactual mode. We can emboss all or some critical features of pictures,

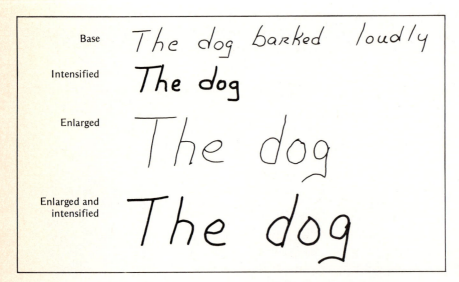

Fig. 6.8
Examples of enlarged and intensified materials.

maps, charts, and other reproductions of reality, as well as print and numerals. Or, we can move from the print code to the braille code. Realize that the print code is a system with particular numerals to represent numbers, particular letters to represent sounds, and particular punctuation devices to give signals about grammar. Braille is a *parallel system*. It uses particular numbers and positions of embossed dots in a six-dot-position rectangular space to represent numbers, sounds, and grammatical signals.

Reading and writing braille are
important skills for blind
pupils to learn.

We can produce braille on a braille writer, or as it is sometimes called, a brailler, or we can produce it on a slate and stylus. One complication is that the writing code is done from right to left in a mirror image of the reading code. This happens because the pupil must punch from beneath the page to get the raised dot with the slate and stylus.

SPECIAL EDUCATION

Our concern here is to differentiate the four special-education components — instructional objectives, settings, procedures, and settings. As always, particulars depend on each pupil's characteristics.

Instructional Objectives

Some visually impaired pupils can see well enough to deal with print and other visual stimuli, *given appropriate magnification and illumination.* These pupils have the same instructional objectives as seeing pupils do. Some pupils cannot see well enough to use print and other visual stimuli. They need some differentiation in instructional objectives. The shorthand phrase "blind" is used hereafter for convenience in referring to these pupils.

Blind pupils need some similarity and some differentiation of objectives in the language arts areas. They have the same objectives for *speech and language* that sighted pupils do. In addition, they may need special objectives for: (1) learning words and concepts for visual phenomena; (2) eliminating verbalisms by learning a base of meanings as a seeing pupil would for such concepts as black holes; and (3) learning to use facial expressions and other body language to send nonverbal messages (Simon, 1974).

In *listening* blind pupils have the same objectives as sighted pupils do. In addition, they may need special objectives for: (1) consciously attending to cues seeing pupils do not use; and (2) holding material in immediate memory (Bischoff, 1979; Hanninen, 1975).

In *reading* blind pupils have, with one exception, the same objectives as sighted pupils do. They need to acquire the structural analysis skills, the comprehension and interpretation skills, and so on. The exception is in the word-recognition skills. Where sighted pupils work with print, blind pupils work with braille. That is, they learn to recognize braille patterns at touch, and they learn to decode braille symbols for sounds and numerals (Craig, 1975; Hanninen, 1975; Caton and Bradley, 1978/79).

In *written production* also, blind pupils have some objectives the same as sighted pupils and some objectives different. Instead of *handwriting* objectives, blind pupils have parallel objectives for learning to use a slate and stylus and a brailler to transcribe information. In addition, as they get older, blind pupils have objectives for learning typewriting skills necessary to communicate with seeing people. Blind pupils' *written composition* and *spelling* objectives do not essentially differ from sighted pupils' objectives; they only include different ways of transcribing material (Bishop, 1971; Henderson, 1974).

Blind pupils have the same objectives as sighted pupils do in the *academic areas*, e.g., mathematics, the social sciences, the physical sciences, and foreign languages. In all of these areas we may need additional objectives for concepts about visual phenomena which we cannot transmit easily through such devices as embossed materials, e.g., space, mass, distance. Further, they would need special objectives for self-protection in such an area as chemistry (Linn and Thier, 1975; Malone and Delucchi, 1979; Struve *et al.*, 1975).

Except in the visual arts, blind pupils have the same objectives in the *arts* as seeing pupils do. Among the visual arts, such activities as drawing and painting would seem closed, but such activities as sculpture and pottery are possible (Napier, 1974; Sinclair, 1975).

Blind pupils have the same objectives as seeing pupils do for many *health*, *physical education*, and *recreation* activities, e.g., rhythms, wrestling, jogging, swimming, and similar activities, which do not involve eye/hand/target activities, such as tennis. Additional activities are possible, given signals on the ball and goal to indicate locations, e.g., beep baseball. Again, pupils need additional objectives for safety (Buell, 1972, 1973; Laughlin, 1975).

To support their learning in other areas, blind pupils may need objectives for training the *other senses* (Barraga and Collins, 1979; Bischoff, 1979; Kimbrough *et al.*, 1976; Stratton, 1977). In addition to training in listening, they need training in using any residual (i.e., remaining) vision. Also they need training in using their tactual, kinesthetic, taste, and olfactory senses to get information about and to deal with the environment.

Generally, pupils who have usable enough vision to deal with print and other visual stimuli should learn at about the same rate as seeing pupils. Blind pupils should learn at the same rate as sighted pupils in areas in which blindness is *not* an impediment, e.g., spelling, social science, and music. They may take more time to learn in areas in which blindness prevents their learning by imitation, e.g., using a sewing machine, tying their shoes.

Instructional Schedules

We do face some problems, and thus decisions, about schedules for instruction. Blind pupils need some special objectives for education, and they need related services — for learning independent travel and for learning tool use. That is, *during school* blind pupils

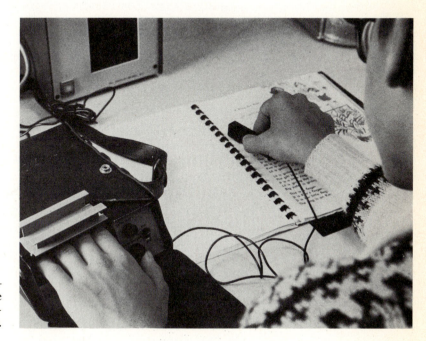

The Optacon (*Optical* to *Tactile Converter*) and other special devices are important in individualizing instruction for visually impaired pupils.

have more to learn than sighted pupils do. Therefore they need to be given more time to learn the total amount of the curriculum learned by sighted pupils. Or, some of the curriculum needs to be dropped for blind pupils so that with the special objectives they must have, the total amount they learn equals that sighted pupils learn.

Instructional Procedures

Generally, we use the same *teaching methods* with visually impaired pupils that we do with sighted pupils. These include the several forms of teacher presentations, student problem solving, group work, individual work, direct experience, and behavior modification (e.g., Curtis and McWhannel, 1972; Douglass and Mangold, 1975; Hayes and Weinhouse, 1978).

Quite rightly, we have repeatedly stressed how visually impaired and seeing pupils' objectives, schedules, and methods of instruction are the same except for some additional objectives for the blind which require extra time. However, *teaching media* and *special devices* are the major places where differences do occur. Fortunately, we have many special media and devices (e.g., Becker and Kalina, 1975; Lamon and Threadgill, 1975; Stratton, 1977). A few examples are:

☐ Communication media — braille, large-print, and audio reproductions (talking books) — of newspapers, textbooks, and other instructional materials, the Bible, and fiction and nonfiction literature. (For instance, Fig. 6.9 has some categories of large-print publications.)

☐ Tangible apparatus — braillers, embossed materials for mathematics, geography, the sciences, and so on, special clocks and watches, sensory training materials, and magnifying devices (see the photographs on p. 249).

The major sources of such media and devices are the Library of Congress, which mails directly to individuals and distributes through regional and local libraries, the American Printing House for the Blind, and the American Foundation for the Blind. In addition, many private publishers and manufacturers produce materials and equipment. These producers and depositories give extensive catalogs directly to visually impaired people as well as to educators and others who work with the visually impaired.

The Optacon scanner (shown on p. 253) deserves special mention. It converts print into vibrations which form the images of letters. A person who can learn to use it can read print material fairly quickly. It is an advantage because it makes a wide range of materials available without the delay and cost of transferring them to enlarged print, talking books, or braille (Bliss and Moore, 1974).

A. *Categories of Large-Type Books in Print*

GENERAL READING

TEXTBOOKS

Fig. 6.9
Examples of media. (*Note:* The print here is in 18-point type. Be sure to look at the various type sizes referred to in the annotations of literature materials.) (*Large Type Books in Print*, 1978, pp. v–vi, x, 355. Reprinted by permission from the R. R. Bowker Company.)

B. *Examples of Items Listed in the Literature Category (Excerpted)*

Literature

ADVENTURES IN LITERATURE PROGRAM. classic
  ed. (HarBraceJ, 1973). 16-18 pt. 11 x 12 1/2. Am
Printing Hse.

  Adventures in American Literature, 8 vols. Early et
  al. gr. 11. Set. 122.80 (4-0052).
  Adventures in Appreciation, 7 vols. Perrine et al.
  gr. 10. Set. 107.45 (4-0051).
  Adventures in English Literature, 8 vols.
  McCormick et al. gr. 12. Set. 112.00 (4-0053).
  Adventures in Modern Literature, 6 vols. Freier et
  al. gr. 11-12. Set. 70.00 (4-0054).
  Adventures in Reading, 7 vols. Connolly et al. gr.
  9. Set. 88.55 (4-0050).
  Adventures in World Literature, 9 vols. Applegate
  et al. gr. 11-12. Set. 138.15 (4-0055).

ADVENTURES IN LITERATURE (THE NEW
  COMPANION SERIES) (HarBraceJ, 1968). 18 pt.
  11 x 12 1/2. Am. Printing Hse.

  Gr. 7. Adventures for You, 4 vols. Pumphrey &
  Johnson. Set. 56.00 (4-0033).

Fig. 6.9 *continued*

Generally, we *allocate personnel* for teaching blind pupils about the same way we do for sighted pupils (Bishop, 1977). These pupils need, and can function with, individual tutoring, independent study, solitary activity, small groups, and large groups. They can use their special media and devices right alongside sighted pupils in these settings. How much they use individual tutoring, solitary activity, or small groups when they are working on their special objectives depends on how many other blind pupils are available to work on the same objectives.

Similarly, we *allocate space* for blind pupils the same as we do for sighted pupils (e.g., Woodcock, 1974). That is, they use common areas, carrels, special centers, and depositories. Carrels and special centers are especially important in their working on their special objectives. In addition, we do need special depositories for storing their special media and special devices.

We must pay special attention to illumination in the settings where partially sighted pupils work. The level usually should range between 70 and 100 foot candles, and the light should be equally diffused over the area.

Instructional Settings

RELATED SERVICES

Visually impaired pupils need medical services and psychological services. Depending on the severity and age of onset of their problems, they may need peripatology/physical therapy, occupational therapy, speech/language therapy, and vocational rehabilitation services. Their families may need information and counseling.

Ophthalmologists treat youngsters who have problems in the structure or function of their eyes. Their treatments include surgery, drugs, and glasses and other types of magnification. In addition, they sometimes pursue orthoptic* exercises.

Medical Services

Orientation and mobility training is given to blind pupils with the aim of their becoming able to travel independently (e.g., Ferrell, 1979; Berla and Butterfield, 1975; Klee, 1975). They must learn to use guides and mechanical aids and to move without aid. Using human guides involves the pupils' being guided by voice directions and by touch and other cues. Using guide dogs, a not too frequent method with youngsters, involves the pupils' being led by a specially trained animal. Using mechanical aids involves the pupils' learning to use canes and various electronic devices such as the sonic torch, a small,

Peripatology/Physical Therapy

---

* Special exercises using prisms.

Blind pupils need orientation and mobility training.

handheld sonar device which emits a gentle vibration and sound when a person or object is in front of it. Movement without aid requires that they learn the positions of things and learn to move around obstacles to get to their destinations.

Such a simple summary doesn't show the extreme complexity of learning enough orientation and mobility skills to travel independently. Pupils need a lot of time and help of specially trained instructors (peripatologists), physical therapists, or teachers working with the pupils and working with families, who in turn work with pupils.

Blind pupils also need to learn *daily living skills*, such as eating, bathing, and dressing. For example, they have to learn such skills as locating food on their plates, serving themselves, and pouring their drinks — all mainly involving learning to place their hands and fingers in a way to give them cues. In addition, they need to learn *tool use*, that is, to use hammers, saws, record players, cassette recorders, TV's, scissors, needles and thread, telephones, knives, pots, pitchers, and so on through the many tools needed for conducting one's daily life. Especially trained occupational therapists or teachers give blind pupils training in the daily living skills and tool use and work with families, who in turn work with the pupils (Sutenko, 1974).

Occupational Therapy

Some blind youngsters — especially younger ones whose blindness is congenital — may have delayed speech and language development. Therefore they probably will need speech/language therapy in addition to the intensive speech/language stimulation and training supplied by their classroom teachers.

Speech/Language Therapy

School psychologists work with visually impaired pupils to get the information we need to do educational planning. Clinical psychologists and psychiatrists work with youngsters who have severe emotional/social problems attendant on their blindness.

Psychological Services

As the visually impaired pupil moves into adolescence and young adulthood, he or she may need vocational rehabilitation services. The VR specialist provides vocational assessment, information, and counseling to the youngster and his or her family. Vocational assessment involves collecting information about the youngster's characteristics related to job success. Vocational information includes material about the nature, benefits, and requirements of occupations. Vocational counseling involves helping the youngster and his or her family mesh interests, aspirations, and capabilities with the job

Vocational Rehabilitation Services

requirements. When the youngster makes his or her vocational choices, the VR specialist may help him or her locate training programs and services needed to succeed in that training program. Also, once the training is completed, the VR specialist may help the youngster locate a job.

Family Information and Counseling

Parents or their surrogates have to make many decisions about their children's education. To do so wisely, they need a great deal of information about the nature and treatment of visual impairment and the rights and protections available to them and their youngsters. Social workers supply much of this information. In addition, many families need help dealing with the trauma attendant on severe handicaps. Social workers, clinical psychologists, and psychiatrists can supply most of this help.

Placing visually impaired pupils in the least restrictive environment

Our last task is to place the pupil in the least restrictive environment he or she can function in for the special education and related services planned. We select the most appropriate placement option and arrange appropriate facilities, transportation, and extracurricular activities, and also attend to safety.

PLACEMENT OPTIONS

We must try especially hard to get the severely visually impaired pupil access as early as possible to infant stimulation and preschool programs (e.g., Adkins and Amsa, 1978). Our goal is to help prevent problems that result indirectly from visual impairment (e.g., excessive dependency) and at the same time to teach pupils skills they need to compensate for the direct effects of visual impairment (e.g., poor spatial orientation). As always, the basic problem we fight is the increasing divergence in growth and development and the snowballing failures in accomplishing the cultural tasks.

As the child gets beyond the preschool period, the range of options we ordinarily use with visually impaired pupils, ranging from the least to the most restrictive alternative, are:

☐ regular class, with a resource teacher/itinerant teacher consulting with the regular teacher and supplying special services, such as braille instruction;

☐ regular class, with part time in a resource room for work on the special objectives, mobility, tool use, and daily living skills;

☐ separate class for visually impaired pupils; and

☐   residential school (Hanninen, 1975).

Figure 6.10 shows how frequently the states were using the placement options in the late 1970s. Generally, regular-class placements were used most frequently, with separate classes and separate schools following and used with about equal frequency.

The placement option chosen for a particular pupil depends on how we answer questions about the pupil, the parents, the teachers, and the school system. For example:

☐   Can the pupil use visual stimuli, given appropriate magnification?

☐   What are the pupil's orientation and mobility skills?

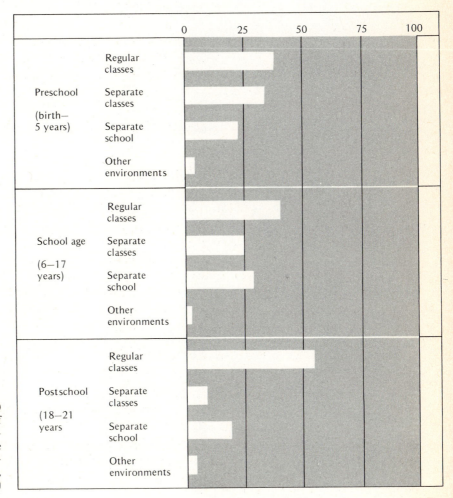

Fig. 6.10
Most frequent placements of visually impaired pupils reported by the states in the late 1970s. (Based on information in BEH, 1979, pp. 169–189.)

Visually impaired pupils can participate in a wide range of activities with other pupils: classroom lessons, physical activities, and vocational training programs.

Again, we must monitor the pupil closely. As his or her capabilities change, we must be prepared to offer a less restrictive environment (e.g., Maron and Martinez, 1980).

In public school placements the resource teacher has a key role in supporting the regular-class teachers. For example:

☐ The resource teacher consults with the regular teacher about the meaning of medical information, procedures for individualizing instruction to compensate for visual impairments, and the ways special devices, e.g., braille readers, can be coordinated with materials seeing pupils use.

☐ The resource teacher takes responsibility for collecting and organizing special equipment — braille typewriters, large-print media, and talking book machines.

☐ The resource teacher delivers instruction in specialized skills, e.g., learning to use a slate and stylus and a braille writer.

EXTRACURRICULAR ACTIVITIES

The visually impaired pupil should be able to participate in most extracurricular activities and community special-interest groups, e.g., glee clubs, school annuals, school newspapers, scouts (e.g., McMullen, 1974). The exception might be those activities requiring skilled eye/hand coordination in relation to targets, as membership on the basketball team does.

TRANSPORTATION AND FACILITIES

Transportation

As we have seen, one goal is to train blind pupils to travel independently. Until the pupil learns the necessary skills, we need to make special arrangements for transportation. These include obtaining companions, making special arrangements with bus drivers, and similar activities. As the pupil becomes more proficient in independent travel, such arrangements can be reduced.

Facilities

We devote a great deal of attention to facilities. One concern is *reducing unnecessary barriers* in the facilities where the visually impaired pupil is placed. For example, we make such adjustments as:

☐ Doing signs in raised letters, raised numerals, and braille letters and numeral(s) and locating them at heights appropriate for the age group in the school.

☐ Using grids in the floor or similar cues signaling approaches to stairs.

SAFETY

Safety precautions for the visually impaired pupil are crucial in both transportation and facilities. Our concern is with the implications of the pupil's visual impairment for guarding his or her safety. As we have seen, visual impairment leads to a number of foreseeable risks in the pupil's interacting with his or her environment. We must anticipate these risks, plan for them, and then continually monitor how our plans are working. Of course, specifics would vary with the pupil: his or her visual impairment and skill in dealing with the environment within the limits of that impairment. However, some examples are:

1. *School premises*
   a) One danger is that a visually impaired pupil could be hit by a flying ball.
   b) The pupil must be kept out of the vicinity of ball games. Other pupils need to be trained to watch for him or her.

2. *Emergencies*
   a) One danger is that in emergencies, e.g., a fire, a visually impaired pupil may not be able to follow evacuation procedures. Further, he or she might interfere with orderly evacuation by others.
   b) Someone needs to be designated as the visually impaired pupil's companion during emergencies. Further, a backup person for that helper needs to be designated and available for times when the helper is elsewhere.

Summary

IDENTIFYING AND PLANNING FOR VISUALLY IMPAIRED PUPILS

Normal Vision   Normal development of visual behavior depends on an intact eye and central nervous system and on adequate functioning of those structures. In turn, accomplishing many cultural tasks depends on normal development of visual behavior.

Visual Impairments   Normal development of visual behavior goes awry when problems occur in the structure and function of the eye or the central nervous system. An impairment exists when these visual deviations make it difficult or impossible for the youngster to accomplish cultural tasks dependent on vision. The Child-Find for visually impaired pupils entitled to the laws' protection includes public awareness campaigns with special emphasis on early detection and treatment, screening for signs of visual impairment, and referral to an ophthalmologist and other specialists for further study. Diagnosis or classification by cause of visual impairment involves determining the source of the problem: *refraction errors* (hyperopia, myopia, astigmatism), *muscular imbalance* (nystagmus, strabismus, amblyopia ex anopsia), and *pathology of the eyeball and nervous tissue* (destruction of optic nerve or the part of the brain controlling vision, traumatic injuries, congenital anophthalmos, retrolental fibroplasia, congenital glaucoma, and cataracts). Diagnosis or classification by degrees of visual impairment involves assessing visual acuity and field of vision. Legal blindness and partial sightedness are the two legal categories. Beyond legal categories, we need to be concerned about visual efficiency.

Visual impairments have a strong impact on pupils' characteristics. They may have limitations in orientation and mobility, tool use, words and language concepts dependent on vision, social skills requiring vision, intellectual tasks requiring vision, and vocational tasks requiring vision. They may or may not show blindisms, emotional difficulties, motivational problems, and academic retardation. They do not have special compensatory senses, but may use certain senses, such as hearing, more efficiently than seeing pupils because they have to depend on them more.

Impact of Visual Impairments on Pupils' Characteristics

Accountability requirements for documenting the Child-Find and developing the IEP guarantee that we use the correct procedures for identifying, and planning for, the visually impaired pupil. The procedural safeguards requiring advocate participation, due process, equal protection, periodic reevaluation, and confidentiality ensure that we protect the pupil's rights as we work with him or her.

Accountability

NONDISCRIMINATORY TESTING OF VISUALLY IMPAIRED PUPILS

Visual impairment may make it impossible to meet the conditions for norm-referenced or criterion-referenced tests. As a result, tests, if we use them, may become another measure of the youngster's visual impairment.

Problems in Testing Visually Impaired Pupils

To get information we need to plan for visually impaired pupils, we use procedures, such as interviews and questionnaires, which we use with other pupils. We use tests if we can meet the necessary conditions pertaining to norm groups and criteria. In all of this information

Procedures for Testing Visually Impaired Pupils

collection, we carefully observe the procedural safeguards against errors which would make testing discriminatory.

INDIVIDUALIZING INSTRUCTION FOR VISUALLY IMPAIRED PUPILS

Communication Media

Communication media for visually impaired pupils include auditory materials, e.g., talking books, magnified and intensified materials, e.g., books printed in 18-point type, and embossed/tactual materials, e.g., braille.

Special Education

Some visually impaired pupils can deal with print, given appropriate magnification and illumination. Others cannot deal with print and thus need differentiation of *instructional objectives* — added objectives for activities such as learning braille, the same objectives for many topics, and dropped objectives when they do not have enough time to master all of the objectives seeing pupils do. Visually impaired pupils have the same *instructional schedules* as sighted pupils in activities where the impairment is not an impediment. They need more time allowed for activities where visual impairment interferes with their learning. For teaching visually impaired pupils, we use the same *methods* as we do for teaching other pupils. However, we use a wide range of special teaching *media* and *special devices* with visually impaired pupils. Visually impaired pupils do not particularly require any special *instructional settings*. The only thing is that we must pay special attention to illumination in settings where partially seeing pupils work and provide depositories for blind pupils' special media and devices.

Related Services

Visually impaired pupils need a variety of related services. All need medical and psychological services. Depending on the severity and age of onset of their problems, they may need peripatology/physical therapy, occupational therapy, speech/language therapy, and vocational rehabilitation services. Also, their families may need information and counseling.

PLACING VISUALLY IMPAIRED PUPILS IN THE LEAST RESTRICTIVE ENVIRONMENT

Placement Options

Visually impaired pupils need access to infant stimulation and preschool programs. Beyond the preschool period, the placement options for visually impaired pupils, ranging from the least to the most restrictive, are regular class, with a visually impaired specialist supplying resource help to the regular teacher; regular class, with part-time resource room help; separate class for the visually impaired; and residential school. The placement chosen depends on the pupil's characteristics.

Visually impaired pupils should be able to participate in most extra-curricular activities without too many adjustments. The exceptions would be activities in which orientation and mobility and skilled eye/hand coordination are at a premium.

Extracurricular Activities

Visually impaired pupils need special transportation arrangements until they learn orientation and mobility skills. We need to devote a great deal of attention to reducing barriers in facilities and guaranteeing the pupils' safety.

Transportation, Facilities, and Safety

7

TOPICS

Identifying and planning for physically impaired pupils

NORMAL PHYSICAL OPERATION

Structure and functioning of the body
Development of normal physical behavior
Physical structure and function and the cultural tasks

PHYSICAL IMPAIRMENTS

Legal definition and prevalence
Finding physically impaired pupils
Diagnosis: Classifying pupils' orthopedic impairments
Diagnosis: Classifying pupils' health problems

IMPACT OF PHYSICAL IMPAIRMENTS ON PUPILS' CHARACTERISTICS

Introduction
Intellectual characteristics
Social/emotional characteristics
Speech and language characteristics
Academic characteristics
Vocational characteristics

Special Needs of Physically Impaired Pupils

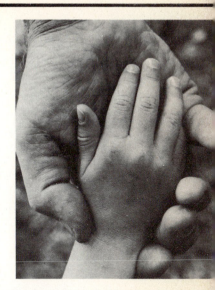

ACCOUNTABILITY

Identifying and planning for physically impaired pupils
Observing the procedural safeguards for physically
impaired pupils

Nondiscriminatory testing of physically impaired pupils

PROBLEMS IN TESTING PHYSICALLY IMPAIRED PUPILS

PROCEDURES FOR TESTING PHYSICALLY IMPAIRED PUPILS

Individualizing instruction for physically impaired pupils

SPECIAL EDUCATION

Instructional objectives
Instructional schedules
Instructional procedures
Instructional settings

RELATED SERVICES

Medical services
Special equipment

Physical therapy
Occupational therapy
Speech/language therapy
Psychological services
Family information and counseling
Vocational rehabilitation services

Placing physically impaired pupils in the least restrictive environment

PLACEMENT OPTIONS

EXTRACURRICULAR ACTIVITIES

TRANSPORTATION AND FACILITIES

SAFETY

Identifying and planning for physically impaired pupils

Again, conducting the Child-Find and organizing the individual education program within the limits of the procedural safeguards is our first task in guaranteeing that physically impaired pupils get a free appropriate public education and an equal educational opportunity. Our activities here are based on our knowledge about normal physical operation and about physical impairments and their impact on pupils' characteristics.

NORMAL PHYSICAL OPERATION

A youngster's bodily structure must be intact, and it must function adequately if he or she is to attain normal development of the physical skills. And, of course, normal physical development is necessary for the youngster's accomplishing the cultural tasks required to meet his or her needs in a socially approved way.

Structure and Functioning of the Body

Our bodies are made up of many systems which work together to enable us to develop physical skills necessary for accomplishing the cultural tasks and thus participating in the world. We have already considered the structure and functioning of the speech apparatus, the eye, and the ear. Here let's consider the bones and joints in the skeletal system, the voluntary and involuntary muscles in the muscle system, the brain and the spinal cord in the central nervous system, the endocrine system, and the organ systems — the cardiovascular system, the gastrointestinal and urinary systems, and the respiratory system.

Figure 7.1 shows two sets of anatomical information: the bony skeleton alone, and the central nervous system. The bones, joints, and muscles in concert provide the mechanics and power for weight bearing and balance in all positions and for movements in all directions at all speeds. The central nervous system is the communications network for receiving the messages the senses provide and for transmitting messages about responses to those sensory messages. Note carefully that the bones, joints, muscles, and nerves control the balance and movement of every part of the body (Bleck, 1975a; Warwick and Williams, 1973).

The internal organ systems — the respiratory system, the gastrointestinal system, and the cardiovascular system — working in coordination process fuel by converting oxygen, food, and liquid into chemicals which nurture the body and also by eliminating wastes. This fuel supplies energy for all of our activities. The endocrine sys-

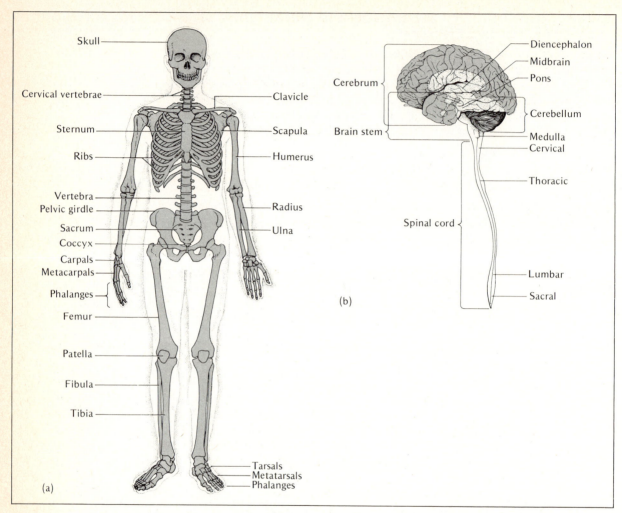

Fig. 7.1
Structure of the (a) skeletal and (b) central nervous systems.

tem controls growth and development of all systems and metabolism of fuel to energy.

Development of Normal Physical Behavior

The infant makes general and uncoordinated movements, but with maturation and learning, he or she masters a wide range of gross movements and fine movements (Ford, 1975; Garwood, 1979*a*). Table 7.1 shows some important milestones in the emergence of normal physical behavior. The earlier, simpler skills again serve as a foundation for the later, more complex skills.

TABLE 7.1 MILESTONES IN DEVELOPING NORMAL PHYSICAL BEHAVIOR.

Age	Gross Motor Skills	Fine Motor Skills
0–12 months	Sits without support. Crawls. Pulls self to standing and stands unaided. Walks with aid. Rolls a ball in imitation of adult.	Reaches, grasps, puts object in mouth. Picks things up with thumb and one finger (pincer grasp). Transfers object from one hand to other hand. Drops and picks up toy.
12–24 months	Walks alone. Walks backward. Picks up toys from floor without falling. Pulls toy, pushes toy. Sets self in child's chair. Walks up and down stairs (hand-held). Moves to music.	Builds tower of three small blocks. Puts four rings on stick. Places five pegs in pegboard. Turns pages two or three at a time. Scribbles. Turns knobs. Throws small ball. Paints with whole arm movement, shifts hands, makes strokes.
24–36 months	Runs forward well. Jumps in place, two feet together. Stands on one foot, with aid. Walks on tiptoe. Kicks ball forward.	Strings four large beads. Turns pages singly. Snips with scissors. Holds crayon with thumb and fingers, not fist. Uses one hand consistently in most activities. Imitates circular, vertical, horizontal, strokes. Paints with some wrist action. Makes dots, lines, circular strokes. Rolls, pounds, squeezes, and pulls clay.

(continued)

TABLE 7.1 Continued

Age	Gross Motor Skills	Fine Motor Skills
36–48 months	Runs around obstacles. Walks on a line. Balances on one foot for five to ten seconds. Hops on one foot. Pushes, pulls, steers wheeled toys. Rides (that is, steers and pedals) tricycle. Uses slide without assistance. Jumps over 15 cm (6″) high object, landing on both feet together. Throws ball overhead. Catches ball bounced to him or her.	Builds tower of nine small blocks. Drives nails and pegs. Copies circle. Imitates cross. Manipulates clay materials (for example, rolls balls, snakes, cookies).
48–60 months	Walks backward toe-heel. Jumps forward ten times, without falling. Walks up and down stairs alone, alternating feet. Turns somersault.	Cuts on line continuously. Copies cross. Copies square. Prints a few capital letters.
60–72 months	Runs lightly on toes. Walks on balance beam. Can cover two meters (6′6″) hopping. Skips on alternate feet. Jumps rope. Skates.	Cuts out simple shapes. Copies triangle. Traces diamond. Copies first name. Prints numerals 1 to 5. Colors within lines. Has adult grasp of pencil. Has handedness well established (that is, child is left- or right-handed). Pastes and glues appropriately.

Source: Hayden and Smith (n.d., pp. 126–133).

At a very minimum, the correct functioning of the physical systems enables us to do many things. For example, we move. We make large, gross movements — walking, running, jumping, throwing, and leaping. We make small, fine movements — talking, chewing, singing, and using tools for writing, cutting, sewing, and so on. We keep the posture and balance we need to lie down, sit, stand, move through space, and change directions as we move through space. We get the energy for all of these activities by processing fuel in the form of air, water, and food. Finally, we generally feel well, that is, free from severe physical pain.

We can learn and perform many cultural tasks because we can move, maintain balance, process fuel to renew energy, and operate free of pain. These cultural tasks are almost endless. For instance, we can take care of our daily living activities. e.g., bathing and dressing, eating, driving a car, cooking, and cleaning. We can take care of our recreational needs, such as playing the piano, playing cards, jogging, swimming, playing tennis, boating, hunting, and going to football games. We can prepare for or engage in vocational and citizenship activities, such as going to school, working at the office, or going to the courthouse to vote. We can do all of these things alone, with family and friends, or in more extended groups. As an illustration, consider again the group of cultural tasks listed in Table 1.1. How many tasks such as these can we accomplish without adequate physical function and good health? Similarly, how many of the later, more complex tasks could we accomplish if we failed to do the earlier, simpler tasks?

Physical Structure and Function and the Cultural Tasks

PHYSICAL IMPAIRMENTS

An insult to one of the body's systems can cause malfunction. The result is inability to perform skills such as those listed in Table 7.1, or inadequate vitality to exercise those skills. These physical problems are labeled impairments if they are severe enough to interfere with the youngster's accomplishing the cultural tasks essential to meeting his or her needs in socially acceptable ways. The legal definitions in PL 94-142 incorporate these relationships in specifying categories we use in identifying youngsters qualified for the rights to special education and related services and the protections of the procedural safeguards. The law covers orthopedic impairments and health impairments:

Legal Definition and Prevalence

1. *Orthopedically impaired* — a severe orthopedic impairment which adversely affects a child's educational performance. The term includes impairments caused by congenital anomaly (e.g., clubfoot, absence of a limb, etc.), impairments caused by disease (e.g., poliomyelitis, bone tuberculosis, etc.), and impairments from other causes (e.g., cerebral palsy, amputations, and fractures or burns which cause contractions).

2. *Other health-impaired* — limited strength, vitality, or alertness due to chronic or acute health problems such as a heart condition, tuberculosis, rheumatic fever, nephritis, asthma, sickle cell anemia, hemophilia, epilepsy, lead poisoning, leukemia, or diabetes that adversely affect a child's educational performance. (PL 94-142, 1977, Sec. 121 a.5)

Look back at Fig. 1.1. About 0.1% to 0.7% of pupils are expected to be orthopedically impaired. As of the late 1970s, about 0.017% had been located and served. Also about 0.1% to 0.7% of pupils are expected to be health-impaired. As of the late 1970s, about 0.27% had been located and served.

Finding Physically Impaired Pupils

The Child-Find identifies those pupils who may be classified as orthopedically impaired or other health-impaired and thus qualified for the entitlements and protections guaranteed by the laws. Some physical limitations are quickly apparent. Some are more hidden.

Extensive public *awareness* campaigns inform people about the various crippling and health problems. The work of the Muscular Dystrophy Association and the Easter Seal Society* are examples of these activities. As with all handicaps, one goal is early detection of physical problems so that the pupil can start in special education and related services soon enough to prevent secondary problems from developing.

Screening for physical impairments begins in the hospital delivery room, and the vigilance continues. Some problems are easy to detect — the pupil is obviously crippled or ill. However, other problems are not so obvious, especially in their earlier stages. Some general danger signs are:

- □ poor coordination shown through awkward movements, frequent stumbling or falling, and frequently dropping things
- □ poor alignment of limbs
- □ pain in muscles and joints or more generalized internal pain
- □ low strength and endurance
- □ excessive paleness
- □ bluish tinge to lips and fingernails
- □ persistent nausea after eating or pallor, sweating, and convulsions near meal times
- □ persistent low-grade fever, and
- □ frequent excessive bleeding and inflammation.

---

* These organizations also raise money for treatment and research.

Some problems are more hidden and require higher vigilance. Petit mal epilepsy and child neglect/abuse need special attention. Petit mal epilepsy often escapes notice because its symptoms are so minimal. We should be especially alert for:

☐ fixed, unblinking, unfocused eyes

☐ short periods of rapid swallowing

☐ repeated small nods of the head, and

☐ apparent failure to hear when spoken to.

Child abuse and neglect are surrounded by uncertainty because people differ in judgments and values about the merits of physical punishment. However, some signs of excess are:

☐ persistent excessive hunger

☐ persistent dirtiness and skin irritations caused by dirtiness — irritations which remain untreated

☐ frequent bruises, cuts, and burns — especially cigarette and cigar burns

☐ unexplained or unusual broken bones — especially on the body in contrast to the arms and legs, and

☐ excessive tension around, and fearfulness of, adults.

Referral for further study occurs in several stages. The first stage is referral to physicians. Depending on the problems, the pupil may see a variety of specialists, e.g., neurologists, orthopedists, cardiologists, endocrinologists, and internal medicine specialists. Once the pupil's condition has been diagnosed and medical treatment completed or at least the pupil is convalescent, related services and special education are considered.

Working with the physician, physical therapists assess motor function and plan training in ambulation. Occupational therapists assess motor function also and plan training in self-help skills and other activities of daily living. Speech pathologists assess speech and language and plan training in communication. Teachers and school psychologists assess whether the physical impairment adversely affects the pupil's educational performance and plan instruction. Finally, for older pupils, vocational rehabilitation or vocational education specialists assess potentiality for occupational training and plan appropriate training programs.

Orthopedic impairments are problems affecting the bony skeleton and muscle systems. They include central nervous system problems, bone, joint, and muscle problems, malfunctions and amputations, and accidents and abuse.

Diagnosis: Classifying Pupils' Orthopedic Impairments

Central nervous system problems

Central nervous system problems are very complex. In addition to controlling movement, the brain controls vision, hearing, consciousness, attention, emotions, and intellectual functioning. Therefore damage to the brain may lead to multiple handicaps. Depending on how much damage occurs and where it happens, we may see a coexistence of movement problems, visual problems, hearing problems, epilepsy, aphasia, learning disabilities, emotional disorders, and mental retardation. The brain damage may happen before, during, or after birth. The damage may result directly from physical injury or indirectly from the brain's being attacked by viruses, from pressure accompanying hemorrhaging or tumor, from too little oxygen over too long a period of time, or from poisoning through substances such as lead.

Cerebral palsy

Cerebral palsy is a movement disturbance resulting from brain damage. Spasticity, athetosis, and ataxia are the most frequently occurring forms of cerebral palsy (Bleck, 1975 d; Denhoff, 1976).

Spasticity is excessive tension in the muscles. This tension prevents movement or makes movement very labored. It also may pull the joints out of shape. Various parts of the body may be affected. In hemiplegia there are spastic muscles in one-half of the body from the midline — either right or left; in paraplegia in the lower half of the body from the waist; in monoplegia in only one limb; in quadriplegia in all four limbs and in the muscles of the face, tongue, throat, and chest. Sometimes spastic eye muscles show up in the form of strabismus (crossed eyes).

Athetosis is involuntary uncontrolled movements of the limbs and the rest of the body when the pupil attempts a purposeful movement. The pupil's limbs flail about and his or her head bobs or jerks. In tension athetosis we see an overlay of spasticity because the pupil tries to control his or her movements by tensing muscles. The eye muscles also may be affected, and we see nystagmus (uncontrolled movements of the eyeballs). Also, athetoids often have hearing impairments.

Ataxia is a difficulty with balance and movement of the body in space. The pupil has trouble walking and falls a lot. He or she also has poor eye-hand coordination and has trouble making purposeful movements with objects.

Two other types of cerebral palsy — rigidity and tremor — happen more rarely. In *rigidity* there is a low level of muscle stiffness that never relaxes. Moving a limb is like bending a lead pipe, that is, bending something pliable but lightly resistant. In *tremor* there is involuntary movement in one extremity — usually one hand or arm. In constant tremor the involuntary movement is continuous. In intention tremor, the involuntary movement happens only when the pupil undertakes to do something.

Spina bifida, a failure of the vertebra to close at the midline during fetal development, may occur at any point in the vertebral column. There are three forms — spina bifida occulta, spina bifida with meningocele, and spina bifida with myelomeningocele (Bleck, 1975*f*).

Spina bifida with *myelomeningocele* is the most serious. A tumor-like sac protrudes through the vertebral opening. This sac holds cerebral spinal fluid and all or parts of the section of the spinal cord in the area. Thus the spinal nerves usually are damaged, and paralysis occurs in any function controlled below the myelomeningocele. For example, a myelomeningocele in the lower back will cause paralysis of leg muscles and the muscles and sphincters important in bowel and bladder control. A myelomeningocele in the neck area could lead to these problems and paralysis in the arm muscles.

Spina bifida with *meningocele* is characterized by the protruding sac, which in this case contains cerebral spinal fluid but no nerve tissue. Therefore there is no spinal nerve damage. In spina bifida *occulta* there is no protruding sac and no nerve damage.

There may also be hydrocephalus accompanying spina bifida with myelomeningocele and with meningocele. The flow of the cerebrospinal fluid is disrupted. Too much fluid might accumulate in the brain area, and the resulting pressure could lead to the pupil's skull enlarging and, more serious, damage to the brain. In turn, brain damage can cause mental retardation, epilepsy, cerebral palsy, learning disabilities, and vision and hearing problems. Which, if any, of these problems occurs, depends on how much damage occurs and where it is located.

Spina bifida

In multiple sclerosis the myelin sheath covering the nerves hardens. This nerve damage leads to muscle problems — weakness, spasticity, or tremor. Depending on which nerves are damaged, the person may have trouble walking and using his or her hands and arms, dizziness, slurring speech, and visual problems. The condition is progressive.

Multiple sclerosis

Muscular dystrophy is a progressive deterioration of the muscles. The more common form is *pseudohypertrophic† muscular dystrophy*,

Bone, joint, and muscle problems*
Muscular dystrophy

---

* In former years we would have included three bone, joint, and muscle problems caused by infections — bone tuberculosis, osteomyelitis (bacterial infection of the bone), and poliomyelitis (viral infection of the spinal cord). Medical advances have almost eradicated these problems.

† *Pseudohypertrophic* means false hypertrophy, i.e., increase in size because of too much fatty or fibrous tissue rather than because of normal growth and development.

which affects only boys. The muscles of the hips and legs and the muscles of the shoulders and arms are affected. Fatty tissue gradually takes the place of muscle tissue, and the pupil progressively loses the power to walk and to use his or her arms and hands. *Facio-scapulo-humeral muscular dystrophy*, as the name suggests, affects the face, the shoulders, and the upper arms primarily and occurs in both boys and girls. It leads to a progressive loss of function of the arm, shoulder, and face muscles (Bleck, 1975 *e*; Brunk, 1975).

Amyotonia congenita

Quite literally, *amyotonia* means a lack of muscle tone, and *congenita* means present at birth. The low muscle tone shows up as extreme weakness. The youngster has trouble sitting, standing, and walking. The condition is not progressive (Garrett, 1975).

Osteogenesis imperfecta

Osteogenesis imperfecta is imperfect formation and growth of the bones; the bones do not develop properly. Also, they break very easily — so much so that the condition is known colloquially as "chalk bones" or "brittle bones" (Bleck, 1975*g*).

Curvature of the spine

We see three kinds of curvatures. *Scoliosis* is a side-to-side curve. There may be a single *c* curve or a double *s* curve. The shoulders are out of line, with one higher than the other. The hips are similarly misaligned. In *kyphosis* the pupil's upper spine is curved forward from back to front, and an excessive rounding of his or her shoulders results. In *lordosis* the pupil's lower spine is curved backward from front to back, resulting in an extensive swaying of the lower back. Pupils with spinal curvatures have trouble with gait and balance. And misalignment of their internal organs may lead to health problems (Katz, 1974; Nagel, 1975*a*).

Arthrogryposis

In arthrogryphosis the youngster's joints fuse. Consequently, there is no movement at the hips, knees, ankles, or waist. As a result, the youngster has trouble changing positions or walking. He or she needs considerable surgery if the joints are fused at odd angles (Bleck, 1975 *c*; Lloyd-Roberts and Letter, 1970).

Perthes disease

In Legg-Calves-Perthes disease, tissue in the head of the pupil's thigh bone deteriorates. As a result, the head flattens and does not fit well into the hip socket, and the pupil experiences muscle spasms and pain. The treatment is complete rest. This rest may be accomplished by confinement to bed or by strapping the leg up and putting the youngster on crutches (Nagel, 1975).

Malformations are improperly formed structures, and amputations are missing structures. Many malformations and amputations result from heredity; from the mother's exposure to disease, drugs, poisoning, and radiation during pregnancy; and from burns and accidents occurring after birth. Some commonly seen examples are club foot, claw hand, webbed fingers or toes, or missing fingers, arms, toes, or legs (Bleck, 1975 *b*; Love and Walthall, 1977).

Malformations and amputations

Fractures are broken bones. Multiple compound fractures lead to temporary crippling.

Accidents and abuse
Fractures

Burns are classified as first, second, and third degree. Third-degree burns have dire consequences. Tissue is charred so much that it is destroyed, and scar tissue forms. The scar tissue, in turn, often causes contractures.* In addition, there may be bad disfigurement. The pupil must recover from the trauma and then go through a long series of treatments — skin grafts to replace destroyed tissue and surgical operations to repair contractures (Cosman, 1974).

Burns

Child abuse and neglect is a complex set of circumstances defined legally as "physical and mental injury, sexual abuse, negligent treatment, or maltreatment of a child under the age of 18 by a person who is responsible for the child's welfare under circumstances which indicate that the child's health and welfare is harmed or threatened" (PL 93-247). Some children are brutalized so badly that they die. Many others suffer permanent, severe physical and psychological injury (e.g., Green, 1978; Green *et al.*, 1974; Martin, 1972).

Abuse and neglect

Health problems are impairments in pupils' physiological functioning. These problems include epilepsy, blood problems, endocrine problems, respiratory problems, cardiovascular problems, and kidney problems.

Diagnosis: Classifying Pupils' Health Problems

Epilepsy is a disturbance of consciousness resulting from disruption of electrical discharges in the brain. The most frequently appearing forms are grand mal seizures and petit mal seizures (Berg, 1975; Bruya and Brolin, 1976).

Epilepsy

In *grand mal seizures* the pupil has a major convulsion — unconsciousness and jerking movements resulting from rapid contraction and relaxation of the muscles. He or she usually falls, may drool or bite his or her tongue when the jaws clench and relax, and may be incon-

Grand mal seizures

---

* Contracture means a permanent shortening of muscles and tendons, producing deformity or distortion.

tinent. The seizure may be preceded by an aura, a forewarning, in the form of a feeling or a sensation, e.g., flashes of light or buzzing in the ears.

Petit mal seizures

Petit mal seizures do not involve so much time or such a heavy motor component. The pupil loses consciousness for a very short time and may also show such symptoms as rapid swallowing or eyeblinking or just fixed staring into space. The seizures often appear to be inattention.

Blood problems

Anemia

In anemia the red blood cells contain an insufficient amount of hemoglobin and therefore cannot carry enough oxygen. Symptoms include weakness, lassitude, paleness, and sometimes jaundice. Sickle cell anemia is an especially severe condition. In addition to the usual symptoms, it may be accompanied by severe pain, headaches, and dizziness (Myers, 1975).

Hemophilia

Hemophilia happens only to boys. The pupil has an absence or a deficiency of the clotting factor in his blood. As a result, he hemorrhages easily and extensively with the slightest injury — a blow, cut, or a sprain. Beyond the direct danger of bleeding excessively or fatally, the pupil's hemorrhaging may lead to inflammation in the bones, joints, and muscles. This inflammation, in turn, can interfere with movement (Leavitt, 1975a).

Endocrine problems

Diabetes

In diabetes the pancreas produces too little insulin, and the body does not properly metabolize sugar. If the sugar level gets too high, the pupil experiences nausea and dizziness. If it gets too low, he or she goes into insulin shock, with pallor, sweating, and convulsions. Unchecked diabetes can lead to blindness, kidney problems, and difficulty with wounds' healing, which in turn may lead to gangrene. Treatment involves insulin injections and control of sugar in the youngster's diet (Christiansen, 1975; Reynold *et al.*, 1972).

Thyroid problems

In *hypothyroidism* the thyroid gland produces too little thyroxin, and metabolism is slowed down. The pupil is lethargic, with little energy for movement or sustained activity, and may become obese. Cretinism results when hypothyroidism is present at birth and remains untreated with thyroxin, the thyroid hormone. The bones and brain do not develop properly, and excessive smallness and mental retardation result. *Hyperthyroidism* goes the other way. There is excessive thyroxin, and metabolism is speeded up too much. The pupil is exceedingly tense and has trouble being still and attentive. He or she usually is quite thin and may have bulging eyes (Garwood, 1979b).

Asthma is a chronic condition in which the pupil has trouble breathing because of spasms in the throat and chest muscles. The symptoms are labored shallow breathing. Asthma is mainly an allergic reaction. However, there is some evidence that it is related to psychological problems (Harvey, 1975*a*).

Respiratory problems

Asthma

In cystic fibrosis the lungs' bronchioles exude an excessively thick and sticky fluid. This fluid can interfere with the youngster's breathing and can destroy lung tissue* (Harvey, 1975*b*; National Cystic Fibrosis Research Foundation, 1971).

Cystic fibrosis

The pupil's heart may be malformed in various ways. For example, there may be holes in the walls or improper connections of the blood vessels to the various channels. In school we see several symptoms traceable to the heart's pumping too little oxygen-containing blood to the extremities. For example, the pupil may show blueness in the fingers and toes and around the mouth and a tendency to tire easily (Baum, 1975).

Cardiovascular problems

Congenital heart defects

The pupil may have heart problems following rheumatic fever. In addition to fever and rash in the acute stages, rheumatic fever may have some difficult aftereffects. The virus may attack the joints, leading to rheumatoid arthritis. If the virus attacks the central nervous system, chorea (sometimes called St. Vitus's Dance) — irregular, spasmodic, involuntary movements of the face and body — may follow. Most life threatening and permanent, however, the virus may attack the lining of the heart and damage the heart structure — most especially the valves (Baum, 1975).

Rheumatic heart condition

Nephritis is an inflammation of the kidneys. The effects manifest themselves in the various signs of inadequate elimination, e.g., puffiness about the eyes and other parts of the body, loss of appetite, fever, nausea and vomiting, headache, lassitude, anemia, high blood pressure, and sometimes convulsions (Love, 1977).

Kidney problems

Nephritis

Nephrosis is degeneration of kidney tissue. As the condition progresses, there is increasingly inadequate kidney function. As a result, the illness shows up in puffiness, loss of appetite, and other signs of inadequate elimination (Love, 1977).

Nephrosis

---

* More generally, cystic fibrosis is a congenital condition in which the secretions of the mucous glands are thick and sticky, causing obstruction and deterioration of the organs involved. The lungs are a very frequent site.

IMPACT OF PHYSICAL IMPAIRMENT ON PUPILS' CHARACTERISTICS

Introduction   Problems in the structure and function of the body systems lead to crippling and ill health, which directly limit or prevent pupils' learning and performing cultural tasks which require movement and balance for any period of time. In addition, these problems may or may not have an indirect impact through their effects on other characteristics, such as emotional behavior or social maturity, which also affect accomplishing the cultural tasks. For example, these comments about cerebral palsied youngsters are general to other physically impaired pupils.

> Intelligent cerebral-palsied individuals meet so many frustrations during their daily lives that they tend to build emotional handicaps as great as their physical disabilities. Fears develop about walking, talking, eating, going downstairs, carrying a tray, holding a pencil and a hundred other daily activities. These often become so intense that they create more tensions and hence more spasticity or athetosis. Thus, one girl so feared to lift a coffee cup to her lips that she could not do so without spilling or breaking it, yet she was able to etch delicate tracings on a copper dish.
>
> Many of these children are so pampered and protected by their parents that they never have an opportunity to learn the skills required of them for social interaction. Their parents are constantly afraid that they will hurt themselves, but as one tension athetoid said to us, "My parents never let me try to ride a bicycle and now at last I've done it. Better to break your neck than your spirit." Many [youngsters] come to a fatalistic attitude of passive acceptance of whatever blow, kindnesses, or pity society may give them. Others put up a gallant battle and succeed in creating useful and satisfying lives for themselves. (Van Riper, 1978, p. 392)

Or, to be more personal, list the activities you have performed in the last twenty-four hours. How many could you have done if your movement, balance, and energy had been restricted or if you had been in pain?

Crippling and chronic health problems show up in many forms. Therefore physically impaired pupils are about as diverse as physically normal pupils are. However, there are some problems related to physical impairment. Whether they appear or not depends on the cause of the physical impairment and how the pupil is treated.

As we have seen, sometimes brain injury causes the physical impairment, as in cerebral palsy, or sometimes the brain may secondarily be damaged, as in spina bifida. When brain injury is present, then coexisting with crippling, the pupil may have impairments in other essential characteristics, e.g., mental retardation, learning

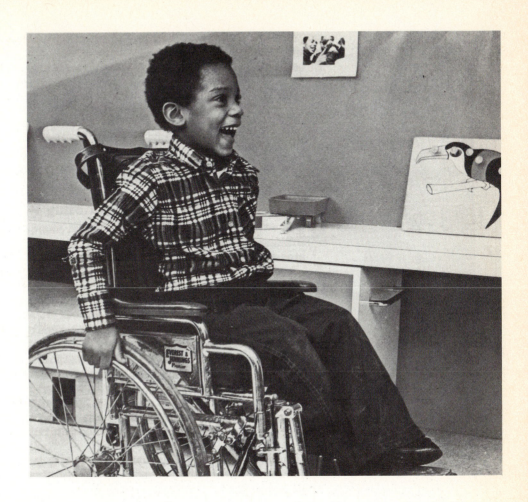

disabilities, speech and language problems, visual problems, and hearing problems.

Crippled pupils face many barriers.

With physical impairments, as in the other types of impairments, labeling and the self-fulfilling prophecy can lead to problems. Pupils who are labeled crippled and treated as crippled may soon learn to act crippled.

Like other impairments, physical impairments can lead to restrictions in experience. Crippling is a barrier to the pupil's doing many activities. A pupil chronically ill, e.g., with sickle cell anemia, may not feel like doing some activities. In protecting pupils with conditions such as hemophilia or brittle bones, we cannot allow them to do many activities. As a result, pupils with these various types of problems may suffer all of the ill effects which follow from restricted experience.

Many crippled pupils face barriers everywhere they turn. Many can't even open doors for themselves. Some cannot get their own drinks of water or put on their own clothes. Some chronically ill youngsters have life-threatening conditions. Many encounter social rejection and other negative public reactions. As a result of such frustration, rejection, and pain, they often show a great deal of anger, anxiety, and feelings of worthlessness.

Finally, there is a more subtle problem. Many crippled pupils are locked up physically, and many chronically ill pupils do not have enough energy or freedom from pain to take much exercise. As a result, they miss opportunities to release tension and to get other benefits of exercise. This situation can affect their intellectual performance and their feelings of physical and emotional well-being.

These are difficult problems. Yet the impact on youngsters' characteristics can be minimized if we give them proper training and support and if they are motivated to perform. This upbeat story about Jason illustrates.

When we [Ms. Allman and Ms. McMahan, team teachers, Fairview Elementary School] were told that Jason would be in our class we were apprehensive. We had observed him when he was in kindergarten and our impression was that his every motion was painful and lengthy. Frankly, we felt it was an imposition to ask us to have a physically handicapped child in a class with fifty-one first- and second-graders. We thought it would be a burden; we didn't know how to cope.

Actually, we have been pleasantly surprised this year. Jason is such a delightful, happy child that we feel fortunate to have him in our class. Our chief problem has been that he must be taken to the bathroom by one of us; this requires ten to fifteen minutes away from the class and may mean that we have to leave in the middle of a lesson. His coordination is poor; writing takes him longer. However, he takes his unfinished work home and his mother helps him, so it's no problem. When he is absent (which is often) his mother helps him keep up. His home situation has been a definite asset.

We have received more help than we expected. Recently we acquired the services of a part-time aide; this helps with the bathroom problem. The special education teacher in our school, who had known Jason previously, reassured us from the beginning and informed us of resources where we could find manipulative materials for children who need special help. We have a high school student who works with Jason in physical education.

Jason is well liked by his peers. They look after him without being protective. For example, during the last fire drill one child reminded us, "Don't forget Jason!" The other children try out

Jason's crutches and are very accepting of his problems. They like and respect him.

Jason wants to be treated like everyone else. At cleanup time, he picks up paper and crawls to the wastebasket with it. He is on grade level and is helping his cousin with his reading.

We think it would be a shame to have Jason in a special class; We think it would be harmful to him. We hope to have him in our class next year! (Turnbull and Schulz, 1979, pp. 13–14)

Intellectual Characteristics

If brain damage is in the picture, mental retardation and learning disabilities may exist side by side with the crippling (e.g., Cruickshank *et al.*, 1976). If brain damage is not involved, we can expect the intellectual characteristics of physically limited pupils to vary as do physically normal pupils' intellectual characteristics. However, physically impaired pupils may score artificially low on intelligence tests and special ability tests because the direct and indirect effects of their impairments may interfere with performance and mask what they are really like and what they can really do. For example, because of their low energy levels and pain, they may not feel like responding to intelligence tests. Their crippling may interfere with their doing intelligence tests involving performance items. Their restricted backgrounds of experience may keep them from having the same learning opportunities as do pupils in the norm groups for the tests.

Social/Emotional Characteristics

Physically impaired pupils show the same range of personality and temperament that physically normal pupils do. However, the indirect effects of crippling and ill health may lead to some strains which show up as social/emotional problems. For example, their restricted experience backgrounds may interfere with their mastering common social skills. Their physical problems may prevent their entering some emotional relationships and some social interactions. Also, they may be unduly angry/hostile or anxious because of so much frustration at innumerable barriers and so few opportunities for tension release. They may develop unnecessary dependency because of all of the care and protection they must have. They may have a great deal of self-hate because of their frustrations, other people's rejection, their physical inadequacies, and their cosmetic problems (physically unattractive disfigurements). Finally, they may feel guilt at the problems they cause their families. Or, most heartbreaking, they may feel, sometimes unconsciously, that their physical problems are retribution for some wrong they have committed, even though they may not be able to figure out what that wrong is (Lubin, 1975; McDaniel, 1976; Sirvis *et al.*, 1977).

Speech and Language Characteristics

When we examined speech and language impairments, we considered the communication problems which brain injury can cause. That is, many cerebral palsied youngsters have speech and language problems.

Beyond problems resulting from brain injury, crippling and other health problems do not directly cause speech and language problems. However, some secondary speech and language problems may happen. For example, excessive overprotection or restricted experience may lead to delayed speech and language development. Excessive emotional strain may lead to fluency and voice-quality problems.

Academic Characteristics

Some physically impaired pupils achieve academically at the level and range we would expect from others their ages and intellectual levels. Others show underachievement which may be traced to several sources. Pupils miss instruction during medical treatment and recuperation. Pupils have more to learn, e.g., ambulation and self-help skills; therefore some things must be dropped from their curricula. Some skills take longer for crippled youngsters to learn; for example, if one has spastic hand muscles, it takes longer to master legible handwriting. Sometimes all of the care and protection required in some cases lead to a dependency and low motivation for achievement.

Vocational Characteristics

Vocational characteristics depend on the pupil's particular physical impairment. Generally, crippled pupils need occupations that require movements they can make. For example, other things being equal, a youngster with a myelomeningocele in the lower back might realistically aspire to being a librarian but not a firefighter. Similarly, they need to look toward less sensitive occupations if their physical problems could endanger others. For example, a pupil with athetosis might more realistically aspire to being an internal medicine specialist than a surgeon. Or, they need to look toward safer occupations if they could be endangered. For example, a pupil with brittle bones might aspire to being an architect but not a brickmason.

The vocational outlooks for chronically ill pupils also depend on their problems. They need more restricted occupations if their activities will be limited. For example, a youngster with a congenital heart problem might aspire realistically to being a bookkeeper but not the operator of a front-end loader. They need to think about less sensitive occupations if they might potentially endanger someone. For example, a youngster with epilepsy might aspire to be an airtraffic planner but not an airline pilot. Or, they might need safer occupations if they might endanger themselves. For example, a youngster with hemophilia might aspire to being a lawyer but not a professional football player.

ACCOUNTABILITY

We are responsible for using correct procedures for identifying and classifying pupils as physically impaired, doing their individual education programs, and protecting them from error.

The first responsibility is to look for every physically impaired pupil who needs help and protection. Consequently, we have public awareness campaigns about physical impairments, their effects, and the possibilities for treating them. In turn, we have programs for screening pupils for possible physical impairments and for referring those who might have physical problems for further study. Again, we report on the activities used for awareness, screening, and referral. Also, we report how many physically impaired pupils we find and serve.

Identifying and Planning for Physically Impaired Pupils

Documenting the Child-Find

We use individual education programs to carefully organize services for pupils who qualify as physically impaired. Here we test pupils' present performance levels to determine how their physical impairments have affected their abilities to learn and to perform the cultural tasks, set goals and objectives for special education and related services on the basis of these present performance levels, choose procedures for accomplishing these goals and objectives, and schedule times for evaluating pupils' progress toward these goals and revising their programs. The IEP team includes the school system representative, the advocates, the teachers, the speech therapist, the physical therapist, the occupational therapist, and other specialists as needed.

Developing the individual education program

We follow the procedural safeguards in every step we take as we identify and classify the pupils as physically impaired and as we develop their individual education programs.

Observing the Procedural Safeguards for Physically Impaired Pupils

Someone advocates for the pupil in all decisions having to do with identifying and classifying them as physically impaired; testing their present performance levels on related characteristics; selecting their goals and objectives for special education, occupational therapy, physical therapy, or other related services they might need; selecting the procedures for reaching these goals and objectives; and evaluating their progress and revising their programs. The pupils' parents or guardians are the logical advocates, but if they choose not to participate, we locate surrogates to stand for the pupils. The parents/guardians or surrogates have the right to call on consultants who have expertise in dealing with physical impairments and their effects.

Advocate participation

Equal protection   We are extremely careful to see that physically impaired pupils have equal protection in classification, testing, instruction and related services, and placement. We treat them as we do all pupils, being especially sure that they are not discriminated against because of their physical impairments or other characteristics. We are especially careful to ensure that they are not discriminated against in testing.

Periodic reevaluation   Periodically, we monitor physically impaired pupils' progress. We catch any previous errors we might have made and rectify them. In addition, we use objective criteria and evaluation procedures to assess the pupils' responses to special education and therapy and to see whether we need to revise their programs.

Confidentiality   Again, confidentiality is mandatory. We restrict all information about the pupils' problems, characteristics, and responses to special education and related services. The advocates have access to all of this information, control over who shall be cleared to see it, and the right to have any erroneous or irrelevant information purged from the pupils' records. Similarly, we destroy all information but their vital statistics after the physically impaired pupils progress through the treatment program.

Nondiscriminatory testing of physically impaired pupils

We undertake our second task, nondiscriminatory testing, once the pupil has been identified as physically impaired. Our goal is to assess the pupil's present performance levels on characteristics essential to learning the cultural tasks and to infer what this information means for individualizing instruction and placement. Our responsibility is to observe the procedural safeguards as we do this assessment.

PROBLEMS IN TESTING PHYSICALLY IMPAIRED PUPILS

The danger is that we will get inaccurate information and make wrong inferences because the pupil will not be able to show in the test situation what he or she is capable of doing. The physical impairment itself, or the problems it causes in other areas such as speech and language, may interfere with our meeting the conditions of norm-referenced testing or criterion-referenced testing. For example, it is extremely difficult to assume that a pupil with moderate to severe spastic quadriplegia has an experience background like that of pupils in the norm groups for most tests or that he or she can take tests under the same procedures as pupils in the norm group. In addition, such youngsters often have high levels of frustration and tension, which can distract them from adequate performance. Problems like these, coupled with problems like unqualified test users, often make testing physically handicapped pupils a suspect business. Again, the danger is that the test will become another measure of the physical impairment.

PROCEDURES FOR TESTING PHYSICALLY IMPAIRED PUPILS

While keeping in mind the problems that can occur, we select our procedures carefully to answer a wide range of questions about a physically impaired pupil's present performance levels. These assessment questions pertain to the pupil's medical diagnosis and treatment, experience background, ambulation skills and other movement capabilities, self-help skills, growth and development in all areas, present psychological status, academic characteristics, and vocational potentialities.

We use a wide range of procedures to collect information for answering these assessment questions. These procedures include collecting records and reports, doing interviews and questionnaires, and observing the pupil in a wide variety of situations. And if we can meet the necessary conditions, the assessment procedures include norm-referenced tests and criterion-referenced tests.

As we use these procedures, we scrupulously guard against the dangers. For example, the participants in the assessment process include physical therapists, occupational therapists, teachers, and others who are qualified by being well trained not only in their specialties, but also in the nature of physical impairments and how they affect pupils' growth and development and their performance of the cultural tasks. We use reliable and valid tests. And we use only norm-referenced tests and criterion-referenced tests that are appropriate. We do not use test modifications that would make the tests' norms inappropriate or the tests' criteria wrong.

Individualizing instruction for physically impaired pupils

Once we have identified the pupil as physically impaired and have assessed his or her present performance levels on characteristics important to learning the cultural tasks, we can undertake the third task, individualizing instruction. We use the test information to plan special education and related services, put the plan into effect, evaluate how well it works, and replan as needed.

We have a lot of information about education and therapy for the physically impaired. Some of this information is presented below as general procedures. Of course, as it always happens, category labels give us some general indications, but the procedures we use for a particular pupil depend on his or her special needs, which in turn depend on his or her physical problems and other characteristics.

SPECIAL EDUCATION

In special education we differentiate the four components — instructional objectives, schedules, procedures, and settings. Again, the way we differentiate depends on the physically impaired pupil's particular characteristics (e.g., Birch and Johnstone, 1975; Cathey and Jansma, 1980; Cratty, 1972; Edgington, 1976; Langley, 1979; Marks, 1974; Myers, 1975; Robinault, 1973; Sherrill, 1976; Silberstein, 1975).

Instructional Objectives

As a general principle, physically impaired pupils should have the same objectives that physically normal pupils have for language arts, the academic areas, the fine arts, vocational education and home economics, and health, physical education, and recreation. The pupils' physical problems and their effects may make us deviate from this general principle in three ways to differentiate objectives. We may need to drop objectives, change objectives, or add objectives. We must stress that this dropping, changing, and adding are temporary for many pupils. As our periodic reevaluations show that the pupil is changing, we change the way we differentiate objectives.

Dropping objectives

Some pupils' physical limitations prevent their attaining some objectives, and those objectives should be ruled out. For example, the pupil who has congenital amputations of both arms cannot perform the movements in cooking and operating the tools in industrial arts. Pupils with moderate to severe athetosis cannot do the movements necessary to music, painting, and other arts with a performance component.

Sometimes limited time requires that we choose among objectives and drop some. For example, some pupils, such as those with moderate to severe spasticity, need a lot of time for medical treatment and convalescence or for physical, occupational, and speech therapy. Some pupils, such as those with muscular dystrophy, anemia, or cystic fibrosis, have limited energy and stamina. The time taken to rest takes away from the time for instruction.

Changing objectives

Some pupils' physical limitations may require that we skin the cat another way by changing objectives. Crippled pupils may not be able to move in ways required by some objectives. For example, a pupil with severe spastic quadriplegia will probably not be able to master handwriting much beyond a signature — if even that much. Therefore our objectives for writing may be that the pupil will learn to type. This pupil also may be severely restricted in speech. Given restriction in possibilities for handwriting and talking, the objective might be that the pupil be able to produce messages through using a communication board. Pupils with brittle bones or arthrogryposis cannot have objectives for strenuous sports and games. They can have objectives for less active pursuits, such as swimming.

Pupils with chronic health problems have similar limitations to objectives for less strenuous activities or safe activities. For example, the pupil with sickle cell anemia might not feel like active play. The pupil with hemophilia or uncontrolled seizures cannot be around dangerous equipment.

Restricted experiences are one bad by-product of orthopedic and health impairments. For example, youngsters do not have a chance to explore their homes and communities. Camps and trips are much more difficult and expensive. Pupils' conceptual development may especially suffer. As a result, we may need to add objectives to compensate for missed experiences. For example, if the pupil has not spent much time on the streets, we may have to devote some extra time to ideas such as community protection and the roles of the firefighter, police officer, and others.

Adding objectives

Crippled pupils should progress at the same rate as normal pupils do on objectives for which their movement problems are not an impediment. For example, a pupil with Perthes disease, clubfoot, or scoliosis should learn to read and write as quickly as any other pupil does. However, we may need to differentiate schedules and to allow more time for pupils whose crippling interferes with their performing the activities required for the objectives they are learning. For example, a pupil without arms and hands may take longer learning to write with his or her feet/toes. A pupil with ataxia may need more time learning to make the eye-hand coordinations required for objectives in writing, painting, cooking, sewing, and sawing.

Instructional Schedules

Some chronically ill pupils also should progress at a normal rate. Pain and reduced stamina may interfere to slow others down. For example, pupils with hemophilia or periodic asthma attacks should progress at the usual rate, whereas pupils who have the pain of a condition such as nephritis or the necessarily restricted activity of congenital heart defects may have to spend less time on school work.

Again, crippled and chronically ill pupils need a lot of medical treatment and time for convalescence following that treatment.

Similarly, crippled pupils often need occupational and physical therapy, and some need speech therapy. All of these related services take time that normal pupils are devoting to their school work. Accordingly, physically impaired pupils may progress more slowly through a set of objectives.

In summary, their problems sometimes cause physically impaired pupils to make slow progress. When possible, we can drop objectives. Beyond differentiating objectives that way, we can differentiate schedules by allowing pupils more time to progress through the objectives in the curriculum.

Instructional Procedures   We do not differentiate our *methods* for teaching crippled and chronically ill pupils. As we do with normal pupils, we deliver instruction through the several types of teacher presentations, group work, individual work, problem solving, and direct experience. Neither do we use special teaching *media*. Physically limited pupils use the same textbooks, tapes, records, and so on, that normal pupils use.

Special *devices* is where we differentiate instructional procedures most. We have a wide range of equipment to compensate for pupils' physical problems and to allow them to participate in school work. Chronically ill pupils need fewer devices than crippled pupils do. For example, if they are confined to bed, they may need a special telephone or TV hook-up or audio- and videotapes which let them participate in

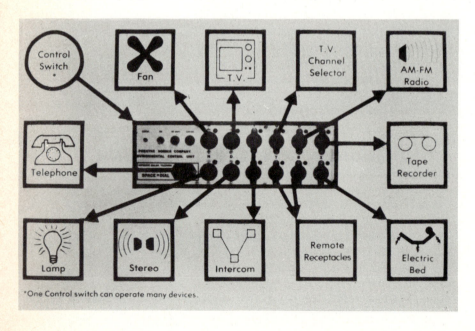

*One Control switch can operate many devices.

We use a wide range of special devices and equipment with physically limited pupils.

their classes' activities at a distance. Also, they may need a variety of racks, bed tables, and lap boards to hold their books and to serve as writing surfaces.

Crippled pupils need many more special instructional devices* to enable them to make the movements required to master their educational objectives. For example, special book racks keep books in the right place, and page turners move the pages. Special large pencils or regular pencils within a ball are available for those who cannot make small hand movements. Special large-handled scissors, crayons, and paint brushes also are useful. As we have seen, communication boards help in communication. Typewriters and mathematical calculators also are essential for some pupils. Also, we need to have available in the classroom such special furniture as standing tables, beds, wheelchairs, and modified chairs.

Instructional Settings

Crippled pupils use about the same instructional settings that normal pupils do. In *allocating personnel* we plan for their having individual teaching, independent study, and solitary activities and for their functioning in both small and large groups. In addition, teacher aides are sometimes necessary to help teachers manage pupils physically, e.g., helping pupils sit down and rise, lie down and rise, get into standing tables, get into wheelchairs, and get up after falling.

In *allocating space* we need to provide common areas as well as carrels and special centers. Depositories are necessary if the pupils use many special devices. We need to provide more space if pupils use much special equipment, e.g., wheelchairs, walkers, standing tables, and crutches.

RELATED SERVICES

Physically impaired pupils probably need more different kinds of related services than do other types of exceptional pupils. Depending on their particular problems, they may need medical services, special equipment, physical therapy, occupational therapy, speech/language therapy, psychological services, vocational rehabilitation services, and family information and counseling services (e.g., Copeland *et al.*, 1976; Downer, 1977; Finnie, 1975; McDonald, 1976; Pearson and Williams, 1977; Tachdjian, 1973; Vandenheiden and O'Grilley, 1976).

Medical Services

Orthopedists treat pupils' bone, joint, and muscle problems. Neurologists treat central nervous system problems. These physicians do

---

* As described below, special devices also are used in occupational therapy, and special equipment is used in physical therapy.

surgery and prescribe drugs, braces, prosthetic devices, and special equipment, such as wheelchairs and walkers.

Internal medicine specialists, neurologists, endocrinologists, cardiologists, hematologists, and urologists, among others, work with pupils who have chronic health problems. They prescribe drugs and do surgical repair. In addition, plastic surgeons repair the effects of third-degree burns and work with the cosmetic problems that some crippled pupils have.

Special Equipment   Physically limited pupils use a lot of special equipment. We have considered special instructional devices. In addition, pupils use equipment to help in their ambulation and performance of daily living activities. To help them get about, they use braces and crutches, along with wheelchairs and walkers of all varieties. To help them manage their daily existence, they use many objects, such as special spoons, plates, and drinking cups, and also dressing and grooming aids.

Physical Therapy   Physical therapists help pupils learn skills for ambulation and independent travel. They use procedures for strengthening and relaxing muscles. And they teach pupils to use movement aids, such as braces and artificial limbs, as well as crutches, walkers, and wheelchairs.

Occupational Therapy   Occupational therapists help pupils learn daily living activities. They work on increasing the strength and flexibility of arm, hand, and finger muscles. And they teach pupils to eat, dress, and groom themselves and to accomplish such tasks as cooking and housecleaning. If necessary in this teaching, they help pupils acquire and learn to use devices such as special spoons, plates, cups, and other equipment.

Speech/Language Therapy   Some cerebral palsied pupils have speech and language problems. We considered these and their treatment in Chapter 4. In addition, some physically limited pupils need therapy for the delayed language which may result from their restricted experiences and from the overprotection they sometimes get.

Psychological Services   School psychologists supply information we need in educational diagnosis. Clinical psychologists and psychiatrists help pupils and their families learn to deal with social/emotional problems attendant on physical impairments. Victims of child abuse and neglect often need special psychiatric attention.

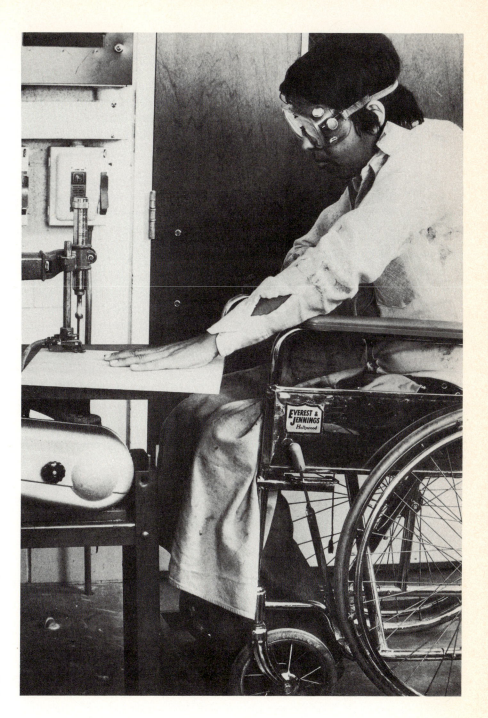

Vocational rehabilitation is
a crucial related service.

Family Information and Counseling Services

Social workers and others supply to parents or their surrogates information they need to make decisions. This information pertains to the nature of the orthopedic or health problems, special education and related services that the pupil needs, and the rights and protections he or she is entitled to. Social workers, clinical psychologists, and psychiatrists supply counseling and other help to families that need support in dealing with the trauma attendant on severe handicaps.

Vocational Rehabilitation Services

As physically impaired pupils move into adolescence and young adulthood, vocational rehabilitation services become increasingly predominant. The VR specialist assesses characteristics important for job selection and success. Then, the specialist supplies vocational information and counseling to the youngster and his or her parents. The vocational information pertains to the benefits and requirements of jobs the physically impaired pupil might do. The vocational counseling involves considering the youngster's characteristics in relation to the job requirements. Subsequently, the VR specialist helps the physically impaired youngster locate sources of training for the job of his or her choice and other services needed to help the youngster benefit from the training and qualify for the job. Finally, if appropriate, the VR specialist helps the physically impaired youngster locate a job once his or her training is completed.

Placing physically impaired pupils in the least restrictive environment

Our final task in providing for physically impaired pupils is to make decisions about placement. We identify and select among placement options, find extracurricular activities, arrange for transportation and facilities, and provide for safety.

PLACEMENT OPTIONS

As with all exceptional youngsters, it is critically important that we get special education and related services to physically impaired children as soon as possible to prevent increasing divergence in their growth and development and to prevent their failing to accomplish increasingly complex cultural tasks (Connors *et al.*, 1978). *Crippled children* need medical treatment early to prevent further orthopedic problems from developing. And depending on their problems, we need as early as possible — during infancy or early childhood — to get them into physical therapy and occupational therapy. Such early therapeutic treatment will help prevent further orthopedic problems, such as contractures, from developing. And they need these therapies to train them in ambulation and hand/arm use and thus head off secondary problems and failures in learning and performing the cultural tasks. Enrollment in special education is important to preschool-age crippled pupils also. Special education activities can help preschool crippled pupils by giving them stimulation they might ordinarily miss because of their restricted opportunities for experience. *Health-impaired children*, of course, need the earliest medical treatment possible. In addition, special education at the preschool level is very important to prevent or make up for the restriction in experience which ordinarily accompanies illness or fragile health.

Physically impaired pupils' conditions do change as they receive treatments and go through convalescence. Therefore beyond the pre-school level, flexibility of placements and flexibility of services are especially important (e.g., Deno, 1978; Green *et al.*, 1980). The place-ment options we ordinarily use with physically impaired pupils, ranging from the most to the least restrictive, are:

☐   instruction within hospitals

☐   instruction within their homes

☐   self-contained special classes

☐   resource rooms where pupils go for special help

☐   regular classes with a resource teacher consulting with the regu-lar teacher and supplying special services.

Figure 7.2 shows how these options were being used in the late 1970s. Regular and special classes were used most frequently, other environ-ments (home, hospital) next, and separate schools least.

Many crippled pupils need access to physical therapy and occu-pational therapy. They may need to be in schools where these related services are available. Of, if another school placement is advisable, they need the service of itinerant therapists. If itinerant therapists are not available, they need transportation to where the physical and occupational therapies may be delivered.

Again, which placement option we select for a particular pupil depends on information about that pupil's needs and capabilities. For example:

☐   How much time needs to be devoted to physical and occupational therapy?

☐   What is the pupil's energy level?

☐   What are the pupil's mobility skills?

☐   Does the pupil have problems in addition to crippling, e.g., epilepsy, learning disabilities?

☐   What safety precautions are necessary?

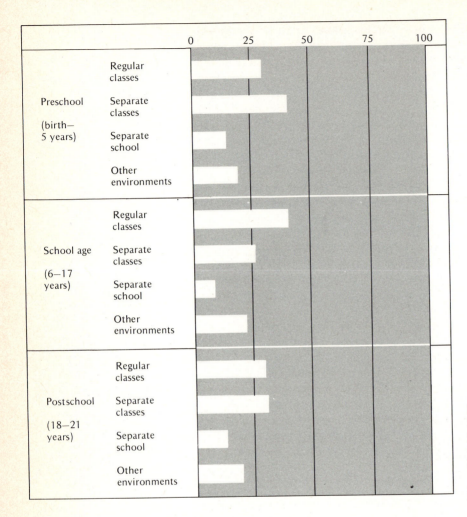

Fig. 7.2
Most frequent placements of physically impaired pupils reported by the states in the late 1970s. (Based on information in BEH, 1979, pp. 169–189.)

And we move the pupil to increasingly less restrictive placements as he or she improves in ambulation and other skills necessary to function effectively and comfortably in a more normal environment.

EXTRACURRICULAR ACTIVITIES

We need to be especially diligent in searching for extracurricular activities, because physical impairments restrict the pupils' experiences so. What pupils can participate in depends, of course, on their mobility, energy levels, and safety needs, as well as on their interests. Therefore we should have available a reasonable range of options for such activities as art, music, drama, school newspaper, table games, swimming, and the body of individual and team sports. Similarly, the pupils should have opportunities in clubs and activities such as the scouts. Again, we should be sure that emphasizing activities that pupils are capable of doing does not isolate them socially.

TRANSPORTATION AND FACILITIES

Some crippled pupils can travel independently, but many do need special transportation accommodations to get to and from school, between school and therapy sites, and around school. Most school

Transportation

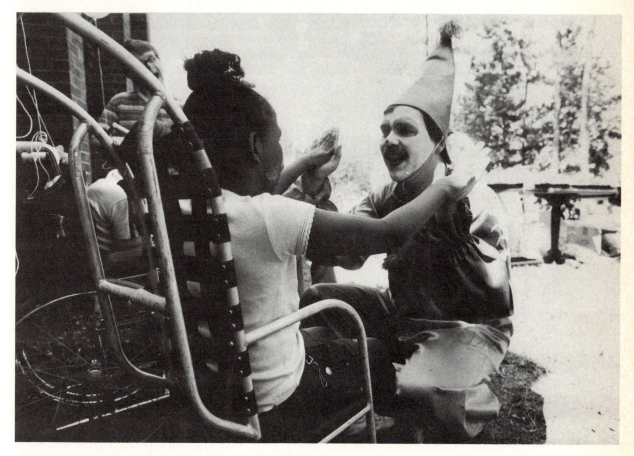

We need to be especially diligent in searching for extracurricular activities because physical activities restrict pupils' experiences so greatly.

systems use special buses and specially trained drivers. If pupils use regular buses, drivers are trained in safety procedures and ways to assist the pupil on and off the bus, to a seat on the bus, and from the bus to his or her house.

Facilities   Facilities are a big problem. However, this problem should lessen as Section 504 of PL 93-112 takes hold and barriers are reduced and access increased. Until then, we attend to and fix any difficulties with such things as curbs, doors, water fountains, rest room facilities, telephones, and stairways. In addition, we obtain for the pupil the special equipment he or she needs, e.g., walkers and wheelchairs.

SAFETY

We are especially vigilant about physically impaired pupils' safety in and around the school and in transportation. We systematically identify foreseeable risks, develop plans for how we will deal with risks and who will be responsible, and then monitor our observations of these plans. Specifics will vary with the pupils' problems. For example, pupils with ataxia fall frequently, so we train them to fall without injuring themselves and have them wear hard hats to protect them from possible further brain injury when they do fall. Epileptic pupils or diabetic pupils whose conditions are not completely controlled medically may go into convulsions. Therefore we restrict their being around moving machinery or using dangerous tools.

Summary

IDENTIFYING AND PLANNING FOR PHYSICALLY IMPAIRED PUPILS

Normal Physical Operation   A youngster's bodily structure must be intact, and it must function adequately if he or she is to attain normal development of the physical skills. In turn, normal development is necessary for the youngster's accomplishing many cultural tasks.

Physical Impairments   An insult to one of the body's systems can cause malfunction. The result is delayed development of physical skills or inadequate vitality to use those skills. These physical problems are labeled impairments if they are severe enough to interfere with the youngster's accomplishing the cultural tasks. The Child-Find includes public awareness campaigns, screening for signs of orthopedic impairments or chronic health problems, and referral to physicians and other specialists for diagnosis and treatment. Pupils are diagnosed or classified as having orthopedic impairments if their problems affect the bony skeleton and muscle systems. Impairments here include: *central nervous system problems* (cerebral palsy, spina bifida, multiple sclerosis); *bone, joint, and muscle problems* (muscular dystrophy, amyotonia congenita, osteogenesis imperfecta, curvature of the spine, arthrogryposis, Perthes disease); *malformations and amputations;* and *accidents and abuse* (fractures, burns, abuse, and neglect). Pupils are diagnosed or classified as having chronic health problems if their physiological functioning is impaired. Chronic health impairments include *epilepsy* (grand mal, petit mal), *blood problems* (anemia, hemophilia), *endocrine problems* (diabetes, hypothyroidism, hyperthyroidism), *respiratory problems* (asthma, cystic fibrosis), *cardiovascular problems* (congenital heart defects, rheumatic heart conditions), and *kidney problems* (nephritis, nephrosis).

Crippling and ill health have a diverse impact on pupils' characteristics. Crippling interferes with physical, speech, academic, social, and vocational activities which require using the crippled structures. Unless brain injury is involved, as it is in cerebral palsy, intelligence level should not be directly affected; however, the frustration and restricted experience that often accompany crippling may lead to social/emotional problems and spuriously low intellectual functioning. Chronic health problems accompanied by the distraction of pain or by reduced vitality generally interfere with functioning in all areas.

Impact of Physical Impairments on Pupils' Characteristics

We ensure accountability in identifying and planning for physically impaired pupils by documenting the Child-Find and developing the IEP. We also ensure accountability by observing the procedural safeguards — advocate participation, due process, equal protection, periodic reevaluation, and confidentiality.

Accountability

NONDISCRIMINATORY TESTING OF PHYSICALLY IMPAIRED PUPILS

The physical impairment or the secondary problems it causes may interfere with our meeting the conditions of norm-referenced or criterion-referenced testing. These and other problems increase the danger that we will get inaccurate information about the pupil.

Problems in Testing Physically Impaired Pupils

Procedures for Testing Physically Impaired Pupils

With the dangers in testing physically impaired pupils in mind, we select procedures for collecting information about a wide range of questions. We circumscribe the use of these instruments very carefully with the procedural safeguards against error.

INDIVIDUALIZING INSTRUCTION FOR PHYSICALLY IMPAIRED PUPILS

Special Education

As much as possible, we use the same *objectives* for physically impaired pupils that we do for normal pupils. However, the pupils' impairments may require that we drop some objectives, change some, and add still others. Some crippled and chronically ill pupils may proceed at the same rate as normal pupils. Others may need adjusted *schedules* to allow more time for them to master some objectives and progress through the curriculum. We usually do not need to differentiate *instructional methods* and *media* for crippled and chronically ill pupils. Special devices is where we differentiate instructional procedures most. *Instructional settings* for crippled and chronically ill pupils need some differentiation. Teacher aides are almost always necessary. So are depositories for special devices and space for special equipment.

Related Services

Physically impaired pupils probably need more kinds of related services than does any other type of exceptional pupil. Depending on their particular problems, they may need medical services, special equipment, physical therapy, occupational therapy, speech/language therapy, psychological services, vocational rehabilitation services, and family information and counseling services.

PLACING PHYSICALLY IMPAIRED PUPILS IN THE LEAST RESTRICTIVE ENVIRONMENT

Placement Options

As with all exceptional pupils, it is critically important that physically limited children get special education and related services as early as possible. Beyond infant-stimulation programs and preschool programs, the placement options, ranging from most to least restrictive, for physically limited pupils are instruction within hospitals, instruction within the home, self-contained special classes, resource rooms, and regular classes with a consulting resource teacher. The particular placement used depends, of course, on the pupil's characteristics and circumstances.

What extracurricular activities physically limited pupils participate in depends on their mobility, energy levels, and safety needs as well as on their interests. We should have available a reasonable range of options.

Extracurricular Activities

Some physically limited pupils can travel independently, but many need special transportation. Facilities for crippled youngsters need careful attention to make them barrier free.

Transportation and Facilities

Safety precautions for physically impaired pupils require a great deal of attention. The task is to identify foreseeable risks, develop safety plans, and monitor the application of those plans.

Safety

8

TOPICS

Identifying and planning for gifted and talented pupils

NORMAL INTELLECTUAL BEHAVIOR

Normal intellectual development
Intelligence, talents, and the cultural tasks

GIFTS AND TALENTS

Legal definition and prevalence
Finding gifted and talented pupils
Sources of gifts and talents
Diagnosis: Classification by type of gifts and talents
Diagnosis: Classification by degree of gifts and talents
Diagnosis: Special problems of particular groups of gifted/
talented pupils

**IMPACT OF GIFTS AND TALENTS ON PUPILS'
CHARACTERISTICS**

Introduction
Physical characteristics
Intellectual characteristics
Speech and language

Special Needs of Gifted and Talented Pupils

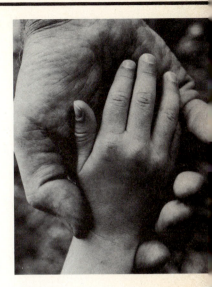

Social/emotional characteristics
Academic achievement
Vocational characteristics

ACCOUNTABILITY

Nondiscriminatory testing of gifted/talented pupils

PROBLEMS IN TESTING GIFTED AND TALENTED PUPILS

The culturally different
The female
The handicapped
The highly artistic
The highly creative

PROCEDURES FOR TESTING GIFTED/TALENTED PUPILS

Individualizing instruction for gifted/talented pupils

SPECIAL EDUCATION

Instructional objectives
Instructional schedules

Identifying and planning for gifted and talented pupils

Gifted and talented pupils are exceptional because they are above average in intelligence and in special abilities, such as sensitivity to color and form. These pupils require special education to more fully develop their talents and to express them through the cultural tasks. Our responsibility is to supply that special education. Identification and planning are our first tasks in carrying out that responsibility. To perform this task, we need to comprehend the nature of normal intellectual behavior, how youngsters manifest their superiority to the normal, and how this superiority affects their other characteristics.

NORMAL INTELLECTUAL BEHAVIOR

Cognition means learning and thinking. Cognitive skills are those involved in learning and thinking. Table 8.1 shows some milestones in the normal development of cognitive skills. As in other functions, the progression, which each intellectual skill building on earlier skills, is very important.

Normal Intellectual Development

Intelligence is central to our learning and thinking. Because we can learn and think, we can adapt to our physical and social environments and, most of the time, control those environments. For example, we can learn to read and in turn use reading as a tool in dealing with myriad tasks, from cooking dinner to planning next Saturday's entertainment to traveling across the country. Refer again to the cultural tasks listed in Table 1.1. Consider how essential intelligence is to learning and performing tasks such as those.

Intelligence, Talents, and the Cultural Tasks

Beyond daily survival, high intelligence, coupled with special talents, makes possible original, creative activity and superb achievement. Examples here could sample our artistic, scientific, social, technological, and sports histories with high points at such events as Michelangelo's paintings in the Sistine Chapel, Darwin's theory of the evolution of species, Ford's development of mass production, Marshall's European reconstruction plan, and Hillary's conquering of Mt. Everest (Bronowski, 1974; Clark, 1969; Michener, 1976; White, 1979). Another way of saying this is that intelligence and special talents enable us to develop new ways of accomplishing the cultural tasks. And they make it possible for us to know and celebrate humanity.

TABLE 8.1 MILESTONES IN NORMAL COGNITIVE DEVELOPMENT.

Age	Skills	
0–12 months	Follows moving object with eyes. Recognizes differences among people. Responds to strangers by crying or staring. Responds to and imitates facial expressions of others. Responds to very simple directions (for example, raises arms when someone says, *Come*, and turns head when asked, *Where is Daddy?*).	Imitates gestures and actions (for example, shakes head no, plays peek-a-boo, waves bye-bye). Puts small objects in and out of container with intention.
12–24 months	Imitates actions and words of adults. Responds to words or commands with appropriate action (for example: *Stop that. Get down*). Is able to match two similar objects. Looks at storybook pictures with an adult, naming or pointing to familiar objects on request (for example: *What is that? Point to the baby*).	Recognizes difference between *you* and *me*. Has very limited attention span. Accomplishes primary learning through own exploration.
24–36 months	Responds to simple directions (for example: *Give me the ball and the block. Get your shoes and socks*). Selects and looks at picture books, names pictured objects, and	Can talk briefly about what he or she is doing. Imitates adult actions (for example, housekeeping play). Has limited attention span. Learning is through exploration

Age	Skills
	identifies several objects within one picture. Matches and uses associated objects meaningfully (for example, given cup, saucer, and bead, puts cup and saucer together). Stacks rings on peg in order of size. Recognizes self in mirror, saying, *baby*, or own name.	and adult direction (as in reading of picture stories). Is beginning to understand functional concepts of familiar objects (for example, that a spoon is used for eating) and part/whole concepts (for example, parts of the body).
36–48 months	Recognizes and matches six colors. Intentionally stacks blocks or rings in order of size. Draws somewhat recognizable picture that is meaningful to child, if not to adult. Names and briefly explains picture. Asks questions for information (*why* and *how* questions requiring simple answers). Knows own age. Knows own last name.	Has short attention span. Learns through observing and imitating adults, and by adult instruction and explanation. Is very easily distracted. Has increased understanding of concepts of the functions and groupings of objects (for example, can put doll house furniture in correct rooms), and part/whole (for example, can identify pictures of hand and foot as parts of body). Begins to be aware of past and present (for example: *Yesterday we went to the park. Today we go to the library*).
	Plays with words (creates own rhyming words; says or makes	Knows own street and town.

(continued)

312 Special needs of gifted and talented pupils

TABLE 8.1 Continued

Age	Skills	
48–60 months	up words having similar sounds). Points to and names four to six colors. Matches pictures of familiar objects (for example, shoe, sock, foot; apple, orange, banana). Draws a person with two to six recognizable parts, such as head, arms, legs. Can name and match drawn parts to own body. Draws, names, and describes recognizable picture. Rote counts to five, imitating adults.	Has more extended attention span. Learns through observing and listening to adults as well as through exploration. Is easily distracted. Has increased understanding of concepts of function, time, part/whole relationships. Function or use of objects may be stated in addition to names of objects. Time concepts are expanding. The child can talk about yesterday or last week (a long time ago), about today, and about what will happen tomorrow.
60–72 months	Retells story from picture book with reasonable accuracy. Names some letters and numerals. Rote counts to ten. Sorts objects by single characteristics (for example, by color, shape, or size if the difference is obvious). Is beginning to use accurately time concepts of *tomorrow* and *yesterday*. Uses classroom tools (such as scissors and paints) meaningfully and purposefully.	Begins to relate clock time to daily schedule. Attention span increases noticeably. Learns through adult instruction. When interested, can ignore distractions. Concepts of function increase as well as understanding of why things happen. Time concepts are expanding into an understanding of the future in terms of major events (for example, *Christmas will come after two weekends*).

Source: Hayden and Smith, n.d., pp. 126–133.

GIFTS AND TALENTS

As we discussed in Chapter 1, gifted and talented pupils are so far above average pupils their same chronological ages on cognitive skills such as those listed in Table 8.1 or other characteristics important to learning and cultural tasks that they do not attain *what they could, what they are able to attain,* when they are exposed to the same instruction as pupils who are closer to average on those characteristics.

Gifted and talented pupils are, of course, not handicapped. Therefore they are not protected by PL 94-142, The Education of All Handicapped Children Act. Rather, they are covered by PL 95-561 (Title IX-A), The Gifted and Talented Children's Education Act of 1978. The legal definition in the statute is:

> Gifted and talented pupils are children and youth who are identified at the preschool, elementary, or secondary level as possessing demonstrated or potential abilities that give evidence of high performance responsibility in areas such as intellectual, creative, specific academic, or leadership ability, or in the performing and visual arts, and who by reason thereof require services or activities not ordinarily provided by the school.

Prevalence figures for gifted and talented pupils are not as available as are those for handicapped pupils. Also, they vary with the types of giftedness investigators include in the samples. However, speaking to the Congress for the U.S. Office of Education, Marland (1972) estimated that 3% to 5% of school pupils are gifted and talented.

Our responsibility is to find gifted and talented pupils whose talents need to be developed. Some gifted and talented pupils are obvious. The problem, however, is that some pupils' gifts and talents are not so obvious. This problem is especially acute for youngsters who come from less favored circumstances.

Awareness campaigns for the gifted and talented have not been stressed a great deal. It is interesting to note that what has been done has been tied to national policy. In the 1950s and early 1960s the United States engaged in cold war diplomacy and as an offshoot entered into technological competition with other countries. Gifts and talents were a great resource in that competition. Consequently, a great deal of effort went into awareness campaigns to find superior pupils. In the late 1960s and 1970s, as national values changed toward concern for the vulnerable populations, awareness campaigns became more devoted to finding gifted and talented pupils from deprived backgrounds who might be unrecognized because they did not have the stimulation to develop and demonstrate their superiority.

Legal Definition and Prevalence

Finding Gifted and Talented Pupils

Screening for gifted and talented pupils includes methods for detecting precocity and superior performance. What we look for are either *demonstrated* or *potential* abilities in intellectual, artistic, social, or physical pursuits (Hagen, 1980; Freeman, 1979; Rodell *et al.*, 1980). These abilities show up in such signs as the following:

☐ *Precocious development* — reaching various milestones earlier than other children of a given age. For example, a pupil who begins retelling stories from picture books at age two to three may be intellectually gifted. A pupil who reaches a high level of coordination early may be physically talented.

☐ *Superior performance* — performance of a particular activity at a higher level than that of other pupils. For example, a pupil who memorizes a poem more quickly, grasps a concept sooner, or solves a problem more expeditiously is potentially gifted/talented. So is a pupil who shows perfect pitch, unusual voice quality, acute sensitivity to color and form, unusual social perceptiveness and ability to organize and lead others, or unusual physical skills.

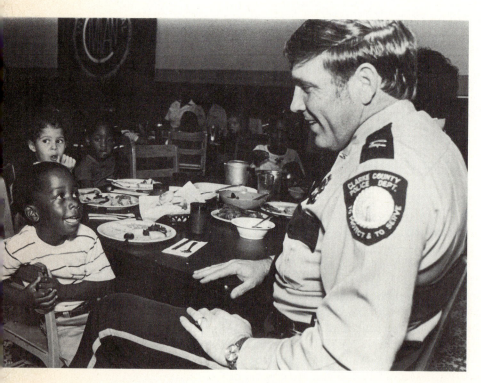

Children begin early to learn motivation and self-concepts that affect the expression of gifts and talents.

☐ *Unusual creativity* — combining ideas or materials in unique ways to develop new products. For example, a pupil who can compose new songs, develop new pictures, structures, or models, produce new ideas, or write new poetry or prose is potentially gifted or talented.

Pupils show precocious development, superior performance, and unusual creativity in many, many specific activities. Our task is to be alert enough to notice these signs. As tools we use observation, checklists/rating scales, and standardized tests. As we have seen, numerous problems can interfere with pupils' test performance and cause us to misjudge their abilities and achievements. Consequently, for screening, most people prefer to use observation with checklists and rating scales to help them observe acutely. For example, Renzuli, Hartman, and Callahan (1975) suggested a scale that focuses attention on learning, motivation, creativity, and leadership characteristics. Since error does occur, of course, we need to use more than one tool in screening.

If our screening indicates possible gifts and talents, *referral* for further study comes next. School psychologists study the pupils' intellectual characteristics. Specialists in working with the gifted and talented weigh their academic and social/emotional characteristics as well as their originality and creativity. Experts in the respective areas — e.g., the pro golfer, the practicing painter, the opera diva — audition youngsters who might have very high gifts/talents in the physical pursuits, the arts, and so on. The pupils' families, of course, are crucial links in collecting information about gifted and talented pupils.

Sources of Gifts and Talents

One question is: Does heredity or environment produce talents and gifts? More colloquially: Are champions born, or are they made? This is a very interesting question, but is not very fruitful for discussion because it is unanswerable. We do not have the tools to separate the two influences with certainty. We can say that usually both a good endowment and a stimulating environment are necessary conditions and that neither is a sufficient condition. Again colloquially: Generally, champions are born to be made.

The evidence that heredity operates in producing superior endowments is fairly conclusive (Newland, 1976). Some families have more gifted and talented members than do others. Of course, families with more gifts and talents produce not only better nature, but also better nurture. Nevertheless, the argument for nature is strengthened by comparisons of identical and fraternal twins. These comparisons show that both twins in identical pairs are more often gifted than both twins in fraternal pairs.

However, the heavy contribution of environmental factors must be recognized. These factors include models to demonstrate possibilities, freedom to explore interests, expectations that shape motivation to high achievement, experiences that provide opportunities for development, instruction that begins to train the talents at a very early age, and most of all emotional support and encouragement.

Some, citing examples such as Abraham Lincoln, may argue that if a true talent exists, it will surface. This is a logical fallacy — the assertion of proof by failure to find the opposite case. For every Abe Lincoln who emerged from bare circumstances, there may have been many who did not. We have a good bit of evidence about underachieving gifted people. For various reasons, some gifted individuals do not develop their talents.

Diagnosis: Classification by Type of Gifts and Talents

People can be gifted and talented in many ways. Again, reflecting our cultural values, we are usually concerned in schools about youngsters who have academic, artistic, social (leadership), and physical superiority. This brief vignette illustrates how many such youngsters can operate.

> The class was composed of around thirty students; they were soon to be joined by the group in the adjoining room and students who dribbled in from the hall to see the show.
>
> Mike was nervous. The prospect of appearing before these people left his teeth chattering, but he refused to call the whole thing off at the last minute. He was introduced as a fourth-grader representing the Lansing schools. Mike sat on a chair in the front of the room, his dangling feet unable to touch the floor.
>
> I watched Mike compose himself and assemble his thoughts. All traces of nervousness disappeared and he viewed his audience objectively. He was in rare form. The students were about to witness an exhibition of the 8-year-old mind of a genius.
>
> Mike was asked to explain the duodecimal system. The piercing voice that answered gave me a mental picture of Woden being ejected from Valhalla. Students jerked to attention. Mike pushed his chair to the blackboard, stood on it and proceeded to illustrate his lecture. The students were excited now and shot questions from all sides.
>
> "Do you know what 'i' is, Mike?"
>
> "Yes, 'i' stands for an imaginary number; it is the square root of minus one."
>
> "What's the Pythagorean Theorem?"
>
> "Well, if you have a right triangle, the hypotenuse squared is equal to the sum of the other two sides squared."

"Do you know the metric system, Mike?"

"In the metric system, the idea is that you measure distance with meters instead of feet, and grams instead of pounds. It's useful because it fits in with the decimal system and there are no messy conversions, like inches to feet."

"Do you like art, Mike?"

"Yes, but not as much as I like science."

"Why?"

"Because it isn't exact—when you are mentally equipped to absorb the exact sciences, you find the unexactness of art less appealing."

"You have a wide command of the English language, Mike."

"Thank you."

"What's a computer, Mike?"

He climbed back into his chair and described the machine with its base two circuits, variables, exponents and components, and told to which numerical powers each circuit could perform.

"You're right, Mike," one of the students said, "I'm studying computer science and couldn't have given a more accurate description."

"Thank you. Of course, any discussion of computers should include cybernetics, the science of 'thinking' machines. This might also involve the principles of statistics, and we should discuss probability and the laws of statistics."

"He's right—he has the idea."

"Do you like astronomy, Mike?"

"Yes, but I don't have enough time for it. Since I left kindergarten, I've been studying some other things."

"Like what, Mike?"

"Like the causes of the Revolutionary War and linguistics and the scientific method—for example there are five steps involved in scientific procedure..." Ten minutes later Mike had exposed the class to the scientific method and thrown in the seven systems of the human body for good measure.

"That's fine, Mike," said a biology major, "but you can't put solids into the pancreas."

"I don't believe I said you could—I said the stomach's acid breaks down the protein into juices, which enter the pancreas."

"That's the idea, Mike. Now in this area of discussion, how would you relate, for example, biology and astronomy?"

"I believe I would say that the entire thought of scientific study has changed in the past ten years. Sciences, especially those involved with the study of life, or biology, can no longer be separated into specific sciences. They must be integrated each into the other as each contributed to the other. Specifically speaking of the relation between biology and astronomy, you are involved in the interworkings of evolution—to be exact, the sun's reaction in the water produced the first forms of life."

There was standing room only; the hall was filling up with students who wanted a glimpse of this crazy little kid. Hey, I'll bet this character can talk until next Thursday.

"Say, Mike, have you ever done anything with the binary system?"

"Oh, yes. I worked 2 to the 80th power once."

"What machine did you use?"

"I just used my blackboard."

"Your blackboard?"

"Yes. Whenever it was full, I'd erase. Then I'd carry the figures in my head and start filling up the board again. I erased many times."

"Gosh, Mike, how long did it take you to get to the 80th power?"

"Approximately two hours. But I had to take time out for lunch."

"When do you grow, Mike?"

"As soon as my father buys my school clothes."

This session lasted for two hours. So that nobody would feel ignored, Mike discussed elliptical orbits, the evolution of the calendar and the differences between the Greek and Roman cultures, with the students waiting in the hall (Grost, 1970, pp. 105–107)

Academically talented

Academically talented pupils achieve extraordinarily in the humanistic and scientific disciplines. They usually show precocity by such acts as learning to read when they are two or three years old. Once their formal education begins, they grasp material quickly and to great depth. In addition, many produce original works. Charles Darwin, John Stuart Mill, and Sigmund Freud are examples of great scholars.

Artistically talented

Artistically talented pupils achieve extraordinarily in the fine arts — painting, sculpture, music, drama, dance, imaginative literature, and the other arts. These talents begin to show up early, and the artists reach excellent levels in performing and interpreting other people's creations as well as in producing new creations themselves. As examples, consider Frank Lloyd Wright in architecture, Leontyne Price in music, and Auguste Rodin in sculpture.

Socially (leadership) talented

Socially talented pupils are those who show extraordinary abilities to organize people and to move them toward a goal. This leadership is demonstrated by people in government, business and industry, and private affairs. Obvious examples are United States Presidents, heads of businesses/industries and labor unions, and chairpersons of volunteer groups.

Physically talented

Physically talented pupils show extraordinary facility in performing in the dance and in sports. They include dancers of all types, specialists in individual sports, e.g., skilled equestrians, gymnasts, and track and field performers, as well as outstanding athletes in team sports, e.g., football, basketball, and so on. Mikhail Baryshnikov, Nadia Comaneci, and Muhammad Ali are diverse examples.

Gifts and talents occur in various degrees. However, it is useful to distinguish between two degrees — moderate and extreme.

Diagnosis: Classification by Degree of Gifts and Talents

There are a few individuals who are extremely gifted/talented. They occur rarely — one in a half million to one in a million cases, but they do occur.

The extremely gifted/talented

The *extremely talented academically* begin to attain very early, and they reach very high levels. We have already alluded to Darwin, J. S. Mill, and Freud. Other examples throughout history are legion — starting with Plato and moving forward (e.g., Bronowski, 1974).

The *extremely talented artistically* also begin to show their precocity very early and number among the great creative artists of their times. Sophocles, Mozart, Picasso, Shakespeare, Isadora Duncan, Eleanora Duse, Caruso, Toscanini, and Steichen are a few examples from among the many (e.g., Clark, 1969).

The *extremely talented physically* become the world-class athletes and dancers. Olympic gold medal winner Eric Heiden operates at such a level. So does the world-renowned prima ballerina Natalia Makarova.

The *extremely gifted for leadership* certainly are among us. However, we may not see them. They may not appear unless a great social crisis* occurs to give them scope for their talents. For example, Martin Luther King, Jr., may have remained a solid, but little-known, preacher had the strands leading up to the civil rights advances not coalesced in the late 1950s and early 1960s.

The moderately gifted are above the average academically, socially, artistically, and physically, but below the geniuses (extremely gifted) in these areas. They occur much more frequently. We see them all around us — learning quickly, solving problems, taking leadership, and turning in highly skilled athletic performances.

The moderately gifted/talented

Several groups may encounter problems expressing their gifts and talents. These include culturally different pupils, female pupils, and handicapped pupils. As a result, their gifts and talents may go unrecognized or, even if recognized, underdeveloped. We consider these

Diagnosis: Special Problems of Particular Groups of Gifted/Talented Pupils

---

* An interesting argument in historical research is whether the great leader's talents would emerge regardless of the times versus the necessity for the great crisis to bring forth great leaders. This very old argument is dramatized in Tolstoy's *War and Peace*.

People can be gifted and
talented in many ways.

problems briefly below. But first let's look at a qualification which
needs reconsidering as we discuss each group: We are now aware of
these problems and their devastations. We are bringing ethical and
legal pressures to bear to alleviate them. However, their traces will
persist through several generations. Therefore it will require several
generations to conquer them.

Culturally different
gifted/talented pupils

"Culturally different" here means pupils who are from the lower
socioeconomic classes or pupils who are from the black, Chicano, and
other racial or ethnic groups which are not of north European ex-
traction.

We can see gifts and talents in every class and every racial and
ethnic group. Yet in the United States educational selections for the
gifted/talented have yielded the reverse of what selections of the
retarded have (e.g., Torrance, 1977). That is, we see a disproportion-
ately lower number of culturally different pupils. Similarly, when we
survey adults who have demonstrated their talents in the public and
private sectors, we again see a predominance of North Europeans.
There are several reasons for this disproportionality. Test bias, selection bias, and different values certainly are major reasons.

We have already considered test bias at some length. In sum, they may disagree on the harm it does or on its solutions, but most experts agree that many standardized achievement, intelligence, and other aptitude tests are biased against culturally different individuals. In the United States the tests are standardized on white middle-class individuals. They contain language and activities characteristic of those used and valued in the white middle-class environments.

This test bias penalizes culturally different pupils in identifications of pupils qualified for special education programs for the gifted and talented in schools. It also penalizes culturally different youth in college admission and advancement in many jobs. They are not selected because they do not earn the test scores required.

Beyond test bias, selection bias has operated. Often in the past, preference has been given to white, North European males. This preference has been blatant in the setting of quotas and in the operation of "old-boy" networks. Or, it has been more subtle, in selecting admission criteria known to favor some groups over others or in failure to systematically recruit minorities and search for nonprejudicial admission criteria.

Beyond test and selection biases, differential values operate in fewer culturally different youngsters' appearing to be gifted/talented as we recognize gifts and talents in our society. Essentially, the dominant United States culture favors the highly rational, can-do approach to life. People who value this approach and excel in it may be considered gifted/talented. Conversely, people who do not value it and excel in it might be overlooked.

Female gifted/talented pupils

Many gifted/talented girls and women go unrecognized. And many who are recognized do not have their gifts and talents developed (e.g., Casserly, 1980; Fox, 1977; Fox and Cohn, 1980; Sells, 1980). Again, there are many reasons. Two major ones are opportunities available to women and the motivational characteristics of females — both coming from deep cultural attitudes.

Almost universally across cultures and throughout history, females have usually had the roles of handmaidens, seldom of lords. That is, females' roles have been different from, and usually inferior to, males' roles. These cultural differences in roles youngsters are expected to and are trained to fill have shaped the way females and males are motivated. Girls learn, often unconsciously, not to value, and even to fear, such things as excelling others; leading others; appearing to be bright; being superior in mathematical, scientific, and technical activities; and reaching high attainments in sports and other physical activities. Boys learn just the opposite — again often unconsciously. These motivational characteristics lead to dreadful problems for both males and females. Among these problems is that females often hide, or at least do not show, characteristics which would enable them to be identified as gifted/talented.

Even if they are recognized, many gifted/talented females' talents are not developed. Many opportunities have been closed to them — starting with the Little League ball teams, which sometimes serve as the first farm clubs for developing youngsters with physical gifts/talents, going through advanced training programs in such areas as medicine and the law, and into leadership positions in the public and private sectors. In short, females have been blatantly or subtly excluded from many programs in which gifts and talents can be trained and expressed.

In addition, the woman's role in childbearing and responsibilities in childrearing have led to restricted opportunities. Not too long ago, pregnant students were expelled from school or college and pregnant workers fired from jobs. Similarly, mothers of young children were not admitted to some schools and colleges or hired in some jobs. Even ignoring these external barriers, internal family values led to the females' staying home with the children and to the males' going out to higher education and higher occupational attainments. Again, the gifted/talented female did not develop her talents or did not have them nurtured by others.

Handicapped gifted/talented pupils

Many handicapped youngsters have gifts and talents; or, reversing it, many gifted and talented youngsters have handicaps. Fortunately, some of these pupils circumvent or overcome the handicap to express the gifts and talents. Probably the supreme example is Helen Keller, who was left blind and deaf in early childhood by encephalitis. Her essays, such as "Three Days to See" (1933), or her books, such as *The Story of My Life* (1903) and *The World I Live In* (1938), reveal a powerful intellect which superb teaching and diligent effort released. This excerpt reveals the magic moment when she connected words spelled in her hands with the things they signified — and consequently got the communication which unlocked her mind. In addition, the excerpt shows the high intellectual level that unlocked mind attained.

> The morning after my teacher came she led me into her room and gave me a doll. The little blind children at the Perkins Institution had sent it and Laura Bridgman had dressed it; but I did not know this until afterward. When I had played with it a little while, Miss Sullivan slowly spelled into my hand the word "d-o-l-l." I was at once interested in this finger play and tried to imitate it. When I finally succeeded in making the letters correctly I was flushed with childish

pleasure and pride. Running downstairs to my mother I held up my hand and made the letters for doll. I did not know that I was spelling a word or even that words existed; I was simply making my fingers go in monkey-like imitation. In the days that followed I learned to spell in this uncomprehending way a great many words, among them *pin, hat, cup* and a few verbs like *sit, stand,* and *walk.* But my teacher had been with me several weeks before I understood that everything has a name.

One day, while I was playing with my new doll, Miss Sullivan put my big rag doll into my lap also, spelled "d-o-l-l" and tried to make me understand that "d-o-l-l" applied to both. Earlier in the day we had had a tussle over the words "m-u-g" and "w-a-t-e-r." Miss Sullivan had tried to impress it upon me that "m-u-g" is *mug* and that "w-a-t-e-r" is *water,* but I persisted in confounding the two. In despair she had dropped the subject for the time, only to renew it at the first opportunity. I became impatient at her repeated attempts and, seizing the new doll, I dashed it upon the floor. I was keenly delighted when I felt the fragments of the broken doll at my feet. Neither sorrow nor regret followed my passionate outburst. I had not loved the doll. In the still, dark world in which I lived there was no strong sentiment or tenderness. I felt my teacher sweep the fragments to one side of the hearth, and I had a sense of satisfaction that the cause of my discomfort was removed. She brought me my hat, and I knew I was going out into the warm sunshine. This thought, if a wordless sensation may be called a thought, made me hop and skip with pleasure.

We walked down the path to the well-house, attracted by the fragrance of the honeysuckle with which it was covered. Some one was drawing water and my teacher placed my hand under the spout. As the cool stream gushed over one hand she spelled into the other the word *water,* first slowly, then rapidly. I stood still, my whole attention fixed upon the motions of her fingers. Suddenly I felt a misty consciousness as of something forgotten—a thrill of returning thought; and somehow the mystery of language was revealed to me. I knew then that "w-a-t-e-r" meant the wonderful cool something that was flowing over my hand. That living word awakened my soul, gave it light, hope, joy, set it free! There were barriers still, it is true, but barriers that could in time be swept away. (Keller, 1903, pp. 22–23)

Beyond Helen Keller, of course, are many others who went beyond handicaps to express gifts and talents. Homer, Van Gogh, Beethoven, Byron, Theodore Roosevelt, Franklin D. Roosevelt, Steinmetz, Vivian Leigh, and Nelson Rockefeller are only a few examples from diverse fields.

Unfortunately, many gifted and talented people do not go beyond their handicaps to realize their potential. We can consider *Look Homeward Angel* and the other work that Thomas Wolfe began and wonder what he might have accomplished if he had grown to full maturity before he was cut off (Berg, 1978). And it is reasonable to believe that there are many others who remain unrealized and unsung. Their emotional problems lead to self-destruction, their motivation is too weak for the great efforts required, or they do not have the appropriate teaching and therapy that will take them over the barriers their handicaps cause.

IMPACT OF GIFTS AND TALENTS ON PUPILS' CHARACTERISTICS

Introduction

Since Greek and Roman times and through the Middle Ages, people have looked to the gifted and talented as servants, or at least as benefactors, of the society. As Hershey (1960) satirized in *The Child Buyer*, the gifted and talented have at times almost callously been regarded as tools or objects to be developed and exploited. These trends reflect the reality that gifts and talents put one in a favored position in learning and using the cultural tasks. Gifted/talented individuals are potentially able to acquire skills earlier and to use them to a higher level.

However, there is also a dark side to the picture. Developing gifts and talents takes a great concentration of attention, energy, and time. By default, the gifted and talented individual may not develop some

Developing gifts and talents takes a great concentration of attention, energy, and time.

skills or perform some tasks as others do. For example, Lombroso (in Blake and McBee, 1978) in discussing the *Eccentricities of Famous Men*, cited some amusing anecdotes; e.g., Newton was so forgetful that he once stuffed his niece's fingers in his pipe, and he seldom returned with what he went after when he left the room to fetch something. Lombroso then went on to make the more serious point that genius may be touched with madness. Today we consider such comments overblown. However, it is difficult to operate at full speed on all fronts. A more contemporary example:

> *Mike was off and running with his usual boundless academic energy. He was quick to establish himself as 60 pounds of baffling inconsistencies. Chronically absent-minded about the mundane responsibilities of life, he was usually the first in the class to finish his assignments, but too preoccupied to hand them in. The teacher made periodic forays into the disorder he called his desk to retrieve his papers. No one could deny the accuracy or inventiveness of his work, providing his work could be read. Mike's penmanship continued to be an abomination and he was fascinated at the prospect of erasing, which added real class to the disreputable looking papers he produced.*
>
> *The study of geography yielded an endless array of painstakingly correct maps, all sloppy and ink-splattered.*
>
> *Artwork was sometimes very good, always messy, and occasionally as incomprehensible as his penmanship. I had the secret hope that Mike might be some new kind of surrealistic nut. So far as music was concerned, he continued to sing like a vulture, but due to the cramped quarters in the gym, the music program was all but abandoned. At least, we assumed this to be the reason. Mike wasn't all bad, however. It's just that what was ordinary and accepted at home, was novel and disconcerting in the outside world. (Grost, 1970, p. 94)*

Generally, we know a great deal about gifted/talented pupils' characteristics. One major source of this information has been the very important *Genetic Studies of Genius* conducted by Terman and his associates over many years.* Some general trends are summarized below.

As a group, gifted/talented pupils are better endowed physically than normal pupils are. They are larger. They develop motor skills, e.g., walking, earlier. They are healthier. In addition, they are often

Physical Characteristics

---

* Terman (1925), Cox (1926), Burks *et al.* (1930), Terman and Oden (1947, 1959), Oden (1968), and Sears and Barbee (1977).

superior in sports and games which require not only physical but also intellectual prowess.

Intellectual Characteristics

Learning and problem solving

Gifted and talented pupils acquire complex discriminations, memorize, and form concepts faster and to a higher level than normal pupils do. They also solve problems better. They show this superiority in learning and problem solving with not only simple materials, but also highly complex and abstract materials.

Intelligence

Intelligence test performance is sometimes used in designating pupils as academically talented. Consequently, of course, they show superior intelligence.

It is important to stress, however, that the artistically gifted/talented, the socially gifted/talented, and the physically gifted/talented also tend to be more intelligent — especially the highly gifted/talented ones. This high intelligence may be missed sometimes. The reasons are fairly straightforward. Most intelligence tests consist of what are sometimes called "convergent thinking" activities. That is, they are closed-ended tasks with particular answers. For example, on the Stanford-Binet, one has to define *orange.* Answers indicating a *fruit* or a *color* are designated correct. Other answers, such as references to the Syracuse University football team or to certain citizens of Northern Ireland, are designated incorrect. Some artistically, socially, or physically gifted/talented pupils do poorly on such convergent tasks. One, they may not be interested in such activities. Two, even though they may be interested, they may not have the types of minds that can deal with such activities.

Creative thinking

Creativity is a complex word derived from the verb "create." It means to generate something new. Common synonyms are "originality," "productive thinking," "divergent thinking," and "inventiveness." Creative activity produces many results, e.g., original mathematical systems, new symphonies, new interpretations of a musical role, new paintings, new coalitions for social action, and new strategies for winning a race. As Stone (1961) suggested with the title of his work on Michelangelo, superb creativity can involve agony as well as ecstasy. William Faulkner gives some insight in this excerpt from his address accepting the 1949 Nobel Prize for Literature:

> I feel that this award was not made to me as a man, but to my work — a life's work in the agony and sweat of the human spirit, not for glory and least of all for profit, but to create out of the materials of the human spirit something which did not exist before. So this award is only mine in trust. It will not be difficult to find a dedication for the

Gifted/talented pupils' intellectual development may outrun their physical development.

money part of it commensurate with the purpose and significance of its origin. But I would like to do the same with the acclaim too, by using this moment as a pinnacle from which I might be listened to by the young men and women already dedicated to the same anguish and travail, among whom is already that one who will some day stand here where I am standing. (Meriwether, 1965, p. 119)

Creative *production** requires particular academic, intellectual, motivational, and physical characteristics.

☐ *Academic:* extensive knowledge and skills to apply to new problems.

☐ *Intellectual:* brightness, special abilities such as facility in remembering and associating diverse bits of information, sensitivity to problems, and skill in evaluation.

☐ *Motivational:* willingness to work long and hard, and also tolerance of ambiguity, frustration, and failure.

☐ *Physical:* stamina and energy level to stay with a problem over a long period.

☐ *Social/emotional:* willingness to face criticism or at least indifference and the ability to tolerate the aloneness, the isolation, required for the concentration and work needed for creative production.

Each of these conditions is a necessary condition for creativity. No one is a sufficient condition. Taken together, if everything works right, they may lead to a creative production (Asimov, 1962; Michael, 1977).

Some gifted/talented pupils are not creative. They can master what others have created, but cannot produce original work of their own. However, some gifted/talented pupils, as they mature, do accomplish creative productions.

Critical thinking   Critical thinking means grasping the nature of something and comparing and contrasting that nature with an external standard. Evaluative thinking is a synonym. Art criticism of the type done by Walter Kerr (e.g., 1967, 1975) and social and political criticism of the type done by George Wills (e.g., 1979) are examples of this type of thinking. Crucial components of critical thinking are a vast knowledge about an area, along with the ability to grasp the nature of a production or activity and to sense relationships and discrepancies. Gifted and talented youngsters can excel in critical thinking.

---

* Production is stressed to distinguish it from the generation of ideas which may not lead to unique results if certain other conditions are not right.

Speech and Language

Gifted youngsters are precocious in speech and language development. They understand spoken language earlier and usually talk earlier than their nongifted age-mates. They master increasingly complex syntactic structures earlier than normal children do. Their vocabularies are larger, consisting of a greater number of words, more abstract words, and more abstruse words.

However, one qualification is important to note. Some gifted/talented people may be almost nonverbal. This may happen because they have different patterns of intellectual abilities, different interests, and different training. For example, some scholars may be adept with mathematics and physics symbols but not with words. Robert Oppenheimer, a highly creative theoretical physicist and leader in developing nuclear power, could not read *Time* magazine with comprehension, partly as a result of his training in logical positivism — which requires an extremely precise use of language, among other things (Davis, 1968). Similarly, some painters can create beautiful landscapes or still lifes, but not tell how to draw a simple table.

Social/Emotional Characteristics

Although some have serious emotional disturbances, the *moderately* gifted/talented generally tend to be better adjusted socially and emotionally than the normal. Like everyone, they have anxieties, depressions, and hostilities. However, these problems interfere with their social interactions and productivity a little less than they do with those of intellectually normal individuals.

Some *extremely* gifted/talented youngsters get along satisfactorily. However, as a group they may have more problems. There are several reasons. One is a constant frustration at the discrepancy between possibilities and accomplishments. George Orwell once commented that any life viewed from within is seen as a series of failures. This generalization is certainly true for the extremely gifted/talented who have the vision to see great problems, the great powers to be developed and applied to these problems, and the acuteness to see limitations. Lord Bertrand Russell's comments and stoicism illustrate this sense of failure, or at least ambiguity, even though he was a Nobel Prize winner and generally a great success by the world's standards.

> My work is near its end, and the time has come when I can survey it as a whole. How far have I succeeded, and how far have I failed? From an early age I thought of myself as dedicated to great and arduous tasks. Nearly three-quarters of a century ago, walking alone in the Tiergarten through melting snow under the coldly glittering March sun, I determined to write two series of books: one abstract, growing

gradually more concrete; the other concrete, growing gradually more abstract. They were to be crowned by a synthesis, combining pure theory with a practical social philosophy. Except for the final synthesis, which still eludes me, I have written these books. They have been acclaimed and praised, and the thoughts of many men and women have been affected by them. To this extent I have succeeded.

But as against this must be set two kinds of failure, one outward, one inward.

To begin with the outward failure: the Tiergarten has become a desert; the Brandenburger Tor, through which I entered it on that March morning, has become the boundary of two hostile empires, glaring at each other across a barrier, and grimly preparing the ruin of mankind. Communists, Fascists, and Nazis have successively challenged all that I thought good, and in defeating them much of what their opponents have sought to preserve is being lost. Freedom has come to be thought weakness and tolerance has been compelled to wear the garb of treachery. Old ideals are judged irrelevant, and no doctrine free from harshness commands respect.

The inner failure, though of little moment to the world, *has made my mental life a perpetual battle.* I set out with a more or less religious belief in a Platonic eternal world, in which mathematics shone with a beauty like that of the last Cantos of the *Paradiso.* I came to the conclusion that the eternal world is trivial, and that mathematics is only the art of saying the same thing in different words. I set out with a belief that love, free and courageous, could conquer the world without fighting. I came to support a bitter and terrible war. In these respects there was failure.

But beneath all this load of failure I am still conscious of something that I feel to be victory. I may have conceived theoretical truth wrongly, but I was not wrong in thinking that there is such a thing, and that it deserved our allegiance. I may have thought the road to a world of free and happy human beings shorter than it is proving to be, but I was not wrong in thinking that such a world is possible, and that it is worthwhile to live with a view to bringing it nearer. I have lived in the pursuit of a vision, both personal and social. Personal: to care for what is noble, for what is beautiful, for what is gentle, to allow moments of insight to give wisdom at more mundane times. Social: to see in imagination the society that is to be created, where individuals grow freely, and where hate and greed and envy die because there is nothing to nourish them. These things I believe, and the world, for all its horrors, has left me unshaken. (Russell, 1969, pp. 329–330, italics added)

Another reason that the extremely gifted/talented suffer is that there are so few of them and they are so different from others. Consequently, it is difficult for them to find other people to relate to. This aloneness can lead to loneliness and possibly cause problems. Or their brilliance and superb achievement can cause feelings of inadequacy and jealousy in less capable people — at least in those who are more insecure. As a result, again, they may have difficulty finding other people to relate to. In award-winning actress Lauren Bacall's words:

> Whatever people have made me in their heads — both from my career and my marriage to [Humphrey Bogart] — is an obstacle to now. They want their memories and fantasies kept intact — they're not interested in the person I am. Every man needs his own identity. His ego will not allow him to be thought of as an appendage to an actress. And though I have never lived my private life like that, I have not found a man secure enough in himself — grown up enough, if you will — to take his chances with me because he knows and values me as I am. (Bacall, 1980, p. 501)

Further, they may not suffer (what seem to them to be) fools gladly. For example, Averell Harriman was nicknamed "The Crocodile" because he made such short work of what he considered to be fuzzy thinkers. Such people are more feared than loved.

Academically, many gifted/talented pupils show precocity and superior performance.

Still further, some extremely gifted/talented individuals are considered socially maladjusted because they "march to a different drummer." They are so perspicacious that they see through to different solutions than the common folk do. For example, Thoreau, from whom the allusion to a different drummer comes, was considered quite cantankerous and certainly was a social isolate.

Academic Achievement

Again, most gifted/talented pupils show precocity and superior performance. They often learn reading and other literacy skills — sometimes by trial and error and without instruction — before they go to school. In preschool and school they learn academic materials faster than other pupils their chronological ages do and, if they are taught, to a higher level.

However, academic underachievement does occur. There are several reasons for this serious problem. One kind of underachievement is the uneven development which must come with the high cultivation of talents. No matter how superior one's endowments are, really superb attainments require a long learning and apprenticeship and continuing work. Consequently, one may be a higher achiever in some areas and an underachiever in others — simply because of time limitations.

Some gifted/talented pupils achieve below normal pupils who are the same *chronological age*. The bases are the usual ones, e.g., poor instruction, physical problems, social/emotional problems, and difficult family circumstances.

Many gifted/talented pupils achieve below their *mental ages*. This happens because they are not taught at the level at which they are capable of learning. That is, they achieve to the level they are taught — their chronological age levels — but this is below their potentiality — their level of mental maturity, which is like that of chronologically older pupils. This underachievement happens because some schools operate in an age-grade lock step and do not do enrichment and acceleration.

> Mike had re-entered school with his usual great expectations. Kindergarten, the kids' stuff, was behind him. Now they would get down to the business (all day) of algebra, astronomy and some semblance of theoretical thought. In Mike's 6-year-old mind this belief was not unreasonable. He was well read, a cognizant and perceptive conversationalist and an articulate speaker. He had mentally absorbed, assimilated and catalogued two sets of encyclopedia, a set of geography books and a wide variety of texts and books from the public library and our own collection. Why was it unreasonable for him to assume that somebody in our educa-

tional system was going to show him how to utilize the vast store of factual material he had hoarded in the boundless area of his mind?

Ironically encumbered with an incredible naivete, Mike had also expected that in some miraculous manner so simple for him, his classmates would return to school in the fall fully prepared to read and to read well. He genuinely believed that whatever form of osmosis he had used to master the reading concept was available to, and applicable by, his fellow first graders. It was with some fear and great misgivings that Mike discovered this assumption to be faulty.

He sat appalled in the small reading circle and came to what was, for him, a reasonable conclusion. The reading textbook was an affront to his dignity.

Remember the Little Red Reader?

> Dick. See Dick. See Dick run.
> The plot thickens.
> Dick is now painting a chair.
> Jane. See Jane run. Run, Jane, run.
> But Jane too sticks around to redecorate.
> Paints another chair.
> Inarticulate Spot does not paint a chair.
> But Sloppy little Sally slops around in the paint for a while.

Mike had not been exposed to this brand of aimless material even in his infancy. As long as he had to do it, he decided to read the book as quickly as possible.

"You may read the next sentence, Mike."

"I will start my recitation at chapter three, as I have already read the previous material."

"What?"

"I said I prefer to read from chapter three, as . . ."

"Mike, our group is reading from the beginning of the book. You will try to read the next sentence."

"I've already read all that."

"You are not supposed to read ahead. You are supposed to follow along with the group . . ."

"Why? I don't expect them to follow me."

"From now on, Mike, you will follow along with the group and not read ahead . . ."

"What are you reading, Mike?"

"Page 30."

"You're reading ahead again. Didn't I tell you to follow the group?"

"Yes."

"Then you will follow the group."

To while away the time in a boring environment, Mike took to *reading the fine print—like the instructions to the teacher in the reading workbook. And he made a fascinating discovery. Now he was prepared to debate an issue where facts were on his side.*

"Why," he asked his teacher, "are you using this workbook incorrectly, and not in the prescribed manner of the curriculum?"

"Because that's the way I'm doing it."

"But it states in the fine print that the teacher…"

"You are not supposed to read the fine print." (Grost, 1970, pp. 58–60)

Vocational Characteristics Gifted/talented individuals can attain higher vocational levels than do normal individuals (Terman and Oden, 1947, 1959). For example, after they reached adulthood, 80% of the youngsters participating in the *Genetic Studies of Genius* had jobs classified as professional, semiprofessional, or business. The rate is 14% in the unselected population, which includes gifted, normal, and retarded people.

Although many gifted/talented adults reach the highest levels in the sciences, the arts, business and industry, education, medicine, the law, public life, and other areas, many others with equal talents and gifts attain much below what they could do. The reasons for such occupational underachievement are many and complex. For example, some weigh the requirements for training and performance and choose not to participate because they do not want to do the hard work and make the necessary sacrifices. Some are never identified and do not realize what potentialities they have. Some do not have the emotional and financial support to get the education and training they need to qualify for jobs at high levels. Some do not have the self-confidence to undertake the tests, auditions, and other stressful activities used to prove merit in our society and to qualify for further opportunities. Some try but do not have the emotional strength and the motivation to stay in the arduous process through training, apprenticeship, and getting established. Some make mistakes and wrong turns that take them away from the training, apprenticeship, and the road to the top. Some just have bad luck and do not make it.

ACCOUNTABILITY

Both legislation and litigation have produced specific requirements about what we must do in identifying and planning for handicapped pupils and in observing the procedural safeguards as we deal with them. We have no such legal requirements about how we must deal with the gifted and talented. No one has brought the appropriate court suits or prevailed on the United States Congress and the several state/territorial legislatures to produce the respective rulings and statutes. However, such litigation and legislation could happen in the future because as citizens, the gifted and talented are protected by the Eighth and Fourteenth Amendments to the United States Constitution and the Privacy Act of 1974. It is reasonable to expect that the precedents and rationales used in ensuring handicapped pupils' rights and protections could be applied to ensure each gifted/talented pupil a free appropriate public education and an equal educational opportunity. For example, the interpretation that equality in education means equal diversity of opportunity certainly might be interpreted to mean that each gifted/talented pupil is entitled to long-term goals and short-term objectives geared specifically to his or her superior present performance levels and potentialities. Again, in the words of the Supreme Court: "There is not equality of treatment merely by providing students with the same facilities, textbooks, teachers, and curriculum" (*Lau* v. *Nichols*, 1974, pp. 553–556).

Nevertheless, in the meantime, beyond legal responsibility, we do have both professional responsibility and moral responsibility — as we do also with the handicapped. Professionally, the ideal is that we should get to know each pupil and then provide him or her the

Morally and professionally, we are accountable for helping ensure gifted and talented pupils a free appropriate public education and equal educational opportunity.

nurture — the education — he or she needs to be as effective and as comfortable as possible. Morally, the ideal is that we owe each pupil respect as a human being and the support he or she needs to develop that humanity. As with all ideals, we seldom reach perfection, but we do constantly strive toward that perfection. We are accountable for no less with the gifted/talented. It is easy to neglect them in the press of other demands. They are so favored — certainly by nature and usually by their environments. Nevertheless, no one can make it alone. Professionally, we are obligated to identify them early, plan their education carefully, and deliver that education effectively.

Nondiscriminatory testing of gifted/talented pupils

Information is essential to the wisest decision making. Our second task, nondiscriminatory testing, can supply information — to use in planning for the gifted/talented pupil, to use in evaluating the pupil's response to the special education and placement decided on, and to use in revising the plans as needed to foster the pupil's growth and development.

PROBLEMS IN TESTING GIFTED AND TALENTED PUPILS

Our root problem in testing *handicapped pupils* is that the handicaps will so interfere with their test responses that the tests become additional measures of their handicaps rather than measures of the characteristics that we are trying to sample. This kind of *Catch-22* situation does not happen too much with the gifted/talented, but we do run into several other types of problems. These problems center on difficulties encountered by gifted/talented pupils who are culturally different, female, handicapped, highly artistic, or highly creative. In each case, we have discussed these pupils' problems earlier as we considered special problems or characteristics of particular groups of gifted/talented youngsters. They are summarized here and are applied to testing.

The Culturally Different   Standardized tests of achievement, intelligence, and other aptitudes are often biased against the culturally different. These biases result from different experience backgrounds, different language patterns, and perhaps different cognitive styles. Such test biases can interfere with pupils' demonstrating their gifts and talents on tests.

The Female   The culture shapes females not to show their brightness or to develop mathematical aptitudes and similar abilities. As a result, they may not develop some skills and talents. Or, if they do develop such skills and talents, they may not express them on tests. This down-playing of gifts and talents may be either conscious or unconscious. Whichever, it may interfere with females' demonstrating their gifts and talents on tests.

Some gifted and talented pupils also have handicaps such as physical disabilities, emotional maladjustments, vision and hearing problems, and learning disabilities. These handicaps can interfere with test performance and, more generally, with their expressing their gifts and talents.

The Handicapped

Most achievement, intelligence, and other aptitude tests sample how well pupils can use language in dealing with cognitive tasks. Also, many such tests sample what pupils learned in school. Many highly artistic pupils can deal extraordinarily well with sounds, colors, and forms, but they are almost inarticulate with words. Also, they have devoted so much time, energy, and interest to artistic pursuits that they have not learned as much academic material in school as they might have. Consequently, they are penalized by many tests.

The Highly Artistic

Most achievement, intelligence, and other aptitude tests involve convergent tasks with one answer. They do not give much room for divergent, original thinking. As a result, many highly creative gifted/talented pupils are penalized by many tests.

The Highly Creative

PROCEDURES FOR TESTING GIFTED/TALENTED PUPILS

We assess the pupil to determine whether he or she is gifted and talented and beyond that to identify characteristics which will enable us to plan most effectively. Specific assessment questions pertain to the pupil's growth and development, family situation, psychological functioning, and education/therapeutic history.

We collect information to answer the assessment questions through the usual procedures. These include examining records and reports, interviewing, and observing the pupil. These procedures may be systematized with checklists and rating scales. As needed, we go beyond these procedures to use criterion-referenced tests and norm-referenced tests — being especially careful to get the right norm groups. Further, a pupil should be tested in his or her native language with more than one test by a multidisciplinary team which includes at least one specialist in working with gifted and talented pupils. And too, it is important to have participation by the pupil and his or her parents in decision making, due process, periodic evaluation, and confidentiality.

Auditions with experts are crucial, of course, when we are dealing with pupils who have special talents. For example, the mathematician should assess the mathematically precocious youngster, and the skilled musician should judge the budding violinist.

Individualizing instruction for gifted/talented pupils

As we think about our third task, individualizing instruction, it is well to remember that gifted/talented pupils have the potentiality for high levels of development in academic, artistic, athletic, and social (leadership) pursuits. By "high levels of development," we mean not only the mastery of what other people have produced before them, but also the creation of new knowledge, new artistic achievements, new social coalitions, and new records of physical achievement. The goal of instruction, then, is to teach them the knowledge and skills they need to reach these high levels of development.*

SPECIAL EDUCATION

Instructional Objectives   We can expect gifted/talented pupils to master all of the instructional objectives that other pupils master. These include the objectives for literacy, the sciences, the arts and humanities, and the vocational subjects.

Beyond the usual levels, the gifted/talented can go on to master more advanced objectives. For any one content area, these more advanced objectives pertain to the structure of knowledge, the principles and abstract concepts in the field, and their applications.

> "And today, children," Mrs. Smith began, "we are going to talk about flowers. What is a flower? What kinds of flowers do we find here in Michigan? You had your hand up, Mike?"
>
> "Yes. I am prepared to give a brief talk on today's subject... In botanical terminology, the word 'flower' refers only to the blossom of a plant. They refer to the blossom, leaves, root and stem as a flowering plant. However, a gardener may refer to the entire plant as a flower.
>
> "In our geographical area we are likely to find a large variety of woodland and prairie flowers, plus, of course, species of the imported or..."

---

* Extensive suggestions about teaching the gifted/talented have been made by such specialists as Freeman (1979), Gallagher (1975), Kaplan (1975), Khatena (1978), Maker (1977), Morgan *et al.* (1980), Newland (1976), Rodell *et al.* (1980), and Stanley (1976).

"That's very interesting, Mike."

"Thank you...even domestic blooms which are foreign, by nature, to this geographical area..."

"Mike, why don't we discuss what you've told us so far?"

"Of course, Mrs. Smith. Which question would you like elaborated?"

"Well, Mike, let's hear what the rest of the class has to say... how fortunate we are to have someone in our room who knows so much about flowers. Mike mentioned some interesting words. Now a botanist is..."

"Well, class, what interesting weather we've been having... rain yesterday, snow today. I wonder what we'll get tomorrow? Yes, Mike?"

"The probability of precipitation tomorrow is 50 percent."

"Oh? I'll bet you'll grow up to be a weatherman, Mike."

"I don't believe I will, Mrs. Smith. I've never considered meteorology as my forte, or as a prime subject for study. I relate to weather only as it affects, or is affected by, my interest in astronomy." (Grost, 1970, pp. 42–43)

Beyond the objectives for knowledge, gifted pupils can master objectives for such processes as creativity and evaluative thinking. For example, they can not only learn to identify and give the characteristics of Michelangelo's sculpture, architecture, and painting, but also evaluate by comparing and contrasting Michelangelo's art with DaVinci's and other contemporaries' art. And beyond such scholarly and critical activity, they can produce some art work incorporating some of the principles and techniques they have learned in their studies of early masters.

Instructional Schedules

Gifted/talented pupils learn faster. This means that they need less teaching and reteaching on a particular instructional objective and also that they need less practice before they master the objective. Once they have mastered an instructional objective, they can do several things.

One thing they can do is to sit through the reteaching and practice the slower pupils need. This unneeded work, called *busywork*, drives some gifted/talented people to the extremes of boredom, desperation, and rebellion. On the other hand, they can be spared the busywork. Once they master an objective, they can turn to another objective. This turning to another objective is called *enrichment* if it is on the same difficulty level as the objective the pupil finished more rapidly. It is called *acceleration* if the new objective is on a more advanced difficulty level.

We need to differentiate schedules for gifted/talented pupils. They should not be subjected to teaching and practice on objectives they have already mastered. Whether we devote the saved time to enrichment or to acceleration depends on the pupil's characteristics and the value systems of all concerned.

Instructional Procedures We use with the gifted the same methods we use with other pupils, i.e., teacher presentations, group work, independent work, and problem solving. However, more emphasis is placed on independent work and problem solving, for two reasons. (1) The gifted/talented are so few that they often have to work alone if they are to learn. (2) The gifted/talented should work at high levels of creativity and critical thinking, and these are solitary activities *sui generis*.

Gifted/talented pupils use the same type of instructional media as other pupils do. They just use more complex media and more of them. That is, they need access to a more extensive library of books, audiotapes, videotapes, and films. They also need access to media and equipment necessary for creative work — recorders, cameras, and special equipment in physics, chemistry, sculpture, music, and other areas.

> *"It's nothing but a piece of junk and I don't want it, Mother. You should have known when you bought this microscope that it was junk. Yet you never told me it wasn't real. You let me think it was a real one. And it was only junk."*
>
> *How unusual for Mike to give in to his emotions. He stood screaming at me, his tear-stained face red with anger. This was a new experience for us.*
>
> *"Mike, I didn't buy that microscope to fool you in any way. It was only a toy—I thought you would find it interesting…putting different things under…"*
>
> *"But you didn't tell me it was a toy. You led me to believe it was a real one, like the scientists use in a laboratory. Only it isn't. I found that out today. It's junk—a junky toy, and I hate it—I'm going to throw it away—I don't want Bobby to have such a junky toy either."*
>
> *"Mike, let's talk about it calmly…"*
>
> *"I don't want to talk about it! I hate it—hate it!"*
>
> *He was screaming at me now. "Mike, why don't you wash your face and we'll talk about it and…"*
>
> *"I said I don't want to talk about it. The teacher is going to get me a real one from the high school lab, and I won't need that junk anymore…"*
>
> *He stomped upstairs to his room and slammed the door. (Grost, 1970, pp. 60–61)*

Gifted/talented pupils use about the same physical arrangements as other pupils do. We must be especially sure that they have ample access to appropriate depositories and to appropriate space for independent work. For example, the pupil who is gifted in languages needs access to a language master and an audiotape library of spoken languages. A pupil gifted in painting needs access to collections of paintings and other graphic arts, as well as a well-lighted, physically attractive place to do his or her own painting.

Instructional Settings

Their teachers are the keystone to developing gifted pupils' talents. These teachers need the talent, knowledge, and experience to reach a high level of attainment themselves. In addition, they need the security, flexibility, and independence of mind to work with other outstanding talents.

The extremely gifted/talented will usually need tutors from outside the school. That is, the budding world-class swimmer needs a special coach; the upcoming political leader needs contact with governors, members of Congress, etc.; and the incipient violinist, orchestra conductor, or soprano requires highly specialized teachers.

RELATED SERVICES

Unless they also have handicaps, gifted/talented pupils do not need special medical services or the various therapies. They may, however, need psychological services, vocational counseling, and family information and counseling.

Psychological Services

As we have seen, some gifted pupils have social and emotional problems. They are subject not only to the usual traumas but also sometimes to isolation and pain caused by their being different. Also, they sometimes have problems because they encounter a great deal of nonsense from less capable people who are in control of their destinies for periods of time. As a result, they often need help from clinical psychologists or psychiatrists to work through their problems. In addition, school psychologists may help in identifying gifted/talented pupils' capabilities in the academic, social, and other areas.

Family Information and Counseling

Making the right decisions about how to develop a big talent or gift is very difficult. It is difficult to find teachers and resources. It is difficult to choose among possibilities for development. Such choices are difficult to make because one often worries, with Robert Frost, about the road not taken. For example, consider the highly gifted pupil who might become a Faulkner, a Roosevelt, an Einstein, a Van Gogh, an

Isaac Stern, a Nureyev, or someone similar. Training must begin early and be highly specialized, e.g., no one life has enough time to develop to the level of both an Einstein and a Stern. In addition, many restrictions must be accepted. For example, a Stern's hands or a Nureyev's body cannot be risked in football — either on a school team or in a backyard pick-up game. Families that must deal with such choices require a great deal of information. Some require counseling.

Vocational Counseling   Many gifted/talented youngsters — especially some of those from less favored backgrounds — need vocational counseling as they go through secondary school. They may need information about the levels of their gifts and talents and what these mean for their occupational choices. They may need information about occupations — their natures, their rewards, and their requirements. Finally, once these pupils have made some choices, they may need information about sources of training, how to get admitted to colleges and universities and other training programs, and where to get the financial and other resources to pay for long training programs.

Placing gifted/talented pupils

PLACEMENT OPTIONS

Of the placement options usually considered for exceptional children, the ones most often considered for the gifted/talented are acceleration, ability grouping, itinerant services, and special tutoring (e.g., Daurio, 1980; Getzels and Dillon, 1973; Hobson, 1980; Meister and Odell, 1980; Stanley, 1973, 1974). In addition, early education is very important for young gifted/talented pupils (e.g., Hall and Skinner, 1980; Rodell et al., 1980).

Deciding about the best place to deliver instruction to gifted/talented pupils is more difficult than you might think. We must look for placements where they can get the instruction and stimulation necessary to develop their gifts and talents. At the same time, we must be concerned about their social and emotional experiences.

With handicapped pupils, the idea is that they will benefit from, and should be in, the least restrictive environment they can get along in. The belief is that they will benefit from stimulation by, and social contacts with, nonhandicapped pupils. That is, when they are placed with higher-functioning pupils, handicapped pupils have a chance to see more mature performance and are motivated to try reaching those more mature levels. And when placed with nonhandicapped pupils, handicapped pupils have a chance to interact with them socially and

emotionally. If we accept development of gifts and talents and satisfying emotional and social interactions as our goals, the same benefits
do not necessarily accrue to the gifted/talented who, by definition,
are superior to the average.

Gifted and talented pupils
need placements where they
can get the instruction and
stimulation necessary to
develop their gifts and
talents.

*"Mother, I've been reviewing some of the aspects of my forthcoming
formal education," Mike was telling me, "and I'm sure it's going to
be challenging. I noticed when we went up to the school for the ice
cream social last year, that they have an extensive library. My
teacher will no doubt lecture us on algebra and astronomy. And the
students make things in kindergarten, so one must conclude that
the teacher is aware of some engineering principles. And Mrs. Fink
said she talked to the kindergarten teacher the other day. This year*

the students will be studying the earth—flowers and rocks and weather—natural science, you know.

"From the charts on the wall of the kindergarten room, it would appear that the students are involved in color perception of the primary, secondary and ternary colors. The study no doubt includes hue, brightness and intensity.

"And from the pictures the children create, I believe they must be studying a school of modern art. This might be difficult—my own work can only be classified with the primitives. Mother, do you think I'm adequately prepared for kindergarten?"

"Mike, I believe you are prepared for any academic contingency."

Mike was obviously headed for trouble. We believed he would be frustrated in kindergarten and my first thought was to visit the teacher and acquaint her with the idea that she had a problem. This smacked of the overprotective mother and apple pie. We decided to let Mike become one of the crowd, regardless of the consequences. As always, we underestimated his aggressive ability to face a problem and cope with it. Or perhaps he considered his own problems as minimal, and the problems of his classmates appalling. Mike was soon to discover that he was cast adrift in a sea of illiterates.

"Good morning, Mike. I'm Mrs. Smith. Welcome to kindergarten."

"Thank you. Good morning, Mrs. Smith."

"Why don't you sit down at one of the tables and work a puzzle, while I talk to Mother?"

Most of the children were strangers to Mike. He obediently went through the motions of putting together a puzzle, but was observing his new companions intensely. The little girl next to him had drawn an apple and was cheerfully coloring it blue. Mike was fascinated.

"That's a very interesting approach to your subject," he told her.

"What?"

"Coloring the apple blue, when usually they're red. It's the kind of approach Picasso would use."

"Who?"

"Picasso."

"Where's he sitting?"

"I really have no idea. I believe he lives in Paris."

"Oh, well, if he isn't here now, he must be in the afternoon class."

"No, I'm not talking about another pupil. I'm talking about Picasso, the Cubist."

"What?"

"Picasso. You see, he went through a period in his artistic career when he painted everything blue. No matter what it was. Just like you're coloring the apple blue, when everyone would expect you to color it red. That's quite creative."

"Oh. Well, I don't know my colors yet. I don't know which crayon is red, so I thought this would look nice."

"You mean you don't actually know one color from the other?"

"No, and I'll bet you don't either. None of the kids do."

Mike picked up the red crayon. "Well, it's really very simple, this is red. But when you get right down to it, you don't really have to know your colors. You see, it tells right on the crayon, what color it is."

"Where?"

"Right here. See, it says, 'R-E-D.' So if you don't know the colors, just look to see what it says on the wrapper."

"How do you know what it says?"

"Well, you read it."

"We learn to read in the first grade. I can't read it now."

"Oh, I'm sorry…" (Grost, 1970, pp. 40–42)

Acceleration

Acceleration, as the name indicates, means moving through school faster. The gifted/talented pupil is placed with other pupils his or her mental maturity level, i.e., those able to learn at the same difficulty and complexity level. In earlier days of the age-grade lock step, acceleration was accomplished by pupils' skipping grades, sometimes called double promotion. Pupils simply bypassed one or two years' work. The assumption was that they knew all of the work covered in the grades they skipped. Grade skipping is the opposite of retaining or failing the slower pupil. Now acceleration is accomplished through three plans: early admission to school, early admission to college, and continuous progress.

Early school admission is allowing the pupil to begin the first grade before chronological age six and kindergarten before chronological age four or five. And quite often pupils are enrolled in infant programs and preschool programs much earlier.

Early college programs are accomplished through three means. *Early admission* is letting youngsters enroll in college before the usual age. *Advanced placement* is allowing pupils to enroll in college courses while they are still in high school — either through programs on campus or through correspondence courses. *Course acceleration* is allowing pupils to take tests over the material in the college courses and giving them one of two benefits: exemption from taking the college course or exemption *and* credit in the course.

In *continuous progress programs* pupils complete all of the instructional objectives as they move along at their own rates. They do not skip any objectives and at the same time are not required to wait for slower pupils. Continuous progress can go on within several settings. It may go on within a class, with the pupil working with other gifted/talented pupils in a small group. It may go on in a primary or in-mediate unit,* with pupils of different ages but similar mental maturity levels working together. Or, in high schools continuous progress may happen by pupils' taking more courses than usual and thus finishing the requirements early.

Acceleration has the advantage of enabling pupils to develop their talents and gifts. Pupils must have good instruction if they are to acquire advanced knowledge and develop complex skills. Most cannot figure out calculus without teaching or develop a champion golf swing without coaching. The disadvantage is that acceleration places the pupil with older pupils, who are more mature physically and socially/emotionally. Therefore although acceleration is beneficial intellectually, it can lead to social isolation and emotional problems. Or it may not.

Another disadvantage from gifted/talented pupils' viewpoints is a mechanical one connected to grading. Grades are an important consideration in college admission. Gifted pupils usually make top grades when they are graded against average and below average youngsters or against objectives selected for these slower pupils. Gifted pupils may not make top grades when they are graded against more mature pupils or more advanced objectives. Thus gifted/talented pupils who master tremendously complicated material in school might be denied college admission unless colleges know the standards they have been graded against.

Ability Grouping

Ability grouping is sometimes used to allow gifted/talented pupils to work together at their own rates and on their particular interests. Three forms are used: self-contained special classes, special schools, and resource room programs.

Special schools are specialty schools for gifted/talented pupils. They are very rare. The models here are in New York: the Bronx High School of Science or the Bronx High School of Music and the Arts.

Self-contained special classes are sometimes used. Here gifted/talented youngsters of the same CA are brought together and are taught on more advanced levels than other pupils. Such classes are frequently used — especially at the middle-school and the secondary-school levels. However, they are seldom labeled as special classes for the gifted. They are just called by such names as *Advanced Mathematics* or *Accelerated English.*

The *resource room* for the gifted/talented is often used for younger pupils. With this plan, youngsters go to a separate room and teacher

---

* Primary units and intermediate units allow several children at several CA levels to be grouped and then subdivided by mental maturity levels.

for work at more advanced levels or on topics not ordinarily covered in the schools.

Ability grouping has two advantages. It allows pupils to develop their talents and gifts. It allows the pupil to be with other pupils of the same CA, i.e., other pupils who have the same levels of physical, social, and emotional maturity. One frequently cited disadvantage is that it fosters elitism. That is, it does not allow pupils to learn to get along with less talented people.

Again, the grading problem and college admission can operate as a disadvantage. That is, the pupil may not get as good grades when he or she is compared to other gifted pupils or to more advanced material.

Itinerant Services

Some teachers specialize in the education of gifted/talented pupils. They deliver enrichment, which is a process of giving pupils experiences not usually done in the schools. These activities are done in the time when gifted/talented pupils are finished with objectives and are waiting for other pupils to complete them.

An itinerant specialist in the gifted/talented may deliver the enrichment experiences to pupils within a particular classroom. Or, he or she may work with groups formed from several classes or schools.

The advantage of the itinerant program is that pupils can receive intellectual stimulation and at the same time stay with other pupils who have the same levels of physical, social, and emotional development. Also, they can learn to live with less capable people.

The disadvantage to itinerant plans and enrichment is that they may be too incomplete and unsystematic. Learning a body of advanced knowledge or a high level of skill requires a great deal of time and intensive instruction. Short time periods and various (miscellaneous) enrichment activities seldom lead to such high levels of development.

Special Tutoring

Some pupils have talents and gifts requiring instruction that most educators do not have the training and experience to deliver. These include high gifts and talents in such areas as mathematics, music, art, and dance. Here pupils need special teachers who begin working with them very early and intensively.

Tutoring has the advantage of saving and developing talent. It has the disadvantage of isolating the student socially and emotionally.

Deciding among Options

We have seen that each type of placement has advantages and disadvantages. Consequently, placements must be decided separately for each pupil, depending on all of his or her characteristics. In making decisions we need answers to such questions as:

☐ What are the pupil's particular gifts/talents? Which ones is he or she most interested in developing?

☐ What is the pupil's social maturity? Does he or she have adequate social skills? Does he or she have opportunities for social development outside of school?

☐ What is the pupil's emotional adjustment like? How much isolation and frustration can he or she tolerate?

☐ What are the pupil's and the parents' value systems? Do they value high accomplishments over social popularity?

EXTRACURRICULAR ACTIVITIES

As with all pupils, extracurricular activities are a valuable avenue for gifted/talented pupils to develop their talents, broaden their interests, and have satisfying emotional and social contacts. They can benefit from work on the school paper and annual, interscholastic and intramural sports, subject-matter clubs (e.g., the Spanish Club), scouts, and similar activities.

TRANSPORTATION, FACILITIES, AND SAFETY

Transportation, facilities, and safety are not particular problems with the gifted/talented. They can usually travel independently and gain access to conventional facilities. They can benefit from the usual safety precautions.

Summary

IDENTIFYING AND PLANNING FOR GIFTED AND TALENTED PUPILS

Normal Intellectual Behavior
Intelligence is central to our learning and thinking. Beyond daily survival, high intelligence, coupled with special talents, makes possible original creative activity and superb achievement.

Gifts and Talents
Gifted and talented pupils are so far above average pupils their same chronological ages on one or more characteristics important to learning and cultural tasks that they do not attain what they could, what they are able to attain, when they receive the same instruction as

pupils who are closer to average on that characteristic. Our responsibility is to find gifted and talented pupils whose special capabilities need to be developed. To do so, we use public awareness campaigns, screening for precocity and superior performance, and referral of possibly gifted and talented pupils for further study. A good endowment and a stimulating environment are both necessary sources of gifts and talents. Neither alone is a sufficient condition. In diagnosis or classification we are concerned about types and degrees of gifts and talents and particular groups that may have special problems. Types of gifts and talents include the academically talented, the artistically talented, the socially talented, and the physically talented. Degrees include the extremely gifted/talented and the moderately gifted/talented. Particular groups that may have special problems are the culturally different gifted/talented, the female gifted/talented, and the handicapped gifted/talented.

Gifted and talented pupils are generally precocious and superior in physical, speech and language, social, emotional, and vocational characteristics. Also, they excel in learning and problem solving, creative thinking, critical thinking, and academic achievement. However, there is a dark side. Their uniqueness can lead to isolation and loneliness. The time and effort required to develop great gifts and talents can also lead to isolation and loneliness as well as deprivation and underachievement in areas not being developed to such a high level.

Impact of Gifts and Talents on Pupils' Characteristics

We have no legal requirements for accountability in supplying adequate programs for the gifted and talented. However, their citizenship makes them eligible, and it is reasonable to expect that the precedents and rationales used in ensuring handicapped pupils' rights and protections could be applied to ensure each gifted/talented pupil's receiving a free appropriate public education and an equal educational opportunity. Meanwhile, beyond legal responsibility, we do have both a professional responsibility and a moral responsibility to supply adequate programs to gifted/talented pupils and to protect them from error and abuse.

Accountability

NONDISCRIMINATORY TESTING OF GIFTED/TALENTED PUPILS

The danger in testing gifted/talented pupils is not the same as the danger in testing the handicapped (i.e., the handicap can interfere with test performance so much that the test becomes another

Problems in Testing Gifted/Talented Pupils

measure of the handicap). Rather, the danger is that the special problems of particular groups — the culturally different, the female, the handicapped, the highly artistic, and the highly creative — can also interfere with their test performance and thus keep them from expressing the full extent of their gifts and talents.

Procedures for Testing Gifted/Talented Pupils

We use conventional procedures for collecting information needed to plan for gifted/talented pupils, always giving due attention to the special problems in testing. In addition, auditions with experts are crucial when we are dealing with pupils who have special talents.

INDIVIDUALIZING INSTRUCTION FOR GIFTED/TALENTED PUPILS

Special Education

We can expect gifted/talented pupils to master all of the *instructional objectives* that other pupils master. In addition, we can expect them to go on to more advanced objectives pertaining to the structure of knowledge, the principles and abstract concepts in a field, and their applications and to master objectives for such processes as creativity and evaluative thinking. Considering *instructional schedules*, gifted/talented pupils can master objectives more quickly than other pupils can, and they should be allowed to do so. Then they should be allowed to turn to other objectives on the same difficulty level (enrichment) or to other objectives on a more difficult level (acceleration). We use the same range of *instructional methods* with gifted/talented pupils that we do with other pupils. However, we generally place more emphasis on independent work and problem solving. They also use the same *instructional media* as other pupils; however, they just use more complex media and more of them — more complex equipment, more extensive libraries, and so on. Beyond the same *instructional settings* used with all pupils, gifted/talented pupils need access to appropriate depositories of media and equipment and to appropriate space for independent work. Also, their teachers need to be capable of high attainment themselves and to have the security, flexibility, and independence of mind needed to work with other outstanding talents. In addition, the extremely gifted/talented need special tutors and coaches.

Related Services

Unless they also have handicaps, gifted/talented pupils do not need special medical services or the various therapies. They may, however, need psychological help, vocational counseling, and family information and counseling.

PLACING GIFTED/TALENTED PUPILS

The most often considered placement options for the gifted/talented are acceleration, ability grouping, itinerant services, and special tutoring. The task is to find the placement where the pupils can get the instruction and stimulation necessary to develop their gifts and talents and at the same time get experiences which are helpful, not harmful, to their social and emotional well-being.

Placement Options

Extracurricular activities are a valuable avenue for gifted/talented pupils to develop their talents, broaden their interests, and have satisfying emotional and social contacts. They can benefit from a wide range of activities.

Extracurricular Activities

Transportation, facilities, and safety are not particular problems for gifted/talented pupils.

Transportation, Facilities, and Safety

TOPICS

Identifying and planning for mentally retarded pupils

NORMAL INTELLECTUAL BEHAVIOR

Normal intellectual development
Intelligence and the cultural tasks

MENTAL RETARDATION

Legal definition and prevalence
Finding mentally retarded pupils
Diagnosis: Classification according to cause of mental
     retardation
Diagnosis: Classification by degree of mental retardation

**IMPACT OF MENTAL RETARDATION ON PUPILS'
CHARACTERISTICS**

Introduction
Physical characteristics
Language
Social/emotional characteristics
Intellectual characteristics
Academic achievement
Vocational and civic adjustment

Special Needs of Mentally Retarded Pupils

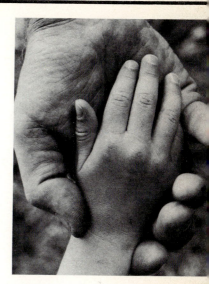

ACCOUNTABILITY

    Identifying and planning for mentally retarded pupils

    Observing the procedural safeguards for mentally retarded pupils

Nondiscriminatory testing of mentally retarded pupils

PROBLEMS IN TESTING MENTALLY RETARDED PUPILS

PROCEDURES FOR TESTING MENTALLY RETARDED PUPILS

Individualizing instruction for mentally retarded pupils

SPECIAL EDUCATION

    Instructional objectives

    Instructional schedules

    Instructional procedures

    Instructional settings

RELATED SERVICES

    Medical services

    Speech/language therapy

Psychological services
Vocational rehabilitation services
Family information and counseling
Physical therapy
Occupational therapy

Placing mentally retarded pupils in the least restrictive environment

PLACEMENT OPTIONS

EXTRACURRICULAR ACTIVITIES

TRANSPORTATION AND FACILITIES

SAFETY

Identifying and planning for mentally retarded pupils

Mentally retarded pupils are below average in intelligence. Some mentally retarded pupils can learn to function independently with some degree of success, given appropriate training and support. More extensively retarded youngsters have more limited prognoses. Yet their functioning can be improved. Our responsibility is to identify mentally retarded youngsters and to marshall all the entitlements and protections they are guaranteed by law. Our first task in this endeavor is to conduct the Child-Find to identify protected pupils and to plan the individual education program, both within the context of the procedural safeguards. As a background, we need to understand normal intellectual behavior, how it comes to be impaired, and the ways these impairments affect pupils' characteristics.

NORMAL INTELLECTUAL BEHAVIOR

We considered milestones in normal development of cognitive skills in Chapter 8 (see especially Table 8.1). Those growth trends, of course, apply also to our understanding of the mentally retarded, who are at the opposite end from the gifted on the distribution of intelligence. Again, intellectual development follows an orderly sequence, with particular skills emerging at approximate ages. Further, intellectual behavior becomes increasingly complex, with more mature intellectual skills being built on simpler ones.

Normal Intellectual Development

As we considered in our discussion of gifted and talented pupils, intelligence is central to learning and performing the cultural tasks. To review: Intelligence determines whether we can acquire the behavior in the cultural tasks and how quickly we can size up situations and consequently how well we can adjust to situations involved in the cultural tasks. Review the cultural tasks in Table 1.1 and consider again how important intelligence is from the very beginning in learning and performing tasks such as those. And, of course, since later tasks are built on earlier ones, the contributions of intelligence to learning and performing the tasks get compounded as the youngster approaches more complex tasks.

Intelligence and the Cultural Tasks

MENTAL RETARDATION

Various problems can cause a youngster's intellectual development to deviate from the sequence of normal intellectual development. This disruption becomes a handicap when it is severe enough to interfere

Legal Definition and Prevalence

with his or her learning and performing the cultural tasks. Over time, we have had various definitions of mental retardation. In later years the American Association on Mental Deficiency has taken the lead in formulating definitions. In current definitions essentially three things are stressed: intelligence level, adaptive behavior,* and presence during the developmental period (i.e., before chronological age eighteen — the approximate age most individuals reach maturity). The federal definition in PL 94-142 closely parallels the AAMD definition: "Mental retardation is significantly subaverage general intellectual functioning existing concurrently with deficits in adaptive behavior and manifested during the developmental period, which adversely affects a child's educational performance" (PL 94-142, *Regulations*, 1977, Sec. 121a.5).

As Fig. 1.1 showed, estimates about how many mentally retarded people there are vary from about 1.3% to 2.4%. As of the late 1970s, about 1.8% were being served.

Finding Mentally Retarded Pupils

The more seriously mentally retarded pupils are obvious. Pupils who are less retarded are harder to spot. Pupils with other problems, such as serious emotional disturbance, and pupils from disadvantaged backgrounds are sometimes misdiagnosed as mentally retarded when they really are not.

Awareness campaigns take two directions. One direction is to alert people to true cases of mental retardation so that treatment can begin early and problems prevented or made less severe. As an example, consider phenylketonuria (PKU), a genetic disorder in which a liver enzyme, phenylalanine hydroxylase, is absent. Phenylalanine hydroxylase metabolizes phenylalanine. When this metabolism breaks down, there is an excessive buildup of phenylalanine, and as a consequence brain structure and function suffer. Severe mental retardation usually results. This cycle can be broken by controlling the infant's diet to reduce the intake of phenylalanine — at least until his or her brain reaches a fairly mature level of development.

The other direction of awareness campaigns is to alert people about youngsters who are in bleak environments — physically, socially, or emotionally — which can interfere with their developing the intellectual potential they have. Again, early detection is important so that treatment and stimulation can counteract these depressing circumstances.

Screening is directed to two problems — delayed development and inferior performance — in relation to other youngsters of a given chronological age. To expand on this idea, note that each chapter in

---

* *Adaptive behavior* and *cultural tasks* are synonyms.

Part II of this book has a set of milestones — those for speech/language, physical function, and so on. Mentally retarded pupils are delayed in reaching such milestones. That is, they usually attain such milestones at later chronological ages than normal pupils do. Part of the same picture is that at any particular age, mentally retarded pupils are usually at lower (inferior) levels on such characteristics. *Examples* of signs are the following:

☐ Slowness and difficulty in developing such self-help skills as dressing oneself.

☐ Slowness and difficulty in walking, talking, language development, and physical development.

☐ Slowness and difficulty in learning play skills and other social skills.

☐ Slowness and difficulty in learning reading, arithmetic, and other topics taught in school.

We have a number of tests and other instruments for screening, e.g., the AAMD scales for assessing adaptive behavior. The Public School Version samples many detailed activities in *independent functioning* (eating, dressing, etc.), *physical development* (vision, hearing, movement), *economic activity* (money handling, budgeting, shopping), *language development* (expression through writing speech, etc., comprehension through reading), *numbers and time*, *vocational activity* (job performance, work habits), *self-direction* (initiative, perseverance, leisure skills), *responsibility* (personal and general), and *socialization* (awareness and social maturity) (Lambert *et al.*, 1975).

Referral for more intensive study follows when our screening indicates that a pupil may be retarded. The essential task is to determine whether the pupil is truly retarded or only spuriously retarded, i.e., whether some outside circumstance is artificially depressing his or her performance. Physicians search for neurological, metabolic, or other physical or sensory disorders which might be causing problems and determine whether these can be treated. School psychologists assess intellectual abilities and adaptive behavior. Teachers inventory the youngster's levels of academic achievement in relation to levels attained by others his or her chronological age. Social workers are concerned with family pathology which might interfere with the youngster's functioning.

Discussions of causes of mental retardation usually focus on medical and psychiatric conditions (e.g., Carter, 1978). The American Association on Mental Deficiency has devoted a great deal of attention to

Diagnosis: Classification According to Cause of Mental Retardation

etiology. In the *Manual on Classification and Terminology*,* the AAMD uses seven categories of causes — infections and intoxications, trauma and physical agents, metabolism or nutrition, gross brain disease, unknown prenatal influence, chromosomal abnormality, and gestational disorders. It also uses retardation resulting from psychiatric disorder, environmental influence, and sensory defects — all three grouped herein under the heading pseudoretardation.

Infections and intoxications

Infections result from invasions by viruses, bacteria, parasites, protozoa, or fungi. They attack nervous tissue and destroy it. This destruction can lead to mental retardation and other dire conditions. Some infections occur prenatally. The mother is the host, and the foreign bodies travel through the placenta to infect the fetus. Rubella infection during the first three months of pregnancy is a specially severe problem. Some infections occur postnatally. The foreign bodies move from the initial site in the body to the brain and cause destruction. This infection of the brain is called encephalitis. Postinfectious encephalitis may follow measles, mumps, varicella, and sometimes influenza or a severe cold.

Intoxications can cause cerebral damage either prenatally or postnatally. The mother's having toxemia during pregnancy, taking drugs or poisons, or being exposed to industrial chemicals can lead to problems by transmission through the placenta to the fetal tissue — especially very early in pregnancy. Postnatally, lead or other heavy metals, carbon monoxide, drugs, or poisons can be toxic to the child and lead to brain pathology. Formerly, so many babies were poisoned by licking lead-based paints or lead toys, e.g., toy soldiers, that now lead is prohibited in just about everything a baby or young child can get to.

Traumas or physical agents

Damage to the brain through trauma can happen before, during, or after birth. It can result from mechanical injuries which tear tissue or cause blood accumulations which in turn cause tearing. For example, a severe blow on the head could cause such injuries.

Brain damage also can result from too long oxygen deprivation (anoxia), which in turn causes the tissue to die. Interruption of the mother's oxygen intake, excessive sedation to reduce labor pains, or suffocation through strangling are examples of problems leading to anoxia.

Formerly, irradiation through X-raying the mother — especially during the early stages of pregnancy — caused a lot of grief. X-ray is used very sparingly now with everyone — especially so with pregnant

---

* The information in this section is based mainly on Grossman (in press).

women. If diagnostic X-rays absolutely must be done for, say, a broken leg, lead shields and other protective devices are used extensively.

Metabolism is the process whereby food is converted in very complex ways to chemicals which enable the bodily systems — including the central nervous system — to survive and function. Difficulties arise when diseases, genetic disorders, or other malfunctions interfere with the youngster's metabolizing fats, carbohydrates, proteins, or minerals. One frequently occurring example is hypoglycemia, or extremely low blood sugar. The result is reduced physical energy and activity, a low level of mental functioning, and emotional depression often appearing in the guise of apathy or low responsiveness.

Metabolism or nutrition

Dysfunction of the thyroid, pituitary, and other endocrine glands can lead to metabolic problems, which in turn may cause disorders in development and inadequate functioning of the brain. As an example, consider cretinism, which is caused by a severe undersecretion of the thyroid gland very early in the infant's development. The result is very delayed development — including delayed intellectual development. Treatment with the thyroid hormone, thyroxin, can prevent the effects of cretinism if that treatment begins early enough.

Slow development and mental retardation also result from nutritional problems caused by dietary imbalances which exist over a considerable period. These dietary imbalances are caused by such conditions as the meal/meat/molasses diets or other inadequate diets that some people subsist on, idiosyncratic diets, e.g., colas and cookies, and infestation with parasites, e.g., hookworms.

A number of conditions, many of them hereditary, can lead to brain pathology, which in turn can lead to mental retardation and other problems. The neurocutaneous dysplasias are usually hereditary, or at least congenital, conditions. There are combined lesions and tumors in the skin, the nervous system, and the visceral organs. Neurofibromatosis and tuberous sclerosis are two conditions in this category.

Gross brain disease

Tumors also occur as new growths within the skull. As tumor growth continues, brain tissue is destroyed.

Sometimes there are congenital lesions of the blood vessels in the brain. Disruption of blood flow, of course, can lead to destruction of brain tissue — through either anoxia or mechanical damage.

Degeneration sometimes occurs in the white matter in the central nervous system or in specific nerve fibers or nerve groups. For instance, in Huntington's chorea, an inherited disorder, emotional disturbance and epileptic seizures occur. At the same time, there is either choreiform movement — involuntary, ticlike circular movements — or muscular rigidity, with no involuntary movements. As degeneration continues, these symptoms get worse until death occurs.

Unknown prenatal influence

Various malformations of the brain and skull, as well as other congenital defects, may lead to mental retardation, cerebral palsy, epilepsy, and related problems. These conditions begin at or before birth, but often no cause can be determined. Microcephaly and hydrocephaly* are frequently discussed conditions.

Microcephaly literally means "small head." The space within the skull is abnormally small. The ears are quite large, and the nose is also large and without a bridge, joining the brow directly. At the same time, the brow is sharply sloping and abnormally furrowed and wrinkled.

Hydrocephaly literally means "water head." There is an excess of cerebral-spinal fluid within the brain's cavities or within the skull but outside of the brain. The pressure may cause the skull to enlarge. Unless hydrocephaly is treated promptly, the fluid's pressure may destroy brain tissue.

Chromosomal abnormality

Sometimes there may be too many chromosomes, malformations in their structures, or both too many chromosomes and these malformed. These chromosomal abnormalities result from many problems, e.g., radiation, drugs and other chemicals, viruses, and gametes from aged parents. These chromosomal abnormalities lead to a number of conditions. Down's syndrome is probably the most frequently occurring. In addition to mental retardation, youngsters with Down's syndrome show particular physical characteristics: a round *head*; *eyes* characterized by speckling of the iris, an upward and outward slant, and inner epicanthal folds; a thick, furrowed *tongue*; markedly low muscle tone in the *arms* and *legs*; short in-curved *little fingers*; and an extraordinarily wide space between the *first and second toes*.

Gestational disorders

Gestation is the process of development to maturity within the womb. The *premature* infant is born before this development is complete — as defined by size at birth (five pounds eight ounces or less) or development time (thirty-seven weeks from the first day of the last menstrual period). The youngster's problems, if any, depend on the structures which did not develop sufficiently. For example, strabismus may occur if the eye muscles did not develop sufficiently. Mental retardation may occur if the brain did not develop sufficiently or if other bodily systems which influence brain function did not develop and so damaged the

---

* Sometimes hydrocephaly occurs without any discernable cause. Other times, however, it is a part of the complex of characteristics in spina bifida.

brain. For example, if the lungs did not operate correctly, oxygen deprivation may occur and brain damage may follow.

The *postmature* infant is one born a week or more after prenatal development is complete. The fetus keeps developing and thus grows larger and more complex. At least two problems may occur if the mother's physiology and anatomy cannot cope with this greater maturity. The fetus may not get enough oxygen and nutrition to sustain his or her large size and more mature development. The largeness may lead to a longer and more difficult birth, with brain injury from anoxia or traumatic injury more likely.

The AAMD has three categories that lead to functional retardation: *retardation following psychiatric disorders, retardation caused by environmental influences,* and *retardation caused by one or more sensory defects, e.g., deafness or blindness/deafness.* Functional retardation means that the emotional disturbance, the environmental deprivation, or the sensory deprivation interferes with the youngster's intellectual behavior or adaptive behavior so much that — whatever the intellectual potential — he or she may appear to be retarded and indeed may actually operate at a retarded level. However, most people believe that the youngster's intellectual functioning would improve if the severe emotional problem, environmental problem, or sensory problem were alleviated or compensated for. Intelligence tests used with such youngsters become another measure of the handicap. Thus they are misused if their results serve as a basis for diagnosing such youngsters as mentally retarded. Similarly, labels are misapplied if they are given to such youngsters. In short, this functional retardation is pseudoretardation — false retardation.

Pseudoretardation

The AAMD has identified degrees of mental retardation; in declining order, these are mild, moderate, severe, and profound. These categories are defined in terms of IQ levels and general levels of adaptive behavior. These criteria are applied with some clinical judgment. That is, a youngster's IQ level could place him or her above a category, but if his or her adaptive behavior were low, he or she might be placed in the category. The material below presents the IQ limits used in the AAMD *Manual on Terminology and Classification* (in press). If the 1979 decision in *Larry P. v. Riles* is upheld in appeal and then extended to states beyond California, we could see marked changes in these classifications by degrees of retardation.

Diagnosis: Classification by Degree of Mental Retardation

Mildly retarded pupils' IQ's fall within the 50–70 range. In adaptive behavior these pupils can acquire some academic material, take care of their personal needs, and live independently as adults.

The mildly retarded

Andrew is a ten-year-old child who has been enrolled in an EMR* program for the past two years. Andrew comes from a family of five children who live in a five-room apartment in one of the lower socioeconomic areas of a large midwestern city. His parents both have limited educational backgrounds — his mother dropped out of school at the end of eighth grade after having repeated several grades; his father completed a little over nine years of formal education.

As a preschooler, Andrew seemed normal in all regards. There were no complications when he was born and his medical history was quite ordinary, with no serious illnesses or accidents. He got along well with other children his age, and he learned to sit, stand, walk, and talk at approximately the ages considered normal. Physically, Andrew was a very attractive child with excellent coordination, making him quite popular with his age peers because he excelled in most sports.

When Andrew was in the first grade it became obvious that he had academic problems. He was unable to keep up with his classmates, particularly in reading. At the end of the year his teacher recommended that Andrew be retained in the first grade, and he was. At the end of his second year in the first grade, he still had educational deficits, but the staff at Andrew's school decided to give him a "social promotion."

Andrew's academic problems were accentuated in the second grade, however, and other students occasionally ridiculed him for his poor academic performance. Andrew began to get in fights. The teacher felt that the fighting was a result of the frustration Andrew was feeling because of his failure and the ridicule. Toward the end of the second grade the teacher conferred with the principal of the school and indicated that she thought Andrew might be better off in an EMR program where there would be less pressure and more individualized attention.... [Among his other characteristics, Andrew's Stanford Binet IQ was 65. Appropriate placement procedures were used, and he was assigned to a class for the educable mentally retarded.] (MacMillan, 1977, pp. 47–48)

The moderately retarded

Moderately retarded youngsters' IQ's are within the 35–49 range. Their adaptive behavior is more limited to rudimentary literacy materials, some ability to take care of their personal needs, simple occupational skills, and semidependent or dependent status as adults.

---

* Educable mentally retarded.

Jonathan is an eleven-year-old child enrolled in a TMR* program in the southeastern part of the country. He comes from a family of two children; his sister is thirteen years older than he is and is married with one child of her own. Jonathan's mother finished high school; his father completed four years of college and is presently employed as an editor for a large newspaper. The family lives in an eight-room house in a middle-class neighborhood.

Soon after he was born, it was apparent that Jonathan suffered from what is known as Down's syndrome (previously it was often called "mongolism"). His skin was quite dry, his eyelids had the characteristic epicanthic folds, and he possessed other diagnostic signs of Down's syndrome. Before he was released from the hospital his parents were told of his condition and that he was mentally retarded.

Jonathan was slow in developing in almost all areas — walking, toilet training, speaking. His parents enrolled him in a preschool program for mentally retarded children when he was three. When it was time for him to enroll in the public schools Jonathan was evaluated and placed immediately in the special program for TMR youngsters, where he has been ever since. Jonathan has been given intelligence tests twice since he entered school; in both instances he achieved an IQ of 40. Evaluation of his social development shows him to be functioning at the level of a normal child half his age.

Jonathan exhibits a pleasant disposition and seems to enjoy school and his classmates. After school and on the weekends he is inclined to stay home, watching TV or playing in his back yard. Other children in the neighborhood are cordial to Jonathan when they see him outside but they do not seek him out to play with him. His mother reports that parents of much younger children become quite anxious if Jonathan plays with them, so she has discouraged Jonathan from playing with these children. (MacMillan, 1977, p. 48)

Severely retarded individual's IQ's are within the 20–34 range. Their adaptive behavior is quite limited, e.g., to rather basic self-care and rudimentary communication. They often have more than one handicap and remain dependent as adults.

Profoundly retarded individual's IQ's fall below 20. In adaptive behavior they are limited almost to rudimentary communication and perhaps simple self-help tasks. They remain dependent as adults. Many profoundly retarded individuals have other handicaps, such as cerebral palsy, epilepsy, visual impairments, hearing impairments,

Severely/profoundly retarded

---

* Trainable mentally retarded.

and fragile health. They may require total life-support systems, e.g., feeding, oxygen, and other services.

Albert is a twenty-six year-old youngster who lives in a large state institution for the mentally retarded, where he has been since he was two. Albert is the first child in a family of three children. His parents both hold graduate degrees — the mother, an M.A. degree in education and the father, a Ph.D. in engineering. The family lives about forty-five miles from the institution where Albert lives; they visit Albert on an average of one day a month and take him home for holidays.

Albert's physicians are not sure of the exact cause of his mental retardation. However, during the first three months of her pregnancy, his mother was exposed to rubella (measles); in addition, during the birth process Albert suffered from a lack of oxygen for about one-half hour.

Within the first two years of his life it became apparent that there was something wrong with Albert. He did not even attempt sitting, walking, and other activities usually developed by the age of two. In addition, he suffered from seizures and was diagnosed as cerebral-palsied.

At the age of two Albert was placed in the state institution for the mentally retarded on the recommendation of the family physician. Since the family lived in a small town where there were no medical services or educational programs for the mentally retarded, and since another child had been born into the family, it was thought that Albert might detract from the attention needed by the baby and that he could be better cared for in the institution than at home.

Albert's development has progressed very slowly since that time. Even now his vocabulary consists of no more than thirty words and he seldom speaks in phrases, let alone sentences. His utterances consist of one- or two-word sentences accompanied by gestures. He was not toilet-trained until two years ago and then only by means of an elaborate behavior-shaping project conducted by faculty members from a nearby university. Dressing remains a problem for him, since the cerebral palsy interferes with the motor coordination he needs to tie shoes, button shirts, and put on a belt. Ward attendants must assist Albert in dressing and usually help him when he is eating. His seizures have been controlled through medication, but his frequent respiratory problems have necessitated hospitalization three times during the past year.

Albert appears to be comfortable in the institution. In fact, his parents noticed that Albert was very anxious when he was at home for a recent holiday.... [P]lacing Albert in a foster care home off the grounds [was considered] but decided against ... due to his medical problems and to his limited personal independence. (Mac-Millan, 1977, pp. 50–51)

IMPACT OF MENTAL RETARDATION ON PUPILS' CHARACTERISTICS*

Introduction

Again, the ability to learn, remember, and solve problems is crucial to survival in our culture. The fact that a pupil cannot be classified as mentally retarded unless he or she has corresponding retardation in performing the cultural tasks (termed adaptive behavior) attests to how crucial intelligence is to surviving in today's world. As our culture becomes more complex and more dependent on the literacy skills, the problems caused by mental retardation increase. And as always, the earlier the insult that interrupts normal intellectual development occurs, the more severe the impact. This snowballing of handicaps happens because later intellectual skills and later cultural tasks are built on earlier ones, and disruptions spill over into all of the youngster's characteristics.

Physical Characteristics

As a group, *mildly retarded* pupils are slightly slower developing and smaller physically than are more intelligent pupils their chronological ages. They have lower proficiency on tests of motor skills. They have considerable difficulty with sports and games that require developing strategies and making decisions as problems arise.

Moderately retarded pupils show more marked physical differences than more intelligent pupils their chronological ages. They are much slower in developing walking, hand use, etc. They are smaller, sometimes poorly proportioned, and sometimes quite underweight or quite overweight. They quite often have neurological problems and malformations such as cleft palate/cleft lip. Their motor proficiency is quite inferior, and their sports and games skills are very limited.

Severely and *profoundly retarded* youngsters are much more limited physically than more intelligent pupils their chronological ages. They are smaller, and their physical function is quite poor. They are often cerebral palsied, have epileptic seizures, and suffer sensory defects. Some have fragile health. Some are able to walk and to use their hands and arms. Others are nonambulatory, have little arm/hand use, and have poor head balance.

Language

Mildly and *moderately retarded* pupils show delayed language development compared to more intelligent pupils the same chrono-

---

* Mentally retarded pupils' characteristics have been extensively reviewed, e.g., Balthazar and Stevens (1975), Berry (1976), Blake (1976), Cobb (1972), Gold (1973), Ingalls (1978), Koch and Dobson (1976), MacMillan (1977), Moore and Moore (1977), Robinson and Robinson (1976). Information in this section is based on material in sources such as these.

logical ages. They are older before they can understand and produce particular sounds, particular words, and particular syntactic structures. In addition, they show more articulation problems, i.e., they more frequently mispronounce and omit sounds. They have smaller vocabularies. Also, they make more syntactic errors.

Severely/profoundly retarded youngsters show much more rudimentary language. Some can use a few words and simple sentences — capabilities which develop late. Others are mute and apparently understand very little that is said to them.

Social/emotional Characteristics

One question is: Do *mildly retarded* pupils show a particular personality pattern that marks them as a group? The answer is no. They show the same range of personal characteristics as other people do. However, as a general rule, they do show more emotional disturbances — more anxiety and more difficulty controlling anger. Such a situation is understandable when we consider the number of problems they face and the limited tools they have to solve those problems. Also, they have more trouble in social situations. They have fewer skills to handle social interactions. They are more often ignored in social situations or actively rejected.

Moderately retarded pupils show a general pattern of emotional and social immaturity. They can operate in groups in simple activities for short periods. Their emotional control is limited, and they may cry or have anger outbursts at simple frustration.

Severely/profoundly retarded youngsters show little social/emotional response. They tend to be apathetic or locked within their own worlds.

Intellectual Characteristics

When we look at intellectual characteristics and academic characteristics, we compare retarded pupils with more intelligent pupils who have the same *chronological* ages. We also compare them with more intelligent pupils who have the same *mental* ages.

Learning and problem solving

The way *mildly retarded* pupils learn has been studied very extensively. Generally, they learn at slower rates and to lower levels when they are compared with more intelligent pupils who have the same *chronological* ages. They also less adequately remember and transfer what they have learned. On the other hand, they respond about the same in learning, remembering, and transferring when they are compared with more intelligent pupils who have the same *mental* ages.

Strategies are conditions that influence how quickly and how well we learn and then remember and transfer what we learned. For example, we memorize material more quickly if we can make it more meaningful by using a principle or what is called a verbal mediator. For example, you can remember this string — 1248163264 — much faster if you use the principle of "double each digit to get the next one" rather than just try to remember an unrelated string. There are many, many such strategies for helping us memorize and for helping us learn discriminations and concepts as well as remember and transfer them. Again, there is extensive information about how well *mildly retarded* pupils can use such strategies. In sum, they can use the strategies about as well as brighter pupils can.*

Creativity and problem solving are another concern. When they are compared to more intelligent pupils who are *chronologically* the same age, mildly retarded pupils are less creative and solve problems less well. Compared to more intelligent pupils who have the same *mental ages*, mildly retarded pupils respond about as adequately to creativity and problem-solving tasks — at least at the younger mental ages.

We do not have such extensive information about the ways *moderately retarded* youngsters and *severely/profoundly retarded* pupils learn and solve problems. However, general observation reveals that they are quite limited in these respects.

The way retarded youngsters' mental ages develop is especially crucial because this development strongly influences how well they can master increasingly difficult tasks as they grow older chronologically. Figure 9.1 shows mental age growth trends for individuals at different levels. The straight broken line on the left shows normal intellectual development — a year's growth in MA for a year's growth in CA. The curves show development attained by individuals with varying degrees of retardation. The numbers within the graph show the numbers of individuals the point is based on. Note that all stay at varying levels below normal. None get above about 132 months (i.e., eleven years) mental age. The borderline retarded continue to show mental growth until about CA 20 and then level off; the mildly retarded, until about CA 15; the moderately retarded, until about CA 12; the severely retarded, until about CA 10; and the profoundly retarded, until about CA 3.

Intellectual growth

Retarded pupils learn academic material more slowly and achieve at lower levels than do pupils who have the same *chronological ages*.

Academic Achievement

---

* Stated another way, this is the matter of the aptitude × treatment interaction. Review the discussion in Chapter 2. In sum, very few consistent interactions of intelligence levels and treatments have been demonstrated, e.g., Blake (1976), Cronbach and Snow (1977), Ysseldvke and Salvia (1974).

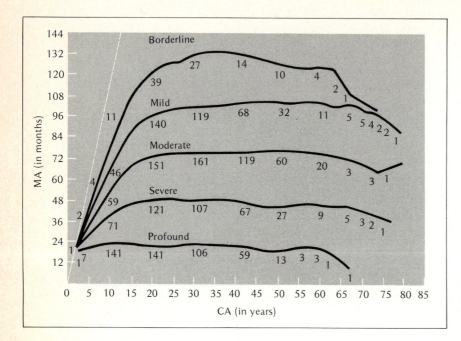

Fig. 9.1
Mental age growth curves for retarded individuals to CA 85. (Reprinted by permission from Fisher and Zeaman, 1970, p. 163.)

They can achieve at the same levels — at least in the literacy skills and math — as brighter pupils who have the same *mental ages.* This similarity between retarded and brighter youngsters of the same *mental ages* happens at the younger mental ages. Retarded pupils fall behind at the older mental ages.

As Fig. 9.1 showed, retarded pupils have slower rates of mental growth. As a result, they are ready for school learning much later than normal pupils are. They master academic materials such as reading and arithmetic much more slowly. They reach a ceiling in the difficulty of material they can master. The limits expected for *mildly retarded* pupils are about fifth to sixth grade level; for *moderately retarded* pupils, about third grade level; for *severely/profoundly retarded* youngsters, the preschool level — other things being equal. These expected limits correspond to the leveling off of mental age growth which we considered above.

Vocational and Civic Adjustment

As a group, *mildly retarded* adults can perform satisfactorily in unskilled and semiskilled jobs. They can participate satisfactorily in community life, and many do. However, more mildly retarded adults than normal adults are unemployed, live as welfare recipients, and have difficulty with law enforcement agencies.

Moderately retarded adults are more limited. They may hold unskilled jobs under close supervision. Or, they may be limited to sheltered workshops, where they do protected work. Similarly, moderately retarded adults have a limited outlook for living independently in the community.

Severely/profoundly retarded youngsters cannot learn or perform jobs — even in sheltered workshops. Nor can they live independently in the community. They need close supervision and care.

ACCOUNTABILITY

Again, and especially with mentally retarded pupils, accountability is a prime consideration. Monitoring covers procedures for identifying and classifying pupils as mentally retarded, developing their individual education programs, and observing the procedural safeguards which protect them from error.

The law requires active searches for mentally retarded pupils entitled to a free appropriate public education. These active searches include procedures for public awareness campaigns focused on mental retardation, screening pupils for signs of mental retardation, and referring for further study pupils who show suspicious signs. The documentation here includes procedures used in the searches and results of the searches as shown by the numbers of pupils who are located and given access to services.

Identifying and Planning for Mentally Retarded Pupils

Documenting the Child-Find

The individual education program is done for every mentally retarded pupil who qualifies for protection and service under the law. It includes, of course, an extensive evaluation of the pupil's present performance levels on all important characteristics, statements about goals and objectives those present performance levels suggest, procedures for reaching those goals and objectives, the least restrictive placement appropriate for delivering instruction to attain those goals and objectives, and schedules for periodically evaluating the pupil's progress toward reaching the goals and objectives. The mentally retarded pupil's advocates (parents or surrogates) and their consultants join the school team — teachers, therapists, psychologists, social workers — as well as physicians, if appropriate, to develop the pupil's IEP and to revise it at appropriate times.

Developing the IEP

As with other handicapped pupils, mentally retarded pupils' civil rights are paramount. We observe the guarantees for advocate participation, due process, equal protection, periodic reevaluation, and confidentiality.

Observing the Procedural Safeguards for Mentally Retarded Pupils

Advocate participation   Advocates for the mentally retarded pupil are critical to getting him or her the best services and appropriate protection. Their role is to see that the pupil's rights are not violated at any point in the process of testing, planning, teaching/treatment, placement in the least restrictive environment, and periodic evaluation of progress with consequent revision.

The advocates may have, and often need, consultants who are versed in the law as well as the nature of mental retardation and its treatment. Although all advocates can use such consultants, they are especially important for unlettered parents — whom we sometimes find with the mentally retarded. These unlettered parents may not realize what the pupil's rights and possibilities are, or they may be intimidated more easily and thus not be as assertive as they should be in attaining the pupil's various entitlements.

Due process   Advocates and their consultants may not agree with recommendations for the pupil — especially the severely/profoundly retarded pupil. If so, they have the right to appeal through the succeeding administrative levels of the school systems and the succeeding jurisdictional levels of the federal courts. Schools are required to inform the advocates and consultants about these due process rights for the mentally retarded.

Equal protection   The equal protection requirement guarantees that every pupil is subject to the same criteria, procedures, and policies regardless of his or her other characteristics. This means that every mentally retarded pupil, regardless of the severity of his or her problems, must be admitted to public education and placed in the least restrictive environment possible. Further, such pupils must receive nondiscriminatory testing procedures and be classified correctly.

Periodic reevaluation   The mentally retarded pupil is reevaluated at frequent intervals. There are essentially two purposes: to search for any errors that may have happened previously and to assess the pupil's progress toward the goals and objectives. Then the mentally retarded pupil's instructional program, placement, and related services are changed in any way that the evaluation results indicate they should be changed.

Confidentiality   All information about mentally retarded pupils and their families is strictly confidential. This means that test information, educational and therapeutic reports, bases for placement, and similar information are available to the pupil's advocates and only those school personnel who have a need to know. Only the advocates can release information. Further, they can require that all erroneous or nonrelevant information be purged from the mentally retarded pupil's file and that all information but vital statistics be destroyed after the mentally retarded pupil reaches the end of his or her schooling.

Nondiscriminatory testing of mentally retarded pupils

Our second task, nondiscriminatory testing, is an integral component of the services we deliver to mentally retarded pupils. Accurate and valid information is our basis for planning the youngster's educational and therapeutic programs, in evaluating the youngster's progress in those programs, and in revising them in a way to further his or her growth.

PROBLEMS IN TESTING MENTALLY RETARDED PUPILS

We have examined the problem of pseudoretardation. In sum, intellectual behavior, or at least intelligence test performance, is extremely sensitive to interference by other problems. Time and again, we have seen, or will see, that some pupils do not show how capable they are on tests because we cannot meet the conditions for norm-referenced testing. These pupils come from different experience backgrounds or different language backgrounds from pupils the test norms are based on. Or, they have handicaps — physical, visual, hearing, language, social/emotional, or learning-disability problems — which interfere with their performing under the conditions the norm groups did. As a result, the tests are not appropriate, and many pupils are labeled retarded when they really are not retarded. They would not show up as retarded if their other problems were taken care of early enough or if their intellectual abilities were measured in ways that did not penalize them for their problems.

Such pseudoretardation and misclassification are a source of a profound legal and ethical concern (e.g., *Larry P.* v. *Riles* 1979; Sarason and Doris, 1978). They are one reason for the strict code regarding nondiscriminatory testing and for the control of intelligence testing in California and other places. At this point, it is relevant to stress that a pupil must not be classified as mentally retarded until other handicaps and also cultural and language differences are ruled out as sources of his or her low test performance.

This difficulty in measuring intelligence accurately is a reason for requiring adaptive behavior as a joint criterion with intelligence for identifying pupils as mentally retarded. Several tests of adaptive behavior have been developed, but they have the same problems that intelligence tests have. That is, it is also difficult to define adaptive behavior and to measure it reliably and validly, and norms appropriate for all pupils are very difficult to establish (e.g., Coulter and Morrow, 1978; Wallbrown, 1980).

PROCEDURES FOR TESTING MENTALLY RETARDED PUPILS

Information collection is aimed at determining whether the pupil is truly retarded and in deciding how to plan his or her educational program. Emphasis is on the pupil's capability in performing the cultural tasks, e.g., self-help skills, physical skills, personal-social skills, academic skills, and prevocational skills. The information collected pertains to the history of the pupil's development as well as to his or her present performance levels.

The procedures here are the usual ones: interviews, observations, and tests if we can meet the necessary conditions. Observations of the pupil's behavior are recorded on checklists, rating scales, or in anecdotal records. As we have considered previously, rating scales for adaptive behavior have been especially developed for working with the mentally retarded — the AAMD scales for sampling adaptive behavior being an example.

In this process of collecting information our strict observation of the procedural safeguards is essential so that we can prevent the many serious errors and abuses which have occurred in the past. We must guarantee the pupil and his or her advocates appropriate participation in decision making, due process, equal protection, periodic reevaluation, and confidentiality. Further, we must use more than one testing procedure, being sure that all are sufficiently reliable and valid and also accurately administered and interpreted by a team of specialists who understand both psychological assessment and mental retardation. Further, we must meet the conditions for criterion- and norm-referenced testing, or we must not use those tests.

Individualizing instruction for mentally retarded pupils

Our third task, individualizing instruction, merits a great deal of attention with the mentally retarded. They need a wide range of special education activities and related services.*

---

* We have many excellent works on procedures for teaching, training, and caring for the mentally retarded: Amary (1975), Blake (1974), Brolin (1976), Burton (1976), Copeland (1976), Deich (1978), Evans and Denney (1974), Ginglend and Carlson (1977), Hannah (1977), Hardy and Cull (1974), Haring and Brown (1976), Frazer and Galka (1979), Galka and Frazer (1979), Humphreys (1979), Kiernan and Woodford (1976), Laus (1977), Lent (1975), Litton (1978), Payne *et al.* (1977), Snell (1978), Sontag (1977), Thompson and Grabowski (1977), Wehman (1977), Wehman and McLaughlin (1980, 1981).

SPECIAL EDUCATION

Several generalizations are important when we consider instruction as it is usually done in the school on the one hand and the intellectual characteristics of mentally retarded pupils on the other hand. These generalizations are that *compared to more intelligent pupils:* mentally retarded pupils are delayed, i.e., they are ready for the objectives at later chronological ages; they learn better at the levels indicated by their mental ages (MAs) than by their chronological ages (CAs); they progress through the objectives at a slower pace; they respond about the same way to learning strategies; they reach the limits of what they can learn sooner; and their adult jobs require less academic knowledge.

Instructional Objectives

One thing that these generalizations mean is that we must select instructional objectives for retarded pupils from among the total body of objectives usually taught in the school. These pupils cannot master all of the objectives that more intelligent pupils do, nor do they need to in view of their potentiality for adult achievement. We make different selections for the mildly retarded, the moderately retarded, and the severely/profoundly retarded. In addition, for each group, we use task analysis to break each objective into its smallest components.

Many retarded pupils can learn some academic materials.

The mildly retarded

For the mildly retarded, we select objectives that will help prepare them to live independently in society. These objectives include objectives for arithmetic, literacy (language, listening, reading, spelling, and writing), social studies (community living), vocational-career education, and health, physical education, and recreation.

Literacy skills are especially crucial. The idea is to teach pupils language and listening, reading, spelling, and writing skills which will enable them to survive, to function successfully, in today's culture — to get along as a family member, consumer, a citizen voting and observing the law, and a worker. This requires listening and reading with some comprehension and then responding critically to the material presented and following directions. It also requires writing legibly with content and structure that communicates (e.g., Kirk *et al.*, 1978).

The moderately retarded

For the moderately retarded, we select objectives that will prepare them to help take care of themselves in a more sheltered environment. These include objectives for self-care (grooming, care of clothes, hygiene), language, speaking, listening, reading for protection (EXIT, GO, STOP, etc.), group living, independent travel if possible, recreation, and skills and habits for working under supervision.

Objectives for self-care are of crucial importance in preparing the moderately retarded pupil to function as independently as possible. They need to learn to eat properly and gracefully, to select their clothes, dress/undress and put up their clothes, to bathe and perform other hygiene tasks, and to engage in recreational activities.

The severely/ profoundly retarded

The stress for the severely/profoundly retarded is on objectives for skills that will make them more comfortable and easier to care for. Objectives for communication aim at their attending to and comprehending messages and their responding with messages about their needs. Objectives for personal-social behavior aim at their reacting to other people and, at more advanced levels, getting along comfortably with others. Objectives for self-help skills are for their assisting when they are dressed, fed, and so on or for their performing basic self-care tasks. Objectives for physical skills aim at their helping in their physical management or at their performing simple physical activities.

Instructional Schedules

We differentiate schedules a great deal for the mildly mentally retarded. First, we delay instruction until they reach mental ages at which they are ready to master particular objectives. Second, we allow them to progress at slower rates. That is, we do more reteaching. For example, we might present an idea to a mildly retarded pupil five times

We select objectives appropriate for retarded pupils' levels of intellectual maturity.

for every three times we might present it to a normal child or every one time to a gifted child. Also, we give them a great deal *more* independent practice. A mildly retarded pupil may need to study a particular word ending, e.g., the *-er* noun former, in twenty different words, whereas the normal pupil would grasp that derivational suffix's meaning in ten repetitions and a gifted pupil in three.

We allow even more time for learning as mental retardation increases, and we wait until even later to begin instruction for particular tasks. That is, moderately retarded pupils would get objectives later, and the severely and profoundly retarded would have them even more delayed. For example, we would expect a normal child to master dressing skills by the time he or she reaches preschool at age three or four. We would work on these with the moderately retarded when he or she is seven or eight and the profoundly retarded when he or she is much older. For the moderately, severely, and profoundly retarded, we would plan on longer sequences of instruction than we use for more intelligent pupils.

To repeat: These delays and extended sequences of instruction as well as the leveling off in mental age mean that the retarded cannot master the body of objectives that more intelligent pupils can. As a result, we drop many objectives usually taught in the schools. The more the pupil's retardation, the more objectives we omit from his or her instructional program.

Instructional Procedures

Methods

Mildly retarded pupils do not do independent problem solving as well as more intelligent pupils of the same CA levels. Beyond that method, they can satisfactorily use the other methods — teacher presentation, group work, tutoring, and solitary practice. Behavior modification techniques are *sometimes* used to focus the pupils' attention and to keep them engaged in tasks until they learn. Whatever the method, the important things are to present very small amounts of material at any one time and to continually check to be sure that pupils are actually learning what we think we are teaching them. Often, they are more passive and do not indicate when they do not understand what is being taught.

The *moderately retarded* do not work well independently. Nor do they benefit very much from large-group instruction. Stated more affirmatively, they require closer teacher direction either in small groups or in a tutoring relationship. Behavior modification procedures are used *widely* to keep their attention focused on a task and to keep them engaged until they learn.

The *severely/profoundly retarded* seldom can profit from small-group instruction. Instead, they need tutoring in one-to-one situations and very close supervision. Behavior modification procedures are used *extensively* to focus their attention and to keep them engaged until they learn.

Media

Mildly retarded pupils can benefit from the types of media used with other pupils. But the particular items must have several characteristics. First, the material is broken down into small steps. For example,

Teaching materials for retarded pupils need to have interest levels appropriate for their chronological ages and difficulty levels appropriate for their mental ages.

to be most productive, their films or tapes are shorter and less complex. If there are three ideas to present, it is more effective to present each idea separately in a different film or tape than to present them together interrelated in a larger sequence.

Another feature to consider in mildly retarded pupils' materials is difficulty level in relationship to interest level. In technical terms we say that their materials need to be *age appropriate* or *low difficulty level and high interest level.* The italicized words mean that the interest levels are appropriate for their CA levels and the difficulty levels are appropriate for their MA levels. That is, the materials need to be suitable to the interests of older pupils, but easier than those older pupils usually deal with. For example, a print story teaching automobile safety rules to teenagers would be about adolescents' using cars in working, dating, and other socializing. Pictures would show teenagers. But the vocabulary and sentences would be like those used with much younger children, and fewer ideas would be presented.

A number of instructional systems have been developed to teach the mildly retarded academic materials. For example, two frequently used kits for the mildly retarded are the Social Learning Curriculum (Goldstein, 1974) and the Project Math materials (Cawley, 1978).

Moderately retarded pupils use a variety of materials at simple levels. Here too materials are broken into small steps. Although generally reflecting relatively mature interest levels in pictures and content, the difficulty levels are even simpler. We have available extensive materials for teaching moderately retarded pupils daily living

Small-group work and tutoring are very appropriate for retarded pupils.

skills (e.g., Goldstein, 1980 *a, b;* Goldstein and Alter, 1980; Lent, 1975).

We do not use too many instructional media as such with the *severely and profoundly retarded.* Instead, we move more toward devices for teaching daily living skills, e.g., button boards and simple electronic language-signaling devices.

Instructional Settings

For the *mildly retarded,* space allocations are about the same as for other pupils. However, because they do need closer supervision, there must be ample provision for small-group work and tutoring. Teacher aides are useful for helping teachers provide the necessary instruction.

The *moderately retarded* have much more specialized needs. The space must be appropriate for small-group work and tutoring. Class sizes must be small enough, and enough teacher aides must be available for very close instruction and supervision. In addition, ample demonstration facilities are very important for moderately retarded pupils. For example, a demonstration house or rooms arranged as a kitchen, living room, and so on, are important for teaching daily living skills to moderately retarded pupils.

Instructional settings for the *severely/profoundly retarded* simulate the home even more. And they include equipment for crippled pupils. For example, there are beds, spaces for watching TV, standing tables, and special chairs. Teachers usually have more than one aide to help in teaching and managing the pupils.

RELATED SERVICES

Retarded pupils require medical services, psychological services, speech/language therapy, vocational rehabilitation services, and family information and counseling. In addition, some severely/profoundly retarded youngsters need physical and occupational therapy.

Medical Services

As we have seen, many pupils' mental retardation stems from physical causes, and some pupils have fragile health. Consequently, at the outset they need diagnoses by neurologists, endocrinologists, and internists and treatment with surgery, diet, hormones, and other drugs as appropriate. Beyond that, they need continued medical monitoring, as all pupils do.

Speech/Language Therapy

Delayed speech and language and also speech and language problems occur widely in the mentally retarded — especially the moderately and severely/profoundly retarded. Consequently, the services of speech/

language therapists are crucial. These specialists work with pupils separately and also work jointly with teachers to ensure a carryover from therapy to the classroom.

Psychological Services

School psychologists are important members of teams responsible for identifying the mentally retarded and for reevaluating them periodically. In addition, since the mildly retarded have more emotional problems than is the norm, clinical psychologists or psychiatrists are needed for psychotherapeutic help.

Vocational Rehabilitation Services

When mentally retarded youngsters reach adolescence, vocational rehabilitation services become important for those who have the potentiality for working independently in the community and for some of those who might attain semi-independent job status. The VR specialist assesses the youngster's status on characteristics having implications for occupational training and performance. He or she provides information to the youngster and his or her advocates about possible jobs and helps them weigh the options. The VR specialist also may help the youngster get special training if that training is delivered outside of the public schools. Or, the VR specialist may work with the special educator and vocational educator if the youngster's training comes through the public schools. Finally, if it is appropriate, the VR specialist helps the mentally retarded youngster obtain employment.

Family Information and Counseling

As it is difficult to deal with any handicapped child, it certainly is difficult for most families to come to terms with mentally retarded children. Family members need information about resources for therapy, education, and training and also about estate planning to provide for the future. They need counseling to help them deal with such emotions as guilt and anger. Social workers and psychiatrists or clinical psychologists often supply such information and counseling.

Physical Therapy

Some severely/profoundly retarded youngsters are not ambulatory. Physical therapists evaluate their sitting, standing, walking and other movement skills, and usually deliver therapy.

Occupational Therapy

Again, some seriously/profoundly retarded have deficits in hand/arm use and therefore inability to perform many self-help skills. Occupational therapists evaluate the youngsters' capabilities in these areas and often deliver treatment.

Placing mentally retarded pupils in the least restrictive environment

Placement for the delivery of services is our final task in providing for mentally retarded pupils. Decisions here are about placement options, extracurricular activities, transportation and facilities, and safety.*

PLACEMENT OPTIONS

In Chapter 2 we considered how in earlier days, mildly retarded pupils were assigned to special classes if special classes were available or to institutions. Moderately retarded youngsters were excluded from public schools as perhaps trainable but not educable. They were kept at home and placed in community programs if such programs were available, or they were sent to institutions. Severely/profoundly retarded youngsters were excluded from public school and usually from community centers. Some were kept at home, some sent to institutions. All of this changed after much discussion and debate and appropriate litigation and legislation. Now the requirement is that every youngster be admitted to public education and placed in the least restrictive environment he or she can get along in — given appropriate services. The effects of these trends in placing pupils are summarized below.

Currently the options for placing the mentally retarded, arranged from the least to the most specialized, are regular classes with the regular teacher being assisted by the resource teacher, resource rooms functioning as part-time special classes, self-contained special classes, and residential schools. Figure 9.2 shows how frequently these options were being used for mentally retarded youngsters as a group in the late 1970s.

For the *mildly retarded*,† the resource room serving as a part-time special class is most often used. Pupils work with the special education teacher on the literacy skills, arithmetic, and the vocational skills and receive tutoring in subjects taught by the regular-class teacher. They work with the regular-class teachers for home economics, art, music, health and physical education, social studies, and general sciences. In the secondary school they participate in work-study programs and after secondary school may enroll in training programs in

---

* Placement of mentally retarded pupils has been widely discussed. Later examples are materials in Blatt *et al.* (1979), Gottlieb (1979), Guralnick (1977), MacMillan (1977), and Scheerenberger (1976).

---

† In former days, when mildly retarded pupils were automatically assigned to self-contained special classes, four levels of classes were used: primary (CA's 6–9), intermediate (CA's 10–13), secondary (CA's 14–16), and work-study (CA's 17+).

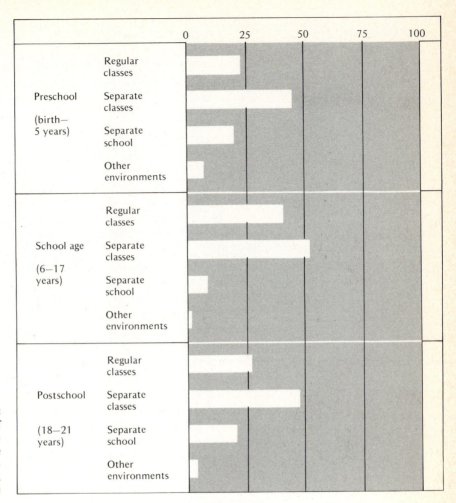

Fig. 9.2
Most frequent placements of mentally retarded pupils reported by the states in the late 1970s. (Based on information in BEH, 1979, pp. 169–189.)

vocational-technical schools. When they get beyond school age, they usually work and live independently in the community.

Moderately retarded pupils are more often in self-contained special classes. Special education teachers and their aides deliver the entire instructional program to the pupils. Pupils may participate with nonretarded pupils in areas such as physical education.

An important thing to note is that even though the moderately retarded pupils are in self-contained special classes, these classes are located in school buildings with other pupils who are about the same ages that the retarded pupils are — a primary school, a middle school, or a secondary school. This is a way of getting to a least restrictive environment and still keep the benefits of special classes.

Inadequate institutions are unnecessary; many individuals can function in less restrictive environments.

As they get older, moderately retarded pupils may go into sheltered workshops for training and work. At the same time, they may live in one of the residential options such as group homes which are available to allow the more seriously retarded youngsters to live outside of institutions but in protected environments.

Severely/profoundly retarded pupils may be in public schools. If so, they are in special classes. Every attempt is made to place these special classes in school buildings where nonhandicapped pupils attend. Some severely/profoundly retarded youngsters may be in residential schools if that appears the best option for the youngster and the family. As they get older, some severely/profoundly handicapped youngsters may live in community facilities.

We have considered repeatedly how important it is to identify handicapped children as early as possible and to begin treatment for them. This early identification and treatment is certainly crucial for mentally retarded children. When remedial physical causes are operating, as, for example, in severe hypothyroidism, medical treatment can prevent or greatly diminish the retardation which might occur. Even in the many cases not amenable to medical intervention, infant stimulation and later special education and related services may be of considerable benefit. Some lost time in development and wrong responses may be prevented, the child may learn to function more adequately than he or she might otherwise, and parents and families may be spared some pain and wasted efforts. In sum, mentally retarded children's development can diverge quickly with corresponding retardation in learning and performing the cultural tasks. Early attention may make this process less extensive.

EXTRACURRICULAR ACTIVITIES

Recreational activities beyond school are very important for all youngsters. They are certainly important for retarded pupils. These youngsters can participate in many activities, such as scouts, and in community programs in which art, dance, dramatic, and play activities suitable for their abilities can be found. Of course, the Special Olympics is an outstanding example of extracurricular activities for the retarded. In the Special Olympics they participate in track and field events and other activities with other youngsters.

TRANSPORTATION AND FACILITIES

Although it takes them a little longer, most *mildly retarded* youngsters can learn to travel independently around town and to some extent out of town. Some can be given sufficient driver training to get a driver's license.

Moderately retarded pupils are more limited in independent travel. With considerable training, most can learn to go about the neighborhood and to use public transportation systems. Out-of-town travel alone and learning to drive a car are seldom realistic.

Special school bus transportation may be necessary to bring moderately retarded pupils to a particular school. This happens because there are so few of them that most medium or small communities do not have a special class in every school or a sheltered workshop in every part of town.

Severely/profoundly retarded youngsters cannot travel independently. Even if they are ambulatory, they need supervision. If they are not ambulatory, they need to be carried and also taken in wheelchairs and special buses.

The mildly and moderately retarded usually have no problem with access to conventional facilities. Neither do those severely/profoundly retarded youngsters who are not physically impaired. Those who are physically impaired, of course, need the same kinds of special facilities that crippled pupils do.

The Special Olympics is an outstanding example of extra-curricular activities for the retarded.

SAFETY

Mildly retarded pupils need special training and some vigilance about safety. Given this training and vigilance, they can learn and observe safety rules.

Moderately retarded pupils need more attention. Most can learn rudimentary safety practices, e.g., how to use a knife correctly and to look both ways before crossing the street. Beyond this, their limited understanding requires *restriction*. For example, they cannot work with power tools. Further, their limited understanding requires *protection*. For example, in a fire evacuation most may need to be taken care of as any very young child would need to be.

Severely/profoundly retarded pupils need close supervision and protection. They cannot be in dangerous situations. In emergencies they need total care.

Summary

IDENTIFYING AND PLANNING FOR MENTALLY RETARDED PUPILS

Normal Intellectual Behavior

Intellectual development follows an orderly sequence, with particular cognitive skills emerging at approximate ages. Intelligence determines whether we can acquire the behavior in the cultural tasks and how quickly we can size up situations and consequently how well we can adjust to situations involved in the cultural tasks.

Various problems can cause a youngster's intellectual development to deviate from the normal sequence of intellectual development. This disruption becomes a handicap when it is severe enough to interfere with his or her learning and performing the cultural tasks. The *Child-Find* for mentally retarded pupils emphasizes public awareness campaigns to alert people to identify true cases of mental retardation early and to find youngsters who are in bleak environments which need to be counteracted. Beyond public awareness, we do screening for signs of delayed development and inferior performance and refer for further study by physicians, psychologists, and other specialists pupils who show such signs. The categories used in diagnosing or *classifying* pupils according to cause of mental retardation include infections and intoxications, trauma and physical agents, metabolic and nutritional problems, gross brain disease, unknown prenatal influence, chromosomal abnormality, and gestational disorders. Also in a larger category — pseudoretardation — are retardation resulting from psychiatric disorder, environmental influence, and sensory defects. Diagnosis or classification by degree of retardation focuses on the mildly retarded, moderately retarded, severely retarded, and profoundly retarded.

Mental Retardation

Mentally retarded pupils tend to show slow development, inferior performance, or problems in other characteristics as well — physical, speech/language, social/emotional, learning and problem solving, rate of intellectual growth, academic achievement, and vocational-civic characteristics. The greater the mental retardation, the more mentally retarded pupils deviate from average in these other characteristics.

Impact of Mental Retardation on Pupils' Characteristics

We observe our accountability for program adequacy for the mentally retarded by documenting the Child-Find and developing the IEP. As we do so, we observe the procedural safeguards by implementing the guarantees for advocate participation, due process, equal protection, periodic reevaluation, and confidentiality.

Accountability

NONDISCRIMINATORY TESTING OF MENTALLY RETARDED PUPILS

Intellectual behavior, or at least intelligence test performance, is extremely sensitive to interference by other problems. Cultural (experience) differences, language differences, or handicaps can keep us

Problems in Testing Mentally Retarded Pupils

from meeting the conditions for norm-referenced or criterion-referenced tests. As a result, youngsters who are not really retarded may earn low scores and be misclassified. Pseudoretardation and misclassification are sources of profound legal and ethical concern.

Procedures for Testing Mentally Retarded Pupils

In collecting information needed to plan for mentally retarded pupils, we use records, reports, interviews, and observation, as we do for all pupils. In addition, we use norm-referenced and criterion-referenced tests when we can meet the conditions for those tests. Also, because of the dangers involved, we tightly circumscribe the process with the procedural safeguards when we collect information about retarded pupils.

INDIVIDUALIZING INSTRUCTION FOR MENTALLY RETARDED PUPILS

Special Education

Mentally retarded pupils cannot master the entire body of *objectives* that more intelligent pupils do. Consequently, we select objectives for retarded pupils gauged to their readiness at any one time and their potentiality for adult achievement. For the mildly retarded, we emphasize objectives preparing them to live independently in adult society; for the moderately retarded, objectives preparing them to help take care of themselves in a more sheltered environment; for the severely/profoundly retarded, objectives for skills that will make them more comfortable and easier to care for.

We differentiate *schedules* a great deal for the mentally retarded. We delay instruction until they reach mental ages at which they are ready to master particular objectives, and we allow them to progress at their own rates. Further, we drop objectives because retarded pupils' slowness causes them to run out of time, and the early leveling off of their mental growth may make some objectives impossible for them to accomplish.

We also differentiate *instructional procedures* considerably for mentally retarded pupils. We extensively use methods involving greater teacher contact and supervision and behavior modification techniques — especially so as retardation increases. Media for the mildly and moderately retarded need to be in smaller steps and appropriate for their mental maturity levels. Also, their materials need to be at low difficulty levels and high interest levels. We use fewer instructional media as such for the severely/profoundly retarded. Instead, we move toward devices for teaching communication and the daily living skills.

Instructional settings for the mentally retarded are increasingly differentiated as retardation increases. Space needs to be adaptable for small-group work and individual work. For the more retarded, facilities for demonstration and actual practice needs to be available — especially facilities to simulate the daily living environment. Also, teacher aides are crucial.

Mentally retarded pupils require medical services, psychological services, speech/language therapy, vocational rehabilitation services, and family information and counseling. In addition, some severely/profoundly retarded youngsters need physical and occupational therapy.

Related Services

PLACING MENTALLY RETARDED PUPILS IN THE LEAST RESTRICTIVE ENVIRONMENT

Today all mentally retarded pupils must have a public education in the least restrictive environment possible and appropriate. Options, arranged from the least to the most specialized, are regular classes with the regular teacher assisted by the resource teacher, resource rooms functioning as part-time special classes, self-contained special classes, and residential schools. As is done with other handicapped pupils, early identification and treatment through infant stimulation, preschool, and other means are essential.

Placement Options

Extracurricular activities are very important for mentally retarded pupils. They can participate in a wide range of activities with some special attention. The Special Olympics is an outstanding example.

Extracurricular Activities

The greater the mental retardation, the less pupils are able to travel independently, and the more protection and supervision they need to guarantee their safety in general. The retarded usually do not have problems gaining access to facilities. The exception is the severely/profoundly retarded pupil who is also physically impaired.

Transportation, Facilities, and Safety

10

TOPICS

Identifying and planning for learning-disabled pupils

NORMAL DEVELOPMENT

Psychological processes
Language
Language, the psychological processes, and the cultural
tasks

LEARNING DISABILITIES

Legal definition and prevalence
Finding learning-disabled pupils
Diagnosis: Classification by type of learning disability
Diagnosis: Classification by cause of learning disability

**IMPACT OF LEARNING DISABILITIES ON PUPILS'
CHARACTERISTICS**

Introduction
Physical characteristics
Intellectual functioning
Social/emotional characteristics
Academic characteristics
Vocational characteristics

Special Needs of Learning-Disabled Pupils

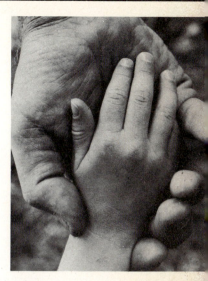

Speech/language therapy
Psychological services
Vocational rehabilitation
Family information and counseling

Placing learning-disabled pupils in the least restrictive environment

PLACEMENT OPTIONS

EXTRACURRICULAR ACTIVITIES

TRANSPORTATION AND FACILITIES

SAFETY

Identifying and planning for learning-disabled pupils

Careful notice of the word *specific* is a key to understanding young-sters who have specific learning disabilities. These problems occur in *particular* psychological and language characteristics — not across the board in all psychological and language characteristics. For LD pupils, as with other exceptional pupils, our first task is to identify them through the Child-Find and to plan for them through the IEP while all the time ensuring them the protection of the procedural safe-guards. Our frame of reference is our knowledge about normal intellectual development and normal language development and also our knowledge about learning disabilities and their impact on pupils' characteristics.

NORMAL DEVELOPMENT

We approach each handicap with two questions: How does the handi-cap deflect the pupil from normal development in the characteristic, and what effect does this deflection have on the pupil's mastering the cultural tasks? For example, when we considered the structure and functioning of the eye, we looked at milestones in visual behavior, the role of visual behavior in mastering the cultural tasks, and the impact of visual problems on pupils' developing visual behavior and master-ing the cultural tasks. It is difficult to do the same thing with learning-disabled pupils because people do not agree what functions go wrong in LD pupils. However, the ones most often mentioned are psychologi-cal processes and language (e.g., Hallahan and Kauffman, 1976; Haring and Bateman, 1977).

Psychological Processes

"Psychological processes" is a term LD specialists use for the intellec-tual functions and inhibitory functions which enable us to learn and to think. The inhibitory functions include focusing our attention on a task and marshalling our motor and other responses to performing that task. The intellectual functions include perceiving stimuli, dis-criminating among stimuli, remembering, forming concepts, and thinking. In Chapter 8 we called these functions cognitive behavior. There we considered the normal development of cognitive functions and especially the increasing complexity of these functions as later functions are built on earlier, simpler ones.

Language

Language includes those functions required for using symbols in dealing with the world. We learn to understand language and to pro-duce it in spoken and written forms. We considered milestones in

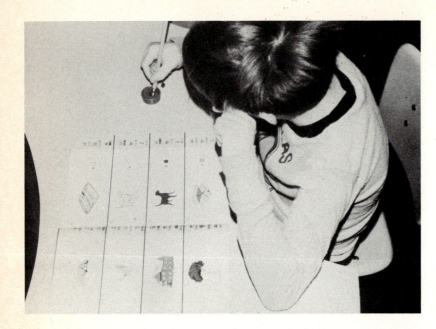

Learning-disabled pupils' problems occur in particular psychological and language characteristics.

language development in Chapters 4 and 5. Again, it is crucial to note the orderly sequence of development, with earlier, simpler speech/ language functions combining to serve as bases for more complex ones.

Language, the Psychological Processes, and the Cultural Tasks

As we have seen, adequate psychological processes and adequate language are essential to our learning the cultural tasks. Our society is so large, it has so many parts, and these parts are so complexly interrelated that it is crucial that we be able to communicate, to learn, and to think and solve problems. These processes are central to almost everything we do — from getting dressed in the morning, to locating a TV program to watch, to taking care of a pet, to interacting with people at school or work, to taking part in an election. Survey again the cultural tasks in Table 1.1. Analyze how important language and the psychological processes are to learning and performing cultural tasks like those. Further, consider how the earlier cultural tasks serve as bases for the later ones.

LEARNING DISABILITIES

Legal Definition and Prevalence

A specific learning disability occurs if something happens, some insult enters in, to deflect the normal development of a psychological process or a language function, or a combination of these and if the deflection is severe enough to interfere with the youngster's learning and performing the cultural tasks. More technically, even though people disagree about the criteria we should use in classifying youngsters as learning-disabled, four characteristics are common to most definitions — underachievement, uneven development, psychological process disorders, and causes excluded (Bryan and Bryan, 1975; Hammill, 1978). The *underachievement* means that the pupil achieves less than he or she is capable of — especially in the literacy skills and mathematics. This underachievement does not happen in all areas, but only in specific functions. Consequently, the youngster shows *uneven development* — achieving up to his or her potentiality in some areas and underachieving in other areas. The *disorders in psychological processes* means that the pupil has problems in some intellectual and inhibitory functions underlying his or her learning to use symbols. *Causes excluded* means that a pupil is not considered to have a specific learning disability if the problems are caused by mental retardation, emotional problems, physical or sensory impairments, or environmental difficulties. PL 94-142 integrates these common characteristics in this definition:

> [Learning disability is a] disorder in one or more of the basic psychological processes involved in understanding or in using language, spoken or written. [This disorder] may manifest itself in an imperfect ability to listen, think, speak, read, write, spell, or do mathematical calculations.
>
> The term includes such conditions as perceptual handicaps, brain injury, minimal brain dysfunction, dyslexia, and developmental aphasia.
>
> The term does not include children who have learning problems which are primarily the result of visual, hearing, or motor handicaps, of mental retardation, of emotional disturbance, or of environmental, cultural, or economic disadvantages. (PL 94-142, *Regulations*, 1977, Sec. 121 a.5)

Figure 1.1 shows that the estimates of prevalence range between 1% and 3%. About 1.9% of the estimated population had been located and served by the late 1970s.

Finding Specific Learning-Disabled Pupils

Our intention in the Child-Find is to identify pupils who qualify as learning disabled and therefore for the entitlements and legal safeguards the law guarantees. LD pupils are often missed or confused with mentally retarded pupils or emotionally disturbed pupils. This confusion happens because of the overlap of their characteristics. For example, mentally retarded pupils achieve below others their chronological ages, and some emotionally disturbed pupils show a breakdown in behavioral control. Consequently, we might misclassify an underachieving, distractible, and hyperactive child unless we look further to see whether he or she shows an uneven pattern of development and disordered psychological processes while at the same time having at least normal intelligence, adequate vision, and so on.

In recent years we have seen widespread public *awareness* campaigns designed to make people sensitive to LD pupils and their problems. An important factor in this increasing awareness is the founding and growth of the Association for Children with Learning Disabilities. The ACLD consists of parents, educators, psychologists, and others who have worked hard for advances in treatment and legal protection for the pupils.

As always, we need to locate youngsters as early as possible so that we can prevent secondary problems from developing. In *screening* we look for signs that a pupil might have learning disabilities. Some common signs are:

☐ Difficulty focusing his or her attention for a reasonable period.

☐ Excessive physical activity.

☐ Tending to manipulate anything that will move — often with a driven, repetitive activity.

☐ Uneven academic achievement, i.e., problems with particular areas such as reading but not with other areas.

Pupils who have severe LD problems show such signs quite obviously. In fact, these youngsters are very difficult to manage if they are distractible and hyperactive. However, some pupils are not so obvious, because they show only uneven achievement and disordered intellectual functions. For example, an intelligent pupil may be quiet and well controlled and focused, but at the same time have problems in visual perception and problems in reading while achieving well in listening, speaking, or mathematics. Consequently, we sometimes need formal screening devices to focus our attention on all important facets of a pupil's behavior. Several procedures help identify high-risk children. For example, the *Developmental Indicators for the Assessment of Learning* and the *Comprehensive Assessment in Nursery School and Kindergarten* help us screen preschool children (Lerner, 1976, p. 31). General behavior rating scales and achievement tests are useful for older pupils.

Referral is our next step if pupils show any of the signs suggesting a learning disability. At a minimum, we refer the pupils to a specialist in learning disabilities for an analysis of their achievement in the literacy skills (listening, reading, spelling, writing), mathematics, and other academic areas. We send them to a school psychologist for assessment of their intellectual abilities and specific psychological processes. We also consult with a speech/language pathologist for a survey of the pupils' language functions. In addition, a physician is consulted if there is a possibility of neurological problems or other medical difficulties.

We classify pupils as learning disabled if they have various problems. These problems may be grouped into two types — problems in psychological processes and problems in language. Youngsters may show only one of these problems, or they may show more than one in various patterns (e.g., Hallahan and Cruickshank, 1973; Ross, 1976).

Diagnosis: Classification by Type of Learning Disability

As we have seen, psychological processes include both intellectual functions and inhibitory functions underlying our learning and using symbols. These processes enable us to become aware of stimuli around us and to act on those stimuli.

Psychological process problems

Inhibition is the process of controlling behavior, i.e., of responding appropriately to stimuli. Some pupils have problems with inhibition (sometimes called disinhibition). Common problems are distractibility, hyperactivity, low frustration tolerance, and perseveration.

Distractibility is trouble focusing on particular stimuli. It happens when pupils cannot control their attention; that is, they cannot focus on some stimuli and ignore others, as we all must do in order to get anything done. For example, as you sit and read, you can hear such noises as the clock ticking, someone walking by, the street traffic, and so on. You could not understand the material you are reading if you could not keep your mind on it and blot out these background stimuli which are extraneous to the book reading.

Hyperactivity is trouble keeping movement focused and productive. It happens when pupils cannot refrain from moving randomly and manipulating every movable object around them. Sometimes the word "driveness" is used to describe this condition. Pupils appear driven beyond their control to random activity.

Low frustration tolerance is trouble dealing with frustration without exploding. It happens when youngsters cannot control their emotions. The term *catastrophic reaction* is a synonym. Pupils become angry or cry when faced with difficulties that others take in stride.

Perseveration comes from the root *persevere* and essentially means perseverance which is not appropriate. That is, the pupil keeps on with something when he or she should stop. For example, if we are spelling "cat," we should stop after one "t." It is wrong to write "catttt...." Some pupils, however, have trouble inhibiting their responses at such boundaries.

The intellectual processes are operations we perform as we learn. LD pupils have problems with perception, memory, conceptualizing, and thinking.

Perception is the process of becoming aware of a stimulus, that is, of grasping something's critical features so that we can identify it and work with it. Some LD pupils have trouble separating a stimulus from its background and working with it. For example, they cannot identify a foreground picture embedded in a busy background. Or an LD pupil who can sew buttons on or put hems in a solid-colored shirt often lapses into error and frustration when sewing a button on or hemming plaid material.

Memory includes the process of learning material and recalling it. For example, we memorize a particular series of digits, e.g., our telephone numbers, or we learn the pairs (words and their equivalents) in a foreign language. We remember these items when we want to use them. Some LD pupils have difficulty memorizing and recalling visually presented associations of words and objects, e.g., a card bearing a picture of a spoon along with the word. They have similar problems with auditory materials, e.g., orally recited songs, spelling words, and verses.

Conceptualizing is the process of working with abstractions, that is, of working with diverse stimuli grouped on common characteristics. Some LD pupils have problems learning and using concepts. For example, they have trouble grouping apparently different objects by a common characteristic such as size or color.

Thinking is the process of focusing on ideas, weighing these ideas, and sometimes using them to solve problems. LD pupils often have problems thinking through things. For example, given the task of fixing a picnic lunch, they have difficulty considering what the lunchers like, how to get the food, how much food to get, when to get it, and how to prepare it.

The case of Tom illustrates some of these problems with the psychological processes — both inhibitory functions and intellectual functions.

> *Having Tom in my eighth-grade language arts class means that there is never a dull moment. At the beginning of the year, his capabilities and performance were not easy to figure out. With some students, all the pieces of information fall into place immediately. Tom puzzled me. I knew he had high ability, yet he demonstrated*

real problems in getting his work done. His math teacher told me that he was having major problems in her class, since his achievement was significantly below the other students'. After observing his behavior closely and talking with the resource teacher in the school, I now seem to have a handle on some of his learning strengths and weaknesses.

In the language arts areas, Tom is able to read just slightly below grade level. Although he does not have the reading proficiency of most of his classmates, he is able to read his textbooks, rarely needing help with a word. In written assignments, his handwriting can be neat; however, he usually approaches a written task in a harum-scarum fashion, writing quickly to get through as soon as possible. More often than not, his papers are messy and difficult to read. When he gets down to work, he is able to make a passing grade on his spelling test. That is the heart of the problem—"when he gets down to work."

It is basically organization that poses extreme difficulty for Tom. He seems almost constantly distracted, having a difficult time sitting down and getting settled. On some days I think he spends more time wandering around the classroom than sitting in his seat. When he goes to sharpen his pencil, he will look out the window and become captivated watching a bird or he will pass the magazine rack and flip through several magazines before returning to his seat. He's fidgety, constantly turning in his seat and moving around. As to his work, he often does not complete it. Since it takes him longer because of his attention span, he sometimes will hand in work several days late. With that much delay and his general difficulty with organization, it is not unusual for him to lose assignments that he has started but not completed. I have to watch Tom about taking short-cuts with his work. If he has ten questions to answer, he sometimes will answer the first, a couple in the middle, and the last, and state that he has finished the assignment. Sometimes I purposefully shorten his assignments so that the length is adjusted to his learning pattern. In this way, he can achieve success and demonstrate a mastery of the content without being penalized for his distractibility. Another approach which seems to help him is for me to write instructions for the class period on the board and sometimes even an outline of class discussions. Since Tom does not always generate his own structure, he seems to benefit from as much as I can impose. I have been pleased with the encouragement and direction he gets from the other students in the class. They tell him things like: "Turn around and do your work." "Come on, Tom, I don't have time to talk to you."

I tried separating him into a part of the room without other desks and students. For Tom, this did not seem to help. He still turned around and talked across the room. Tom does seem to respond to reasoning. He usually knows when he is off track and wants to do better. He often says, "I know, Ms. Allison; I am going to do my work."

His mother and I were talking last week about his overall recent improvement in settling down and following class instructions. She had an insight that made sense to me. During the last month Tom has joined the YMCA swimming program, and he swims almost every afternoon. She thinks that the swimming is a good outlet for a lot of his excess energy. That could possibly be contributing to the fact that some of his classroom restlessness seems to be decreasing.

Tom has his good and bad days, just like all of us. He's got the ability, and it's a continual challenge for me to capitalize on his strengths. (Turnbull and Schulz, 1979, pp. 19–20)

Language problems   As we considered in Chapter 4, the American Speech and Hearing Association uses these definitions: "*Communication* is the process of exchanging messages using any system (not confined to language) and various media (e.g., speech, gesture, facial expression). Language is a conventional system of phonological, syntactic, and semantic rules for encoding and decoding experience. Speech production is the vocal-motor channel of language performance." The symbols we use most often to code our experiences are words, quantities, and geometric forms/shapes. To get along in the world, we must understand and use these language symbols appropriately in both spoken and written forms. That is, we must be adept in *listening* — decoding and understanding spoken language — and in *speaking* — in encoding and producing spoken language by talking. We must be able to *read* — to decode and understand written language and to *write* — to encode and produce a message through spelling, handwriting, and rhetoric. In addition, we must be able to understand and to use mathematical symbols for quantities and spaces/forms, i.e., to do arithmetic, geometry, algebra, and sometimes higher mathematics.

In sum, then, to get along, we have to manipulate all kinds of symbols. Some people have disabilities with particular ones of these language/mathematical functions. Others have problems with more than one. For example, some people can do all right with spoken language, but cannot read. Some can talk, listen, and read, but cannot write. Some can deal with words satisfactorily, but cannot do mathematics. One well-known example is Susan Hampshire, the English actress who performed brilliantly in such demanding roles as Fleur in *The Forsythe Saga* and Sarah Churchill in *The First Churchills*. The actress has dyslexia, a reading disability. She had to use listening and oral recitation to learn her lines and to grasp the characters' natures. She could not use reading, as the other actors did.

Over the years, people have coined various terms for these specific disabilities. Some frequently used terms are:

☐ *Receptive aphasia:* difficulty grasping spoken language

☐ *Expressive aphasia:* difficulty producing spoken language

☐ *Total aphasia:* difficulty grasping and producing spoken language

☐ *Dyslexia:* difficulty reading

☐ *Hyperlexia:* word calling with little or no comprehension

☐ *Anomia:* difficulty producing names of objects

☐ *Dyscalculia:* difficulty doing arithmetic and otherwise using numbers

☐ *Dysgraphia:* difficulty producing material in writing

☐ *Dyspraxia:* difficulty making a specific intentional movement even though no paralysis is present.

This brief comment illustrates these problems — more specifically, dyslexia — especially as they appear from within.

> *Daily I sat staring at a book that would not surrender to me its meaning. In my war with the book, now and again I was victorious over an isolated word, but the endless legion of pages ultimately defeated me. Repeatedly, I looked back over the unfriendly, unyielding rows of print to find a word that I could recognize. In doing so, my failures amassed by the minute, like a swelling mob jeering at me. Finally, the fury rising within me burst from my fists, while from between clenched teeth I silently cursed the head I was pounding. To me, the immutable reality was that my head was bad. It caused my frustration. It sponsored my shame. I knew no alternative but to beat it into becoming a smarter head. That failed, too, adding daily to my feelings of frustration and worthlessness. (Kauffman, 1976, pp. 13–14, citing Rappaport, 1976, pp. 347–350)*

Diagnosis: Classification by Cause of Learning Disability

People certainly do disagree when they begin to discuss causes of learning disabilities. Sometimes there are suggestions of brain dysfunctions and sometimes suggestions of inheritance and environmental problems (e.g., Hallahan and Cruickshank, 1973; Hallahan and Kauffman, 1976; and Quiros and Schrager, 1978). However, quite frequently no cause can be identified.

Brain dysfunction

Some learning disabilities are probably caused by brain pathology. In fact, neurologists, working alone and with psychologists and educators, did much of the early work in the field later named as learning disabilities. For example, Goldstein worked with soldiers who had sustained brain injuries in World War I. He observed that they showed aphasia, low frustration tolerance, inattentiveness, perceptual problems, and conceptual problems. Strauss extended Goldstein's and other neurologists' work to children after World War II.

The problem for diagnosis is this: Not all brain-injured people show learning disabilities, and conversely not all learning-disabled people show brain pathology. There are at least two explanations for this problem. One, the brain is very complex, and therefore some brain injuries do not affect those structures and functions which influence language, intellectual performance, and inhibition. Or two, neurological diagnosis, while good, is not completely sensitive and error-free, and therefore some minimal brain injuries go undetected.

Inheritance   The evidence about inheritance comes mostly from studies of youngsters with dyslexia — reading disabilities. Generally, some families contain more dyslexic people than others do. And there is a greater incidence of dyslexia in identical twins than in fraternal twins and in singletons. However, again, identifying cause is difficult because many times a particular LD pupil is the only member of his or her family to have problems.

Environmental deprivation   Some have suggested that a deprived environment can cause a youngster to be learning-disabled. There are at least three channels. First, children deprived of experience and stimulation at early critical periods may not develop certain perceptual skills. Second, inhibition, or focusing attention and motor activities, also is learned to some extent. Again, missing an opportunity to learn because of a deprived environment can lead to problems. Third, deprived environments do not provide stimulation to language development. In sum, then, deprived environments can lead to problems in perception, inhibition, and language, which in turn may show up as problems in literacy skills and mathematics and thus be classified as learning disabilities.

Unknown causes   Many pupils show learning disabilities but no signs of neurological damage, environmental problems, or family history of learning disabilities. By default, then, we have to infer that the learning disabilities arise from causes which remain unknown to us.

IMPACT OF LEARNING DISABILITIES ON PUPILS' CHARACTERISTICS

Introduction   Our culture, complex and interdependent, requires a high degree of literacy. That is, people must be adept with spoken and written language and with mathematics. It also requires a high degree of social skill; that is, people must be able to inhibit their behavior in the face of a bombardment of stimulation and in the face of high population density.

Learning disabilities can make it very difficult for a youngster to function in this complex, interdependent culture. And the earlier they occur, the more pervasive their influence because of the way later psychological and language skills and cultural tasks are built on earlier ones. For example, distractibility or dyslexia can seriously interfere with a pupil's learning many cultural tasks and using them maturely. Some people learn to circumvent such problems. Many others do not.

There is at present a growing concern for the child with learning disabilities. The enigma of the youngster who has difficulty in learning is, however, not new. Children from all walks of life have experienced such difficulties throughout the years. Indeed, there is evidence that some of the world's most distinguished persons had unusual difficulty in certain aspects of learning.

Thomas Edison, the ingenious American inventor, was called abnormal, addled, and mentally defective. Writing in his diary that he was never able to get along at school, he recalled that he was always at the foot of his class. While his father thought of him as stupid, Edison described himself as a dunce. Auguste Rodin, the great French sculptor, was called the worst pupil in the school. Because his teachers diagnosed Rodin as uneducable, they advised his parents to put him out to work, though they doubted that he could ever make a living. Woodrow Wilson, the scholarly twenty-eighth president of the United States, did not learn his letters until he was 9 years old and did not learn to read until age 11. Relatives expressed sorrow for his parents because Woodrow was so dull and backward.

Nelson Rockefeller, political leader, former governor of New York, and vice president of the United States, suffered from severe dyslexia, which kept him from achieving good grades in school. Moreover, during his political career his poor reading forced him to memorize his speeches. Albert Einstein, the great mathematical genius, did not speak until age three. His search for words was described as laborious, and, until he was seven, he formulated each sentence, no matter how commonplace, silently with his lips before speaking it aloud. School work did not go well for young Einstein. He had little facility with arithmetic, no special ability in any other academic subject, and great difficulty with foreign languages. One teacher predicted that "nothing good" would come of him. Einstein's language disabilities persisted throughout his adult life. When he read, he heard words, writing was difficult for him; and he communicated badly through writing. In describing his thinking process, he explained that he rarely thought in words; it was only after a thought came that he tried to express it in words at a later time.

These persons of eminence fortunately were able somehow to find appropriate ways of learning, and they successfully overcame their initial failures. Many youngsters with learning disabilities are not so fortunate.

Tony is one such case. His parents have long been aware that their son has severe problems in learning. As an infant, Tony was colicky and had difficulty in learning to suck. His early speech was so garbled that no one could understand him, and frequently his inability to communicate led to sudden temper tantrums. The kindergarten teacher reported that Tony was "immature"; his first-grade teacher said he "did not pay attention" and succeeding teachers labeled him "lazy" and then "emotionally disturbed." Tony's distraught parents attempted to find the source of his learning problems to alleviate his misery and theirs. They desperately followed suggestions from many sources that led to a succession of specialists and clinics dedicated to treating such difficulties.

One clinic detected a visual problem, and as a result Tony received visual training exercises for several years. Another clinic diagnosed Tony's problem as a lack of neurological organization and instituted a lengthy series of motor exercises. An opinion of emotional disturbance at another agency led to years of psychotherapy for both Tony and his parents. A reading tutor analyzed the problem as a lack of instruction in phonics, and Tony received intensive phonics instruction for a period of time. The family pediatrician said that the boy was merely going through a stage and would grow out of it. Yet despite this wealth of diagnosis and treatment, Tony still cannot learn. He is unhappily failing in school, and, understandably, he has lost faith in himself. (Lerner, 1976, pp. 2–3)

In sum, the disorders in psychological processes and language can affect the pupil's intellectual, social/emotional, academic achievement, and vocational characteristics; further, sometimes learning disabilities coexist with physical problems.*

Physical Characteristics   If brain dysfunction causes the learning disabilities, it can lead also to physical problems which coexist with the psychological and educational problems. These physical characteristics may be severe enough to be diagnosed as cerebral palsy. Or, they may be more minor and more aptly described as clumsiness. Pupils may appear poorly coordinated and poorly balanced when they undertake such gross motor activities as running, jumping, and skipping. And they may show

---

* We have extensive descriptions of learning-disabled pupils' characteristics, e.g., Bryan (1974, 1977, n.d.), Bryan *et al.* (1976), Critchley (1970), Deshler (1978), Hallahan and Cruickshank (1973), Hallahan and Kauffman (1976), Keogh and Margolis (1976), Knott (1980), Kronick (1976), Silver (1974), Wallach and Goldsmith (1977), Wiig and Harris (1974), and Wiig and Semel (1976).

Male. Age 6 years, 9 months
IQ 106 (Stanford-Binet)

Neurological examination negative.
Poor body image; unintegrated;
developmental lags; immature speech.

"Me dont thin I can write my name."

Fig. 10.1
Figure drawing by a
learning-disabled pupil.
(Reprinted by permission
from Michael-Smith and
Morganstern, 1965, p. 182.)

awkwardness and confusion when they undertake such fine motor activities as writing, drawing, sewing, cutting, and hammering (see Fig. 10.1).

Pupils' learning disabilities can interfere with their performance on intelligence tests. As a result, they may show lower IQ's than they might have if they were free from disorders in psychological processes and language.

**Intellectual
Characteristics**

By definition, LD pupils have disorders in basic psychological processes involved in using language/mathematics symbols. Intelligence tests, of course, are designed to assess pupils' abilities to manipulate symbols in problem solving. Consequently, intelligence test items require pupils to perceive, conceptualize, and think about verbal symbols and mathematical symbols as they solve problems. Further, intelligence test performance requires sustained attention, tolerance of failure/frustration, and ability to restrict one's responses and not persevere inappropriately. Still further, intelligence test performance requires that pupils use spoken and written language and mathematics. As a result, pupils with receptive aphasia, expressive aphasia, or total aphasia simply cannot participate in the administration of most tests. In addition, pupils who have disorders in the psychological processes and with reading disabilities, writing disabilities, or mathematical disabilities have trouble with many items on most tests.

Social/Emotional Characteristics

Many LD pupils have social/emotional problems. Their disabilities can interfere with their establishing satisfying emotional relationships and their participating in social activities.

Inhibition

Obviously, problems with inhibition can interfere with social activities. Distractibility, hyperactivity, low frustration tolerance, and perseveration can make it very difficult for pupils to get along harmoniously with others. Other pupils and adults pretty quickly reject the LD pupil whose attention moves restlessly from one thing to another quickly, who is jittery, jumpy, always moving, who explodes emotionally at the smallest provocation, and who continues a reaction long after that reaction is not appropriate. In turn, as he or she reacts to this rejection by peers and adults, the LD pupil can get more irritable and further out of step with others.

Intellectual functions

Less obviously, perceptual, memory, conceptual, and thinking problems can interfere too with social interaction. To get along socially, we have to be aware of (perceive) and act on social cues — some of them pretty subtle and embedded in complex fields of extraneous stimuli. We have to remember what these cues mean and generalize (conceptualize) about them. Further, we have to use these perceptions and concepts in thinking through and solving social problems. LD pupils who have difficulties with perception, remembering, conceptualizing, and thinking are at a disadvantage in these social situations and often get into trouble. They may miss a cue, such as another person's frown of displeasure, and continue an activity enough to get rejected for it. Or, they may miss a smile of welcome or a friendly tone of voice and not respond to someone they would enjoy being with. They may not be able to remember situations that led to the trouble in the past, to generalize about them, and consequently to understand how they should change their behavior to stay out of trouble in the future. Similarly, their problems with perception and the other intellectual processes can interfere with their analyzing situations which lead to harmony with the other pupils and adults around them.

LD pupils' language problems can lead to social/emotional problems. Obviously, pupils who cannot read or perform other literacy skills may be embarrassed or shamed by other pupils for their (what they consider) inadequacies. Beyond this, they lack a tool. For example, consider how difficult it is to take a trip if one cannot read or to answer a letter if one cannot spell, write, or compose in writing.

Language problems

    Youngsters who have problems only with written language have difficulties, but they can get along if they have oral language skills. Those who have problems with oral language are in much more serious trouble. Youngsters with receptive aphasia cannot understand what is said to them. Those with expressive aphasia cannot produce an oral message for others. Without these oral language skills, they cannot learn written language skills. Thus they are altogether cut off from communicating through language. This being cut off can lead to very serious social/emotional problems.

LD pupils may have trouble learning in such content areas as the sciences, social studies, humanities and fine arts, and vocational subjects. The reason rests in the nature of learning disabilities. Problems with basic psychological processes and problems with language are criteria for identifying a pupil as learning-disabled. The psychological processes and the language functions are, in turn, directly and indirectly involved in academic learning.

Academic Characteristics

    The term *literacy skills* is a synonym for the language functions mentioned in the definitions of learning disabilities. The literacy skills include listening, speaking, reading, writing, and spelling, i.e., the skills of understanding and using written and spoken language. The literacy skills and mathematics also are sometimes called the *tool subjects* to indicate that they are procedures helpful in learning science, social studies, and so on. It is clear that pupils who have disabilities in one or more of the tool subjects can have problems with such content areas as science unless another avenue of learning is discovered and used. For example, applying the principles we saw in the illustrations of Susan Hampshire and Nelson Rockefeller, pupils with dyslexia may have to rely on listening and speaking to learn science and similar subjects and to show what they have learned.

Pupils who have problems with the basic psychological processes are at a disadvantage with not only the literacy skills, which in turn can interfere with learning the content subjects. They also have a direct problem with the content subjects. For example, pupils who have trouble perceiving, memorizing, conceptualizing, and thinking are also going to have trouble learning content in history, music, home economics, or similar subjects as the subjects are usually taught. Pupils who have problems with hyperactivity, distractibility, and perseveration are also going to have problems with these content areas as they are usually taught.

Vocational Characteristics

Adolescent and young adult LD students may have difficulty preparing for jobs and performing jobs. The ability to perform the literacy skills, to use the intellectual functions, and to inhibit inappropriate behavior is crucial to most jobs. For example, youngsters who cannot spell, read, or do mathematics; perceive, form concepts, or think; focus their attention; control their movements; and master their tempers would simply be disqualified for a wide range of jobs, e.g., airline pilots, secretaries, salespersons, teachers, physicians, and others.

The outlook is more favorable for pupils who have fewer problems. For example, if the problem is in only one area, such as mathematics, the youngster could go toward areas that require other skills, e.g., radio announcing or acting.

ACCOUNTABILITY

Specific learning-disabled pupils are protected by the laws. Consequently, we are obligated to use certain procedures in identifying and classifying them, in planning their individual education programs, and in observing the procedural safeguards that ensure their rights.

Identifying and Planning for Learning-Disabled Pupils
Documenting the Child-Find

Our active searches for LD pupils include the usual activities — awareness campaigns, screening, and referral for further study those pupils who seem to have learning disabilities. The procedures used in this Child-Find and the results in number of LD pupils found and served are documented in school reports.

Developing the individual education program

Once pupils are identified as learning-disabled, the IEP comes next in providing them with the services they require. Pupils' present performance levels on a broad range of characteristics are sampled. The results serve as bases for decisions about long-term goals as well as short-term objectives, instructional procedures suitable for those

We are responsible for guaranteeing LD pupils' entitlements and protections under the law.

objectives, and the least restrictive placement appropriate for delivering that instruction. An IEP team makes these decisions about program components as well as about the schedules for reevaluating and revising the IEP. This team consists of the pupil's advocates, the LD specialist, the regular-class teachers, the school psychologist, and also language specialists and other specialists appropriate for the pupil's particular problem.

Pupils who truly have learning disabilities need programs for those disabilities — not some other type of program. Similarly, since there are so many disagreements about the best procedures for working with LD pupils, someone with a discerning eye has to be vigilant so that the LD pupil gets the particular treatments appropriate for his or her particular disabilities. In sum, the procedures for guaranteeing the LD pupil's civil rights bear close scrutiny.

Observing the Procedural Safeguards for Learning-Disabled Pupils

The LD pupil's advocates (parents or their surrogates) have the prime role in every decision — from first screening through the periodic revisions of the IEP. Consultants to the advocates are especially important, since learning disabilities constitute such a complex, multifaceted problem. It is difficult for the advocates alone to know about the many variations of learning disabilities, their combinations, and their treatments — particularly now, when the field is going through the ambiguity of growing pains as a rapidly developing discipline.

Advocate participation

Due process Due process is available to advocates who disagree with recommendations made for their LD pupil. The routes of appeal are clearly made available to them, i.e., the procedures and the levels through the administration of the local/state school system and through the jurisdictions of the federal courts.

Equal protection LD pupils have the rights to the same rules, criteria, and procedures used in dealing with all pupils. In addition, special care is needed to guarantee them nondiscriminatory testing. The appropriateness of the norm group when standardized tests are used and the need for multiple measures are particular areas where vigilance is required.

Periodic reevaluation It is quite important that LD pupils be reevaluated at particular intervals. Their language problems or their psychological process problems, or both can lead to such complexities in testing and teaching that frequent checking for errors and appropriate corrections are necessary. In addition, as the pupil benefits from instruction, this progress needs to be recognized and the IEP altered with new goals/ objectives, procedures, and placements as appropriate.

Confidentiality As it is for us all, confidentiality is a crucial right to be observed for LD pupils. Confidentialilty procedures ensure that advocates control access to the data — to themselves and only to others who have a need to know. Similarly, they may have inaccurate or nonrelevant information purged and all but actuarial information destroyed once the LD pupil completes the special education program.

Nondiscriminatory testing of learning-disabled pupils

Given a pupil referred as learning-disabled, our second task, nondiscriminatory testing, comes to the fore. Tests are used with LD pupils to be sure that they meet the four criteria — academic underachievement, uneven development, psychological process disorders, and exclusion of certain causes. Beyond identification, testing is used to find what pupil disabilities we need to work on or, just as important, to work around and what strengths we can use in this working on and around disabilities.

PROBLEMS IN TESTING LEARNING-DISABLED PUPILS

There are two problems in testing LD pupils: potentiality for error and disagreement about reliability and validity of tests.

One problem in testing LD pupils is the usual problem in testing handicapped pupils. That is, the disability interferes with test per-

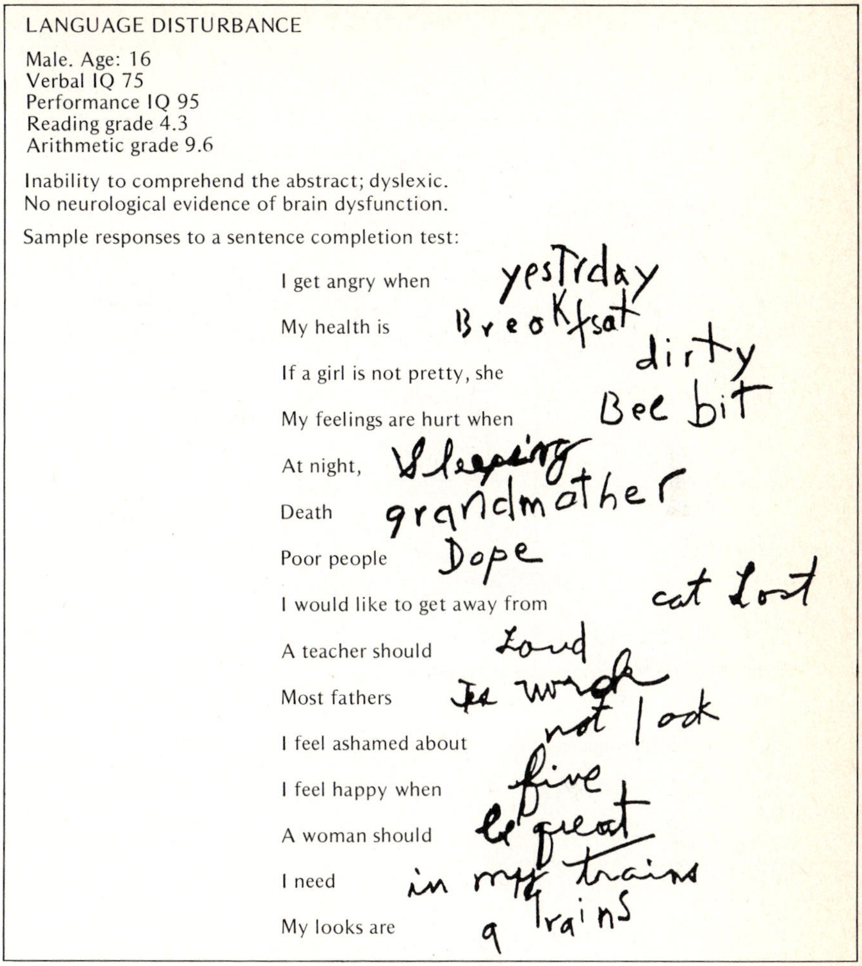

LANGUAGE DISTURBANCE

Male. Age: 16
Verbal IQ 75
Performance IQ 95
Reading grade 4.3
Arithmetic grade 9.6

Inability to comprehend the abstract; dyslexic.
No neurological evidence of brain dysfunction.

Sample responses to a sentence completion test:

I get angry when   yesTrday

My health is   Breokfsat

If a girl is not pretty, she   dirty

My feelings are hurt when   Bee bit

At night,   Sleeping

Death   grandmother

Poor people   Dope

I would like to get away from   cat lost

A teacher should   Loud

Most fathers   Is wrogh
                                       not look

I feel ashamed about   five

I feel happy when

A woman should   be great

I need   in my trains

My looks are   a trains

Fig. 10.2
Written production by a learning-disabled pupil. (Reprinted by permission from Michael-Smith and Morganstern, 1965, p. 188.)

formance. And in turn tests do not measure what they are supposed to measure, but rather become additional measures of the handicap — in this case the learning disability. For example, sometimes sentence-completion tests are used as projective devices for studying emotional adjustment. Look at Fig. 10.2. Note the test items and the potential feelings they could evoke. Note also the youngster's responses. They show a lot about the youngster's language disability, but very little about his emotional adjustment. This type of error can lead to difficulties, especially in diagnosis. The process works this way. One criterion for classifying a pupil as learning-disabled is under-achievement — achievement level below intelligence level. Another criterion is demonstration that emotional disturbances and other problems are not the source of the pupil's underachievement. One

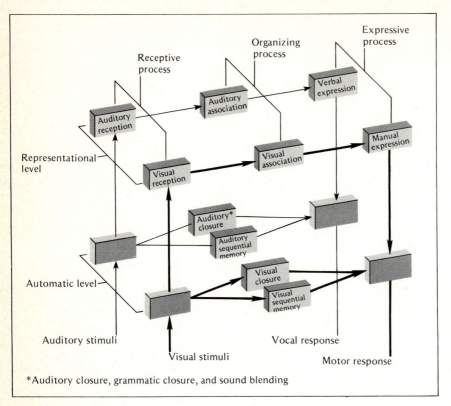

Receptive process

Organizing process

Expressive process

Auditory reception

Auditory association

Verbal expression

Representational level

Visual reception

Visual association

Manual expression

Auditory* closure

Auditory sequential memory

Automatic level

Visual closure

Visual sequential memory

Auditory stimuli

Vocal response

Visual stimuli

Motor response

*Auditory closure, grammatic closure, and sound blending

Fig. 10.3
Structure of the Illinois Test of Psycholinguistic Abilities. (Reprinted by permission from Kirk, McCarthy, and Kirk, 1968, p. 8.)

catch is that the sentence-completion tests may suggest that the pupil has emotional problems when he or she really does not. Another catch is that the pupil's intelligence level may be spuriously low and the discrepancy not apparent because the learning disability interferes with the pupil's showing what he or she can do on an intelligence test. This difficulty is especially a problem in states that require that the youngster must also have at least normal intelligence before he or she can be considered learning-disabled.

Another problem is the disagreement about the reliability and validity of tests people use in identifying LD pupils and getting information to plan their education. An example is the discussion surrounding the *Illinois Test of Psycholinguistic Abilities* (ITPA). Samuel

Kirk and his associates (1968) designed this test to assess information processing. Figure 10.3 shows the structure of the ITPA. Briefly,
the test samples these dimensions:

1. *Levels of organization*
   a) Representational level — the level that uses symbols to carry
      meaning
   b) Automatic level — the level that is habitual and requires less
      translation of a symbol into meaning
2. *Channels of communication*
   a) Auditory-vocal channel — hearing and talking
   b) Visual-motor channel — seeing and doing
3. *Psycholinguistic processes*
   a) Auditory and visual reception

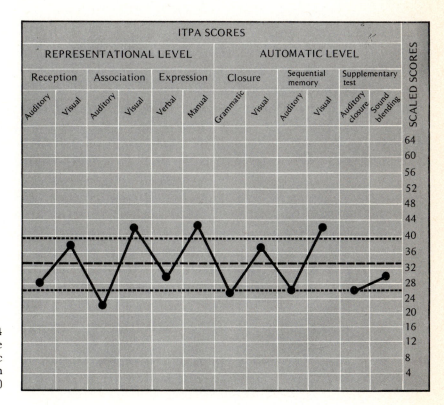

Fig. 10.4
Profile of abilities derived from the
Illinois Test of Psycholinguistic
Abilities. (Reprinted by permission
from Kirk and Kirk, 1971, p. 71.)

b) Auditory and visual association

c) Vocal and manual expression.

These dimensions overlap to yield twelve functions, which the Kirk group sampled with subtests: auditory reception, visual reception, auditory association, visual association, verbal expression, manual expression, grammatic closure, visual closure, auditory sequential memory, visual sequential memory, auditory closure, and sound-blending ability. Figure 10.4 shows the kind of profile of abilities that the test yields.

Some people hold that this test samples behavior very important in diagnosing and treating LD pupils and have developed extensive treatment programs for working with disorders in these processes (e.g., Kirk, 1966; Kirk and Kirk, 1971, 1978; Karnes, 1972, 1975, 1977; Minskoff, Wiseman, and Minskoff, 1975). Others have seriously questioned the validity of the ITPA and the usefulness of psycholinguistic training (e.g., Hammill and Larsen, 1974a, b, 1978; Hammill, Parker, and Newcomer, 1975; Larsen and Hammill, 1975). The argument continues back and forth.

PROCEDURES FOR TESTING LEARNING-DISABLED PUPILS

Collecting Information   Because their problems are so complex, we need a wide range of information about LD pupils, for instance, information about their early development and their current capabilities in physical, sensory, social, emotional, and intellectual behavior — including their abilities to inhibit their behavior and to use perception and other intellectual processes. We get this information through interviewing parents and others who know the pupils, observing pupils in their usual environments, and using such instruments as rating scales and, if we can meet their conditions, criterion-referenced tests and norm-referenced tests — including tests of processes.

Special Procedures for Diagnosis   The two problems — potential for errors in testing LD pupils and disagreement about what characteristics to measure and how to measure them — have led to some very special restrictions on diagnosing pupils as learning-disabled. These restrictions are prescribed in a special set of federal regulations required by PL 94-142. That is, Section 5B of the Statute (1975) requires that the Commissioner of Education "develop regulations that establish criteria for determining whether a particular disorder or condition may be considered a specific learning disability, diagnostic procedures for use in identifying LD children, and monitoring procedures for use in determining whether public agencies are complying with the criteria and diagnostic procedures." Tentative regulations were developed, disseminated, and discussed throughout the United States and then revised. The following additional* regulations were finally adopted (PL 94-142, Regulations, 12/9/77).

1. *Additional team members.* In addition to the people required to diagnose any handicapped child, the team diagnosing an LD pupil must include a regular class teacher† *and* a diagnostic specialist, e.g., a school psychologist, speech/language pathologist, or remedial reading teacher.

2. *Criteria for determining the existence of a specific learning disability.* The team may determine that a child has a specific learning disability if:

   a) The child does not achieve commensurate with his or her age and ability levels in one or more of the areas listed below when provided with appropriate learning experiences; *and*

   b) The child has a severe discrepancy between achievement and intellectual ability in one or more of the following: oral expression, listening comprehension, written expression, basic reading skill, reading comprehension, mathematics calculation, or mathematics reasoning.

   c) The team *may not* identify a child as having a specific learning disability if the severe discrepancy between ability and achievement is primarily the result of: a visual, hearing, or motor handicap; mental retardation; emotional disturbance; or environmental, cultural, or economic disadvantage.

3. *Observation.* At least one team member other than the child's regular teacher shall observe the child's academic performance in the regular classroom setting or other appropriate environment.

4. *Written report.* The team shall prepare a *written* report of the results of the evaluation stating:

   a) Whether the child has a specific learning disability;

   b) The basis for making the determination;

   c) The relevant behavior noted during the observation of the child;

---

* These regulations for diagnosing LD were in addition to those required for all handicapped pupils, i.e., that tests, etc., be in the pupil's native language, that no single procedure may be used, that the evaluation is done by a multidisciplinary team including at least one teacher or other specialist with knowledge in the area of suspected disability, and that there be advocate participation, due process, periodic reevaluation, and confidentiality.

† Or a certified regular preschool teacher if the pupil is below CA 6.

    d) The relationship of that behavior to the child's academic functioning;

    e) The educationally relevant medical findings, if any;

    f) Whether there is a severe discrepancy between achievement and ability which is not correctable *without* special education and related services; and

    g) The determination of the team concerning the effects of environmental, cultural, or economic disadvantage.

5. Each team member shall certify in writing whether the report reflects his or her conclusions. If it does not, the team member must submit a separate statement presenting those conclusions.

Individualizing instruction for learning-disabled pupils

People disagree about most things when they begin to discuss learning-disabled pupils. However, there is usually unanimity on the need for diagnostic/prescriptive teaching — obtaining information describing the pupil's characteristics, planning his or her instruction on the basis of that information, using that plan in teaching, evaluating how well the prescription works, and replanning as needed.* This process, of course, as it is expressed through special education and the related services is our third task — individualizing instruction.

SPECIAL EDUCATION

Instructional Objectives

People differ most about *what* we should teach LD pupils — that is, about instructional objectives. The suggestions are that we should teach psychological processes, language, literacy skills, and mathematics, academic subjects, learning strategies (survival skills), and vocational subjects.

Psychological processes

Proponents of teaching psychological processes maintain that LD pupils should be given training to remedy (treat) the basic psychological processes where they have disorders. The idea is that once the disorder in a psychological process is cleared up, the pupil can perform the instructional objectives for academic material depending on

---

* We have fairly extensive treatises on special education and related services for LD pupils, e.g., Alley and Deshler (1979), Bailey (1975), Baldauf (1975), Bartel (1975), Deshler *et al.* (1979), Goodman and Mann (1976), Hammill and Bartel (1978), Keogh and Glover (1980), Kephart (1971), Myers and Hammill (1976), Myklebust (1975), Wallace and McLoughlin (1975), and Wiig and Semel (1980).

that process. For example, a pupil who has a visual perceptual problem should be trained in visual perception skills. Once this problem is cleared up, he or she should be able to deal with perceptual tasks in math, reading, and other areas.

The main proponents of this approach have been: Strauss, Werner, Lehtinen, Cruickshank, and their associates, who taught perceptual, conceptual, and thinking skills as well as behavior control; Frostig, who taught visual perceptual processes; and Kephart and others, who taught perceptual motor processes. For example, Frostig and Horne (1964) developed a program to treat problems in processes measured by Frostig's Developmental Tests of Visual Perception. This program has activities for teaching *eye-motor skills*, e.g., drawing lines between boundaries; *figure-ground discrimination skills*, such as identifying a particular symbol, say, a square, when it is presented in a different color, size, form, or context; *skills for identifying position in space*, such as avoiding such reversals as *was* for *saw*; and *spatial relation skills*, such as recalling a sequence of items. These activities are combined in a kit, the *Frostig Program for the Development of Visual Perception.*

Language processes

Advocates here suggest that instructional objectives should focus first on language processes. They work on language functions which LD pupils have problems with. The particular functions they stress depend on their ideas about the nature of language. For example, Myklebust and his associates work with expressive and receptive processes in oral language, Kirk and his associates work with the psycholinguistic processes sampled by the ITPA, and Gray and Ryan work with young children in developing very basic syntactic structures, such as producing simple sentences and then increasingly complex forms (e.g., Myklebust, 1975; Kirk and Kirk, 1971; and Gray and Ryan, 1973).

Karnes's materials are good illustrations of these language programs. She developed activities that parents and teachers can use for teaching the psycholinguistic processes to young children who have particular problems, e.g., visual reception disability (the inability to gain meanings from visual symbols and interpret them). Karnes has presented these teaching materials in three kits: the Karnes Early Language Activities, Learning Language at Home, and Goal: Language Development (Karnes, 1972, 1975, 1977).

Literacy skills and content

People who focus on the literacy skills and mathematics have objectives for listening, speaking, reading, handwriting, written composition, mathematics computation, and mathematics problem solving.

They assess the pupils' literacy and select as objectives those in which the pupils have deficits, i.e., the objectives they have not yet mastered.

Beyond the literacy skills — especially with older LD pupils — some people believe in working directly on instructional objectives for content. They use alternative channels of communication and instructional media to circumvent the disability. For example, if the pupil cannot read, they teach him or her orally. They teach LD pupils physical science, social studies, art, and other subjects with their age-mates. Or, if a pupil has been retained and is behind his or her age-mates, they tutor the pupil to help him or her catch up. That is, they do not delay instruction in the content areas until the pupil solves his or her other problems.

Traditionally, this approach has been known as remedial education. Among LD specialists and some other special educators, it is sometimes called the *task training* approach to distinguish it from the *process training* approach. Among the advocates of this approach are Arena (1968, 1972), Gillingham and Stillman (1965), Hammill and his associates (e.g., Hammill and Bartel, 1975), and Lerner (1976), as well as Ysseldyke and Salvia (1974).

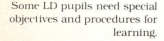

Some LD pupils need special objectives and procedures for learning.

For example, Ysseldyke and Salvia (1974) contrasted the task analysis model and the processes model and concluded that the task

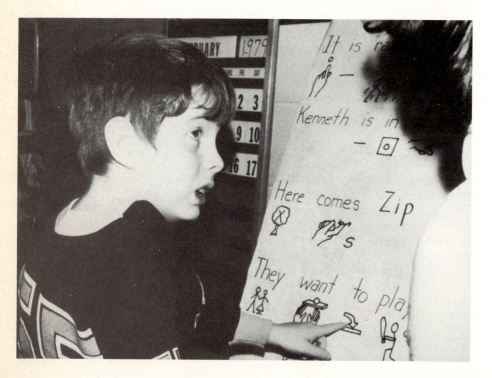

analysis model is the more direct. Task analysis means taking a particular objective — i.e., the terminal behavior — such as learning to differentiate between types of triangles, breaking that objective down into its component parts, and arranging these component parts as a sequence of steps to be achieved. Given the task analysis, proponents of this approach would identify what steps a pupil has mastered and what steps he or she needs still to master and then systematically teach him or her to master each step until he or she reaches the instructional objective serving as the terminal behavior.

Learning how to learn and teaching *study skills* are old approaches. Today the term "learning strategies" is used to describe a variety of techniques for learning and remembering material. An example of a very specific technique is using mnemonic devices as verbal mediators to aid memory, as we do when we use the acronym SALT to help us remember Strategic Arms Limitation Treaties — the series of negotiations and treaties between the United States and the Soviet Union. An example of a more general study skill is a method such as the SQ3R (*Survey, Question, Read, Recite, Review*) method for learning material.

Learning and social strategies (survival skills)

In addition to learning strategies, we also have a set of social strategies which help a pupil progress in school. These range from subtle behavior, e.g., maintaining eye contact with the teacher, to broader behavior, e.g., using appropriate gestures to signal friendliness and appropriate procedures to start and maintain a conversation.

People concerned with educating LD pupils often use the term "survival skills" to refer to these objectives for learning strategies and social strategies. Alley and Deshler (1979) and Bryan and Bryan (1975) are leaders in this approach. For example, Alley and Deshler propose that we teach pupils such skills as: *reading skills* (vocabulary development, word recognition, reading comprehension, varying reading rate, and study skills); *writing skills* (rhetorical modes and mechanics); *mathematics skills* (number and numeration, computation, and problem solving); *speaking skills* (word finding, syntax, oral discourse); *thinking skills* (time management, organizing, and problem solving); and *social skills* (self-awareness and social relationships).

Adolescent and young adult LD pupils need objectives for vocational content and skills — especially if they still have not mastered the literacy skills to a fairly mature level. That is, a teenager who is still reading, writing, and spelling on a primary level needs some intensive help to identify possible jobs and to prepare for those jobs. In programs emphasizing vocational preparation, pupils systematically

Vocational subjects

study job requirements, identify skills they need to learn in order to meet those job requirements, work on those skills in the classroom, and practice those skills in on-the-job training.

Instructional Schedules

Many people use the term "specific learning disabilities" and emphasize the adjective *specific.* The idea is that the pupil has trouble learning in some areas but not in others. Two generalizations about scheduling follow. First, the pupil should progress at a normal rate in academic areas unaffected by the disability and in academic areas where he or she can use alternative skills. Again, consider Susan Hampshire, who could not learn her roles through reading, but could learn them when she heard them orally. Second, the pupil will progress more slowly in academic areas affected by the disability. A pupil who has a mathematics disability (dyscalculia) will progress more slowly in arithmetic, geometry, and algebra. One who has a specific word-recall or naming disability (anomia), will progress more slowly in listening, speaking, reading, and other language arts.

Some difficult decisions about scheduling may be necessary as LD pupils move through school. For example, again, if dyscalculia slows down a pupil's math progress, we need to allow more time for math and science instruction if all concerned consider it important that the pupil master these objectives. This allowing more time may slow the pupil down so much that he or she may need to progress more slowly through school. The other alternative is to let the pupil progress through school at the same rate as other pupils by omitting some objectives. This action may have serious consequences for his or her later development, e.g., it is serious to omit math and science instruction, because the pupil then will not have them available for adult roles.

Instructional Procedures

We teach learning-disabled pupils through such methods as teacher presentations, problem solving, group work, and individual work. Materials range from books to tapes, and so on. What particular methods and materials we use depend on the pupil's particular disability and on the objectives we choose.

Some pupils require alternative means for getting information. This is called circumventing the disability. For example, suppose that a pupil is dyslexic. Certainly we will work on teaching him or her reading. However, we may decide that we cannot hold up teaching social studies, science, literature and other subjects while we wait for him or her to acquire sufficient reading skills for these areas. Consequently, we would use tutors reading to the pupil, audio tapes, and video tapes to transmit information in social studies, science, and the other content areas which non-LD pupils would get through reading.

Sometimes we choose special objectives for LD pupils and use specially designed programs containing methods and materials for those objectives. For example, we mentioned the kits that Karnes and Frostig developed for teaching their programs. There are many other such instructional systems, e.g., the *MWM Program for Developing Language Abilities* (Minskoff, Wiseman, and Minskoff, 1975) and *Building Spelling Skills in Dyslexic Children* and *Building Number Skills in Dyslexic Children* (Arena, 1968, 1972).

We also need special procedures if pupils have such inhibition problems as distractibility, hyperactivity, and perseveration. Two approaches have been used: the stimulus control approach and the behavior modification approach.

Stimulus control has been used by one group that looks to brain injury as a cause of learning disability and perceptual training as a treatment. This group, which started with Goldstein and included Strauss, Werner, Lehtinen, Cruickshank, and their students, developed an extensive set of methods and materials for focusing pupils' attention and breaking perseveration. For example, Cruickshank and his group (1961), in their model training program for brain-injured and hyperactive children, worked out a set of procedures to achieve structure and attention focusing, to remove extraneous stimuli, and to capitalize on the pupil's drive to manipulate things. To achieve *structure*, they used a high degree of control by closely directing the pupils' activities. As pupils learned self-direction, they gradually reduced the supervision. To achieve *attention focusing*, they modified teaching materials to emphasize features pupils should attend to. For example, in handwriting they used heavy black lines or colors to show the pupil the lines he or she should write on and the boundaries where he or she should stop. To *remove extraneous stimuli*, they eliminated extra items whenever possible. For example, to help pupils stay in place in reading, they would use page covers which exposed only the line to be read; in arithmetic they presented only one problem per page. To *capitalize on the pupils' drive to manipulate things*, they used teaching devices with moving parts as much as possible. For example, they used an abacus in teaching pupils arithmetic operations.

Behavior modification has been used by some — especially to help youngsters work on their distractibility and hyperactivity (e.g., Prout, 1977). They use tokens and other reinforcement to help LD pupils stay on task — that is, to focus their attention and not be distractible and to persist in the desired responses rather than be hyperactive. At the same time, they achieve structure by breaking the tasks to be learned into small steps, starting pupils at their levels (i.e., at the steps they are ready for) and carrying them through to the finished performance.

Instructional Settings

Instructional settings for LD pupils — personnel and space needs for working with them — vary with what pupils' particular problems are and whether other pupils have similar problems. Again, for example, suppose that a pupil is dyslexic but able to keep up or excel in all other areas. Then he or she needs someone to read to him or her and a space for working with audio- and videotapes, but no other particular space and personnel adjustments.

Specialists who emphasize procedures to control inhibition problems suggest that the instructional environment be highly structured also. For example, Cruickshank and his predecessors/ successors in the stimulus control group suggested removing or minimizing environmental stimuli as much as possible (e.g., Cruickshank *et al.*, 1961). In such classrooms walls are bare of pictures and bulletin boards, cabinets and bookcases are covered, walls and ceilings are sound-proofed and floors are carpeted, and instructional materials and equipment are kept out of sight. In addition, cubicles are available for pupils who are distracted by other people in the room. These three-sided or fully enclosed booths become offices pupils can retire to for work or for rest when "things begin to get on their nerves" — to put it colloquially.

RELATED SERVICES

Learning-disabled pupils may need medical services, speech/ language therapy, psychological services, vocational rehabilitation, and family information and counseling services.

Medical Services

Not all specific learning disabilities are traceable to brain pathology, but some are. Consequently, pupils need the services of a neurologist to see whether a neurological disorder is present and whether it needs, and can benefit from, treatment.

In addition, the services of an internal medicine specialist may be useful in evaluating the feasibility of drugs and dietary treatment. Considerable controversy has surrounded using drugs to treat LD pupils, especially those with severe distractibility and hyperactivity. For example, some have recommended drugs such as Ritalin, but others have roundly condemned such practices. Physicians should certainly be a crucial part of the team making such decisions.

Oral language problems cited in the federal definition are often called "aphasia" by speech/language pathologists. Difficulty in understanding through listening is sometimes diagnosed as receptive aphasia, and difficulty in using spoken language is sometimes diagnosed as expressive aphasia. Speech/language pathologists are specially trained to work with the aphasias and should be primary members of the treatment team when pupils have these disabilities.

Speech/Language Therapy

Vocational and career education, integral services for learning-disabled pupils, need to begin early.

Psychologists are as important members of the team serving LD pupils as they are with pupils who have other handicaps. School psychologists participate in the various complex diagnostic processes. Clinical psychologists and psychiatrists help pupils and their families work with social/emotional problems which learning disabilities cause.

Psychological Services

Vocational Rehabilitation   The LD pupil in secondary school may need vocational counseling. The VR specialist collects evidence about the pupil's characteristics that are relevant to job performance. In addition, he or she provides information about jobs to the LD youngster and his or her advocates, if appropriate. Then all work to mesh the LD youngster's characteristics with the job requirements. Once the youngster has made some choices, the VR specialist may help him or her locate sources of training and get admitted to a training program. In addition, if needed, the VR specialist may help the LD youngster locate a job.

Family Information and Counseling Services   Specific learning disabilities can be particularly baffling. Pupils are normal in so many areas, but have holes in particular areas such as reading or math. Also, distractibility, hyperactivity, and perseveration can be particularly trying. The pupil has trouble controlling himself or herself or is impossible to control in situations, e.g., church or the grocery store, where control is essential. These situations require that LD pupils' families get information about how best to deal with them and help in dealing with social and emotional disruption in the family. Social workers, psychiatrists, and clinical psychologists can supply this information and help.

Placing learning-disabled pupils in the least restrictive environment

Once the pupil has been identified as learning-disabled and his or her instruction has been planned, our final task is to make decisions about placement for the delivery of special education and related services. These decisions are about placement options, extracurricular activities, transportation and facilities, and safety.

PLACEMENT OPTIONS

Identification and treatment during infancy or the preschool period are as crucial for the LD child as they are for children with other handicaps. Problems with the psychological processes, the language skills, and control of behavior certainly can deflect pupils' development and cause failures in their mastering more and more complex cultural tasks. Consequently, it is important that teachers, speech/language therapists, and psychologists start working with the pupils as soon as possible.

Figure 10.5 shows how LD pupils were being placed in the late 1970s. Options of keeping pupils at home or placing them in special schools or institutions are usually not considered. Self-contained special classes formerly were often used, but they are not too frequent

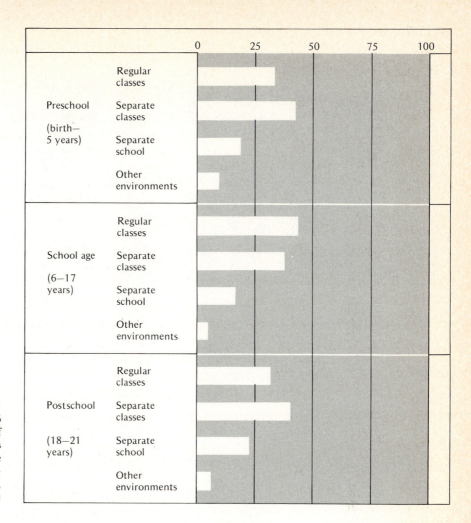

Fig. 10.5
Most frequent placements of learning-disabled pupils reported by the states in the late 1970s. (Based on information in BEH, 1979, pp. 169–189.)

any more. Instead, LD pupils are usually placed in regular classes as their primary bases. They may go to an LD teacher's resource room for special education, to a speech/language therapist's area for language therapy, or to both of these. In some cases the regular teacher works with the pupil in the regular classroom, and the LD teacher and speech/language therapist consult and supply special services and materials.

Several factors are important in deciding among the LD pupils' placement options. These can be stated as questions.

☐ Is the pupil distractible? Hyperactive? How seriously? How well does he or she tolerate frustration?

☐ Does the pupil have a disorder of perception? Conceptualizing? Memorizing? Thinking? More than one process? How seriously?

Extracurricular activities for LD pupils must be chosen with care.

☐ Is the pupil underachieving in listening? Spoken language? Reading? Spelling? Handwriting? Written composition? Mathematics? More than one? How seriously?

☐ Is the pupil underachieving in the content areas? Which ones? How seriously?

Of course, the pupil with more than one problem or a very serious single problem needs more specialized placement, e.g., more time in the resource room. As treatment works and the problems come more under control, the pupil should spend more time in the less specialized environments.

EXTRACURRICULAR ACTIVITIES

Finding extracurricular activities can be quite a problem for a pupil who has serious distractibility, hyperactivity, receptive aphasia, expressive aphasia, or problems perceiving and understanding social cues. Activities that allow plenty of movement and yet require a minimum of group work or teamwork are often used. Swimming and track are examples. However, we need to be careful that the pupil is not unduly isolated by such activities.

Pupils who have dyslexia, problems writing, or similar disorders which are not too disruptive usually have more options for extracurricular activities. For example, most sports are feasible. So are such activities as working on the school yearbook. The pupils simply process information through other means; for example, they use listening instead of reading.

TRANSPORTATION AND FACILITIES

Most LD pupils can travel independently around school and to and from school. Nonreaders soon learn to rely on other means of communication. Seriously distractible or hyperactive pupils or those with aphasia are more limited and need more supervision.

Access to facilities is not a particular problem either. However, some youngsters may have problems with safety signs and warning signals and need special instruction.

SAFETY

Highly distractible or hyperactive pupils need special vigilance and care. They need to be protected from moving cars, high places, and dangerous tools and machinery. Their failure to attend to dangerous stimuli and safety signs and their impulsive behavior can lead to injury.

Aphasic pupils and those who cannot read also need close supervision. They may be injured because they cannot interpret messages indicating danger.

Summary

IDENTIFYING AND PLANNING FOR LEARNING-DISABLED PUPILS

Psychological processes are those intellectual functions and inhibitory functions which enable us to learn and think. Language includes functions required for using symbols in dealing with the world. Adequate psychological processes and adequate language are essential to our learning and performing the cultural tasks.

Normal Development

A specific learning disability occurs if something happens to the normal development of one or more psychological processes or language functions or a combination of these and if the deflection is severe enough to interfere with the youngster's learning and performing the cultural tasks. Four characteristics are common to most definitions of LD pupils — underachievement, uneven development, disorders in psychological processes, and causes excluded. The Child-Find activities to locate LD pupils include public awareness campaigns designed to make people sensitive to LD pupils and their problems, screening for signs suggesting that a pupil might have a learning disability, and referral to physicians, LD specialists, and other specialists for further study. In diagnosis we classify the pupils by type of disability — *psychological process problems* (distractibility, hyperactivity, low frustration tolerance, perseveration, perceptual difficulties, memory difficulties, conceptual difficulties, and thinking difficulties) and *language problems* (difficulties in oral production, oral reception, written production, and written reception). In diagnosing LD pupils we also classify the cause of their problem — brain

Learning Disabilities

dysfunction, inheritance, environmental deprivation, or unknown causes.

Impact of Learning Disabilities on Pupils' Characteristics

LD pupils show difficulties in other characteristics also. If brain dysfunction causes the learning disabilities, it can lead also to physical problems which coexist with the psychological and educational problems. These physical problems may range from mild to severe. In addition, the disorder in intellectual function, language, or inhibition can interfere with the pupil's intellectual, social/emotional, academic achievement, and vocational characteristics.

Accountability

To ensure accountability in identifying and planning for LD pupils, we document the Child-Find and develop the IEP as part of our efforts to provide adequate programs. At the same time, we safeguard the LD pupils' rights by observing the procedural safeguards, including advocate participation, due process, equal protection, periodic re-evaluation, and confidentiality.

NONDISCRIMINATORY TESTING OF LEARNING-DISABLED PUPILS

Problems in Testing Learning-Disabled Pupils

One problem in testing LD pupils is the potentiality for error because the learning disabilities may interfere with test performance. Another problem is the disagreement about the reliability and validity of tests people use in identifying LD pupils and getting information to plan their education.

Procedures for Testing Learning-Disabled Pupils

Because their problems are so complex, we need a wide range of information about LD pupils. Because of the two problems — potential for errors in testing LD pupils and disagreement about what characteristics to measure, we have some very special restrictions in diagnosing pupils as learning-disabled. These restrictions are prescribed in a special set of federal regulations about the members of the team doing the diagnosis, the criteria for determining the existence of a learning disability, and procedures that must be used in the diagnosis.

INDIVIDUALIZING INSTRUCTION FOR LEARNING-DISABLED PUPILS

Special Education

People disagree about what *instructional objectives* we should select for LD pupils. The suggestions range over objectives for the psychological processes, language, literacy skills, and mathematics, academic subjects, learning and social strategies (survival skills), and vocational subjects. Pupils should progress at a normal rate — and need no adjustments in *instructional schedules* — for areas unaffected by the learning disability or for areas in which they can circumvent the problem. They will proceed at a slower rate — and need adjusted schedules — for affected areas they cannot circumvent. The extra time required may necessitate some difficult decisions about dropping objectives from the curriculum. LD pupils potentially can use the full range of *instructional procedures* we use with all pupils, and we select particular methods and media, depending on the pupils' characteristics. In addition, some pupils require alternative means for getting information, some require special procedures for controlling inhibition problems, and some need special objectives and specially designed methods and materials for those objectives. Generally, *instructional settings* for LD pupils vary with what the pupils' particular problems are and whether other pupils have similar problems. In addition, specialists who emphasize procedures to control inhibition problems suggest that the instructional environment be highly structured also.

Learning-disabled pupils may need medical services, speech/language therapy, psychological services, vocational rehabilitation services, and family information and counseling services.

Related Services

PLACING LEARNING-DISABLED PUPILS IN THE LEAST RESTRICTIVE ENVIRONMENT

Identification and treatment during infancy or the preschool period are as crucial for LD pupils as they are for pupils with other handicaps. At school ages, LD pupils are usually placed in regular classes as their primary bases. They may go to an LD teacher, a speech/language pathologist, or both of these for special help. Or the LD teacher may consult with the regular teacher, working with the pupil in the regular classroom.

Placement Options

The particular extracurricular activities selected depend on the LD pupils' specific problems. They should have activities in which they are not penalized by their problems. At the same time, they should not be unduly isolated by such activities.

Extracurricular Activities

Most LD pupils can travel independently, and they do not need special adjustments of facilities or supervision for safety. However, seriously distractible or hyperactive pupils and those with aphasia may need special help in transportation and special precautions for safety.

Transportation, Facilities, and Safety

11

Identifying and planning for seriously emotionally disturbed pupils

NORMAL SOCIAL/EMOTIONAL BEHAVIOR
Development of normal social/emotional behavior
Social/emotional behavior and the cultural tasks

SERIOUS EMOTIONAL DISTURBANCE
Legal definition and prevalence
Finding seriously emotionally disturbed pupils
Diagnosis: Classification by degree of emotional
   disturbance
Diagnosis: Classification by degree of emotional
   disturbances
Sources of emotional disturbances

IMPACT OF SERIOUS EMOTIONAL DISTURBANCES ON PUPILS' CHARACTERISTICS
Introduction
Physical functioning
Speech and language
Intellectual functioning

Special Needs of Seriously Emotionally Disturbed Pupils

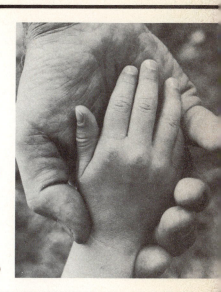

Academic achievement
Vocational functioning

ACCOUNTABILITY

Identifying and planning for seriously emotionally
disturbed pupils
Observing the procedural safeguards for seriously
emotionally disturbed pupils

Nondiscriminatory testing of seriously emotionally
disturbed pupils

PROBLEMS IN TESTING EMOTIONALLY DISTURBED PUPILS

**PROCEDURES FOR TESTING EMOTIONALLY DISTURBED
PUPILS**

Individualizing instruction for seriously emotionally
disturbed pupils

SPECIAL EDUCATION

Social/emotional behavior
Academic skills

RELATED SERVICES

> Medical services
> Psychological services
> Vocational rehabilitation services
> Family information and counseling
> Speech/language therapy

Placing seriously emotionally disturbed pupils in the least restrictive environment

PLACEMENT OPTIONS

EXTRACURRICULAR ACTIVITIES

TRANSPORTATION AND FACILITIES

SAFETY

Identifying and planning for seriously emotionally disturbed pupils

Seriously emotionally disturbed pupils are usually upset youngsters who in turn often cause others around them to feel distress. Our responsibility is to get these pupils to the treatment that will help them be more emotionally comfortable and more socially harmonious. Identification through the Child-Find and planning through the IEP come first as we set about carrying out this responsibility within the protections of the legal safeguards. Our work is based on our understanding of normal social/emotional development, the problems that deflect this normal development, and the impact of these problems on other characteristics that influence how the pupil learns and performs the cultural tasks.

NORMAL SOCIAL/EMOTIONAL BEHAVIOR

Development of Normal Social/Emotional Behavior

Emotional and social behavior go together in very complex ways to influence how happy we are and how well we get along with people around us. Our emotional responses influence our getting along socially with other people, and in turn our social experiences influence our emotional status. *Emotions* essentially are feelings. An infant starts out expressing two kinds of responses: general reactions of pleasure, which develop into such positive responses as love and happiness, and general reactions to distress, which differentiate into such negative responses as fear and anxiety and anger and hostility. *Social behavior* is a coordinated set of responses to other people. An infant starts with a noticing response, attending to other people. Thereafter, social responses become increasingly complex. As the child matures, he or she learns to enter into interactions that will lead to the pleasure reactions. Similarly, the child learns to express his or her negative feelings in ways that cause a minimum of disruption to these social interactions. Table 11.1 lists representative milestones in the development of normal social/emotional interactions. Again, it shows how simple responses serve as building blocks for later, more complex social/emotional behavior.

Social/Emotional Behavior and the Cultural Tasks

As John Donne so wisely said, "No man is an island." We simply cannot make it alone. In turn, benefiting from and contributing to an increasingly complex social environment require that we handle our negative emotions appropriately and maintain a certain degree of happiness and good nature most of the time. Happiness gives us the clarity of mind to concentrate on, and the energy to undertake, the full range of cultural tasks, from studying, to exercising, to performing

Emotional and social behavior go together in very complex ways to influence how happy we are and how well we get along with people around us.

TABLE 11.1 MILESTONES IN THE NORMAL DEVELOMENT OF SOCIAL/EMOTIONAL INTERACTIONS.

Age	Skill	
0–12 months	Smiles spontaneously. Responds differently to strangers than to familiar people. Pays attention to own name. Responds to *no*.	Copies simple actions of others.
12–24 months	Recognizes self in mirror or picture. Refers to self by name. Plays by self, initiates own play.	Imitates adult behaviors in play. Helps put things away.

TABLE 11.1 Continued

Age	Skill	
24–36 months	Plays near other children. Watches other children, joins briefly in their play. Defends own possessions. Begins to play house.	Symbolically uses objects, self in play. Participates in simple group activity (for example, sings, claps, dances). Knows gender identity.
36–48 months	Joins in play with other children. Begins to interact. Shares toys. Takes turns with assistance.	Begins dramatic play, acting out whole scenes (for example, traveling, playing house, pretending to be animals).
48–60 months	Plays and interacts with other children. Dramatic play is closer to reality, with attention paid to detail, time, and space.	Plays dress-up. Shows interest in exploring sex differences.
60–72 months	Chooses own friend(s). Plays simple table games. Plays competitive games.	Engages with other children in cooperative play involving group decisions, role assignments, fair play.

Source: Hayden and Smith, n.d., pp. 126–133.

the daily chores. Good nature is the oil that smoothes the interactions, and sometimes the clangs, among people. Consider again cultural tasks like those illustrated in Table 1.1. Which ones could we learn and subsequently perform in the absence of emotional equanimity and social harmony to make possible attention, energy, and teaching? And which of the later, more complex tasks could we learn if we had not mastered the earlier tasks?

SERIOUS EMOTIONAL DISTURBANCE

Legal Definition and Prevalence

Sometimes circumstances occur or problems arise to deflect a youngster's social/emotional development from the course of normal development portrayed in Table 11.1. When this deflection is severe enough to interfere with the youngster's learning and performing the cultural tasks, we consider that he or she is seriously emotionally disturbed.

We run into some ambiguity when we seek to translate this generalization into specifics needed for serving the pupil (e.g., Garmezy, 1978; Kauffman, 1977; Kelly *et al.*, 1977). If all classification is difficult, identifying emotionally disturbed pupils is especially difficult. People simply do not agree on how we can or should define emotional/social health and disturbance. These disagreements happen for at least four reasons. *One*, throughout history people have had different theories about what social/emotional disturbances are, what causes them, and how to treat them. For example, the followers of Freud, the father of psychoanalysis, have one set of ideas, and the followers of Skinner, the father of behaviorism, have another. *Two*, people with different responsibilities see pupils' behavior differently. For example, it was shown a very long time ago that teachers considered aggressive behavior a serious problem, whereas clinical psychologists were more concerned about withdrawing behavior. *Three*, people from different socioeconomic, ethnic, sex, and social groups differ in what social/emotional behavior they will accept. For

Sometimes circumstances occur or problems arise that deflect a pupil's social/emotional development.

example, lower-class boys accept, and often require, in one another behavior that middle-class teachers, especially women, consider to be quite a problem, and vice versa. *Four*, even within groups, families have different ideas about what makes the good life. For example, some stress social success, outgoing behavior, joining social groups, and leading those groups. Others stress self-reliance and turning inward more. Such families shape their children differently, and in school we may see pupils with very different types of behavior. Sometimes we may confuse social assertiveness with aggressiveness, or introspection with withdrawal.

In special education today we have different definitions of social/emotional disorders. However, there are several common features: The social/emotional problem persists over a long period, is severe, and interferes with performing school work and other cultural tasks. The legal definition in PL 94-142 puts it this way:

Serious emotional disturbance is a condition exhibiting one or more of the following characteristics over a long period of time and to a marked degree, which adversely affects educational performance:

☐ An inability to learn which cannot be explained by intellectual, sensory, or health factors;*

☐ An inability to build or maintain satisfactory interpersonal relationships with peers and teachers;

☐ Inappropriate types of behavior or feelings under normal circumstances;

☐ A general pervasive mood of unhappiness or depression; or

☐ A tendency to develop physical symptoms or fears associated with personal or school problems.

The term includes children who are schizophrenic or autistic.

The term does not include children who are socially maladjusted, unless it is determined that they are seriously emotionally disturbed. (PL 94-142, *Regulations*, 1977, Sec. 121a.5)

It is important to note qualification about socially maladjusted youngsters in the final sentence. This means that asocial youngsters — those sometimes called delinquent — are not included in the federal definition, and thus the entitlements and protections of PL 94-142, unless their troubles with society stem from personal problems rather than only a failure to conform to society's customs and laws.

Prevalence estimates are in Fig. 1.1. Estimates range from between 1.2% and 2%. By the late 1970s, approximately 0.5% of the estimated population had been located and served.

---

* That is, emotionally disturbed pupils' failures are not attributable to mental retardation, etc.

Finding Seriously Emotionally Disturbed Pupils

In the Child-Find we identify pupils who qualify for services and protections under the law because they are emotionally disturbed. In *awareness* campaigns three ideas are crucial. One idea is that many aggressive, acting-out pupils do not need punishment because they are unpleasant. Instead, they need help. These youngsters can be so disruptive and cause so much trouble that the human reaction is to strike back at them. Or, we may move too quickly in repressing acting-out pupils or expelling them from school in order to keep other pupils from being physically hurt or their time from being wasted by someone else's explosions or to keep school property from being damaged. Awareness campaigns can help us see that such striking back, repression, and expulsions are not the best treatment for a seriously emotionally disturbed pupil.

Another idea in awareness campaigns is that some quiet, apparently passive pupils are not model pupils who can be ignored or at least accepted and not given special attention because they do not make trouble. Instead, they too need help. "Still waters run deep." Many youngsters are so withdrawn and compliant that it is easy to miss them in the hurly-burly of the school world. They may be desperately sick youngsters who are retreating further every day or getting angrier and angrier even though they do not show that anger.

Still another idea is that some pupils (sometimes called psychotic) are so profoundly disturbed that they show only minimal responses or no responses to people and events around them. As a result, they are sometimes wrongly considered profoundly mentally retarded or suspected of being profoundly deaf. Youngsters with the three types of profound problems — emotional disturbance, deafness, and mental retardation — need to be treated differently, and this different treatment needs to start very early. Awareness campaigns, then, make people conscious of the need to identify and to respond differently to such problems very early in infancy.

In *screening*, then, we look for acting-out, withdrawing, and psychotic pupils (e.g., Crow, 1978; Kohn, 1977; Newcomer, 1980). As the name suggests, the *acting-out* pupil's attacks are an expression of an emotional conflict within him or her. Here we begin to distinguish between the pupil who attacks to act out and the pupil who attacks because he or she does not know about or does not accept social norms. Signs such as the following indicate that we need to refer the pupil for further study:

☐ Poor self-control, e.g., frequent temper tantrums, irresponsibility, and irritability

☐ Attacks on other pupils, e.g., fighting, teasing, quarrelling

☐ Resistance to adults, e.g., arguing, disobedience

☐ Inappropriate behavior in groups, e.g., profanity *where it is not accepted,* frequent interruptions, consistent rule breaking

☐ Destruction of property, e.g., breaking windows and furniture, destroying toys.

The *withdrawing* pupil keeps the serious emotional problem within. Here we begin to distinguish between the pupil who has a serious emotional problem which is paralyzing him or her and the pupil who is marching to a different drummer, so to speak. Such signs as these indicate that we need to refer the pupil for further work:

☐ Excessive quietness and shyness, e.g., difficulty initiating conversations or speaking up in groups, very soft voice

☐ Extreme self-consciousness, e.g., refusal to look in mirror or try new clothes

☐ Very anxious and fearful, e.g., reluctance to try new things

☐ Frequent depression and sadness, e.g., a general appearance of unhappiness

☐ Quick dips in interest, e.g., some show of response to others with a sudden withdrawal

☐ Frequent illnesses, e.g., upset stomach, allergies, and asthma

☐ Seriously inaccurate perception of the nature of reality and its demands, e.g., cruelty in social situations, such as "truth-telling" about an unattractive dress.

The *psychotic* pupil's behavior is out of touch with reality. He or she simply does not perceive the environment accurately and frequently shows bizarre behavior. Such signs as the following are indications of danger:

☐ Social isolation, e.g., apparent unresponsiveness to other people

☐ Excessive immature behavior, e.g., poor eating habits beyond the time when they should be acquired

☐ Behavior leading to self-injury, e.g., constant head bumping

☐ Unusual physical habits, e.g., rumination (regurgitating partly digested food and continuing to chew it — as a cow chews her cud)

☐ Delusions, e.g., "Some rats are inside chewing my stomach up"

☐ Language consisting of parroted repetitions, jargon, and bizarre statements, e.g., "Sally sum Susie, Sally sum Susie."

These signs of possible social/emotional disturbance can be observed pretty directly. Acting-out behavior is painfully obvious. So is bizarre behavior. Withdrawing behavior is not too difficult to spot, once we are sensitive to it. However, it is sometimes helpful to have screening tools to focus our attention. The Quay-Peterson Behavior Problem Checklist (1967), the Kohn Social Competence Scale, and the Kohn Symptom Checklist for the Preschool Child (1977) are examples of screening tools.

If the pupil shows signs of having a serious emotional disturbance, our next step is *referral* for further study. The primary referral is for psychological evaluation by a psychiatrist or clinical psychologist. This person describes the pupil's problem, tries to unravel its causes or at least conditions contributing to it which need changing, and specifies what kind of therapy might help the pupil. School psychologists assess how much the emotional disturbance is interfering with the pupil's intellectual behavior and academic achievement. Teachers — specialists in educating emotionally disturbed pupils — evaluate how much the emotional disturbance interferes with the pupil's functioning comfortably in a group and his or her responding to instruction in the classroom. Social workers may be needed to join all of these other specialists in getting information about the youngster's family circumstances.

Diagnosis: Classification by Type of Emotional Disturbance

Again, over the years we have accumulated different typologies — listings of types. These classification systems differ because people with different specialties have diverse backgrounds and purposes in classification. Psychiatrists have two major systems: *The Diagnostic and Statistical Manual of Mental Disorders* (DSM-III), done by the American Psychiatric Association (1980), and the categories done by the Group for the Advancement of Psychiatry (Committee on Child Psychiatry) (1966). For example, the GAP proposed these classifications: healthy responses, reactive disorders, developmental deviations, psychoneurotic disorders, personality disorders, psychotic disorders, psychophysiological disorders, brain syndromes, and mental retardation. The GAP gave extensive descriptions for these categories.

Such classification systems are useful to psychiatrists and other specialists. However, some educators and psychologists propose describing behavior in ways that are more helpful in planning educational treatments and judging whether a pupil's behavior is improving or deteriorating (e.g., Folz, 1980). Quay (1972, 1975) and Spivack and his associates (1971) have done some frequently cited work on this problem. These specialists have taken what is called a *dimensional* approach. They do not have numerous different labels and categories, but instead look for the common threads running through many apparently different categories and statements about problems. For example, Quay (1972, 1975) identified four patterns — personality disorders, conduct disorders, immaturity, and socialized delinquency. Spivack, Swift, and Prewitt (1972) labeled one group of symptoms impulsive (e.g., externalized symptoms such as defiance), another group, internalized disturbance (e.g., high dependency), and a third group, classroom disturbance, irrelevant responses, and tendency to externalize blame (e.g., fighting).

As we examine these and other studies in which the investigators used factor analysis,* we see two main patterns emerge — the acting-out pupil, who *externalizes* his or her problems, and the withdrawing pupil, who *internalizes* problems. In addition, some special educators work with psychotic pupils.

Acting-out pupils externalize their problems. These unhappy pupils are restless and subject to frequent temper tantrums. They are angry pupils, attacking other pupils, damaging or destroying any property which may get in their ways, and fighting adults — parents, teachers, and other people in authority. They generally keep their surroundings in an uproar. They are usually loners who do not relate to other youngsters or to adults. And others often actively reject them. This description illustrates.

Acting-out pupils

> Donna is fourteen years old but looks eighteen. She is socially adept, particularly in her relations with boys. She has been socially promoted to the seventh grade. She was referred for disruptive, defiant, and aggressive behavior. She has been involved in frequent fights in school, and her rages have led her to physically injuring others. Recently, she was expelled for attacking a 23-year-old teacher who had made her mad.
>
> Donna is a very pretty, physically precocious girl. She is pseudosophisticated in terms of activities she involves herself in, things she talks about, and her mannerisms. These belie her emotional immaturity. Her approach to problem solving is rigid, confrontive, and belligerent. Once she has made a decision as to how to cope with a situation, she stubbornly and defiantly maintains her position. If her inflexible and defiant confrontation does not lead to resolution, she becomes enraged and attacks.
>
> When Donna loses control, her rage is so intense that she has to be restrained physically to protect herself and others. Often it takes hours for Donna to calm down. After such episodes she can review the events, see how others reacted to her, and give reasons why the others acted and felt as they did. She generally is not able to give alternative ways of acting, but would agree that "The next time I'll do better."

---

* Factor analysis is a statistical procedure for processing many separate test scores and identifying the basic general trends (factors or dimensions) that those test scores have in common.

At home, Donna is subject to much stress. Her mother and stepfather have a tenuous, volatile relationship. Donna has learned her coping strategies directly from her mother, who is hostile and inflexible in her approach to problem solving. Donna has ambivalent feelings toward her mother, depending on her as a much younger child would, feeling very insecure about her mother's love and approval of her, and at the same time feeling a rebellious hostility toward her for not meeting her needs. Her parents have added to her stress by placing unrealistic expectations on her. They see her as having superior intelligence when she actually operates at a barely acceptable intellectual level. They expect that someday she will become a pediatrician, and Donna feels a need to meet this expectation. At home she is expected to care for three younger sisters, and much adult responsibility is placed on her....

Her academic achievement scores put her at the fifth-grade level in math and the sixth-grade level in reading. She has much difficulty in applying math processes to actual problem solving except in reference to money, which she handles with ease.

Below is a story Donna wrote for her English teacher.

About my temper

My Report   *By Donna*

When i get mad at someone, I don't care who it is because I will stay mad at that person for ever and there are some ways to cool your temper when you get mad at someone you can tell some one that you are mad at that person Like yesterday when I got mad at a girl in my class yesterday but my teacher took me out of the room she ask me what the matter with you I got madder at her when she said that to me yesterday she said for me to tell my father hello I was so mad I forgotten to tell him what said when I got home I talk to my father about I did yesterday the center. When me and my little sister named sonia get mad at are parents forget all about what we was mad at them, we get with them to see my grandmother When I get mad at terey like when he call me like this morning like something after ten o'clock I was making up my mother's bed when he called me but when I get finish make up her bed but when I went over my brother's house this morning he was outside when I was going down the road so I said this to him but he walked where I was going this morning then he kiss me good so I put my arms around him and the same thing happened to me so I told him good bye. So he got upset with me because that I said good-bye and I don't like to say good-bye no one like him because I have him just because he is someone in my mine and I do love him just like he love me But when I get mad at him he make me sick to my butt and I will not for give him. When I get mad at my sisters and brothers I don't like my school or the teacher. (Wood, 1979, pp. 63–65)

Withdrawing pupils internalize their unhappiness, or at least they do not express it openly. They are sad youngsters and fearful — especially in social situations. Often they are very angry. But they do not express this anger openly. Instead, they take the passive-aggressive approach of noncompliance and school failure. This means that even though they appear compliant, they refuse to carry out directions, accept leadership, or participate in group activities. They often have severe feelings of inferiority and self-consciousness. They also appear to be loners. They do not establish close relationships with other children or with adults. Often other children and adults reject them or at least ignore them. Consider this illustration.

> Victor's teachers describe him this way: Victor has learned that it is best not to talk at home; you do what you are told. In school he spontaneously offers brief comments about his own activities. He will answer in two word phrases any questions put to him by other children or adults. He will not share his supplies or materials. He participates in all activities but always passively. He has difficulty understanding verbal directions if no visual demonstration is provided to him. When he fails at a task or anticipates that he might fail, he withdraws and refuses all help. Usually he tries to run out of the room or destroys the materials. Sometimes he attacks other children. When others act out he usually gets involved and models them. After such episodes he refuses to talk about the incident or his own role in it. When Victor is praised for something he has done, he quickly destroys it. This same sensitivity is displayed when he recognizes that he has accomplished something. (Wood, 1979, p. 172)

School phobia needs special discussion. Pupils with this problem have a severe reaction to attending school. They do not want to go, and they appear highly anxious while in school. Often they express their anxiety through such physical symptoms as nausea, vomiting, sore throats, allergies, dizziness, or the need for an extraordinary amount of sleep. For example:

> From the start, I hated school, deeply, irrevocably, and silently. Kindergarten was anathema. Rather than take me to the doctor every other day with sore throats and stomach aches that were strictly school-induced, my mother finally capitulated and let me stay at home. First grade was no better, however, and as my sore "threats" would no longer work, and as the compulsory school laws prevented my mother from withdrawing me, I had no alternative but to start off for school daily and then divert myself to the rocks and crevices that then underlay the Hellsgate Bridge in the new and growing suburb of Queens, twenty minutes away by subway from the lower East Side where I was born. (Rothman, 1974, p. 221 — also cited in Kauffman, 1977, p. 12).

Psychotic pupils   The acting-out and withdrawing pupils we considered above are seriously emotionally disturbed, but most do manage to make it — albeit ineffectively and unhappily. However, some others are so profoundly disturbed that they cannot manage to get along. "Psychotic" and "schizophrenic" are terms that have been used over the years to describe these youngsters. In sum, these youngsters are so divorced from reality that they cannot function in society. They show pathology in every area of functioning — physical, motor, perceptual, intellectual, emotional, or social. Severe disorders include early infantile autism and childhood schizophrenia (Kestenbaum, 1978). Table 11.2 contrasts the characteristics of youngsters in these two categories.

TABLE 11.2 DIFFERENTIAL CHARACTERISTICS OF CHILDHOOD SCHIZOPHRENIA AND EARLY INFANTILE AUTISM.

Early Infantile Autism	Childhood Schizophrenia
Lack of affective contact and warmth in relations	More appealing/responsive in human relations
Low family incidence of psychosis	High family incidence of psychosis
Stable, professional home background	Unstable home background
Occurs in both of monozygotic twins	Does not occur in both of monozygotic twins
Not easily conditionable	Easily conditionable
Language disturbance (pronominal reversal, affirmation by repetition, delayed echolalia, metaphoric language, part-whole confusion)	Language development, but may be abnormal
Idiot-savant performance	No special skills
High level of motor skill	Motor skill poor/bizarre movements
No hallucinations or delusions	Hallucinations/delusions occasionally
Perseveration of sameness	Variability
No social interaction	Dependency on adult
No physical moulding when carried	Physical moulding possible
Present from birth	Early development normal
Good health/appearance	Many ailments/frail appearance
EEG usually normal	EEG often abnormal

Adapted by Swanson and Rinert (1979, p. 121) from Herbert (1974, p. 214). (Used by permission.)

Elly, whom we considered in Chapter 1, was diagnosed as autistic (Park, 1972). George illustrates childhood schizophrenia.

> *She [George's mother, Mrs. Johnson] reported that in spite of an uneventful planned pregnancy and full-term normal birth, she noticed that George was different from the other children "from the first day." He rarely cried and seemed content to remain in his crib or playpen. Mrs. Johnson noted that he either felt very soft to pick up—floppy at times—or very stiff, arching his back and seeming to dislike being held. George liked to rock and smiled when he rocked himself. At two, he spoke only 15 words. He did cuddle with his mother, to whom he became deeply attached and demanding. "He'd scream a lot, pulling my hand to reach for things he wanted. Away from me, he was fearful of anything or anyone new, or of being left alone in his room." Tantrums became a daily occurrence. He was punished at first by being left alone "but it only made him scream louder." George was very resentful of his two-month-old brother Tim and became more demanding of his mother's attention. The Johnsons attributed this to normal sibling rivalry in a sensitive child. The pediatrician assured the family that George was a slow starter and "would outgrow it."*
>
> *By age four it was clear that George was not about to "outgrow" his difficulties. He was increasingly withdrawn or, when not clinging to mother, enraged and out of control each time his desires were frustrated. His vocal production was limited to echolalic imitations and strange noises, e.g., imitations of automobile horns, trains, or vacuum cleaners. He could not play with other children, relating only to his mother and older sister. Declared "retarded," he was sent for a work-up at a local clinic. The child psychiatrist noted that he could be absorbed in music for hours, watching the turntable while he listened to records; also that his speech—unintelligible jargon—was delivered in a monotone and that he had no understanding of pronouns. He was preoccupied with turning light switches on and off, or with locking doors and pushing elevator buttons....*
>
> *There was a question about George's diagnosis. The neurologist found incoordination, poor balance, spinning, flailing arm movements and "soft signs" like those associated with minimal cerebral dysfunction. The psychologist, although George was untestable by usual criteria, noted perceptual deficits and overall retardation but felt he was only "pseudo-retarded" and capable of intellectual growth. A working diagnosis was finally established—childhood schizophrenia, organic type, with symbiotic psychotic syndrome. (Kestenbaum, 1978, pp. 364–365)*

Sometimes we roughly classify pupils according to the severity of their social/emotional disturbances. Three conventional levels are mild, moderate, and profound.

Diagnosis: Classification by Degree of Emotional Disturbances

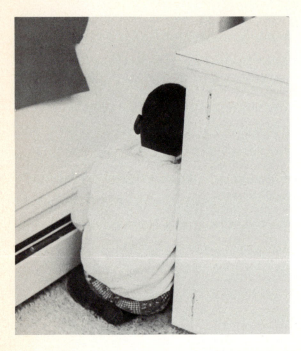

Some youngsters experience a
great deal of pain and unhappiness.

Mild disturbances   As most people do, many pupils have problems that cause them pain and limit their effectiveness. As Freud said, "Neurosis is the price we pay for civilization." However, these mild problems do not cause the youngsters to run into too much trouble, and they grow into reasonably harmonious and productive adulthoods. We are not discussing this group when we are considering seriously emotionally disturbed pupils.

Moderate disturbances   Generally, moderately disturbed pupils experience a great deal of pain and unhappiness. Their characteristics clang pretty hard with their social environments and limit their effectiveness in interpersonal relationships, school, and other cultural tasks. They grow into troubled adults who perform the cultural tasks much less effectively than they might if they did not have their social/emotional problems. Donna and Victor, whom we considered above, could be classified as moderately disturbed.

Profound disturbances   Some youngsters' disturbances are so profound that they find it very difficult to learn and perform the cultural tasks. They are in another world. Pupils whose conditions are classified as autism and childhood schizophrenia are at this profound level of disturbance. Elly and George, whom we also considered above, could be classified as profoundly disturbed.

As we might expect with such complex behavior, it is unbelievably difficult to pinpoint the causes of serious emotional disturbances (e.g., Bazar, 1980). Genetic influences, brain pathology, family influences and school, and other group influences all interact in diverse ways, and, of course, many forces determining behavior remain unconscious, i.e., below the level of awareness (e.g., Buss and Plomin, 1975; Heatherington and Martin, 1979; Loehlin and Nichols, 1976; Schwarz, 1979; Thomas and Chess, 1977).

Sources of Emotional Disturbances

Heredity operates generally through its influence on temperament and more specifically through predispositions to particular disorders. Heredity has a moderate role in determining temperament. This influence shows up as predispositions in such characteristics as sociability, emotionality, activity, and impulsivity. For example, the dimension of sociability has behavior going from the positive side — extremely outgoing, friendly, responsive — through the middle range and on to the negative side — extremely withdrawn, indifferent, and unresponsive. Such predispositions in temperament cause the child to respond in certain ways to his or her environment. In turn, people in the environment react back in ways determined by their own temperaments and needs.

Genetic influences

In addition to a general influence of heredity on temperament, heredity considerably predisposes to specific disorders such as early infantile autism, hyperactivity, antisocial personality, manic-depressive problems*, as well as depression alone and schizophrenia. These genetic predispositions put the child much more at risk to develop problems — especially in environments where there are difficulties.

The brain, of course, controls behavior. Accidents and infections that destroy nervous tissue and toxic (poisonous) substances that disturb brain physiology can disturb the way the brain functions. One effect can be a breakdown in sensitivity and responsiveness, showing up as an inertness and passivity. Another effect can be a breakdown in inhibition, showing up in hyperactivity, distractibility, and a tendency to explode easily into apparent temper tantrums. The breakdown in inhibition and the breakdown in sensitivity/responsiveness may both be considered problem behavior. In addition, they may lead the youngster into conflict with his or her environment, and further problems may develop.

Brain pathology

Volumes have been written in the sciences (e.g., Ainsworth *et al.*, 1978; Levinger and Raush, 1976) as well as the humanities (e.g., Lawrence,

Family influences

---

* People who have manic-depressive problems have periods of high excitement and abusiveness to others which alternate with periods of extremely low spirits and apathy.

1960; Hayward, 1978) about how family members influence one another's happiness and responses to the world. These influences operate in complex ways. Many studies have led to a dead end (e.g., Jacob, 1975). However, as time goes by and we develop more sophisticated ideas about what to look for and more advanced tools to use in our research, we are beginning to unravel the tangle. For example, in a review of seventy-two studies, some of these very up to date, Doane (1978) identified five dimensions that discriminate between families of disturbed and normal individuals. These were patterns of conflict, family coalition patterns, flexibility versus rigidity, family effectiveness and efficiency, and styles of communication. Pathological configurations of these dimensions can certainly lead a pupil to pain and problem behavior.

In addition, the family pathology surrounding child abuse and neglect is a special instance of family contributions to emotional disturbance (e.g., Barker, 1979; Belsky, 1980; Smith, 1978; Williams and Smith, 1980). The abuse and neglect he or she encounters affects a youngster directly. Further, growing up in contact with people who can commit such heinous acts can affect the youngster indirectly. These direct and indirect effects can take the form of moderate or profound emotional disturbances. Or, these effects can be more subtle and produce an apparently sound individual who on closer observation proves to be unable to form close relationships and assume the responsibilities of adult life.

School and other group influences

A pupil's experiences in school and other groups outside of the family certainly influence his or her behavior. Some situations are very favorable and growth-enhancing. Teachers and other adults, as well as other pupils, are open and caring and give the pupil unconditional regard. That is, they treat him or her as a valuable human being. He or she does not have to earn anything or do anything to deserve care and consideration. Other situations are jungles which leave the youngster wounded and hurt psychologically. Teachers and other adults may be indifferent or punishing or at least so inept that they cannot deal with the pupil in the ways needed. Other pupils may ignore the pupil or reject him or her with hostility. Most situations are in between. They have some good elements and some bad elements, and the pupil has to thread his or her way in between.

Interactions among influences

Things would be more simple if any one set of causes operated singly to cause serious emotional disturbances. We could identify the problem and concentrate on treatment. However, multiple causation is the rule, and no one set of influences determines all of a pupil's behavior. There are different theories about how this complex interaction happens (e.g., Bell, 1979; Parke, 1979; Schwarz, 1979). Essentially, the pupil acts on his or her environment, and the environment acts back on the pupil. At critical junctures, branches are reached, and the pupil and those around him or her are deflected along a course that leads to further complications. For example, a pupil might inherit a tendency to be highly impulsive. This impulsiveness may be unpleasant to family members. Depending on their own needs and value systems, they may punish the pupil by rejecting him or her or by withdrawing. This punishment could cause the pupil pain and lead him or her to begin punishing back. This fighting back can lead to more unpleasantness in the family and in the school and other groups. The pupil might fight back harder. And so the vicious cycle continues. In this context, decisions are made about schooling and other matters that affect the course of the pupil's development.

Freud made many contributions to our understanding people. Perhaps his greatest contribution was the concept of the unconscious mind. The unconscious mind, which operates below the level of our awareness, is a collection of impressions, motives, emotions, and thoughts which we do not remember or realize, but which operate to influence our behavior. Some unconscious material can be brought up to more conscious levels through art, techniques such as free association, and projective tests such as the Rorschach or the Children's Apperception Test. However, some material perhaps can never be brought to consciousness. For example, impressions and desires that were repressed before we had words to code them for memory might stay inaccessible because we have no words to express them through.

The role of the unconscious mind

　Unconscious processes operate to influence the behavior of us all — for good and for bad. They certainly contribute to the problems that seriously emotionally disturbed pupils experience. And they make treating serious emotional disorders more complicated.

IMPACT OF SERIOUS EMOTIONAL DISTURBANCES ON PUPILS' CHARACTERISTICS

Again, our culture is growing increasingly complex and interdependent. To get along, people must have the skills and emotional control to handle their fears and angers, to interact reasonably well with others, to form personal relationships, and to maintain some degree of happiness or equanimity. Every one of us has raw spots which cause us pain and interfere with how well we get along. Seriously emotionally disturbed pupils have more extreme problems. They are

Introduction

in pain themselves — consciously or unconsciously — and they have trouble with the common tasks of our culture.

> [They] arouse negative feelings and induce negative behaviors in others. These children are not typically popular among or leaders of their classmates and playmates. They usually experience both social and academic failure at school. Most of the adults in their environment would choose to avoid them if they could. Their behavior is so persistently irritating to authority figures that they seem to invite punishment or rebuke. Even in their own eyes these children are usually failures, obtaining little gratification from life and chronically falling short of their own aspirations. They are handicapped children — not limited by diseased or crippled bodies but by behaviors that are discordant with their social and interpersonal contexts.
>
> Some of the behaviors that handicapped children exhibit are recognized as abnormal in nearly every cultural group and social stratum. Muteness at age 10, self-injurious behavior, and eating of feces, for example, are seldom considered culture-specific or socially determined problems. Such disorders are most likely to be viewed as discrepancies from universally applicable psychological or biological developmental norms. On the other hand, many behaviors handicap children because they violate standards peculiar to their culture or the social institutions in their environment. Academic achievement, types of aggression, moral behavior, sexual responses, language patterns, and so on will be judged as normal or disordered depending on the prevailing attitudes in the child's ethnic and religious group, family, and school. For example, failure to read, hitting other children, taking the belongings of others, masturbating, and swearing are evaluated according to the standards of the child's community. Thus, a given behavior may be considered disordered in one situation or context and not in another simply because of differences in the behavior that is expected by the people the child lives with. (Kauffman, 1977, pp. 5–6)

Social/emotional problems may seriously disrupt pupils' development in other areas — their physical functioning, intellectual functioning, academic achievement, vocational functioning, and perhaps language functioning — and thus directly and indirectly interfere with their learning and performing the cultural tasks.* Earlier problems, as usual, are more pervasive. An important qualification: The generalizations below apply to some emotionally disturbed pupils, but not to others. For example, some pupils show physical symptoms,

---

* We have a great deal of information about the characteristics of children who have emotional disturbances, e.g., Clarizo and McCoy (1976), Halmi (1974), Hicks (1972), Jones (1980), Kauffman (1977), Long *et al.* (1976), Mason (1976), Stewart and Gath (1978), Reinert (1976), and Walker (1979).

but others do not. Some have artificially depressed intelligence test performance, whereas others perform brilliantly.

Physical Functioning

Psychosomatic relationships are well established. Briefly, emotional problems may be expressed through physical illness. Some frequently observed problems which may have emotional origins include asthma, colitis, eczema, ulcers, enuresis, and ecopresis.

Some pupils inflict harm on themselves. These self-injuries may be direct; for example, a pupil may pound his or her head against the floor until it bleeds or until a skull fracture or concussion results. Or, the self-injuries may be more indirect. For example, in anorexia nervosa the youngster — usually a teenage female — refuses to or cannot eat. The starvation leads to severe emaciation and sometimes death.

Beyond psychosomatic illness and self injury, in some pupils emotional disturbance can affect physical development and adequacy of physical skills. In physical development, prolonged intense stress may deflect a pupil from the growth trend he or she was following before the problem occurred and thus lead to a shorter stature than he or she would have attained in the absence of the stress (e.g., Gardner, 1972). The mechanism here is stress affecting parts of the endocrine system which mediate growth. The effect of emotional disturbances on *physical skills* is more direct and obvious. Such reactions as extreme withdrawal, fearfulness, or loss of control certainly can interfere with the smooth performance of physical skills. For example, a physically inert youngster may have trouble hitting a baseball. And chances are that through the years, he or she does not participate in activities that might lead to developing and refining such physical skills.

Speech and Language

Some profoundly emotionally disturbed pupils have speech and language problems. Some do not use language or seem to understand it; they are mute. Some give bizarre meanings to words. Some show bizarre language habits — inappropriate repetition, jargon, and echolalia (echoing or repeating what is said to them).

Less seriously disturbed youngsters less often show speech and language disruption. However, some do have problems in the area called pragmatics. That is, they have difficulty receiving cues and adjusting their speech and language to those cues as they use language in social discourse.

Intellectual Functioning

A little introspection will show you that it is very difficult to keep your mind on intellectual matters when you are emotionally upset. More formally, both theory and research tell us that the emotions and the intellect influence each other strongly. This interaction shows up in intelligence test performance and in learning and thinking.

Intelligence test performance   Emotionally disturbed pupils are not less intelligent than other pupils. However, they may have problems responding to intelligence tests because their emotional problems distract them. As a result of muteness, echolalia, and jargon, some pupils simply cannot be tested. Others score lower than they might if they were not emotionally disturbed.

Generally, some pupils function on tests in the retarded range. The term "pseudoretarded" has been used for a long time to refer to these pupils. As a group, they score spuriously low. A greater than expected number of mildly and moderately disturbed pupils score a little below average. Many more profoundly disturbed youngsters score in the lowest ranges. Figure 11.1 shows how Kauffman illustrates these relationships.

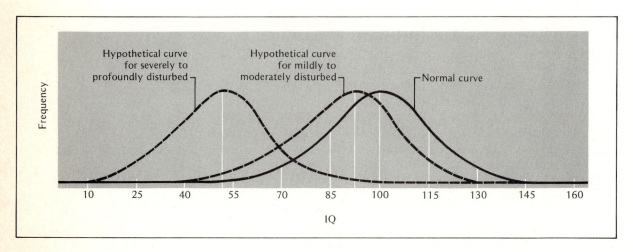

Fig. 11.1
Hypothetical frequency distribution of IQ for mildly to moderately, and severely to profoundly disturbed pupils compared with a normal frequency distribution. (Reprinted by permission from Kauffman, 1977, p. 119.)

Some pupils show uneven patterns of performance. For example, highly anxious pupils may show particular problems with subtests, such as repeating digits, which tap immediate memory.

Learning and thinking   As it does with intelligence test performance, serious emotional disturbance may interfere with intellectual responses for more extended periods of time. We can expect some emotionally disturbed pupils to learn more slowly, to remember less well, and to solve problems less adequately.

And, of course, profoundly emotionally disturbed pupils hardly enter into learning and problem-solving tasks. In addition, some autistic and schizophrenic youngsters show bizarre thinking. That is, their thinking is irrational and shows very little contact with reality.

Academic Achievement

Seriously emotionally disturbed pupils generally underachieve academically. There are two sets of reasons. One, it follows from their difficulties with intellectual tasks that seriously emotionally disturbed pupils might achieve below nondisturbed pupils. Again, one may not have the energy to deal with school tasks when one's attention and strength must be focused on dealing with emotional pain. Two, it follows from their problems interacting with others that they often do not show behavior that teachers reward with good grades or the extra attention needed to learn material pupils find difficult.

In addition, the effects of emotional disturbances may show up in subtle ways. For example, a pupil might achieve very well in reading and language but poorly in math and science, because his or her motivation for the two subjects differs. Or, a pupil might score very well on achievement tests showing that he or she has learned, yet get failing grades from teachers because of poor responses to classroom activities and failures on classroom tests.

Profoundly disturbed pupils show extreme underachievement. In fact, they usually are so far out of contact that they master only the most fundamental skills — even with very carefully structured long-term teaching. There are exceptions, like Elly described in Chapter 1. But these exceptions are rare.

Vocational Functioning

Unless there is strong intervention and that intervention is markedly successful, seriously emotionally disturbed pupils' problems continue into adulthood. And, of course, then they have more difficulties, since they are less protected as adults than they were as children. In addition, their academic underachievement snowballs, getting worse each year.

Many seriously emotionally disturbed pupils become disturbed adults who are *un*employed. Quite a few more are *under*employed. Their social/emotional problems and their academic underachievement interfere with their training for jobs they are capable of doing. And even given the appropriate training, serious emotional problems interfere with their holding jobs they are capable of doing.

ACCOUNTABILITY

Ensuring accountability is sometimes difficult with emotionally disturbed pupils: Acting-out pupils usually elicit so many negative reactions, withdrawing pupils often are overlooked, and psychotic pupils are so far removed from reality. However, quite rightly these youngsters are protected by the laws, and accountability with the Child-Find, the IEP, and the procedural safeguards are a concern.

Identifying and Planning for Seriously Emotionally Disturbed Pupils

Documenting the Child-Find

The Child-Find procedures include awareness campaigns with information about the various kinds of emotional disturbances, careful screening for emotional disturbance — especially the not so obvious withdrawal and passive aggression, and referral of pupils who perhaps have problems to specialists for further evaluation. The reports on the Child-Find include descriptions of procedures used in this active search and the numbers of emotionally disturbed pupils located and served.

Developing the individual education program

The IEP organizing service is essential for each pupil who qualifies for protection as seriously emotionally disturbed. This IEP is based on information about the youngster's characteristics in the social/emotional, the academic, and the other areas so influential in determining his or her responses to therapy and education. The IEP team sets long-term goals and short-term objectives for social/emotional behavior and for academics, suggests procedures for reaching these goals and objectives, specifies the least restrictive placement which seems most appropriate for delivering the education and therapy, and schedules dates for periodic reevaluation and revision. Advocates, psychiatrists/psychologists, school personnel, and social workers are crucial members of the IEP team.

Observing the Procedural Safeguards for Seriously Emotionally Disturbed Pupils

Advocate participation

The procedures for safeguarding seriously emotionally disturbed pupils' civil rights are crucial accompaniments to the Child-Find and the IEP development.

The advocates — the parents or their surrogates — have a central role in decisions about evaluation, programing, and placement. And consultants who are well versed in the nature of emotional disturbances and their treatment are important adjuncts in providing the pupil treatment — especially since the pupil's problems are often so complicated, so vexing, and so apparently intractable. That is, a neutral opinion is usually helpful and probably essential.

Due process

The advocates have a clear line of appeal through the school system and through the courts if they disagree with recommendations for

ED pupils' rights are guaranteed
by law, and we are accountable
for ensuring those rights.

the emotionally disturbed pupil — especially on whether the pupil should receive special services and where those special services should be delivered. It is mandatory that these due process rights and procedures be explained to the emotionally disturbed pupil's advocates.

One important facet of equal protection for the seriously emotionally disturbed pupil is to ensure nondiscriminatory testing. Errors are so likely because of the nature of the pupil's problems that special vigilance is required to be sure that the requirements for more than one test, appropriate norm groups, and the other safeguards are observed. Similarly, care must be devoted to classification and labeling — with special assurances that youngsters from minority groups are not subjected to different criteria and procedures or unjustly penalized because their behavior differs from the conventions of the majority group.

Equal protection

Objective criteria and evaluation procedures are used at frequent intervals to gauge progress — to see how pupils are moving toward the objectives for social/emotional behavior and academics and to help decide whether changes in objectives, instructional procedures, and placements are appropriate. On the basis of these evaluations, the pupil's IEP is revised and thus kept up to date.

Periodic reevaluation

Confidentiality procedures surround the seriously emotionally disturbed pupil — and they should. These confidentiality procedures give the advocates control over information about the pupil and his or

Confidentiality

her problems, treatments, and response to treatments. No one, except people who have a need to know because they are working with the pupil, may have access to the pupil's records without the advocates' release. Further, the advocates can have the emotionally disturbed pupil's records purged of false or unessential information and ensure that all but actuarial data are destroyed once the pupil progresses through the programs.

Nondiscriminatory testing of seriously emotionally disturbed pupils

We turn next to our second task, nondiscriminatory testing, once we have identified a pupil whose social/emotional problems are interfering with his or her learning and performing the cultural tasks. Reliable and valid information is useful in planning therapy and education and in evaluating the pupil's response to those services. Getting such reliable and valid information is fairly complex (e.g., Blau, 1979; Eaves and McLaughlin, 1977; Erickson, 1978; and Patterson, 1977).

PROBLEMS IN TESTING EMOTIONALLY DISTURBED PUPILS

We have two major problems in collecting information about emotionally disturbed pupils. They have to do with underestimating what the youngsters are like intellectually and socially/emotionally.

It is extremely difficult to get even an approximately accurate measure of an emotionally disturbed pupil's intellectual abilities. Again, ability tests are another measure of the handicap. For moderately disturbed pupils, their acting-out behavior or their withdrawing behavior, as the case may be, may make it difficult for them to follow the directions in the test and to answer the questions. For example, the aggressive, hostile, fighting child will seldom sit still for an intelligence test — especially if any frustration or constriction is involved. For profoundly disturbed pupils, their divorce from reality and their mutism or bizarre language make them essentially untestable. In short, and again, the emotions and the intellect interact in very complex ways, and seriously emotionally disturbed pupils usually do not test as well as they might on ability measures.

Beyond ability measurement, it is very difficult to get information about pupils' social/emotional characteristics and about family and other influences contributing to their problems. Even though they may be useful for screening, quick and inexpensive survey instruments are not sufficient to get information for either diagnosis or planning. Social/emotional disturbances are complex, and the roots are deep, often unconscious, and even if conscious, often covered up. Even to begin to understand the problems and their roots takes years of acute observations and close reasoning. Instruments like the Rorschach Ink Blot Test or the Children's Apperception Test help. However, these instruments require highly skilled specialists and much time and money. Schools and community mental health organizations often do not have the time, personnel, and money to do such extensive studies. However, substituting more surface-level procedures is not the answer, because they often do not yield sufficient information.

PROCEDURES FOR TESTING EMOTIONALLY DISTURBED PUPILS

Working with seriously emotionally disturbed pupils requires a broad base of information. Certainly we need a careful description of the pupils' characteristics — their strengths as well as their problems and also their medical backgrounds, therapeutic histories, and developmental histories. Beyond this description, we need more information about, for example:

1. *The seriously emotionally disturbed pupils.* How well do the pupils understand their problems? Do they want to change? Do they know how to change? How do they view other people's actions and reactions toward them?

2. *Other people — families, teachers, pupils,* and *others.* Who are significant to the pupils? How well do they understand the pupils? How do they want the pupils to change? What are their problems and values and what do they want from the pupils? How willing are they to change their own behavior in order to make the pupils more comfortable and effective? Can they, and will they, make such changes?

3. *The resources.* What resources do the families have for making changes that will make the pupils more comfortable and effective? What resources does the community have? What services and facilities do the schools have to help the emotionally disturbed pupils?

We get such information by interviewing, observing, and recording the results on rating scales, checklists, and anecdotal records; by examining other specialists' records; and by using criterion-referenced and norm-referenced tests if we can meet these tests' conditions.

Because of the difficult problems in evaluating seriously emotionally disturbed pupils, safeguards to achieve nondiscriminatory testing need to be observed closely. The pupil must be evaluated with more than one test, those tests must be administered in the pupil's native language, and the evaluation must be done by a multidisciplinary team which includes at least one specialist who has knowledge about serious emotional disturbances and how they affect a pupil's functioning. Further, the tests must be valid and reliable, and the norm groups and criteria must be appropriate for the pupil being tested. Also, there must be advocate participation in decision making, due process, periodic reevaluation, and confidentiality.

Individualizing instruction for seriously emotionally disturbed pupils

Individualizing instruction, our third task, includes both special education and related services for seriously emotionally disturbed pupils, as it does for all pupils.* It is built on the results of the non-discriminatory testing.

SPECIAL EDUCATION

Special education for seriously emotionally disturbed pupils includes both social/emotional behavior and academic skills. And it involves the diagnostic-prescriptive approach of fitting instruction to the pupil's characteristics. Mahon and Blattin's description of activities in a therapeutic nursery school illustrates.

> Let us return to the door of the therapeutic classroom. The mother arrives here with her handicapped child. The child has schizophrenia or brain damage or aphasia: the child has a poor grasp of who he is or who his mother is; he has no language, no reliable set of inner symbols that he can call on to communicate his needs. When he wants something he may kick or scream; when he walks into the classroom he does not carry with him an inner sense of self or the constancy of self and of objects. When he becomes frustrated, angry, or fearful, he may have to return to the door, the place he last saw his mother. If she is there he can refuel and, having pulled himself together, can return to the classroom. . . .
>
> Once inside the classroom the child's anxieties will prevent any meaningful psychoeducational work from being done unless the teacher is resourceful and intuitive and unless the curriculum can be geared at any moment to the needs of the child. Any rigid curricu-

---

* We have many excellent resources to help us build programs for emotionally disturbed pupils, e.g., Apter (1977), Blanco (1977), Ellis (1973), Fagen *et al.* (1975), Feagans (1974), Gallagher and Wiegerink (1976), Hewett and Taylor (1980), Hobbs (1974), Jones (1980), Kazdin (1979), Lewis (1975), Morse (1977), Newcomer (1980), Rhodes and Paul (1978), Shea (1978), Stevens (1977), and Thurman (1977).

lum would make no sense at all. How can you teach an obsessional child to enjoy making a mess; how can you teach an impulsive, messy child to enjoy order and cleanliness; how do you teach an angry child who bites you or bites himself to put his feelings into words; or an aphasic, angry child, to express his feelings in symbolic play or other nonverbal communication: How do you teach a child to make eye contact with you? The teacher is confronted with these difficult tasks — to be the auxiliary ego at all times to children whose egos are immature and fragile. Finding the proper approach to fit the needs of each individual child is a matter of skill, intuition, patience, and perseverance. The teacher is better able to approach this formidable educational challenge when she is armed with all the information about the child that can be made available to her by the rest of the therapeutic nursery team....

Let us try to imagine the scene from inside the child's head. The teacher is singing a song about the names of all the children and the day of the week it is. The child is sitting on a rug with the others trying to feel comfortable. The song is reminding him where he is, who he is. He is beginning to feel safe. He looks at himself in the mirror. The teacher is in the mirror too, naming the parts of his body for him, helping him to get a sense of himself. Suddenly he becomes sad seeing himself in the mirror without his mother. The sadness quickly turns to anger. He tries to punch the teacher. She says no. But he cannot stop. Now he is running around trying to punch everybody and the children are punching back. The adults are separating child from child trying to restore order. The child climbs up on the shelf and jumps. He repeats this. The teacher encourages him. He enjoys this new game with the teacher. The anger has been rechanneled and forgotten for awhile. But now the sadness returns; he is missing mother again. He takes the towel and covers his head with it. The teacher removes it and says peek-a-boo; he laughs — he covers his head again; he enjoys this game too. It is as if he can make the teacher go away and come back again. This makes him feel less helpless. He throws a ball under the table, he retrieves it. He opens and closes the door of the dollhouse. He can make things go away and come back. He can open doors and close them again. Now the teacher wants him to paint. He cannot grasp the brush well with his immature neuromuscular reflexes. He tries to make a circle but the paint splashes all over — he is about to have a tantrum when the teacher begins to admire the splashes. He splashes some more, the teacher applauds. Now he lies down on the brown paper, that the teacher has spread under him. The teacher makes a line of paint all around his body; he stands up. He can see the shape of himself outlined on the paper. The teacher hangs it up on the wall and puts his name under it. He never realized his body could create such an outline. He stands amazed looking at it with his own name written under it. Now the teacher is singing another song, about going home soon and not returning until tomorrow. (Mahon and Blattin, 1978, pp. 73–74)

Social/Emotional Behavior

Objectives

Essentially, there are two goals for social/emotional behavior. One is for the pupil to become more comfortable emotionally. The other is for the pupil to become more effective socially. The specific objectives here depend on the pupil's particular problem and how it keeps him or her from performing the cultural tasks. For example, suppose that a pupil is an isolate who wants social contact but whose aggression and social ineptness cause other pupils to ignore him or her. In the emotional sphere the objectives are for the pupil to understand why he or she is so angry and to find ways to express that anger which do not lead to trouble. In the social sphere the objectives are for the pupil to: learn problem-solving techniques to help resolve conflicts and frustrations, learn how to identify social cues and personal feelings which can guide his or her behavior with others, and learn interpersonal skills, e.g., conversing, making requests, accepting others unconditionally, and enhancing others' feelings of self-worth.

Schedules

It's frustrating to all concerned. However, many social/emotional problems are almost intractable, almost impossible to alleviate — especially when unconscious factors are involved. Therefore progress in reaching objectives for social/emotional behavior is often very slow. It may take years to reduce the severity of emotional problems to such an extent that they do not interfere too much with pupils' performing the cultural tasks. Schedules have to be planned accordingly.

Procedures and settings

If people differ on the best way to teach reading or mathematics or social studies — and they do, you can depend on it — they differ on the best way to help pupils achieve objectives for social/emotional behavior. Some frequently used approaches (procedures and settings) are the psychodynamic, psychoeducational, humanistic, behavioristic, and ecological approaches.* Within each approach, proponents have developed particular variations. The material below is a brief overview.

The *psychodynamic approach* follows the traditions Freud started and his students and others extended over the years. Psychodynamic specialists see the external behavior, which we label problems, as symptoms of deeper traumas — usually unconscious ones. Their methods aim at *catharsis* (the person's expressing the pain the trauma causes), *insight* (the person's understanding the trauma and its effects), and *constructive action* (the person's moving toward personality reorganization, leading to more effective relationships and productive activities). They use such methods as therapeutic interviews, play therapy, and the creative arts. They encourage open

---

* Some writers on approaches to treating serious emotional disturbances also include the learning-disability approach. That approach is described in Chapter 10.

settings which allow pupils freedom to express what they feel and to behave as they wish so long as they stay within certain limits which prevent injury and destruction. Adults are seen as therapists. They help pupils understand their feelings, reach toward insight, and accept limits to behavior. Kestenbaum (1978) represents those working in the psychodynamic tradition today.

The *psychoeducational approach*, as the name implies, gives weight both to the behavior the pupil must express to live in his or her environment without pain and also to the traumas which cause the pupil to come into conflict with his or her environment. Psychoeducational specialists consider that problems begin with diverse causes. At the same time, they consider that further complications will follow if the original difficulties deflect the youngster from accomplishing the tasks appropriate for his or her stage of development. Their work with the youngster is essentially two-pronged. They try to change the people and circumstances around the youngster which might have led to the original problems or which operate on the youngster currently to increase his or her problems. At the same time, they work with the youngster to help him or her learn the behavior appropriate for his or her age group. They do this work in individual sessions and in small-group sessions. They use a wide range of media and materials, with special emphasis on the arts — music, painting/drawing, and drama at levels appropriate for pupils' development. One IEP used as illustration in Chapter 2 is based on the psychoeducational approach. The particular version is called developmental therapy. Note that developmental milestones serve as the focus of the pupil's program. Developmental therapy is the variation of the psychoeducational approach which Wood and her associates originated (e.g., Wood, 1975, 1979; Williams and Wood, 1977; Purvis and Samet, 1976; Bachrach and Swindle, 1978). Many of Wood's ideas come from her work with Long, Morse, and Newman (1976), who were among early proponents of the psychoeducational approach.

The *humanistic approach* owes a great deal to the Freudian tradition. The originators, e.g., Maslow and Rogers, were concerned about self-actualization — the more effective expression of human potential. The humanists aim at helping pupils get in touch with their feelings and work out their destinies in ways to be part of the world but not possessed by it. Stating it in Thoreau's terms, they help youngsters to learn what tune their drummers are playing and to have the courage to march to that drummer regardless of how other people are marching. They stress exploration and individual creativity. Therefore their methods include a great deal of individual work and small-group activity. And, of course, they have accessible a wide range of media — materials and devices — for pupils to use as they need them in their explorations. Space and facilities are flexible, and teachers and other adults serve as consultants to be contacted as needed. This approach is often called open education. Ellis (1973) and Knoblock (1973) exemplify proponents of using humanistic approaches with socially/emotionally disturbed pupils.

The *behavioral approach* has developed out of Skinner's work on principles of instrumental conditioning and what they mean for shaping people's behavior. The behaviorists concentrate on the disturbances. They consider that pupils have learned the responses — the problem reactions — and that the task is to help them extinguish those problem reactions and learn appropriate responses. Briefly, their methods include studying what antecedent conditions led pupils to particular responses and what reinforcement (consequences) those pupils respond to. They manipulate the antecedent conditions and the rewards and punishments in ways that cause the pupils to make the desired responses. There are many specific procedures. One frequently used procedure is behavior shaping, e.g., starting by getting the destructive pupil to make a positive response to frustration and rewarding him or her for the positive response and continuing this process until the pupil consistently makes the positive response even in the absence of reinforcement. Another frequently used procedure is desensitization, e.g., starting by getting the pupil who has a phobia about dogs to play with an attractive toy dog while at the same time getting a desired reward, such as candy, and continuing to associate pleasure with nonthreatening dogs until the pupil can be around an average dog which has both pleasant and unpleasant characteristics. The behaviorists use whatever media are necessary — especially materials that serve as reinforcers. Teachers and other adults are seen as the leaders who control the environment and the pupils — determining what behavior will be manipulated and what reinforcements and environmental manipulations will be used. Facilities too are manipulated as necessary. Haring and Hewett and their followers are among leading proponents of the behavioristic approach for seriously emotionally disturbed pupils as well as other handicapped pupils (e.g., Lovaas, 1977; Hewett *et al.*, 1977; White and Haring, 1976).

The *ecological approach* emphasizes the interaction between the youngster and the many forces in his or her environment. It follows the traditions of ecological biology and ecological psychology. Proponents consider that the youngsters' problems arise because they disturb the social system they are a part of. In turn, the disrupted social system acts back on the youngsters to further disturb them. Treatment, then, focuses on all elements of this interacting system.

Certainly the ecologists work with the youngsters — helping them learn socially appropriate behavior and get rid of some of their discomfort. At the same time, the ecologists work with the many facets of the youngsters' environments — families, schools, and other social groups — to reduce the environment's contribution to the youngsters' problems and to prepare the environment to support the youngsters as they develop new, less disturbing behavior patterns. They work with pupils in small groups to help them gain competence in activities necessary for living in their environments without disturbing them. They use whatever media and materials are appropriate to master these learning tasks. Teacher/counselors work with the small groups, helping them to master academic tasks important to competence, to understand human relationships, and to develop appropriate social skills. Liaison teachers work with people in the youngsters' environments. Space and facilities are kept flexible. Hobbs (1974) and Lewis (1975) represent proponents of the ecological approach.

Academic Skills

Objectives

For *moderately disturbed* pupils, the intention is that they should achieve academic skills at a level appropriate for their capacities as best we can determine those capacities. Consequently, these pupils have objectives for the literacy skills, the content areas, and the vocational subjects. Because seriously emotionally disturbed pupils often underachieve academically, their instructional objectives necessarily start at their current performance levels, but the emphasis is on moving the pupils to where they could be. For example, suppose that a twelve-year-old pupil were achieving in mathematics like most nine-year-old pupils. We would start with the younger pupils' objectives. But we would move the emotionally disturbed pupil along as quickly as possible.

For *profoundly disturbed pupils*, instruction is much more rudimentary. The objectives focus on communication — starting with making contact with others and ranging to more and more normal speech and language. Beyond communication, objectives are for self-care skills such as dressing and eating procedures and intellectual activities such as basic perceptual and conceptual tasks as the youngster becomes ready for them.

Schedules

As we have seen, serious emotional problems can interfere with academic achievement and cause underachievement. These emotional problems' persistence, or the slowness in reducing them, can continue to make academic progress slow, and the pupil may get further and further behind. As he or she goes into adolescence and less time is left in school, we have to consider the matter of dropping objectives. That is, the youngster may not have time to master the entire curriculum. Consequently, priorities for objectives have to be established. For example, all concerned may consider it more appropriate for the teenage pupil to focus on the literacy skills and pre-vocational topics.

Scheduling for profoundly emotionally disturbed youngsters takes into account their very slow progress. Sufficient time is allowed for them to master the essential skills for communicating and living within their environments.

Procedures   As we select *methods*, we need to consider the pupil's problem and maturity level. For example, suppose that a pupil were extremely hostile and acting out. He or she may not be able to tolerate even small-group work and be so disruptive that other pupils could not benefit either. Such a pupil might need more individual tutoring as a method for delivering instruction on academic skills. In such cases we would select individual tutoring. However, such a decision would need to be made very judiciously and to be reevaluated frequently. Its purpose would be to help the pupil attain his or her academic objectives, and it is justified for that. However, it may interfere with the pupil's attaining his or her goals for social/emotional behavior, e.g., learning

Teachers work with individual pupils and small groups, moving toward objectives and handling problems as they arise.

to work with others without an anger outburst. Therefore it should be used as a method only as long as he or she needs it — and no longer.

Materials for teaching academic skills to seriously emotionally disturbed pupils are the same as those appropriate for nondisturbed pupils.

Settings

The settings we considered as we discussed social/emotional behavior apply to settings for instruction in the cognitive skills. Essentially, teachers work alone and in concert with other specialists as they deal with individuals and small groups, moving toward the objectives and handling problems as they arise. Space and facilities have to remain flexible. The idea is to adjust the environment in ways appropriate to enable the pupils to move toward their instructional objectives.

RELATED SERVICES

Seriously emotionally disturbed pupils will need medical services, psychological services, vocational rehabilitation services, and family information and counseling services. They may need speech/language therapy.

Medical Services

Drug therapy, psychiatric services, and neurological services are all important medical services.

Some psychiatric problems respond to *drug therapy*. For example, an extremely acting-out pupil may need tranquilizers to calm down enough to begin to respond to other types of therapy. Quite rightly, the prevailing opinion is that drugs should not be used only to make a youngster more manageable. Instead, they are used to make the youngster more comfortable and more able to work toward the therapeutic and instructional objectives. In addition, physicians should monitor the effects very closely and discontinue the drugs when they are no longer helpful.

Psychiatrists are physicians specializing in social/emotional problems. With seriously emotionally disturbed pupils, their role is to identify whether physical problems are causing the emotional disturbances. Further, they determine whether drugs and other biochemical therapies are possible and whether they should be used.

In addition, psychiatrists deliver therapy to seriously emotionally disturbed pupils and their families. As with educators, the approaches they use depend on their orientations. For example, some may be more psychoanalytic; some more humanistic.

Neurologists enter cases if brain pathologies are suspected. For example, if there is reason to expect that a brain tumor is causing bizarre behavior, neurological or neuropsychiatric diagnosis and treatment are required.

Psychological Services

Clinical psychologists often play key roles in identifying and treating seriously emotionally disturbed pupils. They use diagnostic procedures to search for the nature of the pupils' problems. And they use counseling with pupils and their families to work on those problems.

School psychologists assist in evaluating seriously emotionally disturbed pupils. They collect information about pupils' social/ emotional behavior and intellectual behavior in school. They also assess pupils' academic achievement levels.

Vocational Rehabilitation

As the moderately emotionally disturbed youngster moves into adolescence and young adulthood, vocational rehabilitation services become very important. The VR specialist's first task is to assess the youngster's strengths and problems in characteristics that influence job performance. The next phase is to supply the youngster and his or her parents with information about occupations and their requirements and to help them weigh those requirements with the youngster's strengths, limitations, and interests. Then, once some choices have been made, the VR specialist may help the youngster get the training needed and find a job if necessary.

If the profoundly disturbed youngster has any possibilities of working at a job, the VR specialist would use similar procedures with him or her.

Family Information and Counseling

We know that family members can cause or at least aggravate emotional disturbances in one another. As a result, dealing with a seriously emotionally disturbed pupil's problem usually requires supplying information to his or her family and counseling family members with respect to behavior which may cause the pupil problems.

In addition, seriously emotionally disturbed pupils can be very hard on family life. They often engender hostility, guilt, and fear in many guises. Consequently, family members often need information and counseling to help them deal with these problems and thus to give them relief from their pain and suggestions about how to deal with the youngsters in helpful, growth-enhancing ways.

Speech/Language Therapy

Some seriously emotionally disturbed pupils' speech and language problems might clear up when the social/emotional problems clear up. On the other hand, helping the pupil learn to communicate more accurately might contribute to lessening the social/emotional problems. Therefore speech/language therapy is necessary when communication problems are present.

Placing seriously emotionally disturbed pupils in the least restrictive environment

Finally, we turn to our fourth task, placing seriously emotionally disturbed pupils. We attend to placement options, extracurricular activities, transportation and facilities, and safety (e.g., Budson, 1978; O'Leary and Schneider, 1977; Quay *et al.*, 1972; Shea, 1977).

PLACEMENT OPTIONS

Like other exceptional pupils, the emotionally disturbed pupil needs to be identified and treated as early as possible. The idea is to keep the pupil's development from being deflected from normal trends and in turn to save the pupil problems with the cultural tasks. Early childhood special education opportunities are increasing for young seriously emotionally disturbed pupils.

Work with ED pupils must begin early.

During the school-age period, seriously emotionally disturbed pupils are placed in regular classes and special classes with about equal frequency. Separate schools and residential placements are used less frequently. (See Fig. 11.2.)

When the pupil is enrolled in the regular class, the regular teacher requires consultation from resource teachers, psychologists, and speech and language therapists. Sometimes the resource teacher acts as a crisis teacher, i.e., the person who helps the pupil through it when the stress gets too great and he or she loses control.

The separate class may be a self-contained special class. More frequently, however, it is a resource room where the pupil and the teacher work together on particular objectives for social/emotional behavior or for academic skills.

The separate facilities may be a residential school where the pupil gets twenty-four-hour care. However, such institutions are being used much less frequently as time goes by.

Obviously, seriously emotionally disturbed pupils need to be in the least restrictive environment possible. Many can deal successfully with a regular class or with a resource room. However, some pupils need a more protected environment until they get some of their problems solved. They simply cannot deal with their social/emotional traumas and compete in the society with other pupils — especially as they get older, and adolescent mores and peer pressures start operating. As Hewett put it in his discussion of mainstreaming, they need a place they can go to for R and R — respite and renewal (see Hewett's discussion in Chapter 3). For example, Elly, whom we considered at the outset of the book, was able to make it. Another autistic youngster might need a more protected public school environment. Similarly, an extremely withdrawing pupil might be lost in the bustle and overlooked. Or, a pupil with a severe acting-out problem might be so bombarded with stimuli that he or she would frequently break down into explosions, disrupting himself or herself and everyone else in the surroundings.

Again, the placement can and should change as the pupil improves. Review the case of Joseph in Chapter 3. Note that he moved back and forth some, but kept up a steady trend toward the least restrictive environment.

Several criteria are important in deciding about emotionally disturbed pupils' placement:

☐   how closely they are in touch with reality

☐   how adequately they communicate with others

☐   how adequately they relate to others

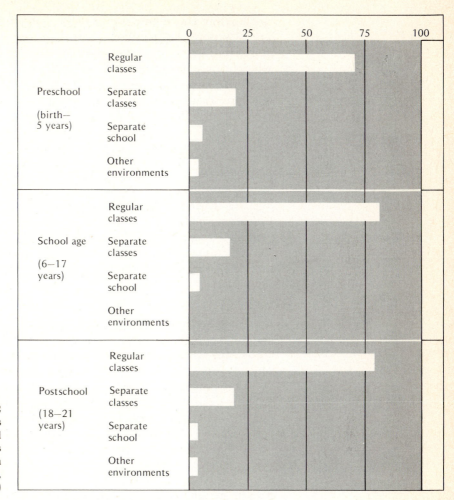

Fig. 11.2
Most frequent placements of emotionally disturbed pupils reported by the states in the late 1970s. (Based on information in BEH, 1979, pp. 169–189.)

☐ how adequately they perform the daily living skills
☐ how much frustration and social stimulation they can tolerate
☐ how much social/emotional support and guidance they need, and
☐ how close their academic achievement levels are to other pupils' achievement levels.

EXTRACURRICULAR ACTIVITIES

Seriously emotionally disturbed pupils certainly need extracurricular activities. Such activities can be less structured and demanding and thus provide pupils with the chance for social and emotional contacts with other youngsters their ages. The trouble, of course, is that the social/emotional problem can interfere with the extracurricular participation. For example, acting-out behavior can cause so many disruptions that the pupil is rejected, or withdrawal behavior can keep the pupil from getting into the situation. Consequently, finding an appropriate extracurricular activity for a pupil takes a great deal of care and effort.

TRANSPORTATION AND FACILITIES

Most moderately emotionally disturbed pupils do not require too much attention in transportation and facilities. Their problems will remain evident, but they can usually manage.

Most profoundly emotionally disturbed pupils do need help in transportation. They are so far divorced from reality that they cannot travel independently without danger of injury or of being lost. They usually do not have problems with access to facilities.

SAFETY

Most moderately emotionally disturbed pupils do not need special safety precautions. A possible exception could be acting-out pupils, who might lose control of themselves so completely as to injure themselves or others when they are around tools and moving machinery.

Most profoundly disturbed pupils might require special safety precautions — especially around tools and moving machinery. They might just be unaware of possible dangers.

Summary

IDENTIFYING AND PLANNING FOR SERIOUSLY EMOTIONALLY DISTURBED PUPILS

Normal Social/ Emotional Behavior
Emotional and social behavior go together to influence how happy we are and how well we get along with people around us. Emotional and social reactions become increasingly differentiated and complex as youngsters grow older. Emotional equanimity and social harmony are very important in youngsters' learning and performing the cultural tasks adequately.

Serious Emotional Disturbance
Sometimes circumstances or problems arise to deflect youngsters' social/emotional development from the course of normal development. When this deflection is severe enough to interfere with their

learning and performing the cultural tasks, we consider that the youngsters are seriously emotionally disturbed. People disagree on how to define social/emotional disturbances, but most agree on these common features: the social/emotional problem persists over a long period, is severe, and interferes with performing school work and other cultural tasks. In the Child-Find for identifying youngsters qualified for service and protection as seriously emotionally disturbed, we engage in extensive public awareness campaigns to alert people to the real nature of social/emotional disturbance, we screen pupils for signs of serious problems, and we refer those with apparent problems for further study. People have developed a variety of categories and labels for *classifying*, or diagnosing, pupils *by type* of social/emotional disturbance. People disagree about the usefulness of many categories and labels. Some prefer a dimensional approach — looking at common threads running through many categories rather than looking at discrete categories. Factor analyses and other analyses yield two main patterns — the acting-out pupil, who externalizes his or her problems, and the withdrawing pupil, who internalizes his or her problems. Further, some special educators work with psychotic pupils. Three approximate levels are used in *classifying degree* of social/emotional disturbance: mild, moderate, and profound. Seriously emotionally disturbed pupils fall into the moderate and profound categories. Because they are so complex, it is very difficult to pinpoint the causes of serious emotional disturbances. Genetic influences, brain pathology, family influences, and school and other group influences all interact in diverse ways, and many forces determining behavior remain unconscious.

Social/emotional problems may seriously disrupt pupils' growth and development in other areas — their physical functioning, intellectual functioning, academic achievement, vocational functioning, and perhaps their language functioning. Earlier problems are usually more pervasive. Different pupils are affected by social/emotional problems in different ways. Some show no effects; others show various patterns of effects.

Impact of Serious Emotional Disturbance on Pupils' Characteristics

We ensure accountability in identifying and planning for seriously emotionally disturbed pupils through documenting the Child-Find and developing the IEP. We guarantee the pupils' rights by observing the procedural safeguards for advocate participation, due process, equal protection, periodic reevaluation, and confidentiality.

Accountability

NONDISCRIMINATORY TESTING OF SERIOUSLY EMOTIONALLY DISTURBED PUPILS

Problems in Testing Seriously Emotionally Disturbed Pupils

Two major problems in collecting information about seriously emotionally disturbed pupils cause us difficulty in finding out what seriously emotionally disturbed pupils are like intellectually and socially/emotionally. First, it is extremely difficult to get even an approximately accurate measure of the pupils' abilities, because their social/emotional problems interfere with meeting the conditions of norm-referenced and criterion-referenced testing. Second, it is very difficult to get information about pupils' social/emotional characteristics and about family and other influences contributing to their problems, because of the requirements for confidentiality, the complexity and often unconscious or hidden nature of the problems, and the resources needed for extensive psychiatric diagnoses.

Procedures for Testing Seriously Emotionally Disturbed Pupils

We need a broad base of information to plan adequately for emotionally disturbed pupils. We get this information through using techniques for observation, reviewing records and reports, and using tests that we can meet the conditions for. Again, because of the problems in collecting information here, we need to circumscribe our activities very carefully with procedural safeguards to prevent discrimination and error.

INDIVIDUALIZING INSTRUCTION FOR SERIOUSLY EMOTIONALLY DISTURBED PUPILS

Special Education

We are concerned about social/emotional behavior and academic skills as we plan special education for seriously emotionally disturbed pupils. The goals for *social/emotional behavior* are for pupils to become more comfortable emotionally and more effective socially. Specific objectives depend on each pupil's particular problems and how it keeps him or her from performing the cultural tasks. In scheduling we have to accept the reality that for some pupils, progress toward the objectives may be very slow and therefore plan accordingly. People differ a great deal on the best way to help pupils attain the objectives for social/emotional behavior. Some frequently used approaches (instructional procedures and settings) are the psychodynamic, psychoeducational, humanistic, and ecological approaches. Proponents have particular variations within each approach.

The *academic goals* for moderately disturbed pupils are that they should achieve at levels appropriate for their capacities as best we can determine those capacities. Consequently, we have objectives for the literacy skills, the content areas, and the vocational subjects gauged at pupils' present performance levels. For profoundly disturbed pupils, instruction is much more rudimentary. Objectives focus on communication, self-care, and basic intellectual activities. As with social/emotional objectives, pupils' progress with academic subjects may be quite slow. We have to schedule accordingly — sometimes with the result that the youngster may not have time to master the entire curriculum, and priorities among objectives have to be set. We may need to differentiate methods considerably for seriously emotionally disturbed pupils to make them appropriate for their problems and maturity levels. Materials for teaching academic skills are about like those appropriate for nondisturbed pupils. In planning settings we adjust the environment in ways appropriate to enable the pupils to move toward their instructional objectives — using team teaching, flexible space and facilities, and other techniques as appropriate.

Related Services

Among the related services, seriously emotionally disturbed pupils usually need medical, psychological, vocational rehabilitation, and family information and counseling services. They also may need speech/language therapy.

PLACING SERIOUSLY EMOTIONALLY DISTURBED PUPILS IN THE LEAST RESTRICTIVE ENVIRONMENT

Placement Options

Like other exceptional pupils, emotionally disturbed pupils need to be identified and treated as early as possible. Placement options, from least to most restrictive, are regular classes, resource rooms, separate classes, and hospital/residential facilities. The options chosen depend on the pupils' characteristics and needs.

Extracurricular Activities

Seriously emotionally disturbed pupils strongly need extracurricular activities. However, their problems interfere here, just as they do in other activities. Consequently, finding an appropriate extracurricular activity for a pupil takes a great deal of care and effort.

Transportation, Facilities, and Safety

Most moderately disturbed pupils do not need too much supervision and adjustment in transportation and safety. Profoundly disturbed pupils need considerable special supervision and adjustment in transportation and safety. Access to facilities generally is not a problem for seriously emotionally disturbed pupils.

Sample IEP's Appendix

REFERRAL INFORMATION

Tommy, nine and one-half years old and enrolled in the third grade, has attended three different schools. He was referred by his foster mother because of her concern about his misbehavior, resistance to her direction, and stealing. He fights with the few friends he has in the neighborhood and has problems getting along with others at home.

His third grade teacher also expressed concern about his behavior. He is very aggressive toward other children (especially on the playground), resistant, verbally abusive to teachers, and disrespectful to others. Tommy's home life has been in constant turmoil. He and his younger half sister live with a widowed foster mother and her elderly mother. Tommy's natural mother has emotional problems and although she reportedly loves the children, she has neglected them physically and psychologically. She voluntarily gave the children to the foster mother a little over a year ago, but still retains legal custody of them. She visits weekly, and the children look forward to her visits. Tommy's natural father was reared by the foster mother's mother and is reported to be "always in trouble." Tommy's father does not live in this area, and Tommy has never seen him. Tommy's current step-father (his half-sister's natural father) has very little contact with the family.

The foster mother did not know any specific developmental history, except that Tommy walked and talked by age two. Enuresis and encopresis at night are lingering problems. His foster mother has been punishing him for this. He was taken to a urologist, who ruled out physical problems as the cause of this problem. With respect to behavior management at home, the foster mother says that nothing she does works for any length of time. He and his sister fight constantly, and he refuses to do his chores. His foster mother took him to Boys' Club and the city's Parks and Recreation Department basketball program. He was suspended for one week from both Boys' Club and school (on different occasions) for fighting. He was enrolled in swimming lessons last summer, but was "kicked out" for dunking and holding other children under water. He told everyone that he could swim, but the staff reported that he was really afraid of the water.

Tommy's foster mother says that Tommy loves watching television, especially sports and "The Rookies," playing kickball, jumping rope, gymnastics, and "running around." He also likes to play checkers with her, but she says it is hard for him to lose.

SUMMARY OF PRESENT PERFORMANCE LEVELS

Educational   The Durrell Analysis of Reading Difficulty placed Tommy's oral reading skills at the low second grade level, silent reading skill at middle second grade level, and listening comprehension at the high third grade level. He could spell several first grade words, but seemed to have no word analysis skills. The Peabody Picture Vocabulary Test (PPVT) indicated a receptive vocabulary comparable to that for other children his age. On the Key Math diagnostic profile, Tommy achieved a 2.9 grade level in content, 2.6 in operations, and 2.3 in applications.

Tommy's eye-hand coordination is age-appropriate, and his left–right orientation is good. He can write in cursive, but prefers printing.

In response to projective pictures, Tommy did not identify with appropriate children, but with the "loner" in school and social situations. He measured happiness in material things rather than in personal relationships and expressed hostility, alienation, and denial when confronted with difficult social situations.

Observation of Tommy in the classroom and playground confirmed the test results and reports from his foster mother and teacher. Tommy worked well on his assignment if the teacher stayed nearby or checked him from time to time. Without this structure, he could not complete a task, lost control, and expressed his anxiety by attacking another child. In the less structured recess time he seemed eager to be a part of a group and tried to participate in group games and discussions. However, he constantly bragged about his own ability to fight or beat others in games. This invariably ended in fights and trips to the principal's office.

Tommy's communication skills are not well developed for his age. He cannot describe events and people. He seems to understand rules and expectations, but cannot give reasons for rules. He also refuses to recognize alternative ways to behave and always blames others. His most frequently used expressions are "That's not fair" and "I told you he was mean."

He tries to assume the leadership and direction of other children, constantly reminding them or the teacher of the rules. When he is not recognized as the leader, Tommy loses control or tries to disrupt the group activity. He seems to be unable or unwilling to recognize the feelings of others, refuses to participate when others determine the activity, and selects several equally disruptive children as models. With those he selects as friends, Tommy will share everything he has. His teacher suspects that much of the "stuff" Tommy shares with his friends has been stolen. In contrast, Tommy bitterly refuses to share supplies or equipment used in the classroom for group projects, unless the teacher asks him to do so.

Psychological

The school psychologist administered the WISC-R and reported a verbal score of 84, a performance scale of 81, and a full-scale score of 81 ± 3. On the psychological evaluation Tommy worked very hard and answered questions carefully, thinking over each question before responding. He had good eye contact with the examiner and seemed to enjoy the individual attention. According to this session, Tommy's current level of cognitive performance falls in the low-average range. He can solve some simple oral math problems. His other verbal skills (reasoning, social judgment, long-term memory, and language) and his nonverbal skills (reasoning, perceptual organization, and psycho-motor speed) are equally developed and fall in the low-average range. His major weaknesses fall in two areas. He has trouble with non-verbal problems concerned with spatial reasoning ability and some trouble in visual-motor integration skills. The projective assessment indicated impulsivity, high anxiety, egocentrism, and an excessive need for nuturance and attention. He uses denial extensively when he is unable to achieve immediate success.

Psychiatric

The results of the psychiatric evaluation were consistent with the other test results and also showed a tendency for Tommy to blame others for his problems. He commented that he likes everything about third grade, especially physical education, but that writing is the hardest. He mentioned some trouble with the children at school, specifically that the children hit him and he hits back. Then they tell the teacher and he gets in trouble. He also said that he does not do his work and talks back to the teacher sometimes. When discussing Boys' Club, he mentioned that he used to go, but does not now because his mother would not take him anymore.

The tentative diagnostic classification was a chronic (severe) anxiety reaction with excessively low self-concept, low ego strength, and moderately developed superego.

Behavioral

The Referral Form Checklist (RFCL) was used independently by Tommy's foster mother, third grade teacher, and the diagnostic team to identify "high priority" behavior problems. The teacher, foster mother, and diagnostic team agreed on several problems: aggression toward other children and property, carelessness, disorganization, problems expressing feelings, and manipulative behavior. Tommy's foster mother also felt that the following problem areas were of high priority: forgetfulness, perseveration, ritualistic behavior, self-aggression, lack of comprehension, not following directions, lack of confidence, failure of attention, repetition, echoing, limited self-help skills, stealing, and reading. His teacher marked five other areas as being high-priority problems: resistant to discipline, silliness, temper, obscene language, and suspicious. The diagnostic team felt that two additional areas were problems of high priority: easily frustrated and immature behavior.

Social/Emotional

Tommy's present level of social/emotional development was assessed by Tommy's teacher, the diagnostic team, and his foster mother together, using the Developmental Therapy Objectives Rating Form (DTORF). As can be seen in the sample DTORF that follows, they identified his current level of social/emotional development, marking objectives already mastered with parentheses ( ), objectives needing work with an (X), and objectives which Tommy is not ready to work on as (NR). The rating indicated Tommy's present social/emotional average level of development to be at the beginning of Stage Three. The overall social/emotional goal for Stage Three of Developmental Therapy is "Learning Skills for Successful Group Participation."

Summary

At the IEP conference, the diagnostic team members discussed the educational, psychological, psychiatric, and developmental findings with Tommy's foster mother, natural mother*, principal, and third-

---

* It was important to have Tommy's natural mother present because she remains the legal parent and must sign the IEP. Also, the parent worker on the diagnostic team felt that her participation could be a first step toward assisting her in reassuming her role as mother with some degree of success.

grade teacher. Together they agreed on an estimate of the severity of Tommy's present problems. The estimate was recorded this way:

	Degree of severity		
	Mild	Moderate	Severe
Behavior	1 2	3	④ 5
Communication	1 2	3	④ 5
Socialization	1 2	③	4 5
(Pre)academics	1 ②	3	4 5
Overall	1 2	3	④ 5

The next step in the IEP conference was to prepare the goals and objectives for Tommy and to identify particular methods and materials for accomplishing them.

GOALS, OBJECTIVES, AND METHODS/MATERIALS

Goal: To successfully participate in routines.   **Behavior**

Objectives:

Suggested Methods, Materials, and Experiences

To participate verbally and physically in movement activities such as playtime, mat time, games, and music activities without physical intervention by adult (B-11).

Tommy should respond with enthusiasm to movement activities, but will lose control unless there is maximum structure. Avoid activities that require taking turns. Simultaneous action of all group members will work best: an obstacle course, role play, a "disco" period, athletic-type calisthenics, playing rhythm instruments in unison, group murals, etc.

To spontaneously participate verbally and physically in activities without physical intervention (B-12).

Tommy's most difficult time is during transitions. Structure the ending of each activity carefully. Communicate exactly what is expected and ask the aide to be nearby to restructure and assist Tommy in accomplishing a smooth transition.

To complete short, individual tasks with familiar material independent of any teacher intervention (B-13).

During individual assignments, circulate near Tommy. Don't interrupt until he pauses, but when he does, respond to the task content and to Tommy's success with it, before he activates for attention. Try to catch Tommy's eye from time to time to communicate support.

To give simple reasons for home, school, and community expectations (B-16).

In a group meeting before each new activity, review or demonstrate the step-by-step procedure. Include only one or two major expectations. Ask the group, "Why do it that way?" At the end of the activity, have another group meeting and ask, "Did it go well by doing it that way?"

Communication   *Goal:*   To use words to express oneself in the group.

Objectives:

Suggested Methods, Materials, and Experiences:

To describe simple, tangible characteristics of both self and others (C-12).

Use *Sports Illustrated*, the local newspaper, and televised sports events to describe the sports heroes. Follow up these units with a parallel unit which provides opportunities for group members to describe what they did during a physical skills unit.

To use words or gestures to show appropriate positive and negative feeling responses to environment, materials, and people or animals (C-15).

Expand these units to include the feelings sports heroes have in highly dramatic moments.

To participate in group discussions in ways not disruptive to the group (C-16).

Introduce role play and dramatics as ways to reenact these notable moments, express the heroes' feelings, and redesign the endings. Have a group meeting to outline the alternative endings. Then structure a group meeting to evaluate the results of each alternative after the various alternatives have been role-played.

To describe characteristic attributes, strengths, and problems in self (C-17).

Follow up the units on sports heroes with units that describe the actual physical skills activities of the group. Encourage the group members to describe their best personal characteristics which contributed to the group's success.

Goal: To find satisfaction in group activities.

Socialization

Objectives:

Suggested Methods, Materials, and Experiences:

To participate in cooperative activities or projects with another child during organized activities (S-18).

Provide highly structural small-group projects and physical skill activities with carefully assigned tasks that require some small amount of interaction between Tommy and a particular child.

To model appropriate behavior of another child (S-19).

For team work, pair Tommy with a child he admires who has appropriate behavior. Give them a project to produce together for the others. Be sure that it results in a highly successful outcome for both children.

To share materials and take turns without verbal reminders (S-20).

Be sure that the activity requires each child to ask the other for a material in order to get the job done.

To participate without inappropriate response in activity suggested by another child (S-23).

Encourage the group to create "adventure" units involving a dramatic incident, role-play, music, art, and movement. Be certain that every child contributes a suggestion that is followed by the others.

Academics   *Goal:* To participate in the group with basic expressive language concepts, symbolic representation of experiences and concepts, functional semiconcrete concepts of conservation, and body coordination.

Objectives:

Suggested Methods, Materials, and Experiences:

To perform physical skills in group games or other activities typically played by elementary school children (A-41).

Plan a daily physical skills program for the group (twenty minutes). Include jogging, climbing, jungle gym, relay running, and ball-handling games. Participation will be enhanced by using a dramatic theme.

To identify illogical elements in simple situations (A-42).

Begin a collection of jokes and riddles and ask group members to bring in their favorites. In art time do "mixed-up pictures" — where each child cuts out pictures from magazines and pastes them in an arrangement that tells a "mixed-up" story. Ask the group to guess what the "mixed up" part is in each picture.

To write primary words and sentences from memory and dictation (A-44).	Expand the "mixed up" pictures to include a title the children each create and write for their own pictures. After titles, introduce "the caption" idea to be written under the picture. Eventually, all classroom units could have a brief "documentary note" by each class member.
To do simple numerical operations of multiplication and division (including arrays) to 25 (A-45).	Continue the second grade arithmetic sequence in place value and regrouping. Use concrete materials and introduce multiplication and division as operations involving regrouping. Pair Tommy with another child of equal skill and have them think of word problems for each other to solve.

PLACEMENT

1. Recommended developmental therapy placement:

    Projected enrollment date: *October 20, 1978*

    Stage: *Stage Three group*

    Time: *1:00–3:00 P.M.*

    Team: *Mrs. Z. and Mr. B.*

    Long-term goals:

    Projected terminating date: *August 1979*

    Projected terminating stage: *Beginning Stage 4*

2. Type and amount of regular education:

    Tommy needs to continue his participation in his third grade class, using academic materials at the second grade level. Because his reading and arithmetic groups are in the morning, he should come to the special education class in the afternoon for an intensive developmental therapy program in the social/emotional areas.

Staff person: *Ms. K.*
Third grade teacher

3. Type and amount of physical education:
Physical skills development should be included in the special education program until Tommy is able to be successful in group processes and games within the small, structured group.

> Staff person: *Ms. Z.*
> Special education teacher

4. Medical/diagnostics/medication needed:

None indicated at this time.

Provide psychological and psychiatric reassessment in June 1979.

> Staff person: *not applicable*

5. Other related services:
Assist Tommy's foster mother in reenrolling Tommy in the Boys' Club or the recreation department's Saturday basketball program. Identify a "crisis" person on that staff who can assist Tommy in being successful and appropriate.

> Staff person: *Mr. O.*
> Social worker

6. Recommended home focus:

Goals: To successfully participate in family routines; to use words to express oneself in the family; to find satisfaction in family activities.

The following suggestions should work toward the accomplishment of these goals. The most important messages for Tommy's family to give him are that they *really* like him and they *really* think he can do things well.

a) Develop a home management plan with Tommy's foster mother and her mother for helping Tommy follow through on his chores. Include no more than two chores at first, and work with Tommy to see that he knows each step in the process. Maintain a spirit of "collaboration" and teamwork during this time.

b) Plan a short time each day when Tommy and his foster mother share an activity which Tommy really enjoys. Keep it very special! Focus on talking together and having fun together during this time. Use the paperback book *Between Parent and*

Child as a guideline to help Tommy's foster mother develop her skill in interacting with him. Games that have a winner and a loser should be avoided for a while. Guessing games, discussions about current sports events, and television stories might be used.

c) Consider the possibility of a community course in effective parenting with Tommy's foster mother.

d) Plan each step to be used in response to Tommy's intermittent enuresis and encopresis. Review the plan with Tommy. Completely avoid recriminations or punishment. Approach the incident as a situation which simply needs a cleanup, and expect Tommy to carry a large portion of responsibility for the cleanup. Also review Tommy's evening diet to reduce excessive eating or drinking.

On a calendar, record each time an incident occurs. If there is not a decrease within two months, consider several other procedures, including awakening Tommy during the night.

e) When an overt stealing incident arises at home, assist Tommy's foster mother in dealing with it in a nonpunitive but firm way. The object should be returned with the statement to Tommy, "This is not ours. We cannot keep it." Encourage her to avoid discussions about the incident with Tommy.

f) Begin meeting with Tommy's natural mother twice a month to see how she is getting along. As she begins to feel better, plan with her ways to begin gradually to assume a parenting role again.

Recommended level of parental participation: (Check one)

Minimal _____

Intermittent ____**X**____

Extensive _____

Staff person: *Mr. O.*
Social worker

SCHEDULE FOR REEVALUATION

Tommy's progress will be reevaluated with the DTORF every ten weeks by a team composed of his special education teacher and teaching aide, his regular third grade teacher, and his foster mother. These rating periods will coincide with the school's regular grading periods. To summarize and document Tommy's progress, three of the DTORF ratings will be recorded on the bar graph (Fig. A.1): the Baseline (entry DTORF), Mid-Year, and End-of-Year.

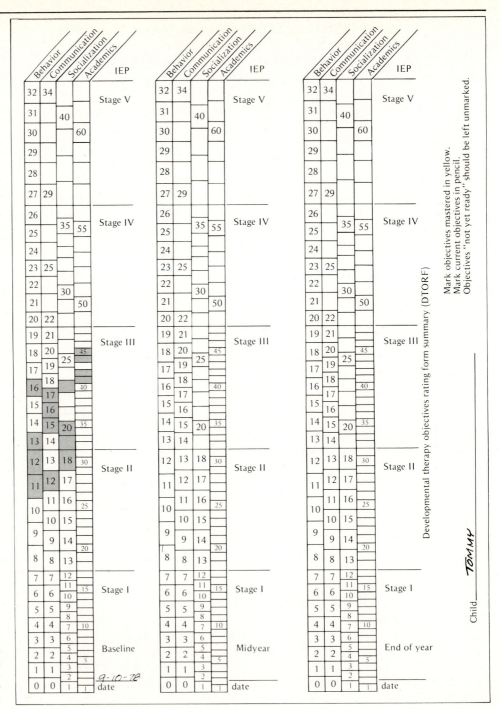

Fig. A.1
Tommy's progress
on Developmental
Therapy Mile-
stones. (Courtesy
of Mary M. Wood.)

John — learning-disabled

Checklist

Date	Event
9-1-77	Referral by Louise Borden
9-3-77	Parents informed of rights; permission obtained for evaluation
9-15-77	Evaluation compiled
9-16-77	Parents contacted
9-18-77	Total committee meets and subcommittee assigned
9-28-77	IEP developed by subcommittee
9-30-77	IEP approved by subcommittee

Committee Members
Mrs. Louise Borden Teacher
Mrs. John Thomas (Sp. Ed.) Coordinator
Other LEA representative
Mrs. John Doe
Parents:
Mrs. Mary Franks
Mrs. Joan Bambara
Mrs. Alice King
Date IEP initially approved 9-30-77

Identification Information

Name	John Doe
School	Beecher Sixth Grade Center
Birthdate	5-15-65 Grade 6
Parents: Name	Mr. and Mrs. John Doe
Address	1300 Johnson Street, Raleigh, N.C.
Phone:	Home none Office 932-8161

Testing Information

Test Name	Date Admin.	Interpretation
PIAT	9-10-77	spell—1.7, math—5.7, read recog—1, read comp—N.A., gen. info—6.3
test of initial consonants (CRT)	9-11-77	knows eight out of twenty-one initial consonant sounds total 2.0
CRT Reading Checklist	9-12-77	oral comprehension—6th grade reading skills—primary level
Carolina Arith. Inventory (Time)	9-2-77	Level IV
Carolina Arith. Inventory (Number concepts)	9-2-77	Level IV

Health Information

Vision:	good
Hearing:	excellent
Physical:	good
Other:	

Yearly Class Schedule

1st semester

Time	Subject	Teacher
8:30–9:20	math	Franks
9:30–10:20	language arts	Bambara (Resource)
10:30–11:20	social studies	Bambara
11:30–12:20	science	Franks
	lunch	
1:10–2:00	art	Shaw
2:10–3:00	P.E.	King

2nd semester

Time	Subject	Teacher
8:30–9:20	math	Franks
9:30–10:20	language arts	Bambara (Resource)
10:30–11:20	social studies	Bambara
11:30–12:20	science	Franks
	lunch	
1:10–2:00	art	Shaw
2:10–3:00	P.E.	King

Continuum of Services

	Hours per week
Regular class	20 hours
Resource teacher in regular classroom	6 hours
Resource room	4 hours
Reading specialist	
Speech/language therapist	
Counselor	
Special class	
Transition class	

Others:

Student's Name   John Doe

Subject Area   Reading

Level of Performance   primary reading recognition, 6th grade comprehension of oral material.

Teacher   Mrs. Bambara—resource teacher

ANNUAL GOALS: 1. John will successfully complete the primer level of the Bank Street Reading Series.

2. John will recognize and correctly say 90 new sight words.

3. John will master 14 initial consonants.

	SEPTEMBER	OCTOBER	NOVEMBER	DECEMBER	JANUARY
OBJECTIVES	Referred	1. Recognize and correctly state the sounds of the initial consonants *b* and *f* 100% of the time. 2. Recognize and correctly say ten new sight words 100% of the time. 3. Complete the first three stories of the primer, reading the material with 50% accuracy.	1. Recognize and correctly state the sounds of the initial consonants *s* and *m* 100% of the time. 2. Recognize and correctly say ten new sight words 100% of the time. 3. Complete the next three stories in the primer, reading the material with 50% accuracy.	1. Correctly recognize and state the sound of the initial consonant *g* 100% of the time. 2. Recognize and correctly say five new sight words 100% of the time. 3. Complete the next story in the primer, reading the material with 50% accuracy.	1. Review and correctly state the sounds of the initial consonants *b, f, m, s,* and *g* 100% of the time. 2. Recognize and correctly state the sound of the initial consonant *h* 100% of the time. 3. Review and correctly say 25 previously learned sight words 100% of the time. 4. Recognize and correctly say five new sight words 100% of the time. 5. Review the previously read stories in the primer, reading the material with 60% accuracy.

MATERIALS	Bank Street Basal Reading Series, Hoffman Phonetic Reading Program, teacher-made materials	Bank Street Basal Reading Series, Hoffman Phonetic Reading Program, teacher-made materials	Bank Street Basal Reading Series, Hoffman Phonetic Reading Program, teacher-made materials	Bank Street Basal Reading Series, Hoffman Phonetic Reading Program, teacher-made materials
AGENT	regular teacher resource teacher	regular teacher resource teacher	regular teacher resource teacher	regular teacher resource teacher
EVALU-ATION	1. informal assessment 2. Criterion Referenced Test (CRT)	1. informal assessment 2. CRT	1. informal assessment 2. CRT	1. informal assessment 2. CRT

Student's Name   John Doe

Subject Area   Reading

Level of Performance   reading recognition (1.2 PIAT), 6th grade comprehension of oral material (CRT).

Teacher   Mrs. Bambara—resource teacher

ANNUAL GOALS:
1. John will successfully complete the primer level of the Bank Street Basal Reading Series.
2. John will recognize and correctly say 90 new sight words.
3. John will master 14 initial consonants.

	FEBRUARY	MARCH	APRIL	MAY	JUNE
OBJECTIVES	1. Recognize and correctly state the sounds of the initial consonants l and d 100% of the time. 2. Recognize and correctly say 15 new sight words 100% of the time. 3. Complete the next three stories in the primer, reading the material with 60% accuracy and mastering the skills that accompany the stories.	1. Recognize and correctly state the sounds of the initial consonants r and w 100% of the time. 2. Recognize and correctly say 15 new sight words 100% of the time. 3. Complete the next three stories in the primer, reading the material with 60% accuracy and mastering the skills that accompany the stories.	1. Recognize and correctly state the sounds of the initial consonants c and t 100% of the time. 2. Recognize and correctly say 15 new sight words 100% of the time. 3. Complete the next three stories in the primer, reading the material with 95% accuracy and mastering the skills that accompany the stories.	1. Recognize and correctly state the sounds of the initial consonants n and y 100% of the time. 2. Recognize and correctly say 15 new sight words 100% of the time. 3. Complete the next three stories in the primer, reading the material with 95% accuracy and mastering the skills that accompany the stories.	Evaluation
MATERIALS	Bank Street Basal Reading Series, Hoffman Phonetic Reading Program, teacher-made materials	Bank Street Basal Reading Series, Hoffman Phonetic Reading Program, teacher-made materials	Bank Street Basal Reading Series, Hoffman Phonetic Reading Program, teacher-made materials	Bank Street Basal Reading Series, Hoffman Phonetic Reading Program, teacher-made materials	
AGENT	regular teacher resource teacher	regular teacher resource teacher	regular teacher resource teacher	regular teacher resource teacher	
EVALU-ATION	1. informal assessment 2. Criterion Referenced Test (CRT)	1. informal assessment 2. CRT	1. informal assessment 2. CRT	1. informal assessment 2. CRT	

Bibliography

Chapter 1   Exceptional pupils

ABA (American Bar Association Categories to Classify Laws). *Mental Disabilities Law Reporter* 1 (1976): 7–9.

BEH. *Progress Toward a Free Appropriate Public Education: A Report to Congress on the Implementation of Public Law 94-142, The Education for All Handicapped Children Act.* Washington, D.C.: U.S. Department of Health, Education, and Welfare, Office of Education, 1979.

Brown v. Board of Education of Topeka. 347 U.S. Code 483, 493, 1954.

Budoff, M. Engendering Change in Special Education Practices. *Harvard Educational Review* 45, 4 (1975): 507–526.

Burgdorf, R. L., Jr. (ed.). *The Legal Rights of Handicapped Persons: Cases, Materials, and Text.* Baltimore: Brookes, 1980(*a*).

———— . Who are "Handicapped" Persons? In R. L. Burgdorf, Jr. (ed.). *The Legal Rights of Handicapped Persons: Cases, Materials, and Text.* Baltimore: Brookes, 1980(*b*).

Burgdorf, R. L., Jr., and D. N. Bersoff. Equal Educational Opportunity. In R. L. Burgdorf, Jr. (ed.). *Rights of Handicapped Persons: Cases, Materials, and Text.* Baltimore: Brookes, 1980.

deBoor, M. F. What Is to Become of Katherine? *Exceptional Children 41* (1975): 517–518.

Dimond, P. The Constitutional Right to Education: The Quiet Revolution. *Hastings Law Journal 24* (1973): 1087–1127.

Dunlap, J. M. The Education of Children with High Mental Ability. In W. M. Cruickshank and G. O. Johnson (eds.). *Education of Exceptional Children and Youth*, 3rd ed. Englewood Cliffs, N.J.: Prentice-Hall, 1975.

Havighurst, R. J. *Developmental Tasks and Education*, 3rd ed. New York: McKay, 1972.

Hewett, F. M. and S. R. Forness. *Educating Exceptional Learners*, 2nd ed. Boston: Allyn & Bacon, 1977.

Park, C. C. Elly and the Right to Education. *Phi Delta Kappan 8* (1974): 535–537.

Public Law 88-352, The Civil Rights Act of 1964 — Statute. *Laws of the 88th Congress — Second Session.*

Public Law 93-112, The Vocational Rehabilitation Act of 1973 — Statute. *Laws of the 93rd Congress — First Session.*

Public Law 94-142. Education of All Handicapped Children Act of 1975 — Statute. *Laws of the 94th Congress — First Session.*

Public Law 94-142. Education of All Handicapped Children Act of 1975 — Regulations. *Federal Register*, August 23, 1977.

Reynolds, M. C., and J. W. Birch. *Teaching Exceptional Children in All America's Schools*. Reston, Va.: CEC, 1977.

Shane, J. G. *et al. Guiding Human Development: The Counsellor and the Teacher in the Elementary School*. Worthington, Ohio: Jones, 1971.

Turnbull, H. R. Legal Implications. In A. J. Papanikou and J. L. Paul, (eds.). *Mainstreaming Emotionally Disturbed Children*. Syracuse, N.Y.: Syracuse University Press, 1977.

Turnbull, H. R. and A. P. Turnbull. *A Free Appropriate Public Education: Law and Implementation*. Denver: Love, 1978.

Tyler, L. E. Individual Differences. In R. L. Ebel, (ed.). *Encyclopedia of Educational Research*. New York: Macmillan, 1969.

_____ . *Individual Differences: Abilities and Motivational Dispositions*. New York: Appleton-Century-Crofts, 1974.

_____ . *Individuality: Human Possibilities and Personal Choice in the Psychological Development of Men and Women*. San Francisco: Jossey-Bass, 1978.

Tyler, R. W., and S. H. White. Chairmen's Report. In R. W. Tyler and S. H. White, chairmen. *Testing, Teaching, and Learning.* Washington, D.C.: HEW — National Institute of Education, 1979.

United States Code, Title 42, The Public Health and Welfare, Sec. 1983. St. Paul, Minn.: West, 1970.

Weatherly, R. PL 94-142: Social Work's Role in Local Implementation. In R. Anderson, M. Freeman, and R. L. Edwards (eds.). *School Social Work and PL 94-142: The Education of All Handicapped Children Act.* Washington, D.C.: National Association of Social Workers, 1977.

Chapter 2   Classification and testing

Aiken, L. R., Jr. *Psychological Testing and Assessment,* 3rd ed. Boston: Allyn & Bacon, 1979.

APA (American Psychological Association and Others). *Standards for Educational and Psychological Tests.* Washington, D.C.: American Psychological Association, 1974.

Armstrong, J. Taxonomies — Special Education. In L. Mann and D. A. Sabatino (eds.). *The Third Review of Special Education.* New York: Grune & Stratton, 1976.

Baldwin, N. Y. Tests Can Underpredict: A Case Study. *Phi Delta Kappan 58* (1977): 620–621.

Bertrand, A., and J. P. Cebula. *Tests, Measurement, and Evaluation: A Developmental Approach.* Reading, Mass.: Addison-Wesley, 1980.

Blake, K. A. *The Mentally Retarded: An Educational Psychology.* Englewood Cliffs, N.J.: Prentice-Hall, 1976.

Blatt, B. Public Policy and the Education of Children with Special Needs. *Exceptional Children 38* (1972): 537–545.

Burgdorf, R. L., Jr. Contracts, Ownership, and Transfers of Property. In R. L. Burgdorf, Jr. (ed.). *The Legal Rights of Handicapped Persons: Cases, Materials, and Text.* Baltimore: Brookes, 1980*a*.

———— . Freedom from Residential Confinement. In R. L. Burgdorf, Jr. (ed.). *The Legal Rights of Handicapped Persons: Cases, Materials, and Text.* Baltimore: Brookes, 1980*b*.

———— , (ed.). *The Legal Rights of Handicapped Persons: Cases, Materials, and Text.* Baltimore: Brookes, 1980.

———— . Voting and Holding Public Office. In R. L. Burgdorf, Jr. (ed.). *The Legal Rights of Handicapped Persons: Cases, Materials, and Text.* Baltimore: Brookes, 1980 *c*.

_____ . Who Are "Handicapped" Persons? In R. L. Burgdorf, Jr. (ed.). *The Legal Rights of Handicapped Persons: Cases, Materials, and Text.* Baltimore: Brookes, 1980 *d.*

Burgdorf, R. L., Jr., and D. N. Bersoff. Equal Educational Opportunity. In R. L. Burgdorf, Jr. (ed.). *The Legal Rights of Handicapped Persons: Cases, Materials, and Text.* Baltimore: Brookes, 1980.

Clements, S. D. *Minimal Brain Dysfunction in Children: Terminology in Identification.* NINDB Monograph No. 3. Washington, D.C.: HEW, 1966.

Cottle, T. J. *Barred from School: 2 Million Children.* New York: New Republic, 1976.

Cronbach, L. J. Five Decades of Public Controversy over Mental Testing. *American Psychologist 30* (1975): 1–14.

Cronbach, L. J., and R. E. Snow. *Aptitudes and Instructional Methods: A Handbook of Research on Interactions,* New York: Irvington/Halstead, 1977.

Divoky, D. Education's Latest Victim: The "LD" Kid. *Learning* (October 1974): 20–25.

Duval County Public Schools. *Individualized Mathematics Curriculum.* Jacksonville, Fla.: n.d.

Fisher, M. A., and D. Zeaman. Growth and Decline of Retardate Intelligence. In N. R. Ellis (ed.). *International Review of Research in Mental Retardation,* Vol. 4. New York: Academic Press, 1970.

Flaugher, R. L. The Many Definitions of Test Bias, *American Psychologist 33* (1978): 671–679.

Gage, N. L. IQ Heritability, Race Differences, and Educational Research. *Phi Delta Kappan 53* (1972*a*): 308–312.

_____ . Replies to Shockley, Page and Jensen: The Causes of Race Differences in IQ. *Phi Delta Kappan 53* (1972*b*): 422–427.

Gee, E. G., and D. J. Sperry. *Education Law and the Public School: A Compendium.* Boston: Allyn & Bacon, 1978.

Gottlieb, J., and G. N. Siperstein. Attitudes toward Mentally Retarded Persons: Effects of Attitude Referent Specificity. *American Journal of Mental Deficiency 80* (1976): 376–381.

Grossman, H. J. (ed.). *Manual on Terminology and Classification in Mental Retardation.* Washington, D.C.: American Association on Mental Deficiency, 1973.

_____ . *Manual on Terminology and Classification in Mental Retardation,* 2nd ed. Washington, D.C.: American Association on Mental Deficiency, 1977.

_____ . (ed.). *Manual on Terminology and Classification in Mental Retardation,* 3rd ed. Washington, D.C.: American Association on Mental Deficiency. In press.

Hammill, D. D., and S. Larsen. The Effectiveness of Psycholinguistic Training. *Exceptional Children 41* (1974): 4–15.

Haring, N. G. Preface and Introduction. In N. G. Haring (ed.), *Behavior of Exceptional Children,* 2nd ed. Columbus, Ohio: Merrill, 1978.

Haring, N. G., and B. Bateman. *Teaching the Learning Disabled Child.* Englewood Cliffs, N.J.: Prentice-Hall, 1977.

Henning, K. K. Public Official Liability: A Trend toward "Administrative Malpractice." *Management Information Service Report,* Vol. 8, No. 1. Washington, D.C.: International City Management Association, January 1976, pp. 1–9.

Hobbes, N. *The Futures of Children: Categories, Labels, and Their Consequences.* San Francisco: Jossey-Bass, 1975.

Hopkins, D. K., and G. H. Bracht. Ten-year Stability of Verbal and Non-verbal IQ Scores. *American Educational Research Journal 12, 4* (1975): 469.

Jensen, A. R. Social Class, Race, and Genetics: Implications for Education. *American Educational Research Journal 5*(1968): 1–42.

_____ . *Genetics and Education.* New York: Harper & Row, 1972.

_____ . *Bias in Mental Testing.* New York: Free Press, 1979*a*.

_____ . *Educational Differences.* New York: Mathuen, 1979*b*.

Johnson, W. *People in Quandaries.* New York: Harper, 1946.

Larry, P. v. Riles. U.S. District Court for the Northern District of California, October 10, 1979.

Leviton, S. P. Freedom of Choice: Competency and Guardianship. In R. L. Burgdorf, Jr. (ed.). *The Legal Rights of Handicapped Persons: Cases, Materials, and Text.* Baltimore: Brookes, 1980.

McCarthy, M. M. Classification of Students: Legal Issues. *Viewpoints 52,* 5 (1976): 33–49.

MacMillan, D. L. Categories and Labels: Hypothesized and Real Effects, In *Mental Retardation in School and Society.* Boston: Little, Brown, 1977.

Mercer, J. A Policy Statement on Assessment Procedures and the Rights of Children. *Harvard Educational Review 44* (1974): 328–344.

Moran, M. R. *Assessment of the Exceptional Learner in the Regular Classroom.* Denver: Love, 1978.

Murphy, J. M. Psychiatric Labeling in Cross-Cultural Perspective. *Science 191* (1976): 1019–1028.

National Advisory Committee on the Handicapped. *The Unfinished Revolution: Education for the Handicapped.* Washington, D.C.: U.S. Government Printing Office, 1976.

National Society for the Study of Education. *Nature and Nurture.* Part 1. *Their Influence on Intelligence.* 27th NSSE Yearbook, 1928.

———. *Intelligence: Its Nature and Nurture.* Part 1. *Comparative and Critical Exposition.* 39th NSSE Yearbook, 1940*a*.

———. *Intelligence: Its Nature and Nurture.* Part 2. *Original Studies and Experiments.* 39th NSSE Yearbook, 1940*b*.

Public Law 93-112, The Vocational Rehabilitation Act of 1973. *Federal Register*, May 4, 1977.

Public Law 94-142, The Education of All Handicapped Children Act of 1975. *Federal Register*, August 23, 1977.

Public Law 88-352, The Civil Rights Act of 1964 — Statute. *Laws of the 88th Congress — Second Session.*

Salvia, J., and J. E. Ysseldyke. *Assessment in Special and Remedial Education.* Boston: Houghton Mifflin, 1978.

Semmel, M. I., and J. I. Heinmiller. The Education for All Handicapped Children Act of 1975; National Perspectives and Long-Range Implications. *Indiana University Bulletin 23*, 2 (1977): 1–16.

Shuger, N. B. Procreation, Marriage, and Raising Children. In R. L. Burgdorf, Jr. (ed.). *The Legal Rights of Handicapped Persons: Cases, Materials, and Text.* Baltimore: Brookes, 1980.

Soeffing, M. Y. New Assessment Techniques for Mentally Retarded and Culturally Different Children: A Conversation with Jane R. Mercer. *Education and Training of the Mentally Retarded 10* (1975): 110–116.

Sorgen, M. S. Labeling and Classification. In M. Kindred *et al.* (eds.). *The Mentally Retarded Citizen and the Law.* New York: Macmillan, 1976.

Swanson, B. M., and D. J. Willis. *Understanding Exceptional Children and Youth.* Chicago: Rand McNally, 1979.

Thomas, E. D., and M. J. Marshall. Clinical Evaluation and Coordination of Services: An Ecological Model. *Exceptional Children 44* (1977): 16–27.

Torres, S. *A Primer on Individualized Education Programs for Handicapped Children.* Reston, Va.: Foundation for Exceptional Children, 1977.

Turnbull, A. P., B. Strickland, and J. C. Brantley. *Developing and Implementing Individualized Education Programs.* Columbus, Ohio: Merrill, 1978.

Turnbull, H. R. Accountability: An Overview of the Impact of Litigation on Professionals. In F. J. Weintraub *et al.* (eds.). *Public Policy and the Education of Exceptional Children.* Reston, Va.: CEC, 1976.

Turnbull, H. R., and A. Turnbull. *Free Appropriate Public Education: Law and Implementation.* Denver: Love, 1978.

Tyler, L. E. *Individuality.* San Francisco: Jossey-Bass, 1978.

Tyler, R. W., and J. H. White. Chairmen's Report. In R. W. Tyler and S. H. White, chairmen. *Testing, Teaching and Learning.* Washington, D.C.: HEW — National Institute of Education, 1979.

Warren, S. A. Special Education Issues in the Seventies. In M. B. Scott, (ed.). *The Essential Profession: Contemporary Issues in Education.* Stamford, Conn.: Greylock, 1976.

Whatever Became of "Geniuses?" Downplaying the Old IQ Numbers Racket. *Time,* December 19, 1977, p. 89.

Wood, M. M. *The Developmental Therapy Objectives,* 3rd ed. Baltimore: University Park Press, 1979.

Ysseldyke, J. E. Diagnostic-Prescriptive Teaching: The Search for Aptitude-Treatment Interaction. In L. Mann and D. A. Sabatino (eds.). *The First Review of Special Education.* Philadelphia: Journal of Special Education, Press, 1973.

Zettle, J. J., and A. Abeson. The Right to a Free Appropriate Public Education. In C. P. Hooker (ed.). *The Courts and Education,* 77th Yearbook. Chicago: University of Chicago Press, 1978.

Chapter 3 Instruction and placement

Abel, D. A. and L. A. Connor. Educational Malpractice: One Jurisdiction's Response. In C. P. Hooker (ed.). *The Courts and Education,* 77th NSSE Yearbook. Chicago: University of Chicago Press, 1978.

Abeson, A. The Right to the Least Restrictive Alternative: In Education. In M. Kindred *et al.* (eds.). *The Mentally Retarded Citizen and the Law.* New York: Free Press, 1976.

Agard, J., M. Kaufman, and M. Semmel. *Mainstreaming: Learners and Their Environment.* Baltimore: University Park Press, 1978.

Aiello, B. (ed.). *Places and Spaces: Facilities Planning for Exceptional Children.* Reston, Va.: CEC, 1976.

Allen, K. E., V. A. Holem, and R. L. Schiefelbusch (eds.). *Early Intervention: A Team Approach.* Baltimore: University Park Press, 1978.

Anderson, R. H. Organizing and Staffing the School. In J. I. Goodlad and H. G. Shane, eds. *The Elementary School in the United States,* 72nd NSSE Yearbook, Pt. 2. Chicago: University of Chicago Press, 1973, pp. 221–242.

Anderson, R. M., J. G. Greer, and W. Mock. Environmental Alternatives for the Severely and Profoundly Handicapped. In J. W. Schifani, R. M. Anderson, and S. J. Odle (eds.). *Implementing Learning in the Least Restrictive Environment.* Baltimore: University Park Press, 1980.

Apolloni, T., J. Cappuccilli, and T. P. Cooke (eds.). *Achievement in Residential Services for Persons with Disabilities: Toward Excellence.* Baltimore: University Park Press, 1980.

Baldwin, V., *et al.* Integrating the Moderately and Severely Handicapped Preschool Child into a Normal Day Care Setting. In M. Guralnick (ed.). *Early Intervention and the Integration of Handicapped and Non-Handicapped Children.* Baltimore: University Park Press, 1978.

Barth, R. S. Beyond Open Education. *Phi Delta Kappan 58* (1976–77): 489–492.

Berliner, D. C., and N. L. Gage. The Psychology of Teaching Methods. In N. L. Gage (ed.). *The Psychology of Teaching Methods,* 75th NSSE Yearbook — Part 1. Chicago: University of Chicago Press, 1976.

Birch, J. W., and M. M. Reynolds. *Teaching Exceptional Children in All America's Schools.* Reston, Va.: CEC, 1977.

Blatt, B. A Drastically Different Analysis. In Mainstreaming: All Sides to an Issue. *Mental Retardation 17* (1979): 303–306.

Blatt, B., and F. Kaplan. *Christmas in Purgatory.* Boston: Allyn & Bacon, 1967.

Blatt, B., A. Ozolins, and J. McNally. *The Family Papers: A Return to Purgatory.* New York: Longman, 1979.

Boggs, E. *Testimony before the 94th Congress.* In Herr (1976).

Braginsky, B., and D. D. Braginsky. The Mentally Retarded: Society's Hansels and Gretels. *Psychology Today 7,* 10 (1974): 18–30.

Brenton, M. Mainstreaming the Handicapped. *Today's Education 2* (1974): 20–25.

Brown, V. Learning about Mathematics Instruction. *Journal of Learning Disabilities 8,* 8 (1975): 8–17.

Bruininks, R. H., and J. E. Rynders. Alternatives to Special Class Placement for Educable Mentally Retarded Children. *Focus on Exceptional Children 3*, 4 (1971): 1–12.

Burgdorf, R. L., Jr., and D. N. Bersoff. Equal Educational Opportunity. In R. L. Burgdorf, Jr. (ed.). *The Legal Rights of Handicapped Persons: Cases, Materials, and Text.* Baltimore: Brookes, 1980.

Burt, R. A. Behind the Right to Habilitation. In M. Kindred *et al.* (eds.). *The Mentally Retarded Citizen and the Law.* New York: Free Press, 1976.

Burton, T. A., S. F. Burton, and A. Hirshoren. For Sale: The State of Alabama (A Comment on Litigation and the Institutionalized Retarded). *Journal of Special Education 11* (1977*a*): 59–64.

_____ . Rhetoric versus Reality. *Journal of Special Education 11* (1977*b*): 69–72.

Callahan, C. M. *Developing Creativity in the Gifted and Talented.* Reston, Va.: CEC, 1978.

CAMS: Curriculum and Monitoring System. Logan: Utah State University, Exceptional Children Center, n.d.

Cawley, J. *Project Math, Levels I-IV.* Tulsa, Okla.: Education Progress Corp., 1978.

CEC. *Policy Statement of the Delegate Assembly.* Reston, Va.: 1976.

Chaffin, J. D. Will the Real Mainstreaming Program Please Stand Up? *Focus on Exceptional Children 6*, 5 (1974): 1–18.

Chambers, D. The Right to the Least Restrictive Alternative: Constitutional Issues. In M. Kindred *et al.* (eds.). *The Mentally Retarded Citizen and the Law.* New York: Free Press, 1976.

Chiba, C., and M. I. Semmel. Due Process and Least Restrictive Alternative: New Emphasis on Parental Participation. *Indiana Bulletin of Education 23*, 2 (1977): 17–29.

Children's Defense Fund. *Children Out of School in America.* Cambridge, Mass.: 1974.

Childs, R. E. A Second Look at Resource Room Instruction by a Resource Teacher. *Education and Training of the Mentally Retarded 10* (1975): 288–289.

_____ . "A Drastic Change in Curriculum for the Educable Mentally Retarded Child," in Mainstreaming: All Sides to an Issue. *Mental Retardation 17* (1979*a*): 299–301.

_____ ." Rebuttal," in Mainstreaming: All Sides to an Issue. *Mental Retardation 17* (1979*b*): 306.

Coleman, J. S. (ed.). *Equality of Educational Opportunity.* Washington, D.C.: U.S. Government Printing Office, 1966.

Coleman, J. S., (ed.) *Equal Educational Opportunity.* Cambridge, Mass.: Harvard University Press, 1969.

Connolly, B., S. J. Odle, and R. M. Anderson. Related Services in the Schools. In J. W. Schifani, R. M. Anderson, and S. J. Odle (eds.). *Implementing Learning in the Least Restrictive Environment.* Baltimore: University Park Press, 1980.

Cook, J. J. Accountability in Special Education. *Focus on Exceptional Children 3*, 9 (1972): 144.

Cox, C. B. Responsibility, Comparability, and the Cult of Accountability in Education. *Phi Delta Kappan 58* (1977): 761–766.

Cronbach, L. J., and R. E. Snow. *Aptitudes and Instructional Methods.* New York: Irvington, 1977.

Deno, E. N. *Educating Children with Emotional, Learning and Behavior Problems.* Minneapolis: University of Minnesota, National Support Systems Project, 1978.

———. Special Education as Developmental Capital. *Exceptional Children 37* (1970): 229–237.

DLM. *Developmental Learning Materials.* Niles, Ill.: 1979.

Dunn, L. M., and J. O. Smith. *The Peabody Language Development Kits — Levels 1–6.* Circle Pines, Minn.: American Guidance, 1965.

Federal Programs Advisory Services. *Handicapped Requirements Handbook.* Washington, D.C.: 1980.

Flaherty, R. EPEC: Evaluation and Prescription for Exceptional Children. In E. Ritvo (ed.). *Autism: Diagnosis, Current Research, and Management.* Holliswood, N.Y.: Spectrum, 1976.

Fredericks, H., *et al.* Integrating the Moderately and Severely Handicapped Preschool Child into a Normal Day Care Setting. In M. Guralnick (ed.). *Early Intervention and the Integration of Handicapped and Non-Handicapped Children.* Baltimore: University Park Press, 1978.

Gallagher, J. J. Planning for Early Childhood Programs for Exceptional Children. *Journal of Special Education 10*, 2 (1976): 171–177.

Gardner, W. I. *Learning and Behavior Characteristics of Exceptional Children and Youth: A Humanistic Behavioral Approach.* Boston: Allyn & Bacon, 1977.

Gartner, A., and F. Riessman. *How to Individualize Learning.* Bloomington, Ind.: Phi Delta Kappa Educational Foundation, 1977.

Gee, E. G., and D. J. Sperry. *Education Law and the Public Schools: A Compendium*. Boston: Allyn & Bacon, 1978.

Gillespie, P. H., and M. C. Sitko. Training Preservice Teachers in Diagnostic Teaching. *Exceptional Children 42* (1975): 401–402.

Glenn, L. The Right to the Least Restrictive Alternative: In Residential Care. In M. Kindred *et al.* (eds.). *The Mentally Retarded Citizen and the Law*. New York: Macmillan/Free Press, 1976.

Goldstein, H. *The Social Learning Curriculum*. Columbus, Ohio: Merrill, 1974.

Goodlad, J. I., and M. F. Klein. *Behind the Classroom Door.* Worthington, Ohio: Jones, 1970.

————. *Looking Behind the Classroom Door*. Belmont, Calif.: Wadsworth, 1974.

Gronlund, N. E. *Individualizing Classroom Instruction*. New York: Macmillan, 1974.

Guralnick, M. J. Early Classroom-Based Intervention and the Role of Organizational Structure. *Exceptional Children 42* (1975): 25–31.

Hambleton, R. K. Testing and Decision-Making Procedures for Selected Individualized Instructional Programs. *Review of Educational Research 44* (1974): 371–400.

Haring, N. G., D. H. Hayden, and G. R. Beck. General Principles and Guidelines in "Programming" for Severely Handicapped Children and Young Adults. *Focus on Exceptional Children 8*, 2 (1976).

Herr, S. The Right to an Appropriate Free Public Education. In M. Kindred *et al.* (eds.). *The Mentally Retarded Citizen and the Law*. New York: Free Press, 1976.

Hewett, F. M. The Orchestration of Success. In A. J. Pappanikou and J. L. Paul (eds.). *Mainstreaming Emotionally Disturbed Children*. Syracuse, N.Y.: Syracuse University Press, 1977.

Hill, E., and P. Ponder. *Orientation and Mobility Techniques*. New York: American Foundation for the Blind, 1976.

Hyer, R. (Personal communication, 1979.)

Jackson, G. B. The Research Evidence on the Effects of Grade Retention. *Review of Educational Research 45* (1975): 613–635.

Jamison, D., P. Suppes, and S. Wells. The Effectiveness of Alternative Instructional Media: A Survey. *Review of Educational Research 44*, 1 (1974): 1–67.

Jenkins, W. M., and S. J. Odle. Special Education, Vocational Education, and Vocational Rehabilitation. A Spectrum of Services to the

Handicapped. In J. W. Schifani, R. M. Anderson, and S. J. Odle (eds.). *Implementing Learning in the Least Restrictive Environment.* Baltimore: University Park Press, 1980.

Jones, R. L. Accountability in Special Education: Some Problems. *Exceptional Children 39* (1973): 631–642.

Kauffman, M., J. Agard, and M. Semmel. *Mainstreaming: Learners and Their Environment.* Baltimore: University Park Press, 1978.

Kirp, D. L. Student Classification, Public Policy, and the Courts. *Harvard Educational Review 44,* 1 (1974*a*): 7–52.

———. On Legal and Educational Questions of Classification in Students. *Harvard Educational Review 44,* 1 (1974*b*): 7–52.

Kliment, S. A. *Into the Mainstream: A Syllabus for a Barrier-Free Environment.* Washington, D.C.: AIA/Rehabilitation Services Administration, HEW, n.d.

Knoblock, P. Open Education for Emotionally Disturbed Children. *Exceptional Children 39* (1973): 358–365.

Knowles, C., P. Vogel, and J. Wessel. Project I CAN: Individualized Curriculum Designed for Mentally Retarded Children and Youth. *Education and Training of the Mentally Retarded 10,* 3 (1975): 155–160.

Kokaska, S. M., and C. J. Kokoska. Individualized Work Centers: An Approach for the Elementary Retarded Child. *Education and Training of the Mentally Retarded 6* (1971): 25–27.

Koons, C. L. Nonpromotion: A Dead-End Road. *Phi Delta Kappan 58* (1976–77): 701–702.

Lance, W. D. Technology and Media for Exceptional Learners: Look Ahead. *Exceptional Children 44* (1977): 92–97.

Larsen, S. C., and M. S. Poplin. *Methods for Educating the Handicapped: An Individualized Program Approach.* Boston: Allyn & Bacon, 1980.

Lau v. Nichols, 483 F 2d 791 (9th Cir. 1973), rev'd. 414 U.S. 563 (1974).

Laycock, V. K. Environmental Alternatives for the Mildly and Moderately Handicapped. In J. W. Schifani, R. M. Anderson, and S. J. Odle (eds.). *Implementing Learning in the Least Restrictive Environment.* Baltimore: University Park Press, 1980.

———. Prescriptive Programming in the Mainstream. In J. W. Schifani, R. M. Anderson, and S. J. Odle (eds.). *Implementing Learning in the Least Restrictive Environment.* Baltimore: University Park Press, 1980.

Lee, D. H. The Role of Teachers in Hospitals. *Special Education/Forward Trends 2,* 3 (1975): 21–23.

Levine, A. *The Rights of Students: The Basic American Civil Liberties Union Guide to a Public School Student's Rights.* New York: Avon, 1973.

McCarthy, M. M. Classification of Students: Legal Issues. *Viewpoints 52* (1976): 33–49.

McGaughey, R. From Problem to Solution: The New Focus in Fighting Environmental Barriers for the Handicapped. *Rehabilitation Literature 37* (1976): 10–12.

MacMillan, D. L., and L. D. Becker. Mainstreaming the Mildly Handicapped Learner. In R. B. Kneedler and S. G. Tarver (eds.). *Changing Perspectives in Special Education.* Columbus, Ohio: Merrill, 1977.

Mann, P. H., P. A. Suiter, and R. M. McClurry. *Handbook in Diagnostic-Prescriptive Teaching,* 2d ed. Boston: Allyn & Bacon, 1980.

Martin, E. W. Integration of the Handicapped Children into Regular Schools. In Mainstreaming: Origins and Implications. *Minnesota Education 2* (1976): 5–7.

Meyen, E. L. Instructional Models. In E. L. Meyen, G. A. Vergasen, and R. J. Whelan (eds.). *Strategies for Teaching Exceptional Children.* Denver: Love, 1972, pp. 9–16.

Moller, H. The Treatment of Childhood Schizophrenia in a Public School System. *Psychology in the Schools 1* (1964): 297–304.

Morgan, M. Beyond Disability: A Broader Definition of Architectural Barriers. *AIA Journal 65* (1976): 50–53.

National Association of State Directors of Special Education. *Functions of the Placement Committee in Special Education: A Resource Manual.* Washington, D.C.: 1976.

Nelson, D. The Ladies Room: An Experience in Personal Rehabilitation. *Journal of Rehabilitation 43,* 4 (1977): 15–16.

O'Connor, G., and E. G. Sitkei. Study of a New Frontier in Community Services: Residential Facilities for the Developmentally Disabled. *Mental Retardation 13,* 4 (1975): 35–39.

Odle, S. J., and B. Galtelli. The IEP: Foundation for Appropriate and Effective Instruction. In J. W. Schifani, R. M. Anderson, and S. J. Odle (eds.). *Implementing Learning in the Least Restrictive Environment.* Baltimore: University Park Press, 1980.

Padzersky, H. R., and J. Gibson. *Goalguide: A Minicourse in Writing Goals and Behavioral Objectives in Special Education.* Belmont, Calif., Fearon, 1974.

Plessy v. *Ferguson,* 163 U.S. 537 (1896).

Public Law 88-352, The Civil Rights Act of 1964, Section 601.

Public Law 93-112, The Vocational Rehabilitation Act of 1973. *Federal Register*, May 4, 1977.

Public Law 94-142, The Education of All Handicapped Children Act of 1975 — Regulations. *Federal Register*, August 23, 1977.

Reynolds, M., and J. Birch. *Teaching Exceptional Children in All America's Schools*. Reston, Va.: CEC, 1977.

Rich, H. L. Establishing the Learning Climate. In J. W. Schifani, R. M. Anderson, and S. J. Odle (eds.). *Implementing Learning in the Least Restrictive Environment*. Baltimore: University Park Press, 1980.

Roos, P. *Excerpts from Testimony of Dr. Phillip Roos in Wyatt v. Stickney*. In B. J. Ennis and P. R. Friedman (eds.). *Legal Rights of the Mentally Retarded and Handicapped*, Vol. 1. Washington, D.C.: Practicing Law Institute: The Mental Health Law Project, 1973.

———. The U.S. Constitution: Is It for Sale? *Journal of Special Education 11* (1977): 65–68.

Roos, P., B. M. McCann, and M. R. Addison (eds.). *Community Based Residential Services and Facilities for Mentally Retarded People*. Baltimore: University Park Press, 1980.

Rosenshine, B. Classroom Instruction. In N. L. Gage (ed.). *The Psychology of Teaching Methods*, 75th NSSE Yearbook — Pt. 1. Chicago: University of Chicago Press, 1976.

Russon, J. R. Mainstreaming Handicapped Students: Are Your Facilities Suitable? *American School and University 47* (1974): 25–32.

Saretsky, G. The Strangely Significant Case of Peter Doe. *Phi Delta Kappan 54* (1973): 589–592.

Segregation of Poor and Minority Children into Classes for the Mentally Retarded. *Michigan Law Review 71* (1973): 1212, 1215–1222.

Semmel, M. I., and J. I. Heinmiller. The Education of All Handicapped Children Act of 1975: National Perspectives and Long-Range Implications. *Indiana University Bulletin 23*, 2 (1977): 1–16.

Silberman, C. E. *Crisis in the Classroom*. New York: Random House, 1970.

Simon, S. B., and R. D. O'Rourke. *Developing Values with Exceptional Children*. Englewood Cliffs, N.J.: Prentice-Hall, 1977.

Smith, S. L. When Learning Is a Problem. *American Education* (November 1978): 18–23.

Sontag, E. Zero Exclusion: No Longer Rhetoric. *Apropos.* Columbus: Ohio State University — National Center on Educational Media and Materials for the Handicapped, Spring-Summer 1976.

Sorbye, R. Myoelectric Controlled Hand Prostheses in Children. *International Journal of Rehabilitation Research 1* (1977): 15–25.

Stanley, J. C. Compensatory Education for Children, Ages 2 to 8: Recent Studies of Educational Intervention. Baltimore: Johns Hopkins University Press, 1973.

——— . The Case for Extreme Educational Acceleration of Intellectually Brilliant Youths. *The Gifted Child Quarterly 20* (1976): 66–75.

Stoddard, G. D. *The Dual Progress Plan: A New Philosophy and Progress in Elementary Education.* New York: Harper, 1961.

Swanson, B. M., and D. J. Willis. *Understanding Exceptional Children and Youth.* Chicago: Rand McNally, 1979.

Tawney, J. W. Programmed Language Instruction for the Severely Developmentally Retarded. *Directive Teacher 21,* 3 (1980): 11–12.

Tebeest, D. L., and J. R. Dickie. Responses to Frustration: Comparisons of Institutionalized and Noninstitutionalized Retarded Adolescents and Nonretarded Children and Adolescents. *American Journal of Mental Deficiency 80* (1976): 407–413.

Treffinger, D. J., *et al.* Encouraging Affective Development: A Compendium of Techniques and Resources. *The Gifted Child Quarterly 20,* 1 (1976): 47–65.

Turnbull, A. P., and J. B. Schulz. *Mainstreaming Handicapped Students: A Guide for the Classroom Teacher.* Boston: Allyn & Bacon, 1979.

Turnbull, H. R., and A. Turnbull. *Free Appropriate Public Education: Law and Implementation.* Denver: Love, 1978.

USOE. *Closer Look.* Washington, D.C.: BEH (Winter).

Van Vechten, D., and I. B. Pless. Housing and Transportation: Twin Barriers to Independence. *Rehabilitation Literature 37* (1976): 202–207, 221.

Vernon, M., and H. Prickett. Mainstreaming: Issues and a Model Plan. *Audiology and Hearing Education 2,* 2 (1976): 5–11.

Vitello, S. J. The Institutionalization and Deinstitutionalization of the Mentally Retarded in the United States. In L. Mann and D. A. Sabatino (eds.). *The Third Review of Special Education.* New York: Grune & Stratton, 1976, pp. 217–243.

Wabash Center for the Mentally Retarded. *Guide to Early Developmental Training.* Boston: Allyn & Bacon, 1977.

Warren, S. A. What Is Wrong with Mainstreaming? A Comment on Drastic Change. In Mainstreaming: All Sides to an Issue. *Mental Retardation 17* (1979): 301–303.

Watts, B. H. Special Education in the Seventies: Promises and Problems. *Slow Learning Child 22* (1975): 67–82.

The Way We Go to School. Boston: Task Force on Children Out of School, 1970.

Wehman, P., and P. J. McLaughlin. *Vocational Curriculum for Developmentally Delayed Persons.* Baltimore: University Park Press, 1980.

_____ . *Program Development in Special Education: Designing Individualized Education Programs.* New York: McGraw-Hill, 1981.

Weintraub, F. J., and A. Abeson. Appropriate Education for All Handicapped Children: A Growing Issue. *Syracuse Law Review 23,* 4 (1972): 1044.

Weisberger, R. A. Planning for the Individualization of Learning with Blind Students. *Education of the Visually Handicapped 7* (1975): 112–115.

Wexler, H. New Technology for the Handicapped. *American Education* (November 1978): 45–46.

Withrow, F. B. Educational Technology for the Handicapped Learner. In Frank B. Withrow and C. J. Nygren (eds.). *Language, Materials, and Curriculum Management for the Handicapped Learner.* Columbus, Ohio: Merrill, 1976.

Wright, R. J. The Affective and Cognitive Consequences of an Open Education Elementary School. *American Educational Research Journal 12,* 4 (1975): 449–468.

Zettle, J. J., and A. Abeson. The Right to a Free Appropriate Public Education, in C. P. Hooker (ed.). *The Courts and Education,* 77th NSSE Yearbook. Chicago: University of Chicago Press, 1978.

Chapter 4 Speech-/language-impaired pupils

Agranowitz, A., and M. R. McKeown. *Aphasia Handbook: For Adults and Children.* Springfield, Ill.: Charles C Thomas, 1975.

Allen, K. E. The Language Impaired Child in the Preschool: The Role of the Teacher. *The Directive Teacher 2,* 3 (1980): 6–10.

American Speech and Hearing Association. *Report of the Task Force on Identifying Children with Language Impairment.* Washington, D.C., 1977.

Aronson, A. E. Dysarthria. In T. J. Hixon, L. D. Shriberg, and J. H. Saxman (eds.). *Introduction to Communication Disorders.* Englewood Cliffs, N.J.: Prentice-Hall, 1980.

BEH. *Progress toward a Free Appropriate Public Education: A Report to Congress on the Implementation of Public Law 94-142, The Education for All Handicapped Children Act.* Washington, D.C.: U.S. Department of Health, Education, and Welfare, Office of Education, 1979.

Boone, D. R. *The Voice and Voice Therapy,* 2d ed. Englewood Cliffs, N.J.: Prentice-Hall, 1977.

———. Voice Disorders. In T. J. Hixon, L. D. Shriberg, and J. H. Saxman (eds.). *Introduction to Communication Disorders.* Englewood Cliffs, N.J.: Prentice-Hall, 1980.

Dalton, P., and W. J. Handcastle. *Disorders of Fluency and Their Effects on Communications.* New York: Elsevier, 1978.

Damste, P. H., and J. W. Lerman. *An Introduction to Voice Pathology: Functional and Organic.* Springfield, Ill.: Charles C Thomas, 1975.

Darley, F. L., and D. C. Spriestersbach. *Diagnostic Methods in Speech Pathology,* 2d ed. New York: Harper & Row, 1978.

Eisenson, J. *Aphasia in Children.* New York: Harper & Row, 1972.

Eisenson, J., and M. Ogilvie. *Speech Correction in the Schools,* 4th ed., New York: Macmillan, 1977.

Emerick, L. L., and J. T. Hatten. *Diagnosis and Evaluation in Speech Pathology,* 2d ed. Englewood Cliffs, N.J.: Prentice-Hall, 1979.

Ewanowski, S. J., and J. H. Saxman. Orofacial Disorders. In T. J. Hixon, L. D. Shriberg, and J. H. Saxman (eds.). *Introduction to Communication Disorders.* Englewood Cliffs, N.J.: Prentice-Hall, 1980.

Filter, M. D. *Communication Disorders: A Handbook for Educators.* Springfield, Ill.: Charles C Thomas, 1977.

Gregory, H. *Controversies about Stuttering Therapy.* Baltimore: University Park, 1978.

Hayden, A. H., and R. K. Smith. *Mainstreaming Preschoolers.* Washington, D.C.: Project Headstart. DHEW Publication No. (OHDS) 78-31117, N.D., pp. 126–133.

Hixon, T. J., and J. H. Abbs. *Normal Speech Production.* In T. J. Hixon, L. D. Shriberg, and J. H. Saxman (eds.). *Introduction to Communication Disorders.* Englewood Cliffs, N.J.: Prentice-Hall, 1980.

Hubbell, R. D. Disorders of Language in Children. In P. H. Skinner and R. L. Shelton (eds.). *Speech, Language, and Hearing: Normal Processes and Disorders.* Reading, Mass.: Addison-Wesley, 1978.

Mower, D. E. *Methods of Modifying Speech Behaviors: Learning Theory in Speech Pathology.* Columbus, Ohio: Merrill, 1978.

Naremore, R. C. *Language Variation in Multicultural Society.* In T. J. Hixon, L. D. Shriberg, and J. H. Saxman (eds.). *Introduction to Communication Disorders.* Englewood Cliffs, N.J.: Prentice-Hall, 1980.

Nation, J. E., and D. M. Aram. *Diagnosis of Speech and Language Disorders.* St. Louis: Mosby, 1977.

Perkins, W. H. *Disorders of Speech Flow.* In T. J. Hixon, L. D. Shriberg, and J. H. Saxman (eds.). *Introduction to Communication Disorders.* Englewood Cliffs, N.J.: Prentice-Hall, 1980.

Polow, N. G. *A Stuttering Manual for the Speech Therapist.* Springfield, Ill.: Charles C Thomas, 1975.

Public Law 94-142, *The Education of All Handicapped Children Act of 1975.* Regulations, *Federal Register*, August 23, 1977.

Rees, N. S. *Learning to Talk and Understand.* In T. J. Hixon, L. D. Shriberg, and J. H. Saxman (eds.). *Introduction to Communication Disorders.* Englewood Cliffs, N.J.: Prentice-Hall, 1980.

Schieffelbusch, R. L. *The Bases of Language Interaction.* Baltimore: University Park Press, 1977.

————. *Language Intervention Strategies.* Baltimore: University Park Press, 1978.

Shelton, R. L. Disorders of Articulation. In P. H. Skinner and R. L. Shelton (eds.). *Speech, Language, and Hearing: Normal Processes and Disorders.* Reading, Mass.: Addison-Wesley, 1978a.

————. Disorders of Phonation. In P. H. Skinner and R. L. Shelton (eds.). *Speech, Language, and Hearing: Normal Processes and Disorders.* Reading, Mass.: Addison-Wesley, 1978b.

Shelton, R. L., and C. A. Wood. Speech Mechanisms and Production. In P. H. Skinner and R. L. Shelton (eds.). *Speech, Language, and Hearing: Normal Processes and Disorders.* Reading, Mass.: Addison-Wesley, 1978.

Van Riper, C. *Speech Correction: Principles and Methods,* 6th ed. Englewood Cliffs, N.J.: Prentice-Hall, 1978.

Wiig, E., and E. Semel. *Language Disabilities in Children and Adolescents.* Columbus, Ohio: Merrill, 1976.

Wingate, M. Disorders of Fluency. In P. H. Skinner and R. L. Shelton (eds.). *Speech, Language, and Hearing: Normal Processes and Disorders.* Reading, Mass.: Addison-Wesley, 1978.

Zwitman, D. *The Dysfluent Child.* Baltimore: University Park Press, 1978.

Chapter 5   Hearing-impaired pupils

Asbed, R. A., *et al.* Early Case Finding of Children with Communication Problems. *Volta Review* 72 (1970): 23–49.

BEH. *Progress toward a Free Appropriate Public Education: A Report to Congress on the Implementation of Public Law 94-142, The Education for All Handicapped Children Act.* Washington, D.C.: U.S. Department of Health, Education, and Welfare, Office of Education, 1979.

Berg, F. S. *Educational Audiology: Hearing and Speech Management.* New York: Grune & Stratton, 1976.

Bess, F. H. *Childhood Deafness: Causation, Assessment, and Management.* New York: Grune & Stratton, 1977.

Birch, J. W. *Hearing Impaired Children in the Mainstream.* Reston, Va.: CEC, 1975.

Bloodstein, O. *Speech Pathology: An Introduction.* Boston: Houghton Mifflin, 1979.

Bolton, B. Introduction and Overview. In B. Bolton (ed.). *Psychology of Deafness for Rehabilitation Counsellors.* Baltimore: University Park Press, 1976*a*.

——— . Rehabilitation Programs. In B. Bolton (ed.). *Psychology of Deafness for Rehabilitation Counsellors.* Baltimore: University Park Press, 1976*b*.

Christopher, D. A. *Manual Communication.* Baltimore: University Park Press, 1976.

Davis, H., and R. S. Silverman. *Hearing and Deafness*, 4th ed. New York: Holt, Rinehart and Winston, 1978.

Frisina, R., chairman. Report of the Committee to Redefine Deaf and Hard of Hearing for Educational Purposes. (Mimeographed), 1974.

Furth, H. *Deafness and Learning: A Psychosocial Approach.* Belmont, Calif.: Wadsworth, 1973.

Glattke, T. J. Sound and Hearing. In T. J. Hixon, L. D. Shriberg, and J. H. Saxman (eds.). *Introduction to Communication Disorders.* Englewood Cliffs, N.J.: Prentice-Hall, 1980.

Hodgson, W. R. Disorders in Hearing. In P. H. Skinner and R. L. Shelton (eds.). *Speech, Language, and Hearing: Normal Processes and Disorders.* Reading, Mass.: Addison-Wesley, 1978.

Hoemann, H. W. *Communicating with Deaf People.* Baltimore: University Park Press, 1978.

Hoemann, H. W., and D. G. Ullman. Intellectual Development. In B. Bolton (ed.). *Psychology of Deafness for Rehabilitation Counsellors.* Baltimore: University Park Press, 1976.

Index to Media and Materials for the Deaf, Hard of Hearing, and Speech Impaired. Los Angeles: University of Southern California, 1978.

Kretschmer, R. *Language Development and Intervention with the Hearing Impaired.* Baltimore: University Park Press, 1978.

Lane, H. S. Academic Achievement. In B. Bolton (ed.). *Psychology of Deafness for Rehabilitation Counsellors.* Baltimore: University Park Press, 1976.

Lassiter, R. A. Work Adjustment for People Who Are Deaf. In R. E. Hardy and J. G. Cull (eds.). *Educational and Psychosocial Aspects of Deafness.* Springfield, Ill.: Charles C Thomas, 1974.

Leslie, P., and B. Clarke. Environmental Alternatives for the Hearing Handicapped. In J. W. Schifani, R. M. Anderson, and J. S. Odle (eds.). *Implementing Learning in the Least Restrictive Environment.* Baltimore: University Park Press, 1980.

Lloyd, L. L., and H. Kaplan. *Audiometric Interpretation.* Baltimore: University Park Press, 1978.

Masland, M. W. Speech, language, and hearing checklist. Appendix I to Asbed *et al.* (1970), pp. 40–42.

_____ . Clinical Audiology. In L. E. Travis (ed.). *Handbook of Speech Pathology and Audiology.* New York: Appleton-Century-Crofts, 1971.

McClelland, K. D. Hearing Mechanism. In P. H. Skinner and R. L. Shelton (eds.). *Speech, Language, and Hearing: Normal Processes and Disorders.* Reading, Mass.: Addison-Wesley, 1978.

Meadow, K. P. Personality and Social Development of Deaf Persons. In B. Bolton (ed.). *Psychology of Deafness for Rehabilitation Counsellors.* Baltimore: University Park Press, 1976.

Moores, D. F. *Educating the Deaf: Psychology, Principles, and Practices.* Boston: Houghton Mifflin, 1977.

Newby, H. A. *Audiology.* Englewood Cliffs, N.J.: Prentice-Hall, 1979.

Public Law 94-142, The Education of All Handicapped Children Act of 1975. Regulations, *Federal Register,* August 23, 1977.

Riekehof, L. L. *The Joy of Signing: The New Illustrated Guide for Mastering Sign Language and the Manual Alphabet.* Springfield, Mo.: Gospel Publishing House, 1978.

Rose, D. E. *Audiological Assessment,* 2d ed. Englewood Cliffs, N.J.: Prentice-Hall, 1978.

Ross, M. *Auditory Management of the Hearing Impaired Child.* Baltimore: University Park Press, 1978.

Simmons-Martin, A. Early Intervention Programs. In B. Bolton (ed.). *Psychology of Deafness for Rehabilitation Counsellors.* Baltimore: University Park Press, 1976.

Skinner, P. H. Hearing. In P. H. Skinner and R. L. Shelton (eds.). *Speech, Language, and Hearing: Normal Processes and Disorders.* Reading, Mass.: Addison-Wesley, 1978.

Streng, A. *Language, Learning, and Deafness: Theory, Amplification and Classroom Management.* New York: Grune & Stratton, 1978.

Van Riper, C. *Speech Correction: Principles and Methods,* 6th ed. Englewood Cliffs, N.J.: Prentice-Hall, 1978.

Wier, C. C. Habilitation and Rehabilitation of the Hearing Impaired. In T. J. Hixon, L. D. Shriberg, and J. H. Saxman (eds.). *Introduction to Communication Disorders.* Englewood Cliffs, N.J.: Prentice-Hall, 1980.

Wiley, T. L. Hearing Disorders and Audiometry. In T. J. Hixon, L. D. Shriberg, and J. H. Saxman (eds.). *Introduction to Communication Disorders.* Englewood Cliffs, N.J.: Prentice-Hall, 1980.

Yater, V. V. *Mainstreaming of Children with a Hearing Loss.* Springfield, Ill.: Charles C Thomas, 1977.

Chapter 6   Visually impaired pupils

Adkins, P. G., and T. D. Amsa. An Early Stimulation Program for Visually Handicapped Infants and Toddlers. *Education of the Visually Handicapped 10,* 3 (1978/79): 75–79.

Aubuchon, M. T. Vision Screening for Preschoolers. *Optometric Weekly 64,* 26 (1973): 630–632.

Barraga, N. C. Utilization of Sensory-Perceptual Abilities. In B. Lowenfeld (ed.). *The Visually Handicapped Child in School.* London: Constable, 1974, pp. 117–154.

Barraga, N. C., and M. E. Collins. Development of Efficiency in Visual Functioning: Rationale for a Comprehensive Program. *Journal of Visual Impairment and Blindness 73* (1979): 121–126.

Bauman, M. K. Psychological and Educational Assessment. In B. Lowenfeld (ed.). *The Visually Handicapped Child in School.* London: Constable, 1974*a*, pp. 93–115.

_____ . Blind and Partially Sighted. In M. T. Wisland (ed.). *Psychoeducational Diagnosis of Exceptional Children.* Springfield, Ill.: Charles C Thomas, 1974*b*, pp. 159–189.

Becker, C., and K. Kalina. The Cranmer Abacus and Its Use in Residential Schools for the Blind and in Day School Programs. *New Outlook for the Blind 69,* 9 (1975): 412–415, 417.

BEH. *Progress toward a Free Appropriate Public Education: A Report to Congress on the Implementation of Public Law 94-142, The Education for All Handicapped Children Act.* Washington, D.C.: U.S. Department of Health, Education, and Welfare, Office of Education, 1979.

Bell, V. H. An Educator's Approach to Assessing Preschool Visually Handicapped Children. *Education of the Visually Handicapped 7,* 3 (1975): 84–89.

Berla, E. P., and L. H. Butterfield, Jr. Teachers' Views on Tactile Maps for Blind Students: Problems and Needs. *Education of the Visually Handicapped 7,* 4 (1975): 116–118.

Bischoff, R. W. Listening: A Teachable Skill for Visually Impaired Persons. *Journal of Visual Impairment and Blindness 73,* 2 (1979): 59–67.

Bishop, V. E. *Teaching the Visually Limited Child.* Springfield, Ill.: Charles C Thomas, 1971.

Bliss, J. C., and M. W. Moore. The Optacon Reading System. *Education of the Visually Handicapped 6,* 4 (1974): 98–102.

Buell, C. How to Include Blind and Partially Seeing Children in Public Secondary School Vigorous Physical Education. *Physical Educator 29,* 1 (1972): 6–8.

_____ . *Physical Education and Recreation for the Visually Handicapped.* Washington, D.C.: American Association for Health, Physical Education, and Education, 1973.

Caton, H., and E. J. Bradley. A New Approach to Beginning Braille Reading. *Education of the Visually Handicapped 10,* 3 (1978/79): 66–71.

Craig, R. H. A Personal Approach to Teaching Braille Reading to Youth and Adults. *New Outlook for the Blind 69* (1975): 11–19.

Currie, L. E. Work Evaluation of the Visually Impaired: A Perspective. *New Outlook for the Blind 69* (1975): 443–444, 446.

Curtis, C. K., and J. D. McWhannel. On the Use of the Inquiry Approach in Social Studies with Blind Children. *New Outlook for the Blind 66* (1972): 223–226.

Douglass, S., and S. Mangold. Precision Teaching of Visually Impaired Students. *Education of the Visually Handicapped 7, 2* (1975): 48–52.

Eichel, V. J. Mannerisms of the Blind: A Review of the Literature. *Journal of Visual Impairment and Blindness 72* (1978): 125–130.

Ferrell, K. A. *Sequence of Visual Development.* Alexandria, Va.: Virginia Commission for the Visually Handicapped, n.d.

———— . Orientation and Mobility for Preschool Children: What We Have and What We Need. *Journal of Visual Impairment and Blindness 73* (1979): 147–150.

Fraiberg, Selma H. *Insights from the Blind: Comparative Studies of Blind and Sighted Infants.* New York: Basic Books, 1977.

Friedman, J., and R. Pasnak. Attainment of Classification and Seriation Concepts by Blind and Sighted Children. *Education of the Visually Handicapped 5, 2* (1973): 55–62.

Fukurai, S. *How Can I Make What I Cannot See?* New York: Van Nostrand Reinhold, 1974.

Hanninen, K. A. *Teaching the Visually Handicapped.* Columbus, Ohio: Merrill, 1975.

Hayes, C. S., and E. Weinhouse. Application of Behavior Modification to Blind Children. *Journal of Visual Impairment and Blindness 72* (1978): 139–146.

Henderson, F. Communication Skills. In B. Lowenfeld (ed.). *The Visually Handicapped Child in School.* London: Constable, 1974, pp. 185–220.

Kidwell, A. M., and P. S. Greer. Sites, Perception, and the Non-Visual Experience: Designing and Manufacturing Mobility Maps. New York: AFB, 1973.

Kimbrough, J. A., K. M. Huebner, and L. J. Lowry. *Sensory Training.* Pennsylvania: The Greater Pittsburgh Guild for the Blind, 1976.

Kinnane, J. F., and A. Siziedelis. *Sources of Interpersonal Anxiety in the Physically Handicapped.* Washington, D.C.: Catholic University of America, 1974, pp. 73.

Klee, K. E. The Long Cane and the Guide Dog as Mobility Aids. *New Beacon 59,* 698 (1975): 141–147.

Kugel, R. B. Vision Screening of Preschool Children. *Pediatrics 50*, 6 (1972): 966–967.

Lamon, W. E., and J. Threadgill. The Papy-Lamon Minicomputer for Blind Children: An Aid in Learning Mathematics. *New Outlook for the Blind 69* (1975): 289–294.

Large Type Books in Print, New York: Bowker, 1978.

Laughlin, S. A Walking-Jogging Program for Blind Persons. *New Outlook for the Blind 69* (1975): 312–313.

Library of Congress, Division for the Blind and Physically Handicapped. *Aids for Handicapped Readers.* Washington, D.C., 1972.

Linn, M. D., and H. D. Thier. Adapting Science Material for the Blind: Expectation for Student Outcomes. *Science Education 59* (1975): 235–246.

Lowenfeld, B. Psychological Considerations. In B. Lowenfeld (ed.). *The Visually Handicapped Child in School.* London: Constable, 1974, pp. 27–60.

McMullen, A. R. (ed.). *Scouting for the Visually Handicapped.* North Brunswick, N.J.: Boy Scouts of America, 1974.

Malone, L., and L. Delucchi. Life Science for Visually Impaired Students. *Science and Children 26*, 5 (1979): 29–31.

Margach, C. B., R. A. Reynolds, and D. J. Wallace. Some Characteristics of Electronic Magnification Systems. *Optical Journal and Review of Optometry 112*, 15 (1975): 16–21.

Maron, S., and D. Martinez. Environmental Alternatives for the Visually Handicapped. In J. W. Schifani, R. M. Anderson, and S. J. Odle (eds.). *Implementing Learning in the Least Restrictive Environment.* Baltimore: University Park Press, 1980.

Merck, Sharp, and Dohme Research Laboratories. *The Merck Manual*, 13th ed. Rahway, N.J.: Merck Company, 1977.

Monbeck, M. E., and M. E. Mulholland. Introduction to Assessment of the Blind. *New Outlook for the Blind 69* (1975): 337–339.

Napier, G. D. Special Subject Adjustments and Skills. In B. Lowenfeld (ed.). *The Visually Handicapped Child in School.* London: Constable, 1974, pp. 221–278.

National Society to Prevent Blindness. *Eye Report for Children with Visual Problems. Blind and Partially Seeing.* New York, n.d.

Public Law 94-142, The Education of All Handicapped Children Act of 1975. Regulations. *Federal Register*, August 23, 1977.

Ritty, J. M. Assessing and Alleviating Visual Problems in the Schools. *Reading Teacher 32* (1979): 796–802.

Rosenthal, A. R. Visual Disorders. In E. E. Bleck and D. A. Nagel (eds.). *Physically Handicapped Children — A Medical Atlas for Teachers.* New York: Grune & Stratton, 1975.

Rusalem, H. *Coping with the Unseen Environment.* New York: Teachers College Press, 1972.

Russell, Y. (ed.). *Sensory Aids for Employment of Blind and Visually Impaired Persons: A Resource Guide.* New York: American Foundation for the Blind, 1978.

Scholl, G. T. Understanding and Meeting Development Needs. In B. Lowenfeld (ed.). *The Visually Handicapped Child in School.* London: Constable, 1974.

Scholl, G. T., and R. Schnur. *Measures of Psychological and Educational Functioning in the Blind and Visually Handicapped.* New York: American Foundation for the Blind, 1976.

Scott, E. P., J. E. Jan, and R. D. Freeman. *Can't Your Child See?* Baltimore: University Park Press, 1977.

Scott, R. A. *The Making of Blind Men.* New York: Russell Sage Foundation, 1969.

Simon, J. D. A Course in Spoken Communication for High School Students Who Are Visually Handicapped. *Education of the Visually Handicapped 6* (1974): 41–43.

Sinclair, D. Art Teaching for the Blind. *Teacher of the Blind 63* (1975): 65–72.

Stephens, B. Cognitive Processes in the Visually Impaired. *Education of the Visually Handicapped 4* (1972): 106–111.

Stratton, J. *The Blind Child in the Regular Kindergarten.* Springfield, Ill.: Charles C Thomas, 1977.

Struve, N. L., H. D. Thier, and D. Hadary. The Effect of an Experimental Science Curriculum for the Visually Impaired on Course Objectives and Manipulative Skills. *Education of the Visually Handicapped 7* (1975): 9–14.

Suen, C. Y., and M. P. Beddoes. Spelled Words as an Output for the Lexiphone Reading Machine and the Spellex Talking Typewriter. *American Foundation for the Blind Research Bulletin 29* (1975): 51–66.

Warren, D. H. Early v. Late Vision: The Role of Early Vision in Spatial Reference Systems. *New Outlook for the Blind 68,* 4 (1974): 157–162.

Weisgerber, R. A. Individualizing for the Handicapped Child in the Regular Classroom. *Education Technology 14* (1974): 33–35.

———. Planning for the Individualization of Learning with Blind Students. *Education of the Visually Handicapped 7* (1975): 112–115.

Woodcock, C. C. A Sensory Stimulation Center for Blind Children. *Phi Delta Kappan 55* (1974): 541.

Chapter 7   Physically impaired pupils

Baum, D. Heart Disease in Children. In E. E. Bleck and D. A. Nagel (eds.). *Physically Handicapped Children: A Medical Atlas for Teachers.* New York: Grune & Stratton, 1975.

BEH. *Progress toward a Free Appropriate Public Education: A Report to Congress on the Implementation of Public Law 94-142, The Education for All Handicapped Children Act.* Washington, D.C.: U.S. Department of Health, Education, and Welfare, Office of Education, 1979.

Berg, B. O. Convulsive Disorders. In E. E. Bleck and D. A. Nagel (eds.). *Physically Handicapped Children: A Medical Atlas for Teachers.* New York: Grune & Stratton, 1975.

Bigge, J. L., and P. A. O'Donnell. *Teaching Individuals with Physical and Multiple Disabilities.* Columbus, Ohio: Merrill, 1976.

Birch, J. W., and B. K. Johnstone. *Designing Schools and Schooling for the Handicapped.* Springfield, Ill.: Charles C Thomas, 1975.

Bleck, E. E. Anatomy — Basic Parts and Terms of the Nervous and Musculoskeletal Systems. In E. E. Bleck, and D. A. Nagel (eds.). *Physically Handicapped Children: A Medical Atlas For Teachers.* New York: Grune & Stratton, 1975*a.*

———. Amputations in Children. In E. E. Bleck and D. A. Nagel (eds.). *Physically Handicapped Children: A Medical Atlas for Teachers.* New York: Grune & Stratton, 1975*b.*

———. Arthrogryposis. In E. E. Bleck and D. A. Nagel (eds.). *Physically Handicapped Children: A Medical Atlas for Teachers.* New York: Grune & Stratton, 1975*c.*

———. Cerebral Palsy. In E. E. Bleck and D. A. Nagel (eds.). *Physically Handicapped Children: A Medical Atlas for Teachers.* New York: Grune & Stratton, 1975*d.*

———. Muscular Dystrophy — Duchenne Type. In E. E. Bleck and D. A. Nagel (eds.). *Physically Handicapped Children: A Medical Atlas for Teachers.* New York: Grune & Stratton, 1975*e.*

_____ . Myelomeningocele, Meningocele, Spina Bifida. In E. E. Bleck and D. A. Nagel (eds.). *Physically Handicapped Children: A Medical Atlas for Teachers.* New York: Grune & Stratton, 1975*f.*

_____ . Osteogenesis Imperfecta. In E. E. Bleck and D. A. Nagel (eds.). *Physically Handicapped Children: A Medical Atlas for Teachers.* New York: Grune & Stratton, 1975*g.*

Brink, J. D. Muscular Dystrophy. In R. M. Peterson and J. D. Cleveland (eds.). *Medical Problems in the Classroom: An Educators Guide.* Springfield, Ill.: Charles C Thomas, 1975.

Bruya, M. A., and R. H. Brolin. Epilepsy. *American Journal of Nursing,* 76 (1976): 388–397.

Cathey, M. L., and P. Jansma. Mainstreaming Orthopedically Disabled Individuals in Various Activities. *The Directive Teacher 2* (1980): 3, 16, 27.

Christiansen, R. O. Diabetes. In E. E. Bleck and D. A. Nagel (eds.). *Physically Handicapped Children: A Medical Atlas for Teachers.* New York: Grune & Stratton, 1975.

Connors, F. P., G. G. Williamson, and J. M. Siepp. *Program Guide for Infants and Toddlers with Neuromotor and Other Disabilities.* New York: Teachers College Press, 1978.

Copeland, M., L. Ford, and N. Solon. *Occupational Therapy for Cerebral Palsied Children.* Baltimore: University Park Press, 1976.

Cosman, B. The Burned Child. In J. A. Doway and L. N. Low (eds.). *The Child with Disabling Illness: Principles of Rehabilitation.* Philadelphia: Saunders, 1974.

Cratty, B. J., and J. Breen. *Educational Games for the Physically Handicapped.* Denver: Love, 1972.

Cruickshank, W. M., D. P. Hallahan, and H. V. Bice. The Evaluating of Intelligence. In W. M. Cruickshank (ed.). *Cerebral Palsy: A Developmental Disability,* 3rd ed. Syracuse, N.Y.: Syracuse University Press, 1976.

Denhoff, E. Medical Aspects. In W. M. Cruickshank (ed.). *Cerebral Palsy: A Developmental Disability,* 3rd ed. Syracuse, N.Y.: Syracuse University Press, 1976.

Downer, A. H. *Physical Therapy Procedures: Selected Techniques,* 2d ed. Springfield, Ill.: Charles C Thomas, 1977.

Edgington, D. *The Physically Handicapped Child in Your Classroom: A Handbook for Teachers.* Springfield, Ill.: Charles C Thomas, 1976.

Finnie, N. *Handling the Young Cerebral Palsied Child at Home.* New York: Dutton, 1975.

Ford, F. Normal Motor Development in Infancy. In E. E. Bleck and D. A. Nagel (eds.). *Physically Handicapped Children: A Medical Atlas for Teachers.* New York: Grune & Stratton, 1975.

Garrett, A. L. Orthopedic Diseases. In R. M. Peterson and J. D. Cleveland (eds.). *Medical Problems in the Classroom: An Educator's Guide.* Springfield, Ill.: Charles C Thomas, 1975.

Garwood, S. G. Physical Development: The Young Child's Growing Body. In S. G. Garwood (ed.). *Educating Young Handicapped Children: A Developmental Approach.* Germantown, Md.: Aspen, 1979*a*.

———— . Physical and Physiological Bases of Handicaps. In S. G. Garwood (ed.). *Educating Young Handicapped Children: A Developmental Approach.* Germantown, Md.: Aspen, 1979*b*.

Green, A. H. Child Abuse. In B. B. Wolmer (ed.). *Handbook of Treatment of Mental Disorders in Childhood and Adolescence.* Englewood Cliffs, N.J.: Prentice-Hall, 1978.

Green, A. H., R. Gaines, and A. Sandgrund. Child Abuse: Pathological Syndrome of Family Interaction. *American Journal of Psychiatry 131* (1974): 882–886.

Greer, B. R., J. Allsop, and J. G. Greer. Environmental Alternatives for the Physically Handicapped. In J. W. Schifani, R. M. Anderson, and S. J. Odle (eds.). *Implementing Learning in the Least Restrictive Environment.* Baltimore: University Park Press, 1980.

Harvey, B. Asthma. In E. E. Bleck and D. A. Nagel (eds.). *Physically Handicapped Children: A Medical Atlas for Teachers.* New York: Grune & Stratton, 1975*a*.

———— . Cystic Fibrosis. In E. E. Bleck and D. A. Nagel (eds.). *Physically Handicapped Children: A Medical Atlas for Teachers.* New York: Grune & Stratton, 1975*b*.

Hayden, A. J., and R. K. Smith. *Mainstreaming Preschoolers.* Washington: Project Headstart, DHEW Publication No. (OHDS) 78-31117, n.d., pp. 126–133.

Katz, J. F. Scoliosis. In J. A. Downey and L. N. Low (eds.). *The Child with Disabling Illness: Principles of Rehabilitation.* Philadelphia: Saunders, 1974.

Langley, M. B. Working with Young Physically Impaired Children: Part B — Educational Programming. In S. G. Garwood (ed.). *Educating Young Handicapped Children: A Developmental Approach.* Germantown, Md.: Aspen, 1979.

Leavitt, T. J. Hemophilia. In E. E. Bleck and D. A. Nagel (eds.). *Physically Handicapped Children: A Medical Atlas for Teachers.* New York: Grune & Stratton, 1975.

Lloyd-Roberts, G. C., and A. W. F. Letter. Arthrogryposis Multiplex Congenita. *Journal of Bone and Joint Surgery* 52-B (1970): 494.

Love, D. H., and J. E. Walthall. *A Handbook of Medical, Educational, and Psychological Information for Teachers of Physically Handicapped Children.* Springfield, Ill.: Charles C Thomas, 1977.

Lubin, G. I. Emotional Implications. In R. M. Peterson and J. D. Cleveland (eds.). *Medical Problems in the Classroom: An Educators Guide.* Springfield, Ill.: Charles C Thomas, 1975.

McDaniel, J. W. *Physical Disability and Human Behavior.* New York: Pergamon, 1976.

McDonald, E. T. Design and Application of Communication Boards. In G. C. Vandenheiden and K. O'Grilley (eds.). *Nonvocal Communication Techniques and Aids for the Severely Physically Handicapped.* Baltimore: University Park Press, 1976.

Marks, N. C. *Cerebral Palsied and Learning Disabled Children: A Handbook Guide to Treatment, Rehabilitation, and Education.* Springfield, Ill.: Charles C Thomas, 1974.

Martin, H. The Child and His Development. In C. H. Kempe and R. E. Helfen (eds.). *Helping the Battered Child and His Family.* Philadelphia: Lippincott, 1972.

Myers, B. A. Child with Chronic Illness. In R. H. A. Haslam and P. J. Valletutti (eds.). *Medical Problems in the Classroom: The Teacher's Role in Diagnosis and Management.* Baltimore: University Park Press, 1975.

Nagel, D. A. Temporary Orthopaedic Disabilities in Children. In E. E. Bleck and D. A. Nagel (eds.). *Physically Handicapped Children: A Medical Atlas for Teachers.* New York: Grune & Stratton, 1975.

National Cystic Fibrosis Research Foundation. *Guide to the Diagnosis and Management of Cystic Fibrosis.* Atlanta, 1971.

Pearson, P. H., and C. E. Wilkens (eds.). *Physical Therapy Services in the Developmental Disabilities.* Springfield, Ill.: Charles C Thomas, 1977.

Public Law 93-247. *Child Abuse Prevention and Treatment Act,* 1974, 93rd Congress — 2nd session.

Public Law 94-142, The Education of All Handicapped Children Act of 1975. Regulations. *Federal Register,* August 23, 1977.

Reynold, A. E., W. Stauffacher, and G. F. Cahill, Jr. Diabetes Mellitus. In J. B. Stanburg, J. B. Wyngaarden, and D. S. Fredrickson (eds.).

The Metabolic Bases of Inherited Disease. New York: McGraw-Hill, 1972.

Robinault, I. P. *Functional Aids for the Multiply Handicapped.* New York: Harper & Row, 1973.

Sherrill, C. *Adapted Physical Education and Recreation.* Dubuque, Iowa: Wm. C. Brown, 1976.

Silberstein, C. E. Orthopedic Problems in the Classroom. In R. H. A. Haslam and P. J. Valletutti (eds.). *Medical Problems in the Classroom: The Teacher's Role in Diagnosis and Management.* Baltimore: University Park Press, 1975.

Sirvis, B., J. Carpignano, and L. J. Bigge. Psychosocial Aspects of Physical Disability. In J. L. Bigge and P. O'Donnell. *Teaching Individuals with Physical and Multiple Disabilities.* Columbus, Ohio: Merrill, 1977.

Tachdjian, M. O. *Pediatric Orthopaedics.* Philadelphia: Saunders, 1973.

Turnbull, A. P., and J. B. Schulz. *Mainstreaming Handicapped Students: A Guide for the Classroom Teacher.* Boston: Allyn & Bacon, 1979.

Vandenheiden, G. C., and K. O'Grilley (eds.). *Nonvocal Communication Techniques and Aids for the Severely Physically Handicapped.* Baltimore: University Park Press, 1976.

Van Riper, C. *Speech Correction: Principles and Methods,* 6th ed. Englewood Cliffs, N.J.: Prentice-Hall, 1978.

Warwick, R., and P. Williams. *Gray's Anatomy,* 35th ed. Philadelphia: Saunders, 1973.

Chapter 8 Gifted and talented pupils

Asimov, I. Those Crazy Ideas. In I. Asimov (ed.). *Fact and Fancy.* New York: Doubleday, 1962.

Bacall, L. *By Myself.* New York: Ballentine, 1980.

Berg, A. S. *Max Perkins: Editor of Genius.* New York: Simon & Schuster, 1978.

Burks, B. S., D. Jensen, and L. M. Terman. *The Promise of Youth.* Stanford, Calif.: Stanford University Press, 1930.

Bronowski, J. *The Ascent of Man.* Boston: Little, Brown, 1974.

Casserly, P. L. Factors Affecting Female Participation in Advanced Placement Programs in Mathematics, Chemistry, and Physics. In

L. H. Fox, L. Brody, and D. Tobin (eds.). *Women and the Mathematical Mystique.* Baltimore: The Johns Hopkins University Press, 1980.

Clark, K. Mc. *Civilization: A Personal View.* London: BBC, 1969.

Cox, C. M. *The Early Mental Traits of Three Hundred Geniuses.* Stanford, Calif.: Stanford University Press, 1926.

Daurio, S. P. Educational Enrichment vs. Acceleration: A Review of the Literature. In W. C. George, S. J. Cohn, and J. C. Stanley (eds.). *Educating the Gifted: Acceleration and Enrichment.* Baltimore: The Johns Hopkins University Press, 1980.

Davis, N. P. *Lawrence and Oppenheimer.* New York: Simon & Schuster, 1968.

Faulkner, W. The Stockholm Address. In J. B. Meriwether (ed.). *Essays, Speeches, and Public Letters by William Faulkner.* New York: Random House, 1965.

Fox, L. H. Identification and Program Planning: Models and Methods. In D. P. Keating (ed.). *Intellectual Talent: Research and Development.* Baltimore: The Johns Hopkins University Press, 1976.

———. Sex Differences: Implications for Program Planning for the Academically Gifted. In J. C. Stanley, W. C. George, and C. H. Solano (eds.). *The Gifted and the Creative: A Fifty-Year Perspective.* Baltimore: The Johns Hopkins University Press, 1977.

Fox, L. H., and S. J. Cohn. Sex Differences in the Development of Precocious Mathematical Talent. In L. H. Fox, L. Brody, and D. Tobin (eds.). *Women and the Mathematical Mystique.* Baltimore: The Johns Hopkins University Press, 1980.

Freeman, J. *Gifted Children: Their Identification and Development in a Social Context.* Baltimore: University Park Press, 1979.

Gallagher, J. J. *Teaching the Gifted Child,* 2d ed. Boston: Allyn & Bacon, 1975.

Getzels, J. W., and J. T. Dillon. The Nature of Giftedness and the Education of the Gifted. In R. M. W. Travers (ed.). *Second Handbook of Research on Teaching.* Chicago: Rand McNally, 1973.

Grost, A. *Genius in Residence.* Englewood Cliffs, N.J.: Prentice-Hall, 1970.

Hagen, E. *Identification of the Gifted.* New York: Teachers College Press, 1980.

Hall, E., and N. Skinner. *Somewhere to Turn: Strategies for Parents of Gifted and Talented Children.* New York, 1980.

Hayden, A. H., and R. K. Smith. *Mainstreaming Preschoolers.* Washington: Project Headstart, DHEW Publication No. (OHDS) 78-31117, n.d.

Hershey, J. R. *The Child Buyer: A Novel in the Form of Hearings before the Standing Committee on Education, Welfare, & Public Morality of a Certain State Senate Investigating the Conspiracy of Mr. Wissey Jones, with Others, to Purchase a Male Child.* New York: Knopf, 1960.

Hobson, J. R. High School Performance of Underage Pupils Initially Admitted to Kindergarten on the Basis of Physical and Psychological Examinations. In W. C. George, S. J. Cohn, and J. C. Stanley (eds.). *Educating the Gifted: Acceleration and Enrichment.* Baltimore: The Johns Hopkins University Press, 1980.

Kaplan, S. N. *Activities for Gifted Children.* Santa Monica, Calif.: Goodyear, 1979.

Keller, H. *The Story of My Life.* New York: Doubleday, 1903.

_____ . Three Days to See. *Atlantic Monthly 151* (1933): 35–42.

_____ . *The World I Live In.* New York: Appleton-Century, 1938.

Kerr, W. *Tragedy and Comedy.* New York: Simon & Schuster, 1967.

_____ . *The Silent Clowns.* New York: Knopf, 1975.

Khatena, J. *The Creatively Gifted Child: Suggestions for Parents and Teachers.* New York: Vantage, 1978.

Lau v. Nichols, 483 F 2d 791 (9th Cir. 1973), rev'd, 414 U.S. 563 (1974).

Lombroso, C. The Eccentricities of Famous Men. In K. A. Blake and M. L. McBee (eds.). *Essays.* Encino, Calif.: Glencoe, 1978.

Maker, C. J. *Providing Programs for the Gifted Handicapped.* Reston, Va.: CEC, 1977.

Marland, S. (submitter). *Education of the Gifted and Talented.* Report to the Subcommittee on Education, Committee on Labor and Public Welfare, U.S. Senate. Washington, 1972.

Meister, M., and H. A. Odell. What Provisions for the Education of Gifted Students. In W. C. George, S. J. Cohn, and J. C. Stanley (eds.). *Educating the Gifted: Acceleration and Enrichment.* Baltimore: The Johns Hopkins University Press, 1980.

Michael, W. B. Cognitive and Affective Components of Creativity in Mathematics and the Physical Sciences. In J. C. Stanley, W. C. George, and C. H. Solano (eds.). *The Gifted and the Creative: A Fifty-Year Perspective.* Baltimore: The Johns Hopkins University Press, 1977.

Michener, J. A. *Sports in America.* New York: Random House, 1976.

Morgan, H. J., M. Tennant, and M. J. Gold. *Elementary and Secondary Level Programs for the Gifted and Talented.* New York: Teachers College Press, 1980.

Newland, T. E. *The Gifted in Socio-cultural Perspective.* Englewood Cliffs, N.J.: Prentice-Hall, 1976.

Oden, M. H. The Fulfillment of Promise: Forty-Year Follow-up of the Terman Gifted Group. *Genetic Psychology Monographs 77* (1968): 3–93.

Public Law 95-561 (Title IX-A), The Gifted and Talented Children's Act of 1978. Statute. Laws of the 95th Congress — Second Session.

Renzulli, J. S., R. K. Hartman, and C. M. Callahan. Scale for Rating the Behavioral Characteristics of Superior Students. In W. B. Barbe and J. S. Renzulli (eds.). *Psychology and Education of the Gifted,* 2nd ed. New York: Irvington, 1975.

Rodell, W. C., N. E. Jackson, and H. B. Robinson. *Gifted Young Children.* New York: Teachers College Press, 1980.

Russell, B. *The Autobiography of Bertrand Russell* (Vol. 3, 1944–1969). New York: Simon & Schuster, 1969.

Sears, P., and A. Barbee. Career and Life Satisfaction among Terman's Gifted Women. In J. Stanley, W. George, and C. Solano (eds.). *The Gifted and Creative: A Fifty-Year Perspective.* Baltimore: Johns Hopkins University Press, 1977.

Sells, L. W. The Mathematics Filter and the Education of Women and Minorities. In L. H. Fox, L. Brody, and D. Tobin (eds.). *Women and the Mathematical Mystique.* Baltimore: The Johns Hopkins University Press, 1980.

Stanley, J. Accelerating the Educational Progress of Intellectually Gifted Youths. *Educational Psychologist 10* (1973): 133–146.

———— . Intellectual Precocity. In J. Stanley, D. Keating, and L. Fox (eds.). *Mathematical Talent: Discovery, Description, and Development.* Baltimore: Johns Hopkins University Press, 1974.

———— . Identifying and Nurturing the Intellectually Gifted. *Phi Delta Kappan 58* (1976): 234–238.

Stone, I. *The Agony and the Ecstasy.* Garden City, N.Y.: Doubleday, 1961.

Terman, L. M. *The Mental and Physical Traits of a Thousand Gifted Children.* Stanford, Calif.: Stanford University Press, 1925.

Terman, L. M., and M. H. Oden. *The Gifted Child Grows Up.* Stanford, Calif.: Stanford University Press, 1947.

_____ . *The Gifted Group at Mid-Life.* Stanford, Calif.: Stanford University Press, 1959.

Torrance, E. P. Creatively Gifted and Disadvantaged Gifted Students. In J. C. Stanley, W. C. George, and C. H. Solano (eds.). *The Gifted and the Creative: A Fifty-Year Perspective.* Baltimore: The Johns Hopkins University Press, 1977.

White, T. H. *In Search of History.* New York: Warner, 1979.

Wills, G. F. *The Pursuit of Happiness and Other Sobering Thoughts.* New York: Harper/Colophon, 1979.

Chapter 9   Mentally retarded pupils

Amary, I. B. *Creative Recreation for the Mentally Retarded.* Springfield, Ill.: Charles C Thomas, 1975.

Balthazar, E. E., and H. A. Stevens. *Emotionally Disturbed Mentally Retarded: A Historical and Contemporary Perspective.* Englewood Cliffs, N.J.: Prentice-Hall, 1975.

BEH. *Progress toward a Free Appropriate Public Education: A Report to Congress on the Implementation of Public Law 94-142, The Education for All Handicapped Children Act.* Washington, D.C.: U.S. Department of Health, Education, and Welfare, Office of Education, 1979.

Berry, P. (ed.). *Language and Communication in the Mentally Handicapped.* Baltimore: University Park Press, 1976.

Blake, K. A. *Teaching the Retarded.* Englewood Cliffs, N.J.: Prentice-Hall, 1974.

_____ . *The Mentally Retarded: An Educational Psychology.* Englewood Cliffs, N.J.: Prentice-Hall, 1976.

Blatt, B., A. Ozolins, and J. McNally. *The Family Papers: A Return to Purgatory.* New York: Longman, 1979.

Brolin, D. E. *Vocational Preparation of Retarded Citizens.* Columbus, Ohio: Merrill, 1976.

Burton, T. A. *The Trainable Mentally Retarded.* Columbus, Ohio: Merrill, 1976.

Carter, C. H. *Medical Aspects of Mental Retardation.* Springfield, Ill.: Charles C Thomas, 1978.

Cawley, J. *Project Math, Levels I-IV.* Tulsa, Okla.: Educational Progress Corp., 1978.

Cobb, H. V. *The Forecast of Fulfillment: A Review of Research in Predictive Assessment of the Adult Retarded for Social and Vocational Adjustment.* New York: Teachers College, 1972.

Copeland, M. *Occupational Therapy for Mentally Retarded Children: Guidelines for Occupational Therapy Aids and Certified Occupational Therapy Assessments.* Baltimore: University Park Press, 1976.

Coulter, W. A., and H. W. Morrow (eds.). *Adaptive Behavior: Concepts and Measurements.* New York: Grune & Stratton, 1978.

Cronbach, L. J., and R. E. Snow. *Aptitudes and Instructional Methods.* New York: Irvington, 1977.

Deich, R. F., and P. M. Hodges. *Language without Speech.* New York: Bruner-Mazel, 1978.

Evans, S., and M. R. Denney. *Reading Achievement Program for the Moderately and Severely Retarded.* Danville, Ill.: Interstate, 1974.

Fisher, M. A., and D. Zeaman. Growth and Decline of Retardate Intelligence. In N. R. Ellis (ed.). *International Review of Research in Mental Retardation,* Vol. 4. New York: Academic Press, 1970.

Fraser, B. A., and G. Galka. *Gross Motor Management of Severely Multiply Impaired Pupils.* Vol. I, *Evaluation Guide.* Baltimore: University Park Press, 1979.

Galka, G., and B. A. Fraser. *Gross Motor Management of Severely Multiply Impaired Pupils.* Vol. II, *Curriculum Model.* Baltimore: University Park Press, 1979.

Ginglend, D., and B. W. Carlson. *Ready to Work? Development of Occupational Skills, Attitudes, and Behaviors with Mentally Retarded Persons.* Nashville: Abingdon, 1977.

Gold, M. W. Research on the Vocational Habilitation of the Retarded: The Present and the Future. In N. R. Ellis (ed.). *International Review of Research in Mental Retardation,* Vol. 6. New York: Academic Press, 1973.

Goldstein, H. *RADEA: A Developmental Program for the Moderately and Severely/Profoundly Handicapped.* Dallas, Texas: Melton Peninsula, 1980*a*.

———. *SAIL: Skills to Achieve Independent Living.* Dallas, Texas: Melton Peninsula, 1980*b*.

———. *The Social Learning Curriculum.* Columbus, Ohio: Merrill, 1974.

Goldstein, H., and M. Alter. *The Perceptual Motor Play Program.* Dallas, Texas: Melton Peninsula, 1980.

Gottlieb, J. (ed.). *Educating Mentally Retarded Persons in the Mainstream.* Baltimore: University Park Press, 1979.

Grossman, H. J. (ed.). *Manual on Terminology and Classification in Mental Retardation* (rev.). Washington, D.C.: AAMD, in press.

Guralnick, M. J. *Early Intervention and the Integration of Handicapped and Non-Handicapped Children.* Baltimore: University Park Press, 1977.

Hannah, M. *SCIL: Systematic Curriculum for Independent Living.* San Rafael, Calif.: Academic Therapy Publications, 1977.

Hardy, R. E., and J. G. Cull. *Severe Disabilities: Social and Rehabilitation Approaches.* Springfield, Ill.: Charles C Thomas, 1974.

Haring, N. G., and T. J. Brown (eds.). *Teaching the Severely Handicapped.* New York: Grune & Stratton, Vol. 1, 1976; Vol. 2, 1977.

Heber, R. A Manual on Terminology and Classification in Mental Retardation. *American Journal of Mental Deficiency, Monograph Supplement,* 1961.

Humphreys, J. C. *Helping the Acutely Handicapped Child: A Guide for Nursing Assistants.* New York: Tiresias, 1979.

Kiernan, C. C., and F. Woodford (eds.). *Behavior Modification with the Severely Retarded.* New York: Elsevier, 1976.

Kirk, S. A., J. M. Kleibhan, and J. Lerner. *Teaching Reading to Slow and Disabled Learners.* Boston: Houghton Mifflin, 1978.

Koch, R., and J. C. Dobson. *The Mentally Retarded Child and His Family. A Multidisciplinary Handbook.* New York: Brunner/Mazel, 1976.

Lambert, N. M., *et al. AAMD Adaptive Behavior Scale, Public School Version,* 1974, rev. Washington, D.C.: AAMD, 1975.

Larry P. v. *Riles.* U.S. District Court for the Northern District of California, October 10, 1979.

Laus, M. D. *Travel Instruction for the Handicapped.* Springfield, Ill.: Charles C Thomas, 1977.

Lent, J. R. Teaching Daily Living Skills. In J. M. Kauffman and J. S. Payne (eds.). *Mental Retardation: Introduction and Personal Perspective.* Columbus, Ohio: Merrill, 1975.

Litton, F. W. *Education of the Trainable Mentally Retarded: Curriculum, Methods, Materials.* St. Louis: Mosby, 1978.

MacMillan, D. L. *Mental Retardation in School and Society.* Boston: Little, Brown, 1977.

Payne, J. S., *et al. Strategies for Teaching the Mentally Retarded.* Columbus, Ohio: Merrill, 1977.

Public Law 94-142, Education of All Handicapped Children Act of 1975 — Statute. *Laws of the 94th Congress* — First Session. Regulations, *Federal Register*, August 23, 1977.

Robinson, N. M., and H. B. Robinson. *The Mentally Retarded Child: A Psychological Approach.* New York: McGraw-Hill, 1976.

Sarason, S. B., and J. Doris. *Educational Handicap, Public Policy, & Social Perspective on Mental Retardation.* New York: Free Press, 1978.

Scheerenberger, R. C. A Study of Residential Facilities. *Mental Retardation 14* (1976): 32–35.

Snell, M. E. *Systematic Instruction of the Moderately and Severely Handicapped.* Columbus, Ohio: Merrill, 1978.

Sontag, E. (ed.). *Educational Programming for the Severely and Profoundly Handicapped.* Reston, Va.: CEC, 1977.

Thompson, T., and J. Grabowski (eds.). *Behavior Modification of the Mentally Retarded.* New York: Oxford University Press, 1977.

Wallbrown, F. H. Adaptive Behavior. *The Directive Teacher 2, 3* (1980): 20–21.

Wehman, P. *Helping the Mentally Retarded Acquire Play Skills: A Behavioral Approach.* Springfield, Ill.: Charles C Thomas, 1977.

Wehman, P., and P. J. McLaughlin. *Vocational Curriculum for Developmentally Disabled Persons.* Baltimore: University Park Press, 1980.

———— . *Program Development in Special Education: Designing Individualized Education Programs.* New York: McGraw Hill, 1981.

Ysseldyke, J. E., and J. Salvia. Diagnostic-Prescriptive Teaching: Two Models. *Exceptional Children* 41 (1974): 181–185.

Chapter 10 Learning-disabled pupils

Alley, G., and D. Deshler. *Teaching the Learning Disabled Adolescent: Strategies and Methods.* Denver: Love, 1979.

Arena, J. I. (ed.). *Building Spelling Skills in Dyslexic Children.* San Rafael, Calif.: Academic Therapy Publications, 1968.

———— . (ed.). *Building Number Skills in Dyslexic Children.* San Rafael, Calif.: Academic Therapy Publications, 1972.

Bailey, E. J. *Academic Activities for Adolescents with Learning Disabilities.* Evergreen, Colo.: Learning Pathways, 1975.

Baldauf, R. J. Parental Intervention. In H. R. Myklebust (ed.). *Progress in Learning Disabilities,* Vol. 3. New York: Grune & Stratton, 1975.

Bartel, N. R. Problems in Arithmetic Achievement. In D. D. Hammill and N. R. Bartel (eds.). *Teaching Children with Learning and Behavior Problems.* Boston: Allyn & Bacon, 1975.

BEH. *Progress toward a Free Appropriate Public Education: A Report to Congress on the Implementation of Public Law 94-142, The Education for All Handicapped Children Act.* Washington, D.C.: U.S. Department of Health, Education, and Welfare, Office of Education, 1979.

Bryan, T. Peer Popularity of Learning Disabled Children. *Journal of Learning Disabilities* 7 (1974): 621–625.

_____ . *Social Skills and Social Relationships of Learning Disabled Children.* Chicago: Chicago Institute for Learning Disabilities, University of Illinois at Chicago Circle, n.d.

_____ . Learning Disabled Children's Comprehension of Non-Verbal Communication. *Journal of Learning Disabilities* 10 (1977): 501–506.

Bryan, T., and J. H. Bryan. *Understanding Learning Disabilities.* New York: Alfred, 1975.

Bryan, T., *et al.* "Come on Dummy": An Observational Study of Children's Communication. *Journal of Learning Disabilities* 9 (1976): 661–669.

Critchley, M. *The Dyslexic Child,* 2d ed. London: Heinemann, 1970.

Cruickshank, W., *et al. A Teaching Method for Brain Injured and Hyperactive Children.* Syracuse, N.Y.: Syracuse University Press, 1961.

Deshler, D. D. Psychoeducational Aspects of Learning Disabled Adolescents. In L. Mann, L. Goodman, and J. L. Wiederholt (eds.). *Teaching the Learning Disabled Adolescent.* Boston: Houghton Mifflin, 1978.

Deshler, D. D., N. Lowrey, and G. R. Alley. Programming Alternatives for Learning Disabled Adolescents: A Nationwide Survey. *Academic Therapy* 14 (1979): 4.

Frostig, M., and D. Horne. *The Frostig Program for the Development of Visual Perception.* Chicago: Follett, 1964.

Gillingham, A., and B. Stillman. *Remedial Training for Children with Specific Disability in Reading, Spelling, and Penmanship*, 5th ed. Cambridge, Mass.: Educators Publishing Service, 1965.

Goodman, L., and L. Mann. *Learning Disabilities in Secondary School*. New York: Grune & Stratton, 1976.

Gray, B., and B. Ryan. *A Language Program for the Non-Language Child*. Champaign, Ill.: Research Press, 1973.

Hallahan, D. P., and W. M. Cruickshank. *Psychoeducational Foundations of Learning Disabilities*. Englewood Cliffs, N.J.: Prentice-Hall, 1973.

Hallahan, D. P., and J. M. Kauffman. *Introduction to Learning Disabilities: A Psycho-Behavioral Approach*. Englewood Cliffs, N.J.: Prentice-Hall, 1976.

Hammill, D., and S. C. Larsen. The Efficacy of Psycholinguistic Training. *Exceptional Children* 41 (1974): 5–14.

———. The Relationship of Selected Relationships of Selected Auditory Perceptual Skills to Reading Ability. *Journal of Learning Disabilities* 7 (1974b): 429–436.

Hammill, D., R. Parker, and P. Newcomer. Psycholinguistic Correlates of Academic Achievement. *Journal of School Psychology* 13 (1975): 248–254.

Hammill, D. D. Adolescents with Specific Learning Disabilities: Definition, Identification, and Incidence. In L. Mann, L. Goodman, and J. L. Weiderholt (eds.). *Teaching the Learning Disabled Adolescent*. Boston: Houghton Mifflin, 1978.

Hammill, D. D., and N. R. Bartel (eds.). *Teaching Children with Learning Disabilities and Behavior Disorders*. Boston: Allyn & Bacon, 1978.

Hammill, D. D., and S. C. Larsen. The Effectiveness of Psycholinguistic Training: A Reaffirmation of Position. *Exceptional Children* 44 (1978): 402–414.

Haring, N. G., and B. Bateman. *Teaching the Learning Disabled Child*. Englewood Cliffs, N.J.: Prentice-Hall, 1977.

Karnes, M. *GOAL: Language Development*. Springfield, Mass.: Milton Bradley, 1972.

———. *The Karnes Early Language Activities Program*. Champaign, Ill.: Generators of Educational Materials, 1975.

_____ . *Learning Language at Home.* Reston, Va.: CEC, 1977.

Kauffman, J. M. *Characteristics of Children's Behavior Disorders.* Columbus, Ohio: Merrill, 1977.

Keogh, B., and A. Glover. The Generality and Durability of Cognitive Training Effects. *Exceptional Education Quarterly 1,* 1 (1980): 75–82.

Keogh, B., and J. Margolis. Learn to Labor and to Want: Attentional Problems of Children with Learning Disorders. *Journal of Learning Disabilities 9* (1976): 276–286.

Kephart, N. *The Slow Learner in the Classroom,* 2d ed. Columbus, Ohio: Merrill, 1971.

Kirk, S. A. *The Diagnosis and Remediation of Psycholinguistic Disabilities.* Urbana: University of Illinois Press, 1966.

Kirk, S. A., and W. D. Kirk. *Psycholinguistic Learning Disabilities: Diagnosis and Remediation.* Urbana: University of Illinois Press, 1971.

_____ . Uses and Abuses of the ITPA. *Journal of Speech and Hearing Disorders 43* (1978): 58–75.

Kirk, S. A., J. J. McCarthy, and W. D. Kirk. *The Illinois Test of Psycholinguistic Abilities,* rev. ed. Urbana: University of Illinois Press, 1968.

Knott, G. P. Communication Competence and Secondary Learning Disabled Students. *The Directive Teacher 2,* 3 (1980): 22–24.

Kronick, D. The Importance of a Sociological Perspective toward Learning Disabilities. *Journal of Learning Disabilities 9* (1976): 115–119.

Larsen, S. C., and D. Hammill. The Relationships between Selected Visual Perceptual Abilities to School Learning. *Journal of Special Education 9* (1975): 282–291.

Lerner, J. W. *Children with Learning Disabilities: Theories, Diagnosis, and Teaching Strategies,* 2nd ed. Boston: Houghton Mifflin, 1976.

Michael-Smith, H., and M. Morgenstern. Learning Disorders — An Overview. In J. Hellmuth (ed.). *Learning Disorders.* Seattle: Special Child Publications, 1965.

Minskoff, E., D. Wiseman, and J. Minskoff. *The MWM Program for Developing Language Abilities.* Ridgefield, N.J.: Educational Performance Associates, 1975.

Myers, P. T., and D. D. Hammill. *Methods for Learning Disabilities,* 2nd ed. New York: Wiley, 1976.

Myklebust, H. R. Non-verbal Learning Disabilities: Assessment and Intervention. In H. R. Myklebust (ed.). *Progress in Learning Disabilities,* Vol. 3. New York: Grune & Stratton, 1975.

Public Law 94-142, The Education of All Handicapped Children Act of 1975, Regulations, *Federal Register,* August 23, 1977.

Public Law 94-142, *The Education of All Handicapped Children Act of 1975,* Statute, 94th Congress, 1st Session.

Public Law 94-142, Regulations, Special Procedures for Evaluating Specific Learning Disabilities. Sec. 121a. 541. *Federal Register,* December 29, 1977.

Prout, H. T. Behavioral Intervention with Hyperactive Children: A Review. *Journal of Learning Disabilities 10* (1977): 141–146.

Quiros, J. B., and O. L. Schrager. *Neuropsychological Fundamentals in Learning Disabilities.* San Rafael, Calif.: Academic Therapy Publications, 1978.

Rappaport, S. R. Sheldon R. Rappaport. In J. M. Kauffman and D. P. Hallahan (eds.). *Teaching Children with Learning Disabilities: Personal Perspectives.* Columbus, Ohio: Merrill, 1976.

Ross, A. O. *Psychological Aspects of Learning Disabilities and Reading Disorders.* New York: McGraw-Hill, 1976.

Silver, L. B. Emotional and Social Problems of Children with Developmental Disabilities. In R. E. Weber (ed.). *Handbook on Learning Disabilities.* Englewood Cliffs, N.J.: Prentice-Hall, 1974.

Turnbull, A. P., and J. B. Schulz. *Mainstreaming Handicapped Students: A Guide for the Classroom Teacher.* Boston: Allyn & Bacon, 1979.

Wallace, G., and J. A. McLoughlin. *Learning Disabilities.* Columbus, Ohio: Merrill, 1975.

Wallach, G. P., and S. C. Goldsmith. Language Based Learning Disabilities: Reading Is Language Too. *Journal of Learning Disabilities 10* (1977): 178–183.

Wiig, E. H., and S. P. Harris. Perception and Interpretation of Nonverbally Expressed Emotions by Adolescents with Learning Disabilities. *Perceptual and Motor Skills 38* (1974): 239–245.

Wiig, E. H., and E. M. Semel. *Language Assessment and Intervention for the Learning Disabled.* Columbus, Ohio: Merrill, 1980.

_____ . *Language Disabilities in Children and Adolescents.* Columbus, Ohio: Merrill, 1976.

Ysseldyke, J., and J. Salvia. Diagnostic-Prescriptive Teaching: Two Models. *Exceptional Children* 44 (1974): 181–186.

Chapter 11   Emotionally disturbed pupils

Ainsworth, M. D. S., *et al. Patterns of Attachment.* Hillsdale, N.J.: Erlbaum, 1978.

American Psychiatric Association Task Force on Nomenclature and Statistics. DSM-III. Washington, D. C.: American Psychiatric Association, 1980.

Apter, S. Application of Ecological Theory: Toward a Community Special Education Model. *Exceptional Children* 43 (1977): 367–373.

Bachrach, A. W., and F. L. Swindle. *Developmental Therapy for Young Children with Autistic Characteristics.* Baltimore: University Park Press, 1978.

Barker, P. *Basic Child Psychiatry,* 3rd ed. Baltimore: University Park Press, 1979.

Bazar, J. Major Project Launched on Childhood Psychosis. *APA Monitor 11,* 1 (1980): 6, 13.

BEH. *Progress toward a Free Appropriate Public Education: A Report to Congress on the Implementation of Public Law 94-142, The Education for All Handicapped Children Act.* Washington, D.C.: U.S. Department of Health, Education, and Welfare, Office of Education, 1979.

Bell, R. Q. Parent, Child, and Reciprocal Influences. *American Psychologist 34* (1979): 930–931.

Belsky, J. Child Maltreatment: An Ecological Integration. *American Psychologist 35* (1980): 320–335.

Blanco, R. F. *Prescriptions for Children with Learning and Adjustment Problems.* Springfield, Ill.: Charles C Thomas, 1977.

Blau, T. H. Diagnosis of Disturbed Children. *American Psychologist 34* (1979): 969–972.

Budson, R. D. *The Psychiatric Half-Way House: A Handbook of Theory and Practice.* Pittsburgh: University of Pittsburgh Press, 1978.

Buss, A. H., and R. Plomin. *A Temperamental Theory of Personality Development.* New York: Wiley, 1975.

Clarizo, H., and G. McCoy. *Behavior Disorders in Children.* New York: Thomas, 1976.

Committee on Child Psychiatry. *Psychopathological Disorders in Childhood: Theoretical Considerations and a Proposed Classification.* New York: Group for the Advancement of Psychiatry, 1966.

Crow, G. A. *Children at Risk: A Handbook of Signs and Symptoms of Early Childhood Difficulties.* New York: Schocken, 1978.

Doane, J. A. Family Interaction and Communication Deviance in Disturbed and Normal Families: A Review of Research. *Family Process 17* (1978): 357–376.

Eaves, R., and P. McLaughlin. A Systems Approach for the Assessment of the Child and His Environment: Getting Back to Basics. *Journal of Special Education 11* (1977): 99–111.

Ellis, A. *Humanistic Psychotherapy: The Rational Emotive Approach.* New York: Julian Press, 1973.

Erickson, M. T. *Child Psychopathology: Assessment, Etiology, and Treatment.* Englewood Cliffs, N.J.: Prentice-Hall, 1978.

Fagen, S., N. Long, and D. Stevens. *Teaching Children Self-Control.* Columbus, Ohio: Merrill, 1975.

Feagans, L. Ecological Theory as a Model for Constructing a Theory of Emotional Disturbance. In W. Rhodes and M. Tracy (eds.). *A Study of Child Variance.* Ann Arbor: University of Michigan Press, 1974.

Folz, D. Judgement Withheld on DSM-III, New Child Classification Pushed (by the American Psychological Association). *APA Monitor 11,* 1 (1980): 1, 33.

Gallagher, J., and R. Wiegerink. Educational Strategies for the Autistic Child. *Journal of Autism and Childhood Schizophrenia 6* (1976): 15–26.

Gardner, L. I. Deprivation Dwarfism. *Scientific American 227* (1972): 76–83.

Garmezy, N. DSM-III: Never Mind the Psychologists, Is It Good for the Children? *Clinical Psychologist 31,* 1 (1978): 4–6.

Halmi, K. A. Anorexia Nervosa. *Psychosomatic Medicine 36* (1974): 18–26.

Hayden, A., and R. K. Smith. *Mainstreaming Preschoolers.* Washington, D.C.: Project Headstart, DHEW Publication No. (OHDS) 78-31117, n.d., pp. 126–133.

Hayward, B. *Haywire.* New York: Knopf, 1977.

Heatherington, E. M., and B. Martin. Family Interaction. In H. C. Quay and J. S. Werry (eds.). *Psychopathological Disorders in Childhood*, 2d ed. New York: Wiley, 1979.

Herbert, M. *Emotional Problems of Development in Children*. London: Academic Press, 1974, p. 214.

Hewett, F., F. Taylor, and A. Artuso. The Engineered Classroom: An Innovative Approach to the Education of Children with Learning Problems. In R. Bradfield (ed.). *Behavior Modification, The Human Effort*. San Rafael, Calif.: Dimensions, 1970.

Hewett, F. M., and F. D. Taylor. *The Emotionally Disturbed Child in the Classroom: The Orchestration of Success*, 2d ed. Boston: Allyn & Bacon, 1980.

Hicks, J. Language Disabilities of Emotionally Disturbed Children. In J. Irwin and M. Marge (eds.). *Principles of Childhood Language Disabilities*. Englewood Cliffs, N.J.: Prentice-Hall, 1972.

Hobbs, N. Nicholas Hobbs. In J. M. Kauffman and C. D. Lewis (eds.). *Teaching Children with Behavior Disorders: Personal Perspectus*. Columbus, Ohio: Merrill, 1974.

Jacob, T. Family Interaction in Disturbed and Normal Families. *Psychological Bulletin 82* (1975): 33–65.

Jones, V. F. *Adolescents with Behavior Problems: Strategies for Teaching, Counselling, and Parent Involvement*. Boston: Allyn & Bacon, 1980.

Kauffman, J. M. *Characteristics of Children's Behavior Disorders*. Columbus, Ohio: Merrill, 1977.

Kazdin, A. E. Advances in Child Behavior Therapy: Applications and Implications. *American Psychologist 34* (1979): 981–987.

Kelly, T., L. Bullock, and M. Dykes. Behavioral Disorders. Teachers' Perceptions. *Exceptional Children 43* (1977): 316–318.

Kestenbaum, C. J. Childhood Psychosis: Psychotherapy. In B. B. Wolman (ed.). *Handbook of Treatment of Mental Disorders in Childhood and Adolescence*. Englewood Cliffs, N.J.: Prentice-Hall, 1978.

Knoblock, P. Open Education for Emotionally Disturbed Children. *Exceptional Children 39* (1973): 358–366.

Kohn, M. The Kohn Social Competence Scale and Kohn Symptom Checklist for the Preschool Child: A Follow-Up Report. *Journal of Abnormal Child Psychology 5* (1977): 249–263.

———— . *Social Competence, Symptoms, and Underachievement in Childhood: A Longitudinal Perspective*. New York: Halstead, 1977.

Lawrence, D. H. *Sons and Lovers.* New York: Viking, 1960.

Levinger, G., and H. L. Raush. *Close Relationships: Perspectives on the Meaning of Intimacy.* Amherst: University of Massachusetts Press, 1976.

Lewis, W. W. Project Re-Ed: A Pattern of Residential Treatment for Emotionally Disturbed Children. In A. Dupont (ed.). *Educating Emotionally Disturbed Children,* 2d ed. New York: Holt, Rinehart and Winston, 1975.

Loehlin, J. C., and R. C. Nichols. *Heredity, Environment, and Personality: A Study of 850 Sets of Twins.* Austin: University of Texas Press, 1976.

Long, N. J., W. C. Morse, and R. G. Newman. *Conflict in the Classroom: The Education of Children with Behavior Problems,* 3rd ed. Belmont, Calif.: Wadsworth, 1976.

Lovaas, O. *The Autistic Child: Language Development through Behavior Modification.* New York: Halstead, 1977.

Mahon, E., and D. Blattin. Therapeutic Nurseries. In B. B. Wolman (ed.). *Handbook of Treatment of Mental Disorders in Childhood and Adolescence.* Englewood Cliffs, N.J.: 1978.

Mason, R. L., Jr. *The Emotionally Troubled Child.* Springfield, Ill.: Charles C Thomas, 1976.

Morse, W. Serving the Needs of Individuals with Behavior Disorders. *Exceptional Children 44* (1977): 158–164.

Newcomer, P. L. *Understanding and Teaching Emotionally Disturbed Children.* Boston: Allyn & Bacon, 1980.

O'Leary, S., and M. Schneider. Special Class Placement for Conduct Problem Children. *Exceptional Children 44* (1977): 24–30.

Park, C. C. *The Siege: The First Eight Years of an Autistic Child.* Boston: Atlantic Monthly Press, 1972.

Parke, R. D. Emerging Themes for Social-Emotional Development: Introduction. *American Psychologist 34* (1979): 930–931.

Patterson, G. Naturalistic Observation in Clinical Assessment. *Journal of Abnormal Child Psychology 5* (1977): 309–321.

Public Law 94-142, The Education of All Handicapped Children Act of 1975. Regulations, *Federal Register,* August 23, 1977.

Purvis, J., and S. Samet (eds.). *Music in Developmental Therapy: A Curriculum Guide.* Baltimore: University Park Press, 1976.

Quay, H. C. Patterns of Aggression, Withdrawal, and Immaturity. In H. C. Quay and J. S. Werry (eds.). *Psychopathological Disorders in Childhood.* New York: Wiley, 1972

_____ . Classification in the Treatment of Delinquency and Anti-social Behavior. In N. Hobbes (ed.). *Issues in the Classification of Children,* Vol. 1. San Francisco: Jossey-Bass, 1975.

Quay, H. C., and D. R. Peterson. *Manual for the Behavior Problem Checklist.* Champaign: Children's Research Center, University of Illinois, 1967.

Quay, A., *et al.* The Modification of Problem Behavior and Academic Achievement in a Resource Room. *Journal of School Psychology 10* (1972): 187–198.

Reinert, H. *Children in Conflict.* St. Louis: Mosby, 1976.

Rhodes, W., and J. L. Paul. *Emotionally Disturbed and Deviant Children: New Views and Approaches.* Englewood Cliffs, N.J.: Prentice-Hall, 1978.

Rothman, E. P. Esther P. Rothman. In J. M. Kauffman and C. D. Lewis (eds.). *Teaching Children with Behavior Disorders: Personal Perspectives.* Columbus, Ohio: Merrill, 1974.

Schwarz, J. C. Childhood Origins of Psychopathology. *American Psychologist 34* (1979): 879–885.

Shea, T. M. *Camping for Special Children.* St. Louis: Mosby, 1977.

_____ . *Teaching Children and Youth with Behavior Disorders.* St. Louis: Mosby, 1978.

Smith, S. *The Maltreatment of Children: A Comprehensive Guide to the Battered Baby Syndrome.* Baltimore: University Park Press, 1978.

Spivack, G., M. Swift, and J. Prewitt. Syndromes of Disturbed Classroom Behavior: A Behavioral Diagnostic System for Elementary Schools. *Journal of Special Education 5* (1971): 269–292.

Stevens, T. M. *Teaching Skills to Children with Learning and Behavioral Disorders.* Columbus, Ohio: Merrill, 1977.

Stewart, M. A., and A. Gath. *Psychological Disorders of Children.* Baltimore: Williams & Wilkins, 1978.

Swanson, H. L., and H. R. Reinert. *Teaching Strategies for Children in Conflict: Curriculum, Methods, and Materials.* St. Louis: Mosby, 1979.

Thomas, A., and S. Chess. *Temperament and Development.* New York: Brunner/Mazel, 1977.

Thurman, S. Congruence of Behavioral Ecologies: A Model for Special Education Programming. *Journal of Special Education 11* (1977): 329–334.

Walker, H. M. *The Acting Out Child: Coping with Classroom Disruption.* Boston: Allyn & Bacon, 1979.

White, O., and N. Haring. *Exceptional Teaching.* Columbus, Ohio: Merrill, 1976.

Williams, G., and M. M. Wood. *Developmental Art Therapy.* Baltimore: University Park Press, 1977.

Williams, G. J., and J. Money (eds.). *Traumatic Abuse and Neglect of Children at Home.* Baltimore: Johns Hopkins University Press, 1980.

Wood, M. M. *Developmental Therapy: A Textbook for Teachers as Therapists for Emotionally Disturbed Young Children.* Baltimore: University Park Press, 1975.

———— . *Developmental Therapy Objectives.* Baltimore: University Park Press, 1979.

Glossary

ABR audiometry (auditory brain-stem response audiometry). Audiometric procedure combining electro-encephalographic and computer procedures. The computer sorts the sound-produced brain waves from brain waves produced by other stimuli. The audiologist determines hearing levels by noting whether the testee has brain waves corresponding to sounds at various pitch and loudness levels.

abuse and neglect. See child abuse.

acalculia. See dyscalculia.

accountability. Responsibility to perform a duty and to perform it accurately. Antonyms: negligence, dereliction of duty, nonfeasance, misfeasance, and malpractice.

achievement/ability grouping. Categorizing pupils by the level at which they are functioning or by the level they potentially can function. Forms are acceleration, retention, homogeneous grouping, tracking, streaming, course selection, and program selection.

acoustic method. Method for teaching deaf pupils to communicate through speech. The youngster uses touch and vision to associate particular patterns of vibrations and visual pictures with particular words, pitches, rhythms, accents, inflections, and intensities.

adaptive behavior. See cultural tasks.

adventitious. Adjective referring to a disorder acquired after birth by accident or illness. Antonym: congenital.

advocates. Parents, guardians, lawyers, expert advisors, and, if appropriate, the pupil, who participate in all decisions about the pupil and who have all the rights of due process in that decision making.

affirmative action. Developing and carrying out a plan for activities to make up for the problems caused by discrimination, i.e., the lost opportunities, the wrong development, or both.

air conduction tests. Audiometric tests in which sound vibrations are transmitted through the ears, starting with earphones on the right and left ears.

amblyopia ex anopsia. Functional blindness that may become permanent. To reduce the confusion that occurs with the double vision of strabismus, the brain suppresses the image from one eye, and the youngster uses only one eye.

American sign language. Manual communication used by deaf persons in the United States. Sometimes abbreviated to *Ameslan*.

amicus curiae. Friend of the court. A person or group that helps in a lawsuit even though not a plaintiff or defendant.

amniocentesis. Procedure for analyzing the amniotic fluid, the fluid in which the fetus develops before birth. Used to determine whether the developing fetus has congenital disorders such as Down's syndrome.

amplifying sounds. Increasing the loudness of sounds by electronically boosting their intensity. Used in hearing aids.

amyotonia congenita. Congenital muscle disorder. Lack of, or very low, muscle tone, which leads to extreme weakness and in turn hampers movement.

anemia. Blood disorder. The red blood cells contain an insufficient amount of hemoglobin, and as a result they cannot carry enough oxygen. Symptoms include weakness, lassitude, paleness, and sometimes jaundice. *Sickle cell anemia* is an especially severe form.

anoxia. Lack of or insufficient oxygen. Prolonged anoxia leads to brain damage.

aphasia. Language disability in which the person has an inability or impaired ability to produce or comprehend spoken language.

aqueous humor. Liquid that keeps the eye clear and lubricated in its socket.

arthritis. Orthopedic disorder in which inflammation of the joints leads to pain and impaired movement.

arthrogryposis. Orthopedic disorder in which the joints fuse, leading to impaired or no movement in areas such as the hips, knees, ankles, or waist. The youngster has trouble changing positions or walking.

articulation. Shaping (pronouncing) the speech sounds as the resonant sound waves go through the patterns of the throat, jaws, and tongue muscles acting together and with the teeth.

articulation disorder. Speech disorder in which there is difficulty in pronouncing sounds. Types are substitutions, distortions, additions, and omissions.

asthma. Chronic health condition in which the pupil has trouble breathing because of spasms in the throat and chest muscles. One symptom is labored shallow breathing.

astigmatism. Visual impairment. A structural defect in the lens prevents light rays from converging on a single focal point on the retina. As a result, the images are indistinct and distorted.

ataxia. Type of cerebral palsy. The youngster has difficulty with balance and movement of the body in space, poor eye-hand coordination, and trouble making purposeful movements with objects.

athetosis. Type of cerebral palsy. The youngster has involuntary uncontrolled movements of the limbs and the rest of the body when he or she attempts a purposeful movement. His or her limbs flail about, and his or her head bobs or jerks. In tension athetosis there is an overlay of spasticity because the pupil tries controlling his or her movements by tensing muscles. Athetoids also may have nystagmus and hearing impairment.

atrophy. Degeneration of an organ or muscle as a result of disuse or disease.

audiogram. Chart portraying the results of an audiometric test.

audiologist. Specialist in hearing functions and disorders. He or she evaluates hearing, identifies hearing disorders, assesses hearing aids, and teaches clients to conserve hearing and to use residual hearing.

audiology. Science of hearing, its disorders, and their remediation.

audiometry. Measurement of hearing. Audiologists use various procedures to determine how loud a sound a person can hear at various pitch levels.

auditory brainstem response audiometry. See ABR audiometry.

auditory method. Oral communication method for deaf individuals. Youngsters learn to use amplified sound and residual hearing to get messages. They learn speech production unconsciously through interaction as hearing youngsters do; or, if that does not occur, they receive speech training.

auditory training. Training designed to enable the youngster to perceive and to discriminate among sounds and to enable hearing-impaired youngsters to learn to use residual hearing.

aura. Forewarning that precedes a grand mal epileptic seizure.

auricle. Outer part of the ear, which catches sounds.

autism. Severe/profound emotional/social disorder in children. Autistic youngsters are mute or have bizarre speech, are withdrawn, show thinking disorders, and may engage in self-stimulating behavior.

blindisms. Mannerisms that visually impaired pupils engage in apparently for self-stimulation. They include such behavior as eye pressing, rocking, spinning around in a circle, staring at lights, and finger play. Comparable to thumbsucking in seeing children.

bone-conduction tests. Audiometric tests in which sound vibrations are transmitted through terminals fixed on the mastoid and forehead bones.

bone tuberculosis. Orthopedic disorder in which there is a tuberculosis infection of the bone.

braille. Embossed code paralleling the print system. Uses particular configurations (numbers and positions) of embossed dots in a six-dot-position rectangular space to represent numbers, sounds, and grammatical signals.

braille slate and stylus. Device for producing braille by hand. The stylus is a small awl used for punching dots. The slate, a hinged metal device in which paper is held, consists of rows of rectangular spaces in which the braille configurations are punched.

brailler. Device set up to produce braille on paper.

brain damage. Injury to the brain through trauma happening before, during, or after birth. It can result from infections; mechanical injuries which tear tissue or cause blood accumulations, which in turn cause tearing; or too long oxygen deprivation (anoxia), which in turn causes the tissue to die.

burns. Tissue damage through heat — classified as first, second, or third degree. Third degree burns have dire consequences. Tissue is charred so much that it is destroyed, and scar tissue forms. The scar tissue, in turn, often causes contractures. In addition, there may be bad disfigurement.

captioned films for the deaf. Films and videotapes in which the spoken material is printed at the bottom of the picture. Available to the deaf through the Library of Congress as well as local and regional libraries.

cardiologist. Physician specializing in diseases and disorders of the heart.

carrels. Small enclosed spaces pupils can retire to for working free from distraction.

case law. See common law.

cataracts. Cause of visual impairment. The lens becomes opaque, and as a result, light images cannot get through, and visual blurring and blindness result.

central nervous system problems. Complex set of problems following pathology in the area of the CNS controlling the function impaired. These problems include cerebral palsy and other physical impairments, visual problems, hearing problems, aphasia and other language problems, epilepsy, mental retardation, learning disabilities, and emotional/social disorders.

central tendency. Average performance of a group. The mean, the median, and the mode are indices of central tendency.

central vision. See perimeter.

cerebral palsy. Movement disturbance resulting from brain damage. The forms of CP are spasticity, athetosis, ataxia, rigidity, and tremor.

child abuse and neglect. Complex set of circumstances defined legally as physical and mental injury, sexual abuse, negligent treatment, or maltreatment of a child under the age of eighteen by a person who is responsible for the child's welfare under circumstances which indicate that the child's health and welfare is harmed or threatened.

Child-Find. Active, systematic search for handicapped pupils protected by PL 94-142 and other laws.

chromosomal abnormality. Disorder in which there may be too many chromosomes, malformations in their structures, or both too many chromosomes and these malformed. These chromosomal abnormalities result from many problems, e.g., radiation, drugs and other chemicals, viruses, and gametes from aged parents. These chromosomal abnormalities lead to a number of disorders, such as Down's syndrome.

class action suit. Lawsuit representing an entire group of people having a particular characteristic. For example, in *Larry P. v. Riles*, Larry P. represented all California youngsters placed in special classes for the retarded on the basis of intelligence test scores.

classification. Sorting people into groups on the basis of one or more common characteristics. Synonyms are concept formation, conceptualization, and categorization. In contemporary reference to exceptional pupils, a tool for fitting education to individual differences, that is, identifying what protected category they belong in so that they can receive the safeguards and entitlements of the law.

cleft lip/cleft palate. Congenital malformation in the upper lip, the palate, or both. It takes the form of a split or opening resulting from failure of closure at the midline during fetal development. It leads to articulation and voice disorders.

clinical teaching. See individualizing instruction.

cluttering. Speech impairment in which there is a disorder in fluency. The speech flow is excessively rapid and garbled, with part words and extra words and syllables.

cochlea. Part of the hearing mechanism. It is located in the inner ear and contains the sensory end organs and other mechanisms which convert sound waves into nerve impulses going to the auditory nerve and the brain.

combined ability and CA grouping. Joint use of procedures for within–chronological age grouping and achievement/ability grouping. Sometimes called a dual-progress plan, an integrated plan, or a part-time special class plan.

common law. Set of legal requirements resulting from judicial decisions in lawsuits.

communication disorder. Impairment in using language, speech, and other means for receiving and transmitting messages.

concentric method. Method for teaching deaf pupils to communicate through speech. Pupils concentrate on a limited number of sounds. They learn to produce these sounds orally and with simultaneous finger spelling to help prevent ambiguities in expression or understanding. They proceed to the next round of sounds after they master the first round. They continue until they can produce the necessary sounds with the correct articulation, voice quality, and rhythm.

conductive loss. Type of hearing loss in which the sound vibrations in the air cannot get through the outer ear or the middle ear to the sensory end organs and the auditory nerve. An obstruction or malformation of the outer or middle ear structures causes the block.

confidentiality requirements. Set of requirements governing access to information about a pupil, purging of nonrelevant information, and destruction of information when it is no longer needed.

congenital. Adjective referring to a disorder occurring before birth when an insult causes development to go awry. Antonym: adventitious.

congenital malformations and amputations. Defects in physical structures that occur before birth.

Frequently seen types are congenital anophthalmos (incomplete development of the eye and brain structures), congenital amputations (absence of fingers, toes, arms, legs, and other structures), and congenital heart defects (holes in the walls or improper connections of blood vessels).

contracture. Permanent shortening of muscles and tendons producing deformity and distortion.

convergent thinking. Close-ended thinking, which leads to one correct or best solution for a problem. Antonym: divergent thinking.

continuum of placements. Set of options for locating a pupil for delivery of instruction, therapy, and other services. These options are arranged along a dimension from least specialized to most specialized. Least specialized means nearer to school as nonexceptional pupils experience it; most specialized means the opposite.

cornea. Outside covering of the eye. It bends the visual stimuli to focus them.

creative thinking. Producing new ideas and solutions to problems. It involves discerning the nature of a problem, generating multiple options for solving that problem, and weighing and choosing among those options.

cretinism. See hypothyroidism.

criterion-referenced test. Test weighing a youngster's performance in relation to an instructional or therapeutic objective.

critical thinking. Making a judgment about an idea or product. It involves comparing a work with a standard of excellence and identifying where it meets or fails to meet that standard.

cultural tasks. Knowledge and skills we must have to meet our needs in ways society approves of, e.g., learning to travel independently. Synonym: adaptive behavior.

curriculum. Set of instructional objectives for a particular area of study.

curvature of the spine. Congenital abnormality in which the vertebral column is misaligned. Types include scoliosis (side-to-side curve), kyphosis (back-to-front curve of the upper back), and lordosis (front-to-back curve of the lower back).

cystic fibrosis. More generally a congenital condition in which the secretions of the mucous glands are thick and sticky, causing obstruction and deterioration of the organs involved. One frequent site is the lungs. The bronchioles exude thick, sticky fluid which interferes with breathing and destroys lung tissue.

deafness. Level of hearing loss (usually 70 dB ISO or greater) which prevents understanding speech through the ear alone, with or without use of a hearing aid. It interferes with a youngster's learning language and speech and consequently his or her learning and performing the cultural tasks.

dB. See decibel.

decibel (dB). Unit for measuring intensity (loudness) of sounds. Referenced against a zero point at which normally hearing people can barely perceive a sound.

defendant. Person or group against whom a lawsuit is brought. For example, Riles was the defendant in *Larry P. v. Riles.*

denasality. See nasality.

depositories. Areas for keeping

books, films, tapes, learning packages, and other materials.

dereliction of duty. Failure to perform a duty.

deviance. Pejorative synonym for variation.

diabetes. Chronic health problem in which the pancreas produces too little insulin and the body does not properly metabolize sugar. If the sugar level gets too high, the person experiences nausea and dizziness. If it gets too low, he or she goes into insulin shock, with pallor, sweating, and convulsions. Unchecked diabetes can lead to blindness, kidney problems, and difficulty with wounds healing, which in turn may lead to gangrene. Treatment involves insulin injections and control of sugar in the diet.

diagnostic-prescriptive teaching. See individualizing instruction.

distance vision. Measure of visual acuity. The person is tested with a Snellen chart (a device containing graded sizes of letters, etc.). The results of the test are usually described as a ratio. The denominator refers to what the normal eye can see at a given number of feet; the numerator, what the eye being tested can see, e.g., a 20/100 means that the eye being tested can see at 20 feet what the normal eye can see at 100 feet.

distractibility. Condition in which the pupil has difficulty inhibiting his or her responses to stimuli. Responses to extraneous stimuli interfere with the pupil's focusing on the relevant or foreground stimuli necessary in performing a task.

divergent thinking. Open-ended thinking, which leads to many solutions for a problem. Antonym: convergent thinking.

Down's syndrome. Congenital condition resulting from a chromosomal abnormality. Characteristics include mental retardation and such physical characteristics as a round head; eyes which include speckling of the iris, and upward, outward slant, and inner epicanthal folds; a thick, furrowed tongue; markedly low muscle tone in the arms and legs; short, in-curved little fingers; and an extraordinarily wide space between the first and second toes.

due process. Requirement that we must give the person the chance to contest before a judge any decision which we as government officials make about him or her. And we must give him or her a chance to use lawyers and expert witnesses and to appeal each judgment to higher administrative levels of government and higher jurisdictional levels of the courts.

dyscalculia. Learning disability in which the person has an inability or an impaired ability to do mathematics.

dyslexia. Language disability in which the person has an inability or impaired ability to read.

echolocation. Object-location procedure based on sonar principles. A device emits high-frequency sound waves which bounce back from objects, producing a signal in which loudness indicates size, and pitch indicates distance. Used by blind people to aid orientation and mobility.

ecological approach. Approach to dealing with emotionally disturbed pupils. In diagnosis and treatment it stresses the interaction of the youngster and his or her environment.

electrocardiography (EKG). Procedure for diagnosing heart function. Electrical impulses caused by the heart muscle activity are recorded on an electrocardiogram.

electrodermal audiometry. See GSR audiometry.

electroencephalography (EEG). Procedure for diagnosing brain function. Electrical impulses caused by brain activity are recorded on an electroencephalogram.

electromyelography (EMG). Procedure for diagnosing muscle function. Electrical impulses caused by muscle activity are recorded on an electromyelogram.

encephalitis. Inflammation of the brain caused by viral infection. May lead to destruction of brain tissue (see brain damage).

epilepsy. Disturbance of consciousness resulting from disruption of electrical discharges in the brain. The most frequently appearing forms are grand mal seizures and petit mal seizures.

equal protection. Requirement that we must use the same rules, criteria, and procedures with everyone. We especially cannot use different rules, criteria, and procedures because people differ on unalterable or uncontrollable characteristics such as age, race, sex, or handicap.

etiology. Cause of a problem.

eustachian tube. Passageway between the nasopharynx and the middle ear. One function is to equalize pressure on both sides of the eardrum.

evoked response audiometry. See ABR audiometry.

expressive language. Producing messages through language. Antonym: receptive language.

extraordinary individual differences. Individual differences in pupils' patterns of development that are so extreme that pupils need special help in learning the common tasks of our culture as well as they might.

farsightedness. See hyperopia.

finger spelling. See manual alphabet.

fluency disorder. Disruption in the flow (rhythm) of speech. The main types are stuttering and cluttering.

fractures. Broken bones. Multiple compound fractures lead to temporary crippling.

free appropriate public education. Set of entitlements and protections guaranteed handicapped pupils under PL 94-142, The Education of All Handicapped Children Act of 1975. A handicapped pupil must have the special education, related services, and nonacademic services he or she needs at public expense, under the direction and supervision of the local school system, provided according to an individual education plan, within the context of the procedural safeguards.

functional. Adjective referring to a condition that does not have a physical cause. Antonym: organic.

galvanic skin response audiometry. See GSR audiometry.

genius. A person who has very high intellectual and creative powers.

gestational disorders. Disorders in the process of development to maturity within the womb. Prematurity and postmaturity are two types.

glaucoma. Condition in which excessive pressure within the eyeball leads to hardening of the eyeball and sometimes destruction. It causes visual impairment — sometimes blindness.

grand mal epilepsy. Type of epilepsy in which the person loses consciousness and has a major convulsion. An aura may precede a grand mal seizure.

gross brain disease. A number of conditions, many of them hereditary, that can lead to brain pathology. The brain pathology, in turn, can lead to mental retardation, crippling, and other problems. Major types are the neurocutaneous dysplasias, tumors, and congenital lesions of the blood vessels.

GSR audiometry. Audiometric procedure based on conditioning. The conditioned response is established by following a sound with an electric shock. The unconditioned response — sweating palms/hands — soon occurs when the person hears a sound because he or she expects the shock. Thus sweating palms becomes the response conditioned to the sound. Then the audiologist can assess what sounds the testee is hearing by noting whether palm sweating occurs as sounds are fed in at the various loudness and pitch levels.

hard of hearing. Level of hearing loss (usually 35 to 69 dB ISO) that hinders, but does not prevent, understanding speech through the ear alone, or with or without a hearing aid, and which adversely affects a pupil's educational performance.

hematologist. Physician specializing in diseases and disorders of the blood.

hemiplegia. Paralysis of one-half of the body viewed vertically. Right hemiplegia is paralysis of the right side of the body; left hemiplegia, the left side.

hemophilia. Happening only to males, a condition in which there is an absence or a deficiency of the clotting factor in the blood, resulting in easy and extensive hemorrhaging with the slightest injury — a blow, cut, or a sprain. Beyond the direct danger of bleeding excessively or fatally, the hemorrhaging may lead to inflammation in the bones, joints, and muscles, which in turn can interfere with movement.

hertz (Hz). Unit for measuring frequency (or pitch) of sounds. Referenced against a zero point set at the average pitch of the human voice.

homebound instruction. Instruction delivered in the home to pupils who are recuperating from illness, injury, or surgery.

Hoover cane. Long, lightweight cane used by blind people to detect obstacles and changes in terrain.

hospital instruction. Instruction delivered in the hospital to pupils who are recuperating from illness, injury, or surgery.

hydrocephalus. Condition in which the flow of the cerebrospinal fluid is disrupted. Too much fluid accumulates in the brain area, and the resulting pressure often leads to the pupil's skull enlarging and, more serious, damage to his or her brain. In turn, brain damage can cause mental retardation, crippling, and other problems, depending on how much damage occurs and where it is located. Often accompanies spina bifida with myelomeningocele or meningocele.

hyperactivity. Condition in which the pupil has difficulty refraining from excessive movement and manipulation of objects. It interferes with the youngster's attending to and continuing to work on tasks long enough to complete them.

hypernasality. See nasality.

hyperopia. Farsightedness. It happens when the pupil's eyeball is abnormally short from front to back and the light rays converge behind the retina. As a result, the pupil can see items clearly when they are off at a distance, but not when they are close up.

hyperthyroidism. Condition in which the thyroid gland produces excessive thyroxin, and metabolism is speeded up too much. The person is exceedingly tense and has trouble being still and attentive. He or she usually is quite thin and may have bulging eyes.

hypertrophy. Abnormal growth (and thus enlargement) of a muscle or bodily organ.

hyponasality. See nasality.

hypothyroidism. Condition in which the thyroid gland produces too little thyroxin, and metabolism is slowed down. The person is lethargic, with little energy for movement or sustained activity. He or she may become obese. Cretinism results when hypothyroidism is present at birth and remains untreated with thyroxin, the thyroid hormone. The bones and brain do not develop properly, and excessive smallness and mental retardation result.

Hz. See hertz.

idiopathic. Adjective referring to a condition in which the cause is not known or determinable.

IEP. See individual education program.

incus. Anvil-shaped bone which is part of the three-bone chain in the middle ear which transmits sound waves.

individual differences. Variations among pupils in important characteristics, e.g., physical, visual, hearing, intellectual, speech/language, and social/emotional characteristics.

individual education program. Management tool for organizing the testing, individualized instruction, placement, and procedural safeguards a pupil needs.

individualizing instruction. Tool for fitting education to individual differences. The phases are diagnosing relevant characteristics, prescribing teaching or therapeutic activites, carrying out that prescription, evaluating results, and revising the prescription, if appropriate. Synonyms: clinical teaching, diagnostic prescriptive teaching.

institution. As used with the handicapped, a place where people with a particular handicap are brought together for living, training, and other specialized treatment, e.g., residential school for the mentally retarded.

instructional media. Materials and machines used to help pupils attain instructional objectives, e.g., textbooks, videotapes, and simulations.

instructional methods. Recurring patterns of teacher behavior, used to help pupils reach instructional objectives, e.g., lectures, tutoring, field trips, and precision teaching.

instructional objectives. Statement about what the pupil should be able to do if he or she learns through instruction. They guide the selection of evaluation procedures and instructional procedures.

instructional procedures. Methods and media used to help pupils attain their instructional objectives.

instructional schedules. Time allowances for the direct teaching and independent practice pupils need to reach their instructional objectives.

instructional settings. Ways personnel and space are allocated for instruction.

intelligence quotient. Index of performance on an intelligence test. Used to infer a person's capability for learning and performing a wide range of activities.

intensification. As used with visually impaired pupils, making print, pictures, and other visual materials darker so that they can be seen more easily.

IQ. See intelligence quotient.

iris. Colored portion of the eye; it screens the light.

ISO. Abbreviation for International Organization for Standards. In audiology, used to designate the standards for audiometric scales.

itinerant teacher. Teacher who travels among classes and schools to consult with teachers working with exceptional pupils or to deliver instruction directly to the exceptional pupils.

Jaeger chart. Device for testing near vision for reading. It consists of various print sizes and thus shows what point type a person can see for reading.

kinesthetic sense. Sense of bodily position and movement.

kyphosis. Type of curvature of the spine. The person's upper spine is curved forward from back to front, and an excessive rounding of his or her shoulders results.

language disorder. Disorder in the ability to learn and use symbols for reality in communication. Two types are aphasia and delayed language.

least restrictive alternative. Concept widely applied in government — when government does have a legitimate communal interest to serve by regulating human conduct, it should use methods that curtail individual freedom to no greater extent than is essential for securing that interest. In reference to handicapped individuals, the concept is applied to residential placement and school placement and means that the individual is placed in the least restrictive environment appropriate.

least restrictive environment. See normalization.

legal blindness. Central visual acuity of 20/200 or less in the better eye with correcting glasses or a contraction of the visual field to an angle of 20 degrees or less regardless of visual acuity.

Legg-Calves-Perthes disease. See Perthes disease.

lens. Part of the eye that focuses the stimulus through the vitreous humor to the retina.

liable. Subject to sanctions for failure to perform a duty accurately.

lipreading. See speech reading.

lordosis. Type of curvature of the spine. The person's lower spine is curved backward from front to back, and an extensive swaying of the lower back happens.

magnification. As used with visually impaired pupils, making print, pictures, and other visual materials larger so that they can be seen more easily.

mainstreaming. Placement in the least restrictive environment for schooling. See normalization.

malformations and amputations. Malformations are improperly formed structures; amputations, missing structures. A wide variety of malformations and amputations result from heredity; from exposure to disease, drugs, poisoning, and radiation during prenatal development; and from burns and accidents occurring after birth. Some commonly seen examples are clubfoot, claw hand, webbed fingers or toes, or missing fingers, arms, toes, or legs.

malleus. Hammer-shaped bone, part of the three-bone chain in the middle ear which transmits sound waves.

malpractice. Inaccurate or erroneous performance of duty.

manual alphabet (finger spelling). Finger/hand patterns for numerals and letters. The finger speller holds one hand in front of his or her chest and spells out words and combinations of words. Conversation by sending and receiving finger spelling is done at about the rate of a spoken conversation.

manual communication. Transmitting and receiving messages through the manual alphabet (finger spelling) and sign language.

meningitis. Infection/inflammation of the meninges — the linings covering the central nervous system. May lead to nerve damage and crippling.

meningocele. Form of spina bifida. A sac containing cerebral-spinal fluid, but no nerve tissue, protrudes through an opening in the vertebra.

meningomyelocele. See myelomeningocele.

mental age. Age level at which a person performs on an age-normed intelligence test such as the Stanford-Binet.

mental retardation. Below-average level of intellectual functioning as indicated by performance on tests of intelligence and adaptive behavior.

metabolic disorders. Diseases, genetic disorders, and other malfunctions that interfere with the person's converting food to the substances which enable the bodily system to survive and function. Diabetes and hypothyroidism are frequently occurring types.

microcephaly. Congenital disorder leading to mental retardation. The space within the skull is abnormally small. The ears are quite large. The nose is also large and without a bridge, joining the brow directly. At the same time, the brow is sharply sloping and abnormally furrowed and wrinkled.

mildly retarded. Level of mental retardation in which individuals' IQ's fall within the 50–70 range. In adaptive behavior they can acquire some academic material, take care of their personal needs, and live independently as adults.

minimal brain dysfunction. Term used formerly for a syndrome that is labeled learning disability currently.

moderately retarded. Level of mental retardation in which individuals' IQ's are within the 35–49 range. Their adaptive behavior is more limited to rudimentary literacy materials, some ability to take care of their personal needs, simple occupational skills, and semidependent or dependent status as adults.

mongolism. See Down's syndrome.

monoplegia. Paralysis of one limb.

morphology. Study of structure. In reference to language, it means studying affixes (prefixes and suffixes) — their meanings and rules for their combinations with root words.

multiple sclerosis. Progressive neurological disorder in which the myelin sheath covering the nerves hardens. This nerve damage leads to muscle problems — weakness, spasticity, or tremor. Depending on which nerves are damaged, the person may have trouble walking and using his or her hands and arms, dizziness, slurring speech, and visual problems.

muscular dystrophy. Progressive disorder in which the muscles deteriorate. *Pseudohypertrophic muscular dystrophy* occurs only in boys. It affects the muscles of the shoulders and arms. Fatty tissue gradually takes the place of muscle tissue, and the pupil progressively loses the power to get up and down, walk, and use his arms and hands. *Facioscapulo-humeral muscular dystrophy* occurs in both boys and girls. It affects the face, the shoulders, and the upper arms primarily. It leads to a progressive loss of function of the arm, shoulder, and face muscles.

myelomeningocele. Form of spina bifida. A sac containing cerebralspinal fluid and nerve tissue protrudes through an opening in the vertebra. The spinal nerves usually are damaged, and paralysis occurs in any function controlled below the myelomeningocele. For example, a myelomeningocele in the lower back will cause paralysis of leg muscles and the sphincters important in bowel and bladder control.

myopia. Nearsightedness. The person's eyeball is abnormally long from front to back. The light rays converge in front of the retina. He or she can see items clearly when they are nearby, but not when they are far off.

nasality. The way air is resonated through the nose and nasal sinuses. *Hypernasality* happens when too much air goes through the nose as the person produces the vowels and all of the consonants except the m's, n's, and ng's. *Hyponasality* or denasality happens when too little air goes through the nose.

nearsightedness. See myopia.

near vision. Visual acuity for close viewing. It is measured several ways. The AMA's special Snellen chart, with the reference set at 14 inches, is one way. For example, 14/40 means that the individual can see at 14 inches what the normal eye can see at 40 inches. Another way is by the Jaeger chart.

negligence. See dereliction of duty.

nephritis. Inflammation of the kidneys. The effects manifest themselves in the various signs of inadequate elimination, e.g., puffiness about the eyes and other parts of the body, loss of appetite, fever, nausea, and vomiting, headache, lassitude, anemia, high blood pressure, and sometimes convulsions.

nephrologist. Physician specializing in diseases and disorders of the kidneys.

nephrosis. Degeneration of the kidneys. As the condition progresses, there is increasingly inadequate kidney function. As a result, the illness shows up in puffiness, loss of appetite, and other signs of inadequate elimination.

neurologist. Physician specializing in diseases and disorders of the central, peripheral, and autonomic nervous systems.

nondiscriminatory testing. Tool for fitting education to individual differences. The process of collecting information about a pupil within the protections of the legal safeguards.

norm. Average test performance of a norm group with particular characteristics. The standard against which an individual's test score can be expressed.

normal curve. Symmetrical, bell-shaped curve with certain statistical properties. Large random samples of most physical measures and some psychological measures are distributed in the form of a normal curve.

normal growth and development. Systematic changes in physical, hearing, visual, intellectual, speech/language, and social/emotional characteristics. These changes occur at certain age periods as a result of complex interactions of maturation (biological unfolding) and learning (environmental stimulation).

normalization. Enabling a person to participate in society as much and as independently as possible. Applied to residential placement, normalization involves arranging housing and services so that the handicapped individual can, as much as possible, live in the community as nonhandicapped individuals do participating physically and socially in school, church, recreation, and other activities. Applied to school placement, normalization involves arranging things so that handicapped pupils

can participate in school activities as much as possible as nonhandicapped pupils do.

norm group. Group used in setting standards of performance for a test. Average performance is determined for a group with particular characteristics. Then, an individual's test score is expressed in terms of its position in relation to the norm group performance.

norm-referenced test. Test in which an individual's score is expressed in relation to a norm group's performance.

nystagmus. Continuous, often rapid, movement of the eyeballs. They may go in a circular movement, or they may move side to side in a left-right direction.

occupational therapist. Specialist who evaluates pupils' capabilities for performing activities of daily living, e.g., feeding themselves or dressing themselves, and then provides therapy for pupils who have problems with these activities.

open education. Procedure for dealing with individual differences by allowing, encouraging, and leading the pupil to explore freely and to engage in objectives appropriate to his or her interests and capabilities. Spontaneous groups may emerge, but no particular groups are imposed.

Optacon. Device for converting print into tactile sensations (vibrations) on the fingers, thus enabling blind people to get a printed message.

ophthalmologist. Physician who specializes in diseases and disorders of the eye.

oral-aural method. Communication method for deaf people. Youngsters learn to get messages through amplification and residual hearing. They also learn to use speech reading. In addition, they are intensively trained in speech production. They are not trained in manual communication. Also, reading and writing instruction are delayed until pupils learn oral communication.

oral method. Method for teaching deaf pupils to communicate through speech. Pupils learn to pronounce syllables and then to combine them into words with the appropriate accent.

organic. Adjective referring to conditions due to known physical causes. Antonym: functional.

orientation/mobility. In referring to visually impaired people's independent travel, orientation is getting lined up toward a goal and in relation to the environment in general; mobility is moving from one place to another.

orthopedic impairments. Problems affecting the bony skeleton and muscle systems. They include central nervous system problems; bone, joint, and muscle problems; malfunctions and amputations; and accidents and abuse.

orthopedist. Physician specializing in diseases and disorders of the bone, joint, and muscle systems.

orthoptic exercises. Activities for training eye functions by using prisms and other devices.

osteogenesis imperfecta. Imperfect formation and growth of the bones. The bones do not develop properly. Also they break very easily — so much so that the condition is known colloquially as "chalk bones" or "brittle bones."

osteomyelitis. Bacterial infection of the bone.

otitis media. Infection/inflammation of the middle ear.

otologist. Physician specializing in diseases and disorders of the ear.

otosclerosis. Condition causing a conductive hearing loss. The stapes bone is fused to the oval window. As a result, sound waves are not transmitted adequately.

oval window. Membrane that connects the middle ear to the inner ear.

palate. The hard palate (in front) and the soft palate (in back) are the structures that form the roof of the mouth.

paraplegia. Paralysis of the lower half of the body when viewed on the horizontal plane.

paraprofessional. Person employed to assist teachers or therapists in working with pupils.

partial sightedness. Central visual acuity between 20/70 and 20/200 in the better eye after correction.

perceptive hearing losses. See sensorineural hearing losses.

perimeter. Device used to map out the field of vision in 360 degrees. *Central vision* is the middle of the visual field. *Peripheral vision* is vision above and below and to the sides of the central vision.

peripatologist. Specialist in teaching visually impaired people the orientation and mobility skills to travel independently.

peripheral vision. See perimeter.

perseveration. Abnormal perseverance. The persistance of a response past the time when it is appropriate.

Perthes disease (Legg-Calves-Perthes disease). Disease in which the head of the thigh bone deteriorates. As a result, the head flattens and does not fit well into the hip socket. Muscle spasms and pain result. The treatment is complete rest. This rest may be accomplished by confinement to bed or by strapping the leg up and putting the youngster on crutches.

petit mal epilepsy. Form of epilepsy in which seizures do not involve so much time or such a heavy motor component as do seizures in grand mal epilepsy. The person loses consciousness for a very short time. He or she may also show such symptoms as rapid swallowing or eyeblinking or just fixed staring into space. The seizures often appear to be inattention.

pharynx. Portion of the throat that connects the oral and nasal structures and the larynx.

phenylketonuria (PKU). Metabolic disorder in which the body does not correctly process protein. It leads to abnormal development and function of the brain and thus mental retardation.

phonation. Production of voiced sounds. The muscles in the rib cage contract to begin the outward flow of air. This air flow is shaped as it goes through the larynx, pharynx, and mouth structures.

phonology. Study of the sounds of a language.

physical therapist. Specialist who evaluates pupils' capabilities for standing, sitting, and ambulation and then provides therapy for pupils who have problems with these functions.

PKU. See phenylketonuria.

placement. Tool for providing for individual differences. Formerly, a tool for getting a group of pupils who can be taught the same way (i.e., taught as one) because they were alike on one or more characteristics important to learning. Currently, a tool for locating a pupil so that the service he or she needs can be conveniently delivered to him or her.

placement in the least restrictive environment. Applying the principle of normalization to placement, i.e., arranging things so that the handicapped pupil can participate in school activities as much as possible as nonhandicapped pupils do. Synonym: mainstreaming.

placement in the most enabling environment. Placing pupils in the environment in which they can function with the most comfort and effectiveness.

plaintiff. Person or group initiating a law suit. For example, Larry P. was a plaintiff in *Larry P. v. Riles.*

pneumoencephalography. A procedure for assessing brain structure. Air is injected in the lower spinal cord and tracked by X-ray through the cord and brain. Abnormal routes indicate pathology.

poliomyelitis. Viral infection of the spinal cord. It often leads to paralysis of muscles controlled by the spinal nerves damaged by the infection.

postlingual hearing impairment. Hearing impairment that happens after the child develops speech and language.

precocious. Adjective referring to an individual who develops abilities and skills at younger chronological ages than average individuals do.

prelingual hearing impairment. Hearing impairment that is present at birth or happens before the child spontaneously learns speech and language.

preschool programs. Special education and related services for infants and young children below school age.

procedural safeguards. Regulations protecting the individual's legal rights during an action. For handicapped pupils, they include four sets of protections — advocate participation, due process, equal protection, and confidentiality — with respect to testing, classification, individualizing instruction, and placement.

profoundly retarded. Level of mental retardation in which individuals' IQs fall below 20. In adaptive behavior deviations below the mean — IQ 19 or below, Stanford-Binet, and 24 or below, Wechsler. In adaptive behavior they are limited almost to rudimentary communication and perhaps simple self-help tasks. They remain dependent. Many profoundly retarded individuals have other handicaps such as cerebral palsy, epilepsy, visual impairments, hearing impairments, and fragile health. They may require total life-support systems such as feeding, oxygen, and other services.

prosthetic devices. Artificial replacements for missing body structures.

pseudohypertrophic. False hypertrophy, i.e., increase in size because of too much fatty or fibrous tissue rather than because of normal development.

pseudoretardation. Functional retardation resulting from interference with intellectual functioning by psychiatric disorders, deprived or harmful environmental influences, or sensory defects.

psychiatrist. Physician specializing in social/emotional disorders.

psychotic. Adjective referring to severe/profound social/emotional disorders in which the person is divorced from reality.

Public Law 94-142. The Education of All Handicapped Children Act of 1975, a statute guaranteeing a free appropriate public education to all handicapped pupils.

pupil. Part of the eye. The opening in the iris that expands and contracts to control the amount of light going into the inner eye.

pure-tone audiometry. Audiometric procedure using tones without content. These are transmitted through earphones. The testee signals when he or she hears them.

quadriplegia. Paralysis of the four limbs and the trunk and neck muscles.

receptive language. Receiving messages through language. Antonym: expressive language.

referral. Arranging for individuals with possible problems to be studied further by specialists.

refraction errors. Disorders that influence how the light rays strike the retina. Refraction refers to the eye's ability to bend (refract) light rays entering it in order to form an image on the retina.

regular class. Self-contained class of twenty-five to thirty-five pupils grouped by CA and no other criteria — especially not achievement level and ability to learn.

related services. Therapy, transportation, and other services the pupil needs to help him or her benefit from special education.

residential school. See institution.

residual hearing. Hearing remaining beyond the hearing loss. By definition, hard-of-hearing youngsters have residual hearing. In addition, many deaf pupils have some residual hearing — especially after they learn to use hearing aids and other procedures for amplifying sounds.

resonation. Reinforcement and prolongation of sound by the sound waves' bouncing and vibrating as they pass through the larynx, pharynx, mouth, nose, and sinuses.

resource room. Separate place where a handicapped pupil goes part-time for special help by a resource teacher.

resource teacher. Specialist serving handicapped pupils either by consulting with the regular teacher or by delivering direct service to pupils in their regular classroom or in a resource room.

retina. Part of the eye structure. It consists of nerve fibers which transmit the sensations to the optic nerve, which in turn transmits the sensations to the brain.

retrolental fibroplasia. Visual disorder caused by the formation of scar tissue behind the lens. This scar tissue interferes with the passage of light rays through to the retina and optic nerve. The condition results from excessive amounts of oxygen being given to premature infants.

rheumatic fever sequelae. After-effects of rheumatic fever including rheumatic heart disease, rheumatoid arthritis, and sometimes chorea (St. Vitus's Dance) — irregular, spasmodic, involuntary movements of the face and body.

rhythm disorder. See fluency disorder.

rigidity. Type of cerebral palsy in which there is a low level of muscle stiffness that never relaxes. Moving a limb is like bending a lead pipe, that is bending something pliable but slightly resistant.

Rochester method. Method of communication for deaf people. Finger spelling is combined with the oral-aural media. Pupils learn to receive messages by using amplification, residual hearing, speech reading, *and* finger spelling together. They learn to send messages by using speech and finger spelling together. At the same time, they receive instruction in using reading to receive messages and writing to send messages.

sanctions. Penalties for failure to meet responsibilities covered by accountability requirements. Kinds include loss of public monies, disciplining of public officials, and personal liability.

schizophrenia. Severe/profound social/emotional disorder. Individuals are divorced from reality and show bizarre behavior and muteness or abnormal language.

scoliosis. Type of curvature of the spine. A side-to-side curve in which the hips and shoulders are misaligned.

screening. Surveying individuals' characteristics to see if they show signs of problems indicating a need for further study.

Section 504 of PL 93-112. A section of the Vocational Rehabilitation Act of 1973, guaranteeing handicapped youngsters access to educational and work environments and freedom from discrimination in education and employment.

Section 1983, Title 42, U.S. Code. Civil Action for Deprivation of Rights, which makes *personally* liable for damages any person who deprives another of rights, privileges, or immunities secured by the Constitution or the laws.

seizure. Loss of consciousness sometimes also accompanied by a convulsion involving alternating spasms and relaxation of muscles manifested in falling, jerking, excessive salivation, and incontinence.

semantics. Study of the meanings of words and other expressions.

sensorineural hearing losses. Hearing losses that happen because the sound sensations are not transmitted through the nerves. They are caused by problems in the brain, the auditory nerve, or the structures in the inner ear — especially the hair cells of the organ of Corti — the sensory end organ for the auditory nerve. Sensorineural losses show up on the audiogram as similar levels of losses on both bone-conduction and air-conduction tests.

severe mental retardation. Level of mental retardation in which individuals' IQs are within the 20–34 range. Their adaptive behavior is quite limited, e.g., to rather basic self-care and rudimentary communication. They often have more than one handicap. They remain dependent.

sheltered workshop. Protected work environment in which handicapped people learn occupational skills, find permanent employment, or both.

sickle cell anemia. A severe form of anemia. See anemia.

sign language. Communication method using complex configurations to represent complete ideas. These complex configurations are developed through combinations of hand positions, patterns, and movements. We have various systems of sign language.

simultaneous method. Communication method, sometimes called the total communication method, in which the deaf employ oral-aural media and manual communication at the same time. They receive messages through amplification, residual hearing, speech reading, finger spelling, and sign language. They send messages through speech, finger spelling, and signs. At the same time, they learn to receive messages through reading and to send messages through writing.

slate and stylus. See braille slate and stylus.

Snellen chart. Device for measuring distance vision and near vision. See *distance vision* and *near vision*.

sonic devices. Devices for detecting obstacles and changes in the terrain. These devices are based on sonar principles involving reflected sounds, with loudness indicating distance and pitch indicating size. Specific instruments include the sonic cane, sonic glasses, and the Pathfinder sonic torch.

sovereign immunity. Doctrine that exempts the sovereign and his or her officials from liability for malpractice or dereliction of duty. Extended today to mean that certain public officials cannot be sued under certain circumstances.

spasticity. Form of cerebral palsy

in which there is excessive tension in the muscles. This tension prevents movement or makes movement very labored. It also may pull the joints out of shape. Various parts of the body and the eye muscles may be affected.

special centers. Areas with materials devoted to particular functions, e.g., mathematics centers contain activities and media which enable pupils to work independently on learning arithmetic objectives.

special class. Separate self-contained class where particular types of handicapped pupils are placed for instruction.

special day school. Separate school where particular types of handicapped pupils are placed for instruction.

special education. Specially designed instruction to meet the unique needs of a pupil.

speech audiometry. Audiometric procedure in which audiologists use two-syllable words called Spondee words. The speech reception threshold (SRT) is the level at which the testee can understand half of the words presented to him or her.

speech disorder. Disorder in articulation, voice quality, or rhythm in producing speech.

speech pathologist. Specialist who diagnoses a pupil's speech, language, and hearing problems and then provides appropriate therapy.

speech production. Sending messages by talking.

speech reading (lipreading). A method for decoding oral language by watching and interpreting primarily lip movements and more generally jaw, throat, facial, and bodily movements.

speech reception threshold (SRT). See speech audiometry.

spina bifida. Congenital malformation in which vertebrae fail to close at the midline during fetal development. It may occur at any point in the spinal column. There are three forms — spina bifida occulta, spina bifida with meningocele, and spina bifida with myelomeningocele.

standardization group. See norm group.

standardized test. See norm-referenced test.

stapes. The stirrup-shaped bone of the three-bone chain which transmits sound sensations through the middle ear.

statutory law. Legal requirements resulting from legislative action.

strabismus. Visual disorder that happens when the muscles pull unequally on a lateral plane. Internal strabismus is a directing of the eyeballs inward toward the nose. External strabismus is a directing of the eyeballs outward toward the ears. One eyeball may be in balance and the other out of balance. Both eyeballs may be out of balance. Or in alternating strabismus, one or both eyeballs shift among the balanced, internal, and external positions. More rarely, there is a muscular imbalance on a vertical plane. Then the eye may shift upward or downward.

stuttering. Fluency disorder in speech. In *primary stuttering* the individual's speech flow is interrupted by blocks and prolongations. In *secondary stuttering* the individual engages in struggle behavior, e.g., grimacing and head bobbing, to try to produce speech.

sweep test. Audiometric procedure used to screen individuals for signs of hearing impairment which merit more extensive diagnostic study.

syntax. Study of the structure of the language as shown in word functions (parts of speech) and sentence patterns.

tactile/visual/auditory method. Multisensory method for teaching pupils to communicate through speech. Pupils learn to produce sounds by associating tactual and visual cues and also auditory cues if they can hear anything at all.

talking books. Recordings of printed material for the visually impaired. Often produced in compressed speech to save time.

test. Procedure for systematically taking samples of a pupil's behavior. Tests include standardized aptitude and achievement instruments, diagnostic and evaluation devices, interest inventories, personality inventories, projective instruments and related clinical techniques, and many kinds of personal history forms.

test reliability. Degree to which test scores are free from chance errors of measurement.

test validity. Degree to which test items are true samples of the behavior they are supposed to measure.

tort law. Body of statutes and common-law precedents governing liability for personal damages for having injured another person.

tremor. Form of cerebral palsy in which there is involuntary movement in one extremity — usually one hand or arm. In *constant tremor* the involuntary movement is continuous. In *intention tremor* the involuntary movement happens only when the pupil undertakes to do something.

tympanic membrane (eardrum). Thin structure separating the outer and middle ear. Sound waves vibrate the eardrum, which activates the three-bone chain (stapes, incus, and malleus) in the middle ear.

variation. Distribution of measures around the central tendency. Percentiles and the standard deviation are indices of variation.

verbalism. Blind pupils' using words without meaning, i.e., words for phenomena they have had no direct sensory experience with.

visible speech method. Method for teaching deaf pupils to communicate through speech by essentially portraying how the vocal cords operate to produce sounds in words and sentences. The idea is that the youngster learns to copy what he or she sees. Some use electronic devices that show speech visibly, e.g., oscilloscopes, which translate sound patterns into light patterns, the Bell Telephone Visible Speech Translator, and the Instantaneous Pitch-Period Indicator. The teacher makes the correct sound, and it appears on the display. The pupil continues to modify his or her sound production until his or her sound patterns approximate the teacher's. Thus the pupil learns by successive approximation and proprioceptive feedback (biofeedback).

vitreous humor. The fluid inside of the eye.

voice disorder. Disorder in which the sounds of the voice are abnormal. Types include breathiness, harshness, hypernasality, hyponasality, too high or too low pitch, and excessive loudness or softness.

within-chronological age grouping. An option for placement. Pupils are categorized first by chronological age and then using grouping within class, tutoring by specialists, and independent learning to provide for individual differences. Various processes are labeled regular classes, remedial teaching, continuous-progress plans, nongraded plans, and resource teaching.

Author Index

ABA (American Bar Association), 35, 489
Abbs, J. H., 143, 505
Abel, D. A., 108, 495
Abeson, A., 62, 105, 106, 123, 130, 495, 504
Addison, M. R., 112, 502
Adkins, P. G., 260, 509
Agard, J., 117, 119, 495, 500
Agranowitz, A., 153, 504
Aiello, B., 121, 495
Aiken, L. R., Jr., 72–73, 491
Ainsworth, M. D. S., 445, 530
Allen, K. E., 110, 162, 496, 504
Alley, G., 414, 417, 525
Alley, G. R., 414, 526
Alter, M., 378, 525
Amary, I. B., 372, 522
American Speech and Hearing Association, 144, 505
Amsa, T. D., 260, 509
Anderson, R. H., 121, 496
Anderson, R. M., 100, 113, 496, 498
APA, 70, 491
Apolloni, T., 112, 496
Apter, S., 456, 530
Aram, D. M., 161, 506
Arena, J. I., 416, 419, 525
Armstrong, J., 49, 61, 491

Aronson, A. E., 154, 505
Artuso, A., 460, 532
Asimov, I., 328, 518
Aubuchon, M. T., 232, 509

Bacall, L., 331, 518
Bachrach, A. W., 459, 530
Bailey, E. J., 414, 525
Baldauf, R. J., 414, 526
Baldwin, N. Y., 76, 491
Baldwin, V., 117, 496
Balthazar, E. E., 365, 522
Barbee, A., 325, 521
Barker, P., 446, 530
Barraga, N.C., 242, 243, 253, 509, 510
Bartel, N. R., 414, 416, 526
Barth, R. S., 112, 496
Bateman, B., 54, 391, 493, 527
Battin, D., 457, 533
Baum, D., 283, 514
Bauman, M. K., 243, 246–247, 510
Beck, G. R., 92, 499
Becker, C., 254, 510
Becker, L. D., 117, 501
Beddoes, M. P., 249, 513
BEH, 171, 214, 261, 300, 381, 423, 467, 505, 507, 510, 514, 522, 526, 530

Bell, R. Q., 447, 530
Bell, V. H., 246, 510
Belsky, J., 446, 530
Berg, A. S., 324, 518
Berg, B. O., 281, 514
Berg, F. S., 182, 192, 507
Beria, E. P., 257, 510
Berliner, O. C., 97, 496
Berry, P., 365, 522
Bersoff, D. N., 32, 61, 130
Bertrand, A., 70, 491
Bess, F. H., 187
Bice, H. V., 287
Bigge, L. L., 287
Birch, J. W., 119, 213, 292, 502, 507, 514
Bischoff, R. W., 252, 253, 510
Bishop, V. E., 227, 252, 257, 510
Blake, K. A., 49, 54, 325, 365, 367, 372, 492, 520, 522
Blanco, R. F., 456, 530
Blatt, B. A., 63, 112, 125, 380, 491, 496, 522
Blau, T. H., 454, 530
Bleck, E. E., 271, 278, 279, 280, 281, 514, 515
Bliss, J. C., 254, 510
Bloodstein, O., 154, 199, 507

Subject Index

Classification   Testing

"We hold these truths to be self-evident,
that all men are created equal,
that they are endowed by their Creator
with certain unalienable Rights,
that among these are Life, Liberty, and the
pursuit of Happiness...."

IDENTIFICATION   NONDISCRIMINATORY TESTING